LANGUAGE, LITERACY and EARLY CHILDHOOD EDUCATION

Janet Fellowes and Grace Oakley

OXFORD
UNIVERSITY PRESS

Oxford University Press is a department of the University of Oxford.
It furthers the University's objective of excellence in research,
scholarship, and education by publishing worldwide. Oxford is a registered
trademark of Oxford University Press in the UK and in certain other
countries.

Published in Australia by
Oxford University Press
253 Normanby Road, South Melbourne, Victoria 3205, Australia

© Janet Fellowes and Grace Oakley 2010

The moral rights of the author have been asserted

First published 2010
Reprinted 2011 (twice), 2012, 2013 (twice)

All rights reserved. No part of this publication may be reproduced, stored in a retrieval system,
or transmitted, in any form or by any means, without the prior permission in writing of Oxford
University Press, or as expressly permitted by law, by licence, or under terms agreed with the
appropriate reprographics rights organisation. Enquiries concerning reproduction outside the scope
of the above should be sent to the Rights Department, Oxford University Press, at the address above.

You must not circulate this work in any other form and you must impose this same condition on
any acquirer.

National Library of Australia Cataloguing-in-Publication data

Fellowes, Janet.
Language, literacy and early childhood education / Janet Fellowes, Grace Oakley.
ISBN: 978 0 19 556628 4 (pbk.)
Includes bibliographical references and index.
Children—Language.
Early childhood education.
Literacy.
Oakley, Grace.

372.21

Reproduction and communication for educational purposes
The Australian *Copyright Act 1968* (the Act) allows a maximum of one chapter
or 10% of the pages of this work, whichever is the greater, to be reproduced
and/or communicated by any educational institution for its educational purposes
provided that the educational institution (or the body that administers it) has
given a remuneration notice to Copyright Agency Limited (CAL) under the Act.

For details of the CAL licence for educational institutions contact:

Copyright Agency Limited
Level 15, 233 Castlereagh Street
Sydney NSW 2000
Telephone: (02) 9394 7600
Facsimile: (02) 9394 7601
Email: info@copyright.com.au

Edited by John Mahony
Cover design by Canvas Group
Text design and typeset by Kerry Cooke, eggplant communications
Proofread by Peter Cruttenden
Indexed by Russell Brooks
Printed in China by Sheck Wah Tong Printing Press Ltd

Links to third party websites are provided by Oxford in good faith and for information only.
Oxford disclaims any responsibility for the materials contained in any third party website
referenced in this work.

CONTENTS

About the Authors — x
Preface — xi
Acknowledgments — xii

PART 1 YOUNG CHILDREN AND LANGUAGE — 1

1 Understanding Oral Language — 3
Introduction — 4
Language and communication — 4
Language and speech — 5
Expressive and receptive modes — 6
Properties of language — 6
Components of spoken language — 8
Language is functional — 14
Language register — 20
Language and culture — 22
Language variations — 23
Bilingualism — 25
Code switching — 26
Language diversity and early childhood settings — 26

2 Theories and Phases of Oral Language Development — 31
Theoretical perspectives of language development — 32
Phases and milestones of oral language development — 38
Oral language development in childcare and education settings — 42

3 Early Childhood Settings and Oral Language Learning and Development — 45
Introduction — 46
Language development and the home setting — 47
Language development and the childcare setting — 49
The primary school setting — 54

4 Key Early Childhood Learning Contexts and Oral Language — 58
Play and oral language — 59
Reading aloud to children — 64
Storytelling — 67

		Conversation and discussion	71
		Investigations	76
5		**Learning Experiences and Activities for Speaking and Listening**	**79**
		Introduction: Important considerations	80
		Speaking and listening activities	81
		The importance of listening	99
		Diversity and listening	104
6		**Language, Thinking and Learning**	**106**
		Cognition and language	107
		Language use and brain development	108
		The relationship between language and cognition	108
		Inner speech and thinking	110
		Language and learning	110
		Questioning for cognition and learning	116
7		**Assessment: Speaking and Listening**	**127**
		Introduction	128
		Oral language assessment	129
		Collecting information about children's oral language	130
		Documentation of oral language learning	137
		Interpreting the information gathered about oral language	146

PART 2 UNDERSTANDING LITERACY: READING AND WRITING — 149

8		**Understanding Literacy: Definitions and Theoretical Perspectives**	**151**
		What is literacy?	152
		Why are definitions important?	152
		Theoretical perspectives on the development of reading and writing	154
		The reciprocal relationship between the constituents of literacy	158
		The importance of motivation in literacy learning	158
		Assessing affective factors	159
		Practices of highly effective literacy teachers	160
9		**Understanding Reading**	**164**
		Foundational knowledge for reading	165
		Text use and understanding	166
		Conceptual or topic knowledge	168
		Teaching concepts about print	170
		Assessment of concepts about print	170
		Knowledge about text purposes	172
		Phonological awareness	172
		Knowledge about letters and sounds	174
		Word recognition: phases of development	177

	Sight words	178
	Learning to read	179

10 Phonological Awareness, Graphophonic Relationships and Sight Words — 187

Phonological awareness	188
Teaching phonological awareness	188
Word-level phonological awareness	189
Principles for teaching phonological awareness	202
Assessment of phonological awareness	202
Teaching about graphophonic relationships	204
What do children need to know about graphophonic relationships?	206
Possible sequences of phonics teaching	209
Principles of phonics teaching	211
Strategies and games for teaching phonics	212
Working with letters and sounds	214
Assessment of phonics knowledge	217
Teaching sight words	219
Strategies for teaching sight words	219
Assessment of sight words	221

11 Strategies for Teaching Reading — 224

Introduction	225
Reading aloud to children	225
Language Experience Approach	228
Shared reading	228
Guided reading	235
Buddy reading	238
Independent reading	239
Reciprocal teaching	239
Literature circles	239
Matching texts to children	240

12 Vocabulary for Reading and Writing — 244

What do we mean by vocabulary?	245
Why is vocabulary important in reading and writing?	245
How does vocabulary knowledge develop?	246
Levels of vocabulary knowledge	246
How can vocabulary development be facilitated in the early years?	248
Indirect instruction	249
Explicit vocabulary instruction	251
Word study	252
Using dictionaries	257
Word sorts/classifications	258
Using contextual clues	258
Teaching word consciousness	259

	Some principles of vocabulary teaching	260
	Assessment of vocabulary knowledge	260
	Toolbox of vocabulary strategies	263

13 Reading for Comprehension — 266

Introduction	267
How can reading comprehension be defined?	268
What does a child need to do/know in order to comprehend a text?	269
Reading comprehension: suggested developmental pathway	269
Levels of comprehension	271
What strategic processes does comprehension involve?	273
Teaching comprehension processes and strategies	281
Comprehension of informational texts	281
Providing appropriate texts	283
Vocabulary for reading	284
Comprehension of multimodal texts	284
Assessment of reading comprehension	285
Toolbox of vocabulary strategies	293

14 Developing Reading Fluency — 301

What is reading fluency?	302
Why is reading fluency important?	304
Fluency development	304
Facilitating fluency	305
Key practices for encouraging fluency	305
Improving the elements of reading fluency	310
Improving expressiveness	312
Using ICT to teach reading fluency	312
Pulling it all together	313
Assisting struggling beginning readers	314
Assessment of reading fluency	315
Toolbox of vocabulary strategies	319

PART 3   LEARNING TO WRITE — 323

15 Introduction to Writing — 325

Written communication	326
Four components of writing	327
The physical aspect of writing	330
Writing traits	331
The writing process	331
Children's growth in written communication	337
Using the phases of writing development	341

16 Writing Purpose and Text Organisation — 344

Introduction	345
Writing purpose	345

	Audiences	346
	Written texts	347
	Types of texts	348
	Teaching about texts: beginning and emergent	354
	Teaching about texts in the early years of school	356
17	**The Writing Conventions: Grammar and Punctuation**	**362**
	Writing conventions	363
	What is grammar?	363
	Oral language and grammar as a prelude to writing	364
	Understanding English grammar	365
	Grammar and writing	373
	Teaching the writing conventions	377
18	**Spelling and Handwriting**	**381**
	The importance of good spelling	382
	Introduction to the English orthographic system	383
	Spelling knowledge	385
	Spelling strategies	388
	Children's spelling development	388
	Invented spelling	391
	Teaching spelling	392
	Spelling activities	393
	Spelling lessons	402
	Handwriting	404
19	**Key Strategies for Teaching Writing**	**409**
	Introduction	410
	Modelled writing	412
	Shared writing	416
	Working with the texts produced in shared and modelled writing	419
	Interactive writing	421
	Language Experience Approach	422
	Guided writing	424
	Independent writing	427
	The teaching strategies in use	427
20	**Writing Experiences and Activities**	**432**
	The emergence of writing	433
	Supporting the emergence of writing	434
	Supporting children's further progress as writers	443
	Developing writing lessons for children in the early years of school	444
	Establishing the stimulus for writing activities	445
21	**Writing: Assessment and Evaluation**	**453**
	What to assess?	454
	Collecting information about children's writing	455
	Letter identification	461

Spelling	462
Assessment of writing interest and motivation	466

PART 4 FRAMING LANGUAGE AND LITERACY LEARNING — 469

22 Children's Literature — 471
Helen Adam

What is children's literature?	472
The place of children's literature in the curriculum	472
The role of the teacher	474
Response to literature	475
The environment for reading and response	476
Response through integrated activities	481

23 Visual and Critical Literacy — 488

Multiliteracies	489
Critical literacy	490
Visual literacy and its importance in the twenty-first century	495
Broad approaches to teaching viewing	501
Suggested themes for critical and visual literacy	503
Assessment of visual literacy	506

24 Literacy and Information and Communication Technologies (ICT) — 509

Young children's engagement with ICT in the modern world	510
Using ICT to facilitate literacy learning in classrooms	512
Using ICT to help children learn word identification and graphophonic relationships	519
Word processors	521
Dedicated spelling software	523
Using the internet	524
Interactive whiteboards	527

25 Connecting with Families — 530

Family literacy practices	531
Family literacy practices and emerging literacy	531
Oral language as a component of family literacy	531
Family literacy and emergent literacy	532
Family literacy diversity	533
Family literacy initiatives	535
Parent–teacher partnerships	536
The benefits of parent–teacher partnerships	537
Partnership practices	538
Working with families from culturally and linguistically diverse backgrounds	544

26 Planning for Language and Literacy Learning and Development — 550

Planning development and learning programs	551
Creating a learning program	552

Key features of a learning program	552
Language and literacy learning programs	554
The integrated program	559
Integrated learning and the inquiry approach	561
Language, literacy and the integrated curriculum	562
Reading and writing in an integrated learning program	564
Children in the early years of school (six- to eight-year-olds)	566
Attitude and motivation	568
The informed early childhood professional	570

Appendix: Oxford Wordlist	*574*
Bibliography	*576*
Index	*593*

ABOUT THE AUTHORS

Janet Fellowes is a Senior Lecturer at Edith Cowan University where she teaches Early Childhood Language and Literacy. She spent fifteen years before this working as a classroom teacher in a range of locations and across early childhood and primary classes. Janet continues to work closely with schools and classroom teachers and is regularly called upon to conduct staff professional development sessions in early childhood language and literacy. Her research work is closely linked to the early childhood classroom and has comprised such projects as Small Group Literacy Teaching in the Early Years, Teacher Efficacy and the Teaching of English as a Second Language, The Community of Inquiry and the Oral Language Development of Preschool Children, Boys and Literacy and Focused Intervention for Effective Literacy Development. Janet is passionate about ensuring that early childhood teachers are knowledgeable about, and inspired by, language and literacy teaching and learning, and that they are reflective, resourceful and adaptable practitioners.

Grace Oakley is an Associate Professor at the University of Western Australia and teaches primarily in Language and Literacy. Grace has lectured in this area for over ten years, in early childhood and primary teaching programs, both undergraduate and postgraduate. She has had classroom experience in K–7 classrooms, including LOTE teaching. Grace's research interests focus on the role of ICT in early literacy learning, helping children who struggle in literacy, literacy assessment, literacy motivation and metacognition in literacy learning. She has been involved in several research projects involving literacy in the early years, one of which investigated teachers' methods of assessing reading. She is also interested in home literacy practices and was involved in the Better Beginnings project.

PREFACE

This text presents the latest thinking about early childhood language and literacy learning and development. It also sets out ways in which early childhood educators can facilitate development and learning for children from birth to eight years. It presents a strong focus on theory and research, which is fundamental to the design of suitable learning environments, teaching and learning programs and assessment practices. However, theoretical knowledge is well balanced with a range of activities and strategies; thereby, early childhood educators are provided with a good grounding for their approach to young children's language and literacy learning and development.

The role of play is acknowledged as highly important and central to the way young children learn; however, 'intentional teaching' and the role of the teacher is also recognised as playing a crucial role in effective language and literacy learning and development.

The text is divided into four main parts, the first three of which cover oral language, reading and writing. The separation of these fields is not intended to imply that each of them stands alone; on the contrary, they are closely associated and children's learning in one area may well enhance, or be enhanced by, their learning in others. The areas are dealt with separately because good teaching calls for a discrete and comprehensive understanding in each.

The fourth part on framing language and literacy learning addresses topics that are important to the establishment of language and literacy programs for children in today's world. Visual and critical literacy as well as the use of information and communication technologies (ICT) are comprehensively addressed in recognition of their essential position in today's early childhood language and literacy programs. Likewise, children's literature, with its central role in children's language and literacy learning, is given dedicated attention. This part also deals with the crucial early childhood practice of connecting with, and working in partnership with, children's families, and a range of practices is presented for this purpose.

The text has been written to be relevant to those working in the early childhood settings of childcare, pre-school and the early years of primary school, and to the language and literacy development of infants, toddlers, pre-schoolers and children in the early years of school. In the interest of expediency, the book generally uses the word 'teachers' when making reference to early childhood educators, whether working in childcare, pre-school or school settings.

Although many chapters make clear links to the different groups of children and the different early childhood settings, the need to ensure an adequate coverage of the topics means that the information presented in some chapters may not always be relevant to all groups of children or each of the early childhood settings. Moreover, there is the need for readers to carefully consider the activities and strategies presented and to decide how to adapt them to the different groups of learners and the different educational and care settings.

ACKNOWLEDGMENTS

We would like to thank our families and friends and our literacy and early childhood colleagues for their support and encouragement as we wrote this book. We would also like to thank the editorial staff (past and present) from Oxford University Press who have worked with us to ensure the book's quality and completion, particularly, Michelle Green, Debra James, Tim Campbell, John Mahony, Geraldine Corridon and Jennifer Butler.

We dedicate this book to six beautiful children—Niamh, Charis, Bayley, Kiaya, William and QiQi—who inspire us in our commitment to language, literacy and early childhood education.

The authors and publishers wish to thank copyright-holders for granting permission to reproduce illustrative material. Sources are as follows:

Clean Slate Press for the cover image of *To town* by Joy Cowley; Evans Publishing Group for the cover image of *Eating fruit and vegetables* by Claire Llewellyn, photographer: Liz Price; Alison Lester and Allen & Unwin for the cover image of *Magic beach* ©Alison Lester 1990, published by Allen & Unwin, Sydney; NordSüd Verlag for the cover image of *The rainbow fish* by Marcus Pfister, ©1992 North-South Books Inc., New York, an imprint of NordSüd Verlag AG, CH-8005 Zurich/Switzerland; Penguin Group for the cover images of *Boo to a goose* by Mem Fox; *There was an old lady who swallowed a fly* by S. Taback; *Belinda* and *Who sank the Boat* by Pamela Allen; *Dear zoo* by Rod Campbell; *Brown bear* by Bill Martin and Eric Carle; *Why is the sky blue?* by Geraldine Taylor and Amy Schimler; *Elephants* (part of the Chatterbox series) by Edel Wignall; Walker Books for the cover image of *The hidden forest* by Jeannie Baker, cover illustration © 2000 Jeannie Baker, reproduced with permission of Walker Books Ltd, London SE11 5HJ on behalf of Walker Books Australia, and for the page from *Let's get a pup!* by Bob Graham, Illustration © Blackbird Design Pty Ltd, reproduced with permission of Walker Books Australia on behalf of Walker Books Ltd, London SE11 5HJ; MobyGames for the screenshot from *Just me and my mom*; Phonics Alive! for the screenshot on page 520. Shutterstock Images for photographs © Diego Cervo (page 4); Herjua (page 7); Calek (page 9); Morgan Lane Photography (page 19); John Stee (page 22); Adam Borkowski (page 47); Poznyakov (pages 49 and 53); Matka Wariatka (page 52); Benis Arapovic (page 55); Ingrid Balabanova (page 59); StockLite (page 107); Pavlov Mikhail (first image, page 326); Pavel Losevsky (page 566). Photograph on page 99 courtesy of Alex Mares-Manton/photolibrary. Thank you also to the RAND Corporation for permission to use the RAND model of reading comprehension (Figure 13.1, page 268) and to the California Department of Education, CDE Press, for permission to use the Student Oral Language Observational Matrix (Table 7.11, page 144).

Every effort has been made to trace the original source of copyright material contained in this book. The publisher and authors would be pleased to hear from copyright-holders to rectify any errors or omissions.

PART 1

Young Children and Language

CHAPTER 1

Understanding Oral Language

CHAPTER OBJECTIVES

This chapter will increase your understanding of:

- language and communication
- the different properties and features of the English language system
- the functional nature of language and the need to adapt language use to suit different speaking and listening situations
- the link between language, culture and identity and the need to acknowledge and respect children's home language or English dialect
- varieties of a language.

This chapter provides an introduction to language as a system of communication. It serves to increase your understanding of the nature of language and to provide you with knowledge that is essential to assisting the language development and learning needs of young children. The greater your understanding of language, the better you can identify and address children's language development requirements. The chapter focuses on the ways in which language must be adapted to suit different social and learning purposes, and on the varieties of language children will likely bring to the classroom or childcare setting.

In Australian society, language is used for oral as well as written communication; however, the focus in this chapter is on oral language. Written language (reading and writing) is addressed in the second part of the book.

INTRODUCTION

The nurturing of oral language development is central to early childhood care and education.

Language, consisting as it does of groups and combinations of words (usually sentences), is the prime means of communication between people. Of course, language is not the only means of communication (think, for instance, of signs, symbols, pictures and gestures) but it is certainly the centrepiece of communication in human society. It is an integral component of human activity and plays a dominant part in the experiences and events of everyday life. How, indeed, would the human race manage without language?

Although oral language is a skill that is acquired naturally by the young, the importance of its development in early childhood cannot be overemphasised. It is, after all, the platform on which learning to read and write is built. A child who has a well-grounded ability in oral language will usually be nicely poised to cope with reading and writing. On the other hand, one who has an inadequate language ability may well be at a disadvantage.

Oral language underpins the whole scope of learning. It is employed to question, to seek information and to proffer ideas. It gives voice to the thinking that surrounds learning experiences and leads to the construction of concepts and the generation of new knowledge.

The nurturing of oral language development is central to early childhood care and education. Young children require constant support to acquire the skills required for the effective use of oral language. They need to witness and participate in a variety of talk experiences that call for, and assist them to develop, different types of language competency.

LANGUAGE AND COMMUNICATION

Humans are social beings and have a need for connection to, and communication with, other individuals and groups in society. Oral language meets this need. It is a means for interaction within the family, social groups, classroom, workplace and elsewhere in the general community. It is the principal mode by which people socialise and share and seek information, in the form of ideas, opinions, attitudes, needs, desires and so on. If children (or indeed adults) cannot speak and listen effectively, they are disadvantaged in many ways.

Communication is a process whereby two or more people construct meaning. It is in many ways a complex, interactive process that involves an encoder (who formulates the message and puts it into a code—spoken language) and a decoder (who interprets and endeavours to understand the information conveyed) working together to build meaning. Meaning is first of all constructed in the mind of the speaker, then verbally encoded into language and conveyed to a listener who interprets and ascribes a meaning to it in their own mind. It should be noted, however, that listeners often use additional information to help them make meaning. They use visual information such as the speaker's body language and they also use the knowledge they have about the context, the topic and the speaker. For the communication to be effective, the meaning intended by the speaker and that derived by the listener must be in close harmony. There needs to be a shared understanding of what is being said.

Assigning meaning to words and sentences involves interpretation. However, a listener's interpretation will be influenced by his or her experiences, topic knowledge and attitudes, and they may therefore arrive at meanings which are quite different from these which are intended by the speaker. The more closely aligned are the participants' experiences, the greater is the likelihood of a shared meaning being achieved; in other words, the greater likelihood of effective communication.

Spoken language is the principal means of communication in society, although written language also of course plays a prominent part. But these are not the only means of communication. As noted above, such things as gestures, body posture, facial expression, eye contact and head and body movement can also be means of communication and can be used to support—or even replace—spoken language. Consider how much one person's spoken approach to another can be enhanced or otherwise modified if it is accompanied by an aggressive gesture, a tense body posture, a cheerful facial expression, glaring eye contact or vigorous head or body movement. Spoken language is one thing; the manner of delivery is another. Then again, the mere nod of a head in response to a verbal question may adequately convey meaning.

The various ways in which meaning is communicated between people are referred to as semiotic systems (Anstey & Bull, 2004, 2005). Language, whether used in spoken or written form, is one semiotic system. It, along with other systems (gestures, images, sounds), are employed by people to communicate meaning to others.

LANGUAGE AND SPEECH

Language is expressed orally through the generation of speech. It facilitates speech by employing a system of signs (patterns of sounds that form words) to represent different objects, concepts, actions and so on. It is an intricate physical process involving use of the vocal tract to control and shape moving air in different ways to produce sounds. Speech is made up of articulation (how speech sounds are made), voice (the production of sound using the vocal folds and breathing) and fluency (the smoothness and natural rhythm of speech).

The development of language requires familiarity with speech and becoming accustomed to the different ways that speech can be adapted for greater clarity of meaning.

Speech and language do not begin to develop at the same time. A child will first learn language so as to be able to understand the speech of others; the ability to produce meaningful speech will develop a little later.

Different spoken languages have sounds and sound combinations that are specific to each of them. The mechanisms of human speech are fortunately designed so that everyone has a latent capacity to produce virtually all the sounds of any language. However, through immersion in a particular language environment, a child's speech gradually comes to mirror that used by the people who surround him or her.

EXPRESSIVE AND RECEPTIVE MODES

Oral language is either **expressive** or **receptive** in nature. It is critical that children be supported in the development of both forms. They are equally important to effective communication growth and general academic success at school.

EXPRESSIVE

Speaking is the expressive form of oral language. It involves:

1. the intention to say something for the purpose of conveying information, making an enquiry, proposing an idea etc.
2. the encoding of the intention into language.
3. the transmission from one person to another by means of speech (of course, a communication may also be received by a number of people).

Expressive communication requires the information etc. to be encoded into language to facilitate its transmission; the greater a person's grasp of the language, the greater should be that person's ability to communicate effectively. The converse is, of course, also true: a poor grasp of the language is usually accompanied by a poor standard of communication.

RECEPTIVE

Listening is the receptive form of oral communication. It requires the listener to decode the language used by the speaker and to assimilate the information etc. that has been conveyed. Once again, the listener's competency in language will affect the quality of this decoding and assimilation.

PROPERTIES OF LANGUAGE

Young children have an extraordinary capacity to master the language that surrounds them. In the space of a few years they become reasonably adept in a language which is, after all, brand new to them. Language has a number of defining properties (Ogle & Beers, 2009; Owens, 2005) and an understanding of these gives some insight into this

Young children have an extraordinary capacity to master the language around them.

remarkable learning capacity. Children become aware of these properties during the language learning process.

- *Language is arbitrary*: a language has words that denote the concepts, objects, actions etc. that the speaker wishes to talk about. There is no logical connection between the form of a word (sequence of sounds) and its meaning. As a language develops, words are randomly invented to identify an object, concept or action. The form and meaning of a word are, in effect, simply agreed upon by users of a language. There are no rules which dictate the form that a word should take.
- *Language has structure*: words are grouped or combined in an organised fashion. There are rules to be followed in forming complete sentences and in the joining together of these sentences to create conversation. Different languages are structured according their own rules. Effective communication requires an innate ability to apply these rules.
- *Language is productive*: language has a range of grammatical patterns that can be used in different combinations to produce new utterances. A speaker can produce limitless types of utterances by combining already known word and sentence elements.
- *Language has the capacity for displacement*: language can be used to talk about things that cannot immediately be seen, heard, felt or smelt; things not connected to the immediate environment. It can be used to talk about subjects, objects and events from the past or in the future, whether real or imaginary.
- *Language is linked to thought*: language is a medium through which thought is communicated. It works in tandem with such mental processes as perception, comprehension, attention and memory. Understanding of a concept etc. and the language to talk about it develop simultaneously.
- *Language is natural*: learning of language is an inherent part of being human. People are born with a strong disposition, and the biological means, for acquiring language skills. A child who is given no training or other support in language development will still acquire a basic language skill.

COMPONENTS OF SPOKEN LANGUAGE

The four key components of language are:

- *phonological* component (sound patterns of a language)
- *syntactic* component (system of structuring sentences)
- *semantic* component (meaning of words and sentences)
- *pragmatic* component (use of language in particular contexts).

Communication requires a capacity to integrate all four components simultaneously. Early childhood professionals should consider the language components when planning ways in which to support children's language growth and when monitoring their language development. Over time, and with the appropriate experiences and support, children's oral language development should occur in relation to each of these components.

THE PHONOLOGICAL COMPONENT OF LANGUAGE

The **phonological** component of language comprises the various sounds that are used in speaking. These include **phonemes** (individual sound units that are used to form words), **intonation** (the rise and fall of the pitch of the voice) and **stress** (the emphasis given to certain syllables in words).

Phonemes are the smallest individual sound units of a language. An example of a phoneme is the /s/ sound such as in the words 'sip', 'sand', 'waste' and 'cats'. The /s/ phoneme is also in the word 'ace' but when written it is represented by the letter 'c'.

Spoken words are formed by combining phonemes in different ways. For instance, the word 'cat' is made by combining the phonemes /c/ /a/ and /t/ while the word 'shed' is composed of the phonemes /sh/ /e/ /d/. Changing one phoneme in a word alters that word (for example, the /b/ in the word 'bat' which sets it apart from the words 'cat' and 'fat').

Every language has a set of phonemes. In the English language there are approximately 40–46 different phonemes. In contrast, Polynesian languages have only about 15.

There are both differences and similarities between the phonemes of English and those of other languages. The English /v/ phoneme (as in 'valley') is not present in the Japanese and Thai languages. The /r/ and /l/ phonemes of English are not produced in the Japanese language; in fact, native Japanese speakers usually find it difficult to distinguish between these two phonemes. The /th/ phoneme of English ('this', 'thing') is not used in the French and Italian languages. The English /r/ phoneme is quite different from the /r/ phoneme of Italian and French. In Arabic there are several phonemes that are unknown in English.

Phonemes are produced when air, after being expelled from the lungs, passes through the vocal chords and out through the mouth. During this process, certain changes to the shape of the mouth or the positioning of the tongue, teeth and lips lead to the formation of different phonemes.

Within any country, there may be variations to the way the phonemes of a language are pronounced by its speakers. These variations may be part of a 'dialect' (refer to the end of the chapter for more information about dialect).

Intonation, also a part of the phonological component of language, encompasses pitch (low and high sound) and stress (the emphasis placed on syllables). Intonation can be used in different ways to alter the meaning of an utterance. Take, for example, the sentence, 'She is ready to go.' It can be said as a statement of fact or as a question, depending on whether there is a rise or a fall in pitch at the end.

The meaning of an utterance can be varied through the manipulation of intonation. For example, the statement, 'sure you did,' can be spoken with different intonations to show irony, sarcasm, assertion or humour.

Stress placed on one particular word in a sentence will contribute to the meaning communicated by the sentence. For example, the meaning of 'My cat ran away' will depend on which word is emphasised. Thus:

<u>My</u> cat ran away.

My <u>cat</u> ran away.

My cat <u>ran</u> away.

My cat ran <u>away</u>.

Variations to intonation can also lead to variations to the emotional meaning of what is said. Surprise, disappointment, anger or joy can be expressed depending on the intonation patterns used.

Children's ability to become attuned to sounds of the language and to learn the ways in which speech can be modulated to provide different meanings is important to the development of effective oral communication.

Infants become attuned to the sounds of language and the way language is modulated to provide different meanings.

The development of an ability to discriminate between different sounds begins to develop as soon as a child is born. Children learn to recognise the sounds around them and what they mean, such as taps running, dogs barking and cars driving past. In terms of language, babies quickly learn to discriminate between phonemes. Indeed, there is evidence that children can distinguish certain phonemes as young as one month of age (Gleason, 2005). How to help children improve their phonological abilities is covered in depth in Chapter 10.

THE SYNTACTIC COMPONENT OF LANGUAGE

The **syntactic** component of language refers to the grammar of the language. It involves the application of rules for arranging words to form a meaningful sentence. For instance, the sentence 'Kate threw the red ball to Jack' is recognised as being syntactically correct, whereas 'Threw the red ball Kate to Jack' is not. Effective communication requires the grammatical rules for distributing words throughout a sentence to be known by both the speaker and the listener (or by the writer and the reader).

It would be impossible for a person to memorise all the possible sentences that the person would need to use over a lifetime. Knowledge of the rules for constructing a sentence is therefore an essential prerequisite for effective communication. These rules enable a person continuously to create new and meaningful sentences as the need arises.

Many of the syntactic rules of a language are absorbed subconsciously while the language is being learnt. The sentence 'Jay jumped the fence' applies the correct word order (syntax)—subject-verb-object. 'Jay' is the subject, 'jumped' is the verb and 'the fence' is the object. However, the sentence could be constructed by a person who does not have an *explicit* knowledge of the rules involved. A lot of people know very little about the rules of the English language but are still able to express sentences that require the application of complex grammatical rules.

Morphology is the aspect of grammar that deals with the way in which words can be modified to form new words so as to provide different shades of meaning. It involves a set of rules for modifying a **base word** by adding an **affix**. For instance the word 'laugh' can be used to form the words 'laughable', 'laughing', 'laughs', 'laughed' or 'laughter'.

Table 1.1: Affix types and word modification

Affix type	Base word	New word
Suffixes	thought	thoughtless, thoughtful
Derivational suffixes	week (noun)	weekly (adverb)
	assign (verb)	assignment (noun)
Prefixes	agree	disagree
	make	remake
Inflectional endings	walk	walks, walked, walking, walker
Plural	dog	dogs
	match	matches
Compound words	wheel	wheelbarrow
	barrow	

There are a variety of different affix types. Each is used differently to modify a base word to produce a new word with a new meaning. Table 1.1 shows some of the types of affixes.

By mastering the rules for forming new words from a base, speakers and writers are provided with a far wider range of choices for expressing themselves. For instance, by the application of morphological knowledge the word 'happy' provides access to the words 'happiness', 'unhappy', 'happily' and 'unhappily'.

Moreover, morphology comes into play to enable the listener (or reader) of a sentence to glean the **tense** that it employs; that is, whether the speaker or writer is talking about something that is presently happening or has previously happened. Tense is indicated by modification of the verb as shown in the following sentences.

> The car <u>travelled</u> up the hill.
>
> The car is <u>travelling</u> up the hill.

To some extent, children learn the syntax of a language naturally through the internalisation of rules. This happens when they are exposed multiple times to particular structures. It is therefore necessary for parents, teachers, and carers to use a variety of different sentence structures when speaking to young children.

A good way of exposing children to a variety of sentence structures is through children's literature. Books often feature language that it is not found in everyday interactions and conversations. Another means is through the use of nursery rhymes and songs.

In primary school, children's use of sentence structure gradually becomes more complex. This is demonstrated through their oral language as well as their writing.

THE SEMANTIC COMPONENT OF LANGUAGE

The **semantic** component of language is all about meaning. It refers to the meaning of individual words as well as the sentences which are constructed. The comprehension of spoken information requires an understanding of the meanings of words. However, this is only part of the picture. Words are put together in accordance with syntactic rules to form sentences which should themselves impart a clear meaning. Words may be given more precise meaning by their placement in a sentence. The sentence also indicates the relationship between the different words (for example, who did what to whom). It is important for comprehension that word order in a sentence conforms to the syntactic rules of the language.

Consider the sentence 'Jack followed the cat'. Its meaning is derived from knowing the meaning of the content words—'Jack', 'followed' and 'cat'—and from the way the words are ordered in the sentence (syntax), which indicates the relationship between Jack and the cat. A different word order, 'The cat followed Jack', provides a different meaning altogether while the meaning of 'Jack the cat followed' does not conform to the rules of English grammar (that is, it is syntactically incorrect) and is quite uncertain.

Words and their formations into sentences are important for the expression of precise, unambiguous meaning that meets the intent of the communicator. The words of a language are fundamental to the conveyance of meaning in communication. The entire collection of words that a person knows and understands is referred to as that person's vocabulary. Children start building their vocabulary quite soon after birth. They begin to comprehend the words of others after just a few months and soon (about nine to twelve months from birth) start producing words themselves. By two years of age, a child's vocabulary is typically in excess of 200 words and it develops rapidly thereafter. Three-year-olds have a vocabulary in the order of 1000 words and for five-year-olds it is well over 2000, although most children have an almost unlimited potential to increase their vocabulary. The majority of English language speakers are thought regularly to use only about 8 per cent of all the words that comprise the English language.

There are generally two categories of words in a language. The first is '**content**' **words**, which represent objects (cat, table), events (party, concert), actions (run, skip) and feelings (happy, delighted). Content words also include adjectives (blue, friendly, tall, round), adverbs (easily, slowly, carefully) and numbers. The meaning of a content word can be explained by describing its characteristics. For example, the word 'cat' can be described as a small fluffy animal.

The second category of words is '**function**' **words**. They are used in sentences to establish the relationships between content words in the sentence. They include pronouns (she, they, my, our), prepositions (of, to, in, for), conjunctions (and, but, so), articles (the, a, an) and interrogatives (who, which, where, what). Function words are far fewer in number than content words.

Words can be used to suggest the attitude or emotions of the speaker or writer. An insect can be described as being 'large' or as being 'hideously large'. Consider the meaning of the following sentences:

> Yesterday, while I was cleaning the house, I came across an extremely large insect.
>
> Yesterday, while I was cleaning the house, I came across a hideously large insect.

The inclusion of the word 'hideously' in the second sentence adds to the meaning of the information being communicated. It provides information about the event as well as the speaker's viewpoint on the insect.

Many of the content words of the English language have more than one meaning, which can only be determined when the words are used in sentences. To put it another way, the meaning of those words is derived from the meaning of the whole sentence. For instance, the word 'fast' can mean to go without food or to be quick. A precise meaning of the word 'fast' is easily gleaned from each of the following sentences.

> Jenny ran <u>fast</u> and won the race.
>
> During the <u>fast</u> Hassan ate only one meal a day.

Different words can have similar meanings. The words 'moist', 'watery', 'soppy', 'soggy', 'drenched' and 'wet' do, as do the words 'melancholy', 'sorrowful', 'unhappy', 'cheerless', 'desolate' and 'sad'. However, the meanings are not precisely the same. There are subtle shades of difference and the choice of an inappropriate word in a sentence may make the meaning ambiguous. For instance, the word 'damage' has a similar meaning to the word 'injure', but if it replaces it in a sentence the meaning becomes unclear. To say, 'I was injured when I tripped over', is clear enough. However, to say, 'I was damaged when I tripped over', does not convey such an obvious meaning.

The way in which a sentence is constructed may dramatically influence its meaning, even though it has basically the same words in it; the sentence structure influences what is seen as important to the information being portrayed. For example:

> A cat chased a mouse.
>
> A mouse was chased by a cat.
>
> It was a cat that chased a mouse.

The choice of appropriate words and sentence structures to express intended meaning is important for clear communication.

It is necessary for children to distinguish separate words in a stream of speech in order to understand them. It is therefore essential for young children to acquire an understanding of the pattern and rhythm of a particular language. For example, when we start to learn a foreign language, such as French, it is difficult for us to 'hear' the individual words unless the speaker makes allowances, such as speaking slowly and more clearly than usual. For very young children, it is difficult to hear individual words in speech. First, they need to understand that speech is separated into individual words. They also need to know that such things as words exist, and need a degree of familiarity with the syntax and rhythm of the language. At a very young age, children begin to realise that speech comprises a series of separate words. The fact that young children play with words and rhymes, and that they are able to use words in new contexts, can be taken as evidence of this (Lane, Pullen, Eisele & Jordan, 2002).

Vygotsky (1978) has pointed out that the realisation that everything has a name is an extremely important milestone in children's language development. After this realisation, it is usual for young children to show extreme interest when parents and teachers provide names for objects and actions.

THE PRAGMATIC COMPONENT OF LANGUAGE

In its everyday sense, '**pragmatic**' means to deal with something in a sensible or practical fashion rather than in a theoretical one. That general meaning is carried over when we refer to the pragmatic dimension of language because this deals with the way in which people use language in the various social and cultural contexts in which they find themselves. You could, perhaps, say that it is the practical use of language.

Competency with the pragmatic component of language requires ability to:

- use language for different communicative purposes (e.g. for greetings, making requests, issuing demands, providing information)

- adapt language to the needs of the listener and to the situation in which language is being used; for instance, additional information might be required when a listener is unfamiliar with the topic, informal language might be appropriate in a social situation with peers while more formal language might best be used in the classroom, or modified language might be employed when talking to a toddler
- employ social and cultural norms of behaviour in different talk situations. For example, the conventions for turn-taking during a conversation or for proximity to other speaker/s
- use of non-verbal communication such as facial gestures and eye contact.

An understanding of the pragmatic component of language is further developed in the following sections about the functional use of language and language register.

LANGUAGE IS FUNCTIONAL

There are a great many different purposes for which people use oral language in their daily lives. These purposes are referred to as the functions of language. Some of them are:

- relating personal or factual information
- offering opinions and advice
- developing and adapting ideas and values
- learning about the world
- entertaining others
- clarifying an idea
- describing an experience
- explaining a process
- influencing the actions of others
- maintaining relationships with others.

LANGUAGE FUNCTIONS

The use of language as a means of communication is integrated naturally into life experiences. It is employed so automatically in interaction with others that the various functions served may well be hard to identify. The case study below illustrates the ways in which language functions within life's daily experiences.

PETER'S STORY: IN THE MORNING

Peter is eight. He lives with his mum, dad and two sisters. Most mornings he starts his day early with his mum calling him to get out of bed and get ready for school. He is generally slow at doing so and his mum has to come and remind him a few times. On the third occasion Peter slowly hauls himself out of bed, has his shower and puts his clothes on ready for school. As he does so, he listens to the radio. It is tuned to his dad's favourite station and he listens to the announcer interview a sports commentator about the weekend football games and then, following this, a song. Peter's two older sisters are already showered and dressed. They are in the room next to his, talking about a birthday party they are going to after school. Finally Peter makes his way to the kitchen where his dad helps him to prepare his breakfast. They talk about what he might like for breakfast, considering the different options, before Peter finally settles on egg and toast. Peter and his dad prepare the breakfast. Peter's dad explains what to do and Peter listens carefully as he follows the instructions, asking for help when he needs it. At one stage, his dad warns him of the dangers of the grill and takes over. Peter eats his breakfast and chats with his dad and his two sisters, who have just arrived at the breakfast table. His mum soon joins them at the table and, as she does, she goes through the routine instructions that go with the school day and that generally involves lunch, school forms, sports uniforms, after-school activities and transport home from school. The calm of the breakfast table is interrupted with a bolt as dad, realising the time, fires off questions such as, 'Have you fed the cat?' He responds positively when he realises all the jobs have been done, and adds, 'Hurry up, we are going to be late!' The urgency is noted and the three children grab their things—bags, lunches, bus money—and scuttle out the front door. There is a bit of pushing and shoving and the occasional exclamation of annoyance from the siblings as they leave the house and make their way to the bus stop.

Peter's story illustrates the ever present nature of different **language functions** in the various events of a person's day. It indicates the role that language plays as a means for people to achieve different purposes of communication. Peter's day had just begun but already he had used oral language effectively in many different ways and for many different reasons. He used language to find out, to explain, to express an opinion and for other purposes. He communicated his own wants, thoughts and ideas. In short, he employed a range of different language functions.

The events in which Peter participated before school and the various language functions which were employed are shown in the table below.

Table 1.2: Case study: Events and language functions

Event	Language functions
Wakes up when mum calls him and tells him the time and urges him to get out of bed and get ready for school	Inform Announce Instruct
Listens to the radio announcer talking to a sports commentator about the weekend football games and to a song	Inform Entertain
Older sisters talk about a birthday party they are going to after school.	Socialise Converse Express feelings

Event	Language functions
Talks to dad about what he might like for breakfast. They discuss the different options.	Discuss Seek information Inform
Prepares breakfast with his dad's help. Listens as his dad explains what to do. Follows the instructions. Asks for help when he needs it. His dad warns him of the dangers of the grill and takes over.	Seek information Explain Describe Ask for help Advise
Eats his breakfast and chats with his dad and his two sisters.	Socialise Converse
His mum gives instructions that go with the school day and that generally involve lunch, school forms, sports uniforms, after-school activities and transport home from school.	Instruct Inform Persuade
His dad questions re activities to be done, 'Have you fed the cat?' Responds positively to children.	Seek information Inquire React Praise
Dad gets everyone off to school by exclaiming, 'Hurry up, we are going to be late!'	Direct Inform Instruct
Three children head off to bus stop. There is the occasional exclamation of annoyance from the siblings as they leave the house.	Express feelings

CATEGORIES OF LANGUAGE FUNCTIONS

Different language researchers have devised different systems for categorising language functions. Three such models are those of Halliday (1975), Wilkinson (1982) and Tough (1977). These models are relevant to the language development and learning needs of young children and are therefore useful guides for early childhood professionals in supporting children's growth in language use. They can be used to ensure variety, significance and purpose when planning language experiences within a childcare or classroom setting.

Michael Halliday's (1973, 1975) model focuses on the language use of very young children. He identifies seven distinct categories of language functions that are taken up as children initially acquire language. His model recognises the central role played by language in the development of children as social beings and sees the language growth of young children as being influenced by a need to use language for the range of purposes relevant to their lives. The functions that he identifies relate to the different ways in which language is used by children in their everyday experiences in the home and in the community. They can be summarised as follows:

- *The instrumental function*: use of language to satisfy a need or to get things done; to communicate preferences, choices, wants or needs.

- *The regulatory function*: use of language to control the behaviour of others.
- *The interactional function*: use of language to get along with others; to develop or maintain an activity.
- *The personal function*: use of language to express personal identity; to talk about self.
- *The heuristic function*: use of language to find out and to learn about things; to understand how and why the world works as it does.
- *The imaginative function*: use of language to pretend or to make believe; to create.
- *The informative function*: use of language to pass on or convey information to others; to explain or describe.

Another useful model for categorising language function is that provided by Wilkinson (Wilkinson, 1982, p. 56, cited in Riley, 2006, p. 13). The functions identified in this model are categorised under three questions: Who am I? Who are you? Who or what is he/she/it?

Table 1.3: Wilkinson's classroom language functions

Who am I?	Language use for the purpose of establishing and maintaining self
	Language use for the purpose of analysing self
	Language use for the purpose of expressing self
Who are you?	Language use for the purpose of establishing and maintaining relationships
	Language use for the purpose of cooperating with others
	Language use for the purpose of empathising with and understanding others
	Language use for the purpose of role playing and mimicry
	Language use for the purpose of guiding and directing others
	Language use for the purpose of giving information
Who or what is he/she/it?	Language use for the purpose of recalling past events
	Language use for the purpose of describing past events (present)
	Language use for the purpose of predicting future events
	Language use for the purpose of making statements of intention
	Language use for the purpose of hypothesis
	Language use for the purpose of predicting what might happen
	Language use for the purpose of analysing and classifying
	Language use for the purpose of explaining and giving reason for
	Language use for the purpose of exploring and asking questions
	Language use for the purpose of reflecting on own and others' thoughts and feelings

A model presented by Joan Tough (1976, 1979) comprises seven different functional categories that are significant to the learning of language by children. Tough's model can be used as a guide in assessing children's competency in the use of language for a variety of important social and learning purposes and in planning further experiences to expand children's use of language.

Table 1.4: Joan Tough's seven language functions

Language function	Description	Example
Self-maintaining	Children use language to satisfy their physical and psychological needs. Children use self-maintaining language to support or assert themselves in relation to others.	I am hungry. I feel sad. That's not good.
Directing	Children use language to control themselves or others. They might be directing the actions of other people or monitoring their own actions.	Don't do that! Go away! I am coming.
Reporting (on present and past experience)	Children use language to share experiences. They might label or describe detail or refer to a sequence of events. They can extract or recognise the central meaning of an experience.	Yesterday I went to the park and then I got an ice-cream. That's a cat. It has big whiskers.
Logical reasoning	Children use language to explain a process, recognise cause and effect relationships, recognise problems and solutions, justify judgments and actions, and draw conclusions after reflecting on an event.	First you have to fold the paper. Then cut triangles and then unfold it. I think it will sink because it is heavy.
Predicting	Children use language to anticipate and forecast events, anticipate possible sequences of events, anticipate possible problems and predict the consequence of actions or events.	I am having a birthday next week. We will need to give our pet some water or he will get thirsty.
Projecting	Children use language to empathise with someone or understand how someone is feeling, and to project into the feelings or reactions of others. They can project into a situation never experienced.	She must be sad that her cat ran away. If she does that, then mummy will be cross.
Imagining	Children use language to develop an imaginary situation based on real life or fantasy and to develop an original story.	One day there was a fairy and she could fly. I will be the policeman and I need to put you in jail.

A MODEL OF LISTENING AND FUNCTION

According to Brace et al. (2006), listening occurs in four types of situation, which can be shown as four distinct quadrants. In quadrant A, the type of listening is two-way and to do with interpersonal topics. Examples include chatting to friends in the playground or conversing with someone on the phone. Quadrant B relates to one-way talk about interpersonal topics. A recount of a personal experience such as a visit to the zoo would fall into this quadrant. Quadrant C talk is two-way and related to information-based topics. An example would be receiving directions about how to get somewhere or a conversation with the zoo keeper about looking after the animals. Quadrant D includes one-way information-based topics such as

Children need to learn to listen for interpersonal as well as informational purposes.

Table 1.5: Different types of listening

	Two-way listening	
Interpersonal (social) topics	**Quadrant A** • Taking part in a conversation in the playground • Chatting on the telephone to a friend • Talking to the teacher about the weekend	**Quadrant C** • The teacher giving instructions about a task • A phone call about the time and venue of a sleepover • Interviewing a friend about her likes and dislikes
	Quadrant B • Listening to someone give an account of an incident • Listening to the teacher telling a story • Listening to a friend telling a joke	**Quadrant D** • Listening to the television or the radio • Listening to a lecture or presentation
	One-way listening	**Informational topics**

Source: Brace et al. (2006)

watching a documentary on the television. Children need to learn how to speak and listen in each of the quadrants and to choose and use appropriate strategies for doing so.

LANGUAGE FUNCTIONS AND CHILDREN

Competent oral communication requires an ability to achieve desired language functions. The function is, of course, the purpose of the language; but the degree to which the purpose is achieved (that is, the effectiveness of the language) will depend on the way in which it is delivered. It will depend on the words used, the sentence structures, the intonation and stress, and so on. The effective achievement of communication purposes requires an innate knowledge of language and an ability to draw on that knowledge.

Young children, as they learn language, use it initially for a very limited range of functions. However, as their language development continues and as they experience a greater range of situations in which language is employed, they expand their ability with language to embrace additional functions. Teachers have a critical role in ensuring that children's language continues to grow. Children in care or pre-school and school settings should be provided with experiences which will extend their existing levels of language functionality.

Children require plenty of opportunity to exercise and develop their skills in the purposeful use of language. They should be assisted to appreciate what can be achieved by the effective use of language and should be given a variety of opportunities to use language in different social contexts to achieve different outcomes. Experiences should be rich in purposeful oral communication. The range of functions that children's language can serve should be continually expanded and the quality of language delivery should be cultivated. Conversations, socio-dramatic play, learning enquiries, games and news-telling are just some of a range of experiences that might be provided to allow children to develop their ability to use language for different purposes.

LANGUAGE REGISTER

When people adapt their language use for a particular context they are adopting what is referred to as a language register (Halliday, 1964). A **language register** is a form of language used for a particular purpose in a particular social setting; for instance, the formal language of the interview setting. Different situations call for the use of different language registers and competent oral communication requires being able to use a variety of language registers and being able to choose that which best fits the situation at hand. This necessitates a certain degree of social awareness, with the awareness determining the language register to be adopted.

Following are the five features of a situation that influence a person's choice of language register:

- *Purpose* (For what reason is communication taking place?)
  People communicate for various purposes. People use language socially (for instance, in greeting and exchanging pleasantries) and functionally (to explain, inform, enquire, instruct, persuade and so on).
- *People* (Who are the people involved?)
  People communicate with other people with whom they may have many differences: different relationships (close relations, friends or strangers), different social status, different levels of authority, different ages, different genders, different cultural or social backgrounds etc.
- *Location* (Where is the communication taking place?)
  People communicate in different surroundings; for example, the classroom, a restaurant, the boardroom or a family lounge room.
- *Activity* (What is the format of communication?)
  People communicate in various planned and unplanned ways; for example, through casual conversations or at lectures and debates.

- *Topic* (What is the subject of the communication?)
  People communicate about different topics, present, past and future, concrete or abstract; for example, a television cooking show, a party, holidays (the list is endless).

Each feature is a variable, and in each situation there is a wide range of possibilities for each variable.

Alternatively, Halliday (1964) classifies the three key features of a context that influence register as:

- *field* (the subject matter or content of the interaction)
- *tenor* (the people involved; their social status, relationships and communicative purposes)
- *mode* (the means of communication; for example, a formal speech, discussion or conversation).

Each situation makes its own communicative demands and a language register must be adopted by a speaker to meet those demands. They are generally adapted in terms of:

- the speaker's choice of words
- the tone (attitude) or intonations (rise and fall of voice) adopted by the speaker
- the speaker's pronunciation of certain words
- the speaker's use of syntax (sentence structures)
- the pace of the spoken words
- the speaker's patterns of interaction with the listeners (the degree to which he or she listens without interrupting, the length of pauses between responses etc.)
- the use of gestures and other non-verbal expressions.

The use of different language registers for different situations may not only be directed towards effective communications; it may also be predicated on the need to observe accepted social norms. Thus, it may be important to know the usual social norms relating to:

- initiating and sustaining conversation
- taking turns
- interrupting someone
- changing subjects
- ending a conversation.

Oral language competency involves an ability to switch language registers to meet the particular demands of the situation in which communication takes place. This requires a certain degree of social awareness, a consciousness of the various features of the situation and knowledge of the way in which the situation dictates the language register which should be adopted. Emmitt, Komesaroff and Pollock (2006, pp. 66–7) emphasise the importance of register to effective communication:

> Individuals normally possess a number of codes or registers, which are used in different situations. Generally, we can switch from one register to another, and some can switch from one dialect to another. For effective communication, it would appear important that an individual possesses a number of registers and be able to use them appropriately.

Young children should be exposed to different speaking situations; the wider the range of situations, the greater the opportuniy to develop an understanding of the language register to be used within each of them. Excursions into the community provide one type of opportuntiy. Children begin to experiement with language register as they take on different roles and act out different scenarios in their socio-dramatic play. Their language demonstrates differences in sentence structure, vocabulary and phonolgical features for the different roles of their socio-dramatic play (Makin, Campbell & Jones Diaz, 1995, p. 25).

LANGUAGE AND CULTURE

Children learn language as a member of a social and cultural community.

Australia is culturally diverse and early childhood professionals will undoubtedly work with children from a range of different cultural backgrounds. This requires getting to know the families of the children and developing an understanding of their cultural backgrounds and home and community communication practices and values.

Culture refers to the 'way of life of a particular group of people' (Kidd, 2002, p. 5). It involves a group's values, beliefs and norms of behaviour and encompasses practices around celebrations, food and meal times, child rearing, recreation, gender and family member roles, religion, music, pastimes and so on. It also includes a group's language and communication practices.

Language use—where, when and how to use it—is prescribed by the values and beliefs of a culture (Diaz-Rico & Weed, 2006, p. 280). Some communication practices will be common to many or all cultures while others may be unique to a particular culture or cultures.

Children learn language as a member of a social and cultural community as they observe, participate in and experience their social and cultural environment. Their language, values and social practices are shaped by the people and experiences of their family and community. Learning language involves learning distinctive ways in which to use it; ways that reflect the values and beliefs of the culture of the family and community groups. For instance:

- ways in which to begin a conversation
- the rules for turn-taking

- acceptable times and ways to interrupt
- the appropriate expression of disagreement or apology
- when respectful language is required, assertive language is acceptable and formal language is necessary.

Learning language entails learning how to communicate within the norms of the cultural group. This includes non-verbal communication practices such as hand gestures, facial expression, body stance and eye contact.

The way in which people communicate reflects the norms and values of the cultural group to which they belong. It is an expression of their identity; of their membership of a particular culture group.

LANGUAGE VARIATIONS

Variations in language can occur among people who speak the same language. Any one language (such as English) is not used in an identical way by all its speakers. There can be considerable difference in the way it is spoken among different groups.

DIALECT

A language **dialect** is a variety of a language that is distinctive to a particular group of people. It can be a regional or a social dialect. A regional dialect is a type of language used by people living in a particular geographical area whereas a social dialect is a type of language used by people with certain social characteristics. Different language dialects or types of language can also be used by people of a certain age, of a particular gender or from a distinct cultural group.

The various dialects of a particular language have many common characteristics; however, each has its own distinctive vocabulary, grammar and pronunciation as well as a legitimate rule system. No one dialect is more valid than any other; each operates to meet the oral communication requirements of the community in which it is used (Owens, 2005, p. 400).

STANDARD ENGLISH

Standard English is simply a variety or dialect of English spoken by the people in a country where English is a first language. It is generally regarded as the 'standard' language because it is the variety that is spoken by the majority of people or those people with the most social power, and is used in most of the country's major social and political domains. It is most likely to be the language of educational and political systems, of commerce and of business and the media.

The standard variety of a language is assigned a special status in the country in which it is spoken as a first language. It is usually the most socially valued variety and accepted as the most appropriate for formal situations and educational purposes. It is commonly the language of the socially and economically advantaged in society and those with prestige and power. It is important that children be taught, and that they use, Standard Australian English, as competency will provide them with access to the important domains of the community and, accordingly, to a wide range of life opportunities.

> **DID YOU KNOW?**
>
> Before the fifteenth century, there was no such thing as a Standard English. There was only a range of social and regional variations of the language. The variety of English which came to be the standard of the English language is linked to the rise in power and prestige of a particular social group within a certain region in England. Their language dialect came to be accepted by people in positions of power while other dialects were not. Its use became more widespread and eventually came to be associated with the important and influential institutions of government, administration, law, religion, education and similar.

ABORIGINAL ENGLISH

Aboriginal English is the name given to the various forms of English spoken by Aboriginal (Indigenous) people throughout Australia. Technically, these language varieties are dialects of English. They have much in common with other varieties of Australian English, but there are distinctive features of accent, grammar, words and meanings, as well as language use. The features of Aboriginal English often reflect features of traditional Aboriginal languages.

Aboriginal English is spoken throughout Australia. It is a social dialect in that its speakers are not determined by region but by membership of a particular social group. However, people in different regions of Australia might speak different varieties of Aboriginal English (Department of Education, Western Australia, 2002, p. 90).

Some of the distinctive features of Aboriginal English include:

- *Economy of words*: less words than Standard English but expressing the same meaning.
- *Listener responsibility*: the listener is largely responsible for working out the meaning.
- *Significance of family relations/kinship*: who is being spoken to is of significant influence to what is talked about and how.
- *Absence of direct questioning*: direct questions are not generally asked; language is used differently to seek information.
- *Value of silence*: silence is considered to hold meaning; people talking will wait for each other to speak, knowing they will speak when they are ready to share information.
- *People speaking at once*: it is appropriate for many people to speak at the same time in a conversation.
- *Manners or social niceties*: these are expressed through facial expression and gesture rather than through words such as please and thank you.

Source: Department of Education, WA (2002, pp. 25–7)

> **CONDUCTIVE HEARING LOSS**
>
> ### What is it?
>
> Otitis media is an inflammation of the middle ear that results in intermittent hearing loss. The effects vary from one day to the next so affected children will be able to hear one day but the next day their hearing might be poor.

Who has it?

Approximately 50 per cent of Aboriginal and Torres Strait Islander school children suffer from otitis media and hearing loss. Many other children suffer from this occasionally; for example, when they have a bad cold that results in an ear infection.

How does it impact on literacy learning?

Otitis media and the resultant hearing loss means that children miss out on a lot of what is being said. This impacts on their vocabulary learning and their phonological awareness as well as their ability to comprehend instructions, and therefore their ability to carry out assigned classroom work.

Strategies for teachers:

- Project your voice and face the children. Let affected children have a good view of your facial expressions and lips.
- Stand still so that children can focus on you and see you properly.
- Make sure the class is quiet before giving instructions. Get rid of background noise such as music.
- Make sure you have children's full attention before you give explanations or instructions. Repeat important information and key elements and check children's understanding—ask them to repeat the main points back to you.
- Provide visual cues such as pictures and diagrams.
- Pair children with a buddy who can help them by repeating instructions to them etc.
- Talk to children about hearing loss. Suggest strategies to them, such as friend, keeping the noise down, facing the person who is speaking, and asking questions to clarify information not heard properly.
- Provide explicit phonological awareness teaching.
- Seat children with hearing loss at the front of the class where they have the best chance of seeing and hearing you speak.
- Consider using a sound field amplification system.

Source: Callahan (n.d., pp. 14–15)

BILINGUALISM

Bilingualism is an ability to speak two languages (the term '**multilingualism**' refers to an ability to speak three or more languages). **Bilingualism** might result from growing up in a bilingual home where two languages are spoken and learnt. It might also be that one language (or more) is learnt in the home and an additional language such as English is subsequently learnt at childcare or school. An individual or an entire speech community can be considered bilingual (Trask & Stockwell, 2007).

An individual might also speak two different dialects of a particular language, often his or her own social or regional dialect as well as the standard language. This is referred to as '**bidialectalism**' (Trask & Stockwell, 2007).

People who speak two or more languages with comparable fluency will often use them for different purposes, though their ease in doing so is likely to be influenced by the attitude of the society in which they live. They will switch between languages depending on the appropriateness of the language to the speaking situation. Sometimes words are mixed from the two languages in one sentence. This can occur when children are still learning their second language or when there is no equivalent way to express a concept in the other language.

CODE SWITCHING

Code switching is a highly sophisticated and practical skill that involves changing from the use of one language to the use of another. In order to code switch effectively, children require the ability to recognise the language most appropriate for a speaking situation and have the linguistic repertoire to switch accordingly (Department of Education, Western Australia, 1999, pp. 13, 52).

For children whose home and community language is Aboriginal English or another language or dialect of English, and for whom Standard English is an additional language, the ability to code switch is important to their being able to move between different cultural or social situations.

Berry (1997) identifies four steps for competency in code switching:

- *Awareness*: recognition of the difference between Standard English and the home language or dialect and accepting that both are valid ways of speaking.
- *Separation*: understanding the difference between the two and developing competency in both.
- *Recognition and use*: the ability to recognise when code switching is appropriate and to practise it in real life situations. It requires a certain degree of proficiency in Standard English and in the practice of switching languages to suit different situations.
- *Control*: the ability to switch self-consciously between the two languages/dialects for different speaking situations.

LANGUAGE DIVERSITY AND EARLY CHILDHOOD SETTINGS

Australian society comprises people who speak different languages as well as various dialects of English. The official language is Standard Australian English (SAE). However, a vast number of the approximate twenty-two million people living in Australia have an alternative home language or English dialect. Their home language might be an Australian Indigenous language or one of many different languages from Europe, Asia and Africa.

This has significant implications for early childhood professionals whose choice of practices can influence the confidence, sense of pride and strength of personal identity for many children. Early childhood professionals should display respect for differences including different cultural, language and dialect backgrounds. Children should have the opportunity to use their first language, and a variety of rich social contexts should be provided involving genuine communication and adequate support for children to learn Standard Australian

English. The following childcare and education practices (Early Childhood Australia, 2009) are important to the personal and language development of all children:

- Give special recognition and acknowledgment to Aboriginal people as the descendents of Australia's original habitants and support the awareness, acceptance and understanding of Aboriginal culture, heritage, language and identities.
- Acknowledge the cultural identity of families and communities and children's language and communication styles.
- Devise learning programs that represent the diversity of cultures in the broader community and extend children's knowledge of their own culture as well as of other cultures.
- Plan services and learning programs through ongoing discussions with families and community members; ensure programs reflect the diversity of the community and that they generally value diversity.
- Promote children's use of their first or home language or dialect; acknowledge its critical role in the general language and cognitive development of children.
- Provide the appropriate resources, materials and speakers of a language/dialect to support maintenance and development of children's home language/s.
- Provide the opportunities and the resources, materials and people for children to learn Standard Australian English.

Source: Early Childhood Australia (n.d.)

Teachers need to build an awareness of how cultural, social and economic differences can impact upon how children speak, listen and make meaning. If teachers are to encourage children to build on their strengths, it is necessary to understand the 'funds of knowledge' (Moll, Amanti, Niff & Gonzales, 1992) or different ways of knowing and doing things that children bring from the home. For example, eye contact is important in most English-speaking cultures but children from other cultures may feel a sense of discomfort if asked to display such behaviour. Some cultures think it is rude to ask direct questions so will instead make oblique enquiries and sometimes, as in some Aboriginal groups, it is not compulsory to respond to questions or other statements.

A BRIEF HISTORY OF THE ENGLISH LANGUAGE

Although the Latin-speaking Romans, led by Julius Caesar, conquered the Celtic tribes in Britain about 50BC, Latin did not thereupon become the foundation of the English language. While the Romans continued with Latin, the Celts retained their Celtic language.

The English language had its genesis when three Germanic tribes, Angles, Saxons and Jutes, ousted the Romans in the fifth century. *Old English*, as it is known, developed from the various Germanic dialects introduced by these invaders. Old English, although the base on which modern English was built, would be understood by only very few present-day English speakers.

Old English developed into four major dialects: Northumbrian spoken in the north of England, Mercian in the Midlands, West Saxon in the south and west, and Kentish in the southeast.

The Viking invasion in the ninth century resulted in Old English coming under the influence of the Norse language, which itself was similar to Old English. Many unique Norse words were incorporated into Old English, which also retained a good sprinkling of Celtic and some Latin words.

The next major influence on the language spoken in Britain occurred when the Norman army from France, which was led by William the Conqueror, defeated the English in 1066 at the Battle of Hastings. This victory was followed by many modifications to life in England. French became the predominant language of the aristocracy. Old English continued to be spoken by the general community but the language gradually incorporated many French expressions.

The French influence continued until the fourteenth century when it was again subsumed by English on King Henry IV ascending to the throne. He was the first king since the Norman conquest who spoke English as his mother tongue. So-called *Middle English* came into vogue from that time. Different dialects were still spoken throughout the country but the London dialect became the general standard. Middle English was still far removed from modern English but is more recognisable to present-day English speakers than Old English.

The sixteenth century Renaissance era marked the next surge in the development of English. Influenced by classical learning and other cultural pursuits, *Modern English* gradually developed. A great many words were added to the English vocabulary; Shakespeare himself is credited with adding around 2000 words and expressions to the English language.

Present-day modern English can be traced to the early nineteenth century. Since then the language has grown enormously through the introduction of words from English-speaking countries outside Britain; that is, from America, Australia, African countries and so on. Moreover, the ease with which people now travel around the world, as well as the huge increase in migration, have had a profound effect on the expansion of the English language.

SUMMARY

Language is used for written and spoken communication. As a system of communication it has many significant properties and components, and understanding these is important to knowing what is involved in children acquiring and developing language. Oral language is used in different ways depending on the communicative purpose and the features of the context in which oral communication is taking place. Children require many opportunities to use language for different speaking and listening purposes and in different contexts. Standard Australian English is the variety of English identified as the official language of Australian society and it is important that children develop competency in Standard Australian English. However, for many children, other varieties of English and languages other than English are first languages, and the languages spoken at home. Children's sense of self and their engagement in all aspects of their life require that their home languages are acknowledged, and that they are a valued feature of the teaching and learning environment.

QUESTIONS AND ACTIVITIES

1. Work with a group to write a definition of language that includes all important features. When you have finished, swap your definition with that of another group and discuss similarities and differences.
2. Observe children using language in different situations in a childcare, pre-school or school context. Determine and reflect upon the use of different language functions.
3. Choose a story book that is appropriate to read to a group of young pre-school children and, using Tough's model of language functions, plan questions that you might ask the children as you read the story. Make sure the questions provide them with the opportunity to use language for a range of functions.
4. Observe children during socio-dramatic play and make notes about the roles they adopt and their use of language, with specific focus on the way they adopt suitable language registers.
5. Conduct research to find out about the variety of languages spoken by Australian people as well as by people specific to the state and region in which you live.
6. Consider the ways in which a learning environment might be established so that it reflects a valuing of different cultures and languages.
7. Determine some appropriate ways in which you can find out about children's home and community language.
8. In what ways might children for whom English is a second or additional language need extra support with using language for different purposes?

KEY TERMS

Aboriginal English
affix
base word
bidialectalism
bilingualism
content words
code-switching
culture
dialect
expressive language
function words
intonation
language function

language register
morphology
multilingualism
phonemes
phonological
pragmatic
receptive language
semantic
Standard English
stress
syntactic
tense

KEY REFERENCES

Anstey, M. & Bull, G. (2004). *The literacy labyrinth*. Frenchs Forest: Pearson Education.
Anstey, M. & Bull, G. (2005). *The literacy landscape*. Frenchs Forest: Pearson Education.
Diaz-Rico, L.T. & Weed, K. Z. (2006). *The cross cultural language and academic development handbook: A complete K–12 reference guide*. Boston: Pearson Education.

Emmitt, M., Komesaroff, L. & Pollock. (2006). *Language and learning: An introduction for teaching*. Melbourne: Oxford University Press.

Gleason, J. B. (2005). *The development of language*. Boston: Pearson Education.

Halliday, M. A. K. (1973). *Explorations in the function of language*. London: Edward Arnold.

Halliday, M. A. K. (1975). *Learning how to mean: Explorations in the development of language*. London: Edward Arnold.

Harrison, N. (2008). *Teaching and learning in indigenous education*. South Melbourne: Oxford University Press.

Ogle, D. & Beers, J. W. (2009). *Engaging the language arts: Exploring the power of language*. Boston: Pearson Education.

Owens, R. E. (2005). *Language development: An introduction*. Boston: Pearson Education.

Trask, R. L. & Stockwell, P. (eds) (2007). *Language and linguistics: The key concepts*. Abingdon, Oxon: Routledge.

CHAPTER 2

Theories and Phases of Oral Language Development

CHAPTER OBJECTIVES

This chapter will increase your understanding of:

- the major theoretical perspectives for children's language development and learning
- how different theories can explain and inform children's oral language development
- identifiable phases of early childhood language learning and development

In this chapter you are introduced to a range of language acquisition and language learning theories, each of which has an influence on your understanding of children's language growth and how best to nurture it. The chapter also provides an overview of the phases through which children are likely to progress as they develop into competent language users—each phase indicating knowledge, skill and behaviour milestones achieved. An understanding of developmental phases is useful for the design of learning environments and programs that align with children's present knowledge and abilities, and supports their further learning and development. However, it is necessary to keep in mind that, although it is useful to consider learning and development in terms of phases, each child's language growth is different and is influenced by factors beyond chronological age (Owens, 2005).

THEORETICAL PERSPECTIVES OF LANGUAGE DEVELOPMENT

For the past century or so, several theoretical perspectives have influenced educators' thinking about how language develops and what kinds of practices parents and educators should adopt to foster children's language acquisition, development and learning. In this chapter, six main perspectives of language learning, as listed below, are described and critiqued.

- behaviourist
- nativist
- maturational
- cognitive developmental
- interactionist
- neurobiological.

Language learning requires an environment that is rich in experience.

BEHAVIOURIST PERSPECTIVE

According to the behaviourist perspective, learning is very much shaped by the environment and by personal experience; thus, nurture rather than nature plays the dominant role in language learning. Those who say that 'nature' plays the main role in children's language learning believe that a person's genetic make-up determines the learning. Others believe that the environment and personal experience (nurture) play the greatest role in learning or acquisition of language. In reality, there is complex interplay between nature and nurture, and the simplistic nature–nurture debate is outdated (Christie, 2005). The behaviourist perspective, which was predominant for much of the first half of the twentieth century, posits that people learn largely by receiving rewards for behaviours they exhibit. According to this perspective, language is learnt by means of imitation, practice, feedback or reinforcement of accomplishments (Hulit & Howard, 2006, p. 19; Lightbown & Spada, 1993, p. 9). Central to this perspective is the role of the environment: language learning requires an environment that is rich in experience and language, and that provides much-needed models of language that children imitate and with which they can experiment. It also requires consistent reinforcement (for example, praise from others or successful communication by the child) to ensure that certain behaviours (language) are repeated and that further imitation and practice occurs.

Imitative behaviour requires that children pay attention to, and copy, adult 'models' or examples of behaviour. Adult modelling may be deliberate or unintended. The idea that parents and teachers should provide models of language is still prevalent in education, and many recommended practices involve the provision of models from which children can learn.

Behaviourists claim that **operant conditioning** (Skinner, 1957) accounts for children's expressive (spoken) language learning. This involves children imitating, or experimenting with, the sounds and patterns that they hear and receiving positive reinforcement by parents, siblings and others around them for doing so (Lightbown & Spada, 1993, p. 9). Reinforcement might be attention, praise or positive body language, or it might simply be successful communication—for instance, when infants receive whatever it was they were attempting to ask for. For example, an infant might say, 'Da-da-da!', and be hugged and kissed and rewarded with, 'Yes, Daddy is here!' If children's behaviour is ignored (not positively reinforced) or even punished, it eventually ceases. Young children soon learn if they are rewarded when they imitate adult speech and behaviour. This increases imitative behaviour, which leads to yet more language learning.

According to the behaviourist perspective, children learn to understand language (receptive language) through of **classical conditioning**. The idea is that children learn to associate objects or actions with words because their environment provides them with the repeated opportunity to hear words while at the same time seeing the objects and actions to which they are linked. For example, a child will come to know what *milk* is if it is named each time it is offered. For example, 'Here's your milk. Are you ready for some milk?'

Criticisms of the behaviourist perspective include:

- It does not adequately account for the rapid rate at which children learn language. The opportunities for imitation and reinforcement are not great enough. The performance displayed by children 'far exceeds the input of the adults in the environment' (Campbell & Baker, 2003, p. 41).
- People's ability to understand language does not account for the many words, phrases and sentences that are quite ambiguous and that can have more than one meaning (e.g. Emmitt et al., 2006).
- Another area unsatisfactorily explained by behaviourists is the exact role of reward. Is reward entirely necessary for language growth?
- Finally, speaking and listening are closely interrelated but the behaviourist perspective implies that they are learnt by two different processes (operant and classical conditioning), which is unlikely to be the case.

NATIVIST PERSPECTIVE

According to the nativist perspective, language learning is a biological phenomenon and the role played by the environment and other people is minimal. In other words, *nature* as opposed to nurture largely accounts for its development. Chomsky (1975), a major contributor to the nativist theory of language learning, asserted that the human brain is structured to learn and use language and this is illustrated by its almost astonishing capacity to create and understand syntactic systems, or grammatical rules. Chomsky called this brain capacity a **language acquisition device** (LAD). Because of the LAD, language learning is said by nativists to be essentially different from other kinds of learning. For evidence, nativists have cited the fact that children are adept at generating rules of grammar. The fact that they often 'overgeneralise' grammatical rules is one expression of this. For example, when a child says, 'The dog swimmed', he or she is generating or transferring rules, albeit not appropriately, because of the irregularity of the verb 'to swim'. Another example of children generating rules of grammar is the Nicaraguan deaf children who invented their own sign language because their carers did not know sign language (Senghas & Coppola, 2001, cited in Arshavsky, 2009). The sign language they invented became a full-bodied language with its own grammatical rules.

Chomsky proposed that children are born with the ability to generate grammar, thanks to a **universal grammar** (Chomsky, 1982), which is a set of principles that underlie all languages. He discussed the fact that all children are born with the capacity to learn any language, and that language has a 'deep structure' as well as a 'surface structure'. The deep structure roughly equates to the meaning, while the surface structure is to do with the words and sentences used to convey the deep structure.

Nativists have used the following arguments to support their theory:

- Children learn their native language at a time when such a complex level of learning is not normally expected.
- Imitation and habit formation (behaviourist theory) alone cannot adequately account for the fact that children acquire language quite early and at a fairly rapid rate.
- The language models to which young children are exposed are often more complex and varied than the language that they themselves generate; young children create sentences that they have never heard others use.
- Children show that they are generating their own system of rules when they overgeneralise grammatical rues (e.g. 'I runned away').
- Despite the often quite different environments in which children grow up, most still achieve mastery of the grammatical structures of a language.

A significant assumption of the nativist view of language acquisition is that people's capacity to learn their native language does not continue indefinitely but that there is a critical time in which a person's brain is predisposed for optimal success with language learning. While the exact time at which the critical period ends is not known, it is thought to be around puberty; though there is some argument that it may be even earlier than this.

A major criticism of the nativist perspective is that it does not adequately take into account environmental and social influences or the role of other people in children's language development. If educators adhered strictly to this perspective, it would not be necessary to teach language because children would instinctively learn all they needed to know.

MATURATIONAL PERSPECTIVE

Maturationists have contributed to the debate on how language is learnt by proposing that biological **readiness** is the key to effective learning. According to this view, language develops or unfolds in a predetermined fashion, according to the child's 'inner clock' (Jalongo, 2007, p. 66). The inner clocks of individual children may vary somewhat. Jean-Jacques Rousseau was an influential eighteenth-century theorist who advocated the idea of allowing children to grow naturally, with minimal interference. In early childhood educational contexts, many current practices have their roots in the maturational perspective. When educators speak of developmental phases and developmentally appropriate practice, they are using ideas from maturational perspectives.

This perspective can be criticised because it tends to under-emphasise the role of social input. It also implies that there is a universal developmental pathway that all children will follow, and clearly this is not the case; for example, in the case of children from diverse linguistic and cultural backgrounds. Also, this perspective has led to some questionable practices that have attempted to accelerate 'readiness' so that teaching can commence.

COGNITIVE DEVELOPMENTAL PERSPECTIVE

Another influential perspective has grown from the writing of Jean Piaget, who did a great deal of work on cognitive development in children. The cognitive developmental perspective posits that language development occurs in tandem with cognitive development, and is developed through activity. That is, children *construct* their own understandings through interaction with their environment and participation in experiences, and both the environment and heredity play a part in language development. Unlike the nativist perspective, the cognitive development perspective does not propose that language learning is essentially different from any other type of learning; there is no special language-acquisition device or special innate ability.

This theory is discussed in greater detail in Chapter 6, which focuses on language, thinking and learning. However, it is useful at this stage to understand the stages of cognitive (and language development) proposed by Piaget.

Piaget proposed several stages of cognitive development, the first of which is the *sensorimotor stage*, which involves young children finding out about the world through their senses and movements. It is only once babies realise that there is permanency in the world, and that objects and people exist (even when they are out of sight), that they can begin to attach names to objects or are able to use symbols. Language is a symbolic system and children cannot begin to attach symbols to referents (objects and actions that are represented by the symbols) until they have a sense of what the objects and actions are. Thus, according to Piaget, it is not possible for children to learn language until they have almost passed through this phase.

The second phase of cognitive development, according to Piaget, is the *pre-operational stage*, which usually occurs in children aged between two and seven years. During this phase, children are thought to be fairly egocentric and unable to think on an abstract level. This limits their ability to speak about abstract concepts and to comprehend talk that is removed from the concrete here and now.

The next stage, the *concrete operational stage*, generally spans the ages of seven to eleven or twelve. Here, children begin to think logically (inductive logic) but still have difficulty with abstract concepts or hypothetical 'what if' situations. Inductive logic involves making generalisations from specific examples given. During this stage of cognitive development, children learn much about morphology, syntax, semantics and pragmatics of language.

INTERACTIONIST PERSPECTIVE

The interactionist perspective emphasises social interactions between children and the significant people in their environment as being the key to language learning and development. The focus on communicative intent is important to these interactions; that is, there is a purpose and a desire to put across meaning. Young children who are not yet able to produce words or language forms will apply communicative intent to their interactions with people; for example, a very young child who wants a drink might indicate this by making eye contact with a parent, pointing to the fridge and vocalising an utterance such as 'mi … mi'. Language acquisition is assisted when the parent responds by providing a language model appropriate to the child's communicative objective. In the example provided, the parent might respond by saying, 'You want some milk? Mummy will get you some milk.'

Bruner has proposed that a **language acquisition support system** (LASS) assists children to learn language. By this, Bruner meant to highlight the importance of social interaction in the development of language. For social interactionists, **scaffolding** and support from competent language users is the key driver of language development, and not merely innate cognitive 'wiring' (LAD) as proposed by nativists. 'Scaffolding' involves an adult providing support and guidance to enable a child to achieve something that would be slightly too difficult if he or she tried to do it independently. The notion of providing scaffolding or support, so that a child can achieve at a higher level than he or she would have been able to manage without help, is important.

This perspective integrates and expands ideas from the perspectives already discussed:

- It acknowledges the importance of the environment in that it purports that children learn language as a result of communicative needs, in social contexts, and with social support.
- It acknowledges the role of the human mind; of children's predisposition to learn language easily.
- It proposes that the LAD and the LASS work together in the language development process.

An important feature of child–caregiver interactions is the caregiver's use of *child directed speech*; that is, the ways in which they adjust their language to suit the capabilities of young learners and to make it easier for them to understand (Lightbown & Spada, 2003, p. 22). This generally involves the use of:

- short simple sentences
- substantial pauses
- repetition of the language models provided
- a somewhat higher pitch than usual
- exaggerated intonation patterns
- emphasis on key (meaning words) in a sentence.

According to interactionists, the support provided by caregivers is fundamental to children's language development. In speaking with children, caregivers generally use language that is just beyond that which children could produce on their own. In so doing, they provide the language models which serve to expand the form and meaning of the language children already know and use. Over time, and as children's use of language expands, carers continue to modify their language use. Because language development is seen to develop within social contexts, the *role of play* is highlighted in this context. Through play, children find opportunities to experiment with language and to take on different roles, especially in the context of socio-dramatic play.

The interactionist framework gives some credence to the part biological factors play in children's language development. Such factors as the innate human capacity for language acquisition, as well as maturation and cognitive ability, are viewed as having some influence on children's language development. However, interactionist theory holds that such factors are not as great an influence as the social interactions between children and the people in their lives.

NEUROBIOLOGICAL PERSPECTIVE

Since the beginning of the 1990s, new brain imaging techniques such as fMRI (functional magnetic resonance imaging) and PET (positron emission tomography) have enabled scientists to study the brain and its workings during certain cognitive activities, such as listening and reading. Neurobiologists have determined that the capacity to learn language can be attributed to the structure of the brain. There are, in fact, specialised areas of the brain that are devoted to hearing, speaking and understanding language. The findings of neurobiologists have supported elements of behaviourist, nativist and social interactionist

Table 2.1: Summary: Theoretical perspectives of language development

Behaviourist	• Language is a learnt behaviour
	• Learning is dependent on reinforcement or reward for behaviour
	• The environment, experiences and reinforcement from caregivers is significant
Nativist	• Language learning is different from other kinds of learning
	• It is an innate ability of all humans
Maturationist	• Language unfolds or develops naturally according to an 'inner clock'
	• Adults should interfere with this process as little as possible
Cognitive development	• Language development and general cognitive development occur together
	• Much is determined by the child's stage of cognitive development
Interactionist	• Social interaction, especially interaction with a high level of support to the child, is highly important for language learning
	• Social interaction can speed up cognitive development and language learning
Neurobiological	• The brain is naturally structured for language learning (as shown by brain scans)
	• Brain development is influenced by the environment and social interaction

views of language learning: that the brain is 'hard wired' to learn language, but effective language learning also depends to a substantial degree on social interaction and occurs within communicative contexts. Without quality language input or social interaction with parents or caregivers, babies' neural networks do not develop effectively to enable fluent language use. In other words, connections between brain cells are only made when children are exposed to, and engaged in, language use.

It must be noted that there has been considerable debate about the different theories of language development. It is important to remember that language is complex and its 'development defies any simplistic description' (Fleer & Raban, 2007, p. 27).

PHASES AND MILESTONES OF ORAL LANGUAGE DEVELOPMENT

The notion of language development phases implies that there is a common developmental pathway that all children will follow. However, while phases of development and characteristic language knowledge and abilities can be identified, language learning and development is not identical for all children. There are considerable variations in the way children progress to become competent with oral language; the 'inner clocks' will vary from child to child and there are also environmental factors that influence their language growth. Some children will sometimes seem to 'go backwards' in some areas as they experiment with language.

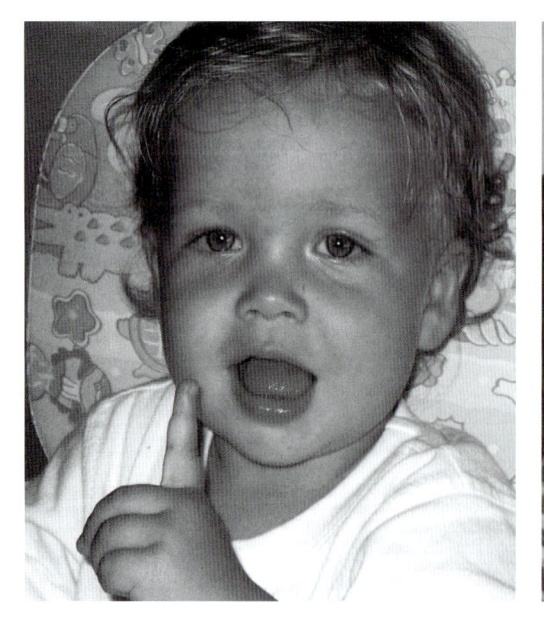

While there is a common developmental pathway, language learning and development is not identical for all children.

The chart below provides an overview of phases of language development and of the typical competencies of each phase. These phases provide teachers with a useful framework for planning and assessment. However, it must be re-emphasised that these are guidelines only, and there will be variations for many children, especially those for whom English is a second or additional language.

Table 2.2: Newborns

Receptive language	Expressive language
Newborns listen to the sounds around them and are soon able to distinguish language sounds from other sounds. They 'startle' at unexpected noises and they respond to new sounds by becoming very still. In order to develop effectively as listeners, babies need to be in environments where they can hear a variety of sounds. They need to be spoken to a great deal by parents and caregivers.	Newborn babies make a range of noises, some of which indicate whether they are experiencing pain or pleasure. Communication with others may not be intentional.

Table 2.3: Up to three months

Receptive language	Expressive language
Very young babies (two to three months) turn towards the source of a voice and smile at speakers. They seem to enjoy listening to familiar voices such as the mother's and father's, especially if comforting tones are used. They quieten and pay particular attention to new voices. Babies may pay more attention to 'parentese' or 'baby talk' (previously known as 'motherese'), where adults speak in an exaggerated way, using simplified language and a high-pitched voice that is somewhat slower and more repetitive than normal speech.	Babies in this age group smile at familiar people when they see them, and smile and gurgle when spoken to. They develop different ways of crying for different purposes, which parents can often 'read'.

Table 2.4: Four to six months

Receptive language	Expressive language
Infants of this age begin to respond to the word, 'No!', although it is not known whether they recognise the intonation or the word. Infants respond to the tone of a speaker's voice. Environmental sounds begin to become interesting, and infants in this age group begin to enjoy toys that make noises, music, and other everyday sounds.	Infants at this age become verbally responsive to the language they hear. They begin to experiment with the sounds that they can make with their mouth and voice, and to mimic speakers. Listening and speaking become intertwined. Babbling becomes very prominent in this age range and infants begin to use the lips to make sounds. They use various sounds in an attempt to communicate.

Table 2.5: Seven to twelve months

Receptive language	Expressive language
Infants in this age group become responsive when spoken to, and pay attention when called by name. Games like 'peek-a-boo' engage them. Infants recognise the names of common objects and will sometimes respond (by looking, pointing or touching) to simple requests such as, 'Where's the doggie?', or 'Give me the doll.' They respond to simple questions, such as, 'More?' Babies in this age group usually have a receptive vocabulary of a few words.	Infants of this age begin to take on conventions of listening and speaking, such as turn-taking and eye contact and, by approximately nine months, they begin to understand and use goal-oriented language and body language, such as indicating that they want more food, or to be picked up. Babies' babbling becomes more complex, and includes more consonants as well as long and short vowels. The first words have, by now, been uttered. They are often words such as 'Mama' or 'Dad-da'.

Table 2.6: One to two years

Receptive language	Expressive language
From twelve months of age to eighteen months, toddlers' oral language capabilities grow very rapidly. They continue to learn conventions, such as turn-taking and looking at the person who is speaking. As well, their comprehension of words and syntactic structures increases dramatically. Indicators of these understandings are children's ability to point to pictures in books when they are named. Children in this age group can also respond to simple commands such as 'Roll the ball.' They enjoy stories and rhymes and will enjoy the repetition of favourites.	Young children in this age group learn many more single words and begin to speak in 'telegraphic' sentences of two words, and sometimes three words. Examples are, 'More milk?' and, 'Daddy gone.' Their pronunciation becomes clearer. By the age of two, children are usually able to say approximately 200 words.

Table 2.7: Two to three years

Receptive language	Expressive language
Young children of two to three years particularly enjoy listening to rhymes and stories, although younger children and babies can also participate in these listening activities. By the age of three, many children have grown in their ability to engage in verbal interactions with others—in short conversations in which they take turns to listen and speak. They comprehend commands that are composed of two steps, such as, 'Get the teddy and put it in the box.' They also begin to understand contrasting concepts or 'opposites', such as hot/cold, big/little, in/out.	At this phase in their oral language development, young children's expressive vocabulary expands at a rapid rate. By the age of three, they have an expressive vocabulary of up to 1000 words. Generally, their utterances are confined to only two or three words but can be understood by others, especially family members. Their sentences are simple and usually have a subject and a verb.

Table 2.8: Three to four years

Receptive language	Expressive language
Three- and four-year-old children can understand a range of sentence structures, including questions that start with 'who', 'what' and 'where'. If a child has a hearing difficulty, it often becomes noticeable at this age.	Children begin to use four or more words in their sentences, and are able to talk about things that are less concrete and immediate. For example, they may talk about friends, places they have been and things they have done. Their speech becomes clearer and more fluent and is easier to understand. Children in this age group ask many questions. By the age of four, they know approximately 1500 words.

Table 2.9: Four to five years

Receptive language	Expressive language
Children in this age group usually enjoy listening to stories and can answer simple questions about them. Their listening comprehension is at the stage where they can understand most things that are said to them. They are able to understand three-step commands, such as, 'Get the crayons out of the box then go to the table and draw a picture.'	By now, children can construct fairly detailed sentences, using compound and complex sentences and using pronouns and past tense. Most sounds are now pronounced correctly. They are able to discuss their feelings and are thus using language for a wider range of purposes. By the age of five, they usually have a vocabulary of approximately 2000 words.

Table 2.10: Five to six years

Receptive language	Expressive language
By the age of six, children have a very large receptive vocabulary of approximately 20,000 words. They understand many sentences, including complex sentences.	By six years of age, children generally have an expressive vocabulary of approximately 2600 words. They can form all types of sentences—statements, commands, questions and exclamations—and can construct simple, compound and complex sentences.

Table 2.11: Six to eight years

Receptive language	Expressive language
By the age of six to eight years, most children have a receptive vocabulary of up to 8000 words. Children of this age have generally learnt that different language behaviour is called for according to the context. Thus, their listening and speaking behaviours will vary according to factors such as the formality of the context.	Children in this age group are able to verbalise for a variety of reasons. They can talk about their feelings and ideas, and can verbalise problems and how they might be solved. They tend to talk a lot.

Sources: Gleason (2005), Jalongo (2007), Owens (2005)

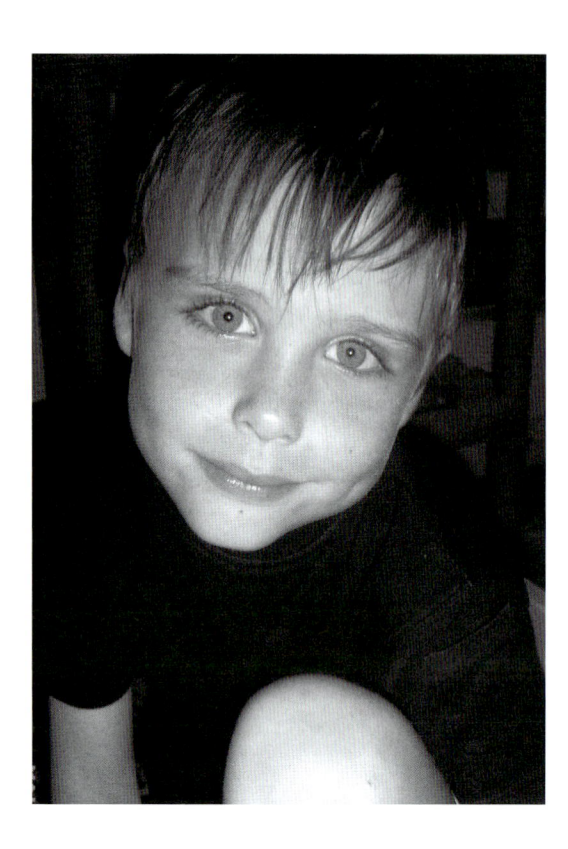

Neurobiologists have determined that the capacity to learn language can be attributed to the structure of the brain.

ORAL LANGUAGE DEVELOPMENT IN CHILDCARE AND EDUCATION SETTINGS

In many ways, the language requirements of children in care and education settings are quite unlike the language they are familiar with at home. 'Classroom talk' is often different from home talk, and more so for children from lower socio-economic and cultural minority backgrounds. Fleer and Raban (2007, pp. 30–2) note that 'home talk' has the following characteristics:

- known patterns of discourse
- usually contains short exchanges
- has an immediate here and now purpose
- supports successful communication
- involves many long interactions and is usually between a child and an adult or a child and other children of various ages
- the audience is usually known to the child.
  In contrast, school talk:
- often uses unfamiliar patterns of discourse
- demands lengthy periods of listening
- often has a 'delayed' purpose
- involves many brief interactions
- is often between children of the same age group
- may involve an unfamiliar audience.

To be successful in school, children are required to learn the discourses of the classroom. There is, in short, a requirement to learn how to use language for learning.

There are many articulations of how children's language development might be conceptualised in terms of phases. A popular one in Australia is the *First steps speaking and listening map of development* (Brace, Brockhoff, Sparkes & Tuckey, 2006) which proposes seven phases of oral language development in children from pre-school onwards. Only the first four are relevant to children in early childhood (pre-school–Year 3) settings and are outlined in Table 2.12.

Table 2.12: Overview: Speaking and listening development

Phase of speaking and listening development (*First steps*)	What children can do
Beginning	Children use and comprehend simple language of the home and community, using non-verbal cues to support their comprehension. They often speak in short utterances and may require considerable support in novel contexts.
Early	Children use their home language to communicate everyday needs, express themselves and their ideas and to enquire through the asking of questions. They understand social and personal functions of language and they respond in 'their own way', but not necessarily in a conventional way, although they are becoming aware of conventions of speaking and listening.
Exploratory	Children in the exploratory phase use standard forms of language (e.g. Standard Australian English) within familiar contexts and are able to communicate in both informal and formal contexts.
Consolidating	Children use most features of the language appropriately in several contexts, and show an increasing degree of audience awareness. They try out different ways of listening and speaking for different purposes. Through use and practice, they consolidate their learning.

In this chapter, you have been introduced to a variety of perspectives about language learning, and you will see practices that are anchored in all of these perspectives in early childhood centres and classrooms throughout the world. Many practices reflect an 'eclectic' approach, which means that more than one theoretical perspective has been drawn upon.

SUMMARY

There is no single fixed explanation for children's language acquisition, learning and development; rather, there are different theoretical perspectives, each of which places emphasis on either nature (biological factors) or nurture (environmental factors) or a combination of both in explaining how children acquire and develop language. Understanding the different theoretical perspectives is important, as each makes a significant contribution to knowing how teachers can support children in developing oral language. It is also important to be familiar with language development phases that signify children's progress along the path to oral language competency.

QUESTIONS AND ACTIVITIES

1. Consider how each of the theoretical perspectives outlined have influenced educators' thinking about language development.
2. Develop a chart that outlines the strengths and limitations of each of the theoretical perspectives of language development.
3. Discuss the notion of 'ages and phases' or developmental milestones in the area of language development and determine its benefits and limitations.
4. With reference to language theories, consider what is meant by the nature–nurture debate.
5. Brainstorm ideas for the use of the information about children's phases of language development to assist with the design of experiences for children.
6. List factors that influence language development and suggest how you might cater for each in the nurturing of children's language development.

KEY TERMS

classical conditioning
language acquisition device
language acquisition support system
operant conditioning
readiness
scaffolding
universal grammar

KEY REFERENCES

Brace, J., Brockhoff, V., Sparkes, N. & Tuckey, J. (2006). *Speaking and listening map of development: Addressing current literacy challenges* (2nd edn). Port Melbourne: Rigby Harcourt Education.

Campbell, R. & Baker, C. (2003). Children learning language. In R. Campbell & D. Green (eds), *Literacies and learners: Current perspectives* (2nd edn). NSW: Prentice Hall.

Emmitt, M., Komesaroff, L. & Pollack, J. (2006). *Language and learning: An introduction for teaching* (4th edn). South Melbourne: Oxford University Press.

Fleer, M. & Raban, B. (2007). *Early childhood literacy and numeracy: Building good practice*. Canberra: DEEWR.

Hulit, L. M. & Howard, M. R. (2006). *Born to talk: An introduction to speech and language development* (4th edn). Boston: Pearson.

Jalongo, M. R. (2007). *Early childhood language arts*. Boston: Pearson.

Lightbown, P. & Spada, N. (1993). *How languages are learned*. Oxford: Oxford University Press.

CHAPTER 3

Early Childhood Settings and Oral Language Learning and Development

CHAPTER OBJECTIVES

This chapter will increase your understanding of:

- important principles of language teaching, learning and development in early childhood education
- the different settings in which young children's learning and development occurs
- general approaches to children's language development and learning.

This chapter provides you with an understanding of the features inherent in each of the different early childhood settings, namely the home, childcare, pre-school and school, and how children's oral language development can be supported within each. In addition, the chapter presents a number of important principles for early childhood language learning and development in general. These principles should guide you in the general design of language experiences that correspond to how young children learn.

INTRODUCTION

Early childhood generally refers to the first eight years of a child's life. These formative years are critical to the quality of children's ongoing oral language development and to their literacy and academic learning, which is itself influenced by their competency in oral language. The knowledge, skills, behaviours and confidence acquired during early childhood provide the foundations upon which children will continue to learn and develop.

In early childhood, children's learning occurs in the settings of the home, childcare, pre-school and school. It is important for each setting to provide children with consistent models of good spoken language, regular opportunities for purposeful and enjoyable engagement in speaking and listening, and positive messages about their oral communication efforts.

Many valuable practices can be employed in supporting and nurturing children's language. Decisions about the use of a particular practice should take into account the children's current levels of oral language learning, their social and physical development and the speaking and listening goals of the curriculum. Decisions should also be influenced by what is known about the ways in which young children's learning and development is best enhanced. The box below outlines a set of principles based on what is understood to be important to ensuring the best opportunity for children's learning.

EARLY CHILDHOOD: LANGUAGE TEACHING AND DEVELOPMENT PRINCIPLES

In early childhood, learning occurs best when:

- Children have a sense of wellbeing, belonging and security, and when positive relationships with others are nurtured.
- The significant adults in children's lives (parents, teachers and carers) hold positive expectations for their learning and development.
- The care, pre-school and school **learning environments** are set up to make links to the children's cultural backgrounds and family experiences.
- Learning experiences accommodate children's interests and backgrounds.
- Learning experiences satisfy children's natural curiosity and tendency towards activity and social participation in the world around them.
- The design of learning programs takes into account *the varying rates of learning and development from child to child* and makes provision for each child's individual needs.
- Learning experiences establish a clear link between children's prior learning and the new knowledge and skills which are being taught.
- Experiences cater for the holistic development of children; that is, they support the simultaneous nurturing of all developmental domains—social, emotional, physical, cognitive, language and creativity.
- Learning programs incorporate play and exploration as the most natural way for young children to develop new understandings and skills.

- Children are given opportunities to explore and play with a variety of different objects and materials.
- Children are provided with opportunities to engage in activities with others.
- Children are able to make decisions about the activities in which they engage; there should be scope and variety in the experiences from which they can choose.
- Children receive regular adult encouragement and feedback and their achievements are acknowledged and valued.

LANGUAGE DEVELOPMENT AND THE HOME SETTING

The home is the first and most significant setting for children's learning.

The home is the first and most significant setting for children, and parents are children's first and most enduring teachers. From the moment of birth, parents and other family members influence children's speech and language acquisition and learning. Through different shared experiences within the family, and the interaction and spoken language of parents and siblings, a child's journey towards competency in oral communication is fostered.

The home provides an ideal setting for children's language learning and development. Verbal interaction is central to the daily activities and events of family life. Typical family routines such as meal times, bed time, shopping and so on provide important occasions for language development. The home also provides children with the people, places, actions and objects to which they can harness their natural desire to explore and learn. It also presents the individual guidance and spoken interaction that serve to enhance learning. Otto (2010) highlights the features of the verbal interactions of the home setting which make it distinctly more advantageous than classroom settings in supporting children's language development. A comparison of home and school language settings is outlined below (Table 3.1).

Table 3.1: Features of children's verbal interactions in the different settings of the home and classroom

The home setting	The classroom setting
Frequent individual adult–child conversations are generally more tailored to the individual child	Adults are shared among a large group of children, which restricts the amount of individual adult–child conversations
Sharing and talking about story books in a one-to-one context	Sharing and talking about story books in a group setting. Less time for individual children
Predominant focus on the immediate context of events, actions and objects present	Degree of de-contextualised language use—language use involving events and objects that are not part of the immediate environment or experiences of the children
Involves a limited number of people with whom children already share close relationships	Involves an adult talking with a large group of children or children talking together in small groups with intermittent adult involvement
Spontaneous and frequently initiated by the children	More frequently teacher-initiated and focused on instructional objectives and procedures
Involves a wide range of topics and generally tailored to the children's needs and interests	Topics driven by the interests of a large group of children and can sometimes be restricted by curriculum requirements
Frequent speaking turns and child-initiated questions	Competing with others for linguistic space in the classroom
Often spontaneous and generally not constrained by established rules and behavioural protocols	Includes ritualised language of routines and social rules; behavioural structures of the large group influence opportunities for, and types of, verbal interactions

Source: Adapted from Otto (2010, pp. 53–4)

It is important, of course, to realise that there is a good deal of diversity between the language experiences from one home to another. There is diversity between families in the language or dialect of English spoken, in the social roles of different family members and in cultural beliefs and their influence on family communication practices. Early childhood educators need to be mindful of difference in children's experience with language and communication in the home and of the validity of each child's experiences and family background.

As well as the family environment, early childhood educators play a vital role in young children's language acquisition and growth. The success of these early childhood settings is enhanced when parents and teachers build strong partnerships and work together. This involves:

- open communication between parents/families and teachers that involves the sharing of information. Methods might include questionnaires, suggestion box, planned and spontaneous conversations, formal and casual meetings, newsletters, arrival and departure greetings, family social days or evenings, notes and message boards.

- family involvement; for instance, providing input into the daily program or in the day-to-day running of the program and assisting with excursions or special events
- parent education programs that serve to empower parents to continue to be their children's first teachers (Estes, 2004, p. 271)
- parent membership in groups of significance to early childhood education and care in general, or of the actual childcare, pre-school or school community (i.e. committees, councils, task forces and advocacy groups)
- responsiveness to families' culture, traditional practices, values and language.

LANGUAGE DEVELOPMENT AND THE CHILDCARE SETTING

Childcare is a service that provides care for infants and toddlers (birth to four years) but that may also provide for the care and education of pre-school children (four to six years). Children in childcare should be grouped by age, and staff should be involved in the care, teaching and development of each group. There should be a basic schedule of care and developmental activities for each group that takes account of the age, interests and needs of the children involved.

CHILDCARE AND BABIES

In childcare, babies are provided with many individual experiences with carers. There should be a focus on developing secure relationships and fostering rich language experiences. Language development is supported by a variety of sensory experiences—opportunities to touch, feel, hear, taste and see—as part of their schedule of care. The carers' continual and

An important focus in childcare is on developing secure relationships and fostering rich language experiences.

consistent use of language encourages optimal language learning and development. Some important practices include:

- talking during different interactions with babies—when changing their nappies, bathing, feeding and nursing them and so on
- talking about the materials, objects and events in the immediate vicinity
- 'verbal mapping' (Otto, 2010) using simple sentences and repetition of key words/talk about what is going to happen or what has happened
- providing a balance between opportunities for babies to hear conversation and sound around them, and quiet times
- language games such as 'peek-a-boo'
- asking questions about people and objects that are in the vicinity; e.g. 'Where is teddy?' or 'Who's that?'
- talking about toys and objects when babies are playing with them
- simple instructions incorporating the identification of words for familiar objects; e.g. 'Show me your nose,' and, 'Look at the lovely flower.'

CHILDCARE AND TODDLERS

As children grow older and become more mobile, they begin to explore their surroundings. This provides new opportunities for the language learning and development of toddlers in childcare. Language development should be integrated with that of other areas of development—physical, social, emotional, cognitive, creative and communication. Children should be given the opportunity to move freely from one play space to another and select from the experiences and materials available. Carers should plan and facilitate the experiences, observe the children at play, mediate when there is a problem and talk with children as they engage in the various experiences provided.

The childcare routine should also include some daily structured time when the children are directed by the carer in activities that call for them to listen to and to understand language. Valuable activities during this time include story book reading, singing, action rhymes and group conversations.

Speaking and listening is integral to the experiences of the childcare setting. Carers should speak to the children clearly and frequently, and encourage them to use language effectively. Some practices for enhancing toddlers' language learning and development in childcare include:

- exploratory activities that invite creative, 'hands-on' interaction with a variety of materials, that allow for 'trial and error' learning and that encourage expressive and receptive language use
- indoor and outdoor play experiences that involve different objects and materials in the immediate proximity and the use of these opportunities for the teacher to communicate with toddlers
- adult responses to toddlers' oral communications that demonstrate the role of language in communicating meaning
- asking open questions (those that don't simply require a yes or no answer)
- showing an interest in toddlers as they communicate and praising them for their spoken communication

- demonstrating conversational practices such as taking turns
- reading stories and talking about the characters, objects and events in a story
- modelling well-structured sentences with enriched vocabulary
- carer talk that involves present, past and future events
- providing commentary on events that are part of the daily routine
- engaging toddlers in pretend play (e.g. use toy animals or teddy bears and create conversations between them, pretend conversations on the toy telephone and pretend tea party with the dolls)
- teaching simple songs and nursery rhymes that incorporate actions or movements
- storytelling using different props (puppets, pictures, objects) to highlight meaning.

Toddlers' development is nurtured through various indoor and outdoor play experiences that involve different objects and materials.

THE PRE-SCHOOL SETTING

The pre-school provides an educational program for children prior to their first year of formal schooling. The program should comprise a mixture of **structured** and **unstructured play** experiences, incorporating both teacher-initiated experiences and activities, and independent indoor and outdoor play. It should also include sessions where the teacher brings the whole class together for certain activities; typically these include roll call, singing, story reading, language games and letter and sound work. Whole of class sessions can also be used as a time to introduce new topics or concepts. For instance, the teacher might conduct a discussion, show pictures, read an informational text or carry out a role play as a way of teaching or reinforcing learning.

The pre-school environment should include a wide range of interesting equipment and materials that can be manipulated and explored. There should be different **play spaces** which can be easily accessed by children and where opportunities to use language for different purposes abound.

The provision of 'real' experiences such as growing plants, cooking, making things and craftwork that are enriched with oral language are significant to children's language development in pre-school. Experiences with a wide range and type of books and other written texts are also important.

Some general practices for enhancing pre-school children's language include:

- oral interactions between teachers and individual children or groups of children during free play time and other child-centred classroom activities
- talking that introduces new vocabulary and grammatical structures to children
- the use of a clear, fluent voice and appropriate intonation as well as good listening practices when talking with children
- responses that focus on the intent rather than the grammatical or word choice errors of children's talk
- the use of open-ended questions that extends children's use of language
- the introduction, demonstration and reinforcement of social courtesies and appropriate speaking behaviour; e.g. turn-taking, listening politely
- encouragement of children's talk during structured group activities
- regular participation in children's play and use of these opportunities to support children's language development
- use of daily routines and activity transitions to support language learning and development.

Children's language is fostered through a variety of structured and unstructured play experiences.

THE PRE-SCHOOL ENVIRONMENT

The environment comprises various aspects of the early childhood education setting. This includes areas for play and learning activities, materials and resources, daily schedules, transitions and routines, as well as the actual teaching and learning programs and activities. Decisions about the design of environmental elements should take into account the need to support and nurture children's language development and learning. Environments should stimulate both the quality and the amount of growth in language (Scafer, Staab & Smith, 1983). Following is a description of different environmental features in relation to their support for children's oral language and learning development.

The physical arrangement of the classroom

The delineation of play and activity areas and the arrangement of furniture should lend itself to talk among children. It should offer opportunities for children to work in both large and small groups as well as with partners and individually. Activity areas need to be set up in a way that minimises children distracting each other. A number of simultaneous talk events should be possible without giving rise to distractions.

Materials and resources

Language materials include objects and items (for example, blocks and construction equipment, magnets and magnetic and non-magnetic items, different sized containers of sand and water, different textured fabric and paper) that can be explored by children and that can be used for cooperative investigations around a range of topics and concepts. They should be age appropriate and of a quantity that is sufficient for the number of children who will need to use them.

Materials for exploration, construction and investigation are central to the pre-school environment.

Learning and teaching programs

Programs outline learning and development outcomes and the experiences, activities and resources to be used in achieving them. They should be designed with regard for the language capabilities of the children for whom they are written and in a way that integrates language use into the different learning and development goals.

Daily schedules

Schedules should be constructed to indicate the range of activities and experiences which are provided and the times at which they will be available for children each day. They should show who will do what and when they will do it. Schedules should ensure that adequate blocks of time are made available for different activities and should provide for a balance between large and small group work and pair and individual activities. They should take account of the time required for different tasks to be carried out for depth of learning. Longer periods of time are often needed for activities where social interaction is a feature and can lead to higher levels of cognitive engagement. Schedules need to show times for children to engage in language-based activities. There should be planned and systematic opportunities for consistent peer interaction.

Transitions

Transitions refer to the methods by which changeover from one teaching activity to another is implemented. They are usually simple and brief and are used to regulate the day and smooth changeovers. Simple language activities can be used during transitions. Songs and rhymes, finger plays, word games and guessing games can assist with smooth and effective transitions while also supporting language learning and development.

Daily routines

Routines in early childhood settings are activities that occur on a regular basis and in a predictable way. Routine activities include such things as meal (snack and lunch) times, the morning roll call, story time, arrival and home times and cleaning-up time. With infants and toddlers they might include nap time. The practices should become habitual and familiar to the children and provide them with a sense of security and comfort. Language should, in some way, be a part of all routine activities. It might be that a routine activity involves songs or rhymes, language or word games, or oral instructions given in a consistent way or engaging in conversations. For instance, toddlers' nap time might begin with a story or song, roll call might involve different questions for children to answer, home time might be marked by a story or a conversation about the day, and meal time might involve conversation and the reinforcement of appropriate social practices.

THE PRIMARY SCHOOL SETTING

During the first few years of primary school, children's learning is directed towards certain discrete subjects (curriculum learning areas). These include English and Mathematics, for which there is strong emphasis, the Arts (music, dance and art), Science, Health and Physical Education, Society and Environment and Information Technology. Lessons should be implemented on the basis of children's developmental levels and curriculum statements of required learning. A class program should be organised so that, for some of the time, separate curriculum learning areas are taught and at other times an integrated approach is used to achieve curriculum learning outcomes.

ENGLISH LESSONS

The English curriculum encompasses reading, writing, listening, speaking and viewing and is given special attention in the early years of primary school. The use and development of

Language experiences in the early years of school should aim to extend children's ability to communicate effectively for a growing range of purposes.

oral language should be integral to all English teaching and learning experiences but should also be given special attention through separate, focused speaking and listening lessons.

The focus should be on extending children's ability to communicate effectively for a growing number of purposes, audiences (people involved) and topics, and attention should be given to the enhancement of children's speaking and listening skills and the strategies to be used for different purposes. Lessons should involve children practicing and developing skills, knowledge and understanding of oral language in authentic oral communication situations and they also should involve explicit skills teaching.

Children's oral language learning and development should be integral to the **learning experiences** of all curriculum areas (for example, Science, Society and Environment, Mathematics). Children need to learn to use language in cognitively challenging ways and for a range of academic purposes; they need to learn to use language to learn. They should be assisted to develop the language knowledge and the communication practices necessary to meeting the demands of academic learning. It is important that they be taught the vocabulary of the topics of study in different curriculum learning areas. They need access to the language that allows them to 'express their thinking, clarify their misunderstandings, or question others' perception' (Otto, 2010, p. 309). The important component of 'language and thinking' is addressed fully in Chapter 6.

There are a variety of practices that teachers can implement to support the language learning and development of children in the early years of primary school, many of which are the same as those of other early childhood settings. However, in order to facilitate learning they might need to be modified to the children's different level of development and language learning needs and to the unique features of the primary school setting. Moreover, to cater for primary school children's more advanced language development and the different features of the primary school class, other practices need also be considered.

In sustaining the oral language learning of children in the early years of primary school teachers should:

- provide a range of exploratory activities that involve children working together to investigate materials and objects and to learn new concepts
- provide opportunities for discussions and conversations in a range of academic and social contexts
- support children in dealing with the oral language demands of academic learning situations
- regularly read books to children and engage them in discussions about the books; the books read should vary in terms of style, genre and complexity of the language features
- model new vocabulary and new ways of expressing thoughts and information for social purposes
- ensure the regular use of oral language activities within different curriculum learning area lessons
- design particular oral language activities (e.g. news-telling, barrier games, group discussions and storytelling) as activities to be routinely carried out as part of the weekly timetable of lessons
- vary the composition of groups when carrying out group work
- extend the children's awareness of, and ability with, the use of the appropriate language registers for different situations; e.g. for giving a presentation on a subject of personal interest to the class, for recounting a story to a class of younger children, for sharing their personal news with a group of classmates or for asking questions of a guest speaker
- use group projects that necessitate children to collaborate with each other to explore topics and concepts and to prepare a presentation that summarises their learning.

Chapters 4 and 5 describe more specific learning experiences and activities for the development of children's oral language. Chapter 4 outlines a number of important language learning contexts that should be characteristic to all early childhood education settings, while Chapter 5 outlines activities and experiences that, while suitable for supporting children's oral language learning, should be adapted to take into account the needs of the learners and the features of the setting. They should be modified to suit the age, experiences and current skills and knowledge of the children with whom they will be used.

SUMMARY

The home is the first and most important setting for children's learning and development and, when working with children in other settings, strong family partnership practices should be established. Children's learning and development also takes place in childcare, pre-school and the early years of school, and their oral development is strongly influenced by the teaching and learning environment which includes the materials, experiences, activities and the people with whom they interact. Each early childhood setting should be established so that key principles about teaching and learning for young children are addressed. Additionally, they should incorporate structures and practices that serve the language development and learning needs of the specific group of children for whom they are catering.

QUESTIONS AND ACTIVITIES

1. Create a chart that shows the unique features of each of the different early childhood settings. Discuss the similarities and differences of these three early childhood education settings and consider the reasons for such differences.
2. Review the 'Language teaching, learning and development principles' at the beginning of the chapter. Identify three that you feel are most important and consider some the practical applications of each.
3. Consider the statement, 'Parents are children's first teachers', and outline how early childhood educators can ensure this is reflected in their practices.
4. What practices for children's language learning are part of each of the three settings of childcare, pre-school and the early years of school?

KEY TERMS

learning environment
learning experiences
play spaces
structured play
unstructured play

KEY REFERENCES

Estes, L. (2004). *Essentials of child care and early childhood education.* Boston: Pearson Education.

Otto, B. (2010). *Language development in early childhood.* Upper Saddle River, New Jersey: Pearson Education.

Scafer, R. E., Staab C. et al. (1983). *Language functions and school success.* Illinois: Scott, Foreman and Company.

CHAPTER 4

Key Early Childhood Learning Contexts and Oral Language

CHAPTER OBJECTIVES

This chapter will increase your understanding of:

- important early childhood learning contexts for children's language learning and development
- the way in which the different contexts support children's language learning and development.

In this chapter you are introduced to five important contexts for young children's language learning and development: *play*, reading aloud to children, *storytelling*, *conversation and discussion* and *investigation*. Each of these contexts performs a significant role in the development of children's language and oral communication while also being important to children's learning and development in general. Each is described in order to provide you with an understanding of their value in promoting children's language and oral communication, though, of course, their natural integration with other literacy areas (reading, writing, viewing) is important and should also be considered when planning. As you read about each context, consider its suitability to different groups of children with different language abilities and diverse language learning and development needs. Consider, also, the ways in which each might be adapted to the different early childhood settings. The five learning contexts presented here do not constitute an exhaustive list, but they are important and, taken together, provide balance in terms of experiences for children's oral language and communicative learning and development. The chapter to follow outlines a range of practical experiences for young children's oral language learning.

PLAY AND ORAL LANGUAGE

Play is a natural learning context for young children; it captures their interest and absorbs their attention (Klein, Wirth & Linas, 2004, p. 28) and children are instinctively drawn to it.

> Play environments enriched with culturally relevant resources provide opportunities to explore processes and concepts, develop positive dispositions to learning and use literacy and numeracy in a range of contexts. Play encourages exploration, risk taking, socialisation and engagement in learning. Through play children can explore and reflect on interests and issues relevant to their lives. (Victorian Department of Education, 2009)

Children's play experiences should be diverse and should involve: physical activity (running, crawling, kicking, catching); exploring the properties of materials and objects; imitating the actions and speech of others; manipulating objects and materials to create something; and creating and acting out imaginary or realistic situations. Children play on their own or with others. When they are more peer-oriented, their play is more likely to include engagement and interaction with others. It might, for example, involve two children using blocks and negotiating the construction of a building or the sharing of observations while using magnifying glasses to examine different materials, or it might entail a group of children 'acting out' a spaceship adventure or retelling a familiar story using puppets.

In early childhood settings, children's play is facilitated by the establishment of **learning centres** (spaces for play), in both the indoor and outdoor environment. The learning centres should contain materials and objects, carefully chosen to encourage children to engage in independent or cooperative play. Learning centres should support unstructured open-ended activity where children determine their own learning and make their own decisions about how to use the materials provided. However, learning centres should also provide for structured activities that serve to guide children's learning in particular ways.

Play provides a valuable context for speaking and listening. The interactive and social nature of many types of play activities necessitate children communicating with each

Play provides a valuable context for speaking and listening.

other, thus learning about and practising oral language. It provides the opportunity for children to learn socially appropriate ways to interact with others and to learn the skills and conventions of conversation. Play regularly requires the use of language for various communicative purposes, and children's ability with the pragmatic component of language is therefore enhanced. There are many reasons for which children might use oral language during play, including:

- Negotiating: deciding on a play theme and roles, sharing materials, choosing activities taking turns, establishing rules and so on.
- Informing: telling others about a play activity which is being undertaken or what has been done or is about to be done.
- Solving problems: discussing and sharing possible solutions to a dilemma, e.g. how will we build a very high bridge? What can we use for the police car?
- Expressing emotions: excitement, happiness, disappointment, frustration and anticipation as their play unfolds.
- Reasoning: why they did or made something.
- Explaining: a play experience or the outcomes of a play experience; what has been done or what is happening when another child joins in.
- Suggesting: how to do or to make something; what to use.
- Describing: what has been made, drawn, wrote or done; qualities or features of objects and materials.
- Asking questions: to seek information or clarification about something.
- Directing: the actions of others.
- Requesting: an item, to join in with others, a change in the direction of the play.
- Instructing: how to do something.

When oral language is a part of children's play, there is also the potential for the enhancement of children's ability with the specific language components of phonology, syntax and semantics as explained below.

- *Syntax*: play supports children in developing increased ability with the structuring of sentences, e.g. composing more complex sentences, using connectives. This is best developed when they can interact with adults during play.
- *Semantics*: play often involves new experiences, materials and objects or involves particular understandings which allow children to further their understanding of their world, themselves and others; they can also learn new words (vocabulary development).
- *Phonology*: play might involve children experimenting with the sounds in words, e.g. making up or practising rhyming chants or identifying words that rhyme or have the same beginning sound. This might occur spontaneously or it might result from specific play activities which are designed to encourage experimentation with words and sounds.

Although independent play activities always have the potential to develop children's oral language, it is important to bear in mind the important role that is played by the teacher. Children's language learning and their ability with oral communication can best be progressed if teachers are actively present and talking with the children during play. They should encourage children to talk for different purposes (for example, describe, explain, find a solution) and assist them to expand or develop their comments and to interact verbally with others to achieve the objective of a play activity (Otto, 2010).

Important to children's oral language learning and development is that teachers engage them in conversations that stimulate and challenge their thinking. Massey (2004) suggests that the talk in early childhood settings is all too frequently lacking in cognitive challenge. When interacting with children during play, teachers should demonstrate, and encourage children to engage in more rich, stimulating talk. This might involve talking to provide explanations, to construct personal stories, to share ideas and opinions, and to reflect on and analyse experiences. Children's language, says Massey (2004, p. 227), needs to be moved beyond the literal 'here and now' and encompass past and future events.

Although the involvement of teachers is important, their intervention during play should only take place if there is a pedagogical reason, so that children's independence, initiative and creativity are not inhibited. Language learning is supported during play when teachers:

- ask questions and make comments about the children's play activity
- reflect the emotions that children express in their play actions
- join in with the play but only for short periods and model the use of language, e.g. for asking for help, explaining what is being done etc.
- verbally reinforce children's actions
- introduce new and interesting words.

Children's language learning is further supported when teachers adopt some quite specific techniques when interacting with children during their play. Some such techniques are:

- *Expansion*: teachers expand what children say, using the correct grammatical structure.
  Example:

> Child: Doggy play.
>
> Adult: Yes, the dog is playing.

- *Extensions*: teachers rephrase children's utterance into a complete sentence, and may add extra information.
  Example:

> Child: Doggy play
>
> Adult: Yes, the dog is playing with his ball.

- *Repetitions*: teachers repeat the child's speech.
  Example:

> Child: The dog's running.
>
> Adult: Yes, the dog's running.

- *Parallel talk*: teachers describe what the child is doing. It is often fruitful to do this in the context of play.
  Example:

  > Adult: You are digging the sand. You have a beautiful red shovel.

- *Self-talk*: teachers describe their own actions to a child. For example, they might provide a commentary of what they are doing while preparing food or tidying up toys. This models sentence structures and vocabulary for the young child.
  Example:

  > Adult: I'm slicing an apple for my lunch. I'm going to get you some toast in a minute.

- *Vertical structuring*: teachers ask questions to encourage children to provide more details.
  Example:

  > Child: Doggy play.
  >
  > Adult: What's the doggy playing with?
  >
  > Child: He play with ball.

- *Fill-ins*: teachers encourage young children to say more by uttering an unfinished sentence and indicating that the child should finish it off.
  Example:

  > Adult: Mummy's yawning because she's …
  >
  > Child: Tired! Mummy tired.

As children mature and develop, their activities will often extend into other types of play. Although learning centres and places for free **exploratory play** should still be part of the learning environment, a more focused and complex exploration of materials and objects should be encouraged (Otto, 2010). Open-ended investigations or projects that are directed towards curriculum outcomes across different learning areas should be established. When these activities are carried out collaboratively by pairs or small groups of children there is the opportunity to enhance a greater variety of language skills.

SOCIO-DRAMATIC PLAY

From about the age of three years, young children readily engage in a type of pretend or imaginative play known as **socio-dramatic play**, which involves the use of whatever materials and resources may be available and adopting roles and developing scenarios and dialogue to act out or role-play realistic or imaginative situations. They might, for instance, adopt the roles of doctors, nurses, patients and receptionists and role-play hospital-related scenarios. They might use a toy cash register and some pretend money to act as shopkeepers and customers or they might put on firemen hats and pretend to be extinguishing fires. Socio-dramatic play is a natural and comfortable pursuit for children. They spontaneously and independently engage in such activity as they seek enjoyment and learning about and understanding of their world.

Children's enjoyment of pretend play provides rich language opportunity.

Early childhood classrooms should provide a special place set up to represent a pretend play setting; for example, a hospital, restaurant, post office or fire station. It should contain a variety of materials representing those typically found in real-life settings so that children are encouraged to take on roles and play out relevant scenarios. For instance, the materials contained in a hospital play setting might contain white coats, stethoscopes, bandages, clipboards, forms, note books, a reception desk, a child-size bed and X-rays.

Socio-dramatic play supports children's use of oral language as they talk to determine the roles they will each play, to label the different materials in the play setting, to discuss and plan their play and to negotiate the direction of the plot. Children use, experiment with and refine their oral language while communicating with others in pretend play situations. When they take on roles and act out scenarios with each other they often need to give directions, ask questions, explain, describe and so on. Children display linguistic ability as they switch between their pretend roles in socio-dramatic play and their real identities (Christie, Enz & Vukelich, 2007, p. 90).

Socio-dramatic play is a powerful context for encouraging and supporting the development of the different components of oral language, as illustrated in Table 4.1.

Children's oral language competency benefits when teachers are involved during their socio-dramatic play. Involvement should encompass:

- Help children to experience the topic first-hand by taking them on excursions to actual places in the community. For instance, before setting up a pretend fire station in the dramatic play area, visit the local fire station. Read the children fiction and non-fiction books about the topic/setting so as to develop their conceptual knowledge and vocabulary.
- Ensure a variety of relevant materials is included in the dramatic play area. These can be real (e.g. fireman's hat) or symbolic (e.g. plastic tubing for the fireman's hose).
- Observe children as they role play and note those who don't engage in talk and those who dominate. Observe children's use of language and decide when enhancement might be achieved by some direct intervention or assist in providing direction in the play episode.
- Become involved in children's play, taking on a role and interacting with them. Model oral language and instigate new conversations or a new direction for the plot. Demonstrate the use of materials in a play scenario.
- Question children and help them consider alternative roles, scenarios and conversations for a setting.
- Demonstrate an interest in the children's dramatic play efforts and show that they are valued.

Table 4.1: Socio-dramatic play and oral language components

Phonology	When playing a role and engaging with others in a role	Apply prosodic features—intonation, tone, loudness/softness
Semantics	Using different items when carrying out activities in an occupational setting	Use vocabulary: use of words such as 'script', 'medicine', 'tablets', 'appointment'
Syntax	Using different sentence types and structuring sentences in oral interactions/conversations	Practise and experiment with sentence structures: giving commands, making statements, asking questions
Pragmatics	Changing use of language to suit the context	Explore functions: change the style of language used to conform to the play setting and scenario; apply social norms of interaction

READING ALOUD TO CHILDREN

Another context central to early childhood learning is the reading aloud of stories to children. It provides an ideal context to develop children's oral language ability and, when it is accompanied by teacher-led discussion, children's oral language learning is even further supported (Trelease, 1995).

The story should be a central resource for the oral language program of early childhood. When stories are regularly read to children, the knowledge acquired assists their oral language development. They learn new words and are exposed to many varieties of sentence structure. The experiences of discussing or retelling a story also aid the development of oral language.

Children's oral language is enhanced when they listen to stories as well as actively participate in dialogue about them (Justice & Pence, 2005, p. 1). Dialogue is encouraged

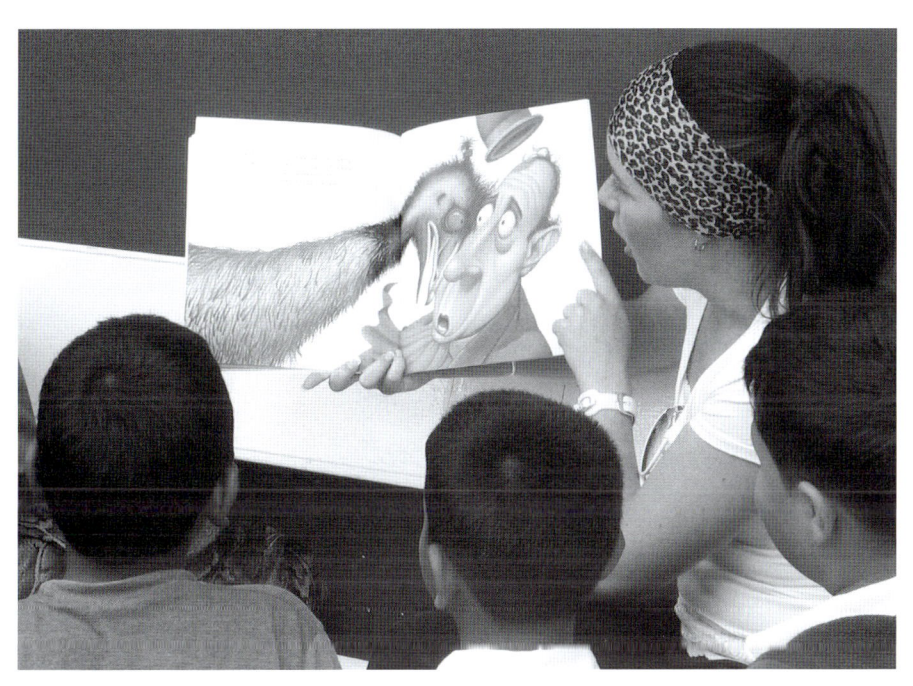

Children's oral language development benefits from regular opportunities to listen to stories being read to them.

when teachers ask questions that require children to do more than just recall facts but also call for them to consider a story more fully; for instance, to explain ideas, predict consequences or justify opinions. To fully extend children's thinking and language, questions should be open-ended and have no right or wrong answer (for example, Which part of the story did you enjoy the most? Why?), and they should include follow-on questions; that is, questions that follow on from children's answers to previous questions (Roe & Ross, 2006). For more about questioning that supports dialogue, refer to Chapter 6. The best language development opportunities are created when sharing and talking about stories is carried out in small groups of about six to eight children.

There are many ways in which the regular reading of stories can progress children's oral language; for instance, phonological knowledge, vocabulary, concepts about the world, a sense of book language and story structure, and understanding about sentences can all be enhanced. The books read should be carefully selected so that they comprise the text features (words, sentences, topics, concepts etc.) that accommodate the children's language learning level.

Young children's stories often use the language devices of rhyme, rhythm, alliteration and sentence repetition. These engage children with the sound of the language in the text and they appeal to their sense of play. Take, for instance, the story book, *Boo to a goose* (Fox, 2001a).

I'd dance with a pig in a shiny green wig
but I wouldn't say boo to a goose!
I'd ride on a 'roo to Kalamazoo
but I wouldn't say boo to a goose
I'd jump from a mountain right into a fountain
but I wouldn't say boo to a goose!

Another well known nonsense rhyme is *There was an old lady who swallowed a fly* (Taback, 1997).

There was an old lady who swallowed a fly.
I don't know why she swallowed the fly,
I guess she'll die.
There was an old lady who swallowed a spider,
that wiggled and wiggled and tickled inside her.
She swallowed the spider to catch the fly.
I don't know why she swallowed the fly.
I guess she'll die.
There was an old lady who swallowed a bird.
How absurd to swallow a bird.
She swallowed the bird to catch the spider,
that wiggled and wiggled and tickled inside her.
She swallowed the spider to catch the fly.
I don't know why she swallowed the fly.
I guess she'll die …

Teachers should exploit the language features of stories to enhance children's phonological learning. They should focus children on the phonological patterns (sound patterns) in the stories which might, for instance, include encouraging children to:

- join in saying the repetitive sections of a story (e.g. '… but I wouldn't say boo to a goose!')
- use the rhyming cue to predict the last word in a sentence when it rhymes with the last word in a previous sentence
- identify pairs or groups of words that rhyme
- identify pairs or groups of words that start or end with the same phoneme (sound)
- clap to indicate the rhythm of the story as it is read
- identify the words in sentences or syllables in words by clapping them.

The use of these activities when reading stories to children tends to focus their attention to the sound of language and to develop their phonological awareness.

Reading aloud to children provides a meaningful context for them to hear words, which is central to their vocabulary development—to their ability to understand and use words in speech. The more extensive is children's vocabulary, the more precise is their oral expression. In other words, deep word knowledge facilitates clear and accurate self-expression (Justice & Pence, 2005, p. 26). The language structure and illustrations in stories help children to work out the meaning of challenging words and when stories are read out aloud they hear and absorb word pronunciations. Moreover, when teachers explain the meaning of challenging words and engage children in actively using the words in conversation, they sharpen understanding of the meanings of those words and, at the same time, are able to better comprehend the story.

Reading stories aloud to children also exposes them to correct grammar and to a range of sentence structures. When children are regularly exposed to language structures which are not yet part of their speech, they develop a stronger awareness of these structures and the ability to use them in their own oral communication.

In order to get the most from reading stories aloud to children, it is essential that the books chosen are appropriate to the culture, interests and the level of their language development. Books should be chosen with topics that are significant to the children's experiences, current understanding and interests. When children can not relate to the topic it is difficult to engage them in listening to the story and in any discussion.

Children require multiple opportunities to listen to stories in order for the experience to affect their ability with clear and precise oral communication. Reading a book every now and then will only provide minimal support to the development of the important oral language components of phonological awareness, vocabulary, grammar and sentence structure knowledge. Children need extensive and ongoing exposure to language, which is provided when stories are regularly and consistently read aloud to them. A minimum of forty-five minutes each day—it can be divided into three smaller periods of fifteen minutes each—is suggested (Dickinson & Tabors, 2002, cited in Massey, 2004, p. 228).

STORYTELLING

Children's experiences telling (or retelling) stories supports their oral language.

Storytelling, which involves the verbal telling of a story (rather than reading one from a book), is a useful means for developing children's oral language skills. The stories told can be well-known children's stories: folk tales from around the world, fairy tales, fables, myths and legends are good sources. They can be real life (something witnessed, experienced or heard about) or imaginary stories prompted by pictures, music or another stimulus. Storytelling comprises the following components:

- *Words*: a story text is created orally and audience understanding requires the storyteller to carefully and distinctly pronounce the words of the story and to develop a well-structured narrative. Through the emphasis of words and phrases and the use of pauses or short periods of silence, emotional suspense can be created.
- *The voice*: the voice is an important tool and should be used in different ways to engage the audience and to support their understanding of the story. Variations to pitch (voice highs and lows), tempo (speed) and rhythm can depict changes to the mood and build suspense in the story and generally enhance story meaning.

- *Gestures, body language and facial expressions*: non-verbal communication methods should be incorporated to further support audience engagement and story comprehension. For instance, when a story reaches a moment of suspense, the teller could lean closer to the audience, widen their eyes and, using a quieter voice and a slower pace, continue the story.
- *Characterisation*: when appropriate, direct speech with characters being given different-sounding voices should be incorporated in the storytelling.

These components are important for effective delivery of the story, but they also serve to enhance meaning by signalling mood and emotion throughout the story and aid listeners' comprehension and maintain their attention.

Storytelling experiences can be further enhanced through the use of one or more of a number of techniques, which include:

- *Props*: the use of pictures, puppets, felt characters or objects are used to tell the story. They help the audience to comprehend the story and maintain interest and attention. They might also be used to signify characters or scenery elements.
- *Audience participation*: the audience can be invited to join in on a recurring phrase or refrain that is part of the storytelling or to provide relevant sound effects.
- *Music or musical instrument*: these can be used to indicate a change to the tone or mood of the story or to signify the arrival or movement of different characters.

The different techniques serve to support children's comprehension of the story in relation to the plot, mood, scene/s, events and characters of the story.

Storytelling can involve the teacher presenting a story to children, the teacher working with the children to compose a story or the children telling stories to each other. Each is important in supporting expressive and receptive language learning that encompasses:

- listening, attention and observation
- ability to mentally map the main events of a story
- use of visualisation and mental imagery to remember and recall detail
- memory and recall of story elements and sequence
- ability to sequence events in a logical order
- new language patterns—diverse ways to construct sentences to express ideas and information
- increased word knowledge (vocabulary)—new words or new contexts for familiar words
- ability to translate information from one medium (e.g. experience, picture, song, story book) to another (oral story)
- clarity of oral expression
- use of voice and body language to engage the audience's interest
- the correct grammar of spoken language
- confidence and clarity with the expression of imaginative ideas
- pronunciation of words
- familiarity with narrative text structures—beginning, middle, end (or orientation, complication and resolution)
- 'story language' such as 'Once upon a time' or 'Long, long ago'
- the use of oral language to entertain
- audience awareness.

> **TEACHER: PREPARING TO TELL A STORY**
>
> - Think the story through as pictures in your mind.
> - Draw a small flow chart or have props that help with the sequencing.
> - Read the story several times before attempting a storytelling session—know it well.
> - Get to know the pacing and rhythm that best fits the story.
> - Incorporate certain phrases that repeat and are key to the story.
> - Explore different voices as you tell the story out loud to yourself.
> - Incorporate pauses that invite participation, build suspense and allow for response.
> - Think of gestures that will add to the story.
> - Consider how you will begin and end the story.
> - Decide if any presentation props will be used.
> - Will any finger plays, rhymes, sounds, songs, refrain or actions be added (to enhance story and audience participation)?
> - Practise the entire story several times.

Children's own storytelling is enhanced when they have the opportunity to observe and listen to the teacher telling stories. They learn about the required features (for instance, that stories need a beginning, middle and end structure), the use of voice, gestures and other components of storytelling and they discover different techniques that can be used in telling stories. The teacher should carefully construct stories so that they expose children to interesting and expressive language for them to emulate.

Moreover, by regularly telling stories to each other, children are provided with the important experience of practising talking, which is essential to their oral language fluency. They can experiment with and refine the use of the different language components—vocabulary, sentence structures, word articulation and morphology—as well as the use of gestures and other non-verbal communication methods.

There are several ways in which teachers can implement storytelling sessions with children. Many of these can also be used by children with their own storytelling experiences. Following are several methods:

- Dress up as a character from a well-known story (e.g. the hare from *The Hare and the Tortoise*) and tell the story from the point of view of that character.
- Tell a known story using puppets, felt board and felt characters, story pictures, magnetic story boards or other supports.
- Draw a series of pictures depicting the sequence of events of a known story and then use these pictures as prompts to tell the story or draw the pictures as the story unfolds.
- Display three pictures that indicate three stages of a story and then orally create the story. This can involve one child saying a few sentences to begin the story, and other children, one at a time, adding sentences to continue it. The teacher should ask questions when necessary to get children to elaborate or provide further detail.
- Hide picture cards around the room where each picture card depicts each part of the plot of a well-known story. Children are provided with a treasure map that indicates the location of each picture and they use it to find them. They then sequence them in the correct order and use them to tell the story.

- Begin with a sentence such as, 'On my way to the shop I saw the most unusual thing!' The children add a few sentences in turn to create a story.
- Using an interesting piece of famous art work (e.g. the *Mona Lisa*) or a piece of music or other stimulus, the teacher works with the children to create a story.
- Tell a story based on a well-known traditional tale but with changes to characters, setting or some aspect of the plot.
- Have community or family members tell the children stories about their lives, about the local community or about major events in history that they remember.
- Audience participation: teach a chant at the beginning of a storytelling session and then have the children join in with this chant at different parts of the story, when indicated by the storyteller.

Successful storytelling sessions require careful planning. The children's age and oral language skills should be taken into account when deciding on story topics, content, length and complexity, and when selecting the props and other aids to be employed. The language (sentence types, structures and vocabulary) should be appropriate to the listening comprehension skills of the children. At the same time, storytelling sessions should provide for the further development of the children's language skills, and new and interesting words and different sentence types and structures should be used.

Table 4.2: Assessing children's oral communication and storytelling ability

Verbal	Beginning	Developing	Competent	Highly competent
Story structure				
Sentence structures used				
Use of vocabulary				
Creativity				
Appropriateness for audience				

Non-verbal	Beginning	Developing	Competent	Highly competent
Gestures and facial expression				
Use of voice				
Use of props				
Additional comments:				

Stories should be told in different ways—in the first person ('One day I was sitting on the beach when suddenly …'); from the point of view of one or other of the characters, i.e. in the third person ('It was not long before Jimmy's aunty arrived …'); and with the use of dialogue ('When my dad showed me the new puppy I asked, "Is she mine to keep?"'). Furthermore, children's language development is best served when storytelling sessions involve a balance of fictional stories and stories about real events, people and places. Children benefit from hearing not just the narrative texts, but also recounts and descriptions that are used for telling factual stories.

Table 4.2 is an example of a guide that might be used for the assessment of children's language, oral communication and storytelling ability. It is designed to provide a clear focus on the information to be gathered about children's oral language during storytelling experiences. Of course, in establishing the information to be assessed, the children's current ability should be taken into account. The information gathered should be used to inform future storytelling experiences and to make modifications to the language program in general.

CONVERSATION AND DISCUSSION

CONVERSATION

Conversations, which are simply the exchange of dialogue between two or more people, should consistently feature as an important part of early childhood settings. They support the achievement of many important social and academic goals (for example, establishing and maintaining relationships, discovering new information, sharing personal experiences and viewpoints and solving problems) and they provide an ideal context for children's oral language development. Conversations might occur between teachers and the children or they might involve children talking with each other.

Early childhood teachers should regularly engage children in conversation in ways that enhance their conversational skills as well as their general speaking and listening ability. Teachers should seek to:

- Talk with children for a variety of reasons; for example, about themselves, what they are doing or are going to do, what they have learnt or discovered.
- Respond positively when children initiate conversation; reply appropriately to their comments and show interest in what they have to say.
- Ask questions that facilitate children's talk.
- Initiate dialogue that involves various thinking processes such as reasoning, predicting or imagining and that requires children to talk about both present situations and past or future events.
- Move to children's level and make eye contact when talking with them.
- Engage in social conversations with children (in addition to conversation that focuses on learning or getting things done); talk with them about their interests, family experiences and friendships.
- Set aside special times for group conversations which are not necessarily directed at children's learning; for example, begin the day with the children in small groups talking for a period of time about topics of personal interest or significance to them or, at the

end of the day, have group conversation time where the children talk to each other about the day's activities.
- Demonstrate good conversation practices, e.g. listening without interruption, responding, keeping to the topic and seeking clarification when a comment is not understood.
- Look for opportunities to initiate interaction with children who seem reluctant to converse, but don't overwhelm them by asking too many questions or putting them on the spot to talk. Allow them to be listeners in conversations or to make non-verbal responses, e.g. smiling, shaking or nodding their head (Kennedy, 2009, p. 11).
- Reinforce appropriate conversation practices, e.g. listening, taking turns and talking at an appropriate volume.
- Ensure that, in group conversations, turns to speak are shared.
- Keep conversations at a relaxed pace and in an enjoyable atmosphere of sharing.
- Demonstrate communication for different purposes, e.g. for commenting on an activity, describing an experience or making a request.
- Capitalise on the different parts of the day including arrival time and meal and snack time. The presence of an adult will ensure that children are engaged in rich and stimulating conversation during these times.

There are many ways in which the experience of conversation benefits children's oral language learning and development. Conversations, when integral to children's daily social and learning experiences, provide the following benefits:

- Children are provided with the regular practice of speaking and listening, which is important to the development of speaking fluency.
- Children increase their language knowledge when, through conversations with teachers, they are provided with models and demonstrations of new words, sentence structures and ways of expressing things.
- When children are provided with appropriate teacher guidance and direction they learn the social protocols and behaviours of conversation—how to initiate, maintain and conclude a conversation, how to politely change the topic of the conversation and the importance of taking turns and listening without interruption.
- Children learn to express different types of thinking. Conversation can call on children to express different types of thinking—reasoning, imagining, predicting and recalling experiences or facts.

DISCUSSION

Discussions share many of the same features as conversations. Like conversations, they involve children talking with each other and/or the teacher and exchanging information, opinions and experiences. They both require children to listen carefully and consider what others have to say and to adhere to certain protocols of group talk situations. Many of the skills necessary for effective conversations are also important to successful participation in discussions.

However, discussions are different from conversations in that they generally have a clear identifiable purpose or goal. They can occur spontaneously as children play and carry out learning activities and they can be carefully planned for achieving a learning goal as well as certain language outcomes. Ideal early childhood environments include plenty of opportunities for children to engage in genuine discussions on a range of topics and for different purposes.

In order to optimise the opportunities for children to learn to effectively participate in discussions and to learn speaking and listening skills on the whole, discussions should regularly be facilitated and supported by the teacher. A number of features should be considered when planning for and implementing discussion. These include the following.

Groups

- Use small groups of between two and six people so as to best allow for the active involvement of all the children.
- For very young children use even smaller group sizes (two to three people).
- Regularly choose the groupings so as to provide balance in terms of the abilities, skills and personalities of the groups' participants.

Purpose

- Provide discussion topics that centre on objects, activities, interests and experiences and that are meaningful for the children and relate to them personally.
- Ensure discussions involve children talking for different reasons: to convey information, share experiences, exchange opinions, report on events, justify actions and ask questions etc.
- Address various topics and purposes over time.

The task

- Integrate discussions into the everyday learning activities of the classroom.
- Set up independent learning centres in the classroom so that they promote discussion among children.

Goal

- Establish and clearly define the overall goal of a discussion. It might, for example, be to work together to solve a problem, to come to an agreement about the likely answers to a set of questions, to share information about a recent experience or to respond to a story.
- Clearly explain what is to be done, the steps to follow and how outcomes are to be recorded or reported back. Children might be required to orally share with the class what was talked about or the conclusions of the group. They might be asked to draw a picture, create a diagram or, if appropriate, to write notes and create written charts. The demands of the task should, of course, reflect the capabilities of the children involved.

Conventions and behaviours

- Use demonstration, explanation and reinforcement to teach the socially appropriate behaviours of group discussion.
- Include behaviours such as eye contact, taking turns, dealing with conflict and listening and responding to others.

Strategies

- Teach and refine children's use of strategies for beginning, sustaining and ending a discussion, and for keeping on task.

Teacher's role

- Ensure there are regular opportunities for discussion.
- Establish groups, set the topic and define the goal.
- Establish the procedures that children are to follow.
- Work with children to construct the rules of group discussion.
- Monitor the talk of individual children and the effectiveness of each discussion group.
- Provide guidance and support for individuals or groups as needed.
- Respond to children who either dominate the talk or don't participate and to groups displaying inappropriate behaviours.

There are different types of discussions, some of which are outlined in Table 4.3. In choosing the types of discussions and the way in which to implement discussions with children, teachers should consider the children's level of oral language development, their speaking and listening skills, the strategies they use and their learning and development needs.

Table 4.3: Some different types of discussions

Discussion type	Description
Sharing	This is sometimes referred to as 'show and tell' and involves one child talking about an object or experience while the others in the group listen and ask questions. To support language development, the teacher should encourage those listening to ask questions, and should also model good questions and support children by helping them to elaborate or by providing clarification when necessary (Christie, Enz & Vukelich, 2007).
Buzz groups	This involves children responding to an experience, story or class activity. It could, for instance, require children to provide as many examples as possible for a given category (e.g. fruit, countries, mammals); to come up with a list of similarities or differences between objects, events, people or places; to recall the steps of a particular procedure; or to place a list of things in order based on a given criterion (e.g. least favourite to most favourite or easiest to hardest). It is useful to provide the items or pictures for such tasks and, perhaps, to begin with a whole class discussion where the teacher inputs relevant vocabulary.
Brainstorm	This involves the children generating ideas on a topic. They work together to produce as many ideas as they can in a given period of time. A brainstorm topic might be worded as a question, e.g. 'What are all the things you remember about the elephants at the zoo?' 'In what ways can the school playground be changed to make it more child-friendly?' In a brainstorm all the suggested ideas are accepted without criticism or evaluation.

Discussion type	Description
Panels	This involves a group of children serving as the experts in a topic and, after preparation time, taking turns to speak about some aspect of the topic.
Committee	Committees are formed to carry out a task or organise an event. A committee might be required to plan and implement a class party or to organise for the equitable use of playground equipment. The committee members work together to make and action decisions for achieving a goal. Different committee members might be given a different role.
Literature circle	This discussion activity centres on children's literature. It involves children being grouped according to the book they have read (or had read to them) and discussing it in terms of its meaning or specific elements (e.g. structure, setting, characters, plot). A specific focus might be provided by the teacher or the children themselves.
Snowballing	This discussion activity begins with different pairs of children talking about a topic. Each pair then joins up with another pair to form a group of four and to share what each pair talked about. Groups of four could then join together to make groups of eight and again share and combine ideas.
Information gap	In this activity two groups are provided with different information on the same topic. For instance, if the topic is 'Life in the desert', one group might be given information about desert plants and another about environmental conditions. The groups have to use talk to share their information and draw it together.
Categorising statements	This involves each group being given a set of cards on which different statements are written (or pictures depicted). For instance, the statements (or pictures) might relate to important foods for health or to 'healthy lifestyle'. The children work together to sort the statements (or pictures) into two piles—those they agree with and those they do not. Alternatively, they can be asked to place the statements in order of importance or relevance.
Giving directions	Groups are provided with a task for which they need to create the oral directions and then use these to direct another group to do the task. This might, for instance, require giving directions for the workings of a simple toy, for making a paper plane or for how a game is played. It might require giving directions for how to get from the classroom to the school tuckshop.

Teachers often facilitate discussions by asking questions. In Chapter 6, a number of questioning frameworks have been provided. They are a useful guide to be used in designing questions that extend children's language and thinking. Of course, the types of questions asked will depend on the purpose for the discussion. It is important to ensure that discussions for children don't simply focus on them answering a teacher's question or on children always directing their thoughts and ideas towards the teacher. It is important that discussion involves children talking with each other and listening and responding to each other's comments.

INVESTIGATIONS

Investigations can be undertaken by children as young as four, either independently or together with others. They should take place in response to the children's particular curiosities about their world and to their wonderments about people, places and things. Investigations involve children interacting with and exploring objects and materials and using different sources of information as they seek to find answers to questions and learn and understand more about their world. For instance, an investigation might involve children finding out about how sound is created using vibrations or determining different natural features of the local parkland environment. Investigations are a type of exploratory play; however, they provide opportunities for more focused engagement and 'more complex interactions with the material provided' (Otto, 2010, p. 315).

Investigations are best when they arise from the curiosities of children and when they serve to answer children's own questions. A simple fascination with the light reflected in a puddle of water after a rainy day provides an opportunity to lead children into finding out about various light or water concepts. Investigations should set in motion new questions and new directions in which to take things. Children have a natural propensity for wonderment and, in harnessing this, their deep involvement in their learning is likely to be assured.

Central to the process of investigation is oral language. Children use oral language for genuine communication purposes as they seek to satisfy their curiosity about objects, places and people and as they learn about topics and develop conceptual knowledge. They use language as they negotiate with others, plan how to find things out, discuss information and ideas and reflect on experiences. Investigations involve:

Oral language is used for genuine communication purposes when it centres around their curiosities about their world.

- *Manipulation*: children explore concepts using a variety of tools, objects and materials. As they do so, they talk and listen to others (children, teachers and adults).
- *Reasoning*: children use facts, properties and relationships to reach new understandings and gain new knowledge. They listen, watch, do, think and talk as they seek to make sense of something and to develop conceptual knowledge.
- *Representation*: children represent information in different ways. They talk, and they tell others what they did or learnt. They also use written and visual language to communicate. They draw pictures and diagrams, create labels, devise symbols, dramatise etc.

The teacher's role is fundamental to the successful use and development of oral language in investigations. Teachers should continually guide children by asking questions, providing demonstrations, explaining and making suggestions. They should input new vocabulary and assist children to express their growing understandings. They might choose to monitor the oral language and interaction patterns that develop when children carry out investigations together.

SUMMARY

Play, listening to stories being read aloud, storytelling, conversations and discussion, and investigations are significant contexts for early childhood language learning and development. Each fosters children's listening and speaking skills and knowledge in distinct ways and each should feature strongly in the different early childhood learning settings.

QUESTIONS AND ACTIVITIES

1. For each of the learning contexts described, identify the opportunities for children's oral language development. In doing so, consider the four components of language (phonological, syntactic, semantic, pragmatic) identified in Chapter 1.
2. How would you ensure play spaces/learning centres are set up so as to be 'enriched with culturally relevant resources'? Why is this important?
3. Create a chart that depicts a possible schedule for infants in care. On the chart indicate the opportunities for reading story books and having 'conversations'.
4. Consider the various ways in which the teacher might support children's use of language when carrying out investigations with young children.
5. Design a story-retelling experience that relates to a children's story book in pre-school or school. Ensure that the language learning focus has been clearly identified.

KEY TERMS

exploratory play
learning centres
socio-dramatic play

KEY REFERENCES

Christie, J., Enz, B. et al. (2007). *Teaching language and literacy: Preschool through the elementary grades*. Boston: Allyn and Bacon.

Justice, L. M. & Pence, K. L. (2005). *Scaffolding with storybooks*. Newark, Delaware: International Reading Association.

Kennedy, A. (2009). Let's talk: Having meaningful conversations with children. *Putting Children First, 32*, 11–13.

Klein, T. P., Wirth D. et al. (2004). Play: Children's context for development. In *Spotlight on young children and play*, D. Koralek. USA, National Association for the Education of Young Children.

Massey, S. L. (2004). Teacher–child conversation in the preschool classroom. *Early Childhood Education Journal, 31*, 4.

Otto, B. (2010). *Language development in early childhood*. Upper Saddle River, New Jersey: Pearson Education.

Roe, B. D. & Ross, E. P. (2006). *Integrating language arts through literature and thematic units*. Boston: Allyn and Bacon.

Trelease, J. (1995). *The read aloud handbook*. New York: Penguin.

Victorian Department of Education (2009). *Victorian early years learning and development framework for all children from birth to eight years*. Retrieved 15/3/2010 from www.vcaa.vic.edu.au/earlyyears/index.html.

CHAPTER 5

Learning Experiences and Activities for Speaking and Listening

CHAPTER OBJECTIVES

This chapter will increase your understanding of:

- considerations for the planning of speaking and listening activities for children
- activities and experiences that serve to develop children's speaking and listening in early childhood
- the role of the teacher in different speaking and listening activities and experiences.

This chapter extends on the previous chapter in which important language learning contexts were discussed. It provides you with a range of experiences and activities that will assist in the development of children's language knowledge and skills and their oral communication competency, and that you might include as part of a comprehensive speaking and listening program for young children (three to eight years). However, it is important to keep in mind that children's understanding about oral communication begins to develop even before they begin to talk. Treat all children (infants, toddlers) as conversationalists and in so doing provide them with the opportunity to learn important understandings about the use of language as a mode of communication. The chapter concludes with a specific focus on listening, the receptive form of oral language. The goal is to draw to your attention the importance of listening as an oral communication competency and to encourage you to consider how to support children as listeners who have the associated skills of attention and concentration. The activities should be complemented by strong teacher guidance and good models of oral language. One final point: as children's language knowledge, understanding and skills develop, they should be introduced to more formal contexts for language use.

INTRODUCTION: IMPORTANT CONSIDERATIONS

For children to become clearer and more effective in their oral communication they require regular experiences in a variety of purposeful talk situations and they need to become competent in both the speaking and listening roles of oral communication. The experiences and activities with which children are provided should serve to facilitate their speaking and listening development. The successful use of any of the experiences and activities suggested in this chapter involves a consideration of the following important points about language and development:

1. *Children's language development and learning is best served when the experiences in which they engage address both oral and written language in an integrated way*. The learning of oral language (speaking and listening) and written language (reading and writing) are inextricably linked and this should be reflected in a teaching program. The activities described here provide for children's speaking and listening development and learning, which is concerned with oral language, as opposed to reading and writing, which are the written language modes. Reading and writing activities should be developed so that they regularly connect to listening and speaking activities.

2. *For many children, the language or dialect spoken at home is different from that of the classroom or care setting*. It is important to establish supportive language environments that recognise and respect children's first language or dialect as a valid system for communication and as integral to children's identity, values and experiences of their family and community. Children should be encouraged to use their first language or dialect as they participate in oral language activities of the classroom or care setting. Practices accommodating this should be established; for instance: involving community members who speak a child's first language; and providing the opportunity for children with a common first language to work together. Methods that support children to understand and learn English should also be used; this might include use of visuals, objects, gestures and facial expressions to support comprehension when talking with children, use of demonstration to accompany explanation, use of small groups to provide a less intimidating environment for talk, and respect for the '**silent period**' as a natural phase in learning a new language.

3. *Not all speaking and listening activities are appropriate for all children*. The activities described in this chapter have not been aligned with particular ages and phases of development or different care or education settings. They vary in terms of their suitability for different groups of children. Decisions should be made about the appropriateness of activities for a group of children as well as the teaching strategies and techniques to be used with particular activities and particular groups of children. Such decisions should take into account the ability and learning needs of the children, the features of the educational setting and the type of program to be implemented. Additionally, one group or class of children will likely present with varying oral language development needs and it is important to provide the range of experiences necessary in catering for these differences. **Open-ended activities** where children can be involved at their own level are useful.

4. *The activity is the vehicle for children's learning.* For it to serve optimal learning and development, teachers need to employ various **scaffolding techniques** (actions taken to support children in completing an activity successfully). Scaffolding might take the form of:

- modelling the activity with emphasis on the language required for the activity (carry it out while the children observe)
- using suitable materials and equipment
- simplifying the activity
- separating an activity into smaller activities or steps and giving step-by-step instruction and demonstration
- using explanation and demonstration to provide the children with direction
- asking questions that serve to direct the children's thinking in a way that is needed for the activity
- making comments that prompt children into taking an activity in a direction that will assist their learning
- participating in an activity with children and, by so doing, directing their learning or demonstrating particular skills.

Regular experiences in purposeful talk situations are important for children to become clearer and more effective in their oral communication.

SPEAKING AND LISTENING ACTIVITIES

TELEPHONE ROLE PLAYS

Telephone role plays involve children carrying out pretend telephone conversations with different people and on various topics (for example, passing on information, establishing a social engagement, discussing a problem or describing an event). They should usually be based on realistic situations, though imaginative scenarios that relate to story book events, topics or themes might also be used. Telephone role plays emphasise the need to use language itself rather than gestures or facial expressions.

The children must listen carefully to the words being spoken since they cannot see the person speaking. Children can learn the social conventions appropriate to different types of telephone conversations.

Children should be encouraged to compose their own telephone role plays, though older children might be directed to role-play specific scenarios that help to achieve precise conversation, speaking and listening goals.

CHARACTER INTERVIEWS

This activity involves the children role-playing an interview with a story book character. In conducting the interview the teacher or a child takes on the role of the story character and answers questions posed by the other children. The process might involve the following steps:

- *Tell the story*: the teacher reads or tells a story to the children while helping them to identify the attributes and actions of a specified character as well as the events in the story.
- *Discuss the character*: a description of the specified character is built up. This might involve the teacher assisting the children to do this or the children working in small groups. Words or phrases that describe the character's traits and actions might be written down.
- *Devise questions*: children work in pairs or small groups, or with the teacher's guidance, to devise questions that they would like to ask the story character.
- *Character interview*: the teacher or one of the children takes on the role of the character and answers the questions posed by the rest of the children. The character might first be required to retell the story from the character's own perspective (in the first person) before the interview begins.

When children take the role of the character and answer questions provided by other children they develop the ability to infer meaning, which is important to both listening and reading comprehension.

Character interviews support children's learning with regard to:

- listening to and understanding a story
- questioning skills
- comprehension, recognising inferential meaning, and thinking beyond the literal level of a story
- understanding story characters
- recalling detail specifically with regard to story characters.

BARRIER GAMES

A barrier game begins with two children sitting opposite each other and having some kind of screen or barrier (often a large piece of cardboard) between them so that they are unable to view what each other has or is doing. The game involves one of the children describing what is on his or her side of the barrier or giving instructions for the other child to follow, draw or create. For example, the children might both have identical farmyard models and several of the same plastic farmyard animals, with the objective being for them to position their animals in identical places in the farmyard model.

The game begins with one of the children positioning his or her farmyard animals and then instructing the other child about where to position his or her animals so that they are placed the same in the farmyard. The child might, for instance, instruct, 'Put the brown cow and the black cow next to each other and put them both above the pond.'

Instructions continue to be given until all the animals have been placed. The child receiving the instructions must listen carefully and follow them and try to reproduce the first child's scene as accurately as possible. He or she might need to ask clarifying questions, such as, 'Do you mean the big pond or the little pond?'

Other barrier games include: one child threading different types of beads onto string and then instructing another child to thread the same type of beads in the same order, or both children being given the same picture but with some small differences in the detail (for example, number of buttons on a person's coat, colour of an animal) and one child asking questions about the other child's picture in order to determine the differences (for example, 'How many buttons does the boy's coat have?').

At the conclusion of a barrier game, the children remove the barrier to see how accurate they have been in creating identical pictures, scenes or constructions or to determine if they have located all the differences.

Barrier games generally involve sequencing activities, assembling and constructing scenes or items, locating a place or following a route on a map, matching activities, or spotting differences. The teacher might first model how the activity proceeds as well as the effective use of descriptive language and the need to give precise instructions.

There are many types of barrier games, some of which include:

- *Colouring*: each child is given a laminated picture and a set of coloured markers. One child colours an item located in the picture and then instructs the other child to do the same. Their instructions should name the item and the colour (e.g. 'Colour the ball green').
- *Adding characters and items to a scene*: each child is given a picture of the same scene (e.g. under the sea, a zoo, farmyard, park, playground or supermarket) and a set of picture cards or items that belong to the scene. For instance, the undersea scene might include picture cards of sea creatures, a shipwreck, a diver, a treasure chest and so on. One child begins by placing an item on his or her scene and then instructs the other child to place the same item in the same location on the scene. The instructions continue until all items have been placed by both the children.
- *Dressing the doll*: each child is given a cardboard cut-out of a doll and a selection of paper clothes. The aim is for the children to dress them in identical clothes and is achieved by one child choosing from the selection of clothing items and placing one item at a time on their doll and then instructing the other child to do the same.
- *Threading*: one child makes a necklace by threading a number of different types of beads onto string. She or he then instructs the other child on each bead to be threaded so that both the children end up with identical necklaces.
- *Spot the difference*: the children are each given pictures which are the same except for a few differences in the detail. By describing their pictures and asking questions, the children try to identify the differences. At the end of the game they lay their pictures side by side and check that they have identified all the differences.
- *Construction*: using construction material such as Duplo and Lego (children's plastic building blocks) or play dough, the children can use the barrier game activity to construct similar objects.

Barrier games are highly motivational and offer a range of learning opportunities. They can be used to develop both listening and speaking in young children and they are effective for working with children for whom English is a second or additional language (ESL/EAL). Barrier games require the giving of clear and detailed instructions, clarifying questions to be posed, taking turns and the use of descriptive (for example, adjectives) and positional (for example, prepositions) language.

Barrier games offer a range of language learning opportunities.

Although barrier games are commonly carried out in pairs, there are many variations. For example, they can be done with the teacher or one child giving the instructions to a small group or even the whole class, or by children playing together in teams. A teacher playing a barrier game with the class and giving the instructions has the opportunity to model the language of instructions and descriptions. This is important for children in developing such use of language themselves.

SORTING AND CLASSIFYING

This involves children sorting and grouping objects (or pictures) according to their attributes and then explaining the process they followed and the basis on which they decided the grouping of the objects. The classification of objects might be done in relation to the objects' colour, shape, use, type of movement or some other attribute. It might involve sorting the objects into two or more groups and it might involve the children finding other ways in which the same set of objects could be sorted.

In order to identify the way in which to sort a set of objects, children need to compare the objects and determine their similarities and differences. The comparison of two objects is a good starting point when helping children to develop classification skills. Talk should begin with, 'What is the same and what is different?'

Sorting and classifying activities might involve the teacher deciding the categories for the sorting; for example, the teacher asks the children to sort all the big things into one group and the small things into another. They might also require the children to decide their own categories. As children sort, they should be assisted to talk about their sorting categories—explaining why they are putting something into a certain group.

A great deal of oral language development can occur when children engage in regular sorting and classifying activities. However, the teacher's guidance and demonstration is important to the development of both classification ability and the language use for classification. Language learning opportunities encompass the areas of vocabulary development, syntax, speaking for different purposes and talking with others to achieve a goal. They include learning about:

- nouns: names of objects (e.g. peg, clip, ball) and labels for attributes (e.g. colour, shape, size, movement)
- adjectives: words that describe the different objects (e.g. blue, tall, big, fast, hard, bumpy)
- adjectives of comparison (comparatives and superlatives): big, bigger, biggest and fast, faster, fastest etc.
- opposites (e.g. soft and hard, big and little, fast and slow)
- sentences that clearly describe and compare objects (e.g. 'The teddy is soft but the peg is hard', 'The ruler and the clip are hard and the other things are soft') and that describe categories of objects (e.g. 'In this group everything is blue')
- speaking for different purposes (e.g. to explain, to recount, to reason, to describe)
- talking with other children and the teacher about how to sort and classify objects.

PICTURE TALKS

Picture talks are a type of discussion that involves the use of a picture as the stimulus for talk. The picture used might be one from a children's story book or it might be a photograph or piece of art. It should be of a size that all the children in the group can easily see.

A picture talk can be carried out with the teacher working with the class or a small group of children, and asking questions of the children about the picture. The questions should be carefully considered so that they prompt the children to observe, and think in different ways about what they see in the picture. The children might be asked to identify and describe people and items in the picture or to locate and name items belonging to a specific category, to make connections between what is in the picture and what they know or have experienced themselves or to imagine other events and scenarios that might relate to the picture.

Example of a set of questions asked during a discussion of a photograph.

> Describe some things you see in the picture.
>
> What does this (point to an object) look like to you?
>
> What objects in the picture are similar, and how?
>
> Why do you think the person took this picture?
>
> If this picture was in an art gallery, what would you call it?
>
> If this picture was in a story book, what would the story be about?
>
> How does the picture make you feel when you look at it?

Questions that the teacher asks are important to developing and extending opportunities for the children to use language to observe, think and talk about a picture and so develop their language skills. It is useful to plan these questions ahead of time to ensure that there is a variety of types, requiring children to express their observations, interpretations, opinions and judgments of a picture and to use language for different purposes and in different ways.

There are many models of question categories that can be used to assist teachers in designing questions for picture talks (as well as for other purposes) that serve to extend children's use of oral language. Some examples are described in Chapter 6 (Language and thinking) and Chapter 13 (Reading comprehension).

Picture talks should also give children the opportunity to ask questions, as the ability to do so is important to a comprehensive development of their oral language ability. Teachers can support children's ability to ask questions by providing good models for them to emulate. Children need to hear examples of different types of questions and of the way in which they can be structured.

Picture talks can also involve small groups of children talking with each other about a given picture or set of pictures. Their task might be open-ended, allowing the children to direct the content of their discussion, or it might be teacher-directed, requiring the children to produce their answers to a set of questions or achieve a specific goal (for example, deciding on the five most interesting or unusual things about a picture). The group might also be given two pictures for which they are required to determine the similarities and differences. Whatever the case, the task and the associated speaking and listening demands should be designed to suit the children's current oral language ability and learning needs.

Picture talks can be established to support children's speaking and listening competency in many ways, including their ability to ask and answer questions, to use complete sentences and descriptive words and phrases, to use oral language to clearly and cohesively express their thoughts, and to speak for such purposes as to name, describe, explain, rationalise or imagine.

ACTION RHYMES

Action rhymes involve children carrying out actions as they recite poems or rhymes. The poems and rhymes should be characterised by the use of rhythm, rhyme and repetition, which enhance their appeal to children as well as their effectiveness in supporting children's language development and learning. The actions should be performed in a way that highlights the meaning of what is being said.

The rhyme *Monkeys on the bed* (refer to the text box) is an example of an action rhyme that has all the elements important to ensuring children's participation and to fostering their oral language development and learning.

Action rhymes should be an integral part of the day in the various early childhood settings. They can be undertaken at different times throughout the day—during group mat sessions, when moving children between learning experiences or contexts, to begin or end an activity or lesson, to settle children before talking with them, and so on.

Action rhymes draw on young children's motivation to play and be active, and the playfulness of the language and the actions should provide all the encouragement children need to become involved. Children can participate at some level regardless of

> ### MONKEYS ON THE BED
>
> Five little monkeys jumping
> on the bed
> one fell off and bumped
> his head.
> Mama called the doctor and
> the doctor said,
> 'No more monkeys
> jumping on the bed!'
> Four little monkeys jumping on the bed … Three little monkeys jumping on the bed …
> [and so on].

their oral language proficiency. When reciting action rhymes with children, teachers should clearly articulate the words, give emphasis to their natural rhythm and use an interesting and lively voice. The actions and words should be recited at a pace that allows the children to keep up.

The rhymes used with different groups of children should be carefully chosen to match the children's interests and capabilities and to provide opportunities for them to learn language. The language development and learning opportunities provided by the regular performance of well chosen action rhymes are extensive, and include:

- phonological awareness (awareness of the rhythm and rhyme)
- sounds of language and of word articulation
- syntax knowledge (structuring sentences and clauses)
- semantics (associate words and phrases with meaning)
- language fluency (practice gained through repetition)
- supporting the development of children's ability to listen with attention, to follow directions and to understand order and sequence.

SURPRISE BAG

The surprise bag activity involves the children determining the identity of an item that has been placed in a bag and cannot be seen. The children ask questions in an effort to gain adequate information to identity the item. There are many ways of implementing this activity; it could begin with a collection of items being displayed and discussed before one is chosen to be placed in the surprise bag. The teacher should model the use of descriptive language and specific vocabulary when talking about each item. Another option is for the children to bring in personal or favourite items from home and to provide clues about them after placing them in the surprise bag.

The surprise bag activity can be carried out with the whole class, although it is best suited to a small group; the smaller the group the greater the amount of speaking practice for each child. It supports children in developing their listening skills, their use of descriptive language and their ability to ask questions to seek or clarify information.

An alternative method for the surprise bag activity is for one child, who knows the identity of the object, to describe it to the other children, being careful not to name it, while the others try to arrive at its identity. When familiar with the process, the children can work in pairs or small groups to carry out the activity with each other. In this case, the teacher would not lead the activity but would provide support that addresses the needs of the groups or pairs of children.

ACTION RHYMES

Finger puppets support children in understanding the meaning of different action rhymes.

Heads and shoulders

Heads, shoulders, knees and toes,
knees and toes, knees and toes;
heads, shoulders, knees and toes,
we all clap hands together.
Eyes, ears, mouth and nose,
mouth and nose, mouth and nose;
eyes, ears, mouth and nose,
we all clap hands together.

[Children touch parts of the body as they sing the song, which can be sung faster and faster.]

Grandma's spectacles

Here are grandma's spectacles,
and here is grandma's hat,
and here is the way she folds her hands,
and puts them in her lap.

Here are grandpa's spectacles,
and here is grandpa's hat,

and here's the way he folds his arms,
and takes a little nap.

[Alternative ending to grandma's verse]:
Grandma claps her hands like this,
and folds them in her lap.

For the spectacles, put thumb and forefinger together on each hand and take them up to eyes. For the hat, with hands make the shape of a hat on top of head. For grandma, put one hand on top of the other to 'fold her hands' and then place them on lap. For grandpa, just fold arms and tilt head forward, eyes closed.

Two little apples

Two little apples hanging in a tree,
two little apples smiling at me.
I shook the tree as hard as I could.
Down came the apples,
mmm—they were good.

Two little dickie-birds sitting on a wall

Two little dickie-birds sitting on a wall,
one named Peter, one named Paul.
Fly away Peter, fly away Paul,
come back Peter, come back Paul.

If you're happy and you know it

If you're happy and you know it, clap your hands.
If you're happy and you know it, clap your hands.
If you're happy and you know it,
and you really want to show it,
if you're happy and you know it, clap your hands.

[In subsequent verses, sing:]
Stamp your feet
Nod your head
Shout 'WE ARE!'
[Do all four.]

Raise your hands

Raise your hands above your head,
clap them one, two, three.
Rest them now upon your hips,
slowly bend your knees.
Up again and stand up tall,

put your right foot out.
Shake your fingers,
nod your head,
and twist yourself about.

There was a little turtle

There was a little turtle, [hold out rounded hand, like turtle shell]
who lived in a box. [place other hand, flat, underneath]
He swam in the puddles, [make swimming motions with hands]
and he climbed on the rocks. [Make climbing motions]
He snapped at the mosquito, [emphasise the word 'snapped,' and clap hands]
he snapped at the flea, he snapped at the minnow, and he snapped at me!
He caught the mosquito, he caught the flea, he caught the minnow,
but he didn't catch me! [Point both thumbs at self]

THE LISTENING POST

Children can go to listening posts to listen to audio recordings of stories.

Listening posts are areas set aside in the classroom where the children can go to listen to audio recordings (often through headphones) of stories, poems and other oral language texts. There is a diverse range of suitable recordings available commercially, but teachers can easily prepare their own recordings using published stories or those that the teacher or the children, or both, have created.

Groups of children or individual children can listen to an audio recording while others are carrying out other activities. Children might simply listen to the recording or they might carry out a related activity afterwards such as to draw, write, talk with others, answer questions or retell or explain the listening text.

A useful listening post activity is to have the children listen to a recording of everyday sounds such as a tap running, a dog eating its food, a clock ticking or rain falling and to identify the sounds orally or by matching them to one of the pictures provided. The ability to notice and discriminate between everyday sounds is an important early listening skill, which usually precedes the development of understandings and skills in phonological awareness.

Talking books are a type of audio recording. They are played on a computer and, as a story is read, the matching written text is displayed. Listening to the story is therefore accompanied by following the written text. There are many commercially available talking books, but book recordings prepared by teachers and the children themselves are an option. The use of information and communication technologies (ICT) to facilitate literacy development in young children is covered in Chapter 24.

Listening to stories read by fluent readers is beneficial to children's speaking and listening development and learning. It encourages vocabulary development, familiarity with text and sentence structures, and the development of positive attitudes towards stories.

NEWS-TELLING

News-telling is a common early childhood listening and speaking activity. It involves children orally recounting a personal experience or event and listening to other children as they do the same. Children's news-telling might be about such things as the weekend's activities or a special family celebration or outing. When children are a little older, the events they recount during news-telling might also include those of a more public nature such as local, national or world events.

During news-telling children orally recount a personal experience or event to other children.

Traditionally, news-telling involves the children sitting on the mat area and taking turns to share their news. A group of children will tell their news each day so that, by the end of the week, each child has had a turn. However, this can be time-consuming and tedious and other ways of organising news-telling should be considered. For example, children might tell their news to a partner (partner news-telling) or to a small group. It is also worthwhile to get the children to retell someone else's news or to audio record their news as a 'news report'(Roberts & Nicholl, 1996).

Children's oral recounts are assisted when they involve a plan that helps them to remember the main components or the sequence of events. A plan might include information about the 'who', 'what', 'where' and 'when' of the experience to be recounted and it might also include a personal response. A plan might be prepared pictorially or in words. It can be used as a memory aid or prompt when telling news.

Figure 5.1: An example of a news-telling plan for young children

WHO	WHAT	WHEN	WHERE
Mum	ck	S D	

My name is

My news today is about …

Where?	When?	What?	Who?	Response
This is where I went …	This is when I went …	This is what I did …	These are the other people who were with me …	This is what I felt/ thought …
		1st 2nd 3rd		

News-telling supports children's oral language development and learning in a variety of ways. They learn about an oral recount and the important elements to include. They learn to:

- speak to an audience for a particular purpose (to share an event or personal experience)
- sequence information in the right order when speaking about events that have happened
- use the past tense
- listen, question and respond.

Children's ability with news-telling and their speaking skills are best enhanced when they are provided with considerable support from the teacher. The development of listening skills and behaviours—for example, looking at the speaker, paying attention, listening without interruption and thinking about what the speaker is saying—requires clear, consistent teacher guidance.

Teachers should assist children to use language (words and sentences) as well as the voice (volume, pitch, speed) and non-verbal language (eye-contact, facial expression, gestures) in a way that provides for clear and meaningful oral communication. An ideal way of doing this is to model the telling of news themselves. Children learn from seeing and hearing good language models. Another useful teacher support is the use of explicit feedback. Teachers should regularly indicate to children the different positive features they demonstrated when telling their news. This might be streamlined by having a specific speaking and listening goal for the week (for example, 'This week we are going to concentrate on using a voice that everyone can hear') and focusing feedback on this aspect.

MEMORY TRAY

In this activity the children are required to observe and recall a number of everyday items that have been placed on a tray and that, after some time, are hidden from view. After observing the items, the children talk together to recall them. The activity can be extended by asking the children to recall attributes of the items (for example, colour, shape, size, use). The memory tray supports children's learning in regard to:

- the use of observation and methods to aid memory
- vocabulary (nouns and descriptive words and phrases).

CLASS MEETINGS

In class meetings, children meet on a regular basis (for example, weekly) to talk together about relevant events or issues or to decide how to get something done. A class meeting might involve children considering how to deal with a problem (for example, bullying), deciding on how to share play equipment fairly or organising a class event.

The teacher's role in classroom meetings is vital to children learning how to successfully participate. They should set out the meeting rules with the children (for example, turn-taking listening attentively to the child speaking, expressing alternative opinions or disagreeing in a respectful way). They should also take the opportunity to model appropriate use of language, particularly for such uses as offering an opinion, making a suggestion, disagreeing with someone or presenting an issue for discussion; for instance, 'I am very worried about …' or 'I would really like to find a way to solve this problem.' Teachers should also demonstrate attentive listening.

THINK, PAIR, SHARE

In this activity children are given time to think and talk about ideas or topics with a partner before sharing them with the larger group. Providing time for children to share their thoughts, ideas and knowledge with one another is important to their language development and learning. The partner situation for talking provides a more secure option for sharing ideas, thoughts and understanding than does the whole group situation. It also means that all the children are given the opportunity to talk whereas in large groups only a few children might get to do so. The activity procedure involves the children:

1   Thinking: after being given a topic or question, the children should be provided with individual time to think. During the thinking time, they might also be asked to draw pictures or write notes as memory aids.
2   Talking in pairs: the children are put in pairs to talk about their ideas, thoughts and knowledge in relation to the topic or question. Each partner should take a turn to talk while the other listens.
3   Sharing: the pairs of children share what they talked about with the larger group.

CELEBRITY HEADS

In this activity, two or three children sit with their backs to the board, and an object, animal or person is identified to the rest of the group but not shown to the children sitting with the board behind them. They must ask questions that require only yes or no replies and that help them to identify the object, animal, or person. The other children answer the questions with a yes or no.

PAIRED IMPROVISATION

In this activity, pairs are given character roles (for instance, a shopkeeper and customer) and they carry out a dialogue appropriate to their roles, making the conversation up as they go along. It is important that the children are familiar with the type of character who they are required to represent.

SEQUENCE CHART

In this activity the children need to verbalise a sequence of instructions that explain how to do something (for example, how to ride a bike, how to make a chocolate milkshake, how to assemble a toy). The children should always have had experience in the process about which they are required to provide instructions. The teacher should indicate or reinforce the language (vocabulary, sentences) that is appropriate for the purpose.

HIDE THE OBJECT

One child is asked to leave the room and, while he/she is gone, another child places an object somewhere in the classroom—in, on, under, above or next to another item in the classroom. The child outside is then called to come in and find the object. As he/she looks, they need to ask the class, 'Is it on the desk?', 'Is it in the bin?' etc.

The following activities have a specific listening focus.

LISTENING WALKS

This activity entails taking children for a walk around the indoor or outdoor environment to listen to, and identify, the sounds heard. The activity might involve stopping the children in different places and having them stand still (or sit or lie down) with eyes closed, focusing aurally on the environment. The sounds heard might then be shared and discussed either immediately or on return to the classroom. The teacher might record the sounds, which can be played back later to stimulate discussion. To provide emphasis on the listening aspect of the activity, young children can be required to cup their hands around their ears or even to wear large, cardboard ears (Primary National Strategy, 2007b).

MAKING SOUNDS

This activity involves children playing and experimenting with simple musical instruments such as drums, pots and pans, toys that make sounds, spoons, shakers, tapping sticks, tambourines, bells, and so on, to create sounds. Many types of simple instruments can be made in the classroom. The activity can also involve children using everyday objects to find out what sounds they make (Primary National Strategy, 2007). A discussion about the sounds made and favourite sounds should follow.

SOUND LOTTO

In this activity the children are assisted to recognise and discriminate between sounds. Each child is provided with a card that has been divided into squares with each square showing a picture of a different object (for example, a card might show pictures of a car, a shower, a cat, a violin, a thundercloud, a pair of scissors cutting through paper, and so on). The objects should all have an associated sound. The teacher plays an audio recording of the sounds associated with the items on the cards. One sound at a time is played and the children decide if they have the item associated with that sound on their card; if they do, they place a counter over the picture.

> **WEBSITES FOR HOW TO MAKE CHILDREN'S MUSICAL INSTRUMENTS**
>
> There are many websites that have instructions on how to make children's musical instruments, some of which instruct on how to make instruments from different cultures.
>
> - Songs for Teaching: www.songsforteaching.com/articles/makingmusicalinstrumentsathome.htm
> - Storytime Songs: www.storytimesongs.com/instruments.html
> - Nine easy-to-make musical instruments: www.kinderart.com/teachers/9instruments.shtml
> - Homemade instruments: www.nancymusic.com/PRINThomemade.htm

SIMON SAYS

Simon says is a very well-known and simple game that develops children's ability to listen and respond to instructions. It involves the teacher (or a child) giving an instruction which, if it begins with the phrase 'Simon says', must be followed by the children. For example, the teacher (or child) might say, 'Simon says, blink your eyes twice,' and the children must perform this action. However, the instruction 'Put your hands on your hips' should be ignored as it doesn't begin with the phrase 'Simon says'.

The game can be adapted to suit the language competency of different groups of children. For more capable language users, the instructions can be extended to include two or three commands which require being carried out in sequence. For example, 'Simon says, put your hands on your hips, then stamp your feet twice, then put your hands on your head.'

When the children are involved in those roles—giving and following instructions—they obtain practice in giving clear simple instructions (commands), listening with understanding and responding to instructions.

Children learn to listen, understand and respond to instructions through such games as 'Simon says'.

PASS IT ON

This activity involves children standing or sitting in a circle with one child sending a message (sentence) to another by whispering it to the adjacent child and it then being whispered from child to child until it arrives at its destination. The aim is to get the message to the recipient using the exact same words and sentence. A sentence such as 'Sally went to the shop and bought twenty green apples' might arrive at the end of the line as 'Sally went shopping and got twenty apples.' When the message has passed through to the finish, the teacher and children discuss what occurred:

- Did the sentence retain its meaning? Why? Why not?
- Which words were missed out?
- Were any words added?
- Were any words substituted by a similar sounding word?

A variation of this game involves two lines (teams) of children. The team that passes a message along without any changes gains a point.

WHAT AM I?

For this activity, children are provided with a set of picture cards (one identical set per child) of different familiar items. The children work in pairs and one child chooses a picture from the set and describes it while the other child tries to determine what is being described. The child who is determining the picture that is being described needs to listen carefully to the description given and, if necessary, ask questions to glean more information. For example, 'Is it big, medium sized or small?', 'Is it red, spotted or stripy?', 'What is its shape?', 'Where would you find it?' The activity develops children's ability to use language to describe and to find out information. It has a strong speaking as well as listening component.

QUICK QUESTIONS

Children need to answer yes or no in response to each of a series of questions asked at a fairly rapid pace. This requires listening carefully to the questions. Example questions:

- Do balls bounce?
- Do all girls have long hair?
- Do doors open and close?
- Is an elephant bigger than a whale?
- Do you have three feet?
- Can a fish talk?
- Is a ball round?
- Do fish live in water?
- Can you pick up a tree?
- Do you write with a ruler?
- Do you rule with a pencil?
- Can you swim in sand?
- Can a boy cook?

DICTOGLOSS

This activity requires children to listen to the teacher read a short text aloud and then to talk with others to remember and recall the content. Older children might also be asked to reconstruct the text in writing. The activity has a strong listening comprehension focus; it assists children to attend to and recall meaning when listening.

It is important to choose a text which has a content and length appropriate to the children's ability. The children should be given the opportunity to first predict the content of the text based on the title and some key content words. The text should be read at a medium to slow pace with appropriate pauses for the children to consider the meaning. After the reading has been completed the children talk in pairs, helping each other to recall the content. Each pair might then join with another pair to pool their recollections.

ACTIVITY SHARING

Activity sharing involves children explaining about an experience or an activity which they have carried out. It might call for the children to share what they have done with the teacher or another adult or with one other child or a group of children. The sharing is done after the experience or activity, requiring the children to recall what they used, what they did and how they did it. It might also involve children drawing conclusions about what was learnt or achieved. For older children, sharing time might be a formalised routine of the day—for instance, after group activities or free play, and using a set framework such as:

- the materials used
- the actual experience or activity (where relevant, the steps involved)
- the outcome (what was made, discovered or achieved).

Additionally, teachers should encourage children to share about an activity while they are engaged in it. They should interact with children and ask questions that require them to share what they are doing. Such questions might include:

- What are you doing?
- What else did you do?
- How did you do that?
- Why did you do that?
- What did you use?
- Why did you use those things?
- How did you work that out?
- What are you going to do next?

LISTENING EXPERIENCES FOR TODDLERS

- engaging in rhymes (including nursery rhymes) and finger play
- sound-making such as clapping to rhythm, drumming and tapping (using a variety of objects)
- listening to music such as The Wiggles, classical music, traditional songs and instrumental music; moving and dancing to music
- engaging in action songs such as 'Head, shoulders, knees and toes', 'I'm a little teapot', and 'If you're happy and you know it'
- locating environmental sounds
- talking about how certain sounds make them feel
- listening to instructions and following them, e.g. 'Please take this block and put it in the box'
- listening to stories
- listening out for mistakes when the teacher reads a well-known story, such as: 'Little Red Riding Hood was on her way to see her grandmother, who lived up a beanstalk'
- expressing feelings or imaginings about sounds or music through drama and art.

Source: Machado (2007, 2010)

THE IMPORTANCE OF LISTENING

Listening is an important part of the communicative process. If children (or indeed adults) cannot listen effectively, they are disadvantaged in many ways. It is important that children are provided with the support that ensures their development in both speaking and listening. Of course, if they engage in purposeful oral communication experiences, both listening and speaking are involved.

Listening involves searching for meaning. The listener constructs meaning using the spoken language heard, combined with what they already know. Thus, listening is essentially a hearing–thinking process. It should be noted, however, that listeners often use additional information to help them make meaning. They use visual information such as the speaker's body language

SOUND DISCRIMINATION ACTIVITIES

Listening walks

This activity involves groups of children going for short walks (indoors or outdoors) and consciously listening to environmental sounds, such as birds singing, aeroplanes or helicopters flying above, and cars, trains and trucks driving past. Children should be taught listening behaviours such as keeping quiet and paying attention while participating in listening walks. They may wear large cardboard 'listening ears' for this activity.

Drum outdoors

This activity integrates with music education and involves children going on a walk and tapping a stick on different objects and surfaces to find out what sound they make.

Sound lotto

This is a game that involves children matching recorded sounds to picture cards.

Source: Primary National Strategy (2007)

and they also use the knowledge they have about the oral language context, the topic and the speaker. Machado (2007, p. 238) defines listening as 'a learned behaviour, a mental process that is concerned with hearing, attending, discriminating, understanding and remembering.' As a learnt behaviour, there is much that educators can do to facilitate its development.

Many of the oral language experiences previously described provide a particularly strong opportunity to support the listening ability of children in pre-school and early years of school. These include but are not limited to:

- listening posts and centres
- sharing of activities and 'news-telling'
- listening walks
- making sounds
- sound lotto
- Simon says
- pass it on
- dictogloss.

CONSIDERATIONS FOR CHILDREN'S LISTENING COMPETENCY

Young children are not always able to discriminate between different sounds. Discriminative listening involves listening for differences in pitch, volume, and so on. This involves listening to environmental sounds and music. The ability to discriminate between speech sounds, such as phonemes, is a skill that can also be developed through discriminative listening experiences.

Cramer writes that good listeners respond to what they hear 'selectively, sensibly and sensitively' (Cramer, 2004, p. 136). That is, they think about their responses and show respect to the speaker. It is necessary for teachers to help children realise that listening can involve several components, namely: listening, thinking about the message, responding and reflecting.

The setting and communicative context in which language occurs will affect the ways in which children listen. Audience is an important factor in speaking and listening contexts. Listeners need to be aware of their role as audience and what is expected of them. As explained in Chapter 1, the register (field, mode and tenor) is important and children need to learn to listen in different ways depending on the purpose for listening as well as other features of the context.

Good social listening is characterised by such behaviours as maintaining appropriate eye contact, focusing on the speaker's meaning, remembering and acting upon the speaker's message, and giving a well thought out and considered response. Needless to say, in order for children to learn good social listening skills and attitudes, it is necessary for parents, caregivers and teachers to model these.

Listening for enjoyment and appreciation might involve listening to stories, poems and rhymes, songs and music and can involve the appreciation and enjoyment of the meaning of the text or of the sounds and rhythms.

Listening for information, or 'efferent' listening, involves listening for factual information or ideas. This includes listening to instructions, and learning about ideas and concepts through listening to presentations, speeches or spoken components of lessons at school. Sometimes, this type of listening is referred to as 'listening to learn'.

Having the ability to listen critically is important to children's development as effective speakers and listeners. It is necessary for members of society to be able to assess the validity of spoken messages and the values and intention of speakers. The ability to make inferences (going beyond what is actually said and determining the implied meaning) is an important part of critical listening, as is the ability to evaluate information. The ability to recognise opinion as opposed to fact is also an important element of critical listening. It is important to realise that critical listening is not the domain of older children's experiences. It should be a consideration in the conversations and general oral communication experiences of children in the early childhood settings of pre-school and the early years of school. The pre-primary conversation (refer to the text box) that took place during the reading of the story *I took the moon for a walk* demonstrates the children's capability for critical listening and response. However, it goes beyond critical listening to children's wonderings and 'big questions' about life. It involves children listening and responding to each other (not just the teacher).

PRE-PRIMARY CONVERSATION DURING THE READING OF THE STORY *I TOOK THE MOON FOR A WALK* (CURTIS & JAY, 2004)

The following is a conversation that took place between pre-primary children as their teacher read to them the story *I took the moon for a walk*. The teacher has been fostering the children's ability and confidence to express their thoughts and wonderings, to ask 'big' questions and to listen and respond to each other's comments and questions.

Sam:	How can you take the moon for a walk?
Bayley:	Take a rocket and grab the moon and bring it down.
Sam:	How can you grab the moon? The moon can't just move down.
Bayley:	You'd have to do it.
Hayley:	You couldn't really [take the moon for a walk], it's just in the book. It's just non-fiction.
Bayley:	You could. You make a rocket and have robot arms which could grab it.
Sam:	But how would the arms be big enough?
Bayley:	You could make the arms twice as big as the school.
Sam:	You couldn't do it on one day.
Chloe:	You could get the fire engine men and they could get to the moon with their ladder.
Davido:	But their ladder doesn't go high enough.
Hayley:	I know you could get a big rock that was really heavy, and put it on the moon and it could push the moon down. It would need to be 10,000 pounds.
Sidney:	Why not cut the moon in half? Then you could bring one half down, then the other; then glue them back together.
Sam:	Moons can follow you but not in the daytime.

Sidney:	How can the moon turn around when it's so heavy?
Cameron:	Well the moon is really moved by the sun's and Jupiter's gravitational pull.
Sofia:	I know how the moon follows you. When you go somewhere at nighttime the moon is so high it looks like it follows you; but it doesn't really. It just looks like it does.
Sam:	I know it does move.
Mitch:	It does move because it circles in the air.
Finn:	To get to the moon you need to put spacesuits on and go in a rocket. When they go to the moon they bounce because of their spacesuits.
Emma:	The moon doesn't have any gravity so it's not the suits, it's the gravity that makes them bounce.
Sidney:	I have actually seen the moon in the sky in the day. So how does gravity move the moon to get the earth into the moon?
Sam:	How does the moon change colour? Because the moon is usually white.

There is some disagreement over whether the moon is actually white, yellow or cream in colour.

Bayley:	The clouds change the colour because the light bounces off the clouds.
Cameron:	The moon is smaller than the earth, so how does the earth go into the moon?
Bayley:	It does because it comes into the atmosphere.

The teacher continues reading from story: '… we tiptoed through the grass where the night crawlers creep'.

Sam:	What are they?
Steph:	Bugs.
Bayley:	No, arachnids.

Teacher reading: '… and the moon called the dew so the grass seemed to weep …'

Sidney:	What does 'weep' mean?
Cameron:	Cry.
Sidney:	Why does it cry?
Cameron:	Grass could cry from happiness or sadness.
Bayley:	My mum cried when I was born.
	So why aren't some of us crying now?
	Because some of us are happy now.
Finn:	Some people cry when they get hurt and some people cry like Matt said because of …
Davido:	Why does that moon have arms and legs?

Pybe:	It's a magic moon.
Teacher:	Is that moon in the book the same moon as the one in our sky?
Davido:	No, because that's round and sometimes the moon is triangle.
Pybe:	There's an African moon and a Netherland's moon and they're different.
Bayley:	Imagine if the moon was stinky.
Teacher:	Could you say that again but change that to a question?
David:	I wonder if the moon smells like gas?
Josh B:	I wonder if you can be friends with the moon?
Teacher:	What are friends?
Teacher:	Can you be friends with things that aren't alive? Like the moon or a wall?
Josh B:	You can be with a teddy.
Teacher:	But isn't a teddy like a wall? Is it alive?
Cameron:	You can because it's lovable.

To teach young children critical listening, the use of media texts such as radio and television advertisements is effective. These spoken texts often contain bias, hidden agendas and persuasive devices. Some of them are plain deceptive.

Children's literature can also be used as read-alouds for the purpose of encouraging critical listening. There are many quality children's books that espouse strong (or subtle) views and biases, which could be used to develop critical listening. Examples include:

- *Drac and the gremlin* by Allan Baillie
- *George and the dragon* by Chris Wormell
- *The violin man* by Colin Thompson
- *Pobblebonks* by Garry Flemming
- *Not now Bernard* by David McKee
- *Square eyed Pat* by Liz Pichon
- *My dad* by Anthony Browne
- *Willy the champ* by Anthony Browne
- *Black dog* by Pamela Allen
- *Window* by Jeannie Baker
- *Grandmother* by Jeannie Baker.

The teacher's use of language is important to the success of children's listening. To ensure children understand, teachers should consider the way in which they use language. They should make sure that sentences are of an appropriate length and complexity. It is also necessary to use language that is comprehensible to children in terms of vocabulary—the teacher needs to judge children's listening comprehension levels and speak accordingly. The use of intonation, pitch, rate and volume, as well as non-verbal communication, needs to be appropriate in order to gain and hold children's attention and facilitate their listening.

DIVERSITY AND LISTENING

Cultural, social and economic differences can impact upon the ways children speak, listen and make meaning. If teachers are to encourage children to build on their strengths, it is necessary to understand the 'funds of knowledge' (Moll et al., 1992) or different ways of knowing and doing things that children bring from the home. For example, eye contact is important in most English-speaking cultures; however, children from other cultures may feel a sense of discomfort if asked to display such behaviour. Some cultures think it is rude to ask direct questions so will make oblique enquiries instead and, sometimes, as in some Aboriginal groups, it is not compulsory to respond to questions or other statements.

IDENTIFYING CHILDREN WHO HAVE REDUCED HEARING

Sometimes children do not make expected progress in speaking and listening and it is important to rule out reduced hearing as a contributory factor. This checklist will help you identify children who may need to be referred to an audiologist for further assessment.

- [ ] Is the child visibly frustrated or anxious?
- [ ] Does the child respond inconsistently or inappropriately to speech?
- [ ] Does the child need to visually track conversations?
- [ ] Does the child tend to turn a particular ear towards a speaker?
- [ ] Is the child easily distracted and disengaged from classroom activities?
- [ ] Can the child follow verbal messages without visual clues?
- [ ] Does the child look to others for confirmation of directions?
- [ ] Can the child keep up with playground games that are based on verbal arrangements?
- [ ] Does the child choose to sit near, or turn up the volume control, when using the radio or television?
- [ ] How confident is the child at joining in classroom discussions?
- [ ] Does the child use strategies to request clarification?

Source: Robinshaw (2007, p. 666)

SUMMARY

There is a range of possible experiences and activities that serve to enhance children's speaking and listening development and learning. Many of these also contribute to children's growth in other important domains of learning and development. In making choices about the learning experiences with which to provide children, or about the way in which to adapt an experience to suit a specific group of learners, early childhood teachers should consider a number of factors. They should take into account the children's speaking and listening abilities and their learning and development needs, the features of the educational setting, program goals and the type of program to be implemented. Experiences and activities for speaking and listening should align to the many features of the learning context and to the unique characteristics of the children.

QUESTIONS AND ACTIVITIES

1. Select one of the speaking and listening activities described in this chapter and decide how you would use it in different ways with two different groups of children at different phases of language development.
2. What are the ways in which you can support children for whom English is an additional language or dialect?
3. Make a list depicting the range of materials and resources that would enrich the speaking and listening component of a program for children in the early years of school.
4. Scan the range of activities presented in this chapter and identify those that would be appropriate for toddlers in a childcare setting. Consider how they might work with the important characteristics of this type of setting.
5. What is meant by the statement, 'The activity is the vehicle for children's learning and development'?
6. Think about how teachers' language use may sometimes be a barrier to children's listening comprehension. Can you think of any examples of when you have seen this happen?
7. In what ways might children for whom English is a second or additional language need extra support with listening?

KEY TERMS

open-ended activities
scaffolding techniques
silent period

KEY REFERENCES

Cramer, R. L. (2004). *The language arts: A balanced approach to teaching reading, writing, listening, talking and thinking.* Boston: Allyn & Bacon.

Curtain, H. & Dahlberg, C. (2010). *Languages and children, making the match: New languages for young learners, Grades K–8.* Boston: Pearson Education.

Machado, J. M. (2007). *Early childhood experiences in Language Arts: Early literacy.* Emerita: Thomson.

Moll, L., Amanti, C. et al. (1992). Funds of knowledge for teaching: Using a qualitative approach to connect homes and classrooms. *Theory into Practice, 31*(2), 132–41.

Primary National Strategy (2007). *Letters and sounds: Principles and practice of high quality phonics.* Retrieved 11/6/2008, from nationalstrategies.standards.dcsf.gov.uk/node/84969.

Roberts, V. & Nicholl, V. (1996). Making the most of traditional newstime. In P. Jones (ed.), *Talking to learn.* Sydney: Primary English Teaching Association.

CHAPTER 6

Language, Thinking and Learning

CHAPTER OBJECTIVES

This chapter will increase your understanding of:

- the relationship between language, thinking and learning
- the importance of oral language to children's learning
- the unique features and demands of talk for academic purposes
- the role of adult talk in facilitating children's language and thinking
- the importance of asking children questions during learning experiences
- different questioning frameworks to guide learning and thinking.

The first part of this chapter presents various theoretical insights into the relationship between language, thinking and learning. While there are some quite complex concepts to be understood, they are important to your becoming an informed and effective practitioner. Early childhood educators are continually required to make decisions about the type of environment that will nurture children's growth and development. They should be able to do so with the decisiveness that resides in deep knowledge about children, their development and learning. In the latter part of the chapter some important practical considerations for supporting children's thinking and learning are discussed. This includes features of effective teacher–child interactions and the use of questioning that extends children's ability to use oral language to express different types and levels of thinking.

COGNITION AND LANGUAGE

Cognition is the mental process whereby knowledge is acquired and understood, whether through thought, experience or the senses, or a combination of these factors. Put simply, cognition is knowledge together with understanding (although knowledge without understanding is hardly knowledge at all). It involves the three important processes of attention, perception and memory (Cook, Klein, Tessier & Daley, 2004).

A child's **cognitive development**—that is to say, the growth of the child's ability to acquire and understand knowledge—will be influenced by both biological and environmental factors (Estes, 2004). The biological aspect relates to genetics; a child's capacity to absorb knowledge is partly influenced by the child's genetic base. In other words, the level of a child's innate ability to assimilate knowledge is founded on the child's biology. The environmental factors relate to the child's sensory and other experiences, particularly experiences based on interaction, oral or otherwise, with adults and other children, and of their observation of the world around them. With the right experiences and supports, children gradually develop in their cognitive ability, learning the processes that assist them to remember, discriminate, compare, classify, plan, sequence, evaluate, analyse, predict and so on (Kearns & Austin, 2007).

The processing and comprehension of language occurs in the brain. The language system of the brain manages the necessary information—words and syntactic (grammar) constructions as well as the connections between meaning and syntax, speech recognition and movement of the muscles that produce speech (Lamb, 2006). Like cognition, language development is influenced by a combination of the individual's genetic core and engagement in their physical and social environment, including oral interaction with other people.

The child's immediate language environment has bearing on brain development.

LANGUAGE USE AND BRAIN DEVELOPMENT

Language used by others in a child's immediate environment has a significant effect on the development of the child's brain. The brain grows significantly during the prenatal stage but is still not fully developed at birth and continues to develop during the first years of life. The brain has a complex circuitry system with billions of neurons (brain cells). It is said that, with the influence of a stimulating language environment, the cells (neurons) of the brain produce greater and more robust neural connections, which leads to more sophisticated pathways (or message transmitting fibres). The type and amount of environmental stimuli (oral language experiences and interactions) is thought to be significant in influencing the formation of neural pathways and thus how the brain develops and functions (Estes, 2004; Kearns & Austin, 2007).

THE RELATIONSHIP BETWEEN LANGUAGE AND COGNITION

It has long been recognised that there are relationships between the development and use of language on the one hand and thought on the other. The most obvious of these is that language (oral and written) is the primary vehicle through which the public expression of thought occurs. However, there are other important relationships that have been brought to light through various investigations. Of particular importance are the work and ideas of the twentieth century psychologists Jean Piaget (1896–1980) and Lev Vygotsky (1896–1934). Although there are some differences between the conclusions they arrive at, they nevertheless provided the foundation for current knowledge about the relationship between language and cognition and they have influenced the teaching and learning practices of early childhood settings.

LANGUAGE AND COGNITIVE DEVELOPMENT

For about the first two years of a child's life, spoken language and cognition develop along separate independent paths. Cognitive development can be said to have a 'pre-language stage' and, likewise, language development to have a 'pre-cognitive phase' (Kozulin, 1986, p. 80). When children reach the age of about two years and they have attained certain levels of growth in cognition and speech, the separate paths of development merge and influence each other. By this time children have also developed an understanding of the relationship between signs (words) and their meanings and so language and cognition are in a position to work together. Thoughts begin to be spoken and speech begins to reflect logical thought (Kozulin, 1988). It is no coincidence that, at this time, children suddenly begin to show greater curiosity in the things in their world and an interest in words and their meanings.

PIAGET ON LANGUAGE AND COGNITION

Piaget put forward the proposition that language is one of several abilities that rely on cognitive maturation. The sequence of children's cognitive development is what determines the sequence of their language growth. His theory suggests that children need first to develop the concept of 'object permanence'—that is, they need to see objects (cat, spoon, ball etc.) as being separate in themselves and to each other and as existing even when they can no longer be seen. This perception allows children to develop conceptual understandings of them (mental categories—such as all cats have four legs, two eyes, fur). As they develop understanding of different objects, they begin to use the symbols (words) to represent them (Gleason, 2005). (Note that, in the early stage of the development of a concept, a child may generalise—for example, using the word 'cat' in reference to all observed animals. Over time the concept is refined—more features are used to categorise cats and to create separate categories for other animals.) Another example of how language follows cognition is that, while children might learn that a needle, scissors and other objects are sharp, it will be some time afterwards before they acquire sufficient language to describe the concept of sharpness (Cramer, 2004).

Piaget saw children as being active learners who develop conceptual knowledge and language through the exploration of their physical and social environments.

Piaget placed emphasis on the importance of objects in the environment and on children's self-talk. Other theorists draw conclusions which are different from those of Piaget and maintain that, although there is a connection between the development of language and cognition, it cannot be concluded that cognitive development precedes language development or that language development relies on cognitive development (Gleason, 2005; Radius, 2006).

VYGOTSKY ON LANGUAGE AND COGNITION

Vygotsky's perspective on the relationship between language and cognitive development differs from that of Piaget. He believed that it is the people, conversations, experiences and objects of the various situations in which a child comes into contact that lead to the emergence and development of children's language and cognition.

Vygotsky held that children are born with a few basic mental functions—attention, sensation, perception and memory—and that, over time, these are transformed to more sophisticated mental processes. He saw both experience and language as being essential components in this process and in the general development of children's cognition. He highlighted the importance of the language of adults and believed that adult language use and adult–child interactions assisted children to shape their thinking and learning (Kearns & Austin, 2007; Kozulin, 1986). When adults participate with children during their play and other exploratory experiences, the adults verbally pass on meanings, convey information and guide children's mental processes. Consider, for instance, a parent's use of language as a young toddler is playing with a ball (for example, 'Where is the ball?' 'Can you roll it to me?' 'Look, it can bounce!' 'Oh dear, it has rolled behind the tree'). The parent's talk supports the child in forming certain conceptual understandings (for example, characteristics of a ball, movement, and object-permanency).

INNER SPEECH AND THINKING

Inner speech is what connects language and thought (Kozulin, 1988). It is an instrument of individual thought which in young children begins as vocalised self-talk. Young children go through a stage of development where their play and activity involves the use of monologic speech or vocalised self-talk. Self-talk assists children to adjust their mental focus and to develop consciousness of their understandings and helps them with self-direction, self-control and problem solving (Kearns & Austin, 2007). When children are confronted with a difficult task, the use of self-talk escalates (Kozulin, 1986). The self-talk of young children is similar to their social speech. It sounds just like the talk they use to communicate with others. However, unlike social speech, it does not serve any social communicative function. It is talk for oneself and, despite it occurring most often when others are around, it is not actually directed to anyone. At about the age of seven years, children's self-talk ceases to be vocalised and becomes internal or inner speech. Children show a new ability—to 'think words' as an alternative to speaking them. The language of **inner speech** has unique structural features. It is abbreviated talk with disconnected and incomplete sentences. The subject of the sentence (and all words connected with the subject) is rarely used (Kozulin, 1986).

LANGUAGE AND LEARNING

HOW CHILDREN LEARN

Children are born with the desire to learn. They learn about themselves and their world, not just by being passive recipients of the knowledge presented to them but through the active construction of knowledge and understanding. That is, they explore, play, observe, try things out, think and check with others, and in so doing build up knowledge about their world.

It is therefore important to children's learning that they are immersed in interesting and stimulating environments which include a variety of materials, objects, events and people, and various social interactions along with the verbal input of adults.

Children use their different senses to learn. They use touch, taste, sight, sound and movement to learn in rich and sensory-stimulating environments. They also learn by means of observation whereby they determine how to do some things by observing and imitating adults and other children. They use repetition and practice to confirm developing understandings and to master new skills and strategies.

Children explore and engage in activities with objects, materials and other people, they process new information, understand new ideas and concepts, learn new skills and store new knowledge. The processing and storage of information occurs in the brain's mental structures, which are referred to as **schemata** (plural) or **schema** (singular). Schemata can be likened to a filing system. It is the brain's filing system containing summaries of information about different **concepts** and topics for which understanding has been gained. When new learning activities and other experiences lead to new understandings, schemata are modified. New information updates existing schemata so they are more accurate and complete (Hulit & Howard, 2006). When new information does not bear any connection to existing schemata, it is usually soon forgotten.

> 'Knowledge is not a commodity existing in some pure and abstract realm independently of particular "knowers", but a state of understanding achieved through the constructive mental activity of individual learners … learners progressively construct their own knowledge by bringing what they already know to bear on new information in order to … extend or modify their initial understanding.' (Norman, 1992, p. 286)

Learning involves the formation of new ideas or concepts that build on the knowledge and ideas already acquired. It is important to children's learning that learning activities acknowledge and use as their basis what children already know (Barnes, 1992). Learning occurs when experiences and learning activities connect to children's existing knowledge (or schemata). Moreover, in order for children to be able to effectively process new knowledge, the relevant schema first needs to be stimulated or brought to the surface.

ORAL LANGUAGE AND LEARNING

Talk is an important endeavour in the process of learning.

Children are assisted in shaping their thoughts and forming knowledge and skills when they are provided with learning environments that involve practical experience as well as talk with each other and with adults (Foley & Thompson, 2007). As children work together to plan, reflect, share ideas and opinions, make suggestions, ask questions and so on, their learning is enhanced. When adults verbally interact with children, when they use focused and deliberate conversations and when they use questions, suggestions, statements of facts and demonstration to guide thinking and learning, the knowledge which children have already acquired is expanded and further strengthened.

Talk is an important endeavour in the process of learning. Speaking and listening practices which support children's learning include conversations, discussions, problem solving, brainstorming, play, games, debates, storytelling, drama, sharing experiences, asking questions and oral reporting. Many of these activities are described in Chapter 5. The following are some of the ways in which these and other talk practices support learning.

- Talk leads children to deeper understanding of topics, ideas and concepts. When children verbalise their thoughts and develop ideas to others they can discover the degree to which they actually understand. Furthermore, they can be assisted by the responses of others to clarify or expand on their ideas. When other people provide feedback, ask questions or share new or alternative ideas, the accuracy and clarity of children's understandings can be brought into focus.
- Talk provides children with increased opportunity to derive meaning from experiences and classroom activities. When children talk with others as they carry out activities together, understandings can be clarified or extended. When they listen to the perspectives of others they have the opportunity to reinterpret and reanalyse their own understandings. Talk allows for concepts to be refined, modified and accurately shaped and constructed.
- Talk stimulates new thoughts. Conversations around an experience can trigger ideas which have not otherwise been considered. The verbal guidance of adults and the more knowledgeable of their peers allow children to learn things which they might not learn on their own.
- Talk influences children's approach to thinking (how they go about it and what they think about). It enhances their ability with different **cognitive processes**. In response to what children say, adults can use questions, verbal prompts, focusing statements and suggestions to direct children to think in different ways or about different aspects of an experience. Thus, children are able to refine their thought processes, elaborate on their ideas and on the concepts being formed and think about something in a more reflective and innovative way.
- Talk helps children to form abstract concepts. Learning based on concrete experiences can move into abstract thinking when children are encouraged to verbalise their learning or to respond to the questions of adults. For instance, the exploration of 3D shapes can lead children to make concluding statements about the shapes' features (e.g. 'An angle is …' 'A cube has …').
- Talk supports the development of children's schemata. Important to the development of schemata are the connections between new information and pre-existing knowledge. Talk is a convenient and expedient means by which these connections can be made. Previous experiences and pre-existing knowledge can be called to mind through talk and they can be linked to ensuing information (Foley & Thompson, 2003).

The greater the variety of talk situations that children experience, the more opportunity they will have for acquiring a wide range of cognitive processes. It is the unique features of the social setting—the people, activities, materials, location and dialogue—that will drive children's use of cognitive processes.

Cooperative learning is a popular teaching approach that involves children working and talking together to accomplish a group learning activity (Herrel & Jordon, 2004). Learning activities focus on group cooperation and interaction and support children in learning new knowledge as well as developing new skills. Members of a cooperative learning group might each be assigned a role—leader, reporter, note taker, timekeeper etc.—which assists the group in completing the activity in a way that ensures their learning and skills development. The teacher monitors group participation, ensuring each member is being given a chance to talk, and intervenes when necessary.

ACADEMIC LANGUAGE

As children get older they have to deal with learning situations that place greater demands on their language and cognition. These situations extend beyond the familiar use of social language (language use in everyday conversations) to include the use of academic language (language use in more structured academic learning situations).

Academic language is a distinct use of language associated with completing the learning tasks for different school curriculum areas; for example, Science, Maths, and Society and Environment. It can be distinguished from social language in many ways. Academic language contexts require the development of new language knowledge and a new repertoire of communication practices.

The most significant differences between social and academic language relate to the cognitive requirements, the contextual features and the vocabulary and syntactic structures. The differences are explained as follows:

- *The cognitive requirements*: Academic language is more cognitively demanding than social language. Where social communication might necessitate the use of such cognitive processes as identification, recall, comprehension and explanation, academic settings necessitate a greater range of, and more challenging, thinking processes (e.g. application, synthesis, analysis and evaluation). Furthermore, in academic situations, children are often required to cope with several different levels of information. They are not just learning new ideas but also are simultaneously learning new tasks, new language and new concepts.
- *The context*: Talk for academic purposes generally involves what is referred to as 'de-contextualised language'; that is, language about things that have not been experienced by the people communicating or about things not in the immediate environment. When language is de-contextualised it is used in a situation where there are few cues to assist understanding, and therefore there is a particular reliance on language clarity. This is quite different from the contextualised language use in most social situations. Contextualised language usually focuses on recent events and familiar people, and can draw on sources of meaning that come from the environment; for example, pointing to and looking at people, objects and activities (McGee & Richgels, 2008). Academic language tends to be relatively abstract and does not usually benefit from the presence of context clues.

The language features

Academic language calls for a more specialised and more complex level of language which is different from that encountered by children in their out-of-school social contexts. Academic topics often require children to learn some specialised vocabulary and technical terms. Sentence structures are often longer and more complicated than those used in social situations (Tompkins, 2006).

School success calls for more than proficiency in social language. It requires children to extend their talk repertoire to the use of academic language with its unique features and demands. As children progress through the primary grades, academic tasks and talk contexts become more complex. Children need instruction that focuses on developing familiarity with, and competency in, the language of school learning situations (Cummins, 1996).

Table 6.1: Features of social language use and academic language use

	Social language	Academic language
Context	Familiar, everyday topics Meaning cues from the immediate environment Usually connected to familiar subjects—the materials, people and experiences of the immediate environment	New and unfamiliar topics Few meaning cues from the immediate environment May not involve familiar subjects
Cognitive demand	Usually a singular subjective viewpoint More likely to be concrete	Multiple viewpoints Many levels of new learning More likely to be abstract
Words and sentences	Everyday familiar words Repetition of words Incomplete sentences. Articles, prepositions, pronouns are often not used Simple sentence structures	Variety of words More subject-specific and technical vocabulary Complete sentences with few abbreviated forms Complex sentence structures

Children may make slow academic progress if the teacher does not provide sound support with language development. It is important for teachers to aim at specific language goals.

ADULT TALK AND CHILDREN'S LEARNING

Adults have important roles to play in the facilitation of children's learning. The techniques available to help children to gain new levels of understanding as a result of the activities in which they engage are particularly significant. These techniques are commonly referred to as **scaffolds**—they are a form of temporary assistance to help children achieve a task, to use and develop cognitive processes, to gain new understandings and concepts, and to acquire new strategies and skills. Scaffolds are only temporary measures and have served their

Adults play important roles in the facilitation of children's language use and learning.

purpose once competency has been reached. Once learning has been achieved and scaffolds are no longer required, they are withdrawn (Department of Education and Training, 2006; Hulit & Howard, 2006).

Talk is an effective scaffold during learning activities and experiences. Conversations and verbal interventions such as questions, prompts, redirecting statements and suggestions are effective scaffolding practices. Consider how a teacher might communicate with children as they carry out a learning task that requires them to determine how to make a plasticine boat with maximum load capacity. What questions could be asked or comments provided that would support children in successfully completing the activity and learning as a result? Likewise, consider a parent's use of language when interacting with a toddler who is playing with a ball. What talk could the parent use to extend the young child's understanding of the associated ideas (movement, characteristics of balls, object permanency)?

Adult talk will not be effective if it dominates learning experiences. It is not the main source of children's learning but rather it is something which should be used to assist. Moreover, when adult talk dominates that of the children's, it inhibits their initiative and sense of ownership of an activity. Learning requires that children's own talk be given a fairly free rein.

The observation of children as they take part in learning activities is important if they are to be provided with the appropriate supports to guide learning. Assistance needs to be given in response to the children's needs and to the goals of the learning program. It needs to be employed in such a way as to encourage continued curiosity and enquiry and children's desire to learn and understand.

Following are a number of different ways in which teachers can use talk effectively in order to scaffold children's learning.

- *Joining in as co-learners*: teachers can participate in the conversations that occur between groups of children as they carry out a learning activity. They can listen to and observe the children as they work and make contributions that assist children's learning while also demonstrating respect for the children's viewpoints. Through participation, teachers can introduce the children to new language, new ideas or new ways of thinking and thus help the children to overcome difficulties should they arise (Norman, 1992) and to acquire the knowledge that is to be derived from accomplishing the activity.

- *Directing attention*: in order to support the children in learning as they carry out a learning activity, the teacher might need to draw children's attention to certain unnoticed but important elements of the task.
- *New information*: the teacher can provide children with supplementary information when it is needed to overcome confusion or to clarify an issue that is impeding progress. Children view the teacher as one source of information that can be used to progress with a learning activity.
- *Extend understanding*: the teacher can guide children's learning by assisting them to achieve clarity and depth in regards to the learning that is to be derived from completing an activity. In order to do this the teacher can invite children to talk about the learning activity—to describe what they are doing or have done or to explain what they have learnt—and provide further information if necessary. Children's learning can be extended when the teacher encourages them to use a different and more applicable cognitive process as they talk about what they have learnt. For instance, the teacher might ask the children to 'categorise the different characteristics of the plants that you have described' and, in so doing, direct their application of the cognitive process of classification. Another way in which teacher can extend children's learning is by encouraging them to ask their own questions. 'What would happen if …?'
- *Demonstrate*: teachers can demonstrate new techniques for carrying out an activity and in so doing they can 'think aloud' (verbalising of the thinking that would normally be carried on inside the head) and demonstrate the mental processes used and how they are used to complete an activity and to achieve learning.
- *Question*: teachers can use questioning techniques to extend and expand children's thinking. They can get children to look at activities in different ways, to pursue different lines of enquiry or to extend understandings drawn from experiences. Teachers can employ questioning to activate and refer children to related prior experiences and knowledge, helping them to make connections between that and new learning.

QUESTIONING FOR COGNITION AND LEARNING

QUESTIONING

Questions are an important tool in the learning process. They serve both language and cognitive development and learning. Questions should call for children to talk for the purpose of exploring ideas and for making sense of, and gaining knowledge from, learning activities. They should encourage the expression of new thoughts and new ways of thinking; for instance, they might require children to verbally describe or categorise objects, predict outcomes, explain possibilities, justify opinions or conclusions, or construct explanations.

As highlighted by Splitter and Sharp (1995, p. 48), 'those questions which are deemed to be most worthwhile will, on the one hand, draw upon and extend knowledge and, on the other, "probe the logic" which makes knowledge and thought itself possible.'

Questions that are effective in supporting children's language and cognitive development and assisting their learning of concepts and knowledge should:

- involve the use of language that children understand
- focus on an activity, experience or topic at hand
- make reference to current or recent experiences or to materials and objects
- require children to use language for a variety of purposes (to describe, explain, reason, create, predict, justify, and so on)
- require children to construct full responses as opposed to simply answering yes or no
- sometimes cater for a range of possible responses rather than a single correct one
- call for children to access different sources of information as they construct their responses.

Children's thinking and language use can be supported by the questions asked.

QUESTION FRAMEWORKS

There are a number of **question frameworks** that categorise question types in terms of the thinking and language that each encourages. These frameworks can be used to assist with the design of questions that contribute to thinking and learning outcomes for children. When children's thinking is encouraged by the questions asked, so too is their language. Children are motivated to seek the appropriate language to express their thinking adequately in response to a question. The following outlines three of these questioning frameworks.

Blank's Levels of Talk

The Levels of Talk questioning model (Table 6.2) was developed by Marion Blank (1978). It outlines four different categories of the thinking that is believed to be within the capabilities of pre-school children. Her model provides a guide for developing dialogue that encourages young children to use language to express different thinking processes. The four talk categories provided by Blank are *Matching, Selective Analysis, Reordering Perception and Reasoning*. The model describes how the four different categories call for children to draw on information from different sources. It also provides examples of questions that lead to the four different types of thinking.

Table 6.2: Levels of talk

Level	Example questions/interrogatives
Level One: Matching The information for responding to questions at this level is directly available and visible to the children. Questions might be about a picture or object, requiring children to do such things as name something, identify matching objects or describe or indicate what is observed, heard or touched. When responding to questions in this category, very little talk is required of children and non-verbal responses are sometimes all that is required. Responses call on children's word knowledge and observation.	Tell me/Find which one is like this? What is this? What can you see? Tell me what you heard/touched?
Level Two: Selective Analysis The information for responding to questions at this level can be found in available concrete materials or a recent experience. However, children need to attend to and select specific features and they need to call on their understanding of a range of concepts in answering questions; for example, size, colour, quantity, function or object. Questions often ask who? what? or where?	Find one that can [cut]. What is happening? What colour is the [dog]? Tell me which things are [sharp/heavy/for eating]. How are these two things different? Name the things that are growing.
Level Three: Reordering Perception The information for responding to questions at this level does not relate directly to what the children can observe. They are required to attend to information supplied, to consider more than one feature or to think beyond the concrete through the use of such cognitive processes as prediction and categorisation.	What will happen next? What could [he/she/it] say? Tell me the story about [this picture]. How are these … the same? Find the things that are not [animals]. Name something that can [fly] but that is not a [bird]. What is an [apple]?
Level Four: Reasoning In responding to questions at this level, children have to reason beyond what is said, heard or seen. They might need to draw on their past experiences, identify corresponding features or events, make links between cause and effect or provide justification for an idea or action.	What will happen if … ? Why will … ? Why would it … ? What made … happen? What could you do if … ? How can we tell that … ? Why can't we tell that … ?

Source: Blank (1978)

The following transcript illustrates the use of Blank's Levels of Talk to encourage young children's thinking and talking. It involves the teacher asking David (six years old) different levels of questions about a picture.

> ### QUESTIONING DAVID USING MARION BLANK'S LEVELS OF TALK FRAMEWORK
>
> Teacher: David, where is the cat?
> David: Um, I think he's on the roof.
> Teacher: Where is the dog?
> David: He's laying down near the bushes.
> Teacher: Tell me about one thing that you can see in the picture.
> David: Um, the boy with the glasses on is looking at the boy with the pink top on and there's something mysterious about his face.
> Teacher: Describe or tell me about the dog in the picture.
> David: Well, he's, he's sleeping and he's got his tail wrapped around his [inaudible] practically and his two feet are crossed and his ears are hanging down.
> Teacher: What is the same and different about the two boys in the picture?
> David: The different thing is one has glasses and one doesn't and they both have shadows.
> Teacher: What is happening in the picture?
> David: Well, it looks like the dog is sleeping, the boys are playing hide and seek and the cat just woke up from a nap.
> Teacher: Can you make up a story about the picture?
> David: Well, there once was a boy with some glasses and he met a boy in the park so he invited the boy around to his house to play hide and seek and then the boy's dog and cat came and he said, 'Go away, go away,' and then the boy that got invited said, 'Don't worry, they're my dog and cat.'
> Teacher: Lovely. If there was another picture and the story continued, what do you think would happen next?
> David: The car would drive out of the garage and the boy would have gone to the shops.
> Teacher: Why is the dog happy?
> David: Because maybe he's dreaming about something good.
> Teacher: Why is the cat on the roof?
> David: Because cats always get on the roof and stuff.
> Teacher: What danger can you see in the picture? What could go wrong?
> David: The car might drive out and maybe it might be wet on the patio so then it might slip and run over the dog.
> Teacher: Why can't children drive cars?

> David: Because, one, they're not old enough; two, they, um, you have to be sixteen or seventeen; and, three, um, they need a licence and they can't get one.
> Teacher: Why are the gate and the garage door open?
> David: Maybe someone just walked in and they're going to drive the car out to wash it.
> Teacher: What could the boy do if he thought the cat was stuck on the roof?
> David: He could run in and ask his dad, um, the cat's stuck on the roof so then he would say, 'Dad can you get the ladder because the cat's stuck on the roof and we need to get it down.'
> Teacher: Can you ask me a question about the picture?
> David: Why are the boys' faces looking mysterious?
> Teacher: Another question, that's a good one, another one, two more I need.
> David: Why is the garage door open and the boy with the pink top why is his face looking a bit mysterious and the gate is open?

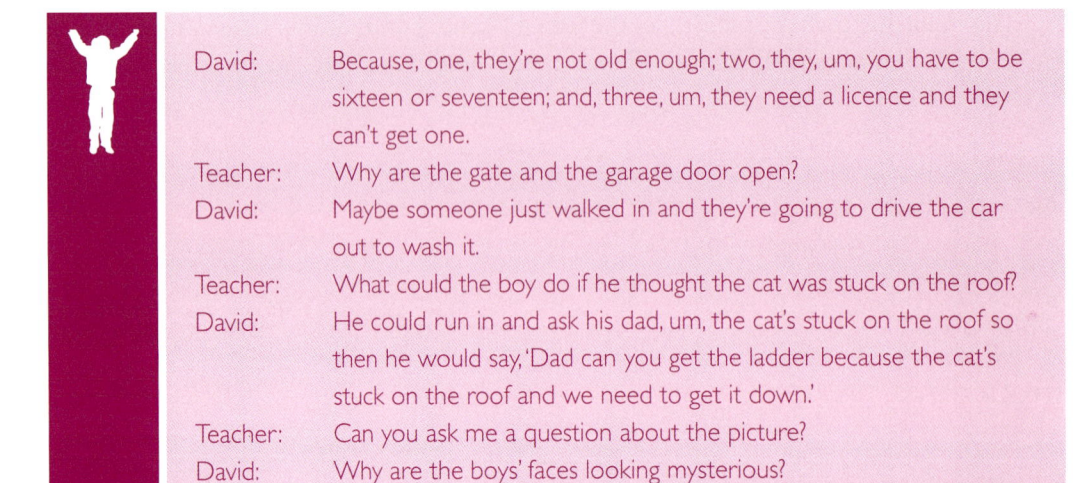

The Splitter and Sharp framework

Splitter and Sharp (1995) provide a useful five-category framework of questions (see box below) that they see as providing different ways to prompt children's reasoning, predictions and viewpoints. Questions are valuable learning tools because they assist children with practices important to learning; they can help children to reinforce what they already know and to use and extend this knowledge to develop new ideas and understandings.

FIVE QUESTION CATEGORIES

Ordinary questions

These types of questions cover the vast majority of ordinary question and answer contexts. These are asked in situations where something which is not held is wanted; for example, information, directions, food. Such a question is directed towards someone who we think will be able to provide us with what we want; for example, the information. They call for a straightforward and determinate answer. Their role in children's learning is limited.

Enquiry questions

These are asked when the questioner does not assume that the person questioned knows the answer. Responses do not usually signal closure, but are likely to stimulate further enquiry. These are the sort of questions asked that support an active quest for understanding.

Rhetorical questions

These are questions for which the questioner usually knows the answer. They are usually asked to determine or appraise what is known about a topic. They do not encourage any level of dialogue that might serve to assist children with their own pursuit of understanding.

Closed questions

These types of questions generally result in short yes or no responses or one-word answers. They are generally used when precise, quick answers are required. They otherwise inhibit thought.

Open questions

This category of questions occurs in a learning environment where the asking of questions is integral to carry out an activity. They require those involved to employ a range of strategies in either asking or answering such questions and in pursuing further enquiry. This category incorporates 'How? What if? and Why?' questions that invite explanation. Open-ended questions might also involve additional follow-up questions that seek elaboration or clarification.

Source: Splitter and Sharp (1995, pp. 48–57)

The following conversation illustrates the language and thinking that can result from good classroom dialogue practices. Children learn to construct their own questions and to respond to each other's questions and comments. The teacher's role is that of facilitator, joining in to direct the dialogue when required. The teacher also works to provide the prompts, cues, questions and language models as necessary to help advance children's thinking and their use of language to express thoughts. The conversation below took place with a group of five- and six-year-olds.

DIALOGUE: YEAR 1 CHILDREN
STIMULUS: PICTURE OF A SPIDER AND A WEB

Anne:	I wonder why spiders make webs—they could make them underground.
Solomon:	Because they haven't got houses, they have to make webs.
Josh:	If they don't have houses, how will they sleep in day or night?
Raffy:	The web is strong and soft.
Sian:	When I have web on my slide and put my finger on it, it is soft and it grows into a flower on my grass because it turns into a red flower.
Isabelle:	Why do webs have silk? Because they look like silky. I don't know if it's silk but it might be.
Louise:	They have no place to like … and soft silky webs and good places to catch and eat and live in.
Liz:	I can answer Isabelle's question. Webs have silk in them—I've felt them.
Josh:	How does spiders make the web?
Caroline:	They find lots of sticky things and get them into strips and make little bags to put their eggs in.

Liliana:	Webs are silky and soft so when you touch them they make your fingers soft—learnt that on the internet. It comes from its bottom.
Sian:	They don't have anywhere else to lay eggs and if it didn't have a web it wouldn't have a soft place to lay eggs.
Sian:	Sometimes I go home after school and see spiders in my garage and I play with it and then I smacked its bottom and a silly toy went to the spider ...
Giani:	Basically not all spiders have webs out of its bum—the spitting spider spits it out of his mouth.
Josh:	If they don't have houses to sleep in they might go in someone's house. One time my cat put the legs of a spider in my house.
Raffy:	Some animals can live without legs—a grasshopper had a leg missing and it stayed alive.
Sian:	Crabs can grow legs back.
Teacher:	Do human legs grow back like that?
Caroline:	My mum said our skin is different from animals—slimy, and ours isn't.
Liz:	Why does Theodore have a thinking box?
Sian:	My floor had to have a polish and we went to a hotel and we saw a man with one leg. He wasn't even hopping to the hotel.
Sian:	He uses a special stick.

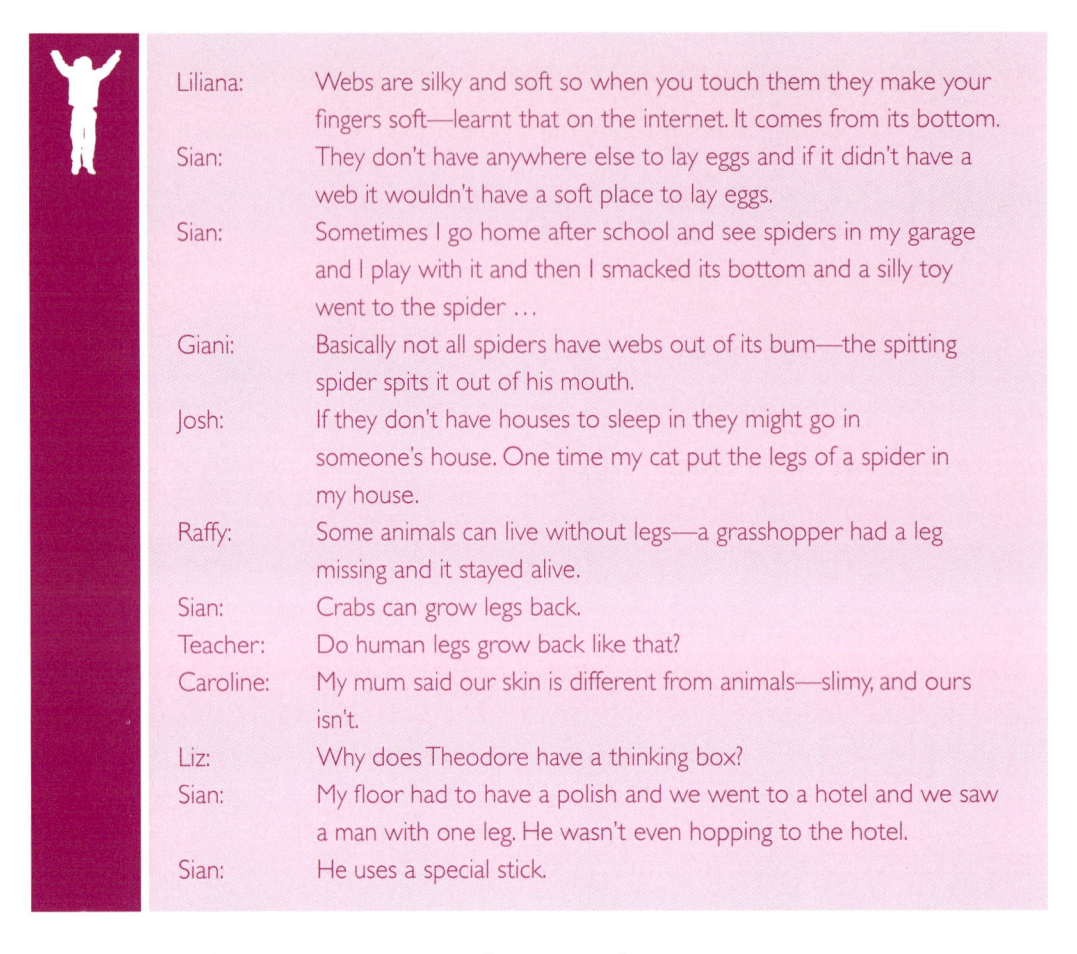

The core and process questions framework

Jill Slack's model (see box below) combines questions that stimulate children's thinking about concepts during conversations with those that assist them to refine their thinking and develop their responses. The two categories of questions are referred to as core and process questions.

Core questions are designed to cue and to direct children's thinking during conversations and discussions. They direct children in using oral language to:

- observe and recall
- group and label ideas
- classify
- make inferences
- predict.

Process questions focus on assisting children with the course of their thinking during conversations and discussions. They might serve to encourage children to:

- refocus their thinking if it gets off track
- express their ideas clearly
- support the ideas or information they present with evidence
- make generalisations based on what they have discovered.

SLACK'S CORE AND PROCESS QUESTIONS

Core questions

These questions cue and direct children's thinking during learning conversations. They should be:

- *clear*—using language that children understand
- *focused*—noticeably connecting to the topic or concept and to the required thought process
- *open*—involving language that provides children with opportunities to use elaborate talk to respond and they should allow for various responses.

Examples

Use questions that invite children to:

- observe
  What do you notice about the … ?
- recall
  What do you remember about … ?
- compare
  In what ways is … similar to … ?
- contrast
  What differences do you find between … and … ?
- group
  Which of the items go together? For what reason?
- label
  What would an appropriate name be? Why?
- classify
  Which of the examples or items belong in the … group?
- establish criteria
  On what basis have the following items of information been ordered?
- infer cause
  What has caused … ?
- infer
  What do you think is true about … ? (Inferring quality)
- predict
  What do you think will happen when/as a result of … ?

Processing questions

These questions direct children to refine their thinking and develop their responses. They entail questions that:

- *refocus*—put children back on track in relation to the type of thinking and talking required in an activity

- *clarify*—assist children to make their ideas/responses clearer or to use more accurate language to express ideas and to define words and bring clearer meaning to ideas expressed
- *verify*—encourage children to provide evidence for their ideas or for the information they present. Children may do this by referring to personal experience or some other means to confirm the validity of their ideas and information
- *redirect*—enhance communication between children. They serve to draw out responses from different children
- *narrow-the-focus*—contain children's responses to content relevant to the thinking called for and the topic
- *support*—help learners to establish relationships between and among statements of evidence.

Examples

Use questions that call for children to:

- refocus
  What makes you say … ?
  You are noticing ways in which … are alike. In what ways are they different?
- clarify
  What do you mean by … ?
  Draw that for me.
  What does the word … mean?
  What are you referring to when you say … ?
- verify
  How do you know … ?
  When or where have you experienced that before?
  Give me an example of ….
- redirect
  In what ways we can group … ?
  What else do you think we will find out when … ?
- narrow the focus
  What do you notice about … ?
  Tell me more about … .
- support
  What is … an example of?
  What is the reason you used for putting then in this order?
  What makes you say … caused … ?
  What makes you say … happened because of … ?
  What is the reason for thinking … will cause … ?

Source: Dantonio (1990)

SUMMARY

A rich language environment is important for the development of children's cognitive ability and, likewise, cognitive maturation influences the development of language. Moreover, talk is fundamental to the process of learning; it assists learners to process information and to develop new skills and conceptual knowledge. The learning experiences in which children engage should foster the use of talk—talk between the children as well as between the children, teachers and other adults.

Asking questions of children as they engage in learning experiences should enhance their thinking, learning and language development; it should direct and extend their thinking and assist them in learning from the experience. Likewise, questioning should support children in their ability to verbally express their ideas and understanding. There are a number of questioning frameworks that teachers can use to ensure that the questions they ask are effective in achieving these objectives.

QUESTIONS AND ACTIVITIES

1. Discuss what you understand to be the relationship between language and cognition.
2. Work with others to create a diagram that demonstrates your understanding of schemata (how children learn).
3. Consider a group of four-year-olds who have diverted from a painting activity to experiment with mixing the paints to discover new colours. What questions could you ask them to encourage them to express the concepts they are learning?
4. Outline a number of different ways in which you can support school-age children in using language as they investigate concepts during a science enquiry.
5. Examine the transcript that involves David (age six) answering the teacher's questions about a picture. Identify the features of the language that the teacher elicits from David through the different question types. Consider specific language elements—vocabulary, syntax and length of utterance.
6. Examine the oral language transcript where five- and six-year-olds are talking about spiders and identify the features of the children's use of language. What do you think the language and learning outcomes might be for this type of dialogue?

KEY TERMS

academic language
cognition
cognitive development
cognitive processes
concepts
cooperative learning

inner speech
question frameworks
scaffolds
schema
schemata

KEY REFERENCES

Barnes, D. (1992). The role of talk in learning. In K. Norman (ed.), *Thinking voices: the work of the national oracy project*. London: Hodder & Stoughton, pp. 123–8.

Blank, M., Rose, S.A. & Berlin, L.J. (1978). *The language of learning: The preschool years*. New York: Grune & Stratton.

Cook, R. E., Klein, M. D., et al. (2004). *Adapting early childhood curricula for children in inclusive settings*. Boston: Pearson.

Dantonio, M. (1990). *How can we create thinkers? Questioning strategies that work for teachers*. Bloomington: National Educational Service.

Estes, L. (2004). *Essentials of child care and early childhood education*. Boston: Pearson Education.

Foley, J. & Thompson, L. (2007). *Language learning: A lifelong process*. London: Oxford University Press.

Gleason, J. B. (2005). *The development of language*. Boston: Allyn and Bacon.

Kearns, K. & Austin, B. (2007). *Working in children's services series: Frameworks for learning and development*. Boston: Pearson Education.

Kozulin, A. (1986). *Thought and language: Lev Vygotsky*. Cambridge: The MIT Press.

Lamb, S. (2006). Being realistic, being scientific. *Linguistic Association of Canada and the United States (LACUS) forum (32)*. Retrieved 29 November 2009 from www.lacus.org/volumes/.

McGee, L. M. & Richgels, D. J. (2008). *Literacy beginnings: Supporting young readers and writers*. Boston: Pearson Education.

Norman, K. (ed.) (1992). *Thinking voices: The work of the national oracy project*. Kent, UK: Hodder and Staughton.

Rathus, S. A. (2006). *Childhood and adolescence: Voyagers in development*. Belmont: Thomson Wadsworth.

CHAPTER 7

Assessment: Speaking and Listening

CHAPTER OBJECTIVES

This chapter will increase your understanding of:

- important processes in the assessment of children's speaking and listening
- the use of various methods to be used in assessing and documenting children's speaking and listening development and learning
- using assessment information to make judgments about children's speaking and listening knowledge, skills and understanding.

In this chapter a range of methods for assessing children's speaking and listening are presented. However, in order to select appropriate methods and to make meaningful interpretations of the information collected, it is important that you have a sound understanding of language, communication and learning and development. It is also important that you understand the curricular requirements. You should refer to the preceding chapters that describe important language components, oral communication features and the ways in which oral language is learnt and developed. Each of the assessment methods described has both benefits and limitations. This usually relates to the early childhood setting and the areas of speaking and listening that you are assessing. As you read about each method, consider its application for different settings and for different aspects of oral language.

INTRODUCTION

The conditions in which children produce oral language can significantly affect how well the language they produce represents their actual ability (Herrera, Murray & Morales Cabral, 2007, p. 58). The **assessment** of children's oral language ideally should be undertaken in natural conditions—that is, it should be carried out during communicative experiences with which the children regularly engage and are familiar (as they play and explore materials, talk about stories, share daily news, investigate topics, have conversations, etc.) and it should involve them using oral language to communicate (speak and listen) for either social or learning purposes. Assessments that involve natural speaking and listening situations are more likely to produce more accurate information about children's oral language ability.

Assessment goals should be based on a reliable understanding of what is known about the natural progression of children's oral language development and the likely variations. A good understanding of typical oral language development will assist in identifying what children already know, what they are capable of doing and what they are ready to do next. It assists with identifying any unusually delayed or accelerated development that can then be addressed. It is important to keep in mind, however, that not all children develop in the same way, since they come from a diversity of home backgrounds and experiences. While social and cultural factors influence language development, so too do personal factors that are determined by genetics. The important thing is to aim for some measure of improvement so that children continue to move forward with their speaking and listening ability.

IMPORTANT ASSESSMENT PRACTICES

- Be knowledgeable about your curriculum, specifically the speaking and listening outcomes and goals.
- Develop a classroom oral language program that has clear goals that align with curriculum and the individual backgrounds of the children. Ensure they are considered in terms of general communicative competence, as well as the specific components of oral language.
- Determine what, who, why, how and when to assess.
- Carry out assessments using a well-managed system for keeping records.
- Reflect on assessment data and evaluate the children's learning and needs.
- Use the information gained from assessments to modify the environment, learning experiences and instruction.
- Communicate the results of your assessment to stakeholders.

State and national curriculum objectives and the more specific goals and objectives of a school or childcare teaching and learning program need to be considered in determining assessment plans. Teachers should seek to measure the current skills, and understandings of children against curriculum objectives and program goals.

ORAL LANGUAGE ASSESSMENT

Assessment of oral language involves the determination of children's general ability with oral communication as well as their competency within the different oral language components—phonological, syntactic, semantic and pragmatic. These have been discussed at length in Chapter 1. They comprise:

1. *The phonological component*: the sound patterns of language
   Teachers need to find out about children's development in the pronunciation of words and specifically determine their ability with the various sounds (phonemes) of the English language. They also need to consider how children use English intonation patterns—pitch and stress—when speaking.
2. *The syntactic component*: the system of structuring sentences
   Teachers need to find out about children's application of the rules for combining words to form meaningful sentences. As soon as a child uses two words together—'More juice!'—the syntactic rule about combining words to convey meaning is being applied. Teachers need to ascertain how young children use sentences. It may involve finding out about the telegraphic speech (modified sentences) of toddlers or the use of simple and more complex sentences by other children, and the use of other elements of syntax such as tense variations and different sentence types (questions, statements, commands).
3. *The semantic component*: the meaning of words and sentences
   Teachers need to find out about children's expressive and receptive vocabulary and their ability to construct sentences and organise their ideas in a way that meets their communication purposes. They also need to find out about their listening comprehension.
4. *The pragmatic component*: the use of language to communicate in different situations
   Teachers need to find out about practical ways in which children use language as they communicate with others. They need to determine children's ability to adjust the ways in which they speak and listen according to the context or situation in which they are communicating, and they need to determine their understanding and use of conventions for different speaking and listening situations (e.g. turn-taking during conversation). Further to this, teachers need to find out about children's confidence when speaking in different situations. It should be noted that these components interrelate.

Figure 7.1: Oral language

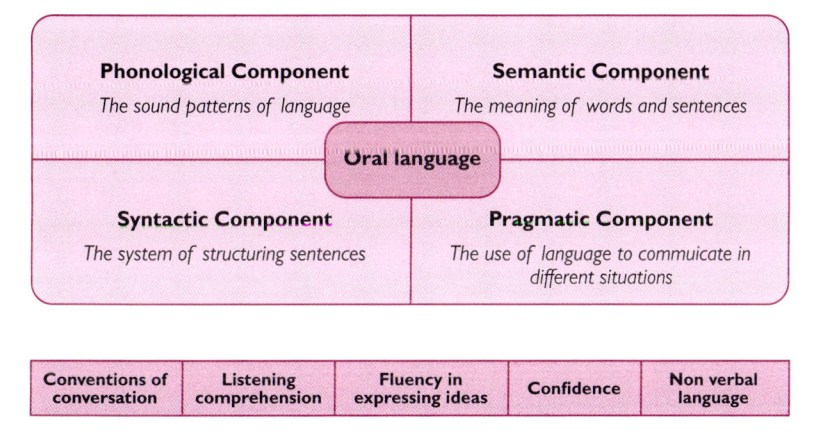

Phonological Component	**Semantic Component**
The sound patterns of language	*The meaning of words and sentences*
Syntactic Component	**Pragmatic Component**
The system of structuring sentences	*The use of language to commuicate in different situations*

Oral language

| Conventions of conversation | Listening comprehension | Fluency in expressing ideas | Confidence | Non verbal language |

COLLECTING INFORMATION ABOUT CHILDREN'S ORAL LANGUAGE

There are a number of ways in which the assessment of children's oral language can be carried out. Some that are most significant to the early childhood context are:

- *Observation*: teachers watch children as they engage in oral language experiences and record the outcomes.
- *Conversations*: teachers gain insights into children's speaking and listening competencies by asking them questions and talking with them.
- *Samples of children's written and visual work*: teachers collect and appraise the written or visual work (e.g. drawing and painting) that children produce as part of their classroom activities when the work involves children's speaking and listening competencies.
- *Children's self-evaluations*: children reflect on their own oral language ability—areas of strength and areas to be improved. After an oral language activity they might be asked to consider the speaking and listening competencies they demonstrated or the degree to which they demonstrated them.
- *Communication with families*: teachers talk with parents and families to ascertain their perspective on their children's oral language ability and to find out about their children's skill in speaking and listening situations outside the school or childcare setting.
- **Formal tests**: children's knowledge and skills are determined through pencil and paper tests that involve answering questions or completing a particular type of written task.

Observation as a means of assessment can be undertaken in a range of activities in which oral language is used.

OBSERVATION

Observation as a method of assessment occurs when teachers monitor children as they engage in speaking and listening activities, in order to find out what they have and have not learnt. It involves looking on without interrupting, and noticing the oral language skills, knowledge and understanding that are exhibited.

Observation is a valuable means by which teachers can collect information or evidence about children's speech and language development and their general **competency** in various speaking and listening situations. Through observation, teachers can learn about children's development and learning across a range of different speaking and listening skills and understandings; for instance, teachers can learn about children's:

- sentence structures—simple, compound and complex
- application of grammatical conventions when forming sentences
- use of different types of sentences—question, command, statement and exclamation
- use of tense when talking in present, past and future
- vocabulary knowledge—general word knowledge and knowledge of words specific to the topic of the speaking and listening context
- functional use of language—using language for different purposes such as to recount, imagine, give reasons, rationalise and solve problems
- attention given to speakers and responses made to the comments of others
- techniques for gaining and maintaining the attention of others
- use of the rules of conversation such as taking turns and listening
- confidence in participating in speaking and listening situations
- fluency and clarity when speaking
- concentration in different speaking and listening situations.

Because observation can uncover a wide variety of information, teachers should establish clearly just what it is they are looking for—what skills, understanding and behaviours they want to find out about. Without a clear purpose for the observation, the task can be overwhelming and end up being a waste of time. Focused observation allows the teacher to concentrate on the exact aspects of oral language about which information is required. It better positions them to identify children's strengths as well as the areas in which development is needed.

Observation as a means of assessment can be undertaken in any one of a range of activities in which oral language is used. It might, for instance, occur as children engage in socio-dramatic play, conversations, indoor and outdoor free play, investigations, storytelling or oral presentations. The important thing to remember is that the activities should be those that are an everyday part of classroom or childcare experiences. They need to be known to the children.

Observation as a means of assessing children's language growth is more effective when a number of situations are observed. When it occurs across a range of situations, there can be greater assurance about the usefulness of the information (data) gathered and that it is a true reflection of the children's abilities. Furthermore, different situations call for children to draw on different skills and understandings as they engage in oral communication. The contextual features to consider in deciding what situations are appropriate for observation are:

- the people present
- the number of people involved
- the activity being carried out
- the subject matter or topic of the talk
- the level of formality or informality of the situation.

Table 7.1: Oral language assessment is most reliable when it takes place over a few different speaking and listening contexts

Socio-dramatic play	Small-group enquiry	Class discussions
Learning centre activities	Introductions and messages	Small group or partner discussion
Small group or class discussions	Conversations	Barrier games
Oral presentations	Making announcements	Indoor and outdoor free play
Listening to and responding to a story	Interviews	News-telling or show and tell
Retelling a story	Role play	Partner investigations
Conversations with teachers and other adults	Problem-solving task	Barrier games

Effective observational assessment requires well-managed procedures, without which they can be unproductive and time wasting. Grisham Brown and Brookshire (2006, p. 48) provide useful guidelines for designing adequately organised observational assessment plans. Their suggestions concentrate on observation during children's play experiences, but they can easily be applied to a broader range of observation situations. They suggest the following steps:

1. Set up two activities that will be used for observational assessment and have these activities available for the children to carry out over a week. Spend time each day assessing the children as they participate in the two activities; attempt to assess all the children by the end of the week.
2. When the activities are available throughout the week, the children are likely to come and go and so there will be ample opportunity to collect the assessment information.
3. If a child is observed performing a skill as they complete an activity additional to the assessment ones, give them credit and make note of this on the information recording sheet.
4. Encourage all the children to participate in the assessment activities at some stage throughout the week.
5. Enlist the assistance of others who regularly work with the children in the class.

An alternative observational assessment system is provided by Raver (2004), who makes clear connections between planning for teaching and learning and assessment methods. The following is an adaptation of her suggested steps:

1. Use curriculum documents to guide the composition of a list of objectives—the skills, understandings and knowledge important to the children's (oral language) learning.

2   Develop a variety of experiences (e.g. play, learning centres and intentional teaching activities), routines and environmental features which will support the development of each of the identified objectives.
3   Work to achieve the identified objectives through the planned experiences, environmental features and routine events, as well as through instructional lessons where needed.
4   Determine how and when assessment will occur. Plan for it to occur throughout a day and over a week. Be clear about how to identify the oral language skills and understanding being addressed. Create forms that can be used to document the children's learning.
5   Assess the children's learning with regard to each of the listed objectives by observing them as they engage in the different experiences. Ensure that observations are relatively quick and do not disturb the flow of an activity. Observe each child at different activities and look for repeated displays of a skill or understanding.
6   Have copies of the recording forms on clipboards and have these placed in different locations in the classroom. It can be difficult to collect data about each objective every day but this allows for easy access when assessment opportunities occur.
7   At the end of the day, transfer the data collected to each child's assessment file.

It is important that the children who are to be the subject of observation be selected in advance; it is unwise to try to observe all children. Perhaps select a group of children with each group being observed on a different day over a period of a week (Boyd Batstone, 2004).

The notes taken should be evaluated in order to determine what they reveal about children's oral language strengths and learning needs. A simple coding system can be used for this purpose. The notes should be used to compile a short summary of each child's strengths and needs, which should help identify the types of learning experiences and instructional lessons that may be required (Boyd Batstone, 2004, p. 235).

Using the story retell

Story retelling is an effective means of assessing oral language. The procedure is to read aloud a story book (at an appropriate listening comprehension level for the child) and then ask her or him to retell it by saying, 'Can you tell me what happened in the story?' or 'Can you please retell the story to me?' Things to look out for when the child retells the story include:

- *Evidence of listening comprehension*: Does the retell indicate that the child fully comprehended the story or is there evidence of superficial comprehension or misunderstandings?
- *Sentence use*: What types of sentences does the child use? Is there a variety? Is the syntax correct?
- *Vocabulary*: What vocabulary does the child use? Does she/he use only simple, high frequency words or is there use of less common words? Are new or less common words from the story used correctly?
- *Organisation of retelling*: Is the retelling well organised? Is it sequenced appropriately, with orientation, complication and resolution given? Is the setting described? Are the characters and their actions faithfully described?
- *Detail*: How much detail is given in the retelling?
- *Expression*: Does the child retell the story with expression and enjoyment?
- *Confidence*: How confident is the child?

Table 7.2: Notes sheet: focused observation of children's language when retelling a familiar story

Story retelling	Yes or no	Story: *The Gingerbread Man.* Date: 19/8/2009 Comments
Aaron	Y	A full recount given, which included all story elements. Recount given with expression and confidence. Full sentences used and good use of vocabulary.
Alisha	-	A few fragmented comments about the story given. Out of sequence. Lots of short phrases used instead of full sentences. Pronunciation of some of the words incorrect.
Fanny	-	No recount offered. Fanny wanted to draw a picture instead. After a few probing questions, Fanny gave short answers or shrugged.
James	Y	Excellent recount. James showed good listening comprehension of the story at literal level. Some inferences made. Fluent retell using simple and complex sentences. Expressive voice and good eye contact.

CONVERSATIONS

Conversation as a method of assessment involves talking with young children and asking them questions about what they know, what they are doing or what they are thinking about. Conversations of this type are easily maintained and are more likely to elicit the children's participation when they occur around topics relating to children's immediate experiences and interests.

Conversations can take different forms and the most appropriate form will depend on the age of the children, the situation in which a conversation is to take place and the information to be gathered. Nilson (2004) identifies conversation as being either informal or structured interviews:

Conversation as a method of assessment involves talking with young children and asking them questions about what they know, what they are doing or what they are thinking about.

- **Informal interview**

  Informal conversations are those which happen regularly in the routine functioning of the classroom or centre. They involve teachers talking to children about the activity in which they are engaged or one recently completed. The conversation should flow in a natural way and allow for the gathering of information about children's spontaneous use of language.

- **Structured interview**

  The interview is a 'little conversation with a purpose' (Nilson, 2004, p. 145). It involves the teacher asking children pre-planned questions about a picture, story book, experience or concept. In this instance, teachers design the questions in order to elicit certain uses of language from the children.

SAMPLES OF CHILDREN'S WORK

The written and visual (drawings, paintings etc.) texts that children produce often reveal insights about their speaking and listening skills and understandings. For instance, after a story is read to young children they might be asked to reflect on a specific element and represent their understanding through a drawing. The content of the artwork produced will often provide an indication of the children's listening comprehension. However, such an assessment is enhanced if the children also talk about their drawing.

The use of work samples to elicit information about children's speaking and listening competencies must be approached carefully. It may be that children lack the necessary skill to produce a piece of work (they may not be able to faithfully represent their understanding through drawing or painting) and it will therefore not provide a fair sample of their competency. To assemble an accurate representation of children's oral language ability, work samples are best used in conjunction with other assessment methods.

CHILDREN'S SELF-EVALUATION

Self-evaluation occurs when children are asked to reflect on their own learning and to make judgments about their ability with different aspects of oral communication. It involves children sharing their thoughts and opinions about their own progress, achievements and needs. It can be carried out through reflective discussions during teacher and child meetings or at other opportune times when the teacher can ask questions that direct the children's thinking about what they have learnt and how they have progressed, and about what they perceive as their oral language strengths and needs. It can also be done after a specific oral language activity where the performance criterion has been established and when the children need to determine the degree to which it has been achieved.

An example of the classroom use of self-evaluation is provided by a class of eight-year-olds who, as part of their learning, were required to conduct oral presentations about a topic. With full knowledge of the task and the oral language competencies to be demonstrated, they were given time to prepare and practise. After their presentations the children were required to rate themselves against five criteria, using three different levels of achievement.

Another scenario involves a Year 1 class that engages in a great deal of small group learning. A regular and familiar practice for these children is to conclude group work activities with an analysis of the group's use of appropriate speaking and listening behaviours. Each group is required to consider and respond to a series of questions; for example, 'Did I look at each person as they spoke?' And, 'Did everyone get a turn at sharing their ideas?' As a group, they determine whether the behaviours were employed or not.

Self-evaluation should be a feature of every classroom. Even very young children can think about their own learning by talking about what they can do and what they know they can't yet do or what they have just learnt to do. Self-evaluation helps children to become more insightful about how they learn and to consider their participation in classroom activities. It helps them to develop the important ability to set their own learning goals and to feel a sense of control over their future learning (Owocki, 2001, p. 28). This is essential to motivation and engagement in classroom activities.

COMMUNICATION WITH FAMILIES

Families are an important source of information about children's oral language. They can provide insights that help to build a comprehensive picture of children's development and learning. They have known their children better and for longer than anyone else (McAfee & Leong, 2002) and have been witness to their children's speech and language development from the outset. The parents' expertise about their children's oral language can expand a teacher's own understanding.

Parents can provide teachers with information about their children's cultural and language backgrounds and they can share experiences of their oral language practices at home and in other contexts outside of the school or childcare setting. Parents and teachers can also work together in setting goals for the children, and parents can provide experiences at home to supplement classroom or childcare centre activities which are intended to help achieve these goals. Teachers can also ask parents to undertake specific assessments of their children's speaking and listening at home. For instance, they could be asked to observe their children when they are in different social situations—with friends, siblings, at the shops or an after-school activity—and note certain skills or behaviours displayed.

Parent–teacher meetings that are timetabled throughout the year provide an obvious opportunity for teachers to source information about children's oral language. However, there are also other opportunities, the choice of which will depend on such factors as parents' availability and the type and detail of the information required. Information can be gained from parents through the use of questionnaires, regular parent–teacher communication folders, casual chats at pick-up time and telephone calls.

FORMAL TESTS

There are many formal, standardised oral language tests that teachers can administer if they have appropriate training in their use. However, many of these are from the USA or the United Kingdom and may thus not be strictly relevant for the Australian context. Furthermore, many of them can only be administered by educators with appropriate postgraduate qualifications, so are not accessible to classroom teachers.

One test that is easily accessible and simple is the Teacher Rating of Oral Language and Literacy (TROLL) (Dickinson, McCabe & Sprague, 2003). This is basically a rubric that teachers use to rate young children in any or all of three areas, namely oral language, reading and writing. Norms are available for three-, four- and five-year-old children (but normed in the USA).

The Comprehensive Assessment of Spoken Language (CASL) (Carrow-Woolfolk, 1999) evaluates receptive and expressive language in great detail and is useful for identifying language delay and disorders. It can be used with children of three years onwards and is an individually administered test that takes thirty to forty-five minutes. This would normally be administered by a speech specialist or school psychologist, or a school-based literacy specialist with postgraduate qualifications. There are many other formal assessments.

DOCUMENTATION OF ORAL LANGUAGE LEARNING

A necessary component of assessment is the documentation of the information which is gathered. Teachers need to keep clear and organised records of their findings with regard to what children can do and what they have learnt. They need to be able to access the assessment information as required—for communicating with others and for revising and changing the teaching and learning program. The documentation therefore needs to be set out in a way that facilitates this.

There are many ways in which children's learning can be documented; some involve the recording of narrative description while others require the presence or absence of a skill or behaviour to be recorded or a rating to be determined. The most appropriate method will depend on the type of assessment being used and the type of information that is being sought. Some useful techniques for documenting assessment information include:

- anecdotal notes
- audio or video recordings
- checklists
- rating scales
- rubrics
- portfolios.

ANECDOTAL NOTES

Anecdotal notes are used to record information gleaned during the assessment process, most often when the means of assessment is observation. They are written accounts of children's use of oral language as noted when they were engaged in speaking and listening experiences. Anecdotal notes can be quite detailed or they can entail the use of only a few words, phrases and sentences. The degree of detail is influenced by the purpose for which the assessment is being carried out.

Anecdotal notes can be a highly effective means of recording the teacher's ongoing observations of children engaged in authentic learning activities. They can be used to build up a very rich and detailed picture of children's progress. It is important to follow an appropriate system. The information recorded should facilitate easy access and should enable informed decisions to be made about children's requirements for their oral language growth.

One simple system for recording observations of children's speaking and listening involves the use of index cards. For each child, assessment data is recorded on a separate index card which also records the date, the child's name and the situation in which the assessment took place. It might also include a reflective or interpretative comment where the teacher writes a summary comment about the child's oral language. An example is provided below.

JAMAL K (FIVE YEARS)

22 June

Situation

Playing at the construction learning centre with Hamish and Karina.

Observations

1. Works silently for long periods. Very focused on what he is doing. Other children playing next to him are talking a lot. Doesn't lose concentration.
2. Asks to borrow pieces of equipment from both children—polite, appropriate volume.
3. Comments on Jamal's building.
4. Stops to listen when Karina tells him about the railway she is building. Shows interest.
5. Tells Karina about his crane by describing to her how he made it.

Reflection

Jamal speaks confidently. He engages in speaking and listening with other children for different social purposes—to obtain things needed, to respond to comments of others, to share personal experiences, to describe. He plays quietly, concentrating on his own endeavours but participates with others when invited or when needing to.

[Observations of each child's social language use were recorded on separate index cards.]

Another effective system for making anecdotal notes is a sheet of paper on which the oral language skills and competencies to be assessed have been written. The paper is divided into about eight to ten boxes and the names of children are written in each. Once the sheet is set up it is placed on a clipboard which is easily accessible to the teacher. Whenever a child is observed, a descriptive note is recorded in the appropriate box. Eventually the sheet is cut up so as to separate the boxes which are then glued into the children's assessment folders.

The assessment chart shown in Table 7.3 provides a more detailed structure for making anecdotal notes during observation. It identifies various aspects of oral language to be assessed and should therefore guide the teacher to make focused observations and anecdotal notes that are of maximum relevance.

Table 7.3: Open-ended anecdotal notes sheet

Focus: Sentences (structures and types) Vocabulary (general and topic)		Stacey	Peter
Zoe	Stephanie	Chad	Kelvin
Antonia	Marcus	Laura	Paulo

Table 7.4: Structured anecdotal notes sheet

Name of child: _____ Year 1:		Oral language	
Aspect	Date	Activity/context	Assessment comments
Language for social interaction Takes turns Listens when others speak Uses appropriate body language Uses appropriate language Sustains conversations Expresses and solicits opinions and feelings			
Speaking to different audiences Changes register			
Speaking for different purposes (e.g. to give information, to question, to satisfy needs, to socialise, to imagine, to express feelings) Uses appropriate oral text type Uses appropriate language or vocabulary Uses appropriate body language			
Attitude Shows confidence Shows enjoyment Uses new words with enthusiasm			

AUDIO OR VIDEO RECORDINGS

Children's engagement in speaking and listening activities can be captured on a video or audio recording. Video or audio recordings can be made as children participate in learning experiences and as they use oral language to communicate with others. Children might be taped while telling a story, recounting an event, dictating a sentence, joining in conversations and interviews with teachers and during partner discussions. Whatever the setting, video and audio tapes of children talking can provide valuable opportunities for careful examination of the language of the children involved. The data can be viewed and documentation made at the teacher's convenience.

The use of video and audio recording as a way of documenting children's performances provides teachers with an opportunity to gain a large amount of detailed and accurate information about children's language competency. Moreover, the video or audio recordings can be shared with parents or families to provide evidence of the children's learning and development. It is advisable to seek parental consent when audio and video recording children for assessment purposes.

CHECKLISTS

A **checklist** is an inventory of competencies (skills or behaviours) where teachers can indicate whether children demonstrate the specified competencies. It is another means by which information about children's oral language proficiency can be recorded. Checklists

Table 7.5: Checklist: observation during free play

	Uses language to communicate preferences, wants and needs	Uses language to enter into ongoing play or join a centre activity	Uses language to resolve or avoid conflicts	Uses language to plan, develop or maintain the play or group activity	Comments
Mavara	✓	✓	✓	✓	
Bradley	✓	✓			Expresses needs but needs to develop socially (manners)
Simone	✓		✓	✓	
Kathleen	✓				Kathy is shy and is beginning to express want and needs She is just beginning to use language to join in play
Gabrielle	✓	✓	✓	✓	

can be created to include a wide range of oral language skills and behaviours; a functional checklist would list only a select range of competencies based on the oral language goals of a specific teaching and learning program.

Checklists can be used with each of the different methods for collecting information about children's oral language ability—observation, conversations and examination of work samples. Teachers observe children carrying out activities, talk with them, seek answers to questions about topics and experiences or look at samples of work and, as they do so, seek to have the children demonstrate competencies itemised on the checklist. The presence or absence of a competency can be recorded by checking the box for each item listed.

Checklists can be combined with anecdotal notes to provide a deeper understanding of the children's oral language skills and behaviours. The example in Table 7.5 allows the teacher to indicate whether a specific speaking and listening behaviour is evident or not and also to make notes that supplement the checklist information.

The checklist in Table 7.6 is more elaborate as it provides for a rating to be given of each oral language competency which is listed. Teachers can do more than indicate the presence or absence of a skill or behaviour; they also can show whether the child can do it independently, with assistance or not at all. This particular checklist also provides for anecdotal notes to be made about the child in respect of each of the listed competencies.

Table 7.6: Checklist 2: includes a rating and area for anecdotal notes, and used while observing children during the 'play dough' learning centre activity

Situation: Small group activity: play dough		Oral language focus:	Rating code: 1 = independent 2 = with assistance 3 = still developing
Name	Skill or behaviour	Observed? (1, 2 or 3)	Comment
Ashija	Passing equipment to other children when asked. Using appropriate language such as, 'You're welcome' or language to clarify other child's request: 'Do you mean the star or the round?'	1	Enjoys being helpful. Ashija always listens to peers and tries to respond to their requests. Always shares
Benny		2	Has to be prompted by the caregiver
Jayden		3	Ignores requests from other children. Today hid a cookie cutter under his chair to avoid sharing
Tiarn		2	Sometimes responds independently but usually has to be prompted by an adult

Checklists, when used to record children's speaking and listening competency, can be maintained and added to over time. The date is noted and a comment is made each time one of the identified skills or behaviours is observed. Table 7.7 is an example of such a checklist.

Table 7.7: Notes sheet: recording children's developing speaking and listening behaviours over time

Name: Angelica DaSilva (ESL)		DOB: 11/7/2005
Teacher(s): Sarah Worton, Mary North		
Listening and speaking behaviour	Date observed	Comments
Listens and acts upon simple instructions, such as, 'Get your shoes'	26/1/2008 MN	Picked up books and put them away when asked
Speaks—uses single words only		
Speaks in short phrases—incomplete sentences	Feb–March	Usually only nouns and verbs used. Also prepositions, e.g. on, in. Some pronouns used—me, you. Possessives heard: mine, his.
Speaks in full sentences	4/4/2008 MN	Said: 'Angie want to play again.' Full sentence but not correct agreement
Can participate in conversations		
Takes turns when engaged in speaking and listening activities	14/9/2008	Still needs development. Does not always listen to other children when spoken to, although she usually listens to adults
Participates in rhymes and chanting activities	5/5/2008 SW	Participated in 'Jelly on a Plate' and seemed to enjoy
Asks questions	19/6/2008 MN	Asked: 'Where Shelley gone?' Functional language OK but syntax needs development
Retells story books	19/10/09	Not yet. When asked what happened in 'The Very Hungry Caterpillar', said, 'He like cake and he like apple'

Source: adapted from Beaty (2009, p. 55)

RATING SCALES

Rating scales are similar to checklists in that they provide a list of oral language competencies (skills or behaviours) to be assessed. However, unlike checklists, they do not merely facilitate the recording of the presence or absence of each competency; they require consideration of quality or frequency. Each competency is ranked along a continuum from low to high quality or low to high frequency. Symbols, words or phrases are used to indicate the different rankings. For instance, the numbers 1–5 might be used, where 1 indicates low quality and the numbers 2–5 show increasingly better quality.

Ratings scales allow teachers to rate children's competency in particular areas rather than simply judging whether a skill or understanding at a particular level is present or not. In many ways, ratings scales are preferable to checklists because they are more informative and positive in that they emphasise what the child *can* do. Below are some examples of ratings scales for oral language assessment.

Table 7.8: Rating scale

Skill or behaviour	1	2	3	4	5
Use of appropriate words					
Use of complete sentences					
Responds to the comments of others					
Expresses own ideas					

Table 7.9: Rating scale

Skill or behaviour	Always	Most of the time	Some of the time	Not yet
Is an active participant in language activities				
Speaks clearly and fluently				
Shares experiences and feelings in relation to the topic				
Understands and uses appropriate body language and gestures				

RUBRICS

Rubrics are a type of rating scale. They comprise a series of descriptors (written statements) to indicate different levels of proficiency for each competency under assessment. Children's ability in each is indicated by considering the different statements and choosing the one that best describes proficiency.

An example of the use of the rubric as a means to record information about children's speaking and listening ability can be seen in Table 7.10. It involved a teacher carrying out a series of interviews with the children in her pre-primary class; one of the purposes of which was to find out about children's use of complete sentences. The following extract from a rubric shows the recording scale used. During the interview, the teacher analysed the relevant information and decided which statement on the scale best described each child's performance.

Table 7.10: Extract of a rubric: demonstrating a scale for one assessment criteria

Sentences	Always uses complete sentences	Usually uses complete sentences; a few minor faults	Uses complete sentences some of the time	Rarely uses complete sentences	Never uses complete sentences

The Student Oral Language Observational Matrix (SOLOM) (California State Department of Education and San Jose (California) Unified School District, (n.d.) is

Table 7.11: SOLOM: Student Oral Language Observation Matrix

Traits	1	2	3	4	5
Comprehension	Cannot be said to understand even simple conversation	Has difficulty understanding what is said; comprehends only 'social conversation' spoken slowly with frequent repetitions	Understands most of what is said at slower-than-normal speed with repetitions	Understands nearly everything at normal speed, although occasional repetition may be necessary	Understands everyday conversation and normal classroom discussions without difficulty
Fluency	Speech is so halting and fragmentary as to make conversation virtually impossible.	Usually hesitant; often forced into silence by language limitations	Speech in everyday conversation and classroom discussion frequently disrupted by the student's search for the correct manner of expression.	Speech in everyday conversation generally fluent, with occasional lapses as student searches for the correct manner of expression.	Speech in everyday conversation and classroom discussions fluent and effortless, approximating that of a native speaker.
Vocabulary	Vocabulary limitations so extreme so as to make conversation virtually impossible.	Misuse of words and very limited vocabulary; comprehension quite difficult	Student frequently uses wrong words; conversation somewhat limited because of inadequate vocabulary.	Student occasionally uses inappropriate terms and/or must rephrase ideas because of lexical inadequacies.	Use of vocabulary and idioms approximates that of a native speaker.
Pronunciation	Pronunciation problems so severe as to make speech virtually unintelligible.	Very hard to understand because of pronunciation problems; must frequently repeat in order to make self understood	Pronunciation problems necessitate concentration on the part of the listener and occasionally lead to misunderstanding.	Always intelligible, though one is conscious of a definite accent and occasional inappropriate intonation patterns	Pronunciation and intonation approximate that of a native speaker.
Grammar	Errors in grammar and word order so severe they make speech virtually unintelligible.	Grammar and word order errors make comprehension difficult; must often rephrase/restrict self to basic patterns.	Makes frequent errors of grammar and word order that occasionally obscure meaning	Occasionally makes grammatical and/or word-order errors that do not obscure meaning	Grammatical usage and word order approximate that of a native speaker.

Reprinted by permission, California Department of Education, CDE Press.

an example of a rubric that is widely used to record the oral language development of children who are learning English as an additional language (see Table 7.11). It clearly demonstrates the way in which the ordered statements for a specific competency signify growth of proficiency.

Rubrics can be developed quite easily. However, effectiveness in their design is largely determined by having a clear and specific understanding of the various elements and qualities of language and of the knowledge, skills and understandings to be developed in supporting children to become competent speakers and listeners. The following steps (from Gunning, 2010, p. 89) can be used in creating a rubric.

1. Write a definition for each skill or behaviour identified.
2. For each skill or behaviour, develop a scale:
    - Establish the highest and lowest ability levels.
    - Fill in the levels that will fall between the highest and lowest level.
3. Check that the skills and behaviours and the difference between each level are clearly specified.

PORTFOLIOS

Portfolios are a way of compiling and retaining a range of documents that provide evidence of children's strengths, changes, growth and progress over time. They are not a method of assessment but, rather, a collection of many assessments that have been carried out. Any combination of documents may make up a portfolio as long as they all serve to inform about children's learning, progress and ability. Portfolios might include checklists, samples of children's work (with each sample including additional information about the activity, goals and abilities demonstrated), anecdotal notes from assessment observations, photographs with notations that complement an assessment document, assessment rating scales and rubrics related to specific activities. All items in portfolios should be clearly identified and labelled. They should, where possible, include information such as the date, situation and activity, time of day and any other information which may assist in the understanding of an assessment item. They might also indicate the amount and type of assistance gained from the teacher if this is the case. Teacher annotations are also useful in clarifying the learning and development demonstrated in each item. A written comment might indicate what the work shows about the child's learning and development.

When portfolios are used to demonstrate children's speaking and listening growth over time, the following materials might be included:

- CDs and DVDs that show the child using oral language in a range of learning settings and activities
- paintings, pictures, craft or written texts that reveal something about a child's listening
- checklists and/or rubrics that indicate language and oral communication knowledge, skills and understanding.
- samples of children's work appropriate annotations
- photographs showing children participating in different speaking and listening scenarios and with annotations that provide information about the settings and the children's participation.

INTERPRETING THE INFORMATION GATHERED ABOUT ORAL LANGUAGE

The information collected about children's oral language requires interpretation. Teachers should carefully examine the assessment information and, in so doing, determine what it reveals about each child's current speaking and listening competencies. Examination should involve different sources of information gleaned from different speaking and listening situations. There are a number of recommended practices to ensure the most accurate interpretation of assessment information. These include:

- Look at the information as a whole and synthesise or summarise it.
- Determine what the information reveals about children's current speaking and listening knowledge, understanding, skill and confidence.
- Match the information against relevant curriculum and program outcomes and the speaking and listening phases of development frameworks.
- Identify the speaking and listening strengths and needs of individual children, groups of children and the whole class in general; create a class profile.

SUMMARY

There is a variety of methods that can be used to gather the information required to make accurate judgments about children's speaking and competency and their learning and development needs. Two significant methods are observation of children and conversations with families; however, others should also be utilised so as to ensure breadth, depth and accuracy of information. Early childhood learning environments, experiences and activities should be planned in the light of a sound knowledge of present skills and understanding, and learning and development needs.

QUESTIONS AND ACTIVITIES

1. How might teachers ensure that children have appropriate opportunities to demonstrate their oral language competencies and growth in a range of areas?
2. How could assessment practices be modified to accommodate children from culturally and linguistically diverse backgrounds?
3. Discuss the role of parents in the assessment of young children's oral language.
4. Identify a set of criteria appropriate to the assessment of the oral language development of toddlers and design a rubric that you could use in gathering and interpreting information.
5. Refer to a daily timetable/routines of the infants in a childcare setting and determine the times when information about their language and communication growth could be observed and noted. What do you consider to be the best method for recording the information?
6. Design a checklist that might be employed to assess the speaking and listening competencies of a class of Year 2 children during news-telling sessions.
7. Consider the types of questions you might ask pre-school or school-aged children to determine their attitude to and confidence with speaking and listening in general.

KEY TERMS

anecdotal notes
assessment
checklist
competency
formal test
informal interview
outcomes
portfolio
rating scale
rubric
structured interview
self-evaluation

KEY REFERENCES

Beaty, J. J. (2009). *50 early childhood literacy strategies*. Upper Saddle River: Pearson.

Boyd Batstone, P. (2004). Focused anecdotal assessment: A tool for standards-based assessment methods. *The Reading Teacher, 58*(3), 230–9.

California State Department of Education and San Jose (California) Unified School District (n.d.) *Student Oral Language Observation Matrix (SOLOM)*. California: CSTE.

Dickinson, D., McCabe, A., et al. (2003). Teacher rating of oral language and literacy (TROLL): Individualising early literacy instruction with a standards-based tool. *The Reading Teacher, 56*(6), 554–64.

Grisham Brown, J., Hallem, R., et al. (2006). Using authentic assessment to evidence children's progress toward early learning standards. *Early Childhood Education Journal, 34*(1).

Gunning, T. G. (2010). *Creating literacy instruction for all students*. Boston: Pearson Education.

Herrera, S. G., Murray, K. G., et al. (2007). *Assessment accommodations for classroom teachers of culturally and linguistically diverse learners*. Boston: Pearson.

McAfee, O. & Leong, D. J. (2002). *Assessing and guiding young children's development and learning*. Boston: Allyn and Bacon.

Nilson, B. A. (2004). *Week by week: Documenting the development of young children*. Clifton Park: Thomson Delmar learning.

Owocki, G. (2001). *Make way for literacy! Teaching the way young children learn*. Portsmouth, NH: Heinemann.

Raver, S. A. (2004). Monitoring progress in early childhood special education settings. *Teaching Exceptional Children, 36*(6).

PART 2

Understanding Literacy: Reading and Writing

CHAPTER 8

Understanding Literacy: Definitions and Theoretical Perspectives

CHAPTER OBJECTIVES

This chapter will increase your understanding of:

- definitions of literacy
- major theoretical perspectives on literacy learning
- the impact various theoretic perspectives have had on literacy teaching
- the affective factors involved in literacy and how to assess them.

In this chapter, you will learn about how definitions of literacy have changed over the years. You are encouraged to think about the relationship between definitions of literacy and the teaching practices that are played out in childcare and school settings. Theoretical perspectives of literacy learning are also discussed, as is recent research on what makes an excellent literacy teacher. Also, we will discuss the motivation of children in the literacy area. The information in this chapter will help you formulate your literacy teaching rationale or philosophy, which will help you develop coherent and effective literacy teaching programs.

WHAT IS LITERACY?

Since literacy evolves with changes in cultural communicative practices and technological developments, so too do definitions of what literacy is. Also, definitions of literacy reflect the theories and perspectives of their authors, and there are several theoretical perspectives of literacy. Having said this, there is some consensus on what literacy entails, and most definitions include reading, writing, speaking and listening and, sometimes, viewing or visual literacy. Also, many definitions mention the importance of critical thinking, critical literacy, flexibility and the ability to choose appropriate means of communication for particular contexts or purposes. The use of a variety of text forms, including new electronic and multimedia texts, is increasingly being seen as an element of literacy.

WHY ARE DEFINITIONS IMPORTANT?

Teachers and pre-service teachers might wonder why definitions matter and how they relate to practical work in the classroom or centre. In fact, definitions matter greatly because they influence curricular decision making, at both macro and micro levels. At the macro level, there are bodies that create curriculum documents that teachers must adhere to, and definitions of literacy play a central part in the setting of these. At the micro level, teachers themselves create a *classroom curriculum* in that they have practices and priorities that shape the classroom environment, as well as teaching and learning priorities and processes.

The Early Years Learning Framework for Australia (EYLF) (DEEWR, 2009, p. 38) defines literacy as follows:

> Literacy is the capacity, confidence and disposition to use language in all its forms. Literacy incorporates a range of modes of communication including music, movement, dance, storytelling, visual arts, media and drama, as well as talking, listening, viewing, reading and writing. Contemporary texts include electronic and print-based media. In an increasingly technological world, the ability to critically analyse texts is a key component of literacy.

Another important document, *The shape of the Australian Curriculum: English paper* (National Curriculum Board, 2009, p. 6), defines literacy as follows:

> Literacy conventionally refers to reading, writing, speaking, viewing, and listening effectively in a range of contexts. In the 21st century, the definition of literacy has expanded to refer to a flexible, sustainable mastery of a set of capabilities in the use and production of traditional texts and new communications technologies using spoken language, print and multimedia. Students need to be able to adjust and modify their use of language to better meet contextual demands in varying situations.

However, the draft Australian National Curriculum (2010) splits the English learning area into three parts: Language, Literature and Literacy. Many other definitions would include the appreciation of literature and knowledge about language as part of 'literacy'.

In contrast to the EYLF, which is concerned with the literacy learning of children from birth to five, the National Curriculum viewpoint does not highlight the arts, such as music and dance, nor does it mention affective factors such as confidence and disposition.

> ### OTHER DEFINITIONS OF LITERACY
>
> - OECD (2005): [Literacy is] students' capacity to access, manage, interpret and reflect on written texts in order to achieve their goals, to develop their knowledge and potential, and to participate effectively in society.
> - Hill (2007, p. 3): Literacy is reading, writing, speaking and listening, and involves the knowledge and skills required to engage in activities required for effective functioning in the community.
> - Makin and Jones Diaz (2002): [Literacy] includes talking, listening, visual literacies such as viewing and drawing, as well as critical thinking ... Children participate in many different literacy practices in their homes, their communities and their educational settings.
> - Luke and Freebody (2000): [Literacy is] the flexible and sustainable mastery of a repertoire of practices with texts of traditional and new communications technologies via spoken language, print and multimedia.

> ### OUR DEFINITION OF A 'LITERATE PERSON'
>
> A literate person has a repertoire of understandings and capabilities that enable effective receptive and expressive communication. A literate person can understand and create, with critical awareness, a range of texts in spoken, written, visual and multimedia modes for a variety of purposes.

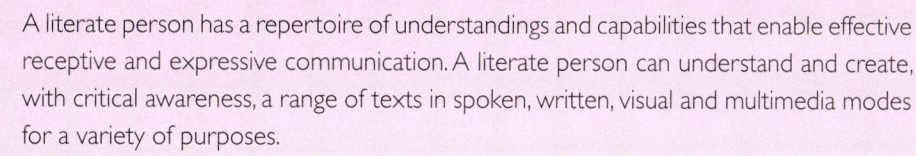

Teachers' own definitions of literacy develop throughout their careers and are influenced by classroom experiences and professional reading and dialogue. Teachers may also be influenced by their own childhood experiences in becoming literate and their personal beliefs about how people learn. It is worth noting that we teachers sometimes have fragmented theories that have conflicting elements. For this reason, it is necessary to reflect regularly on what we do in the classroom and on how our personal definitions and theories relate to our practices. We may have an *espoused theory* (what we say or think we believe about literacy learning) and a *theory in use* (the theory underpinning our actual teaching practices). There should, in reality, be no discrepancy between these two theories.

There is no 'best' way to define literacy, since it is almost a living thing that changes and is moulded according to the needs and practices of groups of people. As Thames and York (2004, p. 603) remind us, 'Literacy is complex; it is a constantly mediated force that can take on a life of its own in different contexts, cultures, and social and political arenas.'

Because of this difficulty, some authors have suggested the use of the term 'literacies', which acknowledges that there are many different ways of 'doing literacy'. The term 'multiliteracies' was coined by the New London Group, who argued that there are many literacies, examples being scientific literacy, critical literacy, visual literacy, computer literacy and so on. Furthermore, different cultural groups have their own literacies.

THEORETICAL PERSPECTIVES ON THE DEVELOPMENT OF READING AND WRITING

Theoretical perspectives on the development and learning of oral language have already been discussed in Chapter 2. It will be most useful for the reader to review these and keep them in mind while reading the current part of this book.

Over the years, there have been many theoretical perspectives on how children learn to read and write. In the context of early childhood education, the following perspectives have been most influential.

MATURATIONAL

The **maturational perspective** on literacy learning informed practice in the early to mid twentieth century and held that children could not learn to read or write until they were biologically mature enough. That is, children had to wait until they had reached a mental age (of six) until they were deemed to be 'ready' to learn literacy. To this end, *readiness* tests, which measured visual, auditory and motor skills, were used in schools to ascertain whether children were ready. According to this perspective, which originated largely in the work of Gesell (1928), influences at home and early communicative experiences had little to do with children's capacity to learn literacy; it was dependent on biological maturation.

Much early research and theory in the area of literacy was generated by psychologists (such as Gesell). The methodologies employed by the psychologists were generally those used in the physical sciences such as chemistry and physics, and therefore focused on aspects of literacy that were observable and measurable. In the name of being objective, much about literacy learning can be missed or overlooked when it is studied from this perspective. Emotions, relationships, cultural factors and even (invisible) cognitive factors were not studied. Not surprisingly, this resulted in a somewhat narrow view of literacy. The National Association for the Education of Young Children (NAEYC) and International Reading Association (IRA) (1998) have expressed concern that a maturational perspective persists among many early childhood teachers today, despite much evidence to the contrary.

DEVELOPMENTAL

The **developmental perspective** was built on the work of psychologists such as Thorndike. This perspective held that, although children need to have reached a point of readiness before being taught to read and write, certain environmental and classroom-based experiences and activities can speed up the maturational process. During this era, a battery of so-called pre-reading activities was introduced to children upon starting school. These had little to do with authentic reading and writing activities. For example, a range of perceptual-motor activities was carried out, which were supposed to prepare children for tracking print with their eyes. Other activities involved the recognition and discrimination of shapes, some of which were letter-like. Many activities were in the form of worksheets, which were not very motivational or meaningful to children. According to many teachers today, these activities were actually a waste of time (e.g. Vukelich, Christie & Enz, 2008), and usually delayed more useful reading activities and instruction until the middle of the first year of school (Year 1).

EMERGENT

The **emergent perspective** constituted a major challenge to the maturational and developmental perspectives, and was based on the work of Piaget. Whereas the maturational and developmental perspectives held that early experiences in the home and community had little to do with successful literacy learning, the emergent perspective proposed that these influences were central. (In fact, the developmental perspective held that if parents tried to 'teach' their children about reading and writing before they reached the point of readiness, they could do more harm than good.) The emergent perspective, which arose in the 1970s, proposed that early literacy experiences in the home, such as talking, singing, drawing and scribbling, lap reading and so on, were central to an ongoing literacy learning *process*, which was seen as active and constructive, not something that simply unfolds. Literacy learning was no longer seen as the acquisition of a series of discrete skills, but as an ongoing process beginning at birth. Major proponents of this perspective were Marie Clay from New Zealand (1979), Ken Goodman (1973) and Frank Smith (1971). This perspective was at the heart of the **whole language** movement, which encouraged teachers to teach reading and writing in the context of real texts and authentic purposes. Skills, such as learning about letter–sound relationships, were learnt within the context of whole texts, not as separate, decontextualised sets of skills.

Some teachers, such as Neuman and Roskos (1998), have argued that the term 'emergent' implies that there is a disjuncture between beginning readers and conventional ('real') readers, and that it is in reality difficult to identify a point at which emergent becomes conventional literacy. For this reason, they argue that the term 'emergent' is of limited usefulness and that it may be preferable to see becoming literate as a lifelong process that begins at birth and usually has no end point. In other words, one continuum is of more value than seeing literacy development as a series of discrete stages.

Cambourne's seven conditions of literacy learning

In the early 1980s, the Australian Brian Cambourne (1988) proposed that many of the conditions that enable the successful learning of oral language should be transferable to written language contexts. In order to learn literacy, children need to be immersed in written language, be exposed to demonstrations and be in environments in which several other 'conditions' are met. The seven conditions are briefly described below.

Immersion
Babies are immersed in oral language from the day they are born. This immersion helps them learn oral language. Cambourne proposed that children need to be immersed in written language in order to learn how to read and write.

Demonstration
Babies hear models of language from the day they are born. All around them, people are speaking and listening for a variety of purposes. Cambourne suggested that children who are learning to read and write need to be exposed to demonstrations and models.

Expectation

Children are expected to learn to speak. They almost always live up to the expectations of those around them and learn to speak and listen for a variety of purposes. Cambourne stated that caregivers and teachers should have the same kinds of expectations that children will learn written literacy. It is well known from research such as Rosenthal and Jacobson's (1968) 'Pygmalion' research that children tend to live up to (or down to) teachers' expectations. In Rosenthal and Jacobsen's research, teachers were given false IQ scores for children. The children tended to achieve at the level expected for the (false) score given to the teacher, not for their real score. This research shows how powerful teacher expectations can be.

Responsibility

When learning how to speak, children are given responsibility for their own learning. That is, they are very often the ones who decide what is attended to, what questions are asked, what is ignored and what is important. They are central in their own learning and they elicit responses and help from those around them through their actions and responses. Cambourne proposed that, in the context of written language, children will achieve more if they are given responsibility for their own learning and more choice about what, how and when they (learn to) read and write.

Approximation

When children learn to speak, they use many approximations. That is, much of what they say is not quite correct but, as long as they 'have a go' and can be understood, their attempts are acknowledged and celebrated. They are not chastised for making 'mistakes' and they are not constantly corrected, although adults around them will constantly model conventional or acceptable forms. Cambourne proposed that approximations should be acceptable in the context of written literacy, as this will enable children to get on and fulfil their purposes without being hampered by the fear of making mistakes.

Employment

Children would not get far in oral language learning if they did not get a chance to use or practise the language learnt. Likewise, in the context of written language, Cambourne has pointed out the importance of numerous opportunities to use and practise in meaningful contexts.

Feedback

Feedback is given to children as they learn to speak, and this feedback is often by means of rephrasing and modelling, as well as by explicit correction that is not disheartening. Children who are learning to read and write also need constructive and positive feedback.

Cambourne's seven conditions of literacy learning, although still influential and highly useful, are now often seen as necessary but not sufficient. The framework has been criticised as not being research-based or 'evidence'-based. However, research has been carried out in recent years by researchers around the world that does support many aspects of the framework. For example, recent research has shown that children often need to be given systematic and explicit teaching in some areas, although it could quite reasonably be argued that this kind of teaching could be included under 'demonstration'.

SOCIO-CULTURAL

Socio-cultural perspectives emerged in the 1990s. This view of literacy learning further highlights the importance of cultural practices in the home and in other social groupings. According to this view, some children go to school with experiences and attitudes that are closely aligned to what is needed in school literacy contexts. These children are advantaged in that they can accommodate easily to the school environment and the literacies that are 'done' in such contexts. Other children, however, may not have the appropriate *cultural capital* (Bourdieu, 1977) to help them get to grips with the literacy practices that are valued and practised in formal educational contexts.

Thanks to the socio-cultural perspective, early childhood professionals have come to appreciate the importance of finding out about, valuing and building upon literacy practices that occur in the home. They realise that they need to find ways to build bridges between home and school literacies.

Barratt-Pugh (1998, p. 5) has described six elements of a socio-cultural view of literacy:

1 Children's learning about the nature of literacy and how to 'do' literacy arises from participating in a variety of literacy activities in the home and the community.
2 Literacy practices are often 'culturally specific' and these practices contribute to children's sense of identity.
3 Children have a variety of understandings about what literacy is and how it is 'done'.
4 There are different literacy practices for a variety of literacy purposes.
5 Children learn literacy in different ways, or have different 'patterns' of literacy learning.
6 Literacy practices are valued differently, depending on the social and educational context.

Freebody and Lukes's (1992) socio-cultural theory of reading asserts that there are four sets of roles, resources or 'practices' that children need to be able to control in order to become effective readers. The four practices are not hierarchical but are equally important and should all be addressed right from the start, although the emphasis will change according

Figure 8.1: Freebody and Luke's socio-cultural perspective

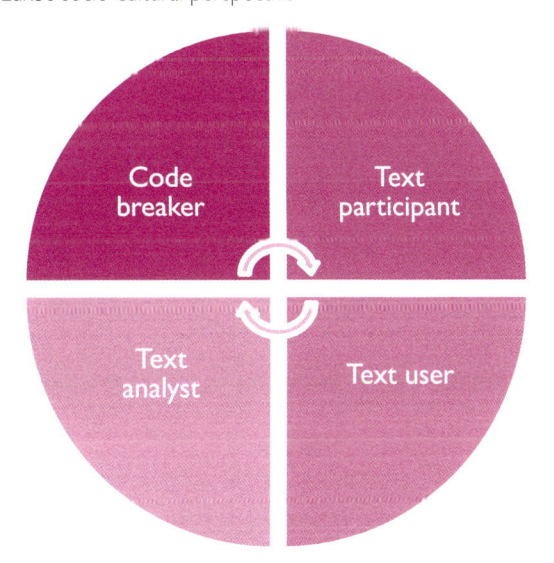

Source: adapted from Freebody and Luke (1992)

to the particular teaching situation. The *code breaker* practice is to do with 'cracking' the codes of letter–sound correspondences and the grammar of particular texts. The *text participant* practice involves making meaning of the text, including making personal connections such as linking the text with prior experiences and knowledge. The *text user* practice is to do with understanding that there are different text types for different purposes, and that there are different audiences with different needs and expectations. The *text analyst* practice involves appreciating that texts are not neutral and that authors have values and agendas that readers need to uncover and think about.

'EVIDENCE-BASED' APPROACHES

More recently, there has been a call for teachers to apply an **evidence-based** approach to the teaching of literacy. This has followed on from large-scale reviews of literacy teaching such as the National Reading Panel in the USA (2000), the Rose Report (Rose, 2006) in the UK and the National Inquiry into the Teaching of Literacy (NITL) in Australia (2005). Although there is certainly no simple recipe for success in teaching literacy, there are bodies of research that are deemed to be good evidence that certain approaches will work with particular groups of children. In order to be successful in ever-changing literacy contexts, it is imperative that teachers keep up to date with new research findings and constantly reflect on their practices in the light of these.

THE RECIPROCAL RELATIONSHIP BETWEEN THE CONSTITUENTS OF LITERACY

It is essential to understand that different constituents or strands of literacy have a reciprocal relationship. For example, reading and writing are intimately intertwined. Without reading, writing would be impossible and, likewise, writing enhances reading skills and knowledge. In short, when children practise and improve in one aspect of literacy, other aspects are also usually enhanced. Although we discuss constituents of literacy separately in this book, the close, reciprocal relationship between these elements must always be kept in mind.

THE IMPORTANCE OF MOTIVATION IN LITERACY LEARNING

It has been mentioned in this chapter that some of the early perspectives of literacy learning may have led to reduced levels of motivation in children, since they dealt with fragmented elements of literacy, sometimes in meaningless contexts. Motivation is of the utmost importance in literacy learning. Children who are not motivated will not read or write very much, will not be drawn to books, magazines, computer-based texts or paper and pencils, and will consequently not achieve at optimal levels.

Intrinsic motivation, which is said to come from within the individual, is what we as teachers should attempt to generate. Guthrie, Wigfield and Perencevich (2004) point out that intrinsically motivated children frequently seek out texts to read in their leisure time, and that these texts will not necessarily be of a trivial, 'light' nature used for 'entertainment' purposes only. Texts selected will often be at a challenging level because young readers are often eager to access the interesting content. In very early childhood contexts, children may not actually read selected text in a conventional way but may engage in exploratory or role-play reading, which is a valuable part of becoming literate.

Guthrie and his associates point out that teachers can most effectively increase children's intrinsic motivation to read by *ensuring success* through the provision of appropriate (scaffolded) instruction and literacy activities. Giving children texts and activities at an appropriate difficulty level is an obvious starting point. Explicitly pointing out to children their successes is also important. Celebration of success and 'having a go' are important elements of a positive classroom environment. Oakley (2006b) summarises some elements of literacy motivation in Table 8.1.

Table 8.1: Elements of literacy motivation

Success	Children are likely to be motivated in literacy when they expect to succeed. In reading, it is necessary to provide the appropriate level of texts and the appropriate level of support. Likewise, in writing, children need to experience success.
Choice	As much as possible, allow children choices in the texts that they will read. Even in content areas, it is possible for teachers to provide an array of books on a topic for children to choose from. In writing, children should have some choice regarding what to write about.
Challenge	In many instances, children enjoy a challenge and can experience a sense of achievement and satisfaction from engaging with challenging texts. It is important that the challenge is not so great as to become 'frustrational'.
Interest	Even very young children have interests and are more likely to be motivated in literacy contexts if there are texts available in topics of interest to them.
Purpose	Reading and writing without a clear purpose is rarely motivational and, furthermore, it is difficult for children to succeed if they are not sure of the purpose of the task.

ASSESSING AFFECTIVE FACTORS

Affective factors include motivation to read, attitudes towards reading and feelings of self-efficacy and confidence about reading, and it is important for teachers to find out about children's feelings about themselves as readers and about their reading interests. Much of this can be done through observation of their reading behaviours, through conversations with them and/or their parents, and through the monitoring of reading logs and reading journals, in which children (or their parents) record what they have read and, hopefully, write brief comments about the books.

An example of a checklist to be used the record observations of children's attitudes is shown in Table 8.2.

Table 8.2: Observational checklist: Reading attitude

Name: Michael Piazza, Year 1. Date: Over the last two weeks, Michael has:	Yes	No	Comments
Seemed happy and relaxed when engaged in reading	✓		
Talked about stories or other texts he's read or had read to him	✓		
Borrowed and talked about library books		✓	Michael has borrowed books but does not get around to reading them at home
Brought in books or other texts from home to share with classmates and teacher		✓	Not yet
Chosen to read instead of engaging in another activity such as puzzles, blocks etc.	✓		
Listened and engaged enthusiastically during story time	✓		
Engaged in reading electronic talking books on the computer	✓		Michael loves ETBs

Source: based on a checklist by Cunningham, Moore, Cunningham and Moore (2004, p. 279)

Structured surveys and interviews are also available to help teachers find out about motivation and attitudes towards reading. A well-known example is the Elementary Reading Attitude Survey (ERAS) (McKenna & Kear, 1990), which is suitable for children in Year 1 and above. This survey contains forty statements about reading, and children have to indicate how they feel about the statement by circling the appropriate picture of Garfield, who looks glum at one extreme of the scale and ecstatic at the other. Examples of statements contained in the ERAS include:

- How do you feel about reading for fun at home?
- How do you feel about reading instead of playing?
- How do you feel when the teacher asks you questions about what you read?
- How do you feel when you read out loud in class?

PRACTICES OF HIGHLY EFFECTIVE LITERACY TEACHERS

What is a highly effective literacy teacher and what practices does such a teacher engage in? In truth, highly effective literacy teachers engage in a wide variety of teaching practices and use them in a purposeful, intentional manner, depending on the situation and the children's needs. For this to occur, constant reflection is necessary. As noted above, there is no simple recipe for literacy teaching, although there are some helpful principles, such as those outlined by Hiebert et al. (1998, p. 7:4):

- Provide literacy activities that all children participate in regardless of abilities, and provide support for struggling children.
- Design literate classroom environments.
- Model and teach decoding and comprehension processes.
- Create extensive and diverse reading opportunities for students.
- Provide engaging literacy instruction so that children are eager to learn to read and write.
- Monitor children's progress in reading and writing.

Eight years later, the Australian National Inquiry into the Teaching of Literacy (2006, p. 9) suggested that there are six important elements that lead to good literacy outcomes in schools:

- A belief that each child can learn to read and write regardless of background;
- An early and systematic emphasis on the explicit teaching of phonics;
- A subsequent focus on direct teaching;
- A rich print environment with many resources, including fiction and non-fiction books, charts and computer programs;
- A strong leadership and management practice, involving whole-school approaches to the teaching of reading and writing; and
- An expectation that teachers will engage in evidence-based professional learning and learn from each other.

There is more emphasis in the NITL on direct, explicit teaching, which has been shown to be advantageous for many children, especially for those from disadvantaged socio-economic and cultural minority groups.

The *In teachers' hands* research (Louden et al., 2005) identified six 'dimensions' in which highly effective teachers were more active, which was later changed to five dimensions (Louden et al., 2008). The most effective teachers ensured a high level of student participation and engagement in the learning activities, differentiated learning activities according to children's needs, provided support and scaffolding at word and text level, and were highly knowledgeable about how children learn literacy. In addition, mutual respect was a characteristic of their classroom environment, and they were excellent at managing and orchestrating the complex demands of the classroom. This research supported Hattie's findings that the teacher plays a pivotal role in children's literacy learning: 'Excellence in teaching is the single most powerful influence' (Hattie, 2003, p. 4). For more in depth information about this research, see the In Teachers Hands website: inteachershands.education.ecu.edu.au.

In this chapter, the various perspectives that underpin practice in early childhood contexts have been discussed. Throughout their careers, teachers use and refine their personal theories of literacy teaching and learning through reflecting on their practice and engaging with the professional literature.

SUMMARY

In this chapter various definitions of literacy have been examined. Definitions are important because, to some extent, they drive literacy instruction. Theoretical perspectives are also important as they underpin teaching strategies and our ideas about how children's literacy development should occur.

The chapter has outlined some general principles of motivation in literacy learning. Very little learning will occur where motivation is absent and attitudes are negative. Finally, practices associated with excellent literacy teaching and learning have been introduced.

QUESTIONS AND ACTIVITIES

1. Why is it important for teachers to be aware of the theories that influence their teaching?
2. Why is it necessary for teachers to constantly re-evaluate their personal theories and reflect on their teaching practice?
3. Which theoretical perspectives have been influential over the last century and what impact have these had on teaching practice?
4. How can a teacher encourage maximum motivation in her/his literacy classroom?
5. Discuss the characteristics of effective literacy teachers. What steps can you take to ensure that you will become a highly effective literacy teacher?
6. Next time you are on practicum, reflect on your practices and the theories that underpin them.

KEY TERMS

affective
developmental perspective
emergent perspective
evidence-based
maturational perspective
socio-cultural perspective
whole language

KEY REFERENCES

Barratt-Pugh, C. (1998). The socio-cultural context of literacy learning. In C. Barratt-Pugh & M. Rohl (eds), *Literacy learning in the early years*. Crow's Nest, Australia: Allen & Unwin.

Cambourne, B. (1988). *The whole story: Natural learning and the acquisition of literacy in the classroom*. New York: Ashton Scholastic.

Department of Education, Employment and Workplace Relations (DEEWR) (2009). *Belonging, being and becoming: The Early Years Learning Framework for Australia*. Barton, ACT: Commonwealth of Australia.

Freebody, P. & Luke, A. (1992). A socio-cultural approach: Resourcing four roles as a literacy learner. In A. J. Watson & A. M. Badenhop (eds), *Prevention of reading failure*. Sydney: Ashton Scholastic.

Gambrell, L. B., Malloy, A. J. & Mazzoni, S. A. (2007). Evidence-based best practices for comprehensive literacy instruction. In L. B. Gambrell, L. Morrow & M. Pressley (eds), *Best practices in literacy instruction*. New York: The Guilford Press.

Goodman, K. S. (1973). *Psycholinguistics and reading*. New York: Holt, Rinehart and Winston.

Guthrie, J. T., Wigfield, A. & Perencevich, K. C. (2004). Scaffolding for motivation and engagement in reading. In J. T. Guthrie, A. Wigfield & K. C. Perencevich (eds), *Motivating reading comprehension: Concept oriented reading instruction*. Mahwah, NJ: Erlbaum & Associates.

Hiebert, E. H., Pearson, P. D., Taylor, B. M., Richardson, V. & Paris, S. G. (1998). *Every child a reader*. Michigan: CIERA.

Louden, W., Rohl, M., Barratt Pugh, C., Brown, C., Cairney, T., Elderfield, J. et al. (2005). *In teachers' hands: Effective literacy teaching practices in the early years of schooling*. Commonwealth of Australia.

Louden, W., Rohl, M. & Hopkins, S. (2008). *Teaching for growth: Effective teaching of literacy and numeracy*. Perth: Department of Education and Training.

National Inquiry into the Teaching of Literacy (2006). *Teaching reading: Report and recommendations*. Barton, ACT: Australian Government Department of Education, Science and Training.

CHAPTER 9

Understanding Reading

CHAPTER OBJECTIVES

This chapter will increase your understanding of:

- the importance of foundational knowledge for reading
- some broad teaching and learning strategies for foundational knowledge
- the development of reading
- theoretical positions on learning to read.

In this chapter we discuss the knowledge and understandings that children need to have in order to begin to read. From the day a baby is born, the knowledge that enables them to learn how to read and write begins to develop. While some of these foundational skills are learnt informally if the environmental conditions are appropriately print- and talk-rich, others need to be explicitly taught in pre-school and lower primary settings. Later in this chapter we discuss the development of reading and some broad theoretical perspectives on how children learn to read.

FOUNDATIONAL KNOWLEDGE FOR READING

> The foundations of learning to read are set down from the moment a child first hears the sounds of people talking, the tunes of songs, and the rhythms and repetitions of rhymes and stories. (Fox, 2001b, p. 13.)

From very early in life, children begin to learn the foundational knowledge that will enable them to grow as readers and writers. When they are babies, they begin to learn oral language, gestures and purposes of communication. A little later, they begin to observe parents and others in their community using print and other symbol systems such as pictures and diagrams for a variety of purposes—for entertainment, to keep in touch with people, to send and receive messages, to learn, to follow recipes, to remember what needs to be bought from the shops and for a host of other reasons.

Interaction with others is the basis of children's language and literacy learning in the early years, and there is much that parents and childcare professionals can do to maximise children's learning. It has been found quite recently that reading to very young babies, perhaps from birth, can be beneficial for many reasons, including increased motivation to read and more successful literacy outcomes in the long term, such as better reading comprehension, writing and spelling by the age of seven (Wade & Moore, 1998, 2000).

It is important to realise that children learn a great deal about literacy in informal settings at home and in the community. It is up to teachers and childcare professionals to find out about this knowledge, to value it and to build upon it. This should be done as early as practicable, and be based on teaching methods that are backed up by research. The Australian National Inquiry into the Teaching of Literacy (2006, p. 36) recommended that there are certain foundational skills, namely phonological awareness and knowledge of graphophonic relationships, that should be taught 'explicitly, systematically, early and well'. *The Early Years Learning Framework for Australia* (DEEWR, 2009) has stated that this learning (for children aged five and under) should largely take place in play-based, social settings. It may seem that there is a contradiction between explicit teaching and play-based learning but the EYLFA has stated that **intentional teaching** should be used alongside play-based learning. Intentional teaching takes place when teachers 'use strategies such as modelling and demonstrating, open questioning, speculating, explaining, engaging in shared thinking and problem solving to extend children's thinking and learning' (DEEWR, 2009, p. 18).

FOUNDATIONS OF READING AND WRITING

- oral language
- vocabulary and conceptual knowledge
- concepts about print and books
- phonological awareness
- the alphabetic principle

It should be noted that there is a degree of uncertainty in the research literature about which skills are, in fact, foundational for early reading success, although it is agreed that *oral language skills* and *code-related skills* are important (NICHD Early Child Care Research Network, 2005). Code-related skills include phonological awareness, letter recognition and naming, knowledge of letter–sound relationships, emergent writing and concepts about print. Oral language skills foundational to reading and writing include receptive and expressive vocabulary, knowledge of syntax (sentence structure) and semantic knowledge (knowledge about the world and a range of topics), as well as some ability to understand and retell narrative stories. It has been found that these foundational skills are interrelated and each skill may vary in its importance over time.

TEXT USE AND UNDERSTANDING

ORAL LANGUAGE

Oral language knowledge is central in helping children learn to read and write, and strong oral language skills in the early years (as young as three years old) predict reading proficiency later on (NICHD Early Child Care Research Network, 2005). In order to access or create print, children need to understand what words mean, how sentences are constructed and how texts work. A great deal of this knowledge is transferred from knowledge of words, sentences and texts in oral language contexts. A whole part of this book has been devoted to oral or spoken language and it is recommended that this part is read carefully before the chapters on reading and writing are studied.

Oral language is important to early reading and writing for two main reasons (Hiebert, Pearson, Taylor, Richardson & Paris, 1998). First, children's knowledge about words and sentences and their phonological awareness influence their ability to learn to read. Having said this, the exact nature of the connection between oral language and reading and writing remains somewhat unclear because research conducted so far has had mixed results (Roth, Speece & Cooper, 2002).

Second, oral language allows children and teachers to discuss reading and writing and texts, and plays a part in teachers' explanations and in being understood by their students. This, of course, facilitates comprehension and learning. Through oral language, children also learn about the purposes and communicative functions of language. This knowledge is highly important in learning and using written language.

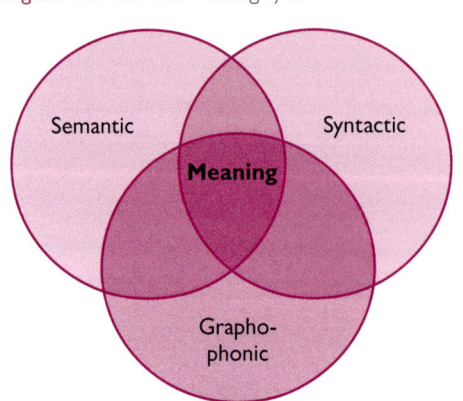

Figure 9.1: The three cueing systems

Children use semantic, syntactic and graphophonic **cueing systems** in order to identify words in texts and gain meaning from texts. This involves them accessing and using their knowledge of syntax and grammar, or how sentences work (*syntactic* knowledge); their knowledge about the world and concepts (*semantic* knowledge); and their knowledge about letters and sounds (*graphophonic* knowledge). Successful young readers use all three cueing systems effectively, in a strategic way, to identify words and to make sure that the text is making sense. Much of children's syntactic, semantic and graphophonic knowledge is built through oral language experiences. In the case of syntactic knowledge, children learn a lot about how sentences work, such as word order and parts of speech and their functions, in oral language contexts. Naturally, at a young age they are not able to articulate what parts of speech they must use in sentences, but they have an implicit knowledge of where in a sentence a verb can go, or where a noun can go, for example. If you were to say to a child for whom English is a first language, 'The dog black is running', they would probably be able to tell you that the word 'dog' (noun) should come after the word 'black' (adjective). Likewise, if you were to say, 'A big running was horse', they would probably find this sentence funny and tell you that the words are in the wrong order. In reading contexts, this syntactic knowledge helps them cross-check their reading. If something they read doesn't 'sound right' syntactically, they know they must have made a mistake.

Children learn much about the sounds in English (and whatever other languages they speak) through oral language experiences. This knowledge about sounds, or phonological awareness, is necessary to learning about letter–sound relationships, which is essential for decoding or 'sounding out' words when reading and writing. Research clearly shows that, in the early years, phonological skills are most important (Scanlon & Vellutino, 1996).

For young children, knowledge and understandings about the world, or semantic knowledge, is also gained largely through oral language contexts. Learning new words and what they mean (vocabulary) is highly important to comprehension. In fact, Roth et al. (2002) found evidence that the semantic ability of young children (in Kindergarten) predicted Second-Grade reading.

It needs to be mentioned at this point that the notion that all good readers use the three cueing systems is contested. It appears that proficient *mature* readers primarily use decoding and their sight-word bank to identify unknown words and rarely need to cross-check using syntactic and semantic cues (Wren, 2001).

It has been pointed out by numerous researchers and teachers that reading, writing and oral language are *reciprocal* (Raban & Coates, 2004). That is, oral language assists the development of reading, as discussed above, but it is also true to say that reading and writing development assist in the improvement of oral language abilities. This is due to the fact that reading and writing encourage the use of wider vocabulary, a variety of syntactic and textual structures, and a good deal of thinking and talking about language.

VOCABULARY

Because vocabulary for reading and writing is such an important topic, a whole chapter of this book (Chapter 12) has been devoted to it. Children can find it more difficult to read individual words if they have not heard them before or are not sure of the meanings. For example, a child may read the sentence: 'The driver saw a sign at the end of the road.'

If the child does not have the word 'sign' in her spoken vocabulary, it will be difficult to pronounce the word as it is not straightforward to sound out because of the presence of the letter 'g'. Thus, in conjunction with increasing knowledge about graphophonic relationships, knowledge of vocabulary is essential to facilitate word identification. It almost goes without saying that vocabulary knowledge is also necessary for comprehension. 'The canine was fearsome' is a sentence that would be difficult for a child to comprehend if she didn't know that a dog can be referred to as a 'canine' or that 'fearsome' means frightening.

CONCEPTUAL OR TOPIC KNOWLEDGE

In order to comprehend texts, whether written, read aloud or oral, it is necessary for children to have a store of conceptual knowledge, or knowledge about the world. Without this *prior knowledge*, it is difficult for readers to link the text with anything meaningful. Teachers and caregivers should continually build children's knowledge about the world through a range of activities, including reading, science activities, discussions, watching videos and television programs, excursions and incursions. (An incursion is a visit to the school or classroom by an individual or group of people for the purpose of educating the children about a particular topic or entertaining them. For example, a snake handler might take snakes and reptiles into the school for the children to view.) Before asking them to read or listen to a particular text, teachers may find it necessary to supplement children's prior knowledge in the particular area. Pre-reading activities designed to 'activate' children's prior knowledge, or to get them thinking along the right lines, are also highly recommended. This will help children effectively use cognitive comprehension processes such as predicting, making connections, visualising and finding the main idea. (See Chapter 13, Reading for Comprehension, for more information about cognitive comprehension processes.) Conceptual knowledge is related to vocabulary knowledge.

CONCEPTS ABOUT BOOKS AND PRINT

Unless children have had some experience with books and other texts, they will not have the basic concepts about print that are necessary to begin reading. These are often learnt incidentally by children in the context of parental and childcare read-alouds and other activities around books and texts, but it is an unfortunate reality that many children start school without this knowledge. Children whose home language is not English may start school with concepts about print that do not relate to books that are in English, although they will often have concepts about print in other languages. Education professionals should assess children's knowledge of print concepts at the earliest opportunity as no assumptions about children's prior experiences can be made. The important concepts about print and books that children need to know are as follows.

Book handling

When they first come to childcare, pre-school or even to school, some children do not know what a book is for or how to open it and turn the pages. All children need to be in possession of these basic concepts about print in order to become readers and writers. Also, they need

Through teacher modelling and hands-on experiences with books, book handling skills generally do not take long to develop

to know where the front of a book is and where the back is, as well as which is the right way up. Through teacher modelling and hands-on experiences with books, book handling skills generally do not take long to develop. However, it is important for teachers to find out about children's existing book handling skills so that appropriate experiences and instruction can be provided. Observation of children's book handling is an obvious means of finding out, although there are also formal assessments that can be used, such as Marie Clay's Concepts About Print Test, which is part of her well-known Observation Survey (Clay, 2002). Talking with the child can also reveal a lot about their concepts about print. It needs to be remembered that children from different cultures may have different ideas about book handling.

Directionality

In the English language, print goes from left to right and starts at the top of the page. For children who have had home experiences of different languages, the directionality of written English may seem strange. In Arabic and Hebrew, for example, writing starts from the right and moves to the left. Chinese and Japanese have traditionally been written from top to bottom in vertical rows, starting on the right hand side of the page and working towards the left. However, these scripts are often written horizontally and left to right these days. Before children can begin to read and write in English, they need to develop understandings about directionality of print, and this can be done by giving them experiences with books and explicitly pointing out the directionality of print during such activities as *shared reading* or the *Language Experience Approach*. These strategies are described in detail in Chapter 11.

Concept of word

When looking at print on a page, children need to know that each word is separated by a space and that there is a one-to-one correspondence between spoken and written words. This concept will be difficult to grasp, however, for children who are not phonologically aware at the word level and who still hear language as a continuous stream of speech with no boundaries between words. Children also need to understand the *permanency* of print; that is, that printed words and texts say the same thing each time they are read. Young children do not necessarily understand this. Children who are still exploratory or role-play readers often pretend to read books, but the words they 'read' can vary with each reading. Repeated readings of the same story book can help build the understanding that the printed word is constant.

Concept of letter

Here, children need to understand what a letter looks like as opposed to a word or a punctuation symbol, or even a numeral. This does not necessarily mean that they will know the name of the letter or the sound(s) it makes. Nor does it mean that they will have a concept of the **alphabetic principle**—the understanding that letters are used to represent sounds. Talking about letters in stories, playing with plastic letters and practising writing letters are all activities that help build up children's concept of letters.

Punctuation

Another concept about print is the ability to recognise punctuation symbols, and perhaps name them conventionally. If a child recognises speech marks but calls them 'talking marks', this indicates that she or he has an understanding of their function and can differentiate them from words and letters. Punctuation such as semicolons and colons would not usually be known by young children, but commas, speech marks, full stops and question marks need to be recognised and understood by the end of the early childhood years.

TEACHING CONCEPTS ABOUT PRINT

There are several broad strategies for assisting children to learn about concepts of print. As noted above, one of the most effective is shared reading (described in detail in Chapter 11), which can be carried out one-to-one (parent and child) or in group contexts in the classroom. Here, the adult points at words as they are read aloud, thereby demonstrating directionality and showing what a word is. Also, adults can talk about print conventions such as letters and punctuation when appropriate.

Another very effective strategy for helping children develop concepts about print is the Language Experience Approach, where adults scribe 'stories' for children, based on children's own experiences. Children's writing experiences also help build their concepts about print; they can practise and experiment with what they know about print.

ASSESSMENT OF CONCEPTS ABOUT PRINT

Assessment of concepts about print can largely be carried out informally, on an ongoing basis; observations of children as they interact with texts, and conversations with them about books, are excellent means of collecting information about their knowledge. Conversations with parents can also be highly informative.

Also, analysis of children's writing can tell the teacher a lot about concepts about print: Does the child leave spaces between 'words'? Is the writing started at the top left? What direction does it go in? (The child's first language needs to be borne in mind here—the home language may have a different direction.) Are letters (or letter-like marks) grouped together to form 'words'? This observational and conversational data can then be recorded on checklists and anecdotal notes (see Table 9.1), which have been discussed in the previous two chapters.

Table 9.1: Concepts about print

Name: _____ Date: _____ Age: _____			
	Consistently	**Sometimes**	**Not yet**
Knows front and back of book			
Knows where to start reading			
Knows left–right directionality			
Knows return sweep (goes to beginning of next line)			
Can point to a word			
Can point to a letter			
Can point to a capital letter			
Opens book and turns one page at a time			
Knows what a full stop is for			
Knows what a question mark is for			
Knows what a picture or illustration is			
Other:			
Comments:			

Formal assessments of children's concepts about print are also available, and these include components of the Early Literacy Test—Stage 1 (Gillham, 2006), the Reading Progress Test—Phase 1 (Vincent & Crumpler, 1997) and Clay's (2002) Concepts About Print (CAP) test. In this assessment, the child is asked to interact with a small reading book and is required to show a letter, show a word, say where reading should begin and which way the reader should progress, among other things. Some of the pages of the reading book have the words and letters mixed up or the picture upside down and the child is asked to identify what is wrong with the words and which is the top of the picture. Examples of questions the teacher asks during the Concepts About Print test (Clay, 2002, pp. 48–9) are:

'Show me the front of the book.'
'Show me the bottom of the picture.'
'Which way do I go? Where do I go after that?'
'Show me a capital letter.'
'Show me *no*.'

Clay's Concepts About Print test is not without criticism, however, and recent criticisms argue that it is rooted in an old definition of literacy that does not take into account the increasing multimodality of texts and the changing role of images in texts.

KNOWLEDGE ABOUT TEXT PURPOSES

Having basic knowledge about the *purposes* and *audiences* of various text types is an area that is important as a foundation for children's reading and writing success. This knowledge comes from having experiences with a range of texts (both oral and written) in various contexts. Generally, children learn about a range of text types in the home, although there are of course great variations in how literacy is used and constructed in different homes.

Children need to know that stories are mainly for enjoyment and entertainment, although they may also have a moral or message. Just as importantly, children need to appreciate that informational texts give facts about the world around us and that we consult them when we want to learn something. There are other texts such as greetings cards, letters, emails, shopping lists, notes, recipes and web pages, all of which have different structures, audiences and purposes. Some texts are persuasive in nature and subtly (or not so subtly) try to persuade us to think, feel or act a certain way. Very young children can learn much about text purposes by observing role models such as parents using texts for a variety of purposes, along with some discussion about texts and their purposes. Older children learn more about text purposes through reading and writing. Different text types, or genres, will be discussed in more depth in the chapters on writing.

PHONOLOGICAL AWARENESS

WHAT IS PHONOLOGICAL AWARENESS?

Phonological awareness involves the understanding that speech can be broken down into smaller parts. That is, a stream of speech can be broken down into words, and words can be broken down into syllables, **onset–rime**, and phonemes. These terms are fully described and defined below, in the section on levels of phonological awareness. A definition of phonological awareness from Yopp and Yopp (2009, p. 13) states that: 'Phonological awareness is the ability to attend to and manipulate units of sound in speech (syllables, onsets and rimes, and phonemes) independent of meaning.'

WHY IS PHONOLOGICAL AWARENESS IMPORTANT IN READING AND WRITING?

Phonological awareness is an important foundation of reading and writing of alphabetic languages such as English. It is a necessary prerequisite for the application of **graphophonic**

knowledge (knowledge about letter–sound relationships). In the case of writing and spelling, children need to be able to *segment* or break words into sounds—for example, be able to segment the word 'tin' into the three phonemes, /t/-/i/-/n/. It is then necessary to represent each phoneme 'heard' with an appropriate letter or grapheme. In the case of reading, phonological awareness, or more specifically the ability to *blend* phonemes together, is necessary in order to 'sound out'. It is necessary to sound out the phonemes (not the letter names) and then to string or blend them all together to form a word. Without phonological awareness, effective code-breaking is not possible. Phonological awareness is a strong predictor of reading success in later years, particularly in the area of decoding (Heath, Fletcher & Hogben, 2006).

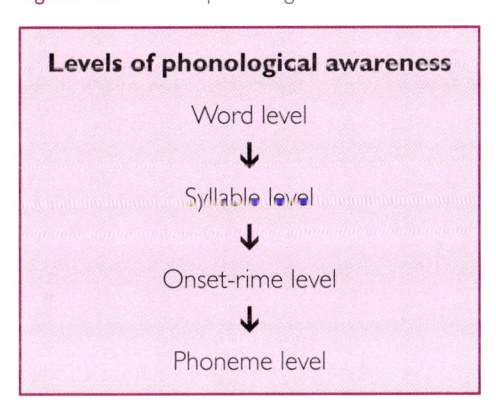

Figure 9.2: Levels of phonological awareness

Levels of phonological awareness

Word level
↓
Syllable level
↓
Onset-rime level
↓
Phoneme level

THE LEVELS OF PHONOLOGICAL AWARENESS

As already noted, phonological awareness is composed of several levels (Lane, Pullen, Eisele & Jordan, 2002). It is important to understand these because the levels impact on the sequence and type of teaching. The less complex aspects of phonological awareness are at the *word level*: the ability to recognise and generate rhyming words, and the ability to break sentences into individual words. More difficult, complex phonological awareness activities involve segmenting, blending and manipulating syllables and phonemes.

The ability to segment and blend at the onset-rime level is the next level of difficulty. An onset is the beginning of a single syllable word and is composed as a consonant or a group of consonants. The rime is the part of the word that comes after the onset, and always begins with a vowel. In the word 'pink', for example, the /p/ is the onset and the /ink/ is the rime. On the word 'string', /str/ is the onset and /ing/ is the rime.

Finally, children learn to segment, blend and manipulate words at the phoneme level. This level is called *phonemic awareness*. It is important to note that some American authors refer to all phonological awareness as phonemic awareness. It is necessary to bear this in mind when reading the international literature.

HOW DOES PHONOLOGICAL AWARENESS DEVELOP?

Phonological understandings and knowledge develop largely outside the context of written literacy, but are consolidated once children begin to learn to read and write and to match letters to sounds (Stuart, 2005).

Torgeson and Mathes (2000) have proposed that knowledge about phonemes tends to develop in the following sequence:

1. can tell when two words rhyme (e.g. 'man' and 'can')—this is rhyme recognition
2. can generate a rhyme for a simple single syllable word (e.g. 'fat' and 'cat')
3. can isolate and say the initial sound of a word (e.g. /s/ in 'sand')
4. can blend the sounds in two phoneme words (e.g. /o/ -/n/ for 'on')
5. can isolate (segment) and say all of the sounds in two- and three-phoneme words (e.g. /p/-/i/-/n/ for 'pin')
6. can blend the sounds in four-phoneme words containing initial consonant blends (e.g. /p/-/l/-/o/-/t/ for 'plot')
7. can isolate and say the sounds in four-phoneme words that contain initial blends (e.g. /s/-/t/-/e/-/m/ for 'stem')
8. can blend the sounds in four-and five-phoneme words that contain initial and final blends (e.g. /c/-/r/-/u/-/s/-/t/ for 'crust').

It is important to remember, however, that not all children develop in the same way. Some children, especially children for whom English is a second language, may not conform to the sequence suggested above.

Strategies for teaching and assessing phonological awareness are dealt with in depth in the next chapter.

KNOWLEDGE ABOUT LETTERS AND SOUNDS

THE ALPHABET

An important foundational skill is the ability to recognise and name letters of the alphabet, both upper and lower case. Letter knowledge is one of the most reliable predictors of later reading success (Scanlon & Vellutino, 1996); that is, children who know their alphabet upon school entry are likely to learn to read without too many problems.

This is another of what Paris (2005) has called a *constrained skill*. That is, children should be able to learn the alphabet fairly quickly, once instruction has commenced. Of course, many children learn about letters at home and may know most of them before formal schooling commences. By the time they reach approximately five years of age, many children will know alphabet letters that are personally significant to them, such as letters from their own name (McGee, 2007).

Unfortunately, there has been relatively little research conducted on how best to teach the alphabet to children (National Institute of Child Health and Human Development, 2000). Bloodgood (1999) has shown that letter alphabet knowledge develops only when children begin to find letters meaningful to them through interaction in contextually relevant activities. This means that they need to be linked to ideas and objects that children already know and are interested in. Their own and their friends' names are an obvious example, as are letters associated with favourite animals, books and places.

WHAT DOES 'LEARNING A LETTER' COMPRISE?

According to *Letters and sounds* (DfES, 2007), knowing a letter entails the following:

- distinguishing the shape of the letter from other letter shapes
- being able to recall and recognise the shape of a letter from its name
- writing the shape of the letter with the correct movement, orientation and relationship to other letters
- naming the letter
- recognising and articulating a sound (phoneme) associated with the letter shape
- recalling the shape of the letter (or selecting it from a display) when given its sound.

There is some disagreement in the literature as to whether letter names or letter sounds should be taught first, or whether they should be taught together. *Letters and sounds* recommends teaching names and sounds together, in a systematic, planned way. As can be seen from the set of skills a child needs to fully know a letter, some of them are to do with recognising the shape of the letter and assigning a name to it and others are to do with assigning sounds to it. The next chapter, which deals with graphophonic knowledge, will discuss assigning sounds to letters. In the current chapter, the focus will be on recognising and naming letters.

TEACHING LETTER NAMES

Children can learn about letters and letter names through games and puzzles, discussion during Shared Book Experience, songs, and the use of charts, posters, software and environmental print. Engaging in writing can also help children learn letter names (McGee, 2007).

There are dozens of alphabet books on the market. Reading them to children and pointing out the letters while doing so can be very beneficial, not to mention enjoyable, and such books can also facilitate early learning of some letter–sound correspondences. Children in pre-school should be encouraged to play with letter tiles and plastic letters, and to make letters out of play dough and other materials. Children can paint, draw and make collages of letters. They can paint them on the pavement with water, they can draw them in sand with a stick and they can make alphabet biscuits during cooking time. Also, they can enjoy alphabet charts and songs. Highly informative informal assessment can take place through observation and conversation during these learning activities. Some teachers make use of commercial resources and schemes, such as LetterLand, and these resources can play a role in teaching the alphabet, but they need to be part of a wide range of resources and practices. LetterLand has pictogram characters, such as 'Clever Cat', to help children remember letter shapes and sounds. By the time they start Year 1, many children will know most letter names.

> **BOOKS TO HELP TEACH THE ALPHABET**
>
> - *ABC I can be* by Verna Wilkins (1993)
> - *Alphabet ice cream* by Sue Heap and Nick Sharratt (2007)
> - *Alphabet poem* by Michael Rosen (2004)
> - *Alphabet wings* by Ilana Kresner (2005)
> - *Alpha bugs* by David A. Carter (1994)
> - *Alpha oops! The day Z went first* by Alethea Kontis (2006)
> - *Bugs and beasts ABC* by Irma Gold (2006)
> - *Dr Seuss' ABC* by Dr Seuss (2003)
> - *Eating the alphabet: Fruits and vegetables from A to Z* by Lois Ehlert (1989)
> - *G is for galaxy: An out of this world alphabet* by Janis Campbell (2005)
> - *Little Aussie alphabet book* by Tamara Sheward (2006)
> - *Little bear's alphabet* by Jane Hissey (2000)
> - *Maisy's ABC* by Lucy Cousins (2006)
> - *My first ABC* by Pamela Allen (2006)
> - *On Market Street* by Arnold Lobel (1989)
> - *P is for peanut: A photographic ABC* by Lisa Gelber (2007)
> - *The dangerous alphabet* by Neil Gaiman (2008)
> - *The icky bug alphabet book* by Jerry Pallotta (1989)
> - *The most amazing hide-and-seek alphabet book* by Robert Crowther (2005)
> - *The Z was zapped* by Chris Van Allsburg (1987)

THE ALPHABETIC PRINCIPLE

As noted above, the understanding that letters represent sounds is fundamental to reading and is known as the alphabetic principle. Children who have grasped the alphabetic principle will generally know a few graphophonic relationships, but will still have a lot to learn. For example, a child might say, 'K stands for /k/ in Kelvin.' They are most likely to know about the letters and corresponding sounds in their name and they may know some letters and sounds from the environment, such as 'M' for McDonald's. Unless children understand that letters symbolise sounds, they will find it difficult to progress. Many children commencing the first year of formal schooling will have an understanding of the alphabetic principle but will not know many letter–sound relationships. For children who come from homes where the language system is not alphabetic but logographic, the alphabetic principle can be particularly difficult to grasp. (A logographic system uses pictograms to represent words or syllables, and not letters. Chinese and Japanese are examples.)

LETTER–SOUND RELATIONSHIPS

In order to become good readers and spellers, children need to know how letters represent sounds, or graphophonic connections. Children who do not have a good grasp of the relationships between letters and sounds are very disadvantaged in reading and writing.

Development of knowledge about letter–sound relationships

Although not all children develop knowledge about letter–sound connections in the same way or at the same pace, some broad generalisations can be useful as frameworks for thinking about how children learn. In *Every child a reader*, Hiebert et al. (1998) point out that most children learn some letter–sound correspondences during the pre-school years. This learning is closely tied to the understanding that words can be segmented into sounds (phonemic awareness) and that letters represent sounds in a systematic way (the alphabetic principle).

Later, children develop the ability to phonetically decode single syllable words. They may also monitor their own reading through using the syntactic and semantic cueing systems in conjunction with their decoding (graphophonic) knowledge. The next stage of phonics development involves the ability to instantly recognise single syllable words through the use of graphophonic knowledge and through the use of analogy (knowledge of word families or rimes). Children in this stage can also decode multi-syllabic words through phonic and structural analysis. Structural analysis involves breaking words down by units of meaning, or prefixes, root words and suffixes.

In the final stage of learning about letter–sound relationships, children can decode most unknown multi-syllabic words that are not in their sight-word store (Hieber et al., 1998). They recognise most words automatically, through rapid decoding and a large store of **sight words**.

As already stated, not all children will develop phonics knowledge at the same rate or in the same sequence as that described above. The sequence of development depends partly on how the child is taught. Because development of letter–sound knowledge depends largely on the teaching program used, assessment should relate to the teaching program.

WORD RECOGNITION: PHASES OF DEVELOPMENT

It is proposed that word recognition develops in phases (Ehri, 1995), starting with a pre-alphabetic phase, in which children recognise some letters by their shape and have an emerging understanding that letters represent sounds (the alphabetic principle). Children in pre-school and some older children in childcare contexts are likely to be in this phase.

During what Ehri (1995) has called the *partial alphabetic* stage, children acquire more graphophonic knowledge and are able to decode some simple words, such as consonant-vowel-consonant words like 'dog'.

Next, children become *fully alphabetic*. Here, they are able to apply graphophonic knowledge to decode more complicated words, including unfamiliar words, and they instantly recognise some words ('sight words'). This usually occurs during the first year of formal schooling.

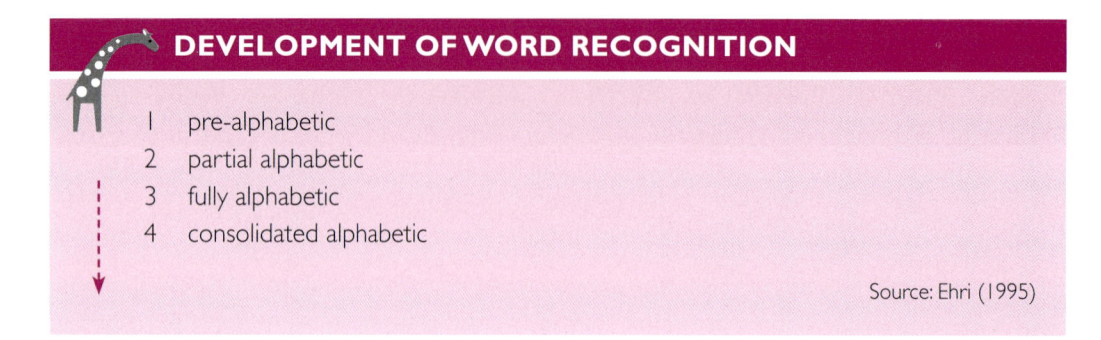

> **DEVELOPMENT OF WORD RECOGNITION**
>
> 1. pre-alphabetic
> 2. partial alphabetic
> 3. fully alphabetic
> 4. consolidated alphabetic
>
> Source: Ehri (1995)

> **GUIDE TO WHAT YOUNG CHILDREN MIGHT BE EXPECTED TO ACHIEVE IN WORD RECOGNITION**
>
> End of the year before First Grade (year before Year 1):
> - has knowledge of many letter–sound correspondences
> - begins to understand that the sequence of letters in a written word represents the sequence of sounds or phonemes in the spoken word.
>
> End of First Grade (Year 1):
> - decodes single syllable words in texts phonetically
> - monitors own reading through using the syntactic and semantic cueing systems.
>
> End of Second Grade (Year 2):
> - decodes most unknown multi-syllabic words that are not in sight-word store
> - recognises most words automatically.
>
> Source: Heibert et al. (1998)

This is followed by the *consolidated alphabetic* stage (Ehri, 1995). Here, children 'chunk' letters together to enable them to decode unfamiliar words more effectively. In the final stage of word reading ('automatic' reading), according to Ehri (1995), students instantly recognise words through sophisticated decoding strategies and the use of context as confirmation. Although clearly representing stages of development, Ehri (1995) acknowledges that children do not necessarily proceed through the phases in a strict sequential manner. As with all phases of development, it is important to remember that not only is the sequence of development a reflection of experiences and cognitive abilities, but also children may 'regress' or appear to be in two phases simultaneously.

SIGHT WORDS

WHAT ARE SIGHT WORDS?

There are some words that children should be taught to read at sight to facilitate quick and fluent reading. When a word can be recognised at sight by a child it is said to be in his or her sight-word store, and children's sight-word stores constantly grow until, as mature readers, most everyday words are sight words. Many words that enter the *sight-word store* are not actively taught—they are read and written repeatedly by children until they are known 'off by heart'.

Words committed to memory as sight words obviously vary from child to child, since each child has had different exposure to words, has different interests and motivation, and has different ways of remembering things. Children should be taught **high-frequency words** so that these become sight words. High-frequency words are those that appear most frequently in the English language. Heibert (1998) has pointed out that there are twenty-five very frequent words that comprise almost 33 per cent of words in texts. These words include 'I', 'the', 'for', 'a', 'that', 'to', 'was' and 'from'. The 100 most frequent words comprise 50 per cent of words in texts, so if children have these 100 words in their sight-word store they are well on their way to becoming accomplished at word recognition.

The most frequent 300 words comprise 65 per cent of words in text, and the most frequent 1000 comprise 75 per cent of words in texts. It should be a goal that children finish Year 1 knowing the first 100 high-frequency words as sight words, although of course some children will not be able to achieve this and others will far exceed this goal. Heibert has pointed out that very few children who do not know the first 100 high-frequency words by the end of Year 3 (3rd Grade) ultimately become good readers.

There are several lists of high-frequency words available, and these are very similar, although not identical because they are based on slightly different samples of texts. Very well known lists are the Dolsch and the Fry lists. These can be found easily on the internet. They are featured in the National Institute for Literacy website at www.nifl.gov/readingprofiles/Dolch_Fry_Pop.htm.

For Australian children, an excellent list of high-frequency words is the Oxford word list, which is in the appendix of this book. The Oxford list features the top 307 words used by children (in their writing) in their first three years at school. Needless to say, it is also important to teach high-frequency words in spelling activities; this will assist children to store them as sight words. The teaching and assessment of sight words will be covered in subsequent chapters, as will the teaching and assessment of phonological awareness and phonics.

LEARNING TO READ

DEFINITION OF READING

Reading is the ability to decode, make meaning from and use a range of texts with purpose and critical awareness. It is acknowledged that all texts are cultural constructs and that reading occurs in a range of socio-cultural contexts, making it impossible to fully separate the act of reading from the contextual situation in which it occurs. It should also be recognised that reading is an integral part of literacy as a whole and that it is somewhat unrealistic to think of reading as separable from writing, viewing, speaking and listening.

In this chapter we focus on reading the written word, although the ability to read pictures and illustrations, as well as television programs and movies and other visual and multimedia texts, are nowadays seen as being part of reading (National Curriculum Board, 2009). For reasons of clarity, we have dealt with the reading and creation of visual texts in a separate chapter. There are also separate chapters on key aspects of reading, such as phonological awareness and phonics, reading comprehension, fluency, vocabulary for reading and key strategies for teaching reading.

READING DEVELOPMENT

Reading, like all other aspects of literacy, begins to develop from infancy. When children listen to rhymes, song lyrics and stories, they are beginning to learn about reading and its purposes. They see parents and other role models read for a range of purposes and this is also important in early literacy development. Children see symbols from very early in life and learn that they have meaning. For example, a young child known to one of the authors knew the meaning of numerous car logos and, by the age of three, could say what car brand went with each logo. As we all know, most children around the world learn all too soon that the big golden 'M' means French fries. From a young age, children enjoy being read to and like to 'read' books independently. They will often make stories up to go with pictures and, before they learn the concept that print in texts represents specific words and has permanency, their spoken stories may well be different each time they 'read' a particular book.

Eventually, children come to understand that letters represent sounds and that words are represented by letters or groups of letters. It is necessary for them to 'crack the code' of letters–sound relationships. As well as decoding words, it is necessary for children to engage in certain types of *thinking* so as to ensure comprehension of texts.

Ideally, most children should be reading simple texts independently by the age of about eight, or the end of Year 3, and there is evidence to show that students who do not achieve this are highly unlikely to 'catch up' in later years (Juel, 1988). It is therefore highly important that teachers of children in their early years do everything possible to help young children learn to read well in order to avert later reading difficulties (Snow, Burns & Griffin, 1998). Having said this, it must be noted that not all reading difficulties can be prevented by excellent early teaching and intervention, although it has been shown that many children do benefit greatly from this approach (Snow et al, 1998). Some children have *specific learning difficulties* or *reading disabilities* that require long-term specialist support.

Reading development does not happen without appropriate environments, interactions and activities, and we as teachers have a duty to provide the best possible learning opportunities for all children. Reading development needs to be carefully nurtured and intentionally taught, although this is certainly not to say that young children should be put under pressure to engage in learning activities that are beyond their capabilities or be subjected to overly formal learning environments. Spontaneous *free-flow play* (Bruce & Spratt, 2008) should also be encouraged, especially in pre-school contexts, since this allows and encourages children to try language out, to find their own props and re-enact stories and life experiences, and to act out possible scenarios and experiment with different roles and projected situations. Play also encourages movement, problem solving and decision making and, through all this, more possibilities for experimentation with language.

Teachers play a major role in helping children do all of this and, no matter how disadvantaged a child might be in terms of socio-economic or cultural background, it has been shown that the teacher can and does make a great difference (Hattie, 2003; Louden, Rohl & Hopkins, 2008).

There are several different articulations in the literature about phases or stages children might pass through when learning to read, and the differences in terminology and divergences in underlying theories can be somewhat confusing, especially since there are separate phases and stages in the literature for word identification, comprehension, phonological awareness, and so on. It is worth noting at this point that references to stages are not meant to be exact or prescriptive, since some children develop in fairly idiosyncratic ways and there is often overlap between the stages. However, phases and stages can provide useful guidance to novice teachers about what might be expected *in general* in children's reading development.

It is beyond the scope of this chapter to discuss all of the influential work that has been carried out in the field of research on reading development (e.g. Chall, 1983; Sulzby, 1984), so we will restrict our discussion to what we see as the most current and relevant ideas. According to the National Association for the Education of Young Children (NAEYC) (1998) and the International Reading Association (IRA) (2009), there are five early childhood phases of reading and writing development, which span from infancy to the end of Grade 3 (grade or year levels are approximate). In terms of reading, these are summarised in Table 9.3.

Table 9.3: Phases of early reading development

Phase	What readers learn to do in this phase
Phase 1 *Awareness and exploration* (infancy through pre-school) Children explore their environment and build the foundations for learning to read and write.	• Enjoy listening to, viewing and discussing texts • Understand that print carries a message • Engage in reading and writing *attempts* (pretend or role-play reading) • Identify labels and signs in their environment and label objects in books • Participate in rhyming games • Identify some letters and make some letter–sound matches
Phase 2 *Experimental* reading (the year before Year 1) Children develop basic concepts of print and begin to engage in and experiment with reading and writing.	• Enjoy being read to and themselves retell simple narrative stories or informational texts • Use descriptive language to explain and explore • Recognise letters and know some letter–sound correspondences • Show familiarity with rhyming and beginning sounds • Understand left-to-right and top-to-bottom orientation and familiar concepts of print (in English) • Match spoken words with written ones
Phase 3 *Early* reading (approximately Year 1) Children begin to read simple stories and can write about a topic that is meaningful to them.	• Read and retell familiar stories • Use strategies (such as rereading, predicting and questioning) when comprehension breaks down • Use reading for various purposes on their own initiative • Orally read with reasonable fluency • Use letter–sound associations, word parts and context to identify new words • Identify an increasing number of words by sight

Phase	What readers learn to do in this phase
Phase 4 *Transitional* reading (approximately Year 2) Children begin to read more fluently and write various text forms using simple and more complex sentences.	• Read with greater fluency • Use strategies more efficiently (rereading, questioning and so on) when comprehension breaks down • Use word identification strategies with greater facility to identify unknown words • Identify an increasing number of words by sight • Spend time reading daily and use reading to research topics
Phase 5 *Independent and productive* reading (approximately Year 3) Children continue to extend and refine their reading and writing to suit varying purposes and audiences.	• Read fluently and enjoy reading • Use a range of strategies when drawing meaning from the text • Use word identification strategies appropriately and automatically when encountering unknown words • Recognise and discuss elements of different text structures • Make critical connections between texts

Source: NAEYC (1998, pp. 15–16)

The Reading Map of Development and the Writing Map of Development (known as the *First Steps* materials) (Annandale et al., 2004), which are commonly used in Australian schools, set out similar phases of reading development, although these do not align exactly with the NAEYC model. The *First Steps* phases describe reading development into adulthood and do not focus on the early years only. They are well worth referring to.

PERSPECTIVES ON HOW TO TEACH READING

Views about how children can be taught to read can be broadly categorised as either part-to-whole or whole-to-part, although many teachers see the benefits of a so-called 'balanced' approach, which borrows from both (Pressley, 2006).

Part-to-whole approach

According to the part-to-whole (also known as 'bottom-up' or 'skills-based') approach, the development of reading begins with children learning about the 'parts', such as letters and individual words. Once children have learnt about letters and sounds and how to decode words, they can move on to reading whole texts. There is an emphasis in the early years of reading on easily decodable texts, and phonics skills are often taught in isolation with the assumption that children will be able to apply these skills to real, connected texts when necessary.

As well as phonics (letter–sound relationships) being taught, children are taught to look for patterns in words so that they can read by *analogy*. This involves identifying *word families*, or words that have a rime in common, such as *g-ame*, *l-ame* and *s-ame*.

The sight words (or whole word) approach is another aspect of the part-to-whole approach. Here, children are taught whole words in isolation, often through the use of flash cards or basal readers containing a tightly controlled vocabulary and much repetition of words. This was the basis of the 'look and say' teaching that was popular in the 1930s through to the end of the 1960s.

Whole-to-part approach

Teachers who use this approach, which is also known as the 'top-down' approach, begin with a whole text, which is generally read aloud to children in a shared reading context. The book, which will usually be in an enlarged format, is likely to be 'real' children's literature, although it may be published by an educational publisher specifically for teaching reading. It may even be a 'big book' written by the teacher or by children. The whole-to-part approach emphasises meaning-making and enjoyment of texts, not decontextualised learning of component skills.

During repeated readings of the book, teachers point out and talk about a range of text features. The meaning of the text is foregrounded, but letters and sounds in the words are also attended to, and a range of follow-up activities are designed to encourage children to explore words and make connections between letters and sounds. Teachers often select books that contain specific letter patterns so that their phonics teaching can be systematic.

Well-known proponents of the top-down approach include Ken Goodman (1973), Frank Smith (1971) and Constance Weaver (1990). In recent years, the whole language philosophy that underpins this approach has been criticised for underplaying the fact that many children need systematic, explicit phonics instruction. This criticism is not altogether fair because excellent teachers who have a whole language philosophy often *do* successfully weave explicit and systematic phonics teaching into the authentic activities that form the basis of their literacy instruction (Dahl & Scharer, 2000). However, there are many interpretations of how a 'whole language' philosophy might be translated into practice (Dahl & Scharer, 2000; Weaver, 1990), leading to a variation in what is taught and emphasised by individual teachers.

Which approach is better?

There is no simple answer to this question and there is evidence to support both perspectives. For example, there is plenty of recent research indicating that systematic, explicit phonics teaching is essential for many children (e.g. Johnston & Watson, 2005). The (Australian) National Inquiry into the Teaching of Literacy (2006, p. 14) recommended that teachers provide 'systematic, direct and explicit phonics instruction so that children master the essential alphabetic code-breaking skills required for foundational reading proficiency. Equally, that teachers provide an integrated approach to reading that supports the development of oral language, vocabulary, grammar, reading fluency, comprehension and the literacies of new technologies.'

There is also ample evidence to show that focus on meaning is important and that teaching children simply to 'bark at print' is fruitless and detrimental to motivation and comprehension; it is imperative that learning to read is enjoyable and that children see the communicative purpose of what they are learning.

Research clearly shows that children learn in different ways (Whitehead, 2007) so it is essential that teachers utilise a broad range of strategies (International Reading Association, 1999), which should be chosen with reference to the needs and aptitudes of the children concerned. In some teaching situations the focus may be on letters and sounds and in others the focus will be on meaning. In order to respond in a timely fashion to individual students' needs, it is necessary for the teacher to have a deep understanding of how children learn to read and also to have current and relevant information about the children's learning in this area. For this, a reflective, responsive approach to teaching is essential.

Child-initiated or teacher-initiated curriculum?

In Australia there is considerable controversy about what should be taught and how it should be taught, especially in pre-school contexts. Some models of early childhood literacy learning favour child-initiated instruction, which involves the teacher facilitating learning rather than explicitly teaching according to a prepared plan. A teacher as *facilitator* encourages learning by providing a rich learning environment where the child can choose activities of interest. In this model, teachers guide children through learning by asking questions that prompt children to engage in problem-solving activities. They encourage children to take ownership of and reflect on their learning (Machado, 2010). A teacher-initiated curriculum, on the other hand, involves the teacher planning what the child will learn and how it will be learnt. It is not usually open to negotiation and may or may not be of interest to the child. In reality, quality early childhood literacy programs entail a combination of child-initiated and teacher-initiated learning.

SUMMARY

In this chapter it has been shown that there is 'foundational knowledge', that enables young children to progress towards literacy success. Although research into which knowledge is the most important to children as early literacy learners is ongoing, there is some consensus that oral language and phonological awareness are greatly important. Knowledge about the alphabet is also essential, as are understandings about how print works and the 'alphabetic principle'. It is important for early childhood teachers to teach and assess foundational knowledge well, as, without a strong grasp of these concepts, children cannot proceed to become effective literacy learners. In this chapter we also defined reading, outlined phases of reading development in early childhood and discussed major perspectives about how reading might be taught. In the following chapters the ways in which children learn various aspects of reading are discussed.

QUESTIONS AND ACTIVITIES

1. What is foundational knowledge for literacy and why is it important?
2. How do children acquire or learn foundational knowledge? How do home experiences impact on this?
3. Go into a childcare centre or pre-school classroom and observe the environment. Think about how its richness in print and talk might facilitate the development of foundational skills for reading and writing. What kinds of toys, resources and manipulatives do you see that might assist in this?
4. How might a teacher who subscribes to a part-to-whole approach to teaching reading differ from a whole-to-parts teacher in terms of the way she or he uses materials and resources for teaching literacy?

5   What are the benefits and limitations of using 'developmental phases' to understand the growth of reading ability in children?
6   Can you see any possible disadvantages of a 'balanced' approach to teaching reading? What are they?
7   Study Table 9.1 and think about how you as the teacher might facilitate children's learning. What could you provide in the classroom or centre environment (for example, picture books, posters, labels, toys, blocks)? What could you do on a day-to-day basis to assist the children's learning (for example, talk, reading aloud)?
8   As you work through the following chapters, keep returning to Table 9.1 and reflect on how the strategies, principles and learning activities discussed might relate to children's accomplishments in the right-hand column of the table.

KEY TERMS

alphabetic principle
cueing systems
graphophonic knowledge
high-frequency words
intentional teaching
onset-rime
sight words

KEY REFERENCES

Clay, M., M. (2002). *An observation survey of early literacy* (2nd edn). Auckland: Heinemann.
Commonwealth of Australia (2009). *Belonging, being and becoming: The Early Years Learning Framework for Australia.* Barton, ACT: Commonwealth of Austalia.
Department for Education and Skills (DfES) (2007). *Letters and sounds: Principles and practice of high quality phonics.* Norwich: DfES.
Ehri, L. C. (1995). Stages of development in learning to read by sight. *Journal of Research in Reading, 18,* 116–25.
Hiebert, E. H., Pearson, P. D., Taylor, B. M., Richardson, V. & Paris, S. G. (1998). *Every child a reader.* Michigan: CIERA.
Johnston, R. S. & Watson, J. E. (2005). A seven year study of the effects of synthetic phonics teaching on reading and spelling attainment. *Insight, 17,* 1–9.
National Association for the Education of Young Children (1998). *Learning to read and write: A joint position statement of the International Reading Association and the National Association for the Education of Young Children.* Retrieved 15/12/2009, from www.naeyc.org/positionstatements.
National Institute of Child Health and Human Development (2000). *Report of the National Reading Panel. Teaching children to read: An evidence-based assessment of the scientific research literature on reading and its implications for reading instruction* (No. 00-4769). Washington, DC: Government Printing Office.

Raban, B. & Coates, H. (2004). Literacy in the early years: A follow up study. *Journal of Research in Reading, 27*(1), 15–29.

Snow, C., Burns, S. M. & Griffin, P. (1998). *Preventing reading difficulties in young children.* Washington, DC: National Research Council. National Academy Press.

Torgeson, J. K. & Mathes, P. G. (2000). *A basic guide to understanding, assessing and teaching phonological awareness.* Austin, TX: Pro-ed.

CHAPTER 10

Phonological Awareness, Graphophonic Relationships and Sight Words

CHAPTER OBJECTIVES

This chapter will increase your understanding of:

- the levels of phonological awareness
- approaches to teaching about graphophonic relationships
- effective methods of teaching phonological awareness, graphophonic relationships and sight words.

The importance and development of phonological awareness, graphophonic relationships and sight words has been discussed in previous chapters. We will now focus on approaches and strategies for teaching these understandings and skills, which form the basis of word recognition ability. In general, phonological awareness, graphophonic relationships and sight-word teaching and learning should be enjoyable for children; the use of a variety of appropriate strategies, both in the context of reading and writing and as separate, explicit lessons, will ensure enjoyment and maximum learning.

PHONOLOGICAL AWARENESS

In terms of language, babies quickly learn to discriminate between **phonemes**, which are the sounds of a language. In English, there are forty-four phonemes (or forty-five, depending on the speaker's accent). Phonemes are blended together to make syllables and words. There is evidence that children can distinguish certain phonemes as young as one month of age (Gleason, 2005). The ability to discriminate between phonemes and to detect rhymes in words is essential for some aspects of listening for enjoyment; many poems, rhymes and finger plays involve word play.

There are four levels of phonological awareness: *word awareness*, *syllable awareness*, *onset-rime awareness* and *phoneme awareness* (Lane et al., 2002). Some phonological awareness skills can and often do develop prior to learning to read, while others develop alongside reading (Stuart, 2005). However, the rate and sequence at which phonological awareness abilities develop varies from child to child. Even so, research suggests that phonological awareness develops through a gradual process of refinement of sounds, starting with broad distinctions between general sounds, moving ultimately towards fine gradations of phonemes (Barratt-Pugh, Rivalland, Hamer & Adams, 2005).

Torgeson and Mathes (2000) (see box below) have suggested a developmental sequence for phonological awareness, with all of the skills ideally being mastered by the end of the first year of formal schooling (Year 1).

SEQUENCE OF PHONOLOGICAL AWARENESS DEVELOPMENT

1. can recognise whether two words rhyme
2. can think of a rhyme for a simple word (such as 'cat', 'dot')
3. can isolate and pronounce the initial sound of a word (e.g. /n/ in 'nose')
4. can blend the sounds in two phoneme words (e.g. /b/-/oi/ for 'boy')
5. can isolate and pronounce all the sounds in two- and three-phoneme words
6. can blend the sounds in four-phoneme words containing initial consonant blends
7. can isolate and pronounce the sounds in four-phoneme words that contain initial blends (e.g. 'crab')
8. can blend the sounds in four- and five-phoneme words containing initial and final blends ('crisp').

Source: Torgeson and Mathes (2000, p. 7)

TEACHING PHONOLOGICAL AWARENESS

Although young children can learn much about phonological awareness informally at home and in school through listening to and chanting rhymes, playing with words, and through songs and clapping games, research clearly shows that most children do benefit from some explicit and systematic phonological awareness teaching. It should be noted that the teaching of phonological awareness alongside phonics is highly effective. As will become apparent throughout this chapter, it is often not possible or desirable to fully separate the teaching of phonological awareness from the teaching of phonics.

> Hey diddle, diddle,
> The cat and the fiddle,
> The cow jumped over the moon.
> The little dog laughed
> To see such sport
> And the dish ran away
> With the spoon.

> Baa, baa, black sheep,
> Have you any wool?
> Yes, sir, yes, sir,
> Three bags full.
> One for the master,
> One for the dame,
> And one for the little boy
> Who lives down the lane.

> Humpty Dumpty
> Sat on a wall,
> Humpty Dumpty
> Had a great fall.
> All the king's horses,
> And all the king's men,
> Couldn't put Humpty
> Together again.

Nursery rhymes are important in the development of phonological awareness.

Phonological awareness can be described as a *constrained* area of knowledge (Paris, 2005), which means that it is a finite area of knowledge and should not, realistically, take a long period of time to master for most children. The majority of children, by the end of the second year of school (Year 2), will be fairly proficient. Many children will commence their formal schooling with a great deal of knowledge about words and how they can be broken down into sounds, while others will start school with very little knowledge about sounds. Regular assessment and ongoing monitoring should therefore be carried out so that children who are already competent in an area are not asked to participate in activities that will not benefit them. Because children's phonological awareness knowledge varies widely in pre-school and the early years of school, much teaching in this area takes place in small group contexts, although there is some scope for whole class teaching.

WORD-LEVEL PHONOLOGICAL AWARENESS

WORDS

Children need to realise that a word and the object or action it refers to are separate; that words are labels. Sometimes they find it difficult to separate a word from its *referent* (a referent is something that is referred to), as evidenced by the fact that they cannot always distinguish the size of a word from the size of the object it refers to. For example, when

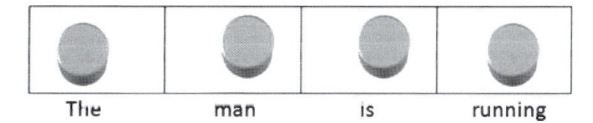

| The | man | is | running |

Counting words activity

asked, 'Which is the biggest word? Car or tricycle?', young children may respond that 'car' is the biggest (Rohl, 2000).

Another understanding that young children need to acquire at the word level is the fact that speech is composed of a series of separate words and is not a continuous stream of sound. To help children learn this, it is a good idea for parents, caregivers and teachers to play games such as clapping hands for each word spoken, or counting words in a spoken phrase or sentence. Sometimes it can help to get children to place a counter or token on a mat or table for each word spoken. This is especially so if they cannot yet count. A string of beads can be used to fulfil this function—children simply move a bead along to the right for each word spoken.

Until children gain these broad understandings about words, it is difficult for them to progress to more difficult levels of phonological awareness. That is not to say they should not be exposed to rhymes, songs, alliterations and other forms of word play.

RHYMES

Identification of rhyming words

A phonological awareness task that children can generally accomplish quite early is the identification of words that rhyme or do not rhyme. Many children as young as three years of age know some nursery rhymes and are able to identify words that do not rhyme with others (known as an *oddity task*) (Maclean, Bryant & Bradley, 1987). Children from home backgrounds where rhymes and nursery rhymes are not common, however, may need explicit instruction in what rhyming words are and in identifying them, and this will involve giving many examples of rhyming words, as well as reading aloud lots of rhymes. There are many nursery rhymes to choose from, as well as an abundance of rhyming books for young children, such as *'I don't care!' said the bear* by Colin West (1996), which tells a *cumulative* story of a moose on the loose and a pig who is big, not to mention a snake from a lake. (A cumulative story is one in which there is repetition, but after each repetition the story is extended.) The Madeline books, such as *Madeline and the bad hat* by Ludwig Bemelmans (1956), are delightful tales about a small schoolgirl, Madeline, all told in rhyme. All of these stories are available on video/DVD so they can be viewed and listened to repeatedly, which can be helpful because children can get to know the rhyming stories and join in.

Rhyming word cards

To a large extent, rhyme identification can be taught and assessed orally, through the teacher asking questions such as, 'Does *sand* rhyme with *hand*?' and, 'Which of these three words rhyme? *Pig, fig, fog*.' Another question variation is, 'Which word is the odd one out because it doesn't rhyme? *Pig, fog, fig*.'

For further practice in the identification of rhyming words, children can be asked to match picture cards. Here, the teacher provides packs of picture cards and asks children to sort these into rhyming pairs (or larger groups). For example, a picture of a *mouse* will be paired with a picture of a *house*, a *snake* with a *cake* and a *dog* with a *frog*. When making or selecting picture cards, it is important to make sure the pictures represent objects that the children will be able to recognise and name. If in doubt about this, go through the cards with them first and discuss the pictures.

Rhyme generation

Rhyme generation is a slightly more difficult task than rhyme identification and, in fact, can be very challenging for some children (Lane et al., 2002), especially children who do not have a large vocabulary or who have English as a second or additional language. This can be overcome somewhat by asking these children to generate *nonsense words* that rhyme, instead of real words. For example, if a child can't think of a word that rhymes with 'sink', it is quite acceptable for her to say 'tink' or 'nink'.

RHYME GENERATION GAME: ROLL-A-RHYME

1. Children sit in a large circle.
2. The first child calls out a word (e.g. '*bag*') and rolls the ball to another.
3. The second child calls out a word that rhymes with the word given by the first (e.g. '*rag*'), then calls out a new word (e.g. '*brick*').
4. She then rolls the ball to another child and the process continues until each child has had a turn.

Source: Scraper (2005, p. 39)

There's a wocket in my pocket (1974) by Dr Seuss is full of rhyming nonsense words, such as: *nupboard* in the cupboard, *ghairs* beneath the stairs, *bofa* on the sofa and *jertain* in the curtain. This book should certainly whet children's appetites for generating nonsense rhymes.

As is the case in the identification of rhyming words, much can be achieved in rhyme generation through oral activities, such as: 'Tell me a word that rhymes with sheep.' Or, the teacher can read out a poem and then reread it, asking the children to supply the missing rhyming words. More examples of oral activities are given below.

Rhyming riddles can encourage children to focus on words that rhyme while at the same time attending to meaning (because the riddle needs to be solved). Examples of rhyming riddles can be seen on the next page.

Rhyming names are engaging and relevant because children can make up funny rhymes about people they know, or even about themselves. 'Grace went to space', 'Sean's pants are torn', 'Chris wants a kiss' and 'Nick is feeling sick' are some examples. Needless to

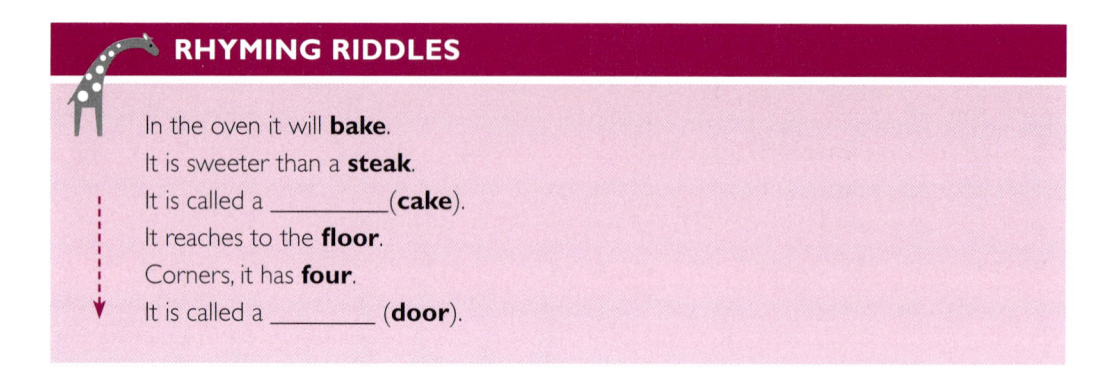

> **RHYMING RIDDLES**
>
> In the oven it will **bake**.
> It is sweeter than a **steak**.
> It is called a _____ (**cake**).
> It reaches to the **floor**.
> Corners, it has **four**.
> It is called a _____ (**door**).

say, rhyming names are a lot easier to make up for single syllable names than for multi-syllabic ones.

Making up new and humorous endings to known songs and rhymes can also be an engaging and useful activity. 'Jack and Jill went to the mill' and 'Twinkle, twinkle little star, how I want to drive your car!' are examples. This activity can also raise children's awareness of syllables since the new version of the rhyme should ideally have the same number of syllables as the original.

Rhyming word hunts involve children collecting pictures of words that rhyme and putting them together in some way; for example, on a rhyming word mobile, bookmark or collage (Fox, 2008). Suitable pictures for word hunts can be found in old magazines, comics and catalogues. Children can do this in pairs or small groups so there is a lot of discussion about which words do and do not rhyme. Children can *make books* of rhyming words by drawing or pasting in pictures of words that rhyme. Adults can help them write the words underneath the pictures.

Isolating the rime in rhyming words

This is the most demanding of the phonological awareness tasks that involve working with rhymes, and actually belongs in the onset-rime level of phonological awareness (discussed below). Essentially, this task involves the child being able to identify the rhyming part in words; for example, being able to say that it is *'op'* that makes the words 'shop' and 'stop' rhyme.

SYLLABLE LEVEL

At the syllable level, phonological awareness involves the ability to detect, count and segment syllables in words, and also to manipulate them. Manipulation involves deleting, adding and substituting syllables to make a different word (or nonsense word, also sometimes known as a 'non-word'). The ability to segment and count syllables has been found to be important to reading and spelling, whereas the ability to manipulate them is less crucial (Adams, 1990; Munro, 1998).

What exactly is a syllable?

The notion of what constitutes a syllable is not as cut and dried, or as simple, as many people think (Munro, 1998). The main area of difficulty for most people is not counting the syllables in a word, but deciding exactly where the syllable boundaries are. What is more, there are different rules about syllable boundaries depending on whether the word is written or spoken. The word 'parrot', for example, can be split into syllables orally as: 'pa-rrot' or 'parr-ot', whereas in writing it should be split between the two consonants in the middle: *par-rot*. There are some quite involved linguistic rules about what a syllable is, which are somewhat beyond the scope of this text. However, a syllable has to contain a vowel or a vowel sound and the consonant or consonant cluster that precedes it, if there is one. There may also be a consonant after the vowel. When teaching and assessing phonological level at the syllable level, it is not necessary for teachers and caregivers of children in their early childhood years to be overly concerned with the location of syllable boundaries as long as the child is able to split words into the correct number of syllables without repeating or omitting any of the sounds (Munro, 1998).

Teaching phonological awareness at the syllable level

Research indicates phonological awareness at the syllable level is fairly unproblematic to teach. It largely involves clapping and tapping activities, which entails a degree of teacher modelling (Lane et al., 2002). Teaching children to segment multi-syllabic words into syllables can begin when children are in pre-school; for example, by helping children to segment their names into syllables. Many of the types of activities described in the section above (on rhyming) can be modified for use with syllables.

Syllable clapping games should involve some teacher modelling, such as, 'I am going to break the word *jacket* into syllables. Listen to how I do it: jack et.' The teacher should clap the two syllables while repeating 'jack-et'. The children then join in.

Munro (1998) has noted that common difficulties in syllable identification include children repeating or omitting parts of the word. For example, a child might say, 'tick-cket' for 'ticket', repeating the /k/ sound when it should only be pronounced once. Children can also have difficulty hearing the schwa sound, which is the 'er' sound in 'mother', which is sounded as a neutral vowel.

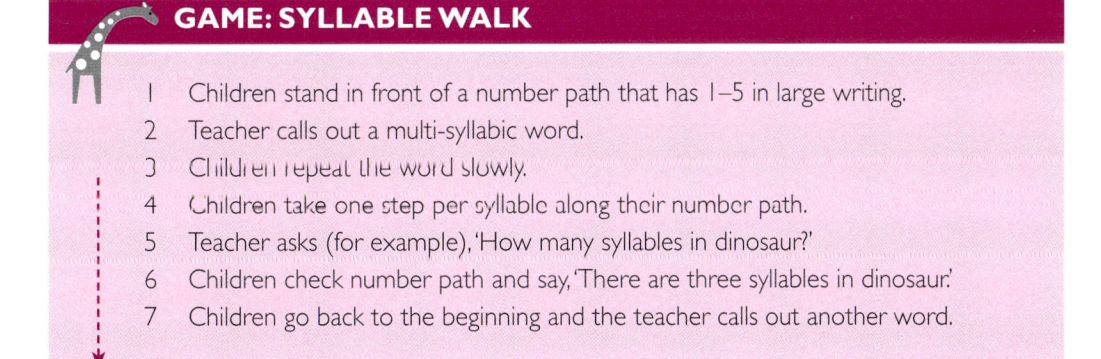

GAME: SYLLABLE WALK

1. Children stand in front of a number path that has 1–5 in large writing.
2. Teacher calls out a multi-syllabic word.
3. Children repeat the word slowly.
4. Children take one step per syllable along their number path.
5. Teacher asks (for example), 'How many syllables in dinosaur?'
6. Children check number path and say, 'There are three syllables in dinosaur.'
7. Children go back to the beginning and the teacher calls out another word.

Source: Scraper (2005, p. 31)

By around five years of age, children who have been given extensive experience involving syllables are likely to able to identify syllables, count the syllables in words, and delete a syllable (usually the first one) from a multi-syllabic word (Cramer, 2006). Here, the teacher would say, 'Say the word *tennis* without the *ten*.' It is often easier to start this kind of exercise using *compound words*, so the teacher could say, 'Say the word *suitcase* without the *case*.' (A compound word is a word composed of two or more smaller words, such as landline, bathroom, backpack and football.)

At home, parents of children as young as four can play syllable games. Yopp and Yopp (2009) describe how they played the *broken word game* with their four-year-old children. The Yopps would say things like, 'We're going to the *mar-ket*', to which the children would respond, 'The market! We're going to the market!' Although their children found it easier to blend syllables into words, as in the example just given, than to segment words into syllables, they were still able to segment before they turned five years of age.

Picture card sorts can be used for a range of phonological awareness activities. At the syllable level, children can be asked to sort pictures into piles or put them into designated containers. Start them off sorting single- and two-syllable words and, as they become more accomplished, add three- and even four-syllable words.

ONSET-RIME LEVEL

This level of phonological awareness involves being able to detect and manipulate the onset and rime of words. The onset is the beginning sounds of a single syllable word, such as the /s/ in 'sat' or the /str/ in 'string'. It precedes the first vowel in a syllable, which is where the rime begins. This is a useful level of analysis for children because it helps them read by analogy (if I can read 'dog', I can figure our 'log') and learn to spell by building **word families**, or words that have a rime in common (Adams, 1990).

It has been shown that being phonologically aware at the onset-rime level is a predictor of children's reading success in later years, and, having had many opportunities to work with onset and rimes at school, most six-year-old children (end of Year 1) are able to recognise onset-rimes (Goswami & Bryant, 1990). Listening to and playing with rhymes and rhyming words at an early age, particularly in pre-school, will give children a good basis for the development of onset and rimes (Cramer, 2006).

Many activities that involve onset-rime are covered in the phonics section of this chapter, below, because they involve letters as well as sounds. Rimes can also be taught in the context of shared reading (Gill, 2006), using texts where there are rhyming words. Gill suggests five steps for teaching rimes in the context of the shared reading of poetry. This is an example of teaching phonological awareness and phonics simultaneously. The steps are outlined below:

1. *Reading the poem*
   The teacher reads the poem aloud with enjoyment and expression. When the poem is read for a second time, the children join in where possible. Here, children become acquainted with the meaning of the poem and have the opportunity to hear the teacher emphasise the rhythm and rhymes when reading aloud expressively. They also get a chance to say the rhyming words themselves.
2. *Introducing a skill*
   The children are asked to listen for rhyming words in the poem as it is read once again. Once they have identified rhyming words, the teacher writes them on a large piece of card, with one word directly beneath the other. The rhyming part may be written in a different colour. Children are then asked to identify any spelling patterns in the rhymes on the list (from this point on, the activity also teaches phonics as it not only focuses on sounds but also on letters). The teacher asks the children to think of more words that rhyme and they are added to the appropriate list. For example, if children identify the rhyming words 'sight' and 'bright', these two words will go in the same list. However, 'sight' and 'bite' will go in

separate lists. Although they rhyme, they do not have the same rime. When the lists are complete, they are hung on the classroom wall for further reference.

3 *Working with words*

This step can proceed in several different ways. The teacher can cut the poem up into sentence strips or separate lines and ask the children to put them together again, or can give children onset-rime cards and ask them to make words by putting an onset and a rime together. Any activity that involves children attending to the rimes and their spellings will be suitable as a working with words activity.

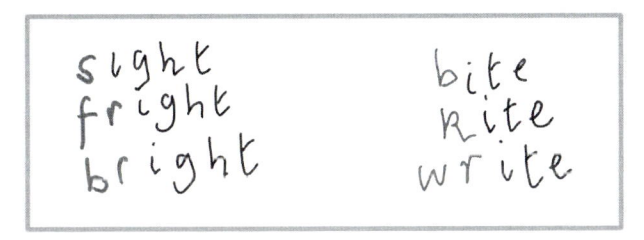

> sight
> fright
> bright
>
> bite
> Rite
> write

Working with word families

4 *Writing*

This step can take several different directions. Children may rewrite the poem using different rhyming words or they may use the poem as a springboard for writing another type of text such as a letter or a story.

5 *Rereading*

This can be done at intervals throughout the school term to ensure revision of the rimes learnt. Each time it is reread, children are able to participate more fully by joining in the choral reading and identifying the rimes.

PHONEME LEVEL

This level of phonological awareness is the most sophisticated and is likely to require the most instruction. It involves the ability to detect, count, segment, blend and manipulate individual phonemes. This is an important ability in that it is a precursor to being able to use graphophonics (letter–sound) knowledge to 'sound out' when reading and spelling. This level of phonological awareness is often referred to as **phonemic awareness** (Lane et al., 2002), although it must be noted that some international authors refer to 'phonological awareness' as 'phonemic awareness'.

The instruction of phonemic awareness involves a variety of activity types, such as sound detection and counting, sound matching, and sound oddity detection. In sound detection activities, children are asked to say which word begins (or ends) with a particular phoneme. This can be done in the context of story reading or through games. The UK Primary National Strategy's *Letters and sounds* materials contain many useful games and activities to teach these aspects of phonological awareness (Primary National Strategy, 2007b). More sophisticated tasks at the phoneme level involve the blending and segmenting of individual phonemes, and phoneme deletion and manipulation tasks.

Research has shown that by the end of First Grade (USA), as a result of both explicit and implicit teaching, the majority of children can count phonemes (Cramer, 2006), and by the time they are six or seven years old most children can delete and add initial phonemes to make new words in words of up to three phonemes (Pratt & Brady, 1988, cited in Cramer, 2006). As in all other aspects of reading and learning, there are many exceptions to this, however.

The phonemes in English are categorised as either vowels or consonants. Vowels are either *short vowels, long vowels* or *diphthongs*. Short vowels are short, such as the /ă/ in 'cat', whereas long vowels are pronounced for a longer period of time. The /ō/ sound in 'boat' is long. A diphthong is a sound where two vowel sounds are sounded together, as in the word 'boy'. There are different symbols and notations for representing long and short vowels but, in schools, teachers often use the macron and the breve (see box below).

Table 10.1: Phonemes in English

Phoneme	Example	Phoneme	Example	Phoneme	Example	Phoneme	Example
/ă/	bat short vowel	/h/	hen	/ō/	boat long vowel	/th/	thick
/ā/ or /ai/	late long vowel	/ĭ/	bit short vowel	/oi/	toy diphthong	/TH/	that
/aw/	caught lawn long vowel	/ī/	bite right long vowel	/oo/	book	/ŭ/	nut short vowel
/b/	big web	/j/	jam lodge giraffe	/OO/	root long vowel	/ū/	cute
/ch/	chin nature beach	/k/	candle kick	/ow/	cow diphthong	/v/	vase
/d/	dog bad	/l/	list pull	/p/	pig, nip	/w/	win
/ĕ/	red short vowel	/m/	mud thumb	/r/	rag	/wh/	white
/ē/ or /ee/	seed long vowel	/n/	nest bin	/s/	sit pass	/y/	yell
/f/	fire tough	/ng/	sing	/sh/	shop	/z/	zoo
/g/	go log	/ŏ/	pot wasp short vowel	/t/	top lit	/zh/	measure
/3/	bird 'r' controlled vowel	/ə/	better schwa vowel				

The chart below (Table 10.1) shows some common phonemes in the English language. It must be remembered that people speak in different dialects and accents and there is variation in the way that phonemes, especially vowels, are pronounced. In some dialects, not all of the phonemes are used. For example, not everyone uses the phoneme /wh/, which sounds the 'h' as well as the 'w'. Scottish people commonly pronounce this, but in Australian English it is not common.

It is useful to be aware of the International Phonetic Alphabet (IPA), as this is used in dictionaries to describe pronunciations. An interactive phonemic chart is available at the BBC's *Learning English* website: www.bbc.co.uk/worldservice/learningenglish/grammar/pron/sounds/chart.shtml. In this website it is possible to click on symbols of the IPA and hear the corresponding sound. This is in Standard English, not Standard Australian English, which has some different vowel sounds. For Australian sounds, refer to: clas.mq.edu.au/phonetics/phonetics/ausenglish/index.html.

MARKING LONG AND SHORT VOWELS

Macrons (ā) are often used to mark long vowels
Breves (ă) are often used to mark short vowels

ISOLATING SOUNDS

The isolation of sounds involves children being able to say what the first sound in a word is, for example. If the word is *trick*, the child will be able to say that the first sound is /t/. They may also be able to tell you that the last (or final) sound is /k/ and the middle sounds are /r/ and /i/.

One simple activity for helping children develop this is a game called 'Same or different'. This game involves children listening for words that have common sounds. Initial consonant sounds are the easiest for children to match, so the teacher or caregiver would start with these, eventually working to common final and then middle sounds. Say to the children: 'Listen while I say two words (from the story) I want you to give the thumbs up if they start the same and thumbs-down if they don't start the same.' A variation of this game is to ask the children to repeat the two words and say either, 'same' or 'different' (Barclay, 2009).

Being able to recognise alliteration involves the recognition of a recurring initial sound. Making up alliterations, such as 'The cute cat caught a clumsy canary' is an entertaining and beneficial learning activity. There are many children's books that feature alliteration. One such book is *Dr Seuss's ABC* (1963), which contains a crazy alliterative story for every letter of the alphabet, such as: 'Willy Waterloo washes Warren Wiggins who is washing Waldo Woo'. *Our daft dog Danny* by Pamela Allen (2009) is another example of a book featuring alliteration, as is *Animalia* by Graeme Base (1986). *Animalia* is suitable for children in the early years of school but is not appropriate for pre-school children, since some of the vocabulary is fairly demanding:

- 'quivering quails queuing quietly for quills'
- 'wicked warrior wasps wildly waving warlike weapons'
- 'great green gorillas growing grapes in a gorgeous glass greenhouse.'

Children can make up their own alliterative stories and picture books, with the help of the teacher. They can cut out from magazine pictures of things starting with the same sound then make up funny stories, such as 'angry alligators attack apples', 'clumsy cows come close', 'lively ladies love lipstick' and 'crazy carrots climb calmly'.

Things that start with the /m/ sound

CHILDREN'S BOOKS WITH RHYME OR ALLITERATION

- *Each peach pear plum* by Janet and Alan Ahlberg (1989)
- *Where's my teddy?* by Jez Alborough (1994)
- *Our daft dog Danny* by Pamela Allen (2009)
- *Animalia* by Graeme Base (1986)
- *Madeline and the bad hat* by Ludwig Bemelmans (1956)
- *Have you seen my cat?* By Eric Carle (1973)
- *'Slowly, slowly, slowly', said the sloth* by Eric Carle (2002)
- *Five little monkeys jumping on the bed* retold by Eileen Christelow (2006)
- *Goodness gracious* by Phil Cummings (1989)
- *Hairy McClary from Donaldson's dairy* by Linley Dodd (1985)
- *All right, Vegemite!: A new collection of Australian children's chants and rhymes* compiled by June Factor (1995a)

- *Real keen baked bean!: A fourth collection of Australian children's chants and rhymes* compiled by June Factor (1995b)
- *Possum magic* by Mem Fox (1991)
- *Don't forget the bacon* by Pat Hutchins (1978)
- *Moses supposes his toeses are roses and 7 other silly old rhymes* retold by Nancy Patz (1983)
- *We're going on a bear hunt* retold by Michael Rosen (1989)
- *The cat in the hat comes back* by Dr Seuss (1958)
- *Dr Seuss's ABC* by Dr Seuss (1963)
- *There's a wocket in my pocket!* by Dr Seuss (1974)

Picture cards, which are useful in all aspects of teaching phonological awareness, can be used to teach initial sounds. Give a child a set of three picture cards, two of them depicting objects with the same initial sound, and ask, 'Which two words have the same beginning sound?' Or, 'Which word is the odd one out? Which word does not have the same beginning sound as the other two?'

Picture sorts can help children improve their initial sound identification ability. They are given a stack of picture cards and asked to sort them according to the initial sound.

Picture hunts can also be of benefit. Here, children search for pictures of objects that start with a particular sound, cut them out and glue them to a collage, poster or bookmark.

The old favourite, *I-Spy*, is a simple game that can be used to help children learn about initial sounds. The player chooses an object in sight and says, 'I spy with my little eye, something beginning with the sound /b/.' In this version of I-Spy, it is important that the phoneme (sound) is used and not the letter name.

Initial sound cards. Ring and rooster start with the same sound, so chair would be discarded.

A sound shop can be set up in the centre or classroom. The shop should be set up so that it only sells things that start with a particular sound. For example, the shop could sell things beginning with the /t/ sound, such as a toy truck, toffee, a Tinkerbell doll, toilet roll, turmeric, tape, and so on. Children can search the classroom for items to put in the shop or can bring things in from home. After a few days, the stock in the shop is changed to objects starting with another sound.

ORALLY SEGMENTING SOUNDS

Oral segmentation involves identifying each sound in a word in the correct sequence. For the word 'trick', the child would be able to segment the word into its four phonemes: /t/-/r/-/i/-/k/. Note that words do not necessarily have the same number of phonemes as they have letters, as many phonemes are represented by more than one letter. This is an important concept for children to learn once they begin to link phonemes with letters.

To help children learn to segment words, teachers can model 'stretching' words by saying them very slowly and emphasising each phoneme. Keep the sounds connected so that the children can still hear the word. When modelling how to stretch the word 'mum', for example, the teacher would say 'mmmuuuummm'. Children should then be given some words to stretch, with teacher assistance if needed. Words made up of *continuous sounds* such as /m/, /n/, /s/, /f/, /r/, /w/ and so on are the best to start with. It is easy to stretch /s/ into 'sssssss' and easy to stretch /f/ into 'fffffff'. Some sounds, such as /p/, /g/, /h/ and /t/ cannot be stretched out and are known as *stop sounds*.

Once children have learnt to stretch words they can begin to isolate the phonemes. Ask them, 'What sounds do you hear when I stretch the word, mum? Mmmmmuuuuummmm.' Another useful activity that can be used to assist children in isolating and segmenting sounds is the *sound box*, sometimes also known as the *Elkonin box* after its Russian inventor. Here, children are asked to place a counter or token into a box for each phoneme they hear in a word. For the word 'pen', for example, three tokens would need to be used, one per box. When children are able, they can be given pictures of objects and they can independently say the word, segment it and place tokens in the sound box for each phoneme heard. The teacher can check the tokens to assess children's ability in segmenting.

Similar to the syllable walk described above, children can participate in a *sound walk* (or phoneme walk). The teacher calls out the word and the children must take a step for each phoneme in the word, pronouncing a phoneme with each step they take.

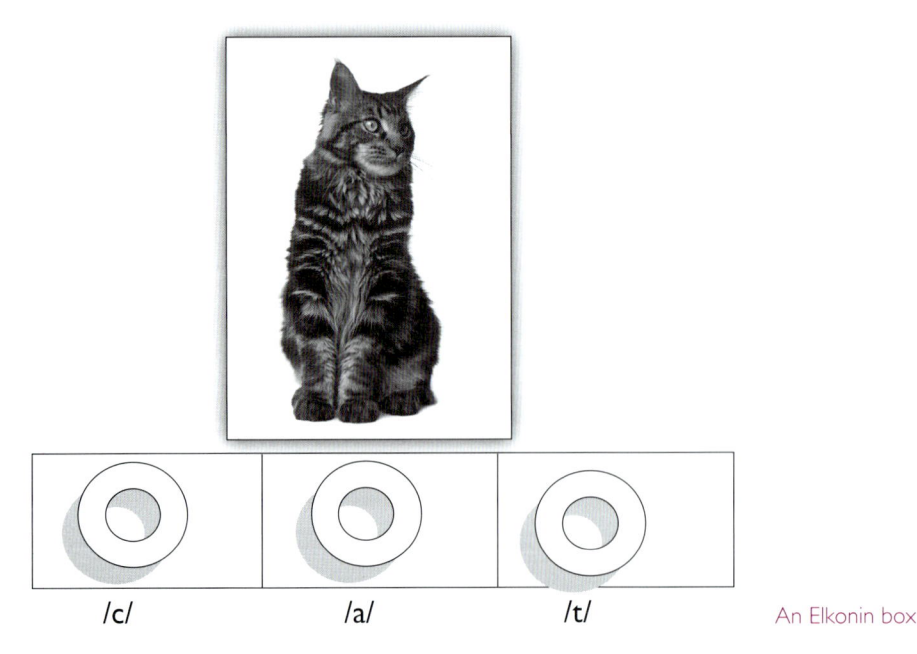

An Elkonin box

ORALLY BLENDING SOUNDS

Oral blending entails being able to put sounds together, in sequence, to make a word. For instance, a child may combine the three phonemes /th/-/i/-/n/ to make the word 'thin'. Teachers should primarily use modelling and questioning to teach blending. For example, a teacher or caregiver might say, 'What word do I get when I blend these sounds together? /sh/-/o/-/k/.' Blending is also taught through phonics activities and within the context of reading and spelling.

Letters and sounds (Primary National Strategy, 2007a) suggests that early childhood teachers should, throughout the day, 'sound talk' selected words. For example, he or she might say, 'Come and /s/-/i/-/t/ on the /m/-/a/-/t/.' Some of the children's names may also be said in this, such as, '/b/-/r/-/a/-/d/, come over here, please.' For extra interest, a soft toy can be used to 'sound talk' to children. It can give instructions such as, 'Put your hands on your /h/-/e/-/d/.'

It is most important that teachers pronounce phonemes clearly and correctly during blending activities. That is, there should be no superfluous sounds that are not actually in the word. When pronouncing the /t/ sound, for example, it should not be pronounced as 't-uh' as the /t/ sound does not actually have the voiced 'uh' sound added to it when it is in words.

MANIPULATING SOUNDS

The ability to manipulate sounds is a more complex and difficult task than isolating and segmenting, and involves *adding*, *substituting* or *deleting* sounds in words to make new words. Children often do not master this until they are six or seven years old. In order to manipulate phonemes, they need the prerequisite skills of isolating, blending and segmenting.

Sound addition

Sound addition means adding sounds to words. For example, 'Say tamp with an /s/ before it', or, 'Say tin and add a /t/ to the end.' As in any other phoneme manipulation tasks, the teacher will need to model and give examples before asking the child to do it.

Sound deletion

This involves being able to say the word but leaving out one of the sounds, which may be the initial, final or a middle (medial) sound. Deletion of initial sounds is the easiest and deletion of a medial sound is the most demanding. Examples of sound deletion tasks would be, 'Say thin without the /th/' or 'Say train without the /r/'.

Sound substitution

This entails changing one of the sounds in a word to make a new word. For example, 'Change the first sound in fog to make an animal (dog)' or 'Change the last sound in bag to make a word that means 'not good' (bad).'

Consonant riddles can also be used as a means of helping children learn about sound substitution. Here, they are required to think of a word that rhymes with a given word and starts with a specified consonant sound: An example of a consonant riddle is, 'What rhymes with *sand* but starts with /b/?'

Picture searches are a useful means of getting children to identify sound omissions, additions and substitutions in words. A group of children should be looking at the same picture; for example, an illustration in a big book. The teacher then explains that she will say the name of something in the picture but (for example) with its first sound changed. The children have to discover what the teacher is referring to. If the teacher wants the children to say 'tree', for example, she might say 'cree'. A more difficult version of this game would be to omit or substitute final or medial sounds. For extra interest, a puppet can be used to incorrectly pronounce the words.

PRINCIPLES FOR TEACHING PHONOLOGICAL AWARENESS

Fox (2008, p. 44) has summarised some principles or 'best practices' for teaching phonological awareness. These principles are based on research findings.

- Teach beginning sounds first, then final sounds, then middle sounds.
- Teach phonological awareness, letter names and phonics together.
- Teach only one or two skills at a time.
- Teach phonological awareness early, in pre-school and the first year of school (Year 1).
- Small group teaching is the most effective.
- The pace of teaching depends on the needs of individual children.
- Help children *use* their phonological awareness knowledge when reading and writing.
- Begin with short words (two phoneme words, then three phoneme words, and so on).

ASSESSMENT OF PHONOLOGICAL AWARENESS

To a large extent, assessment of phonological awareness occurs informally during teaching; children's responses to requests to count, add, delete or manipulate syllables, onsets or rimes, or phonemes often speak for themselves and can be recorded through the use of checklists, ratings scales and anecdotal notes. A quick and easy assessment of early phonological awareness would involve checking the child's ability to identify initial phonemes, to segment three-, four- and five-phoneme words, and to blend three-, four- and five-phoneme words. Table 10.2 shows some examples of items that teachers might include in early phonological awareness assessment checklists.

Other simple means of assessing phonological awareness include the Yopp-Singer (1995) assessment, which requires children to segment words into phonemes. There are twenty-two words in this assessment, including words such as: *lay, grew, dog, keep* and *wave*. Munro's *Assessing and teaching phonological knowledge* (Munro, 1998) is also an excellent resource, as is the Phonological Awareness Literacy Screening (PALS) early literacy assessment, which can be found on the website www.pals.virginia.edu.

Lane and colleagues (2002) have suggested that the best measures of phonological awareness are those that are administered on an individual basis. As already mentioned, informal observation of individual children performing specific tasks, such as the instructional tasks described in this chapter, can be a highly effective means of assessment in this area.

Table 10.2: Quick informal assessment of phonological awareness (example)

Child's name: _____ Age (years and months): _____ Date: _____		
	Task	**Record of responses**
Hearing and identifying individual words in a sentence	**Sam has a small white kitten.** *Child places a counter for each word he/she hears when the teacher reads the sentence.*	
Hearing and identifying each syllable in a word	**finger man pony dinosaur** *Child claps the syllable (or beats) after the teacher says the word.*	
Identifying same initial phoneme in a set of words	**four, fast finger** *Child identifies the same beginning sound of the words said by the teacher.*	
	sun sat dog *Child identifies the word in the set of words that does not have the same initial sound as the others.*	
Hearing and identifying words that rhyme	**shop drop drip** *Child identifies the two rhyming words.*	
Producing words that rhyme	**fish** **day** *Child supplies a rhyming word for each word the teacher says.*	
Separating the onset from the rime in a word (onset-rime)	**can, man, fan, plan** *Child identifies the sound that is the same in three words (rime).*	
Hearing individual phonemes in a word	**fin, shop, dog, man** *Child identifies the beginning, middle and end sounds of words.*	
Segmentation of words into phonemes	Group 1: **bay, top, ship, hat, rock** Group 2: **stop, grab, sleep, train, think** Group 3: **plant, stamp, crust, splash, floats** *Child segments the word into separate phonemes, e.g. b-ay, t-o-p, c-r-u-s-t.* *If child struggles with a group, do not assess the next group.*	
Blending phonemes	Group 1: **o-n, t-i-n, r-a-t, f-ee-l, b-u-g** Group 2: **j-u-m-p, h-o-l-d, b-r-ow-n, s-t-ai-n, ch-i-p-s** Group 3: **sh-r-i-n-k, c-l-a-m-p, p-r-i-n-t, c-r-ee-p-s, s-t-r-aigh-t** *Child blends the phonemes into words, e.g. ch-i-p-s into chips.* *If child struggles with a group, do not assess the next group.*	

TEACHING ABOUT GRAPHOPHONIC RELATIONSHIPS

Phonics can be defined as: 'A method of teaching word recognition or decoding that emphasises the sound–symbol (letter) relationships that exist in a language' (Rasinski & Padak, 2008, p. 14).

A good knowledge of the system of graphophonic or letter–sound relationships used to represent the English language helps children decode (read) words they have not seen before and is important for their spelling development.

Carole Torgerson and her colleagues (2006) carried out a comprehensive literature review on the teaching of phonics and concluded that beginning readers should be taught phonics in a systematic, incremental sequence. In addition, they should be taught how to blend phonemes to facilitate 'sounding out' when reading, and that blending and segmenting are reversible processes.

Torgerson's report outlines effective phonics teaching as being part of a literacy curriculum that also includes speaking and listening skills and phonological awareness. She suggests that, for most children, systematic phonics teaching should commence at (approximately) the age of five, but this is subject to teacher judgment. There will certainly be occasions when phonics teaching should start earlier or later. Other literature reviews on phonics and reading tend to concur with Torgeson's recommendations (e.g. DfES, 2007).

The research indicates that phonics teaching should:

- be explicit and systematic
- be taught daily
- be taught at a brisk pace
- include a variety of multi-sensory teaching and learning strategies
- be constantly practised and reinforced through such activities as shared reading, guided reading and writing
- be informed by careful assessment and monitoring
- be enjoyable.

Although the systematic and explicit teaching of graphophonic relationships is important, it must be stressed that this should be part of a balanced reading program that also attends to vocabulary, comprehension and fluency, using authentic texts. There is probably no 'best' way to do this and much depends on teacher judgment and the particular teaching context. There are several broad approaches to teaching phonics (National Institute of Child Health and Human Development, 2000), and they are briefly described below.

APPROACHES TO PHONICS TEACHING

Analogy approach

This teaching strategy involves teaching children about word families. For example, if a child can read the word *back*, she should be able to read the word *sack* by using analogy. That is, she knows the word 'back' and therefore the '*ack*' *phonogram*, so all she needs to do is replace the /b/ sound with a /s/ sound. To help children spell by analogy, teachers should help them focus on *phonograms,* such as 'uck', 'at' and 'in'. Phonograms are ways of spelling rimes that can be heard in syllables. The analogy approach is all about getting children to see patterns in words, or *word families*. There are approximately 350 phonograms in the English language, so obviously it is not possible to explicitly teach all of these. In *Every child a reader,* it is recommended that teachers teach fewer phonograms well, rather than teaching many phonograms superficially (Hiebert et al., 1998). Children need many opportunities to practise and apply what they have learnt in different contexts. Hiebert et al. have suggested that the following 38 phonograms are worth focusing on, since between them they appear in some 600 words.

Table 10.3: High-frequency phonograms

	Vowel-consonant/ Vowel-consonant-consonant (V-C/V-C-C)	Vowel-consonant-e/ Vowel-vowel-consonant (V-C-e/V-V-C)	Diphthongs, r-controlled and others
a	am, at, ack, ank, ap, an, ab, am	ain, ail, ake, ay	----
e	ell, est, ed	eed	ew
i	ill, in, im, ip, ick, ing, ink	ine	ight
o	op, ot, ock, ob	----	out, ow, ore
u	uck, um, ug, unk	----	----
y	----	----	y (as in try)

Analytic approach

Here, children are taught how to analyse words they have already recognised in order to investigate or discover letter–sound relationships. The *analytic approach* to phonics teaching often occurs in the context of reading books, or during shared reading activities with the teacher, and is essentially a whole-to-parts approach. Although some children seem to be able to analyse words and discover letter–sound relationships for themselves, most need a degree of teacher support. Research indicates that children who have English as a second language and children who have reading difficulties are disadvantaged by this method of teaching phonics; they need explicit teaching.

Embedded phonics approach

In this approach, the teaching of phonics is taught within the context of reading, and children are taught to use context cues such as semantic cues and syntactic cues alongside the graphophonic information to help them identify words. The *cueing systems* of reading have been discussed in Chapter 9.

Synthetic approach

This approach involves explicitly teaching children how sounds are represented by letters. It is essentially a parts-to-whole approach that teaches children how to 'sound out' words by matching letters with phonemes and then blending the phonemes to make a word.

There is some evidence that **synthetic phonics** instruction is superior to other approaches (Johnston & Watson, 2005).

Phonics through spelling

Children can learn a lot about phonics through spelling, particularly *invented spelling*. They segment the word they wish to spell and then use an appropriate grapheme (letter or group of letters) to represent each sound. This gives children the opportunity to practise thinking about the sequence of sounds in words and how they might be represented. Invented spelling involves children spelling words phonetically; that is, they represent the sounds that they hear, using letters that can represent those sounds. They may spell 'dog' as 'dg' or 'monster' as 'montr', but the process is valuable because it encourages them to think about sounds in words and how they can be represented.

This type of phonics teaching starts with the sound, not with the letter, and for many children may be the best way to learn phonics. Moats (1998) has stated:

> One of the most fundamental flaws found in almost all phonics programs, including traditional ones, is that they teach the code backwards. That is, they go from letter to sound instead of from sound to letter … The print-to-sound (conventional phonics) approach leaves gaps, invites confusion, and creates inefficiencies (pp. 44–5).

Hybrid approaches

There are some commercial phonics programs available that are, in fact, hybrids or combinations of the above approaches. Also, in practice, teachers modify phonics teaching approaches to suit their own teaching contexts.

WHAT DO CHILDREN NEED TO KNOW ABOUT GRAPHOPHONIC RELATIONSHIPS?

The Rose Report (2006), which reported on an independent review on the teaching of early reading in the UK, stated that children need the following skills and understandings in the area of phonics, which is best taught in a clearly defined and incremental sequence. His recommendations concur with those of Torgeson.

- Children need to learn the skill of blending (synthesising) phonemes in the order in which they occur, all through a word, in order to read it (the synthetic approach).
- Children need to be able to apply the skills of segmenting words into their constituent phonemes in order to spell.
- Children need to understand that blending and segmenting are reversible processes.

There are other understandings, not mentioned in the Rose Report, that are also important. The fact that a letter can make several different sounds needs to be understood. For example, the letter 'g' can make a /g/ or a /j/ sound. It is also important for children to realise that there are several different ways to spell the same sound. When they first begin to spell, they will often choose a **grapheme** (letter or group of letters that represent a phoneme) that is feasible but not correct (conventional). For example, they might spell

Table 10.4: Common graphemes (consonant sounds)

Consonant Sounds	Common letter combinations (graphemes)				
/b/	b (sob)	bb (rabbit)			
/c/	c (cat)	k (kitten)	ck (rock)	ch (echo)	qu (queen)
/d/	d (dog)	dd (baddy)			
/f/	f (frog)	ff (fluffy)	gh (rough)	ph (phone)	
/g/	g (gold)	gg (foggy)	gh (ghost)	ge (page)	
/h/	h (hat)	wh (whole)			
/dʒ/ /j/	j (jam)	g (giraffe)	dge (fudge)		
/l/	l (log)	ll (dolly)			
/m/	m (mug)	mm (tummy)	mb (lamb)		
/n/	n (nest)	nn (funny)	kn (knife)	gn (gnome)	
/p/	p (pup)	pp (happy)			
/ŋ/ /ng/	ng (ring)				
/r/	r (ring)	rr (sorry)	wr (wrong)		
/s/	s (sun)	ss (miss)	c (circus)	se (nurse)	ce (mice)
/ʒ/ /zh/	s (treasure)				
/t/	t (tub)	tt (cotton)	ght (light)	ed (skipped)	
/v/	v (vase)	vv (savvy)	ve (believe)		
/w/	w (wet)	wh (white)	u (quill)		
/x/	x (fox)	cks (rocks)			
/y/	y (yellow)				
/z/	z (zip)	zz (dizzy)	s (raser)	se (cheese)	ze (breeze)
/tʃ/ /ch/	ch (chicken)	tch (itch)			
/ʃ/ /sh/	sh (ship)	ti (station)	ch (chef)		
/ð/ /th/	th (then)	th (leather)			
/θ/ /th/	th (thin)				

'bread' as 'bred' and 'giraffe' as 'jraff'. Because there are so many ways to represent a phoneme in the English language, it can take some time for children to learn the conventional way to spell particular words. Sadly, some children never fully come to grips with conventional spellings.

Table 10.5: Common graphemes (vowel sounds)

Vowel sounds	Possible letter combinations (graphemes)			
/ă/	a (bat)			
/eɪ/ /ā/	a (baby)	a-e (cake)	ai (nail)	ay (bay)
/eə/	are (mare)	air (hair)		
/ɑː/	ar (bar)	a (banana)		
/ĕ/	e (leg)	ea (head)		
/iː/ /ē/	e (he)	ea (teacher)	ee (bee)	ey (donkey)	y (lolly)
Diphthong /ɪə/	ear (dear)	eer (deer)		
Schwa /ə/	er (diver)	ar (collar)	or (doctor)	ure (treasure)	a (cobra)
/ɜː/	er	ir (bird)	or (worm)	ur (turn)
/ĭ/	i (lip)			
/aɪ/ /ī/	i–e (wife)	igh (tight)	y (fry)	
/ɒ/ /ŏ/	o (dog)	a (wasp)		
/əʊ/ /ō/	o (host)	oa (float)	o-e (pole)	ow (crow)
Diphthong /ɔɪ/	oi (join)	oy (boy)		
/ʊ/	oo (cook)	u (full)		
/uː/	oo (moon)	ew (chew)	ue (glue)	
/ɔː/	or (fork)	a (wall)	au (sauce)	aw (jaw)	oor (floor)
Diphthong /aʊ/	ow (owl)	ou (mouse)		
/ŭ/	u (bus)	o (love)		
/ū/	u-e (tube)			

Tables 10.4 and 10.5 show how some phonemes of the English language can be represented. You will see that some sounds, such as /n/, have more spelling variations than others. Note that the tables are not exhaustive. Not all of the common letter combinations will be encountered in early childhood contexts.

POSSIBLE SEQUENCES OF PHONICS TEACHING

New teachers can feel quite overwhelmed at the thought of teaching young children about letters and sounds and often don't quite know where to start. Children will often be most interested in the letters in their own name and the sounds that they make, and these graphophonic connections can be taught incidentally in the context of reading and writing. It is also useful to point out salient graphophonic features when engaging in shared reading. Here, much depends on what the particular text lends itself to. For example, when reading *Mrs Wishy Washy*, the letter 'w' and the /w/ sound might be pointed out. Other words starting with the /w/ sound might then be collected and written on a classroom chart. Children might also do some art and writing activities that include the use of the letter 'w'.

Table 10.6: Most common sounds of letters

Continuous sounds	As in	Stop sounds	
/a/	cat	/b/	bat
/e/	leg	/c/	cot
/f/	fin	/d/	dog
/i/	sit	/g/	get
/l/	log	/h/	hat
/m/	man	/j/	jet
/n/	net	/k/	kip
/o/	job	/p/	pet
/r/	rat	/q/	quit
/s/	sun	/t/	tap
/u/	nut	/x/	fox
/v/	vet		
/w/	wet		
/y/	yes		
/z/	zoo		

Source: based on Carnine et al. (1997, p. 56)

However, for systematic, explicit phonics instruction, researchers and teachers have proposed possible sequences for introducing letter–sound relationships. This does not mean that discussion of letters and their sounds cannot still happen in contexts such as shared writing and reading—it is important that this happens *as well as* systematic teaching. Below, we outline some suggestions from the literature about how phonics teaching might be sequenced.

Carnine and colleagues (1997, p. 71) have suggested four simple guidelines for sequencing:

- Introduce only the most common sound for a letter, at least initially. So, for the letter C the hard /k/ sound as in *cat* would be introduced before the soft /s/ sound. [See Table 10.7.]
- Letters that might be confused by children, that are visually or auditorily similar, should be taught at separate times.
- Introduce more useful (high frequency) letters before less useful letters.
- Introduce lower case letters before introducing upper case letters because lower case letters are more easily distinguishable from each other.

Carnine et al. have suggested that the sequence for introducing letter combinations should be informed by the frequency of the particular letter combinations in children's texts. They have suggested the illustrated order (see Tables 10.6 and 10.7), although they acknowledge that other orders may work just as well.

Table 10.7: Suggested order for introducing letter combinations

1 th	6 qu	11 oo	16 ay	21 kn	26 au
2 er	7 ol	12 ee	17 igh	22 oi	27 aw
3 ing	8 oa	13 ai	18 ou	23 oy	
4 sh	9 ar	14 ch	19 ir	24 ph	
5 wh	10 ea	15 or	20 ur	25 wr	

Source: Carnine et al. (1997, p. 163)

LETTERS AND SOUNDS ORDER

The letters s, a, t, i, p and n have been identified as good places to start, since they appear in many *phonetic* words (DfES, 2007). (A phonetic word is a word with regular spelling. It is spelt the way it sounds. The words 'cat', 'snip', 'slipper', 'basket' and 'grim' are examples of phonetic words.) See Table 10.8.

LETTERS AND SOUNDS PHASES

The UK Primary National Strategy resource, *Letters and sounds*, has developed a phonological awareness and phonics teaching program for young children that comprises six phases (Department for Education and Skills (DfES), 2007). This is a useful guide to help teachers decide how to sequence phonics teaching.

Table 10.8: Letters and sounds order

1	s	a	t	i	p	n		Phase 2
2	c	k	e	h	r	m	d	
3	g	o	u	l	f	b		
4	ai	j	oa	ie	ee	or		Phase 3+
5	z	w	ng	v	oo	oo		
6	y	x	ch	sh	th	th		
7	qu	ou	oi	ue	er	ar		

LETTERS AND SOUNDS PHASES

- *Phase One* is a foundational phase in which children learn phonological awareness skills such as oral blending and segmenting words. This is preceded by general listening activities, based on recognising environmental and musical sounds.
- *Phase Two* (approximately six weeks' duration) involves learning nineteen letters of the alphabet and one sound for each. Children also learn to blend and segment sounds. (See Table 10.8.)
- *Phase Three* (up to twelve weeks) involves learning the letters of the alphabet not covered in Phase Two, and consolidating those from Phase Two. Blending and segmenting sounds represented by single sounds and graphemes of more than one letter is taught. (See Table 10.8.)
- *Phase Four* (four to six weeks) involves blending and segmenting words with adjacent consonants and consolidating grapheme–phoneme correspondences already introduced.
- *Phase Five* (throughout Year 1) builds on the phonemes and graphemes introduced in Phases Two and Three and is implemented throughout the first year of school. This includes the introduction of more graphemes to represent phonemes already taught and the blending and segmenting of sounds represented by all grapheme–phoneme correspondence taught so far.
- *Phase Six* (throughout Year 2 and beyond) involves word specific spellings of same sounds (e.g. sea/see) and increasingly fluent sounding and blending of words encountered in reading for the first time, alongside spelling of words with prefixes and suffixes.

Source: *Letters and sounds* (DfES, 2007)

PRINCIPLES OF PHONICS TEACHING

Major reports, as we have seen, recommend that phonics should be taught explicitly and discretely (that is, not embedded) as a major approach to teaching early reading. The Rose Report (2006) recommends that high-quality phonic work is most effective when it is part of a broad curriculum that employs a range of multi-sensory activities to develop children's oral language and phonological awareness skills, and that for *most* children it is appropriate to begin this teaching at approximately five years of age.

In the early years of school (from Year 1 or, for children who are ready, prior to this), phonics should be taught every day in at a brisk, snappy pace, and should be reinforced as appropriate across the curriculum, through such activities as shared and guided reading. Careful assessment and monitoring of children's learning is also a key element of effective teaching in this area.

It should be pointed out that, although the Rose Report is based on a synthesis of research findings, it is not without its critics. As in most areas of educational research and practice, there is no consensus on how early reading should be taught.

STRATEGIES AND GAMES FOR TEACHING PHONICS

WORD FAMILY POSTERS

A word family is a series of words with a common rime, such as 'same', 'came', 'dame', 'lame', 'shame' and 'blame'. Making word family posters with input from the children is an engaging and beneficial activity and helps children learn phonics by analogy. For this activity, several word cards that use one or two different phonograms are needed; for example, hat, fat, bat, sat, that; jet, pet, set, get, net; pig, wig, dig, big, fig.

- Show the children the word cards one by one—discuss the meaning of the words and invite the children to make some observations about the spellings. Ask them if they recognise any of the phonograms. Attach the word cards to the board or easel randomly.
- Draw children's attention to the phonograms or rimes that have been pre-written on a poster and read them out (or ask a child what they say).
- Now invite children to look for a card on the board and stick it in the correct column, according to the phonogram. If they put the word into the incorrect channel, ask them to check the letters again. Support as necessary.

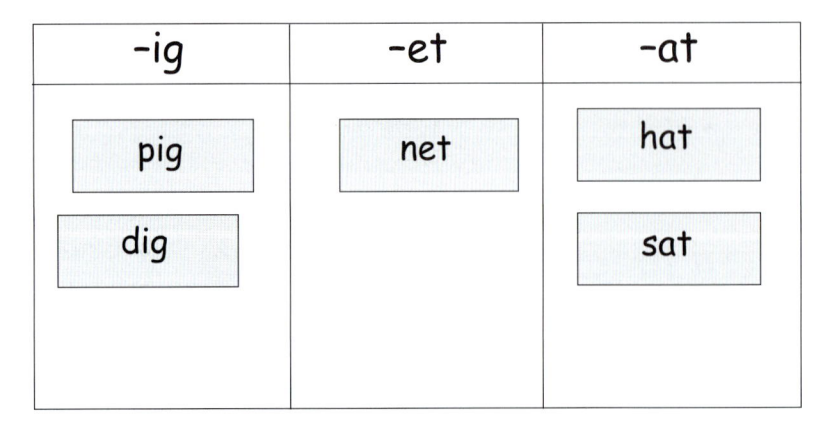

-ig	-et	-at
pig	net	hat
dig		sat

Word family sort

- Once all of the words have been sorted into categories, children work in groups to make their own phonogram posters. Each group has a different phonogram. They write the words using coloured markers and illustrate the words by drawing or sticking on pictures from magazines.

WORD FAMILY SORTS

Children can engage in word sorts to categorise words according to their word families. They must study the phonograms in words and decide which column or pile each word should go into. There are several worthwhile interactive online games that entail sorting words into families, such as the *Read Write Think Word Family Sort* at www.readwritethink.org.

WORD SLIDES

Word slides constitute two pieces of card, the first of which has a fixed onset or rime written on it as well as a window cut into it, and the second of which has several onsets or rimes written on it. The second card is slid along behind the first to make new words. The illustration below shows a word slide with the fixed onset 'sh'. When the second piece of card is slid along behind the window, the words 'shop', 'shin' and 'shell' can be made. It would also be useful to include rimes that cannot make a word with the given onset, as children benefit from discussing whether or not they have made a real word.

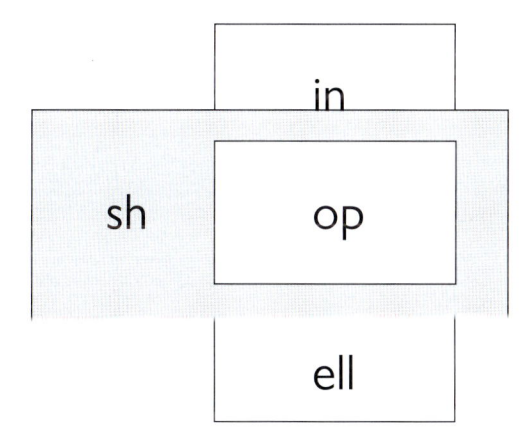

Word slide

ONSET-RIME WORD SPINNERS

In this game, pairs or small groups of children spin two spinners to make words using an onset and rime. One spinner has onsets and the other spinner has rimes. The spinners are made using stiff card. Push a pencil through the centre.

- Each group of children has an onset spinner and a rime spinner.
- Children take turns to spin the two spinners and decide if it makes a word. For example, it may land on '**s**' and '**et**'. This makes the word 'set' so the children would write this down. All words with the '**et**' rime should go in the same column, and so on.

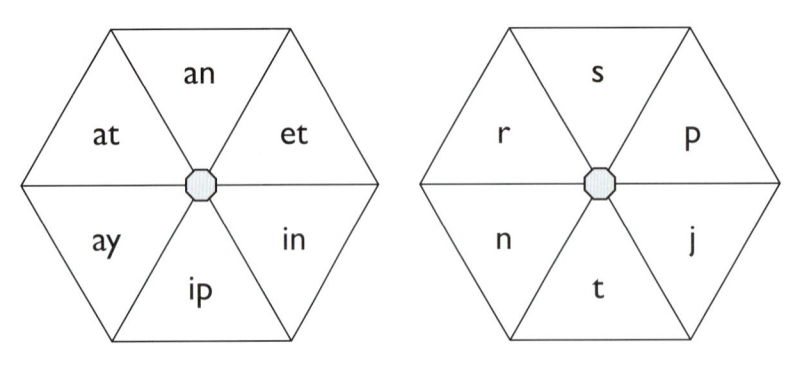

Word spinners

WORKING WITH LETTERS AND SOUNDS

WORD SORTS

In word sorts that focus on phonics, children are given a stack of words on index cards or the like. They are asked to examine the words to find or identify letter–sound correspondences, then sort the cards into piles or boxes according to a particular graphophonic feature.

Closed word sorts

In closed word sorts, the teacher provides some guidance by nominating the graphophonic feature that children must look for when sorting. For example, she might ask the child to put words where the vowel digraph 'ea' says the short vowel sound /e/ (ĕ) as in 'bread' in one pile and the long vowel sound 'ē' as in 'easy' in another.

Word sorts can be done on the computer. Illustrated below is a word sort in which the child must sort words with 'gh' in them into two categories; words where the 'gh' is silent and words where it is not silent. The teacher has made the word cards electronically and the children must drag and drop them into the correct side of the screen.

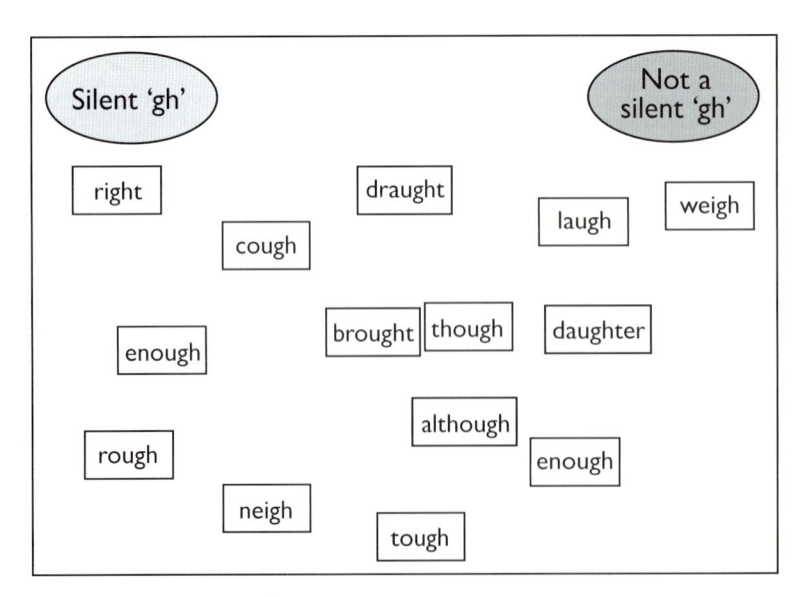

Word-sorting activity

Open word sorts

Open word sorts allow children to choose their own criteria for sorting the cards. This involves the children actively identifying patterns in the stack of words that they have. This is suitable for children who have mastered closed word sorts.

MODELLED WRITING

During modelled writing, which will be explained in greater detail in the chapters on how to teach writing, the teacher writes on the board or on a large piece of paper and thinks aloud as he or she does so, demonstrating to the children how to make decisions about writing. As part of this, the teacher can and should talk about spellings and graphophonic connections.

SHARED READING

Even when a systematic, explicit phonics program is in place, it is still necessary to point out and discuss letter–sound correspondences in the context of real texts, and shared reading is an excellent means of doing this. Words encountered in shared reading can be extracted from the text for use in word sorts and other phonics activities.

MAKING WORDS

This activity involves children making words from letters. The letters may be in the form of letter cards, plastic letters, magnetic letters or simply letters written on wooden tiles. Word making can also be done on the computer with electronic letter cards. As they make words from the letters they have been given, children think about and practise their knowledge about letter–sound relationships and word families. This encourages a problem-solving approach which can assist them to build theories about letter–sound relationships. It is also highly engaging (Cunningham & Cunningham, 2002).

Often, the letters given to the children spell a long word, which may be a compound word such as 'suitcase' or 'chopstick'. The children rearrange the letters to make words, which they then write on a list. Usually, they start by making small words and then make longer words. They should also try to find the big word (for example, 'chopstick'). After they have made the words, they should sort them into letter patterns or word families.

The teacher can provide guidance in word-making activities by asking the children to make specific words. With

Making words

the letters from the word 'chopstick', for example, she could start by saying: 'Make the word *top*. Now take the letter *t* away and put another letter in its place. What word does that make now? Can we make any other '*op*' words from the letters we have?'

Next, the teacher could direct children to experiment with the 'ick' phonogram: 'Make the word *pick*. Now take the letter *p* away try putting the letter *s* at the front. What word does it make? Take away the letter *s* and try another letter at the front. Does it make a word?'

Once children get the idea that they can make new words by simply exchanging one or two letters, they quickly make related words from the letters they have. Through word-making activities, they are encouraged to look at patterns in words.

WORKING WITH MULTI-SYLLABIC WORDS

Many children who appear to excel in the first year or so at school begin to flounder when texts become more complex and words with multiple syllables become more prevalent. An important approach to helping children decode multi-syllabic words is to help them find the phonograms within them. For example, the word 'stacking' contains the '**ack**' phonogram. You will have noticed that it also contains the '**ing**' suffix. Teaching affixes (suffixes and prefixes) alongside continued emphasis on phonograms can greatly assist children in decoding multi-syllabic words.

DECODING WORDS STRATEGICALLY

The use of processes and strategies is an important element of becoming independent learners. It is the effective choosing, using and evaluation of strategy use that allows children to really 'take off' in reading.

To help children learn about and apply decoding strategies, teachers need to model their use during reading and writing, using *think-alouds* to explain what they are doing and thinking. For example, a teacher might say, 'Mmm, I can see the **uck** phonogram in this word. It looks a little bit like the word *duck*, which we all know from the book we read last week. There's a consonant blend before the uck phonogram. I'm going to sound it out … /s/-/t/. I can figure the word out now … /s/-/t/-/uck/. Stuck. And that makes sense because I can see in the picture that the tractor's stuck in the mud.'

The teacher can also model how to use resources, such as classroom charts and personal word books. Again, this can be done in the context of shared reading or writing: 'I'm not sure what this says (fright), but I think that phonogram might be on our classroom chart. Ah, I can see the phonogram there … and it's next to the picture of a light. It must be **ight**. I can put /f/-/r/ in front of it to figure the word out … /f/-/r/-/ight/. It's fright!'

You will see that in the example of a think-aloud, above, the teacher uses quite technical language about letters and sounds, such as 'consonant blends' and 'phonograms'. Giving children the language to talk about (and think about) language is very important. Language about language is called *metalanguage*.

After modelling, there should be a good deal of guided and independent practice. Without this, it will be difficult for children to understand and remember what has been demonstrated.

ASSESSMENT OF PHONICS KNOWLEDGE

Children's knowledge of graphophonic relationships can be assessed by several different means, and much depends on the sequence and way in which it has been taught; assessment of graphophonic knowledge must be in alignment with phonics teaching. According to many educators and curriculum bodies (for example, DfES, 2007 and Tompkins, 2007), children should ideally have been taught all major phonics concepts by approximately the end of Year 2 and should normally be able to demonstrate the skills outlined in Table 10.9 between the ages of approximately four and eight.

The Hearing and Recording Sounds in Words Test (Dictation Test) from the Observation Survey (Clay, 2002) is a standardised test that requires children to write down sentences

Table 10.9: Criteria for assessing knowledge about graphophonic relationships

What the child can do When assessing what children know in this area, the teacher should bear in mind the sequence of their phonics teaching, which may not exactly align with the order of skills shown below.	Examples
Can match the four most frequently used consonant sounds (in the English language) to single letters	e.g. /s/, /p/, /t/, /n/
Knows (can recognise and say) the two most common short-vowel sounds and match them to single letters	/ă/ as in cat, /ĭ/ as in wig
Can match less frequently used consonant sounds to single letters	e.g. /c/, /k/, /h/, /r/, /m/, /d/, /g/, /l/, /f/, /b/
Knows (can recognise and say) slightly less frequent short-vowel sounds and match them to single letters	/ĕ/ as in egg, /ŏ/ as in rot, /ŭ/ as in cut
Can read and spell consonant-vowel-consonant (CVC) words (including non-words)	dad, ten, sat, hip, put, zog
Can recognise and blend consonant sounds (at the beginning and at the end of words)	/pl/ as in play, /str/ as in string, /mp/ as in camp
Can segment CVC and CVCC words into onsets and rimes Can change onsets and rimes to make new words (word family knowledge)	c-at, c-amp, st-amp, sp-ill, c-at can be made into m-at
Knows long-vowel sounds and can match them to common digraphs that represent long vowel sounds	/ā/ as in brain, /ē/ as in feet, /ō/ as in boat, /oo/ as in moon
Can read and spell CVCe words	game, ride, slide, bone, lame
Knows consonant digraphs and can match sounds to letters and read and spell words that contain consonant digraphs	/th/ as in then, ch/ as in chip, /sh/ as in shop and wish, /th/ as in thing and bath, /wh/ as in when, why, what, /ng/ as in thing
Knows that W and Y are usually consonants at the beginning of words/syllables and vowels at the end of words. Can identify the sounds made by these letters	window, yesterday by, baby

What the child can do *When assessing what children know in this area, the teacher should bear in mind the sequence of their phonics teaching, which may not exactly align with the order of skills shown below.*	Examples
Can segment CVCe and other long-vowel words into onsets and rimes Can change onsets and rimes to make new words (word family knowledge)	ch-ase, sl-eep, fl-y, m-ole, b-each b-each can be changed to r-each or t-each
Knows that the letters C and G can make hard and soft sounds. Can read and write words containing these consonants	/g/ as in girl, /g/ as in giraffe /c/ as in cat, /c/ as in circle
Knows vowel sounds of less common vowel digraphs and can read and write words that contain these vowel digraphs	/ô/ as in walk, caught, saw, bought, /ā/ as in weigh, /ē/ as in key, chief /ī/as in pie, eye /ŏo/ as in would, could, should, /ū/ as in stew, blew, fruit
Knows vowel diphthongs and can read and write words using them	/oi/ as in boil, boy, /ui/ as in quit
Knows the sounds made by the less frequently occurring consonant digraphs and how to read and write words containing these digraphs	/ph/ as in phonics, graph /gh/ as in laugh, /ng/ as in sing, hang /tch/ as in switch, match
Can identify r-controlled vowel patterns and read and write words containing this vowel pattern	/âr/—hair, bear, bare, their, there /ar/—star /er/—here, fear, deer /or/—worn, store /û/—first, bird, burn, work
Can read and write words that contain more unusual consonant patterns	/g/—girl, ghost /j/—jet, gem, rage, lodge /k/—cat, kettle, sock /s/—sun. circus, goose /z/—zoo, rise, logs /q/—queen

Sources: Carnine et al, 1997; DfES, 2007; Tompkins (2007)

dictated by the teacher. The teacher then analyses the children's attempts in order to find out which phonemes they have represented in a feasible way. This test can give good diagnostic information about children's beginning knowledge about letter–sound relationships and it also assesses aspects of phonological awareness (segmenting words into sounds).

Teachers can informally assess children's phonics knowledge through listening to them read (and analysing their errors or miscues) and through analysing their spelling. Observation of children as they engage in *word sort* activities can also be highly informative.

In addition, there are many published phonics assessments, both informal and formal. Commercial phonics programs, such as *Jolly Phonics* (www.jollylearning.co.uk) often include assessment instruments. However, some of these schemes and packages have limitations and need to be evaluated carefully before being adopted as part of a teacher's reading program.

Some phonics assessments involve asking the child to read a series of 'nonsense' words, or *non-words*, such as 'zet' or 'zill'. McKenna and Stahl (2003) have created a test called 'The Z Test', which is a non-word test composed of words beginning with the letter 'z'. Non-word tests ensure that children cannot read words as visual wholes (as memorised 'sight words'), but that they use phonics knowledge to decode them. This type of assessment has been criticised, however, as being meaningless to children.

TEACHING SIGHT WORDS

Most words should eventually become 'sight words'. That is, the reader should be able to recognise them instantly without having to consciously decode them. Having a large sight-word vocabulary is important because it frees up cognitive space and enables higher-level comprehension processes to occur. A word becomes a sight word when a child has seen it and worked with it several times. For some children, a word needs to be seen only a few times before it enters their sight word store. For others, though, it takes much longer. Engaging in a good deal of reading and writing will help children learn sight words and for some children this will result in a large sight-word store. For many others, teachers need to provide explicit teaching and a range of activities that require children to study, analyse and use the words.

WHICH WORDS NEED TO BE TAUGHT AS SIGHT WORDS?

As indicated in the previous chapter, it is important that high-frequency words, or words that occur most frequently in the English language, become sight words, since this will increase children's ability to read and write fluently. Also, words that are difficult to decode should be taught as sight words, especially if they are high-frequency words.

STRATEGIES FOR TEACHING SIGHT WORDS

SENTENCE STRIPS

Children write a sentence from language experience or other activities that they have engaged in onto a strip of paper. To do this, they will often need some support. Once the sentence has been written the child cuts it into individual words and then reassembles the sentence correctly.

WORD SHAPES

For some children, the shape of words helps them recognise them quickly. This applies for words written in lower case because upper case words are not easy to distinguish from one another on the basis of shape. For example, the word 'happy' has quite a distinctive shape in lower case

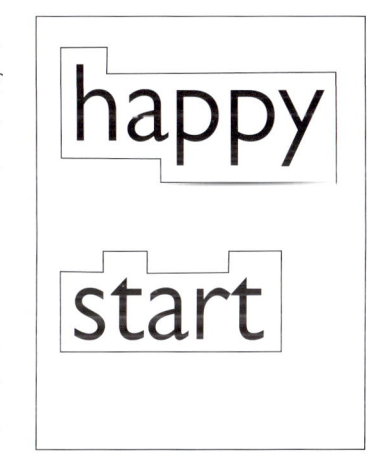

Word shapes

because it has three descenders and one ascender. Drawing 'frames' around words can assist children in noticing and remembering the shape of a word.

TRACING ACTIVITIES

For some young children, the use of multiple senses can assist in learning sight words and spellings. Children who find learning difficult can benefit from tracing activities, which involve writing words in or with a variety of materials, such as writing with the finger in shaving cream or in sand trays, or making words with play dough or modelling clay. While tracing out the word, the child should say the word out loud. Tracing activities are time consuming and are only useful in cases where a child is having difficulties.

WORD SORTS

Word sorts, which have been mentioned above as a means of teaching phonics, can also be an excellent means of assisting children in building their sight-word store. Here, children categorise or sort words in various ways, such as by final sound, number of syllables or meaning, or whether or not they contain a certain sound or a particular letter pattern. As Bear and his colleagues (Bear, Invernessi, Templeton & Johnston, 2004) have noted, word sorts can help significantly in the learning of sight words, as well as phonics, spelling and vocabulary.

WORD WALLS

Word walls can be used in a variety of ways in the early childhood classroom. Often, they are alphabetised collections of words that the teacher and children build up through their reading and writing activities. Having these words on display on the wall can assist children in their reading and writing, although it is necessary for the teacher to model how to use word walls effectively. Children will not always use such resources without being reminded.

DOMINOES

Word dominoes can be used to help children learn sight words. Each domino has two words to be learnt written on it, one at each end. The game dominoes is then played in the normal way, with children matching words in order to proceed. In pre-school contexts, the dominoes can have words as well as pictures on them.

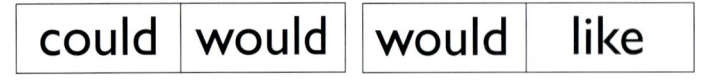

| could | would | would | like |

Word dominoes

BINGO (WORDO)

Each child is given a bingo card, which will show several words to be learnt. Of course, each card needs to be slightly different so that only one child (or possibly two) can win. To save time, give children blank bingo cards that have one or two 'free spaces'. Write all of the words

WORD BINGO		
which	many	could
make		down
like	two	said

Word bingo

on the board and ask children to *randomly* copy words onto their cards. The teacher or a child calls out words from the list one at a time and children search their card for the word, covering it with a counter or laminated square if they have it. The winner is the first to get a row of words in either direction or diagonally. The illustration below has only nine squares and has the square in the centre as the free space, but another option is to have a 5 x 5 card, and the free space does not have to be in the centre.

MATCHING GAMES

Each word to be learnt is written onto two cards. Between ten and fifteen words (20–30 cards) will be needed for each game, which is usually played in pairs. Pairs of cards are placed upside down on the floor or on a table and then shuffled around. Children take turns to turn over two cards. If the cards match, they keep them. If not, they put them back (upside down) and the partner takes a turn.

EXTENSIVE READING

It has been known for many years that if children do not read a lot, they do not get 'good' (Allington, 1977). Children's learning of sight words can be enhanced by shared reading, especially of texts that are predictable, since seeing and hearing the teacher repeatedly read a word can help children memorise words. For example, *Have you seen my cat?* by Eric Carle (1973) repeats the word 'cat' many times. Repeated reading of the same text is also an effective means of helping children learn sight words. For children who can read independently, regular independent reading can also assist in the expansion of their sight word vocabulary. Writing can also help children consolidate their sight-word knowledge.

ASSESSMENT OF SIGHT WORDS

Teachers can usually gain a rough idea of how their young students are progressing in terms of sight-word knowledge through listening to their oral reading; children with a good bank of sight words generally read quicker and with more fluency than those who don't. Another 'authentic' way to monitor sight-word knowledge is to keep an eye on students' word banks. A word bank is a physical store of words that a child is learning or knows by sight. The words are generally written on cards. Words that are deemed to be 'sight words' of the child should be moved to a 'My Sight Words' or 'Words I Know' compartment of the word bank. To be counted as a sight word, a word needs to be recognised instantly on at least three separate occasions.

Asking children to read words in isolation from word lists such as the Fry Instant Word list (Fry, Polk & Fountoukidis, 2000) and the Dolsch lists is another means of assessing sight-words. These are lists of high-frequency words, or words that are used the most frequently in the English language, and can easily be accessed on the internet by keying in 'Dolsch words' or 'Fry's instant words'. Most informal reading inventories also include graded word lists, which can help teachers make a judgment about children's sight-word attainment.

If a formal assessment is deemed to be necessary, the OSELA (Clay, 2002) includes high-frequency word lists, as does the DIBELS (Good, Kaminski, Smith, Laimon & Dill, 2001) and many other published assessments.

The practice of having children read lists of words in isolation has been criticised as being a relatively meaningless task for children, since it may not be the kind of reading task normally carried out in the classroom. Furthermore, children cannot use all cueing systems when reading words in isolation.

SUMMARY

In this chapter we have discussed some important issues in the teaching of phonological awareness, phonics and sight words, and have described some ways of teaching these skills. There are many other teaching strategies and games to assist in the teaching of these areas, but it is beyond the scope of this book to describe them all. Follow up the many excellent references we have cited to further your knowledge.

QUESTIONS AND ACTIVITIES

1. What is the relationship between phonological awareness and phonics?
2. How can phonological awareness help children learn to spell?
3. How can early childhood teachers weave phonological awareness teaching into everyday routines?
4. Return to Table 9.1 in Chapter 9 and think about how phonological awareness, phonics and sight-word teaching and learning fit into each phase of development.

KEY TERMS

grapheme
phoneme
phonics
phonogram
synthetic phonics
word family

KEY REFERENCES

Bear, D., Invernessi, M., Templeton, S. & Johnston, F. (2004). *Word their way: Word study for phonics, vocabulary and spelling instruction*. New Jersey: Pearson, Merrill Prentice Hall.

Cunningham, P. M. & Cunningham, J. (2002). What we know about how to teach phonics. In A. E. Farstrup & S. J. Samuels (eds), *What research has to say about reading instruction* (pp. 87–109). Newark: DE: International Reading Association.

Fox, B. J. (2008). *Word identification strategies* (4th edn). Upper Saddle River, New Jersey: Pearson.

Gill, S. R. (2006). Teaching rimes with shared reading. *The Reading Teacher, 60*(2), 191–3.

Hiebert, E. H., Pearson, P. D., Taylor, B. M., Richardson, V. & Paris, S. G. (1998). *Every child a reader*. Michigan: CIERA.

Johnston, R. S. & Watson, J. E. (2005). A seven year study of the effects of synthetic phonics teaching on reading and spelling attainment. *Insight, 17*, 1–9.

Lane, H. B., Pullen, P. C., Eisele, M. R. & Jordan, L. (2002). Preventing reading failure: phonological awareness and instruction. *Preventing School Failure, 46*(3), 101–10.

Munro, J. (1998). *Assessing and teaching phonological knowledge*. Camberwell: ACER.

National Institute of Child Health and Human Development (2000). *Report of the National Reading Panel. Teaching children to read: An evidence-based assessment of the scientific research literature on reading and its implications for reading instruction* (No. 00-4769). Washington, DC: Government Printing Office.

Rohl, M. (2000). Learning about words, sounds and letters. In M. Rohl & C. Barratt-Pugh (eds), *Literacy learning in the early years*. Crows Nest, NSW: Allen & Unwin.

Yopp, H. K. & Yopp, R. H. (2009). Phonological awareness is child's play. *Young Children, 61*(1), 12–21.

CHAPTER 11

Strategies for Teaching Reading

CHAPTER OBJECTIVES

This chapter will increase your understanding of:

- key procedures for teaching reading in early childhood contexts
- how to link theoretical positions with key reading procedures
- the gradual release of responsibility and how it applies to reading instruction.

In this chapter, you will build on the understandings you have gained in the previous two chapters. We describe some common teaching strategies for reading, and you will see these practices being used in many classrooms. As a teacher, you will learn how to use teacher judgment in order to modify strategies to make them more suitable for particular teaching contexts. For example, most can be modified for use with slightly older or younger children or for use with children for whom English is a second language. When you are working with children who have reading difficulties it will also be necessary to modify strategies and materials.

INTRODUCTION

There are several key teaching and learning strategies, approaches or procedures which can be utilised to help children learn to read texts. It should be noted here that there is sometimes confusion about the word 'strategies'. On some occasions this term is used to refer to teaching and learning procedures that teachers put into place to help children learn, and this is what we mean by the term 'strategies' in this chapter. Children also use reading 'strategies', which are ways of thinking and behaving to help them read texts.

In some of these strategies, most of the reading responsibility lies with the teacher as she or he models to the children how and why reading is done. Modelling entails demonstrating to children how to read, and usually includes a degree of thinking aloud about how to make reading decisions while reading a text. Thinking aloud should enable, as far as possible, children to see inside a proficient reader's head as they read so that internal cognitive processes can be observed.

Over time, the teacher gradually releases responsibility to the children, through guiding them through texts ('guided practice') and then, finally, encouraging independent reading. This model of teaching is based on the notion of 'scaffolding' (Bruner, 1990) and is known as the **gradual release of responsibility**.

This model is utilised in good teaching across the curriculum, not only in the teaching of literacy, and is illustrated in Figure 11.1.

Figure 11.1: Gradual release of responsibility from the teacher to the child

READING ALOUD TO CHILDREN

Reading aloud to children is a form of *modelled reading*, since the educator is demonstrating how to read to the children and providing a high degree of support. The children listen and are able to concentrate on enjoying and comprehending the story without the burden of trying to decode words. This type of reading does not generally involve children attending to print, although the teacher or caregiver may show the book cover and illustrations and ask children to make predictions about the story.

Texts selected to be read aloud are usually too difficult for the children to read on their own and, quite often, too difficult for them to read in **guided reading** contexts. However, the texts should be at children's listening comprehension level and be of interest to them. Their listening comprehension can be greatly enhanced through listening to teachers reading aloud, since they gain exposure to new vocabulary, concepts, sentence structures and text types.

> ### READING TO INFANTS (0–18 MONTHS)
>
> - Newborn babies will enjoy the sound of a calm yet expressive voice. They particularly tune in to the primary caregiver's voice.
> - Physical contact (cuddling, tickling) is an important part of reading to young infants.
> - Ensure that you are in a quiet and comfortable place when you read to infants.
> - Don't be afraid to use expressive voices and silly sounds while reading to capture attention and maintain interest.
> - Keep reading sessions brief for younger infants. It doesn't matter if you don't finish the book.
> - Make sure that the older infant can see the pictures so that you can point to, label and talk about illustrations.
> - Allow the infant to respond by pointing and naming objects (even those who cannot articulate clear words can respond in this way).
> - Encourage the infant to touch the book. Babies also enjoy exploring physical objects with their mouths and books are no exception. Cloth books and board books that can be washed or wiped are best.
> - Where possible, allow the child to turn the pages themselves.
> - If the child can talk, ask them simple questions such as:
>   - What is this?
>   - What is happening?
>   - Who is this?
>   - What happens next?
>
> Sources: Makin & Whitehead (2004); Whitehead (2007)

Children's comprehension or *thinking* processes can be enhanced through caregivers and teachers reading aloud to them, as they can encourage children to make connections between what is in the book and what they already know. Consult the chapter on reading comprehension for more information about making connections (text-to-self, text-to-text and text-to-world). When reading aloud to children, teachers can also encourage other comprehension processes such as inferring, summarising and asking questions of the text.

Reading aloud to children is also beneficial to children in learning about reading fluency, as they hear the teacher read fluently and with expression. Without access to models of fluent reading, children are not able to learn to read fluently or to assess their own reading in terms of fluency.

The research shows many benefits of read-alouds, but research evidence about how best to implement read-alouds is scarce. However, teachers identified as excellent at read-alouds do tend to have some common practices, such as setting a purpose for the reading, selecting books that are highly interesting to the children, becoming familiar with the book before starting to read it aloud to children, reading in an animated and fluent fashion, making connections to children's independent reading and also to their writing, as well as encouraging discussion about the book before, during and after reading (Fisher, Flood, Lapp & Frey, 2004).

An important element of real-alouds is the **expressive engagement** of children. According to Sipe (2002), the *responses* of young children to stories assist and reflect their comprehension.

> ### READING TO TODDLERS (18–36 MONTHS)
>
> - Toddlers love rhythm, rhyme, alliteration and stories with repetitions. They enjoy familiar themes in stories and simple storylines.
> - Non-fiction books with pictures of objects that toddlers can point to and attempt to name are appropriate.
> - Toddlers enjoy books that will stimulate multiple senses, such as 'feely' books or books with mirrors or parts that make noises.
> - Make book reading interactive—encourage toddlers to ask questions and make comments about the book as you go along. Talk about the books and relate them to the toddler's experiences.
> - Point out and name some of the letters and numerals in books (to older toddlers).
> - Books selected should be clear with a strong storyline and have pictures or illustrations that support the storyline.
> - Toddlers enjoy hearing stories repeatedly and have favourite books. Be prepared to read favourites many times.
> - Two- and three-year-olds can participate by pointing at pictures and naming them, making the noises of animals or machines in the story, acting out some of the scenes or repeating some of the dialogue. They can also engage in simple conversations about the story.
>
> Sources: Makin & Whitehead (2004); Machado (2010)

Sipe has suggested a typology of expressive engagement, which includes dramatisation, talking back, critiquing or controlling, inserting and, finally, taking over (see box below). Teachers should actively encourage such responses from young children, although this needs to be done in an orderly way so that behaviour management problems do not arise.

Read-alouds are an important component of a balanced literacy program and should not be seen as something that only very young children need; they are beneficial throughout the pre-school and school years, although it can be increasingly difficult to select texts that are of interest to every child in the group.

> ### EXPRESSIVE ENGAGEMENT
>
> - *Dramatisation:* children often spontaneously dramatise parts of texts. For example, if there's a wolf in the story they may bare their teeth. During the telling of the story they will often use facial expressions and gestures that reflect a dramatisation of the story, and after the story they may enact the story with the whole body. For example, after hearing *Jack and the beanstalk* they may stomp around like a giant.
> - *Talking back:* 'talking back' is a type of engagement that involves children talking to the characters in the book. For example, they might yell out to Red Riding Hood, 'Look out, there's a wolf hiding behind the tree!' or, 'Don't listen to him—he's trying to trick you!'

- *Critiquing/controlling:* this type of expressive engagement involves children commenting about what they would do if they had some control over the plot, characters or setting of the story. For example, using *Little Red Riding Hood* again, a child might say, 'I would make Red Riding Hood do some kung fu on that wolf!' or 'I would give the Grandma a fierce husband … he would chase the wolf away.'
- *Inserting:* this is an interesting type of expressive engagement in which children insert themselves or people they know into the story. For example, they might say to a friend, 'You are the mummy bear and I'm Goldilocks because I've got gold hair.' This can indicate that children are making connections between their own lives and the text.
- *Taking over:* this involves children going beyond the text and, in fact, using it as a basis for creating a completely different story. This occurs when children feel empowered enough to take a story and twist it, play with it or subvert it, and involves a high degree of creativity.

Source: Sipe (2002)

LANGUAGE EXPERIENCE APPROACH

The Language Experience Approach (LEA) (Stauffer, 1970) has already been briefly mentioned in Chapter 7 with reference to the teaching of speaking and listening. This strategy is also highly useful for teaching children about reading and writing and is often used in pre-school and Year 1 contexts. (Reading and writing are closely interrelated and have only been separated in this book for the sake of clarity.)

Children learn much about reading and writing from this experience, not least some concepts of print, such as the fact that print can be written down, and is written from top to bottom and left to right. Children also learn that letters represent sounds and that words have spaces between them. Because the scribed text should use the child's own words and syntax, the theory is that it should be a meaningful text to read back, using language and syntax that the child understands. After the teacher has scribed the text, the child is asked to read it. It is beneficial for the teacher to ask the child to repeatedly read the text over a few days. The text should be available for the child and peers to revisit throughout the term, thus ensuring revision and consolidation of learning.

SHARED READING

This strategy was originally introduced by New Zealander Don Holdaway (1979) and is sometimes referred to as Shared Book Experience (SBE). There are variations of **shared reading** but all involve the teacher reading aloud while children follow along and join in where possible.

The rationale behind shared reading is that, since young children love to sit on parents' laps and listen to stories being read aloud, it should be possible for teachers to read aloud to several children at once through the use of enlarged or big books, thus extending the benefits of 'lap reading' beyond the home. The idea is to mimic the way in which parents read to their children—with warmth, intimacy, enthusiasm and gestures. The use of big books also enables teachers to point at words as they go along, using a special pointer, and in the process helping children learn concepts about print such as directionality, one-to-one correspondence between spoken and written words, and some simple punctuation like full stops, commas and speech marks. Also, shared reading helps children develop listening comprehension, learn some sight words through repeated exposure, and also learn some letter–sound correspondences, either through problem-solving approaches or a degree of explicit teaching.

Because shared reading is a holistic approach, starting with a whole text and, only once the story is told and understood, moving to sounds and letters, it has become associated with the *whole language* philosophy, which has been explained and discussed in Chapter 9. Butler (1987, p. 11) writes: 'Using the Shared Book Experience approach, children can begin reading books from the very first day at school. They do not need to know any "phonics" to begin. They *do* need to know the sound–symbol system of written language eventually, but they can learn this *while* learning to read and write.' Of course, this view about how phonics is best learnt is now contested.

THE HOUSE THAT JACK BUILT: AN EXAMPLE OF A CUMULATIVE STORY

This is the house that Jack built.
This is the malt,
that lay in the house that Jack built.
This is the rat,
that ate the malt
that lay in the house that Jack built.
This is the cat,
that killed the rat,
that ate the malt
that lay in the house that Jack built.
This is the dog,
that worried the cat,
that killed the rat,
that ate the malt
that lay in the house that Jack built.
This is the cow with the crumpled horn,
that tossed the dog,
that worried the cat,
that killed the rat,
that ate the malt
that lay in the house that Jack built.

Shared reading constitutes a high degree of teacher support and modelling and therefore sits at the left-hand side of the gradual release of responsibility (GRR) model that is illustrated above. The child has relatively little control and would not normally be able to read the book independently because of its difficulty level. Through the shared reading context, a *community of readers* (Tompkins, 2009) can be built, which can assist children to see themselves as readers and develop a love of reading, as well as a capacity to share and discuss texts with peers.

SELECTING BOOKS FOR SHARED READING

Books selected for shared reading should contain *repetitive* structures and *predictable* parts so that children can begin to join in as the teacher reads aloud. Books with rhymes and refrains are ideal. Joy Cowley's *Mrs Wishy Washy* (1980) is an example of an excellent book for shared reading that has been popular for many years because of its humour, its relevance and its appropriate language for young children. It includes repetition, and children are able to predict upcoming words, particularly by using syntactic and picture cues. For example, when reading the lines below, children are easily able to provide the names of the animals because of the illustrations. Children are often able to provide the verbs (for example, 'rolled') due to the clear illustrations and the syntactic pattern.

> 'Oh, lovely mud!' said the cow. And she jumped in it.
>
> 'Oh lovely mud', said the pig. And he rolled in it.
>
> 'Oh lovely mud', said the duck. And she paddled in it.

Brown bear, brown bear, what do you see?, written by Bill Martin Jr and illustrated by Eric Carle (1984), also has a repetitive structure that makes the book highly appropriate to read in the early years. The classic tale *The little red hen* is another story with a high degree of predictability. Teachers can also produce their own big books, often with the help of the children in shared writing contexts.

Other books that are appropriate for shared reading are those with a *cumulative* structure. Such texts repeat phrases and sentences and extend them or build on them as the story progresses. A well-known cumulative text is the classic tale, *The house that Jack built*. Another is *There was an old lady who swallowed a fly*.

Texts that feature *rhythm* and *rhyme* are appropriate for shared reading because they are pleasant to listen to and because the rhyming can help children predict words.

Rhythm can also help children predict the number of syllables that might be in unknown words, thus assisting prediction and decoding.

ELEMENTS OF SHARED READING

Holdaway (1979, p. 71) suggests that the stages of discovery, exploration and independent experience and expression should make up the shared reading sequence. These stages are described below. There are other articulations of how shared reading should proceed, and some of these will be discussed briefly after Holdaway's model has been outlined.

Discovery

In the discovery stage, children discover the book through listening to the educator read it aloud, attempting to read along as the teacher points to the words, joining in where possible, and making meaning. They will have been asked to make predictions about the book before the reading, and the teacher will often stimulate predictions by showing the children the cover and reading the title beforehand. She will often do a *picture walk* of the illustrations in the whole book. A picture walk involves the educator browsing through the pictures in the text, making comments and asking the children questions about them. She does this to inspire the children's curiosity and imagination as well as to help them predict the story and the vocabulary. She can use the picture walk to explain and discuss new concepts and vocabulary that will arise during the story.

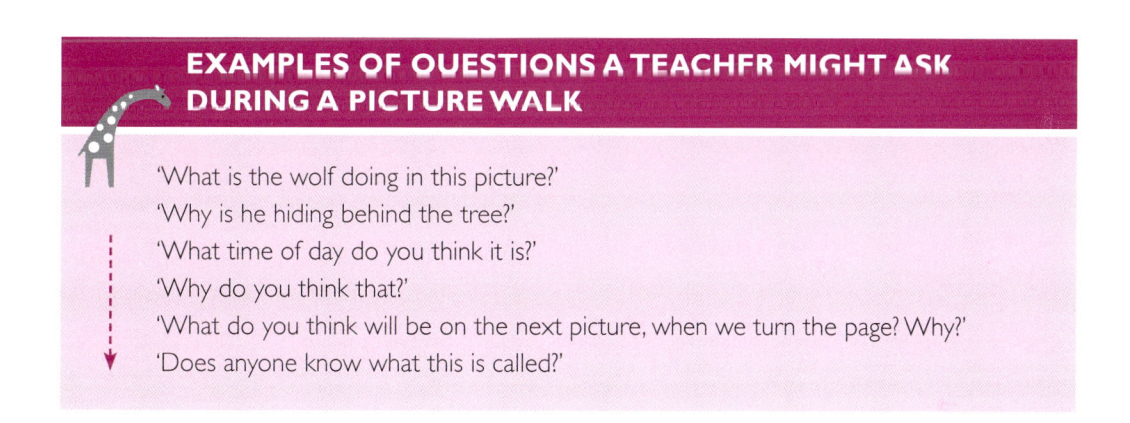

> **EXAMPLES OF QUESTIONS A TEACHER MIGHT ASK DURING A PICTURE WALK**
>
> 'What is the wolf doing in this picture?'
> 'Why is he hiding behind the tree?'
> 'What time of day do you think it is?'
> 'Why do you think that?'
> 'What do you think will be on the next picture, when we turn the page? Why?'
> 'Does anyone know what this is called?'

Enjoyment of the text is paramount in the discovery stage and should be one of the educator's main aims. During the discovery stage, children's interest in the book is gained, and they are encouraged to 'chime in' when they are able—for example, when there are repetitions and refrains in the book, or when they are able to predict or read the words. Because they are able to join in when they feel able and comfortable, there is little pressure on children to perform. Shared reading provides a relaxed environment in which children can 'have a go' at reading.

Holdaway (1979, p. 72) states that *word solving* should be encouraged by encouraging children to make suggestions about letter–sound relationships and by discussing them. This should be done, according to Holdaway, 'at an appropriate skill level and without unduly interrupting the story'. This type of phonics instruction is known as *analytic phonics*, which largely relies on children analysing words and figuring out letter–sound correspondences for themselves. Analytic phonics contrasts with *synthetic phonics*, which begins with teaching children letter–sound relationships and then encourages children to build words from these. Phonics and how to teach it was discussed in depth in Chapter 10.

The discovery stage also involves reader response and reflection. Children are invited to respond to the text after the teacher has read it through, perhaps by providing a comment about their favourite part, by responding to the story as a whole, or by speaking about their own experiences and how these might relate to the story.

Exploration

The next stage of shared reading advised by Holdaway is exploration, which involves rereading of the text. This is often done the day after the initial reading and on subsequent days throughout the week. During rereading, children are increasingly able to participate, since they are getting to know the text and learning how to read the words therein. Repeated readings of texts have been shown to assist children in becoming fluent readers (Samuels, 1979).

Through rereading, children are able to become more familiar with syntactic structures used in the book, to build up sight words through repeated exposure to them, and to further explore how letters and sounds relate to each other. Teachers are able to use rereading to point out or teach concepts about and conventions of print, such as page turning, directionality, spaces, the fact that pictures support the text and that the print usually carries most of the meaning, the fact that print is constant and the story does *not* change from reading to reading (as oral stories sometimes do), the role of punctuation, and so on (Butler, 1987). During this stage of reading, teachers are able to demonstrate or model strategic reading such and making predictions and using the text to confirm or reject them, skipping unknown words to see if the context of the sentence will provide syntactic or semantic cues to enable the word to be predicted, and rereading portions of the text to confirm or clarify meaning.

Also during this stage, teachers can use masking devices to hide certain parts of the text from the children and draw their attention to words and letters under focus. A sliding mask can be used. Sticky post-its are also an option for covering up parts of the text that the teacher wishes to reveal at a later point in the shared reading process.

The rereadings intrinsic to shared reading provide opportunities for children who have some difficulty to learn concepts about print, conventions and reading strategies. However, more recent research has shown that these 'at risk' children also need systematic, explicit teaching (National Institute of Child Health and Human Development, 2000). They often do not learn enough through the problem-solving, holistic approach of shared reading alone.

Independent experience and expression

This, final, stage of Shared Book Experience can involve a range of activities that engage children in responding to and expressing their understanding of and feelings about the story. The expressive arts, including visual arts, drama and music, can be used to facilitate this. For example, after reading *Mrs Wishy Washy*, children might dramatise the book, with one child (or the teacher) taking on the role of Mrs Wishy Washy and others taking on the roles of the farm animals. Other activities suggested by Holdaway include painting and drawing, mural making, mask making, puppetry, mime and writing (possibly with the teacher as scribe). During this stage, children may also have the opportunity to revisit the book independently. This may be through the use of little books and/or audio recordings of the book at listening posts. A range of other activities, including dress-ups and role plays, word recognition games, art activities and others appropriate to the age group, can be set up in literacy centres or stations around the classroom.

Other authors since Holdaway have suggested how shared reading might proceed. Tompkins (2009) has suggested that five generic stages of the reading process, which are applicable to several different reading strategies or procedures, can be used. These stages are: pre-reading, reading, responding, exploring and applying. There are many teaching and learning activities that can be carried out in each of these stages. An example of Tompkins's five stages being used with reference to *Baabooom* (Waddell & Wojtowycz, 2000) is given below in Table 11.1.

Pre-reading

Here, the purpose for reading is set, predictions about the story are made, and connections are made to prior knowledge, to other texts that have been read and to the children's personal experiences and feelings. The teacher may do a 'picture walk' to help children use the pictures to help them make predictions and connections.

Table 11.1: Plan: Shared reading of *Baabooom!* by Waddell and Wojtowycz (2000)

Sample sequence of activities Year 1 (Term 1) (experimental and early readers)		
Day	**Stage**	**Activity**
Monday	Pre reading	Sing an animal song such as 'Old MacDonald' and talk about animals that might be found on a farm
		Talk about blowing up balloons. The teacher blows up a balloon until it is very large (but not too large). Talk about small, medium, large or large, larger and largest (integration with maths)
		Prediction about the text using the front cover and the title
		'What is the bull doing with the balloon? What are the other animals on the cover doing? What sort of expressions do they have on their faces … are they happy or worried? What clues does the title give us? Does the word 'baabooom' sound like any words you know?'
	Reading	Teacher reads the story aloud using pointer/actions. Quick discussion of story and its meaning, then reread
	Responding	Exploratory and early readers: teacher reads statements aloud and children help decide if they are true or false. Sort into two groups on whiteboard
		Examples of statements:
		Clucky-Cluck found a balloon (T)
		Big Cousin Bull ran away (F)
		Clucky-Cluck wanted her balloon to grow bigger (F)
		Cousin Bull was polite to everybody (F)
Tuesday	Reading	The teacher rereads the story using pointer, and children participate by joining in repetitive parts: 'The balloon grew and GREW until …'
		Early readers: children work in pairs or groups of three to sort statements into true/false
	Responding	Discussion about bullying (cross-curricular links)

Sample sequence of activities		
Year 1 (Term 1) (experimental and early readers)		
Day	Stage	Activity
Wednesday	Reading	Teacher reads the story again. Children participate by reading aloud.
	Exploring	Exploratory readers: Listen for initial sounds: /b/ and /k/. Do children know any words with /b/ or /k/ at the end? Listen to story again for rhyming words Segment selected words into phonemes using counters Early readers: discussion of rhymes. Focus on the /OO/ sound in 'grew' and 'blew'. Write some –ew words on the large paper with children's input. /OO/ words not spelt –ew (e.g. 'blue') are written in another column
Thursday	Reading	Reread the story. Choose children or groups of children to read parts of the story (choral reading)
	Applying	Teacher models writing (write in speech bubbles). Choose a picture from the story and consider the question, 'What would Big Cousin Bull be saying?'
Friday	Reading	Reread the story. Children take different parts and read.
	Applying	Small books: independent reading Children write, 'What would Big Cousin Bull be saying?' (Speech bubble activity). Literacy centres: word games, write letters to animals

Reading

Here, the text is actually read. In the context of shared reading, the teacher reads the book aloud with expression. She or he rereads it one or two times end encourages children to join in.

Responding

Children are encouraged to respond to the story during this stage. Responding may be carried out orally, through discussions, or through reading logs and journals. Responses can also be made through the arts.

Exploring

During this stage, children reread the text and explore it or analyse it in some way in order to focus on the meanings and words it contains. They may also examine how the author has crafted the text. Through this exploration, their understandings are deepened and elaborated.

Applying

During the applying stage of the reading process, children are given the opportunity to use the text in some way. They may do this through a combination of writing, drama, music or art projects.

GUIDED READING

This reading strategy, suitable for lower primary, essentially involves selecting a book at the reader's **zone of proximal development** (Vygotsky, 1978) and providing targeted support so that the child can read it, learn from it, and grow as a reader. The 'zone of proximal development' (ZPD) is where a child, with the support of another, can achieve a task that would be too difficult to achieve alone. Children are grouped according to specific reading needs and given texts at an *instructional* level—when a child can read 90–94 per cent of the words accurately—so that the level of challenge is 'just right' (Clay, 1991). With an instructional level text, children can read most but not all without support. Essentially, guided reading enables children to practise using reading strategies that they already know; the teacher helps them apply this knowledge to new reading contexts, rather than teaching them new strategies (Hornsby, 2000). Groupings change according to the focus of the teaching and are thus *dynamic*.

Hornsby (2000, p. 33) lists some reading strategies (see box below) that children can practise in *guided reading* contexts, although these must be taught through modelling and demonstration (modelled and shared reading). Not only should guided reading assist children to *use* reading strategies but they also need to learn how to *choose* appropriate strategies for the reading situation. This can involve a high degree of *metacognitive awareness*, or knowledge about one's own thinking and reading processes.

Guided reading has become increasingly popular in recent years, with authors such as Fountas and Pinnell (1996a) writing comprehensive texts on the subject and conducting a good deal of work to help teachers 'level' children's books. Much research has been carried out on guided reading, although some of this should be viewed with caution since guided reading is conceptualised and implemented in many different ways, some of which may be more effective than others, depending on the context.

SUGGESTED PROCEDURE FOR GUIDED READING

A suggested procedure for guided reading has been provided by the Victorian Department of Education (1998), although many variations of this can be found in the literature. The procedure below can and should be varied according to the circumstances.

SELECT AN APPROPRIATE TEXT

The teacher should first select a text that is appropriate to the group of children's needs. Texts used for guided reading need to be well written, interesting to the child and at an instructional reading level. They should be short enough to be read in one session and multiple copies should be available so that children can be taught in small groups (often of about six).

Texts need to be *matched* to the group of children's specific literacy needs, which teachers should have acquired through careful observations, the use of running records and through a range of other assessments. Texts used for guided reading should not have been read by the children before, as this will negate any benefits of this approach, such as learning to predict and using appropriate strategies to decode unknown words and make meaning. Teachers need to carefully read the texts before the teaching session to familiarise themselves with the challenges they may hold and how they may be used to teach the teaching points.

> **READING STRATEGIES FOR CHILDREN TO PRACTISE DURING GUIDED READING SESSIONS**
>
> - using background knowledge
> - using context to make predictions
> - confirming, adjusting and rejecting predictions during reading
> - self-monitoring own reading by asking questions such as, 'Does this make sense?' and, 'Does this sound right?'
> - using graphophonic cues and asking, 'Does it look right?'
> - recognising errors or 'miscues' that disrupt meaning
> - using visual or pictorial cues
> - rereading, looking back and reading ahead when needed
> - rereading text before an unknown word and reading around the unknown word before beginning to decode it using sounding-out strategies (in order to activate all three cueing systems)
> - cross-checking information
> - asking for help when necessary.
>
> Source: Hornsby (2000, p. 33)

TUNING IN TO READING

The tuning in stage of guided reading is about stimulating children's motivation to read and 'activating' the prior knowledge that may help them read the text. Children's related experiences should be discussed. The discussion should, if possible, mirror the tense used in the text, as this will supposedly help children make meaning.

BOOK INTRODUCTION

During the book introduction, teachers should prepare children to successfully read the text. This may involve discussions and demonstrations about specific reading strategies, or may involve using features of the book such as the title, the table of contents or the index. The teacher may conduct a picture walk to help children predict the contents and vocabulary of the text, and may explicitly discuss some of the vocabulary or language features of the text. Teachers can, at this stage, ask children some directing questions so that they will have a purpose and a focus for their reading.

INDEPENDENT READING

During this step of guided reading, children read independently, either silently or in a quiet voice. They do this at their own pace and the teacher is available to provide assistance in the form of prompts, if needed. The teacher also observes the children's reading behaviours during this time. Whether or not the child uses a finger to track reading, reads aloud or silently, rereads parts of the text, and general body language such as facial expressions are observed. It is during this step of guided reading that the teacher takes the opportunity to conduct running records of selected children's reading. Through running records, she can ascertain the suitability of the text in terms of level (it should be at an instructional level), and which cueing systems the child is using. Reading rate (or speed) and the proportion of errors and self-corrections is also calculated. How to conduct running records is dealt with in Chapter 13.

DISCUSSION

After reading, the children and teacher discuss the text and its meaning. They may also discuss strategies they used to read the text and any problems they had during the reading. The teacher may direct the children to reread specific parts of the text in order to consolidate a teaching point. Children are encouraged to provide their responses to the text: their feelings about it, what connections they made with it, and their thoughts about it.

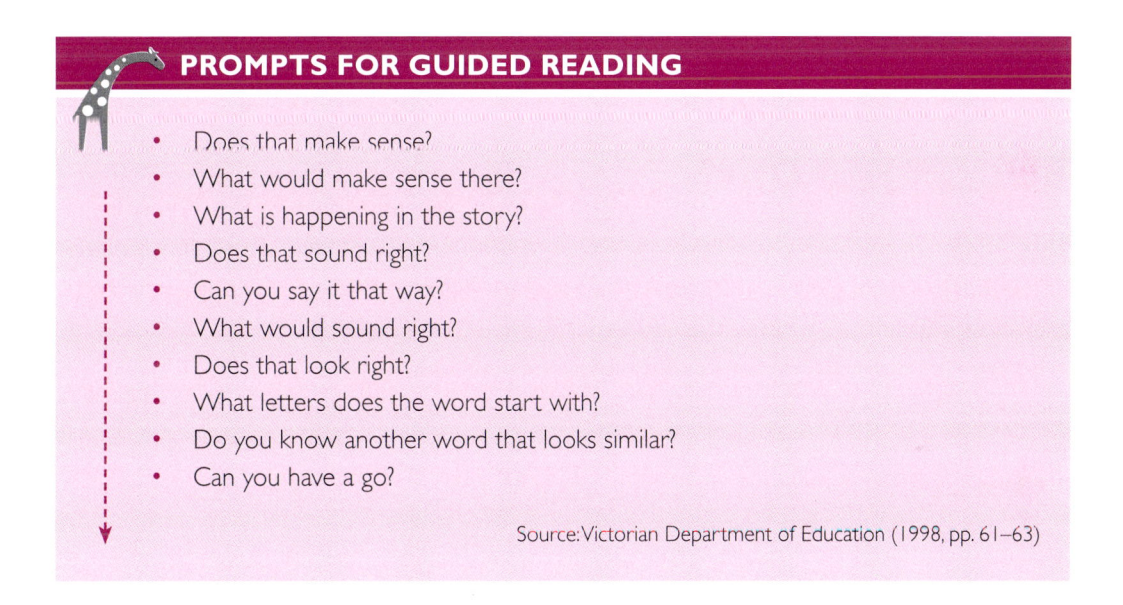

PROMPTS FOR GUIDED READING

- Does that make sense?
- What would make sense there?
- What is happening in the story?
- Does that sound right?
- Can you say it that way?
- What would sound right?
- Does that look right?
- What letters does the word start with?
- Do you know another word that looks similar?
- Can you have a go?

Source: Victorian Department of Education (1998, pp. 61–63)

FOLLOW-UP ACTIVITIES

The teacher provides follow-up activities that require the child to return to the text and explore it at a deeper level or look at it from a different angle. There are numerous activities

Sentence strips

that can fit into this category, such as writing, working with words and sentences, art, music and drama activities. Much depends on what the children's particular needs are.

WHAT DOES THE REST OF THE CLASS DO WHEN THE TEACHER IS WITH A GUIDED READING GROUP?

In order for guided reading to run effectively, it is necessary for teachers to be highly organised. Engaging and useful activities need to be provided for the rest of the children in the class, and these must be such that the children can work independently. A range of *literacy learning centres* or 'kidstations' can be set up for this purpose (Ford & Opitz, 2002; Guastello & Lenz, 2005). These can include listening posts, phonics games and activities, word sorts and writing activities, as well as reading activities such as sequencing tasks, cloze tasks and paired reading. Children can be involved in recreating stories using puppetry, felt boards or Readers' Theatre. Learning centre activities are limited only by the teacher's imagination, and should be highly enjoyable for children. A task board (sometimes known as a work board or chart) needs to be used to schedule children into particular activities.

BUDDY READING

Buddy reading involves two children reading or rereading texts together. One of the readers is usually more advanced than the other and is thus able to provide some support, often by reading aloud and encouraging the less advanced reader to read along either aloud or silently. Meetings usually occur once a week for approximately half an hour.

The two readers collaborate to make sense of the text, and are encouraged to talk about it to deepen and elaborate understanding. Together, they should engage in a problem-solving process to decode unknown words and work out the meanings of new vocabulary. In essence, one of the readers acts as a peer tutor. Peer tutors can benefit through needing to think about reading fluently with expression, the articulation of their reading strategies and responses to the text, and through the process of asking questions about the text (Block & Dellamura, 2001).

The 'tutee' benefits on many counts. First, she or he receives individualised attention from a reader who is more experienced and who can provide a model of good reading. It is important that children realise that children, not just teachers, can become reading experts. Furthermore, reading with a buddy with whom they have built up a relationship can improve children's attitude towards reading. It may also be the case that explanations given by other children, instead of by teachers, are more comprehensible to children as they can 'hear literacy strategies explained in words that are more closely attuned to their own oral vocabularies' (Block & Dellamura, 2001, p. 365).

A potential disadvantage of buddy reading is that the more advanced reader may do the lion's share of the work, reducing opportunities for the weaker reader to gain from the experience. This problem can be avoided, however, if the children are carefully taught how to turn-take and collaborate (Tompkins, 2009). The reading buddy can be improved for both partners if book buddy reflections or journals are kept. This can help teachers monitor what is happening during buddy reading sessions (Block & Dellamura, 2001).

INDEPENDENT READING

Independent reading is highly important because children can become proficient readers only through many hours of practice, which requires a good deal of independent reading. This is carried out in the classroom during independent or silent reading time and, for this to work, children need to feel comfortable and settled enough to focus on their reading. It is a good idea to get them to select their book(s) for independent reading prior to reading time, since many children spend a lot of time choosing their book, leaving little time for actual reading. If independent reading is conducted on a small group (rostered) basis, children can sit in the reading corner or centre on beanbags or cushions. In whole class independent reading it is often easiest to have them sitting at their desks, although this may detract somewhat from the pleasure.

Children should be strongly encouraged to engage in a good deal of independent reading at home. For this to succeed, they need to have access to texts that are at an appropriate (easy) level and about topics that are of interest to them. Parents' cooperation in this is highly desirable, as they can facilitate children's home independent reading by providing a quiet time and space for this to happen. They can also model reading for a variety of purposes, including reading for pleasure. However, not all parents will have the capacity to assist in this way, for a variety of reasons.

It is also common in the early years for children to take graded or levelled readers home to practise their reading skills. Parents listen to their child read the 'home readers' and it is highly advantageous if they are read more than once. Teachers can send special bookmarks home with tips for parents on how to assist their child if he or she 'gets stuck' or makes a mistake. It is also fruitful to hold information sessions at school to inform parents about how they can help their children in literacy learning.

RECIPROCAL TEACHING

Reciprocal teaching is a strategy that helps children learn how to use four important comprehension processes: summarising, questioning, clarifying and predicting. This strategy, devised by Palincsar and Brown (1984), is strongly supported by research findings. Traditionally, this strategy has been used primarily to help children in middle primary and older to read, but has more recently been successfully in young children in (USA) kindergarten (e.g. Meyers, 2006). This strategy was originally developed to teach struggling readers but research shows it to be effective in many contexts. Reciprocal teaching can help children comprehend either fiction or non-fiction texts. Reciprocal teaching is explained fully in the chapter on comprehension.

LITERATURE CIRCLES

Literature circles are a context for sharing texts after they have been read independently so are suitable for lower primary classrooms. Small groups of children who are reading the same book or book section meet to discuss it. This helps them think deeply about the text and enables them to share their thoughts, questions and reflections about it in a context where normal classroom discourse patterns, which may often be teacher led, are cast off (Greene Brabham & Villaume, 2000). Children take responsibility for the discussion and construct the questions to be asked, and should be encouraged, where possible, to select the books to be read. This will help enhance motivation and interest.

Sometimes, each group member has a specific role to play which will help the group look at the book thoroughly. One member may visualise what is happening in the text through providing drawings to bring to the meeting. Another child may bring a short summary of the reading to the circle, while another might bring a list of interesting words from the text. The teacher can set the roles as appropriate to the age and ability of the group, and roles can be given funny names, such as *Wow Words Collector* or *Super Summariser*. Roles should be rotated on a regular basis, if not each time the group meets.

MATCHING TEXTS TO CHILDREN

It is important to match texts to children's reading ability and interests. The reading task will also influence the choice of text. For example, a book being used for guided reading can be more difficult than a book selected for independent reading because, in guided reading, the child will be given a level of support from the teacher, whereas in independent reading this is not the case.

LEVELLED TEXTS

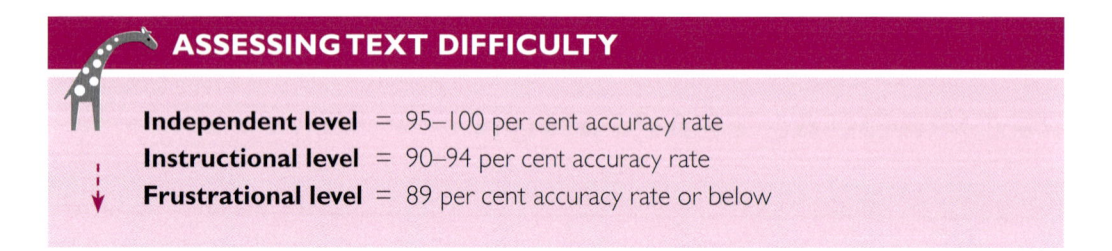

ASSESSING TEXT DIFFICULTY

Independent level = 95–100 per cent accuracy rate
Instructional level = 90–94 per cent accuracy rate
Frustrational level = 89 per cent accuracy rate or below

It has been argued (e.g. Clay, 1991; Fountas & Pinnell, 1996b) that texts need to be finely graded or 'levelled' in terms of their complexity and reading difficulty to assist teachers in providing appropriate texts for children. Without **levelled texts**, it would be difficult for teachers to estimate which texts would be at an *instructional* level for guided reading, for example, or at an independent or easy level for independent reading. Texts at a *frustrational* level for a particular child should only be used in high-support contexts, such as shared reading. Commercial reading schemes are usually levelled, although there is unfortunately no consistent levelling method, so a Level 20 book in one reading scheme will probably not be the same as a Level 20 book from another publisher. Scholastic's guided reading levels are graded from A to Z, as are Fountas and Pinnell's levels. The Reading Recovery levels, originally devised by Dame Marie Clay, range from 1 to 30. Some organisations and individuals have devised 'correlation charts', where attempts have been made to make meaningful comparisons between different levelling schemes. One such correlation chart can be found on the Reading A–Z website at www.readinga-z.com/guided/correlation.html. These correlation charts need to be viewed fairly critically, however, as publishers may not use common criteria for levelling so direct comparisons are not possible.

Children's literature is not levelled at all, so novice teachers can find it difficult to gauge a book's difficulty. However, several groups have attempted to grade children's literature by assigning each book a number called a Lexile (see the Lexile Framework for Learning at www.lexile.com). Lexiles can assist teachers somewhat in deciding on the *readability* and suitability of a children's book.

Readability can be estimated by teachers themselves, and several methods or formulae have been suggested in the literature to facilitate this. However, all of these have limitations. The RIX Readability Formula is a quite simple although fairly crude measure. There is an online RIX calculator at www.standards-schmandards.com/exhibits/rix/. It is generally agreed that the RIX and others like it, which assess readability by measuring average word and sentence lengths, are too crude to assist teachers in levelling texts for children in the early years of reading.

The reliability of the various means of levelling used by publishers has also been questioned (Pitcher & Fang, 2007). Texts are levelled according to criteria such as length and complexity of sentences, sophistication of vocabulary, length of words, whether or not words in the text are considered to be *high frequency* words (words that are used frequently in spoken language and/or written texts) and the degree to which the reader needs to make inferences in order to comprehend the text. Other factors that may be taken into account are the degree of predictability in the text and the usefulness of pictures and visuals in assisting readers to make sense of the text, as well as the subject matter. When using a reading series, it is worth finding out what methods were used by the publisher to level the books; some publishers have detailed information about this on their websites.

Rog and Burton (2002) suggest that, if schools wish to set up their own levelling system, they should use the following five criteria:

- vocabulary (the number of words per page and proportion of high-frequency words)
- size and layout of print
- predictability of text (rhyme or pattern)
- illustration support
- complexity of concepts (familiarity of objects and actions).

Using Rog and Burton's guidelines (refer to their article for more detail), it is possible to set up a levelling system (10 levels) that can incorporate a whole range of early childhood texts.

FINDING OUT ABOUT CHILDREN'S READING INTERESTS

There are several ways of finding out about children's interests, the most obvious ones being to ask them directly and to observe their reading selections. It is often a good idea to speak to parents also.

There are several published 'Interest Inventories' available, which can assist teachers in finding out about their students' interests in reading. However, many of these are not appropriate for children in their early years. Teachers often devise their own inventories to suit their particular contexts and, as already noted, supplementary information can be gathered through observations of children and discussions with their parents. It is worth noting that this information-gathering needs to be ongoing as children's interests change.

> **EXAMPLE INTEREST INVENTORY**
>
> Child's name: _____ Age: _____ Date of interview: _____
> Interviewer's name: _____
>
> 1. What do you like doing at weekends?
> 2. What is your favourite book?
> 3. What is your favourite television program?
> 4. What is your favourite movie?
> 5. Which animals do you like best?
> 6. Which games and sports do you like?
> 7. Who are your best friends?
> 8. Is there anything you don't like?
> 9. What would you like to learn more about?
> 10. Can you tell me about the most exciting thing you've done this week?
>
> Comments and observations:

SUMMARY

In this chapter, a range of popular reading procedures have been discussed. These form the backbone of instruction in reading connected texts. Through these procedures, teachers can help children learn about word level, sentence level and text level features of texts in the context of meaningful reading activities.

It must be remembered that it is necessary to *explicitly* address such areas as letter–sound relationships, the role of punctuation, word meanings, and comprehension strategies. Some of this work can be done in context through the key procedures explained in this chapter, but in some cases the teacher will decide to teach certain concepts out of context through other strategies, described elsewhere in this book.

QUESTIONS AND ACTIVITIES

1. What role do you think shared reading can play in the teaching of letter–sound knowledge?
2. What assumptions about how children learn to read underlie guided reading?
3. What are the benefits and limitations of levelling books for children?
4. How might you set up your classroom to allow for small group teaching, such as guided reading? What might the rest of the class be doing when you are with the reading group?
5. What kinds of reading centres or 'stations' might you set up in your classroom? Think about your last school practicum: What centres did you observe? (for example, reading corner, listening post, matching games and sentence strips activities, and so on). How might reading centres be varied to accommodate the needs of a variety of children?

KEY TERMS

analytical phonics
expressive engagement
gradual release of responsibility
guided reading
levelled texts
shared reading
zone of proximal development

KEY REFERENCES

Ford, M. P. & Opitz, M. F. (2002). Using centers to engage children during guided reading time: Intensifying learning experiences away from the teacher. *The Reading Teacher, 55*(5), 710–17.

Fountas, I. C. & Pinnell, G. S. (1996). *Guided reading: good first teaching for all children.* Portsmouth, NH: Heinemann.

Holdaway, D. (1979). *The foundations of literacy.* Sydney: Ashton Scholastic.

Palincsar, A. S. & Brown, A. L. (1984). Reciprocal teaching of comprehension-fostering and comprehension-monitoring activities. *Cognition and Instruction, 1,* 117–75.

Pitcher, B. & Fang, Z. (2007). Can we trust levelled texts? An examination of their reliability and quality from a linguistic perspective. *Literacy, 41*(1), 43–51.

Rog, L. J. & Burton, W. (2002). Matching texts and readers: Leveling early reading materials for assessment and instruction. *The Reading Teacher, 55*(4), 348–56.

Sipe, L. R. (2002). Talking back and taking over: Young children's expressive engagement during storybook read-alouds. *The Reading Teacher, 55*(5), 476–83.

Tompkins, G. E. (2009). *Language Arts: Patterns of practice* (7th edn). Upper Saddle River: Pearson.

Victorian Department of Education (1998). *Teaching readers in the early years: Keys to Life early literacy program.* Melbourne: Longman.

Vygotsky, L. (1978). *Mind in society: The development of higher psychological processes.* Cambridge: Harvard University Press.

CHAPTER 12

Vocabulary for Reading and Writing

CHAPTER OBJECTIVES

This chapter will increase your understanding of:

- why vocabulary is important to young readers and writers
- the development of vocabulary knowledge
- how to plan for vocabulary teaching in early childhood settings
- assessing vocabulary for reading and writing.

Oral language is the basis of literacy, and knowledge of words and their meanings is particularly important in reading and writing since it facilitates reading comprehension and word identification, as well as the writing of clear, interesting and accurate texts. Teachers and childcare professionals should provide experiences and environments that maximise children's exposure to, and use of, rich vocabulary. As discussed in the first part of this book on oral language development, there needs to be a lot of talk for a variety of purposes and in a variety of contexts. Also, it is necessary to include some explicit, structured teaching of vocabulary in the classroom. The provision of appropriate experiences and vocabulary instruction for a diversity of children needs to be carefully planned, so in this chapter you will be introduced to some key guidelines and strategies, based on theory and research. At the end of the chapter, we have provided some additional vocabulary teaching strategies for you to try (see Toolbox of Vocabulary Strategies). These are mostly suitable for children in their lower primary years.

WHAT DO WE MEAN BY VOCABULARY?

As is so often the case, there is confusion around the definition of vocabulary and what, exactly, it entails. Simply put, a vocabulary can be seen as a collection of words known by a particular person. A person's **receptive vocabulary** is the collection of words that they recognise and understand when listening or reading, while their **expressive vocabulary** is the collection of words that they are capable of using appropriately in speaking and writing. Generally, people have many more words in their receptive vocabulary than in their expressive vocabulary—they understand more words than they actually use themselves. People's expressive and receptive vocabularies constantly grow and change, and words can be superficially known or well established (deeply understood) in a person's vocabulary store or mental lexicon.

A *sight vocabulary*, which is the collection of words that a person recognises on sight when reading ('sight words'), should not be confused with the notion of vocabulary as understanding word meanings, or **meaning vocabulary**, which is what we are dealing with in this chapter. A sight vocabulary is to do with word identification or recognition, not word comprehension. Sight words are discussed in Chapter 10.

WHY IS VOCABULARY IMPORTANT IN READING AND WRITING?

Needless to say, it is difficult for young children to comprehend texts if they encounter too many words they do not know the meaning of. Quite often they will be able to infer (deduce) word meanings from the context of the text, using syntactic and semantic cues, but sometimes inadequate receptive vocabulary will lead to a breakdown in text comprehension, whether the text is read by the child or read aloud by a teacher or caregiver.

For example, if a child has not heard of the word 'magnet' or has heard it but is not sure about its meaning, the following sentence may be difficult to comprehend, even though young children in lower primary school may well be able to decode it: 'The big magnet sucked the toy cars up.'

Having a good receptive vocabulary also facilitates a reader's ability to decode words, as it contributes greatly to the semantic cueing system. For example, a child may be presented with the following sentence: 'The gigantic monster lived at the top of the hill.' Unless the word 'gigantic' is in the child's receptive vocabulary, it is possible that the word will be mispronounced when sounded out, as something like 'gig-an-tic'. However, if the word is in the child's receptive vocabulary, this mispronunciation may still occur initially, but the child may then link it with the known word 'gigantic' and hence be able to correct the mispronunciation, associate the written word with the word meaning, and go on to comprehend the text.

In writing, having a wide vocabulary helps children write interesting and precise texts, no matter what the genre. In narrative writing, children need access to a wide variety of adjectives and verbs in order to describe attributes and actions in their stories. In non-fiction texts, it is essential to be able to use the technical vocabulary associated with the topic of the text. For example, a report about horses might require children to understand and use the word 'mammal', as well as many others such as 'diet', 'behaviour', 'hock', 'crest', 'fetlock', and so on. Also, children need to know words that connect clauses, sentences and paragraphs, such as 'although', 'third', 'sometimes' and 'next'.

In short, vocabulary is important for thinking, learning and communicating, and children who do not acquire a wide vocabulary will likely be less successful in school, as well as in their social and working lives, than children with wider vocabularies. It is crucial for children to build a good vocabulary in the early years as it stands them in good stead for later years. It has been found, in fact, that children who are behind in their vocabulary in Third Grade are not likely to catch up (Beimiller & Slonim, 2001), so excellent early teaching in this area of literacy is absolutely necessary. As in all areas of literacy learning, it is crucial to make sure that children do not fall behind. This can be achieved through the provision of good **first-wave teaching** and early intervention, if required. First-wave teaching is good, explicit, appropriate teaching in the early years. Such teaching can play a part in preventing reading difficulties (Snow, Burns & Griffin, 1998).

HOW DOES VOCABULARY KNOWLEDGE DEVELOP?

The development of vocabulary knowledge is complex and incremental and has to a large extent already been discussed at length in the chapters on oral language development (semantic development). Essentially, vocabulary is learnt through interacting with others, participating in activities with others, reading and listening, and through direct modes of instruction, such as deliberate word study and vocabulary lessons. The vast majority of words are learnt informally and incidentally.

Some children know 5000 words or more by the time they start formal schooling in Year 1, and it is estimated that they learn between 1500 and 8000 a year during their school years (see Brantley, 2007). Many others know considerably fewer than this when they start school, largely as a result of differences in home experiences. Hart and Risely (1999) found that three-year-olds from advantaged homes had oral vocabularies five times larger than those from less advantaged, lower socio-economic homes. Since many words are learnt incidentally, outside of formal schooling, it is extremely difficult for teachers to close this gap. Entering into partnerships with parents can be most fruitful.

Many children from less advantaged homes will not have had a wide variety of books read to them by parents, and will have experienced a different quantity and quality of talk in the home. These children are at a considerable disadvantage from day one of their formal schooling and will need a great deal of intervention from teachers if they are ever to close the gap or catch up.

Other children, upon starting school, will not have many English words in their vocabulary, but will know words (and the associated concepts) from their first language or mother tongue. These children may be at a disadvantage if teachers do not investigate and capitalise on their prior knowledge about language and about the world.

LEVELS OF VOCABULARY KNOWLEDGE

What does it mean to know a vocabulary word? According to Harmon, Hedrick, Soares and Gress (2007, p. 138), 'Knowing a word means not only knowing the meaning, but knowing the contexts in which it is used; it means knowing related words and ideas; it means knowing when and where to use a word.'

It has been suggested that word learning follows two broad phases. First, a general idea of the word meaning is formed. This is often sufficient for getting 'the gist' of spoken and written texts. In the second phase, after multiple exposures to the word in multiple contexts, a word is known at a 'deep' level, and can be used in different contexts and may be defined in several ways. It takes a long time and multiple contacts with a word for the second phase to be attained. However, as noted above, it is not always necessary to know the meaning of a word at a 'deep' level, and in early childhood contexts not very many words will be known at this level.

Nagy and Scott (2000) have suggested finer gradations of word knowledge, which may be more useful to the educator than the two broad phases outlined in the previous paragraph. The following grades of knowledge are suggested:

1. *Unknown word*: the child has never heard the word before or has no recollection of hearing it.
2. *Knowledge that the word exists*: the child has heard the word before and recognises it but doesn't know what it means.
3. *Partial knowledge*: the child has a vague or general understanding of the meaning of the word.
4. *Complete knowledge*: the child has a good enough knowledge to use the word appropriately and comfortably in multiple contexts.

Sometimes, children will have little or no knowledge relating to the *concept* that a particular word labels, whereas they will now and again be aware of the concept but not know the words relating to it. For example, it would be of limited use teaching young children the word 'magnetic' until they have had a chance to play with magnets and explore the concepts. Hence, when teaching vocabulary it is important to build up associated conceptual knowledge through a range of science, mathematics, drama and other activities. It is necessary to build on and relate to known concepts.

Teachers, when planning their vocabulary teaching, need to decide what depth children need to learn a particular word, and in order to make this decision may take the questions below into consideration.

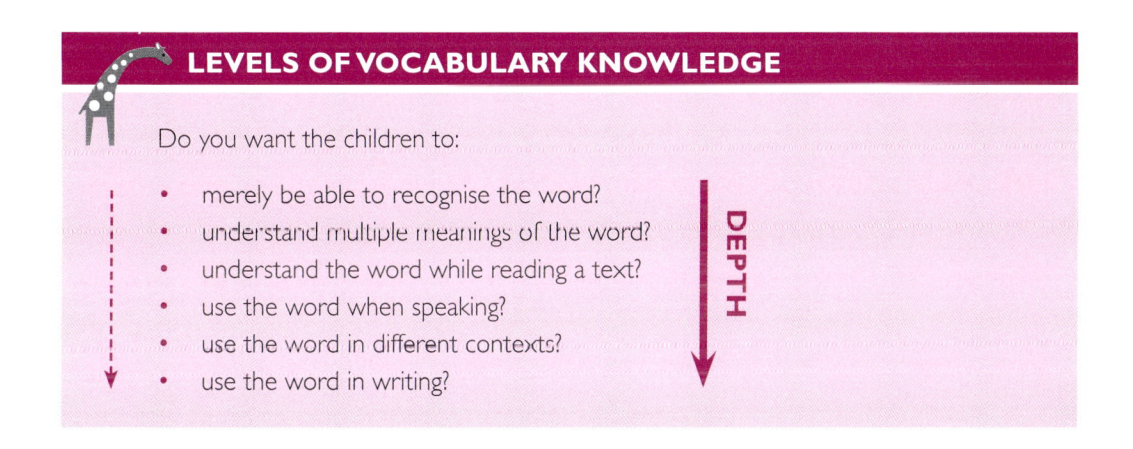

LEVELS OF VOCABULARY KNOWLEDGE

Do you want the children to:

- merely be able to recognise the word?
- understand multiple meanings of the word?
- understand the word while reading a text?
- use the word when speaking?
- use the word in different contexts?
- use the word in writing?

DEPTH

Naturally, teaching approaches will vary according to the depth of knowledge needed. For more depth of knowledge, generally the word should be encountered and used in a wider variety of contexts. Children's metacognitive processes should be developed in order to assist in the learning of vocabulary words in depth. There is a section on metacognition in vocabulary learning below.

HOW CAN VOCABULARY DEVELOPMENT BE FACILITATED IN THE EARLY YEARS?

Relatively little research has been conducted on the instruction of vocabulary in the early years of school, but the evidence available indicates that a 'balance' of explicit and indirect or incidental teaching of vocabulary is necessary (NICHD, 2000).

Three main factors are involved in word learning (Blachowicz, Fisher & Watts-Taffe, 2005):

- characteristics of the learner
- characteristics of the word
- the depth or level of word knowledge required [see previous part].

CHARACTERISTICS OF THE LEARNER

As in any teaching and learning context, the characteristics of the learner are paramount. Caregivers and teachers need to consider a number of important questions, including the following:

- What is the child's home and linguistic background?
- What are the child's prior experiences and understandings?
- What are the child's interests?
- What is the child's learning style?
- Is the child motivated to learn new words?
- Does the child have any literacy learning difficulties?

The educator will find it necessary to gather such information on an ongoing basis, with data coming from multiple sources such as observations, conversations and interviews, and the analysis of work samples (including transcripts of oral texts). More formal types of assessments such as vocabulary inventories and tests may also be useful, although these are certainly no substitute for ongoing classroom assessment.

CHARACTERISTICS OF THE WORD

Whether or not the child knows the concept underlying the word influences the ease with which the word is learnt. For example, most children will have experienced 'exhaustion' and will therefore find this word easier to learn than 'gravity', which is an abstract concept outside their personal experience. Not only will children have personal experiences to hook the word 'exhaustion' onto, but teachers and caregivers will find this word easier to model and explain than 'gravity', as they will be able to relate it to the word 'tiredness' and role-play being exhausted. Furthermore, words grounded in everyday experience are easier to repeatedly use for a range of authentic purposes.

The word may be related to a word already known in that it may have the same root word; this will facilitate learning. For example, the word 'telescope' may be easier to learn if the child already knows 'telephone', especially if it has been explained that the root word 'tele' means 'far'.

Another word factor that may influence ease of learning is word length. Longer words may be harder to remember, unless they can be split into meaningful parts, as in the case of compound words, such as bathroom. Words that have been borrowed from languages such as French may be difficult to learn because of difficult pronunciations. The word 'blancmange' is an example.

Words with multiple meanings can sometimes cause confusion, thus caregivers and teachers need to make sure that children are exposed to words with multiple meanings in multiple contexts, and that the multiple meanings are actually discussed and used by children. Homophones may also cause confusion. These categories of word, and how to teach them, are described later in this chapter.

INDIRECT INSTRUCTION

'Indirect instruction' refers to the vocabulary learning that occurs through other activities within the classroom, and not through focused, explicit vocabulary instruction. The majority of word learning in the classroom will occur through indirect instruction, especially if the environment is rich in language use and is designed to encourage language use in a range of authentic contexts.

STORY BOOK READING

Story book reading as an indirect means of building vocabulary has significant research backing, especially if the target word is more frequently encountered in a particular text. Repeated readings of a text and discussion, especially that initiated by the child, are also helpful in building vocabulary in young children. Children over the age of four are more likely to benefit from story book reading as a means of developing vocabulary than are younger children and this strategy is greatly enhanced if the story books are also used as a context for *discussion*. Simply reading to the children is less effective. Small group contexts are more effective than whole class contexts (Neumann & Dickinson, 2001, cited in Blachowicz et al., 2005).

Repeated exposure to new vocabulary has been shown to increase vocabulary learning. One way of ensuring repeated exposure is through repeated readings, which has been shown to help young children's vocabulary development (Senechal, 1997). The number of repetitions needed seems to vary according to the child, but two to three readings seems to be most appropriate. However, repeated exposure ideally needs to be through different means of exposure. For example, the word might first be encountered in a story, then reread and discussed, then used in a modelled writing session, and then used again during a role play or a content area lesson.

Shared reading is an ideal means of exposing children to rich vocabulary in story books. It entails repeated readings, which is known to be beneficial, and can be used as a springboard for discussion and, if appropriate, a variety of word study activities.

Books are important in vocabulary learning because they use different language from everyday social and instrumental language. Children's literature is a rich source of figurative language and language for a range of different purposes that many children will not encounter in everyday life. For example, in *A sausage went for a walk* by Ellisha Majid and Peter Kendall (2008), the cornflakes 'fluttered' and 'scampered'. Wide reading constitutes indirect instruction and is a major means of building vocabulary. In many cases, children are able to learn new words through inferring meanings from the context of the text. How to infer word meanings from context needs to be modelled by the teacher in modelled reading, and then scaffolded in shared and guided reading contexts.

Picture labelling activities are important, even for the youngest children. Here, an adult and a child sit together and the adult points at pictures and labels them by saying, 'What's this? Oh, I saw one of those at the farm! It's a *tractor*. Do you remember when we went to the farm and saw a *tractor*?', or, 'That's a *zebra*. Look at its lovely black and white *stripes*. One day we'll go to the zoo and you can see a real *zebra*.' It is important to return to these picture books as many times as possible so that the child can be repeatedly exposed to the words. Through books, children can learn names of things they have not personally experienced.

THE HOME CORNER

The 'home corner' (which is known by many different names around the world) is a place where young children can *play with language* and experiment with new words and ways to use them. It is crucial for children to be given opportunities to use words that are already in their receptive vocabulary so that these words can move into their expressive vocabulary also. Home corners can be designed to encourage the use of particular target words. For example, if words associated with health are being targeted, it may be appropriate to have the home corner set up as a hospital. Words such as 'stethoscope', 'temperature', 'recover', 'bandages' and 'medicine' may be practised.

DRAMA AND ROLE PLAY

Drama can be used as a means of allowing children to try out roles and contexts that are usually outside their experience, thus allowing them to try out new words. The teacher, either in role or out of role, can model the use of words that might be used in the context concerned. For example, the child may role-play being a shop assistant and have the opportunity to use words such as 'assist' in sentences such as, 'How can I assist you, sir?' The teacher can extend children's grasp of partially known words through drama, by modelling their use and by prompting children to use them.

INDEPENDENT READING

Once they can read independently, children learn many words through this. For maximum benefit, they need access to a wide range of texts, both fiction and non-fiction, at an appropriate level. They also need to possess a repertoire of vocabulary learning strategies as well as a metacognitive stance towards reading. Vocabulary learning strategies include use of context (clues in the text) and structural analysis (breaking words into morphemes), which are explained in more detail below. Unfortunately, though, many children do not do much voluntary reading, which hampers their vocabulary growth. Teachers and caregivers therefore need to be creative in motivating children to read as much as possible.

EXPLICIT VOCABULARY INSTRUCTION

Explicit instruction is necessary for words that are not likely to be 'picked up' incidentally. However, it is not possible to explicitly teach a great many words in the crowded curriculum that exists in many educational contexts, so teachers need to be extremely selective about which are the best words to teach so as to ensure the best use of time.

DECIDING WHICH WORDS TO TEACH

It can be difficult to decide which words to teach, but some factors to consider include (Blachowicz et al., 2005):

- the importance of the word to the theme or topic(s) that the children are currently working on
- what words the children already know
- whether or not the word will significantly affect the comprehension of a text to be read
- the level of interest the children might have for the word
- the frequency or utility of the word in the English language
- the degree to which the learning of the word will help children learn other words.

Teaching children words that they are not likely to hear or see again or use is not the best use of classroom time. Furthermore, it is counterproductive to explicitly teach vocabulary words if the children are likely to be able to infer the meaning through the use of context, as practice in using context to learn word meanings is very important and should be maximised.

It is often fruitful to engage children in selecting words to be learnt as this ensures interest. When reading stories to young children, teachers and caregivers can ask them to listen out for new or interesting words, which can then be discussed, investigated and written down, either in the children's personal dictionaries or on a word wall. The children can draw pictures to illustrate the new words.

Word lists such as Fry's word lists (Fry et al., 2000) may be useful as they show which words appear most frequently in written English. In Fry's fifth hundred list, for example, words like 'produce', 'surface' and 'material' appear. These words are quite common in written English and children will need to understand their meaning in order to comprehend and write texts. Needless to say, it is important also to teach high-frequency words as sight words and in spelling lessons.

WORD STUDY

When studying words and their meanings, there are several categories of words that should be included, such as compound words, synonyms and antonyms, root words and affixes, and words with multiple meanings. Since it is important that children become metacognitive and strategic in learning vocabulary, it is important that teachers *use terminology* such as 'synonym', 'compound words', 'prefixes', and so on. Without the necessary language and terminology, it is difficult for children to think about and discuss their learning. Furthermore, teacher explanations become easier and more effective when they can make use of relevant terminology. Word study activities are in general most suitable for children in lower primary, although some of the oral activities may be modified to use in pre-school, depending on the abilities of the children concerned.

IDEAS FOR TEACHING ABOUT COMPOUND WORDS

- Have children brainstorm compound words and then talk about the word parts.
- Point out and discuss compound words in shared reading.
- Play games such as compound word bingo.
- Make compound words by joining two small words (e.g. draw lines or put two cards together).
- Have a compound word hunt (look for compound words in texts).
- Use computer games and web resources.

COMPOUND WORDS

Compound words are those that are composed of two smaller words. For example 'plug' + 'hole' = 'plughole' or 'news' + 'paper' = 'newspaper'. The meaning of compound words is usually not too difficult to gain, once children are able to break the word into its parts, although some compound words, such as 'foot' + 'hills' = 'foothills' and 'break' + 'fast' = 'breakfast' may be more difficult to understand because children may not know the meaning of the component parts, such as 'fast' in 'breakfast'.

SYNONYMS

It is important for children to explore synonyms. A synonym is a word with almost the same meaning as another. For example, 'large' might be seen as a synonym of 'big'. However, the meanings are not quite identical. It is important for children to realise that there are shades of meaning, and that the context will influence the choice of words. Words often have connotations that children need to understand. For example, we may associate the word 'pig' with smelly, greedy and unpleasant. Unless they understand the connotations of words, which are often culturally determined, they will often not be able to infer meanings.

Teachers and children can put synonyms into a *sentence frame* and then discuss the slight differences in meaning and whether or not the sentence context is appropriate (Blachowicz et al., 2005).

> The little girl *yelled* at the top of her voice.
>
> The little girl *screamed* at the top of her voice.
>
> The little girl *roared* at the top of her voice.
>
> The little girl *shrieked* at the top of her voice.
>
> The little girl *howled* at the top of her voice.
>
> The little girl *squeaked* at the top of her voice.

By the time children reach Year 3, most should be able to use a children's thesaurus to find synonyms. They can also find synonyms using word processing software such as MS Word.

Synonym webs are useful to help children explore and think about synonyms and their usage. A full description of this strategy can be found in the toolbox of teaching strategies section at the end of this chapter.

Cloze can be used to help children think of synonyms. Simply blank out selected words in a text and ask children to brainstorm as many words as they can think of that would make sense in the blank space. The teacher can then provide the word that was blanked out, which may be a word that is new to the children. However, since they have already engaged in a brainstorm it is likely that they will have generated some synonyms for the target word.

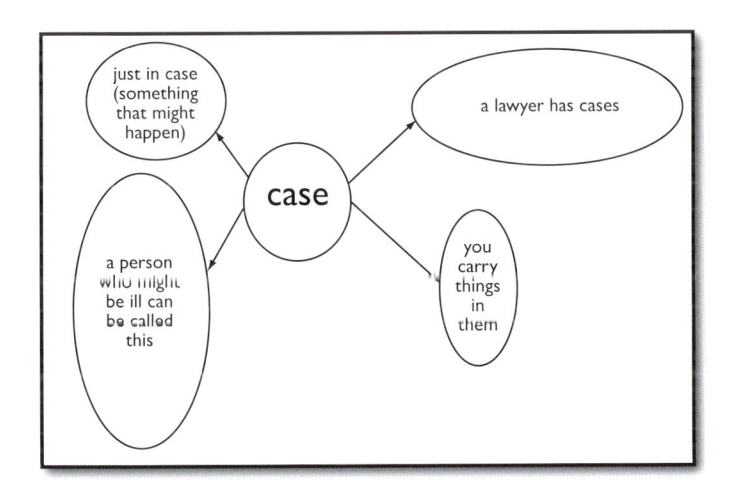

A synonym web

USEFUL WEBSITES FOR TEACHING SYNONYMS

- BBC Schools Bitesize Literacy: www.bbc.co.uk/schools/ks1bitesize/literacy/synonyms/index.shtml (The child needs to be able to read.)
- BBC Schools Magic Key: www.bbc.co.uk/schools/magickey/adventures/code_game.shtml

ANTONYMS

An antonym is a word with an opposite meaning. For example, 'little' is an antonym or opposite of 'large', and 'light' is an antonym of 'dark'. Many words do not have antonyms.

Vocabulary cline

A vocabulary cline is a sequence of words, showing the gradation of meanings between a word and its antonym. For example, the words 'sizzling' and 'freezing' could be used in a vocabulary cline as illustrated.

A vocabulary cline

HOMOPHONES OR HOMONYMS

Homophones (or homonyms) are words that sound the same but have different meanings and spellings. Examples include 'fare' and 'fair', 'dear' and 'deer', 'rain' and 'reign', and 'hole' and 'whole'.

Homophone poster

Children can make charts, drawings or posters of homophones, with pictorial illustrations. It is usually necessary for teachers to draw particular attention to the differences in spelling so that children can clearly distinguish the visual differences between the two words.

TEACHING ABOUT MORPHEMES

Table 12.1: Common root words

Root	Meaning	Origin
aqua	water	Latin
cent	hundred	Latin
pod	foot	Greek
scope	see	Greek
therm	heat	Greek
phon	sound/voice	Greek
port	carry	Latin

Morphemes are the parts of words that bear meaning, namely root or base words, prefixes and suffixes. Using information about morphemes to unlock word meanings is called *structural analysis*. In the early childhood years, analysis of word parts is largely informal, although there is absolutely no reason that most pre-primary and lower primary children should not be able to learn, for example, that the thermometer used by the nurse in the story book is made up of the word parts 'therm', meaning heat and 'meter', meaning measure. Traditionally, discussion of word parts is held off until later (middle primary) but research shows that discussion about meanings of word parts with lower primary children can be highly beneficial (Nunes, Bryant, Pretzlik & Hurry, 2006). Much of this will be incidental discussion.

Root words

English words are derived from various sources, such as Latin, Greek, Norman French and Anglo-Saxon, so it is highly useful to teach children the meanings of root words. Children aged seven or over will particularly benefit from learning about morphemes. Incidental teaching about morphemes and their meanings is effective and appropriate for younger children, although some direct teaching can be used also.

Affixes

Affixes are composed of prefixes and suffixes, and are added to root words to change meaning. There are several high-frequency affixes that are commonly used in texts that young children might encounter. Caregivers and teachers can attempt to describe what these mean, using language that the particular child will understand. However, it is generally not until approximately Year 3 that structural analysis, or the breaking apart of words into morphemes (root words and affixes), becomes a focus.

Table 12.2: Affixes

Prefixes		Suffixes	
un- undone	not	-less sleeveless	lacking
semi- semicircle	half	-ness coolness	condition
sub- submarine	under	-able Lovable	capable of being
multi- multicoloured	many	-ward westward	in the direction of
dis- distressed	not, away, apart	-en shorten	cause to be

FIGURATIVE MEANINGS

Figurative meanings can cause confusion, especially for children who have not had many stories read to them or for children who have English as a second or additional language. A figurative meaning is when a metaphor or a figure of speech is used.

Similes such as 'hard as nails' or 'daft as a brush' fall into this category. Anthony Browne's picture books, *My dad, my mum* (Browne, 2006) and *My brother* are all full of excellent similes and can be used to introduce children to this type of language.

Metaphors include such sentences as 'It was bucketing down' and 'She was frosty'. Understanding metaphors can be particularly difficult for children for whom English is a second language.

Idioms are sayings such as 'a drop in the ocean', 'a piece of cake' and 'all in the same boat', and are very common in the English language. Some idioms and sayings arose many years ago. For example, the idiom 'It's raining cats and dogs' is said to have originated from the grim old days in London, when it was so filthy that heavy rain would wash dead animals along the streets, including cats and dogs.

The *Amelia Bedelia* series of books by Peggy Parrish are hilarious children's books that are full of idioms. The main character, Amelia, gets into constant trouble by taking things literally. For example, when she is asked to draw the curtains she draws them with a pencil.

MULTIPLE MEANINGS

Many words have more than one meaning. For example, the word 'sink' can be a kitchen sink, which is a noun, or it can be a verb as in 'sink a ship'. When children encounter a second meaning for a word they already know, they may be somewhat confused. However, they soon realise that words can have more than one meaning, and it is up to the teacher or caregiver to assist them in learning multiple meanings. Children can draw pictures of the two (or more) different meanings on a word poster.

MAKING CONNECTIONS

Get students to think about where they have heard a word or similar/related words. Getting children to make connections between words increases their word awareness and helps them see relationships between words, their meanings and their origins. It has been suggested that up to 50 per cent of new words encountered by young children are, in fact, related to words already known (Anglin, cited in Graves, Juel & Graves, 2007).

USING DICTIONARIES

Dictionaries are used fairly widely in schools and, while it is important for children to use this important resource, the practice of asking children to refer to dictionary definitions in order to learn new words is not always efficacious. For one thing, many dictionary definitions are hard to understand and do not make sense to young children, even when children's dictionaries are used. Furthermore, children often misinterpret dictionary definitions and use the words incorrectly.

It is necessary to use a variety of methods to enhance vocabulary learning—and the use of dictionaries as a major strategy is not likely to be very useful (NICHD, 2000), especially in younger children.

Having said this, there are useful dictionaries available for young children, such as picture dictionaries and multimedia dictionaries. These can be helpful because they provide visual and other information to help young children understand word meanings. *My first, incredible, amazing dictionary* by Dorling Kindersley is a multimedia dictionary that provides pictorial illustrations, animations and simple definitions that the child can click on to hear a narrator read aloud.

The young learner's picture dictionary is an example of a simple picture dictionary that shows words in categories, such as 'At home'. Such dictionaries can be particularly useful for children who have English as a second or additional language. It may be necessary for teachers and caregivers to point to the pictures and pronounce the written words, depending on the child and the word. There are many picture dictionaries, some specifically for young children, online. Some of them have audio, so that when the picture is clicked the word is pronounced. An example is the Language Guide website at www.languageguide.org/im/fruits/eng/.

Dictionary skills need to be explicitly taught. Children need to learn how to find words in alphabetical order, starting with the first letter, and then moving on to the second letter, and so on. They also need to know what they can do if they can't find the word in the dictionary. Is there another spelling they might try (the Have-A-Go-Pad can help here). Other dictionary skills include thinking about and understanding definitions, and understanding the symbols for pronunciation and parts of speech used in dictionaries. Children in their early years need to begin to acquire a general understanding of these things. One good way of doing this is to assist the children in making and illustrating their own personal dictionaries. Personal digital dictionaries, which include pictures and audio, can be developed by young children using the Clicker 5 (Crick Software) software.

There are several good websites to assist children in learning dictionary skills, including one at BBC for Schools Bitesize, where children play an animated game to match words with their definitions. This website can found at: www.bbc.co.uk/schools/ks2bitesize/english/activities/dictionaries.shtml.

WORD SORTS/CLASSIFICATIONS

Donald Bear and his associates (Bear et al., 2004) have shown how word sorts can facilitate literacy learning at the word level in several ways, and one of these ways is vocabulary learning. Words can be sorted according to meaning (concept sorts). For example, they can be put into different piles according to teacher-specified classifications. For example, a set of words could be classified into 'living' and 'non-living', whether or not they have anything to do with homes and houses, or whether or not they are to do with parts of the body. Words can also be sorted according to whether or not they share a morpheme. There are many possibilities.

Table 12.3: Concept sort

Living	Non-living
Horse	House
Cabbage	Container
Anemone	Shower
Teacher	Computer
Cockatoo	Seashore

USING CONTEXTUAL CLUES

It is important for children to learn to use the context of the text, whether spoken or written, to infer the meanings of unknown words. Blachowicz et al. (2005, p. 18) have pointed out that it is important to begin teaching how to use contextual cues in the early years, moving from the familiar and simple to the unfamiliar and complex. It is suggested that children need to gain the following understandings:

- Some word meanings are explicitly defined in texts but often the surrounding text will contain clues or cues.
- Context cues may be in the form of words, phrases or sentences.
- Context cues may be in another sentence or even another paragraph.
- Context cues may appear before or after the unknown word.
- There may be multiple cues as to the meaning of a word.
- Illustrations can contain clues.
- Some texts are not rich in contextual cues and the reader may need to look elsewhere for word meanings (such as their own prior knowledge).

During modelled reading, teachers should demonstrate how to use contextual cues to work out the meaning of words. This involves the teacher *thinking aloud* about how she or he solves the problem of inferring an unknown word using textual cues, which may be at the sentence or the text level. Children can then be involved in solving such problems within interactive contexts such as shared and guided reading, before they will eventually be able to use contextual cues independently. As with the teaching of any cognitive strategy, the gradual release of responsibility is recommended.

> **RIDDLES**
>
> - What do sea monsters eat? *Fish and ships.*
> - Why was the baby ant confused? *All of its uncles were ants.*
> - What gets wetter the more it dries? *A towel.*
> - Why didn't the skeleton cross the road? *Because he had no guts.*
> - What did the little plate say to the big plate? *Dinner's on me!*
> - What goes up when the rain comes down? *Umbrellas.*

TEACHING WORD CONSCIOUSNESS

Word consciousness can be thought of as being aware of words, interested in them and curious and motivated enough to want learn about them. Word consciousness also involves being metacognitive and using various processes to understand and learn about words. It is important to foster this disposition during the early years as, without it, children are unlikely to be avid word learners. One of the most important things teachers and caregivers can do is to model word consciousness; that is, to show an interest in words and an eagerness to learn about them.

In order to inculcate an interest in words, teachers and caregivers can engage in *word play* as this requires children to think about words and their meanings. Riddles constitute word play, such as puns, and are excellent for stimulating word consciousness. Teachers can have a daily riddle, where she or one of the children presents a riddle. If you examine the riddles in the textbox above, you will notice that, in many cases, they work because of the multiple meanings of some of the words or because they contain homophones or near homophones. There are many books and websites that provide riddles for children. Games such as charades, as well as commercial games such as Pictionary and Scrabble (or Junior Scrabble), also may be used to generate word consciousness.

Word walls are large areas of the classroom wall where words written clearly on pieces of card are displayed, often for the whole term. These are presented attractively, often with a border and illustrations, to help maintain children's interest. The collection of words on the word wall grows as the term progresses, with words from a variety of sources being added to it. Words relating to the theme being studied should certainly be added, as should high-frequency vocabulary words, high-interest words, potentially confusing words, and any others that the teacher (or children) deems necessary. Many words will be taken from books being read by the class, whether fiction or non-fiction. Some classrooms have more than one word wall; a main one and one or two smaller ones for different purposes.

Interactive word walls are word walls that are actively used as tools. This constitutes a multi-sensory approach to learning about new words—their meaning, letters, sounds, morphemes, syllables, and so on. New words can be clapped and chanted as they are added to the interactive word wall, and many activities and games centre on the words on the interactive word wall. Essentially, an interactive word wall is a word wall that is not controlled by the teacher and is used by the children.

Interesting word charts are a form of word wall. Children 'collect' the interesting words they encounter and take them into the classroom to share, define and illustrate, and display. Prepare to be amazed at the words young children find interesting—they are often big and complex words!

Word of the day activities involve looking at a particular word throughout the day—its meaning, its letters, the way it looks, the way it sounds, how it originated, and so on. Children can engage in role plays, art work, poetry writing and other forms of artistic expression around the word (Graves, Juel & Graves, 2007). Words of the day can be added to the word wall or the interesting word chart, and need to be revisited regularly for purposes of revision, enrichment and making connections to other words.

Word histories and origins can be investigated to help stimulate and develop children's word awareness. Looking at where words came from and how they might have been used differently in the past can be fascinating to children. There are many websites on etymology that you can refer to for ideas.

SOME PRINCIPLES OF VOCABULARY TEACHING

In this chapter, we have discussed the development and the importance of vocabulary for reading and writing, as well as speaking and listening. In summary, there are several principles that should be borne in mind when planning vocabulary teaching for the children in your class:

- Vocabulary should be taught both directly and indirectly, but most will be learnt indirectly through the provision of stimulating and language-rich environments.
- Repetition and multiple exposures to vocabulary words, in different contexts, are important.
- Learning in rich contexts is valuable for vocabulary learning.
- Where possible, vocabulary learning should entail active engagement in learning tasks.
- Vocabulary can be acquired through incidental learning.
- Dependence on a single vocabulary instruction method will not result in optimal learning.
- Revisiting and revision of new words is important.
- The home can be the best place for vocabulary learning and teachers should inform and support parents in this.

ASSESSMENT OF VOCABULARY KNOWLEDGE

An important question to ask in assessing vocabulary is: Which words do children *need* to know? The usefulness and importance of a word to a child should certainly be a factor in the teaching and assessment of vocabulary (Harmon et al., 2007). Once it has been decided *what* to assess in vocabulary, decisions about *how* and *when* to assess need to be made. According to Harmon et al. (2007), three effective ways of assessing vocabulary are:

- asking children to *provide synonyms and antonyms* of the word
- asking children to *categorise words* under headings
- observing children's *use of words* in oral and written contexts.

Receptive vocabulary (listening and reading) has traditionally been assessed through questioning and asking children to provide definitions in their own words. However, this may give limited knowledge about whether or not children have a 'deep' concept of the word. Asking children to categorise words or sort them according to meaning can often provide a clearer picture of children's understandings.

Picture vocabulary assessments can also be used to assess receptive vocabulary. Here, children are shown pictures and are asked to point at the picture that matches the stimulus word that is pronounced by the teacher. A formal test of this type is the Peabody Picture Vocabulary Test—Revised (Dunn & Dunn, 1997). However, this assessment is from the USA and may not always be culturally appropriate for all Australian children, especially culturally diverse children. The PAT-R (Australian Council of Educational Research, 2008) also has a receptive vocabulary test, which is in the multiple choice format.

The assessment of expressive vocabulary (speaking and writing) can be achieved through the analysis of texts, both spoken and written, produced by the children. Teachers can also use informal assessments, such as picture cards that children are asked to name (label) orally. They can also ask children to think of synonyms and antonyms for words.

Formal tests include the Expressive Vocabulary Test (Williams, 1997), which is for children who are five years of age or more. In this test, the student responds with a one-word answer to two types of items: they must label items (pictures) and provide synonyms.

SUMMARY

In this chapter we have discussed the importance of teaching vocabulary to children in the early years, through the use of implicit and explicit strategies. Children who do not have a wide listening or receptive vocabulary will inevitably find it difficult to comprehend texts. In the early childhood years, hands-on experiences, supported by lots of talk between adults and children, will play a large part in vocabulary learning.

QUESTIONS AND ACTIVITIES

1. How can teachers maximise opportunities for children to learn vocabulary incidentally?
2. What issues might children for whom English is a second or additional language face?
3. What advice can teachers give parents about their children's vocabulary learning at home?

KEY TERMS

expressive vocabulary
first-wave teaching
meaning vocabulary
receptive vocabulary
structural analysis
word consciousness

KEY REFERENCES

Bear, D., Invernessi, M., Templeton, S. & Johnston, F. (2004). *Word their way: Word study for phonics, vocabulary and spelling instruction.* New Jersey: Pearson, Merrill Prentice Hall.

Beimiller, A. & Slonim, N. (2001). Estimating root word vocabulary growth in normative and advantaged populations: Evidence for a common sequence of vocabulary acquisition. *Journal of Educational Psychology, 93,* 498–520.

Blachowicz, C. L. Z., Fisher, P. J. & Watts-Taffe, S. (2005). *Integrated vocabulary instruction: Meeting the needs of diverse learners in grades K–5.* Naperville, Illinois: Learning Point Associates.

Brantley, D. K. (2007). *Instructional assessment of English language learners in the K–8 classroom.* Boston: Pearson.

Graves, M. F., Juel, C. & Graves, B. B. (2007). *Teaching reading in the 21st century* (4th edn). Boston: Pearson Education.

Harmon, J. M., Hedrick, W. B., Soares, L. & Gress, M. (2007). Assessing vocabulary: Examining knowledge about words and word learning. In J. R. Paratore & R. L. McCormack (eds), *Classroom literacy assessment: Making sense of what students know and do.* New York: The Guilford Press.

Hart, B. & Risley, T. R. (1999). *The social world of children learning to talk.* Baltimore: Brooks.

Nagy, N. M. & Scott, J. A. (2000). Vocabulary processes. In M. B. Kamil, P. B. Mosenthal, P. D. Pearson & R. Barr (eds), *Handbook of reading research: Volume III* (pp. 269–84). New York: Longman.

National Institute of Child Health and Human Development (2000). *Report of the National Reading Panel. Teaching children to read: An evidence-based assessment of the scientific research literature on reading and its implications for reading instruction* (No. 00-4769). Washington, DC: Government Printing Office.

Richek, M. A. (2005). Words are wonderful: Interactive, time-efficient strategies to teach meaning vocabulary. *The Reading Teacher, 58*(5), 414–23.

TOOLBOX OF VOCABULARY STRATEGIES

SEMANTIC FEATURE ANALYSIS

Materials

Whiteboard and marker (or IWB) or chart paper.

Description

The semantic feature analysis involves children filling in or creating a grid that pertains to a particular category. For example, it might be about Australian animals. This activity helps to clarify and deepen children's understanding of word meanings.

Procedure

- Choose some category names—for example, Australian animals.
- The children brainstorm. 'What words fit into the chosen category?' For Australian animals, we might expect quokka, kangaroo, possum and wombat.
- List some of the features of the items in the category. For example, features of Australian animals might include: pouch, four legs, vegetarian and nocturnal.
- Create a grid and complete this as a group. When children become more proficient at semantic feature analysis, the teacher may step back and allow them to take on more responsibility for completing the task.
- After having created the grid, discuss this and the features of the words/items being analysed.

Example

Table 12.4: Australian animals

	Marsupial (has pouch)	Nocturnal	Herbivore (eats vegetables only)	Lives on the ground
Kangaroo	✓	✓ (mostly)	✓	✓
Quokka	✓	✓ (mostly)	✓	✓
Koala	✓	✓	✓	✗
Tasmanian devil	✓	✓	✗	✓

SEMANTIC MAPPING

Materials

Whiteboard and whiteboard markers or paper/card and marker pens. The software Kidspiration can be used.

Description

Semantic mapping, also known as semantic webbing, helps children to think about the relationships between words and concepts, thus deepening their understanding of the vocabulary concerned. The semantic map is in the form of a graphic organiser, where lines connect a central idea to several related ones. These can be done either as a pre- or post-reading activity.

Procedure

- The teacher writes the target word on the whiteboard or a large piece of paper.
- In small groups or pairs, children brainstorm as many words as they can that relate to the target word.
- The teacher writes these words on the board, working interactively with the children to put them in broad categories, which are grouped together.
- Titles for the categories are formed, either by the teacher or the teacher and children together.
- Lines are drawn between the groups of words to indicate relationships.
- When children are able to, they can create semantic webs without this level of teacher support.

SYNONYM WEBS

Materials

Whiteboard and markers, paper/card and markers, or Kidspiration software (materials vary).

Description

Through this strategy, children think about synonyms for words, thus deepening their understanding of word meanings.

Procedure

- The teacher (or class member) nominates a target word.
- The children brainstorm synonyms and may use a thesaurus to find others.
- The teacher and children collaborate to decide which words 'go together' in categories and discuss reasons for the categories or classifications (if there are any).

VOCABULARY VISITS

(Blachowicz et al., 2005)

Materials

At least five teacher-selected books about a theme; a group of theme-related words identified by the teacher; posters and pictures relating to the theme.

Description

This strategy constitutes a 'virtual field trip', since it is usually not possible for teachers and their classes to go on as many field trips or excursions as would be desirable. Books and pictures are used as a basis for discovery and discussion.

Procedure

- The teacher supplies many books about a theme (for example, weather) for children to read and discuss.
- The children do a brainstorm around the theme—looks like, feels like, sounds like.
- The words brainstormed are written on a large chart by the teacher.
- The teacher reads a book aloud. Children are then asked for 'thumbs up' when they hear any of these words from the list.
- Words are added to the theme-word chart as the class progresses through the thematic unit.

VOCABULARY WORD MAPS

Materials

Vocabulary word map handouts.

Description

In this strategy, children work in pairs or independently to discuss and explore a particular word. They do this through writing a definition of the word, putting the word into a sentence, drawing a picture to illustrate the word, and thinking of synonyms and antonyms of the word. This activity deepens students' knowledge of a word. It can be done in small groups, with the teacher as scribe.

Procedure

- A target word is chosen, either by the teacher or the children.
- Children discuss the word in order to arrive at a definition in their own words, some synonyms and (perhaps) antonyms, and a sentence containing the word.
- They then draw a picture to illustrate the word. This activity can be modified, depending on how much teacher support the children need.

Example: Vocabulary word map template

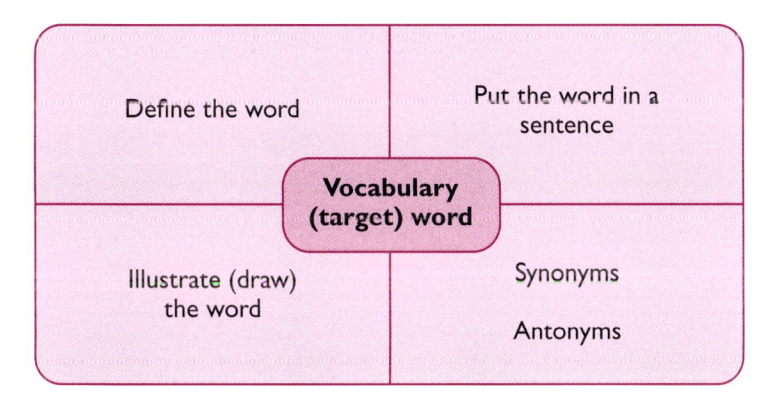

Define the word	Put the word in a sentence
Vocabulary (target) word	
Illustrate (draw) the word	Synonyms Antonyms

CHAPTER 13

Reading for Comprehension

CHAPTER OBJECTIVES

This chapter will increase your understanding of:

- different definitions of reading comprehension
- the elements of reading comprehension
- strategies for teaching reading comprehension
- different means of comprehension assessment.

In this chapter you will be introduced to reading comprehension and how to teach it. Of course, reading comprehension is strongly linked to listening comprehension, which is developed in oral language contexts. Please refer to Part 1 of this book to refresh your memory about how children come to understand spoken language. The link between listening comprehension and reading comprehension can be facilitated by lots of reading aloud by the teacher as well as activities such as storytelling and through a good deal of talk about texts. Because many children do not begin to read texts for themselves until late pre-school or lower primary, the emphasis in this chapter is largely on children in these age groups. As in the vocabulary chapter, there is a toolbox of additional teaching strategies at the end of the chapter.

INTRODUCTION

Without comprehension, reading is a meaningless and pointless exercise. However, some young children do not realise they are supposed to make meaning from the texts they read, and many more do not have appropriate skills and strategies to help them make meaning. Most children who are not good at comprehension also have weaknesses in word identification. Yet it has been shown that approximately 10 per cent of children who have good decoding skills have problems in comprehending texts (Nation & Snowling, 1997), which demonstrates that there is a lot more to reading comprehension than simply being able to read the words.

For children who have trouble comprehending texts, reading is a tedious task that may involve little more than sounding out words or 'barking at print'. It is not surprising that such children soon become unmotivated, avoid reading, and usually fall behind in their reading abilities relative to their age peers. Once they fall behind in their reading, it is almost inevitable that they will fall behind in other subject areas. Furthermore, it can be extremely difficult for children to 'catch up' in reading once they have fallen behind. It is therefore crucial that teachers and caregivers give children in their early years as much support and appropriate instruction and guidance as possible to enable them to succeed in comprehension. Some children will require intensive early intervention.

In order to be successful at reading comprehension, it is of course necessary for children to know that texts are supposed to make sense and to fulfil some sort of purpose, but it is also essential that they possess a range of other word-level literacy skills as well as a degree of knowledge about language, texts and the world. Furthermore, they need to be able to self-monitor and *orchestrate* the skills and knowledge they have. Reading comprehension is, thus, a highly complex activity that needs to be *taught*. The assumption that children will learn to comprehend simply by listening and reading is erroneous (Snow, 2002).

Of crucial importance is knowledge of the syntax and vocabulary of the English language, which children initially gain through oral language experiences, which we have discussed at length elsewhere in this book. Put simply, children who do not have the ability to comprehend spoken language are very unlikely to comprehend written texts. It is therefore necessary to read aloud to young children on a regular basis and to help them make sense of the texts read. It is extremely helpful to talk about the meaning of the texts read aloud and, also, to talk about the language.

Background knowledge about the world and conceptual knowledge are essential for effective comprehension, and children need to be able to call upon this knowledge to help them understand the texts they read. Effective teachers and caregivers constantly help children increase their world knowledge and conceptual knowledge through a range of activities, including discussion. They also help children make connections between their existing knowledge and what is encountered in texts.

As mentioned above, a degree of competence in word identification is a requirement for reading comprehension, as is knowledge about text types, structures and purposes. Finally, children need to learn **cognitive processes** and strategies to help them make meaning. These are essentially *thinking* activities, and must usually be carefully modelled and scaffolded by the teacher.

HOW CAN READING COMPREHENSION BE DEFINED?

Definitions of literacy and of reading are subject to some debate and there are several different theoretical models of literacy and reading that underpin these definitions. It should come as no surprise, then, that there is no consensus on how 'reading comprehension' should be defined.

It is, however, agreed that reading comprehension is a *complex* meaning-making process that involves thinking. The RAND Reading Study Group (Snow, 2002, p. 11) suggests that comprehension is 'the process of simultaneously extracting and constructing meaning through interaction and involvement with written language'. This particular definition emphasises the importance of recognising that reading comprehension is a *process* that leads to a product (an understanding of a text), and that meaning is both constructed by the reader and extracted from the text. (A process can be defined as a sequence or series of actions or behaviours that lead to a product or a specified end-point.) According to this definition, the comprehension process involves the *reader*, the *text* and the particular reading *activity*, which to a large extent depends on the reading purpose. Furthermore, the comprehension process cannot be divorced from the socio-cultural context in which it occurs, since it is this context that influences children's background knowledge, their experiences and their attitudes towards literacy. Successful comprehension depends on the interaction between reader, text and activity factors; a particular child may be able to comprehend certain types of texts in certain situations but not in others.

Figure 13.1: RAND model of reading comprehension

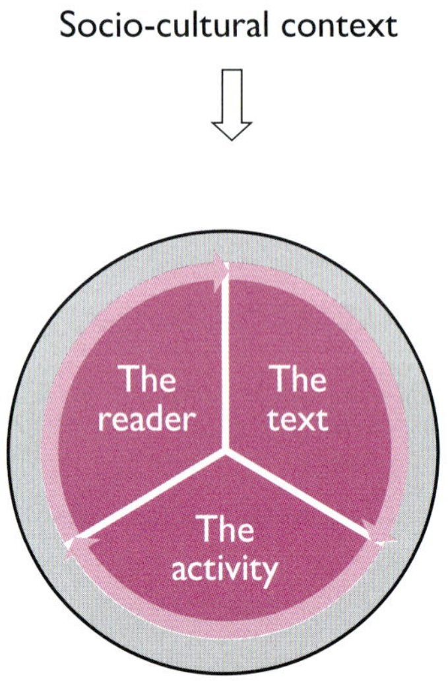

Source: Snow (2002). Reprinted with permission.

> [Comprehension is] the process of simultaneously extracting and constructing meaning through interaction and involvement with written language. (Snow, 2002, p. 11)

> Comprehension can be seen as the processes of using one's own prior experiences and the writer's cues to construct a set of meanings that are useful to the individual reader reading in a specific context. (Irwin, 1991, p. 9)

The RAND conception of reading acknowledges complexity, and contrasts with Gough's 'simple' view of reading, which regards reading comprehension as the product of word recognition and comprehension of oral language/vocabulary knowledge (Gough, 1996). According to the simple theory, reading problems can arise from a child's limited knowledge in either word recognition or oral language comprehension, or both. However, some argue that this theory oversimplifies the complexity of reading (Stahl & Yaden, 2004). Nevertheless, the simple model of reading has recently been given some weight in the

United Kingdom, where it is currently the government-endorsed conceptual framework for the teaching of reading (Primary National Strategy, 2005).

Irwin (1991, p. 9) has provided a useful definition of reading comprehension that highlights the importance of the reader's prior knowledge and comprehension processes, but unlike the RAND definition, it only mentions *construction*, and not *extraction* of meaning. This is an important distinction because it reflects underlying beliefs about where the meaning comes from—from the reader's head, from the text or from a combination of the two. Some definitions foreground the fact that readers *construct* meaning, which may lead to insufficient attention being paid to the author's intended meaning. After all, meaning is constructed from what is written and illustrated in the text as well as what the reader already knows.

All of the above definitions of comprehension have something to offer, but we define comprehension as a complex, strategic process that involves the reader using prior knowledge about the world, about language and about texts to construct and extract meaning from texts. In this definition, there is no specific reference to 'written' texts because many texts are now multimodal and include diagrams, illustrations and even hypermedia elements such as video clips, animation and sound. All of these textual cues can be used to construct and extract meaning.

WHAT DOES A CHILD NEED TO DO/KNOW IN ORDER TO COMPREHEND A TEXT?

In order to fully understand a text, readers must bring into play a repertoire of skills and practices. Luke and Freebody's four practices framework (Luke, 2001; Luke & Freebody, 1999), which was introduced in an earlier chapter, is useful in that it reminds us that readers need to be simultaneously cracking graphophonic and syntactic codes (code breaker), engaging in semantic practice (text participant), understanding text purposes and audience (text user) and engaging in critical reading (text analyst) in order to fully comprehend a text.

According to McKenna and Stahl's cognitive model of reading (2003, p. 8), comprehension is dependent on three separate components, namely *automatic recognition of words* in the text, *comprehension of the language* in the text and the ability to choose and use the *strategies* needed to achieve specific reading purposes. This model adds to the simple model (word identification and listening comprehension) in that it recognises the importance of strategic processes and, most importantly, *thinking*.

In order to recognise words automatically, children need phonological awareness, graphophonic skills, a bank of sight words and the ability to use context cues to identify words. All of these elements have been covered in previous chapters. Comprehension of language (listening comprehension) has been dealt with in the chapters on oral language and vocabulary. In the current chapter, the focus will be on the *strategies* good readers use to help them comprehend.

READING COMPREHENSION: SUGGESTED DEVELOPMENTAL PATHWAY

Reading comprehension development begins in the context of children listening to texts being read aloud. This may be at home with parents, grandparents and siblings or in childcare contexts with childcare professionals. Children in childcare, pre-school and the early grades of primary school are often read to during read-alouds and shared reading.

Children also learn a lot about texts and their purposes through observation of, and interaction with, family members and others. The purposes of newspapers, shopping lists, greetings cards, religious texts, story books and a range of other text types are often learnt at home through informal means.

Table 13.1: Reading comprehension

Childcare and pre-school	The focus is on listening comprehension (which has been discussed in the chapters on speaking and listening)
Year before First Grade/Year 1)	Notices when simple sentences do not make sense
	Answers questions out loud
	Demonstrates familiarity with different types of texts, such as story books, informational texts, poems, and newspapers, and everyday print such as signs and labels
	Begins to make predictions based on illustrations
First Grade (Australia: approximately Year 1)	Self-corrects when a word doesn't fit with the context/does not make sense or sound right
	Notices when difficulties are encountered in comprehension—awareness that texts should make sense and some degree of monitoring for meaning
	Makes predictions about what will happen next in stories
	Discusses how, why and what (informational texts)
	Is able to orally paraphrase/talk about new information from texts
	Writes responses to questions after reading
Second Grade (Australia: approximately Year 2)	Goes back and rereads sentences that do not make sense
	Is able to interpret information from graphs, diagrams and charts
	Recalls facts and details of texts (literal comprehension)
	Discusses the similarities and differences in events and characters across stories
	Connects and compares information across informational texts
	Asks how, why and what questions about stories
Third Grade (Australia: approximately Year 3)	Is able to identify words or word parts that impede comprehension
	Summarises main points from fiction and non-fiction texts
	Discusses themes of texts
	Asks how, why and what questions of informational texts
	Has knowledge about structure of texts; i.e. cause–effect, fact–opinion, main ideas and supporting details of informational texts
	Examines hypotheses and perspectives of texts—critical literacy

Source: *Every child a reader* (Hiebert, 1998)

When children begin to read, they need to think about what they are reading to ensure it makes sense and to decide how it fits in with any predictions they may have made. Also, early readers should be able to give a simple retell of what has happened in a narrative text. In the case of informational texts, they should be able to paraphrase what they have read to show that they have interpreted and understood the information.

By the end of Year 3 at school, most children will have achieved different **levels of comprehension** (see below for explanation of these) and be able to *monitor* their own reading to ensure it makes sense to them; if a text is not making sense, the child should be aware of this and be able to apply some simple 'fix up' strategies.

Although there are many pathways to literacy and it is acknowledged that children come from a diversity of socioeconomic and linguistic backgrounds, and that these factors influence their literacy learning, researchers have devised 'typical' sequences of comprehension development such as the one shown below, which was developed by Heibert et al. (1998) as part of *Every child a reader*.

LEVELS OF COMPREHENSION

There are different levels of comprehension, which apply to both listening and reading comprehension:

- literal—on the lines
- inferential—between the lines
- evaluative—beyond the lines
- critical—beyond the lines with an emphasis on critical literacy.

The *literal level* of comprehension simply involves noticing and remembering what the text actually says. This is sometimes referred to as 'on the lines' or 'right there' comprehension. Using the 'Red Riding Hood' text below, answering the question 'Who was dressed up as Little Red Riding Hood's grandma?' would involve comprehension at a literal level because the answer can be obtained from the story—it is clearly stated that *the wolf* dresses up as grandma.

The *inferential level* of comprehension involves the reader or listener making an inference or 'reading between the lines' to find meaning. A question that would require the reader to make an inference is, 'Why did the wolf dress up as grandma?' In order to answer this question, the reader needs to think about *why* something happened or about the motives of one of the story book characters. This may also involve working out what a pronoun in the text refers to. The answer is not directly stated in the text. An acceptable answer to the question posed above would be, 'The wolf dressed as grandma to trick Little Red Riding Hood so that he could get close enough to eat her.' Pre-service and early career teachers often find it difficult to construct inferential questions, which often begin with:

- The main idea of this story is …
- Why did the …?
- What did the author mean by …?
- Who was the author referring to when she wrote, 'They (pronoun) …'
- How do you think (name the character) feels when …?

LITTLE RED RIDING HOOD

Retold by Grace Oakley

Once upon a time there was a brave but rather careless little girl. She had a beautiful red cape with a hood, which she always wore on cold days. The girl's name was Little Red Riding Hood. She lived on the edge of a big, dark forest, where a sneaky wolf lived. One day Little Red Riding Hood decided to visit her grandmother. In her basket, she packed a small birthday cake, some grapes and some of her grandmother's favourite chocolates.

As she walked through the woods she picked some beautiful flowers. She was so busy picking flowers that she didn't see the wolf peeping at her from behind a tree. The wolf's mouth was watering. Someone was chopping wood nearby, so she didn't hear the wolf whisper to himself, 'Yummy!'

When she arrived at her grandmother's cosy little cottage, which was full of pink and lilac furnishings, she called, 'Where are you, grandmother? Are you ready to celebrate?'

She heard a loud cough coming from the bedroom so she went up the stairs. Her grandmother was wearing her white nightgown and bed cap and looked very sick and ugly. 'My, what big ears you have today, grandmother', Little Red Riding Hood said, concerned.

'All the better to hear you with, my dear', came the hoarse reply.

'And what big, bloodshot eyes you have, grandmother', Little Red Riding Hood said, rather nervously. 'Perhaps you should see a doctor.'

'All the better to see you with, my dear', the bed-ridden figure replied.

'What big, big, teeth you have!' Little Red Riding Hood said, even more nervously. 'Perhaps you should see a d…d…dentist!'

'All the better to EAT you with', the wolf yelled as he jumped out of bed.

Little Red Riding Hood screamed loudly and began to run. The wolf's mouth was wide open and he was just about to take a big juicy bite when a burly woodchopper burst through the door and saved the day. In one mighty swoop he chopped off the wolf's head.

Grandmother crept out from the wardrobe, where she had been hiding. 'My, my, what a big axe you have!' she said.

The End

The next level of comprehension is the *evaluative level* of comprehension, which requires the reader to read 'beyond the lines'; that is, to make judgments, to think about their responses and feelings towards the text, and to relate it to their own life experiences and beliefs. An evaluative question relating to the 'Little Red Riding Hood' text is, 'How do you think the woodcutter might have felt after he saved grandma and Little Red Riding Hood from the wolf?' There is no 'correct' answer for evaluative questions as they require children to think about the qualities of the text and how it makes them feel, what it reminds them of, and how it might connect to the world, to the self and to other texts. Sometimes teachers refer to a *critical level* of comprehension, which involves the reader thinking about the author and the ways in which he or she has crafted or constructed the text to achieve a particular purpose. In the chapter on Visual and Critical Literacy (Chapter 23), the devices authors use to influence and even manipulate readers will be discussed.

WHAT STRATEGIC PROCESSES DOES COMPREHENSION INVOLVE?

In the last decade or two, attention has been called to the cognitive (thinking) processes that readers must use in order to make sense of texts. Good readers use multiple strategies and are adept at choosing appropriate strategies for the task at hand. All of these processes can be taught to young children, including older pre-school children (Gregory & Cahill, 2010) through teacher modelling and think-alouds, followed by guided practice (the gradual release of responsibility model). When introducing a new strategy, it is important that teachers tell the children what the strategy is called, why it is important, and when and how to use it (Hill, 2007). Some of the most important cognitive strategies are described below.

MAKING PREDICTIONS

When children are asked to make predictions about a text, this entails setting a purpose for reading. Also, making predictions may result in children becoming more motivated to read the text to find out if their predictions are correct. Predicting what a text might be about encourages readers to look for evidence in the text and to revise initial predictions if necessary. It is also important to be able to predict what the next words might be, what the next sentence might say, and what the next paragraph might say. Thus, prediction can occur at word, sentence or text levels. Making predictions about texts gives readers a hypothesis to use to guide their reading, which in turn necessitates active thinking. Also, making predictions involves using existing knowledge and linking it to possible occurrences in the text, which facilitates making connections.

Teachers can model predicting by stating their predictions and explaining what information their predictions are based on. For example, 'I predict this book is going to be about a dog that gets lost. I think this because the girl on the front cover is hugging the dog and she has tears in her eyes. They look as though they've just found each other again! There's also a clue in the title, *Where's Scotty?*'

Before reading aloud to children, caregivers and teachers can ask them for predictions and list these on the board. It is important to ask children to substantiate their predictions: 'What makes you think that might happen?' Children can also predict particular words they think might be in the text. The prediction process can be facilitated by flicking through the book and looking at the pictures together prior to reading.

Once predictions have been made, it is important that they are referred to throughout the reading. Sometimes they will prove to be incorrect, in which case new predictions will need to be made.

MAKING CONNECTIONS

Making connections to the text, to the world, to background information and to personal experiences is an important aspect of comprehension. Indeed, it is not possible to make meaning without making these connections. As Luke and Freebody (1999) have suggested, readers need to constantly be asking themselves, 'What does this mean to me?'

Keene and Zimmerman (2007) have pointed out that it is necessary to make *text-to-self*, *text-to-text* and *text-to-world* connections when reading or when being read to. Even young children are capable of doing this, although Cunningham and Shagoury (2005) have pointed out that emergent readers will have limited knowledge in some of these areas. For example, children who have had little exposure to books will find making text-to-text connections difficult. Children who are from diverse cultural backgrounds may find it difficult to make text-to-world connections if they are presented with culturally inappropriate texts to read or listen to. However, this should not prevent teachers modelling how to make such connections with reference to books read in class. The text connections described by Keene and Zimmerman are elaborated below.

Text-to-self connections

Text-to-self connections involve the reader relating the text to their personal experiences. Children can be prompted to make text-to-self connection by being asked to complete *connecting statements* such as the following. These, of course, can be modified to suit the age group and needs of the children:

- That reminds me of when I …
- Something like that happened to me to me when …
- If that happened to me I would …

Children can also ask themselves questions in order to make connections. For children who can read, teachers can make lists of relevant questions and write them on posters. Questions might include:

- Does this remind me of anything that has happened to me?
- Has the same thing ever happened to me?
- What would I do if this happened to me?
- How did I feel when I was reading this?

Text-to-world connections

In order to comprehend texts, it is necessary for readers to link what they know about the world (their general conceptual knowledge) to what the text says. Children can be prompted to make such connections by being asked to complete connecting statements, such as:

- This story reminds me of [something] that happened in the real world …
- Something happened in this story that would not happen in the real world. It was the part …

Questions children could ask of the text to prompt text-to-world connections could include:

- How is the story (text) the same as the real world?
- How is it different from the real world?
- What did this text remind me of in the real world?

Text-to-text connections

As the name implies, text-to-text connections involve the reader thinking about the text in terms of other texts read. For example, a child who says, 'I read a book about ogres and they were mean, not kind like Shrek', is making text-to-text connections.

Connecting statements:

- This reminds me of a story I read called …
- The same thing happened in another story I read …
- This is different from [another story] because …

Questions to ask:

- How does this remind me of other texts/stories I've read?
- How does it remind me of movies I've watched?
- How is this different from other texts I've read?

QUESTIONING

Good readers question the text and themselves before, during and after reading. Young children ask many questions about the world, but do not, without prompting, tend to ask questions of texts they read. Even when they are prompted, young children will often describe texts or make statements instead of posing questions (Cunningham & Shagoury, 2005). Answering and generating questions is central to comprehension and can operate at different levels. Questions can generate lower- and higher-order levels of thinking as they move from the literal to the deductive and evaluative, making increasing cognitive demands. Making up literal questions is obviously much easier than generating inferential or evaluative questions, and young children should gain plenty of practice asking literal questions before moving on to the inferential level.

The teacher needs to scaffold questioning by modelling questioning and answering. As in all aspects of literacy teaching, guided practice is necessary after modelling and demonstration has taken place. Teachers can model questioning through think-alouds. For example, while reading aloud 'Little Red Riding Hood', the teacher could think aloud:

- 'Why has the grandma got bigger ears than usual?'
- 'Why has Little Red Riding Hood got birthday cake in her basket?'
- 'Why is the wolf's mouth watering?'
- 'What will happen next?'

While reading texts to children, teachers can periodically stop and allow children to think up a question. Children can share these questions with the whole group or with a partner. Every now and then, they should be asked if their questions have been answered by the text. Children should be asked to explain their answers where possible.

Question–answer relationships (QARs)

Taffy Raphael (Raphael, 1984; Raphael & Au, 2005) has outlined the importance of helping children understand that there are different types of questions that can be asked of texts in order to 'get at' different types of information; that is, there are different relationships between questions and answers. There are questions that can be answered by looking 'in the book' and those that can be answered using information 'in my head'. These two main categories are subdivided as shown in Table 13.2.

The QAR framework is useful as it can help lower primary children understand where they should look in order to answer questions. It also provides a shared language so that children and teachers can talk and think about strategies for understanding texts. QARs may seem somewhat complicated for children in the early years, but research has shown that by

Second Grade (Year 2), students can easily learn to distinguish between Right There and Think & Search. Anecdotal data from teachers suggests that even younger children are able to talk about all four QARs (Raphael & Au, 2005). They are certainly able to distinguish between 'in the book' and 'in my head'.

Table 13.2: Question–answer relationships

In the book	OR	In my head
Right There: the answer is stated explicitly in the text, often contained within a single sentence Or		**On My Own**: the answer is not to be found in the text. The reader must think about their own experiences and background knowledge in order to find the answer Or
Think and Search: the answer can be found in the text but some summarising and searching is required. The answer can be across sentences or paragraphs. Sometimes the answer may even be across chapters		**Author and Me**: the answer is not in the text but not entirely in the reader's head either. The reader needs to think about how the text and their own ideas fit together

BUILDING MENTAL IMAGERY OR VISUALISING

Building mental imagery, or 'picturing' objects and actions in texts, helps deepen and personalise meanings. Cunningham and Shagoury (2005) refer to mental images as 'mind pictures'. Young children often find it easier to communicate these through art and physical movement than through words.

Even children who are not yet at the stage of decoding can be encouraged to close their eyes and construct 'pictures in their head' when they are read to. They can then externalise these through descriptions or through expressive arts such as art or drama. Teachers and caregivers can think aloud about what they are picturing as they read and can ask children to describe their mental imagery. Tompkins (2007) has pointed out that good visualisers are often disappointed with movie versions of books because the movies do not match the wonderful images that they had visualised.

DETERMINING IMPORTANCE

It is crucial to be able to differentiate 'big' or *main ideas* from *supporting detail*, and this can be difficult to do because often main ideas are not plainly stated in texts but need to be inferred. In order to get the main idea, it is usually necessary for the reader to understand the text as a whole as opposed to understanding smaller chunks, such as sentence-level or paragraph-level comprehension. Zimmerman and Keene (1997) have referred to the main idea as the 'essence' of the text.

One way of helping children organise their thoughts and represent the relationships between ideas in texts is by having them create 'webs' (see Figure 13.2). Cunningham and Shagoury (2005) have used these with children in (US) kindergarten, although a lot of support is needed by children this young. Children whose writing is still at a role play or experimental stage can draw pictures to represent the ideas in texts, or they can use software such as Kidspiration to help them. When they are reading informational texts, children can use *graphic organisers* such as Venn diagrams and flow charts to organise and represent ideas in the text. These are discussed in the section on informational texts, later in this chapter.

Wood, Lapp and Flood (1992) suggest a *tour guide strategy* to assist children in finding the main idea. It is suitable for young children and is a pre-reading activity that involves the 'tour guide' (a child) taking a 'tour' through a book, looking at pictures, headings, captions and important words, such as words that are in bold font. Tour guides should talk about text features that they notice by making comments such as, 'In front of you is a photograph of a slow loris. This animal lives in Asia.'

There are many other ways of teaching young children how to determine importance, but it is beyond the scope of this introductory text to describe these.

Figure 13.2: Concept web

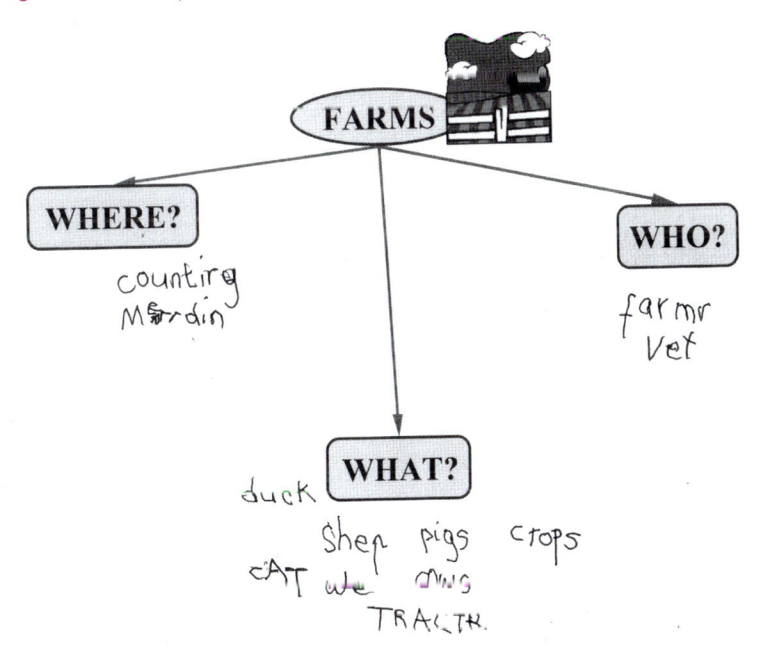

MAKING INFERENCES

Good readers make inferences when reading, and this is often done automatically, without conscious awareness. As explained earlier in this chapter, inferencing involves using information or clues from the text to make meaning that is not directly stated in the text. This involves reading 'between the lines', or using a combination of clues from the text and background 'in head' knowledge. Good readers make inferences without being conscious of it.

Tompkins (2007) suggests four steps for teaching children how to make inferences. First, get them to think of *background knowledge* they have that relates to the story. Second, help the children look for clues the author has written in the text. Third, teach the children to generate inferential questions that tie together information from steps one and two. Finally, children answer the inferential questions that they have generated. A good deal of teacher modelling, think-alouds and questioning are important in teaching this strategy, as in all of the other strategies.

SUMMARISING

Summarising involves thinking about the main ideas of the text and how they relate to each other, and conveying the text's 'essence' without giving supporting details and explanations. Children who have learnt about text structures usually find this easier because they have a framework to put their summary into. For example, knowing that a story has a beginning, a middle and an end (or an orientation, complication and resolution) will help children decide which parts of the text are important and which are merely supportive. They can then delete the supporting details from their summary.

RETELLING AND SYNTHESISING

Retelling plays a role in synthesising because it necessitates identifying key points or events in the text. Synthesising involves retelling, analysing, evaluating, summarising, inferring, and linking to personal experiences and knowledge. Synthesis is probably the most difficult part of comprehension because it requires all of the others to be operating effectively and in some ways it involves 'adding' something to the text.

SELF-MONITORING AND FIX-UP STRATEGIES

Good readers use self-monitoring for meaning and use 'fix-up' strategies when meaning is lost (for example, rereading, placing a finger under the difficult parts, subvocalising, locating the page where the tricky part was first mentioned, cross-checking with a picture or diagram etc.) (Ketsch, 2005, p. 9). Young readers who self-monitor well are able to identify the part/s of the text that they do not understand. They should also be able to articulate what the difficulty is ('I don't get what the author means when she writes, "Arriving in Australia was an important milestone in my Uncle John's life."')

Whereas the strategies above are cognitive strategies because they involve thinking, self-monitoring is a *metacognitive* strategy because it entails thinking about thinking. Good readers may do this at a subconscious level, but children who are novice readers often have to ask themselves questions to self-prompt. Questions might include (Pressley, 2002):

- Do I understand this word?
- Is the text making sense to me?
- Am I using background knowledge to help me?
- Am I reading a book that's too hard?
- Do I know why I'm reading this book?
- Am I asking the right questions?

Being aware of where and what comprehension problems are can help children decide how best to 'fix up' breakdowns in meaning-making. Teachers need to equip children with a range of fix-up strategies and show them when and how to use them. This is best done through modelled reading followed by guided reading. Key fix-up strategies are described below.

Rereading the text

The reader can decide to reread parts of the text in order to fix up a particular confusion or to answer a question: 'It said something about what the birds eat on page three. If I read that bit again, maybe it will help me figure out what "pellets" means.'

Read forward

The reader can look forward to another part of the text for information that might help solve the comprehension problem: 'The book says, "A dog can nurse her pups for a few weeks. The pups are said to be weaned when they start to eat solid food." I'm not really sure what nursing means or what solid food is but the next paragraph might tell me. I see its subheading is called More about Weaning.'

Restate the difficult sentence or passage

Sometimes, restating the difficult sentence or passage in their own words (paraphrasing) can help children comprehend: 'Oh, so the author means that coming to Australia was a very important event in her Uncle John's mother's life.'

RECIPROCAL TEACHING

During reciprocal teaching, students read segments of text (or have segments of text read aloud to them if they have not started to read) and orally make predictions about, question, clarify and summarise the segments of text. There are several models for doing this—whole class, guided (by teacher) or small independent groups.

Through reciprocal teaching, children are taught how to use four important comprehension processes: summarising, questioning, clarifying and predicting. Although this strategy has in the past been used primarily to help children in middle primary and older, it has in recent years been successfully used in early childhood contexts such as in (USA) kindergarten (e.g. Meyers, 2006). The four components of reciprocal teaching are described below.

Predicting

- Students make predictions about what is going to happen in the next section of text, using available clues (such as pictures, headings, titles and text structure) and their background knowledge.

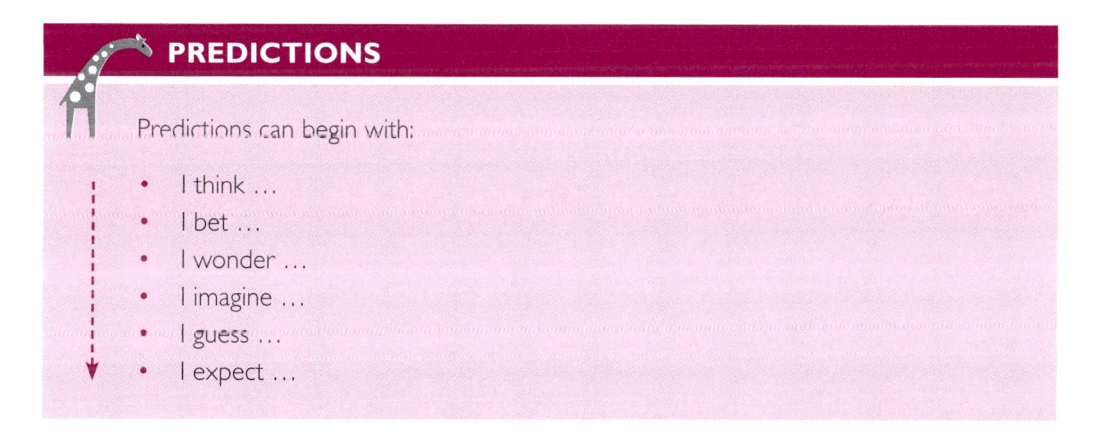

PREDICTIONS

Predictions can begin with:

- I think …
- I bet …
- I wonder …
- I imagine …
- I guess …
- I expect …

- This involves students forming hypotheses.
- Making predictions provides a purpose/focus for reading.

Clarifying (monitoring)

- involves defining unknown words
- explaining ideas
- thinking about something not understood and using 'fix-up' strategies such as reading on, rereading, looking at pictures, consulting dictionary.

Questioning

- involves students asking questions that can be answered by the text
- involves identifying content worth asking questions about
- children can self-test to make sure they can answer their own questions from the text.

Summarising

- involves students putting text information into the own words
- involves identification of main ideas, paraphrasing, and integration of main ideas in the text.

Implementing reciprocal teaching in early childhood classrooms

- Initially, the teacher carries out whole class lessons involving modelling and think-alouds. In pre-school contexts, this will be the main emphasis. Teachers will model the strategies when reading aloud.
- Guided practice comes next, in which the teacher supports students by adjusting the demands of the task based on the students' level of proficiency.
- Next, students learn to conduct discussions in small groups with little or no teacher assistance. In many early childhood contexts, this stage may not be reached. In the later years of lower primary, it can be implemented with some children.
- Finally, students carry out the strategies 'in head' during reading independently.
- The four strategies can be done in any order, but all four must be present in a reading session in order for it to count as reciprocal teaching.
- It is essential for teachers to use materials that are challenging but not overly difficult. In other words, texts should be at the zone of proximal development (ZPD).
- It is necessary to incorporate content area texts that need to be read for other curriculum areas.
- Texts can be fictional and the reciprocal teaching can focus on aspects such as settings, characters and plot.
- Once students are familiar with the procedures, groupings can be somewhat heterogeneous as stronger students can help the weaker ones.

Reciprocal teaching can be used in various forms in the early years. In pre-school years, there is obviously an emphasis on listening comprehension, and children can be asked to: make predictions about the text to be read aloud to them (prediction); talk about parts they didn't understand (clarifying); ask questions about the text before, during and after the reading (questioning); and attempt to summarise the text or say what it was about. Teachers must model these processes before expecting young children to be able to do them. For example, a teacher might say before reading a text: 'I predict this book is going to be about dogs. I think this because of the pictures. Also, the title is *One hundred and one Dalmatians*, and I know a Dalmatian is a dog.'

TEACHING COMPREHENSION PROCESSES AND STRATEGIES

Based on a review of the research, Duke and Pearson (2002, p. 208) have suggested a framework for all comprehension strategy instruction, which is based on Bruner's (1990) notion of 'scaffolding' or 'gradual release of responsibility' (GRR). We have referred to elements of the GRR throughout this chapter.

1. an explicit description of the strategy and how and when it should be used
2. modelling of the strategy in action
3. collaborative use of the strategy
4. guided use of the strategy
5. independent use of the strategy by child (without support).

COMPREHENSION OF INFORMATIONAL TEXTS

Informational (non-fiction) texts differ from fiction or narrative texts in several ways that impact on children's ability to comprehend them. First, they are likely to contain content-specific or technical vocabulary that may not be in young children's receptive (listening) vocabulary. For this reason it is necessary for teachers to provide pre-reading instruction to help children comprehend the text at the word level. New words may be introduced and spoken about prior to the reading. See Chapter 12 for ideas about how to teach vocabulary to young children. Second, such texts are structured according to the type of message and its purpose.

When assisting young children to comprehend informational texts, important considerations include:

- text structure
- vocabulary
- types of illustrations.

EXPOSITORY TEXT STRUCTURES

Text structures of informational texts vary according to the type of message. For example, the intent of the text may be to compare and contrast two or more entities, perhaps ducks and swans, or frogs and toads. The ways in which informational texts are organised can and should be taught to children, as this helps them predict what the text may say, and helps them organise the information in their heads. The organisational structures—sometimes called *top level structures* or expository text structures, include:

- sequence or time order
- cause and effect
- description
- compare and contrast
- problem and solution.

Figure 13.3: Sequence structure

cocoon → caterpillar → butterfly

One of the best ways of helping children identify and understand expository text structures is through the use of *graphic organisers*. These are diagrams that assist children to see the organisation of the text and thus to connect the ideas in the text. Teachers can show and discuss the blank or partially complete graphic organiser before reading to prepare children for reading the text. During reading, graphic organisers can be referred to by children to keep them 'on track', and they can be used to help structured note-taking. Graphic organisers can be utilised after reading, too; the teacher or children can complete the chart to present the information contained in the text.

Sequence

The sequence or time-order expository text structure is similar in many ways to children's narratives or stories because events are often shown in time order. Books about history and biographies follow this type of structure, as do some science texts that describe life cycles and processes. There are certain words, known as *signal words* or cue words/phrases, that can assist readers to decide on the expository text structure. Signal words associated with texts that have a sequence or time-order expository structure include: 'next', 'then', 'after', 'first', 'second', 'finally', 'before', 'until', 'later', 'on' (date), and 'at' (time). There are many other, more sophisticated, signal words that are not likely to be found in texts for young children. The graphic organiser that is commonly used to represent the time sequence structure is the flow chart.

Compare and contrast

In the compare and contrast expository text structure, the author discusses how two or more things are alike or different. Two or more types of animals or birds may be compared and contrasted, or two cultures may be compared. Signal words associated with the compare and contrast structure include: 'differs from', 'although', 'yet', 'but', 'however', 'contrast', 'similar', 'same' and 'different'.

Compare and contrast text structures can be graphically represented in several ways, but a popular graphic organiser is

Figure 13.4: Venn diagram: compare and contrast

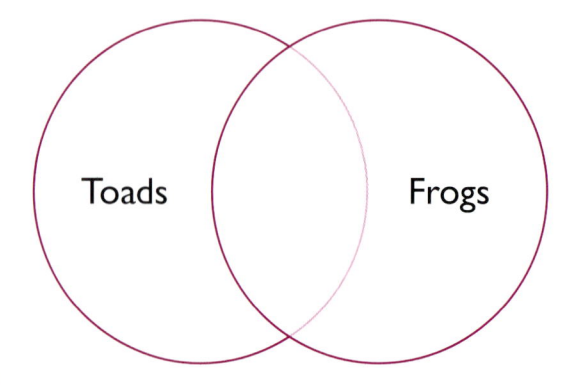

Toads   Frogs

the Venn diagram. Information and communication technologies (ICT) such as Kidspiration can be fruitfully used in the construction of graphic organisers.

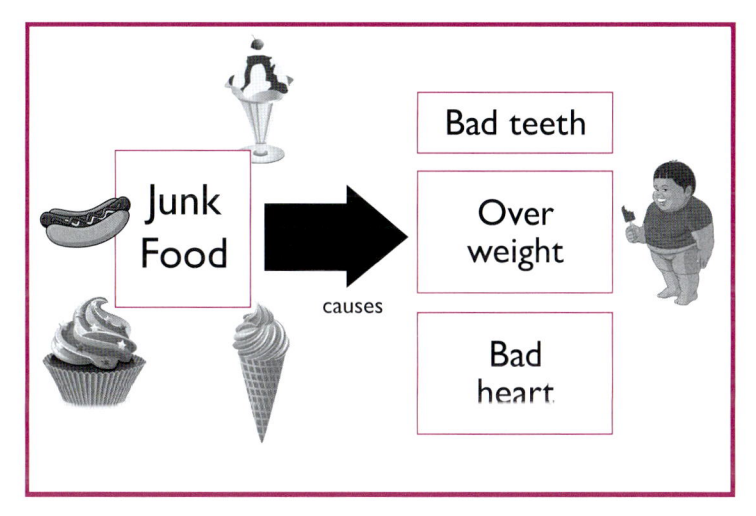

Cause and effect graphic organiser

Description

A very common expository text structure that children in the early years are likely to encounter is the description. This structure is employed to describe a topic; for example, monkeys, France, aeroplanes or rainforests. The features or characteristics of the entity being described are outlined in this expository text structure, and examples are given. Signal words and phrases include: 'for example' and 'such as'.

Cause and effect

The cause and effect expository structure involves the delineation of a cause and effect relationship. For example, texts about the effects of the sun on unprotected skin, the effects of pollution, or the effects of unhealthy foods or poor personal hygiene may be encountered by young children. Cause and effect texts for young readers of Year 3 and below might include signal words such as: 'because', 'makes', 'the reason', 'result', 'leads to', 'creates', 'so that', 'effect', 'cause', 'if … then' and 'therefore'.

Problem and solution

Another common expository text structure is the problem and solution. This is where a problem is outlined and possible solutions are given. Signal or cue words for this structure include: 'problem', 'question', 'solution', 'answer', 'solve' and 'puzzle'. The issue of pollution could be discussed in this text structure, with possible solutions to the problem. Occasionally, elements of the cause and effect expository structure can be mingled with the problem solution, which may impede or complicate comprehension.

PROVIDING APPROPRIATE TEXTS

As mentioned above, the RAND group has stressed the importance of the text in the reading process. To maximise comprehension, it is of crucial importance that the text is matched to the reader's abilities and interests as well as to the reading purpose. Graves, Juel and Graves (2004, p. 270) have suggested that the following factors should be considered in assessing text suitability or 'readability':

- How familiar is the child with the content of the text?
- Does the child have appropriate background knowledge?
- What is the organisational structure of the text?
- Is the text coherently written?
- Will the text be of interest to the child?
- Is the sentence complexity appropriate for the child?
- Is the vocabulary appropriate?
- Is the length of the text appropriate?

There are several other means of assessing readability, some of which are rather questionable. For example, the RIX (Anderson, 1983) is a tool that teachers can use to judge text difficulty according to the number of 'big' words of seven letters or more per sentence. However, this technique does not take into account that some long words are easy enough to read and understand, especially if they are easily decoded or are compound words. Conversely, there are smaller words that may be difficult to decode and understand; for example, 'yacht' or 'skulk'. In deciding upon text appropriateness, the teacher also needs to think of the reading activity. Will the child be reading independently or will they be receiving support? What will they be expected to do after reading?

VOCABULARY FOR READING

Children's development in text comprehension is dependent, in part, on their vocabulary development. Readers cannot understand what they are reading without knowing what most of the words mean. Children use words that they have encountered in oral language contexts to make sense of the words they see in print.

As children learn to read more advanced texts, they must learn the meaning of new words. This can and does occur through the reading, writing and oral experiences of the classroom. However, effective vocabulary development also requires the direct and explicit teaching of words and their meanings, and the introduction of strategies for learning new words. Repetition and multiple exposures to words and the use of computer technologies will assist vocabulary development. Instruction should be based on a combination of methods and be ongoing. In the context of reading a text, comprehension can be supported when new vocabulary within a text is identified and taught before reading occurs. For more detail about teaching vocabulary, please refer to Chapter 12.

COMPREHENSION OF MULTIMODAL TEXTS

Multimodal texts are becoming more and more prevalent and nowadays young children, even in their pre-school years, have considerable contact with multimodal texts, such as websites and CD-ROMs. In short, they are usually quite familiar with multimodal texts, and this extends to children who do not have a computer in the home but who may have other devices such as electronic games or handheld devices (Levy, 2009). Multimodal texts are composed of multiple symbol systems, not just printed words and pictures as is the case in 'traditional' texts. It is therefore necessary for children to be able to 'crack the code' and comprehend each symbol system and to think about how the symbol systems *work together* to create meaning. To make meaning of multimodal texts, children must use a variety of cues from different symbol systems simultaneously. It appears that children are to some extent developing these proficiencies at home, informally, but research clearly needs to be carried out so that pedagogies and practices can be developed for schools and childcare centres.

ASSESSMENT OF READING COMPREHENSION

It is difficult to assess comprehension in young children for many reasons, including possible limitations in their expressive vocabulary, short attention spans, and their limited world experience (Stahl, 2009). Assessment of comprehension should take into account a range of reading comprehension outcomes and it should be based on a 'rich and elaborated theory of reading comprehension' (Snow, 2002, p. xix). A variety of assessment techniques should therefore be used, and these should assess both the comprehension process and the product (end result). A combination of formal and informal assessments should be used on an ongoing basis. Assessment should also be able to identify those children who might be having difficulties in specific areas and be sensitive to the diverse needs and cultural backgrounds of children (Snow, 2002). There are several ways to assess reading comprehension, including word comprehension measures, passage comprehension measures, story retelling measures, cloze procedure measures and curriculum-based measurement of reading comprehension (Rathvon, 2004).

WORD COMPREHENSION ASSESSMENTS

Word comprehension assessments are also known as reading vocabulary tests, which assess whether children comprehend the meaning of individual words. These assessments are useful because comprehension depends on good knowledge of vocabulary. They do not assess comprehension per se, however. Vocabulary assessment has been discussed, above.

PASSAGE COMPREHENSION ASSESSMENTS

Passage comprehension assessments involve the child reading a passage of text, either silently or orally, and then answering questions, either orally or in writing. In some formal passage comprehension assessments, such as the Progressive Achievement Test-Reading (PAT-R) (Australian Council of Educational Research, 2008) children are permitted to reread and refer to the text before answering questions, whereas in others they are not. When not allowed to refer to the text, children may be disadvantaged as rereading and looking back may well be part of their normal reading process. Teachers need to exercise care when using comprehension assessments that require children to provide written answers to questions because writing ability and motivation may affect their answers—meaning that it is *writing* being assessed, not just reading comprehension.

QUESTIONING

Questions relating to the levels of comprehension (literal, inferential, evaluative/critical) are often used to assess comprehension (McKenna & Stahl, 2003). This can be problematic because whether or not the child's answer is deemed to be good or poor often depends on teacher judgment, which may not always be reliable. Another problem with comprehension questions is that the child may answer them correctly without having read or understood the text, using 'in the head' information only. For example, after reading a text on birds, the teacher might ask, 'Where do birds lay their eggs?' Many children would know the answer to this without reading a book.

RETELLINGS

Retellings require children to retell in their own words a story they have read (Rathvon, 2004). Reading comprehension is judged according to the amount of detail provided and the correct sequencing of events. The teacher may use a generic or a text-specific checklist to record the child's retelling (Oakley, 2006a) and can ask probing questions to jog the child's memory. In the early childhood years, children are asked to do oral retells as their low writing level may limit answers. It must be remembered that children with expressive language difficulties or immaturity may not be able to show their comprehension adequately through oral retells (Gunning, 2006).

CLOZE

Cloze assessment of reading comprehension involves children supplying missing words in texts that have had selected words deleted. In early childhood contexts, this is often done orally. Words may be deleted at random or may be key words. In some cloze assessments (called the modified cloze procedure) children are given several words to choose from with which to fill in the gaps.

Drawbacks of the cloze procedure include the fact that it is a fairly 'unnatural' format that can be confusing for some students, especially if they have had little experience with this type of activity (Irwin, 1991; McKenna & Stahl, 2003). If the cloze is a written assessment, results can be affected by the child's levels of writing ability and motivation. Cloze measures generally only assess sentence level comprehension and usually do not adequately assess children's ability to integrate information between sentences and paragraphs (paragraph- and text-level comprehension).

THINK-ALOUDS

Think-alouds can be used before, during or after reading as a means of making children's thinking observable. This technique is particularly useful for assessing children's comprehension processes. In this procedure, children are asked to 'think aloud' at certain points in their reading. This may be facilitated by 'stop and think cards' (Annandale et al., 2004b) or sticky tags being placed at certain points in the text. Think-alouds are a good means of assessing comprehension *processes*.

CONVERSATIONS AND INTERVIEWS

Having conversations or 'conferencing' with children about their reading can be a fruitful way to find out about their knowledge about and attitudes towards reading. Teachers may ask a range of questions about the text and how the child is going about the task of reading it.

ANALYSIS OF WRITTEN WORK

This is a very common means of assessing children's comprehension. Here, a product such as story map or written retell is examined for evidence that the child has comprehended a text. Written works and other artefacts do not give many clues about the processes the child has used to comprehend, however.

RUNNING RECORDS

Running records (Clay, 2002) are a means of informally assessing young children's reading processes and accuracy, and are an important component of Reading Recovery programs and many guided reading programs (Fountas & Pinnell, 1996). The teacher records the errors and 'self-corrections' made as the child reads aloud and then calculates accuracy self-correction rates. The self-correction ratio can be useful in indicating the extent to which the child is reading for meaning. Teachers also use running records to gain a glimpse into how a child seems to be using the cueing systems (meaning, syntactic, visual/graphophonic), thus giving them insight into some of the child's reading strengths and areas of needs. Running records can also be used to help teachers select texts at appropriate levels for learning.

Administering a running record

To administer a **running record**, the teacher sits beside the child, who is asked to read aloud a text of (preferably) 100 words or more. The text can be either 'unseen' (new to the child) or one that has been encountered only once before. It should be a text that the teacher estimates to be at an instructional level for the child. As the child reads, the teacher records correct words and errors on a blank sheet of paper, using a tick for each word correctly read and special codes for any errors. These codes are shown in Figure 13.5. A teacher who is inexperienced in taking running records may prefer to use a transcript of the text to mark while the child reads. She or he may also audio record the child's reading so that the accuracy of the markings can be checked.

PERCENTAGE ORAL READING ACCURACY

$$\frac{\text{Total words correct}}{\text{Total words}} \times \frac{100}{1}$$

After the child has read the text, accuracy and self-correction rates are calculated using the formulae shown. If the child achieves an accuracy rate of 95 per cent or more, the text is

Running Records	
Marking Conventions	
Accurate reading:	✓ ✓ ✓
Substitution : (Error)	sank leg sink log
Repetition: (Not an error)	R or ✓ ✓ ✓ R
Self correction (SC): (Not an error)	sank SC sink
Omission: (Error)	— sink
Insertion: (Error)	legs —
Told: (T) (Error)	T mice
Appeal (A):	A mice
Try That Again	[ ] TTA

Running records coding system

Summary of Running Record

Name: _____ Date: _____ DOB: _____ Age: _____ yrs: 6 mths: 2
School: _____ Recorder: JC

SUMMARY OF RUNNING RECORD
Text Titles | Running Words Errors | Error Rate | Accuracy | Self-Correction Rate
1. Easy _____
2. Instructional _____
3. Hard Ben went to school | 22/5 | 1:4.5 | 77% | 1:2.6

Directional Movement: This is fine. Good return sweep. Still uses finger.

ANALYSIS OF ERRORS Cues used and cues neglected

Easy: _____
Instructional: _____
Hard: Not attending to all of the letters in words. Using initial & end letters & guessing. Over-reliance on use of illustrations. Needs to cross-check for meaning. CROSS CHECKING ON CUES: although usually makes sense. Now beginning to self-correct. SC rate improving. She did comprehend most of text. Work on grapho-phonic cues.

Ben went to school
1. On Friday, Ben went to school.
2. He painted a picture.
3. He wrote a poem.
4. He ate an apple.
5. He sang some songs.

Page		E	SC	Cues used E	SC
1	✓ ✓ ✓ wet/went | SC ✓ ✓	1		M S V	M S V
2	✓ did/painted ✓ Painting/picture	1	1	M S V / M S V	
3	✓ white/wrote ✓ p-o-m/T poem	1	1	m s V / m s V	
4	✓ had/ate ✓ ✓	1		M S V	
5	✓ ✓ a/some SC song/songs SC R		1 1	M S V / M S V	m s V / m s V
Totals		E: 5	SC: 3	Cues used	

Example of a running record

deemed to be at an *easy level*, whereas with an accuracy rate of 90–94 per cent, it is deemed to be at an *instructional level*. In cases where the child achieves an accuracy rate of 89 per cent or below, the text is at a *frustrational level*. For most teaching/instructional purposes, texts at the instructional level are ideal, and texts chosen for independent reading would usually be at the easy level. Frustrational-level texts can still be used, but a high level of teacher support is needed. Shared reading would be an appropriate context in which to use a text at a frustrational level.

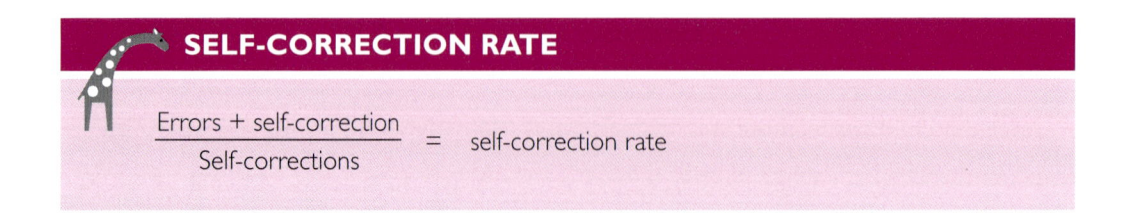

SELF-CORRECTION RATE

$$\frac{\text{Errors + self-correction}}{\text{Self-corrections}} = \text{self-correction rate}$$

The self-correction ratio can help teachers decide the extent to which the child is reading for meaning; a child who makes errors and does not correct them, even if they do not make sense, is clearly not self-monitoring for meaning. A high self-correction rate of 1:2 or 1:3 is deemed to be indicative of good self-monitoring. A low self-correction ratio or no self-correction of errors is cause for concern and corrective teaching is necessary.

It is beyond the scope of this chapter to discuss running records in depth and the reader is referred to Clay's work (2002) to gain a deeper understanding.

Errors are analysed from running records and this analysis leads to hypotheses about whether the child concerned seems to have used 'meaning', 'visual' or 'structural' cues, or a combination of the three, at the point of making the error. For example, if a child read: 'The cat sat on the hat' instead of, 'The cat sat on the mat', the teacher might infer that she or he used 'meaning' (semantic) cues because what was read ('The cat sat on the hat') does indeed make sense. Also, it might be inferred that 'structural' (syntactic) cues were used because the sentence is syntactically correct. Visual (that is, graphophonic) cues were partially used because the end of the word was read accurately.

What does the research say about running records?

Research shows that the most effective early years teachers do, in fact, use running records with graded texts to monitor the progress of their students (Pressley et al., 2001). However, a range of other assessments need to be used alongside running records because they are not fully reliable.

Research on the reliability of running records indicates that, in order to arrive at truly reliable results, each student should read a minimum of three passages to different teachers and the three scores should be averaged (Fawson, Reutzel, Smith, Ludlow & Sudweeks, 2006). This is obviously not practicable in most busy schools. Research has also revealed inter-scorer reliability may be an issue in running records, with raters scoring running records inconsistently, according to different levels of experience and understandings about the reading process (Blaiklock, 2003; Fawson et al., 2006). This indicates that novice teachers should probably not be placing too much reliance on running records. Clay herself has stated that thorough training is needed in order to administer and evaluate running records effectively.

Text factors vary greatly from one text used for a running record to another, and this further limits reliability: linguistic and conceptual features of texts can vary greatly, even when they have been 'levelled' by teachers or commercial organisations. The levelling of texts is an inexact process in many school contexts, although some good advice on how to do this is available in the literature (Fountas & Pinnell, 1996). The fact that levelling is inexact means that the use of running records to measure growth or progress is not exact. Some educational publishers now supply assessments with their reading schemes and packages, many of which incorporate variations of running records. The PM Benchmark Kit is an example.

INFORMAL READING INVENTORIES

Informal reading inventories (IRIs) (Burns & Roe, 1999; DeKonty Applegate, Benson Quinn & Applegate, 2008; Johns, 2005; Manzo, Manzo & McKenna, 1995; Temple, Crawford & Gillet, 2009) are based on graded reading passages that children usually read aloud. As in the case of running records, the child's reading rate and accuracy are recorded. Also, comprehension is assessed through several (approximately eight to twelve) oral questions after the text has been read. Questions assessing literal, inferential and critical comprehension are often included, as are questions designed to assess vocabulary knowledge, sequencing of events and identification of the main idea.

Walpole and McKenna (2006, p. 592) have suggested that IRIs can help teachers find out about a child's reading level (independent, instructional or frustrational), listening level, decoding strategies and sight-word knowledge, as well as reading rate. Furthermore, error analysis can provide insight into a child's use of the cueing systems.

Paris and Carpenter (2003) have pointed out some limitations of IRIs, and these include problems in assessing comprehension adequately, the fact that they are relatively time-consuming, and that they are not accurate enough to track reading progress over time. Walpole and McKenna (2004) point out that the results of IRIs are, in themselves, not specific enough to inform planning, particularly in beginning or struggling readers. However, IRIs can be highly useful as 'screening' instruments that are intended to 'raise the alarm' that there may be a problem that needs to be followed up with more specific diagnostic assessments. In short, IRIs can be useful as part of a comprehensive system of assessment tools, for use with children of approximately five years old or more. A useful assessment of this type is the Handy Informal Prose Inventory (Ayrey, 1999), which can be obtained from: www.handyres.com/p/530414/informal-prose-inventory-1-.html.

PORTFOLIOS

Evidence about reading abilities and attitudes that can be included in portfolios includes anecdotal notes, observational checklists, literature questionnaires, audio and video clips (on CD or DVD), story retelling records, records of think-alouds, running records, informal reading inventories, reading lists and logs, reading attitude surveys and interviews, and rubrics (Cohen & Wiener, 2003), as well as children's work samples that have been marked and analysed. It is important for teachers to consider the purpose of each item included and the aspect(s) of reading that it assesses. Ideally, a portfolio should show reading growth and the child should to some extent be included in deciding what goes into the portfolio. The negotiation with the child about what should be included can enhance their knowledge about themselves as readers, as well as their sense of ownership over their learning, and can greatly assist them in self-assessing their own reading.

SUMMARY

In this chapter, reading comprehension has been discussed in terms of development, processes and teaching. Also, some strategies for the assessment of reading comprehension have been outlined. It has been pointed out that it is important to teach comprehension from very early on in a child's life; it is not fruitful to wait until a child can decode until comprehension is addressed. In the early years, comprehension is taught primarily through talk, in the context of real texts being read for genuine purposes.

QUESTIONS AND ACTIVITIES

1. What is comprehension and how does it relate to the foundational skills of literacy?
2. How can comprehension processes be taught to young children?
3. How does reading comprehension relate to listening comprehension?
4. Using what you learnt in the chapters on oral language and foundational skills, think about what parents and childcare professionals can do to pave the way for successful comprehension once children start to read.

KEY TERMS

cognitive strategies
informal reading inventories
multimodal texts
levels of comprehension
running records

KEY REFERENCES

Cunningham, A. & Shagoury, R. (2005). *Starting with comprehension: Reading strategies for the youngest learners*. Portland, Maine: Stenhouse Publishers.

Duke, N. K. & Pearson, P. D. (2002). Effective practices for developing reading comprehension. In A. E. Farstrup & S. J. Samuels (eds), *What research has to say about reading instruction* (3rd edn, pp. 205–42). Newark, Delaware: International Reading Association.

Irwin, J. W. (1991). *Teaching reading comprehension processes* (2nd edn). Englewood Cliffs, NJ: Prentice Hall.

Keene, E. O. & Zimmerman, S. (2007). *Mosaic of thought: The power of comprehension strategy instruction* (2nd edn): Heinemann.

Levy, R. (2009). 'You have to understand words … but not read them': Young children becoming readers in a digital age. *Journal of Research in Reading*, 32(1), 75–91.

Luke, A. & Freebody, P. (1999). A map of possible practices: Further notes on the four resources model. *Practically Primary*, 4(2), 5–8.

Pressley, M. (2002). Metacognition and self-regulated comprehension. In A. E. Farstrup & S. J. Samuels (eds), *What research has to say about reading instruction* (3rd edn, pp. 291–309). Newark, Delaware: International Reading Association.

Primary National Strategy (2005). *The new conceptual framework for teaching reading: The 'simple view of reading'—overview for literacy leaders and managers in schools and Early Years settings*. Retrieved 25/11/2008 from DfES: www.standards.dfes.gov.uk/primaryframework/downloads/PDF/Paper_on_searchlights_model.pdf.

Raphael, T. E. & Au, K. H. (2005). QAR: Enhancing comprehension and test taking across grades and content areas. *The Reading Teacher*, 59(3), 206–21.

Snow, C. (2002). *Reading for understanding: Towards an R & D program in reading comprehension*. Santa Monica, CA: RAND.

Stahl, S. & Yaden, D. B. (2004). The development of literacy in pre-school and primary grades: Work by the Center for the Improvement of Early Reading Achievement. *The Elementary School Journal, 105*(2), 141–65.

Tompkins, G. E. (2007). *Literacy for the 21st century: Teaching reading and writing in prekindergarten through grade 4.* Upper Saddle River, NJ: Pearson, Merrill Prentice Hall.

TOOLBOX OF COMPREHENSION STRATEGIES

A selection of useful classroom activities.

ANTICIPATION GUIDES

Materials

Teacher pre-prepares an anticipation guide, which is a series of six to ten statements about a topic. The statements will be answered as 'true' or 'false'.

Description

Anticipation guides are useful in that they can help children activate prior knowledge, or get them thinking along the lines of the text they are preparing to read. Anticipation guides can also give children a purpose for reading and help them question the text as they read it, therefore improving reading for meaning. More able children can write anticipation guides for other children to use.

Procedure

- Children discuss the statements on the anticipation guide. This can be done as a whole class, as a small group or in pairs, depending on the needs and abilities of the children.
- They tick 'true' or 'false' for each statement (in the 'before reading' column). In pre-school contexts the 'true/false' statements can be done orally.
- Children read the text (or teacher reads it to them) and then review their initial responses.
- Children discuss the statements and decide on responses 'after reading'. They should go back the text to check their answers.
- Compare 'before reading' and 'after reading' responses.

Example anticipation guide

Table 13.3: Anticipation guide for *Bats*

Before reading		Statements	After reading	
True	False		True	False
		Bats sleep with their eyes open.		
		Fruit bats eat nothing but fruit.		
		Bats are blind.		
		Bats can eat half their weight in food in one day.		
		Bats sleep at night like humans do.		

BLURB WRITING

Materials

Pencils, paper, art materials for illustration (optional). Blurbs can be written on a computer, if preferred.

Description

To write a good blurb it is necessary for children to understand the main ideas of the story, to have identified main characters and their traits, and to be able to summarise the story. A good blurb is short and persuasive.

Procedure

- Children read book or multimedia text (or watch a movie).
- Discussion of the text.
- Children write 'blurb' about the text and draw an illustration (in either order).
- If the blurb is written on the computer (e.g. PowerPoint), additional elements such as sound effects can be added. Electronic blurbs can be posted on school or class intranet to encourage peers to read the book in question.

CHARACTER MAPPING

Materials

Paper, pencil (or computer and concept mapping software).

Description

Character mapping involves identifying traits of characters from books read. Supporting evidence must be given.

Procedure

- Children read book or it is read aloud by the teacher.
- Character traits are identified by the children. This can be done as a whole class, in small groups or in pairs.
- The character traits are written onto a 'character map'.
- Supporting evidence is supplied for each trait. A rereading of the book (or parts of it) may be necessary.
- Children discuss or share their character maps.

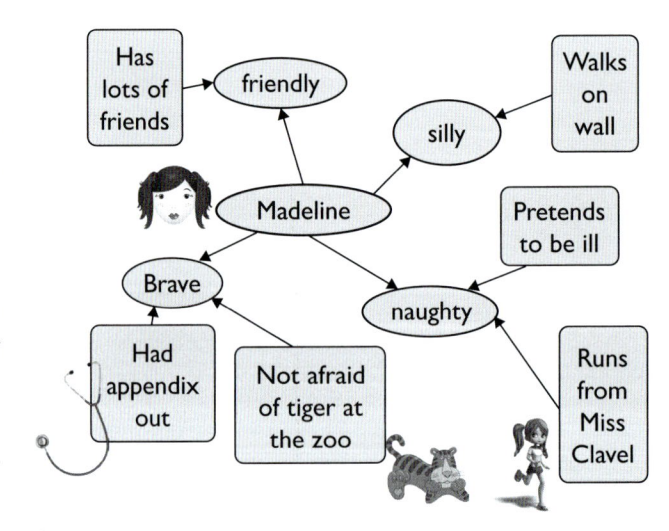

Character map

CHARACTER RANKING

Materials

Story books.

Description

Children rank characters according to traits; for example, kindness, cruelty, sneakiness. This encourages understanding of characters and can involve processes such as making connections and inferencing.

Procedure

- Children list the characters from a story (or from several stories).
- They then rank the characters according to a specified character trait.
- Rankings are then discussed.

CREATING TITLES

Materials

No special materials needed.

Description

The creation of a title necessitates comprehension of the text as a whole, and the identification of the main ideas.

Procedure

- The teacher covers the title of the book and reads the book aloud.
- Children create a suitable title for the book (or for individual chapters of a chapter book). This can be done orally or in writing, depending on the abilities of the child.

DIRECTED READING THINKING ACTIVITY (DRTA)

(Stauffer, 1975)

Materials

Picture book or chapter book story. The children must not already know the story, so fairy tales are usually not appropriate for DRTA.

Description

This activity involves children making predictions about texts before reading them (or before having texts read aloud to them). During reading they confirm or reject their predictions.

Procedure

- The teacher introduces the story by discussing the title with the children and perhaps some of the pictures. It may be necessary to read the first paragraph or so from the story.
- The teacher asks children for predictions about what might happen in the story, based on the title and the pictures.
- Predictions are discussed and all children select a prediction. They explain (to the teacher or to a partner) why they think the predication is a good one.
- The children read (or the teacher reads aloud) a portion of the text, after which they are asked if they still think their initial predictions were good ones. At this point they can change their predictions. The teacher may give some possible scenarios by asking, 'What if [something] happened next? How would the story go then?'
- Continue reading, predicting and re-predicting, stopping at pre-specified points in the story.
- At the end of the story, children discuss their responses and talk about their predictions and the features of the text that they used to help them make predictions.

GUIDED IMAGERY

Materials

A story book to read aloud. This should contain lots of descriptive language.

Description

This activity helps children learn how to visualise characters and events in books.

Procedure

- The teacher reads a story aloud without showing the children the illustrations or the cover.
- Children close their eyes as the book is being read and attempt to create their own pictures in their minds.
- Children are asked to draw one of the 'mind pictures'.
- Discuss pictures in terms of text. Teachers can ask such questions as:
  - 'Who is the boy in the picture? Why did you draw him like that?'
  - 'Where is the boy? Which part of the book did you use to help you draw the setting you've drawn here?'
- The teacher rereads the book, showing the original illustrations. These are compared with the illustrations drawn by the children.

HOT-SEATING/CHARACTER INTERVIEWS

Materials

Seat, and may need props such as hats and spectacles.

Description

Children's questioning skills and inferencing can be enhanced through this strategy.

Procedure

- The teacher takes on the role of a character.
- Children create and ask questions of the character. Children ask questions that are factual—questions about motivations, consequences.
- The teacher gives answers in role.
- Props, such as masks and hats and puppets, can be used by the person in the hot seat to help them get into the character.
- Pairs of children can interview each other (one in role as a character from text).

This strategy requires modelling by the teacher before children will be able to sit in the 'hot seat' and be interviewed 'in character'.

K-W-L CHARTS
Ogle (1986)

Materials

Large sheet of paper or card with three columns drawn on it (see example below). An interactive whiteboard can be used instead of paper or card.

Description

K-W-L charts help children comprehend non-fiction texts by getting them to think about the topic and the text before and after reading. K-W-L means *know*, *want to know* and *learnt*.

Procedure

- Before reading a particular text, children brainstorm what they *know* about the topic in the book. This helps 'activate' and extend their prior knowledge. The teacher writes children's ideas in the 'K' column of the chart.
- Teacher then asks children what they would like to know about the topic and their contributions are written in the 'W' column. Deciding what they *want to know* helps children set a purpose for reading and also helps them think of appropriate questions they might ask of the text.
- After reading the book (or more than one book) on the topic, the 'L' column is completed. The articulation of what they have *learnt* requires children to reflect on the text(s), extract main ideas and summarise.
- Discuss the whole chart. Did the children find out what they wanted to know? Was their prior knowledge accurate? This process can help children integrate existing and new knowledge.

This strategy was designed by Ogle (1986) and can be modified in several ways. For example, a fourth column can be added to the K-W-L, entitled 'still want to know'. Sometimes, a 'T' can be added to make a K-T-W-L. The added column is for information that children *think* they know but aren't sure (Jonson, 2006). Children can do K-W-L charts in small groups, pairs or as individuals when they are able.

What I (we) **know**	What I (we) **want to know**	What I (we) **learnt**

PICTURE WALKS

Materials

Picture book.

Description

The picture walk is useful to teachers because it can help them ascertain what background knowledge the children may have about a topic. For the children, any background knowledge they have can be activated and perhaps extended, and the teacher can raise vocabulary that might appear in the written text. The picture walk can also be a good context for the children themselves to compose questions. Not least, this strategy can engage the children in the text and arouse their interest in hearing the text read aloud or in reading it themselves.

Procedure

- The teacher shows the children the cover of a book and then flicks through the book, looking at and discussing the pictures with the children.
- From the pictures, the children can make predictions about what might happen in the story.
- Throughout the picture walk, the teacher prompts the children by asking questions like, 'What's happening in this picture?', 'What do you think might happen on the next page?' or 'Why do you think that?'
- When the children are able, they can do picture walks in pairs, with each child taking turns to make comments and predictions, and to ask questions about the story.

RESPONSE JOURNALS

Materials

Journals for children. The teacher can design these according to the needs and abilities of the children concerned.

Description

Response journals help children make connections through reflection. They also help children become metacognitive as they think about their reading processes.

Procedure

- Children write their responses to books as they read them or straight after reading them.
- They can also write down the questions they ask themselves, their predictions, their feelings etc.
- The teacher can direct children to write about particular aspects of their reading. For example, 'Today I want you to write about the questions you asked as you were reading', or 'Today I would like you to draw a picture of the character. How did you picture him?'

STORY MAPPING

Materials

Paper, pencils and coloured pencils.

Description

This activity can help children 'pull together' characters, settings and events from stories. It can also facilitate future 'in head' story mapping.

Procedure

- Demonstrate/model how to draw a 'map' of story events.
- Involve children in retelling the story.
- Now ask children to work collaboratively to map other stories (and make comparisons between them).
- Teacher can supply cards/pictures from book for children to map or sequence

TABLEAUX

Materials

A clear space.

Description

Create a tableau, statue or 'freeze frame' of something that happened in the book.

Procedure

- In small groups, children portray a scene or an idea from the book using their bodies. Children will need some time to plan and discuss their tableau.
- The 'freeze frame' can come to life when cued by, for example, a sound.
- The tableau can be supplemented by simple props, written subtitles and signs and sound effects.
- The teacher or another child can tap participants on the shoulder and they can express their thoughts (in character).
- After the tableau, the group can take questions and comments from the rest of the class (the audience).

TALK TO THE AUTHOR/AUTHOR'S CHAIR

Materials

No special equipment.

Description

These activities encourage children to ask and answer questions of authors and texts.

Procedure

- *Talk to the author*: read a text in shared reading and then demonstrate how to note any questions that you would like to ask the author; for example, 'Who was this?' and 'Why did this happen?' Children can then try this for themselves.
- *Author's chair*: one child pretends to be the author and is interviewed by the other children about the text(s).

THOUGHT BUBBLES

Materials

Photocopies of pictures from books with empty thought bubbles on them. Alternatively, children can draw pictures they have visualised and add thought bubbles. Teachers can scribe where necessary (where children cannot yet write conventionally).

Description

This activity encourages inferencing and making connections.

Procedure:

- Children read a book.
- Children add a thought bubble to character.

CHAPTER 14

Developing Reading Fluency

CHAPTER OBJECTIVES

This chapter will increase your understanding of:

- the different definitions of reading fluency
- the elements of reading fluency
- some core strategies for teaching reading fluency to young children
- how to assess reading fluency in (lower primary) children.

This is the final chapter in the part on teaching young children to read. Here, you will learn about fluency and its importance to reading comprehension. Because fluency involves children who have started to read in a conventional sense, the emphasis is on children in the late pre-school and lower primary year, although it is crucial for parents and childcare professionals to model fluent reading to very young children so that they can begin to understand what it sounds like. At the end of this chapter is a toolbox of strategies you can use to help children in your class improve in this area.

WHAT IS READING FLUENCY?

There has been considerable disagreement about what reading fluency is, and hence how it should be taught. Traditionally, fluency has been seen as the ability to read at an appropriate **pace** (speed) with a high degree of accuracy. According to this view, quick and automatic word identification is necessary (but not necessarily sufficient) for comprehension. That is, readers need a large store of *sight words* that they instantly recognise, as well as very efficient decoding strategies for words not in their store of sight words, in order to achieve reading fluency. LaBerge and Samuels (1974) argued that without this **automaticity** of word recognition, a disproportionate amount of a reader's available attentional and cognitive resources are engaged in lower-level processing, leaving insufficient resources for the higher-level thinking needed for comprehension. In other words, children can get bogged down in the hard work of sounding out individual words and therefore find it difficult to attend to the meaning of the text. Their reading can be so slow and word-by-word that by the time they get to the end of the sentence they have forgotten what was at the beginning; they cannot string the words together into meaningful phrases and sentences, much less comprehend whole texts.

> Oral and/or silent reading fluency results when a reader can successfully engage, integrate and self-monitor a repertoire of interactive reading competencies, including automaticity of word recognition, appropriate reading rate, smoothness, phrasing, expression and comprehension. Reading fluency involves the strategic use of graphophonic, syntactic/grammatical, semantic knowledge. (Oakley, 2005, p. 14)

More recently, this view has been questioned, and the relationship between fluency and comprehension has been problematised. Does comprehension necessarily follow on from fluency, or does it also facilitate fluency? Is there a straightforward unidirectional relationship between fluency and comprehension or is there some sort of reciprocal relationship? Are fluency and comprehension two different things that can be separated or should comprehension and fluency be seen as inextricably interrelated (Samuels, 2002)? These questions are not easily answered and research and debate are ongoing.

Some children can read at an appropriate pace with few mistakes yet not comprehend the text, while others read at a fairly slow pace and make quite a few mistakes yet somehow manage to make sense of the text. Children learn in different ways and vary in their areas of strength and need, and there is no single 'correct' or 'normal' path to literacy or fluency. It follows that there are many reasons for children not being able to read fluently or for having problems comprehending. The traditional view of fluency as merely automaticity of word identification and rate of reading may therefore be viewed as somewhat simplistic. Oakley (2005, p. 13) has suggested that reading fluency might be seen as an 'outcome of the engagement, integration and self-monitoring of a repertoire of interactive reading competencies'.

Fluency results when the reader is able to simultaneously perform many literacy processes, including lower-level decoding and higher-order comprehension processes, as well as being able to integrate and self-monitor these processes. Because fluency is complex there can be several reasons for a child finding it difficult. Teachers therefore need to carry out appropriate assessments in order to uncover these obstacles. Assessment of fluency is dealt with towards the end of this chapter.

Having outlined some of the problems with the conceptualisation of fluency, there does seem to be some consensus in the academic literature that the following elements are involved:

- reading rate or pace (speed)
- accuracy and automaticity of word recognition
- smoothness and appropriate **phrasing**
- expressiveness.

It must be noted that reading fluency is often expressed in terms of *oral* reading fluency. However, readers need to be fluent when reading silently, too. Even when reading silently, it is necessary to read at an appropriate pace, with a high degree of accuracy and appropriate phrasing or 'chunking' of groups of words. However, the role of expressiveness or *prosody* may not be important in silent reading, even though people tend to hear an inner voice when reading, which may enhance the reading experience if it is expressive.

ELEMENTS OF FLUENCY

Reading rate/pace

The reading rate is the speed of reading. This is usually expressed as the number of words read per minute (WPM), although sometimes words correct per minute (WCPM) is used. Reading rate depends on the developmental level of the reader *and* the difficulty of the text.

Accuracy rate

This is usually expressed as the number of words read correctly per hundred. An accuracy rate of 95 per cent or more would indicate that the reader finds the text 'easy' and can read it independently. An accuracy rate of less than 90 per cent generally indicates that the text is difficult or 'frustrational' for the reader.

Automaticity

Automaticity is the ability to accomplish a task easily, without conscious thinking. Automaticity of word recognition entails being able to recognise words instantly, without having to expend conscious effort.

Phrasing

Phrasing involves being able to 'chunk' sentences into parts, using meaning and syntax as cues.

Expressiveness

A person who reads with expression uses volume, pitch and intonation to make the reading sound interesting and to convey meaning.

WHY IS READING FLUENCY IMPORTANT?

There are several important reasons for ensuring that children are able to read fluently. The National Reading Panel (USA) pointed out that fluent readers tend to enjoy reading more and have more positive attitudes towards reading; they are therefore more likely to do more reading and thus become better readers and learners (NICHD, 2000). A positive attitude towards reading is crucial and can make all the difference to a child's success as a reader and as a student. Further, a child's self-esteem and motivation can be positively influenced by the ability to read fluently.

There are many occasions in life when fluent oral reading is desirable if not necessary; for example, when reading newspaper articles, jokes or letters aloud to family and friends. Fluent silent reading is also important as it leads to better comprehension and enjoyment of texts, not to mention the ability to read more quickly and efficiently.

As adults, it is often necessary to read fluently in the workplace; for example, when reading out reports and presentations. It is also desirable to be able to read fluently in order to read aloud engagingly to children, thus helping the next generation of readers. There are no doubt many other benefits of being able to read fluently.

FLUENCY DEVELOPMENT

For beginning readers, it is of course not realistic to expect quick and accurate reading. These readers are very much focused on decoding and need to look at each letter in each word in order to do this. They read word by word, which is a slow and halting process that takes a lot of cognitive capacity, leaving little left over for comprehension. Beginning readers cannot generally decode and comprehend simultaneously, and therefore need to switch between one and the other (Samuels, Ediger & Fautsch-Partridge, 2005). At this stage of reading development, the focus should be on improving decoding skills and increasing the children's bank of sight words. It is also valuable to model expressive reading, appropriate phrasing and meaning-making processes during shared reading.

Once children are well into the early phase of reading, they are able to read in two-, and sometimes three- and four-word phrases. This is because their sight-word vocabulary is increasing and their decoding abilities are improving. Also, they are using their semantic and syntactic cueing systems more efficiently to predict what words might be coming next. More cognitive capacity is left over for comprehension processes. Even so, there is still a degree of switching backwards and forwards between decoding and comprehension processes. During this phase, children are able to focus on linking words together into phrases, clauses and sentences—or units that make sense or 'go together'. During this phase it is useful to focus on 'chunking' words together appropriately (phrasing), using punctuation and meaning as guides. See the section below on phrasing for more detail and suggested teaching strategies.

Later, children begin to read in larger 'chunks' of words: three and four words at a time or more. This reflects the fact that their word identification abilities are becoming even more automatic and that their understanding of syntactic boundaries and sentence structure is improving. At this stage, children have more attentional capacity left over to be able to concentrate on comprehension, which in turn facilitates word identification and fluency.

However, there is still little expression in their reading. At this stage, a teaching emphasis on expression, where appropriate, can be extremely fruitful.

When children become truly fluent readers, they have achieved automaticity of word recognition and are able to attend to and use the text's syntactic structure. Because of this automaticity, there is sufficient attentional capacity to allow more focus on comprehension processes. This is when children tend to improve greatly in terms of reading with expression. They are able to control and 'pull together' all of the sub-processes of reading, some of which are occurring automatically.

FACILITATING FLUENCY

It has been suggested that many teachers do not *explicitly* teach reading fluency, perhaps because of a theory in use that fluency will develop as a by-product of word identification and comprehension teaching and learning. However, it should be recognised that specific fluency instruction *does* help children improve their reading overall, including reading comprehension. It should therefore be included in the literacy curriculum in its own right.

Because of a theoretical emphasis on speed of word recognition, teachers and researchers have traditionally focused to a large extent on improving readers' graphophonic (decoding) and sight-word competencies in order to help them improve their fluency. It is indeed true that children need to be taught how to use, engage and control graphophonic, as well as syntactic and semantic, cues in order to identify words. However, as indicated above, there is much more to fluency instruction than this. The metalinguistic and metacognitive awareness that facilitates this coordination and self-monitoring is vitally important (Oakley, 2005); children need to know what fluent reading sounds like and need to develop 'inner models' of fluent reading (Clark, 1995), and be able to compare these to their own reading.

There are some key strategies for facilitating fluency that have research-based backing, namely:

1. *modelling* fluent reading so that children can come to understand what fluent reading is
2. *reading while listening*, which may be through choral reading, paired reading or reading along with an electronic talking book
3. *repeated readings* of the same text
4. learning about *phrasing*.

KEY PRACTICES FOR ENCOURAGING FLUENCY

MODELLING

Many children have few opportunities to hear what fluent reading sounds like, since reading aloud to children at home does not always take place on a regular basis. For this reason, it is imperative that teachers and caregivers read aloud to children often. Also, it is important to give children opportunities to think about and discuss what *sounds* good and conveys the meaning of the text in the best way. Modelling enables children to build 'inner models' of what fluent reading actually sounds like (Clark, 1995), which they can then learn to compare to their own oral reading.

Shared reading

Shared reading is an excellent context for modelling. During shared reading, the teacher can 'think aloud' about how the oral reading should sound, what sort of expression is appropriate, what pace of reading is best, and how words might be chunked together.

Analysis of non-fluent reading

Teachers can occasionally read dysfluently—for example, in a monotone voice, word by word, or in the wrong pitch, volume and speed—and ask children to make suggestions as to how they might 'fix' their reading.

Listening posts

Children can use listening posts and electronic talking books (computer based) to access models of fluent reading. They can also use listening posts for reading-while-listening activities (see below).

Reading buddies

If in a school context, older, fluent readers can visit the classroom and read to individual or small groups of children. This can be of benefit for both the older and the younger children.

Comparing reading to 'inner models' of fluent reading

Oakley (2003) had children record their reading and then listen to it and analyse it in terms of how they thought good, fluent reading should sound ('inner models'). They then re-recorded it and compared their readings to see which version sounded better.

READING WHILE LISTENING

Reading while listening involves the child reading (usually aloud) while listening as a proficient reader narrates the text. The proficient reader may be a parent, teacher, peer or even a taped recording. Different types of reading while listening are described and discussed below. Full instructions for implementing some of these strategies are at the end of the chapter.

Shared reading

Shared reading is an ideal context for reading while listening, as the teacher reads aloud and points at words and phrases as she or he goes along. Shared reading is also a good means of repeatedly reading the same text. Children in the beginning and early phases of reading, who do not have highly developed decoding and sight-word abilities, can enjoy practising reading with appropriate speed, phrasing and expression.

Choral reading

Choral reading involves children reading a story or poem together. Texts used for choral reading often have a refrain as this allows less able students to join in, and sometimes actions are added, such as clapping, clicking fingers and facial expressions. For information about how to implement choral reading, see the toolbox of strategies at the end of this chapter.

TEXTS FOR CHORAL READING

Three little kittens

Group 1:	Three little kittens
	They lost their mittens,
	and they began to cry … *(Sniff three times and wipe eyes)*
Narrator:	So sad! *(Look glum)*
Group 2:	Oh, mother dear,
	We sadly fear,
	our mittens we have lost. *(Look to the left, to the right, and to the left again)*.
Narrator:	So bad! *(Look of shock/horror)*
Group 3:	What? Lost your mittens, *(Put hands on hips)*
	you naughty kittens!
	Now, you shall have no pie.
	(Stamp feet twice)
Narrator:	So mad!
	(Point finger angrily)

Mary had a little lamb

Whole Class:	Mary had a little lamb,
Student 1:	its fleece was white as snow;
Entire Class:	and everywhere that Mary went
Student 1:	the lamb was sure to go.
Class:	It followed her to school one day
Student 2:	which was against the rules;
Class:	it made the children laugh and play
Student 2:	to see a lamb at school. [laugh ha ha ha!]
Class:	And so the teacher turned it out,
Student 3:	but still it lingered near;
Class:	and waited patiently about
Student 3:	till Mary did appear.
Class:	Why does the lamb love Mary so?
Student 4:	the eager children cry.
Teacher:	Why, Mary loves the lamb, you know,
	the teacher did reply.

Echo reading

Echo reading entails a fluent reader, often teacher or caregiver, reading simple texts aloud, (usually only a sentence or two at a time in the early grades) and the children repeating what has been read. Children should read along silently as the teacher reads and actually read the text when they themselves read aloud; echo reading is not a memory game in which children merely parrot what the fluent reader has said.

Echo reading is often most rewarding for the children when the text includes dialogue. The children can then have fun trying out different voices.

Paired reading

Paired reading (Topping, 1987) is a one-on-one technique, whereby an experienced reader pairs up with a novice reader and offers support when needed. Essentially, both read together until the child signals to the experienced reader to fade out. The child reads aloud until he begins to stumble, when the experienced reader joins in again.

Recorded/taped readings

Research into this form of listening while reading has indicated that it can be significantly beneficial to reading (Carbo, 1996). Here, the child listens to a recorded text while following along using the printed version of the text, either reading aloud or silently.

Audio recordings of books can now be downloaded from the internet. For example, a number of Robert Munsch books, including *The paper bag princess*, are narrated by Munsch himself on his official website (www.robertmunsch.com). These can be downloaded free of charge and listened to on iPods. Mem Fox reads *Koala Lou* on her website (www.memfox.net/audio/koala_lou.html). However, this must be listened to sitting by the computer as it cannot be saved.

Digital or electronic talking books can also be used for listening while reading activities. Children sit at the computer and engage in these texts, which are either on CD-ROM or online. Children usually find these multimedia texts highly engaging and motivational (Glasgow, 1996–97) and are often willing to read them repeatedly, which is itself beneficial.

Children listen to a recorded text while following along using the printed version of the text, either reading aloud or silently.

REPEATED READINGS

Repeated reading entails reading the same short text (100 to 300 words) up to four or five times in order to achieve appropriate pace, accuracy, expression and phrasing. Another effect of repeated readings is the repeated exposure of particular words, which can then move into children's sight-word repertoire. The number of times a child needs to see a word before it becomes a sight word depends on a number of factors, such as the child's memory and the features of the particular words.

The traditional view is that children should be provided with 'easy' or independent-level texts for repeated readings, but this view has recently been questioned. Some researchers now think that it is more beneficial to work with slightly challenging or 'instructional' texts. Some teacher support may be required during the first reading.

The main target of repeated reading is often to increase rate of reading. However, in the case of young children, overemphasis of pace of reading can be detrimental. It could be argued that this may give younger children the wrong impression about the purposes of reading; it is not desirable for them to think that 'racing' through texts is the aim. Indeed, children in lower primary grades (Year 3 and below) may be better served by not focusing on rate. This is not to say that the teacher should not monitor changes in rate. Children's reading rate can, indeed, drop, and this may be because they are paying more attention to meaning or have moved to more difficult texts.

READERS' THEATRE

Readers' theatre (RT) involves groups of readers giving an oral performance of a script (adapted from a children's book). This is not like a performance of a play because readers do not memorise the text, but read it to an audience after having rehearsed it several times (repeated readings) to ensure that it is smooth, expressing and entertaining. No stage 'set' or elaborate props are used, although a few simple props such as hats, wands and spectacles might be used.

As well as improving fluency, RT can be effective in boosting children's interest in reading and their confidence. Because RT involves the interpretation of scripts, it can be an excellent means of developing comprehension. Children need to understand the plot, characters and motives in order to perform the script.

Children who are able will enjoy modifying children's books into RT format, but more often in early childhood contexts the teacher will do this. Busy teachers may access free RT scripts on the internet and some examples of worthwhile websites are given below. It will be necessary to select scripts suitable for early childhood classrooms from these script collections, as some are meant for older children.

READERS THEATRE SCRIPTS (WEBSITES)

- Reading a-z.com: www.readinga-z.com/guided/theater_list.html (Free resource but registration required.)
- Teaching Heart: www.teachingheart.net/readerstheater.htm
- Lois Walker website: loiswalker.com/grasshop.html
- Belford Middle School's Drama and Presentation Skills website: bms.westport.k12.ct.us/mccormick/rt/rtscriphome.htm (Includes scripts for Years 2 and 3.)
- Reading Lady: www.readinglady.com/

FOCUS ON PHRASING

According to some researches, **phrasing** is 'at the heart' of fluency (Zutell, Donelson, Bevans & Todt, 2006, p. 269). Phrasing involves knowing how to put words into appropriate 'chunks' as opposed to reading one word at a time, and not 'running on' from one sentence to another without paying attention to punctuation.

Syntactic/grammatical knowledge

It is essential to provide instruction in identifying phrase boundaries. In order to assist students with this, teachers may draw light slash marks in texts at naturally occurring pause points. In addition, it is necessary to explain and model to children that good readers read in phrases. Reading in phrases involves the eye and the brain being several steps ahead of the voice (the so called 'eye–voice span'). This allows the reader to 'plan ahead' somewhat when reading aloud.

In order to help children use punctuation cues when reading, there are some simple techniques that teachers can use. One of these is for teachers to read aloud texts that have had punctuation deleted. This will involve reading with inappropriate expression and with pauses in the wrong places. Children are then asked to comment on what sounded right and what didn't sound right (and *why*). The teacher can then add punctuation, with the children's input, and reread the story until it sounds right. Not only will this activity help children develop their reading fluency but it also will improve their overall understanding of the role of punctuation, and thus their writing.

IMPROVING THE ELEMENTS OF READING FLUENCY

PACE

It is important for children to read at an *appropriate* reading pace: too slow, and it is often difficult for young readers to string the individual words together to make sense of them; too fast, and there may not be enough time for the reader (or listener) to think about the words being read and make links between the text and prior knowledge. Some young children think that fast reading is *good* reading and it is important for teachers and caregivers to impress on them that, in fact, there is no point in reading quickly if this means reading without comprehension. As noted above, an overemphasis on increasing reading rate can be counter-productive, resulting in reduction of meaning making.

When children are at a beginning stage of learning to read, a good way to help them read at a quicker rate is to work on improving their decoding skills (phonics) and building their sight-word vocabulary. These children should also be encouraged to engage in *repeated* readings of texts, even if these are very short and simple texts. This will enable them to concentrate on speed and meaningful phrasing and expression, without being hampered by the 'decoding' bottleneck. It will also help them build their self-concept as readers, as well as helping them consolidate their sight-word repertoire, which will help children improve their reading rate. *Reading while listening* is an effective way of helping children improve their pace of reading, as well as helping children improve their phrasing and word identification.

CALCULATING WORDS CORRECT PER MINUTE (WCPM)

- Ask the child to read an 'easy' level text of at least 100 words.
- Time how long it takes the child to read the text (in seconds).
- Do the following calculation:
    1. number of words read minus errors = number of word read correctly
    2. number of words read correctly ÷ number of seconds taken
    3. multiply by 60 and round to nearest whole number (to convert back to minutes) = WCPM

For example:
98 (TOTAL WORDS)
− 5 (ERRORS)
= 93 (WORDS CORRECT)

93/105 (SECONDS) = 0.88

0.88 × 60 = 53 (WCPM).

So, what is a good reading rate? When should we as teachers be concerned that a child is not reading at an appropriate pace to be able to string words together into meaningful phrases, clauses and sentences? At the beginning of Year 1, we would not be concerned because many children are still learning the basics of decoding and a few high-frequency and high-interest sight words at this point. By the middle of the first year of schooling, however, we might expect children to be reading at least ten to twenty words per minute, and by the end of the first year, fifty words a minute would be a reasonable target. However, *it cannot be stressed enough* that children vary enormously in their reading abilities and these targets can only be taken as rough guides. Many children start school with the ability to read simple texts, whereas other Australian children start school without even rudimentary knowledge of the alphabet. Other children have English as a second language and have knowledge about their mother tongue but no knowledge of reading texts in English.

The following table (from the USA—Australian norms are not available) provides a rough guide of how many words correct per minute (WCPM) children at or above the 50th percentile can typically read when reading grade-level materials. Children reading ten words or more below the 50th percentile might be considered 'at risk' and be given extra support (Hasbrouck & Tindal, 2006). Clearly, it is not appropriate to measure the reading rate of children below Year 1.

Table 14.1: Words per minute guide

	End of year
Year 1	55–110 WCPM
Year 2	90–140 WCPM
Year 3	105–160 WCPM

Source: Hasbrouck & Tindal (2006)

IMPROVING EXPRESSIVENESS

Most adults know what expressive reading sounds like. The voice varies in speed, volume, stress and pitch to convey meaning and emotion. It is difficult to read with expression if the text is not fully understood. Indeed, when a child reads aloud with inappropriate expression it *can* point to an underlying lack of comprehension, which the teacher may care to investigate through probing questions.

However, there are plenty of cases where a child actually does comprehend a text but still does not read with expression. Their voice may be monotone, with little variation in pitch, speed and volume. This can occur if a child has not heard models of expressive reading, taking into account the elements of **prosody**. It is thus highly important for teachers and caregivers to read with expression when reading aloud to children. Reading through the story prior to reading it aloud can make all the difference. Teachers can check their reading for expression by recording themselves and listening to the recording.

It is important to distinguish between fiction and non-fiction, since it is not necessary to read informational texts with the same kind as expression used for stories. Indeed, it is usually preferable to use a more 'matter of fact' voice when reading non-fiction, and children should be made aware of this (Zutell et al., 2006).

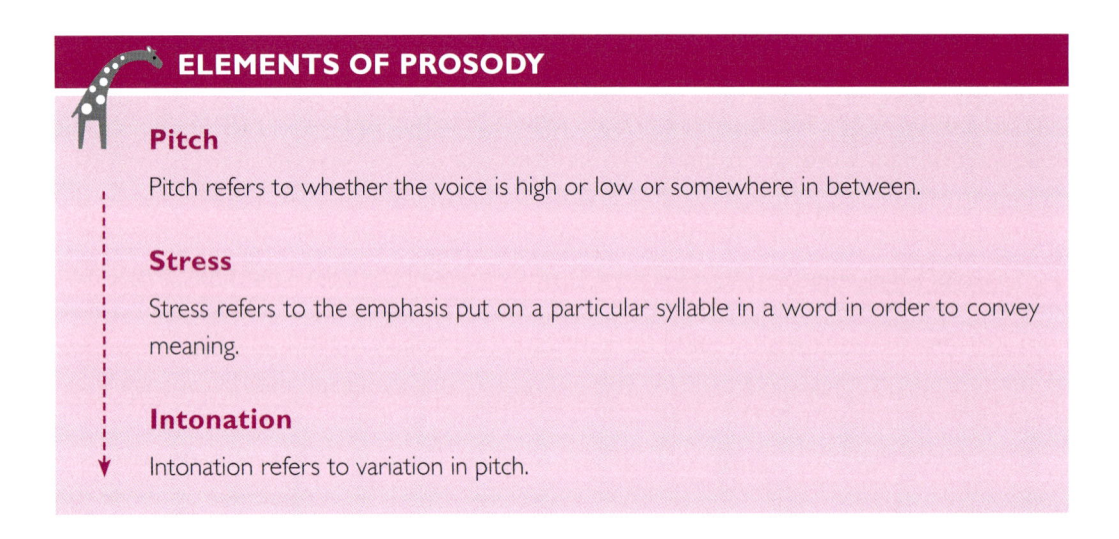

ELEMENTS OF PROSODY

Pitch
Pitch refers to whether the voice is high or low or somewhere in between.

Stress
Stress refers to the emphasis put on a particular syllable in a word in order to convey meaning.

Intonation
Intonation refers to variation in pitch.

USING ICT TO TEACH READING FLUENCY

Information and communications technologies (ICT) can be used to deliver any of the four main fluency teaching strategies: modelling, reading while listening, focus on phrasing, and repeated readings.

READING DIGITAL/ELECTRONIC TALKING BOOKS (ETBS)

Reading digital talking books, such as the *Living books* CD-ROMs, can assist in the development of reading fluency in that they can be used to provide models of fluent reading.

Although many ETBs feature narrators who speak in American or British accents, children from other English speaking countries, such as Australia, can indubitably benefit. Children can access ETBs either in the classroom or at home to supplement other models of fluent reading they hear, which sometimes are few.

Also, reading ETBs can help children learn sight words, since spoken and written words appear together. Children can make correspondences between written and spoken words and, if the ETBs are read several times, the repeated exposure will help them build their sight-word vocabularies, which can assist in improving reading rate.

Another feature of some ETBs is that text highlighting is usually provided. Sometimes this is provided in meaningful 'chunks' or phrases, as opposed to single words or entire sentences, and this can help children understand how to focus on words in groups or 'chunks' instead of on individual words.

WRITING DIGITAL BOOKS

Engaging children in the writing of digital or 'talking' books may help children become fluent readers (Oakley, 2003). This is especially so if writing the digital text is used as a context to think about phrase boundaries. Going through the process of deciding where to place text highlighting can assist children in understanding syntactic boundaries.

Furthermore, the making of digital talking texts involves recording children's reading. It is useful to get them to listen to their recordings, in small groups, and then discuss whether or not they 'sound right'.

Digital talking texts (sometimes known as electronic talking books or story books) are discussed further in Chapter 24 on Literacy and ICT.

DIGITAL BOOKS ONLINE (WITH AUDIO)

- The Farm Animals: www.magickeys.com/books/farm/page1.html
- Read Along Stories and Songs: www.rif.org/readingplanet/content/read_aloud_stories.mspx

PULLING IT ALL TOGETHER

APPROPRIATE TEXTS/READABILITY

When focusing on fluency, it is important that the text is an appropriate level for the child. It has long been suggested that the text should be at an 'independent' or 'easy' level for fluency training (95 per cent accuracy rate or higher), which will free the child to focus on phrasing, appropriate rate, smoothness and expressiveness; there should not be too many word identification 'bottlenecks' to overcome when fluency is the intended outcome. However, Stahl and Heubach (1995) conducted research that suggests a slightly more challenging level of text is more effective for increasing reading progress. Other features of the text that should be considered include the reader's familiarity with the text type, and their level of interest in the topic.

SELF-MONITORING

Because of a theoretical emphasis on speed of word recognition, teachers and researchers have traditionally focused to a large extent on improving readers' graphophonic (decoding) and sight-word competencies. However, children need to be taught how to use (engage and control) graphophonic, syntactic/grammatical, semantic and strategic information, and how to *integrate and self-monitor* these competencies in order to achieve reading fluency (Oakley, 2005). In order to self-monitor, children need to know what fluent reading sounds like, and to compare their own reading to inner models (Clark, 1995) of fluent reading. Explicit teaching is usually necessary in order for children to achieve this metacognitive awareness, and this is done through modelling, discussion and analysis of readings.

PRACTISE, PRACTISE, PRACTISE

As Allington has pointed out pointed out (1977) children need to read a lot to become good at fluency, so anything that increases motivation to read may indirectly increase fluency. To practise, practise, practise is highly important. For this to occur, it is necessary for teachers to provide a variety of appropriate and interesting books for children to read, and to foster motivation to read as a desired disposition. A key means of doing this is by modelling enthusiasm for reading.

ASSISTING STRUGGLING BEGINNING READERS

For beginning readers who are struggling in terms of fluency, Zutell et al. (2006, p. 271) have developed a five-day cycle that uses elements of Reading Recovery, which is a technique used to help young children (usually aged six) who struggle with reading. Reading Recovery involves children engaging in daily one-on-one sessions with a specially trained Reading Recovery teacher. In these 20- to 30-minute sessions, children read and reread books, work with words and sentences and write stories and sentences (Clay, 1993).

Zutell et al.'s cycle pulls together many of the fluency techniques already discussed in this chapter.

- On the first day of the cycle, an appropriately levelled book is discussed and then read through for the first time by the teacher, although the child may join in at times. The child then reads the text, at least once, although it will usually be necessary for the teacher or tutor to provide support—for example, through prompting or reading along.
- On day two of the cycle, the book read the previous day is briefly discussed and the child rereads it. There is more focus on day two on decoding strategies, if the student needs this kind of support. Also, the tutor extracts words from the text and the child works with them out of context. Sentence strips are matched to the text and then are cut into individual words for the child to reassemble.

- On days three and four, the child should be ready to reread the text *with a focus on fluency*. Here, the teacher or tutor may discuss with the child what fluent reading sounds like and may model fluent reading, using portions of the text. If needed, the teacher may commence by engaging the child in echo reading. As in day two, words and sentences are manipulated and reordered using sentence strips and word cards. Words easily identified (as sight words) are put into a word bank and will be frequently revisited and consolidated through games.
- On day five of the cycle, the teacher asks the child to read a copy of the text that has been typed onto plain text (with no pictures and a different layout) and the child rereads the text. The purpose of removing the pictures is to ensure a focus is on the words. At this time, the child's accuracy rate and reading rate (speed) are measured and recorded. Again, words from the text are read out of context and some are put into the child's word bank.

There is another cycle for children beyond beginning stages, which is similar in many ways, but also includes listening to taped recordings of previous readings and a greater emphasis on teacher modelling. For more information, refer to Zutell et al (2006).

ASSESSMENT OF READING FLUENCY

There is no clear agreement of what fluency is and therefore no consensus about how it should be taught. This has, not surprisingly, led to some ambiguity as to how best to assess it. However, the literature suggests that the following elements can be assessed:

- reading rate (speed)
- accuracy and automaticity of word recognition
- smoothness and appropriate phrasing
- expressiveness and prosody.

The assessment of these four elements, alongside assessment of comprehension and metalinguistic knowledge and metacognitive processes, will provide a very in-depth picture of what children can do in this area. Naturally, it is best to start off with simple assessments and delve deeper only if there appears to be a problem.

Assessment of reading rate is a simple matter of calculating how many words per minute (WPM) the child can read. Some teachers prefer to measure words correct per minute (WCPM), which combines the assessment of accuracy and rate. The instructions for doing this are earlier in this chapter. Accuracy and automaticity of word recognition can be assessed in several ways.

Informal reading inventories (IRIs), which have been discussed above, can be useful in the assessment of fluency because that they contain short texts at various levels of difficulty and 'quick calculation' guides to save teacher time. The number of words in the texts is pre-counted for the teacher as are accuracy guides. IRIs also contain comprehension questions that teachers can ask to obtain a quick idea about a child's comprehension. The teacher can also assess phrasing and smoothness when children read these texts.

The NAEP Oral Reading Scale (see box) is a very simple scale that enables teachers to place children in levels, from Level 1 to Level 4. A child in Level 1 still reads primarily word by word, although may occasionally chunk words into two or three word phrases. However, these 'phrases' do not preserve the meaning or syntax of the text. A Level 4 oral reader has achieved fluent reading and reads in large meaningful chunks most of the time, with expressiveness most of the time.

> ### NAEP'S ORAL READING FLUENCY SCALE
>
> #### Level 4
> - Reads primarily in larger, meaningful phrase groups.
> - Although some regressions, repetitions and deviations from text may be present, these do not appear to detract from the overall structure of the story.
> - Preservation of the author's syntax is consistent.
> - Some or most of the story is read with expressive interpretation.
>
> #### Level 3
> - Reads primarily in three- or four-word phrase groups.
> - Some smaller groupings may be present.
> - Majority of phrasing seems appropriate and preserves the syntax of the author.
> - Little or no expressive interpretation is present.
>
> #### Level 2
> - Reads primarily in two-word phrases with some three- or four-word groupings.
> - Some word-by-word reading may be present.
> - Word groupings may seem awkward and unrelated to larger context of sentence or passage.
>
> #### Level 1
> - Reads primarily word-by-word.
> - Occasional two-word or three-word phrases may occur—but these are infrequent and/or they do not preserve meaningful syntax.
>
> Source: US Department of Education, National Center for Education Statistics (1995). *Listening to children read aloud*. Washington, DC.

The Multidimensional Fluency Scale (MFS) (Zutell & Rasinski, 1991) is a rubric that teachers can use to guide and record their assessments of children's fluency in the following dimensions:

- expression and volume
- phrasing
- smoothness
- pace.

Students' capabilities in these four areas are rated 1 to 4. The modified MFS can be found, in full, at www.timrasinski.com/presentations/multidimensional_fluency_rubric_4_factors.pdf.

When assessing fluency, it is crucial to use appropriate texts. Samuels (2002) has suggested that teachers should assess students' fluency by selecting *two* unfamiliar passages at the student's estimated reading level. Passage length should not be too long, ranging from half a page to two pages. Both passages should be approximately the same length.

Self-assessment and peer-assessment should also be used, as this will help children judge their own reading fluency and help build their self-monitoring ability. This can be done by asking them to complete checklists, listen to tape and video recordings, and engage in discussions about fluency.

SUMMARY

In this chapter we have discussed what fluency is and how it can be taught in the early childhood years. Fluency is closely related to comprehension, and depends on rapid and accurate word identification, among other things. It is important to start teaching fluency in the early years and not wait until children are older. This can be done through modelling and discussion of what fluent reading sounds like.

QUESTIONS AND ACTIVITIES

1. How are fluency and word recognition related?
2. How does comprehension affect fluency and vice versa?
3. How can teachers help children who do not have word recognition difficulties improve their fluency?
4. What are prosody, pitch and pace?
5. Listen to a child read and assess their reading in terms of smoothness, pace, prosody and accuracy. What feedback might you give them and how will you help them improve their fluency?

KEY TERMS

automaticity
pace
phrasing
prosody

KEY REFERENCES

Hasbrouck, J. & Tindal, G. A. (2006). Oral reading fluency norms: A valuable assessment tool for reading. *The Reading Teacher, 59*(7), 636–44.

Hoffman, J. V. & Crone, S. (1985). The oral recitation lesson: A research-derived strategy for reading basal texts. In J. A. Niles & R. A. Lalik (eds), *Issues in literacy: A research perspective. Thirty-fourth yearbook of the National Reading Conference* (pp. 76–83). Rochester, NY: National Reading Conference.

National Institute of Child Health and Human Development (2000). *Report of the National Reading Panel. Teaching children to read: An evidence-based assessment of the scientific research literature on reading and its implications for reading instruction* (No. 00-4769). Washington, DC: Government Printing Office.

Oakley, G. (2003). Improving oral reading fluency (and comprehension) through the creation of electronic talking books. *Reading Online, 6*(7), n.p.

Oakley, G. (2005). Reading fluency as an outcome of a repertoire of interactive reading competencies: How to teach it to different types of dysfluent readers (and how ICT can help). *New England Reading Association Journal, 41*(1), 13–21.

Samuels, S. J. (2002). Reading fluency: Its development and assessment. In A. E. Farstrup & S. J. Samuels (eds), *What research has to say about reading instruction* (3rd edn, pp. 166–83). Newark, Delaware: International Reading Association.

Samuels, S. J., Ediger, K. & Fautsch-Partridge, T. (2005). The importance of reading fluency. *New England Reading Association Journal, 41*(1), 1–9.

Stahl, S. A., Heubach, K. & Holcomb, A. (1995). Fluency-oriented reading instruction. *Journal of Literacy Research, 37*, 25–60.

Zutell, J., Donelson, R., Bevans, J. & Todt, P. (2006). Building a focus on oral reading fluency into individual instruction for struggling readers. In T. Rasinski, C. L. Z. Blachowicz & K. Lems (eds), *Fluency instruction: Research-based best practices* (pp. 265–78). New York: Guilford Press.

TOOLBOX OF FLUENCY STRATEGIES

CHORAL READING

Materials

Books that have been previously read. Nursery rhymes can also be used.

Description

Choral reading involves children (and often the teacher) reading a story or poem aloud in unison. This allows less able students to join in without feeling threatened.
Choral reading works best with texts that have repetitions and refrains, dialogue or poetry.

Procedure

- The teacher should first model reading of the text, showing how to read with expression and appropriate rate.
- The teacher allocates parts to groups of children. Different sections of the story or poem can be read in the following ways:
  - unison (the whole group reads at the same time)
  - refrain (an individual reads the narrative and a group reads the refrain)
  - antiphonal (small groups instead of individuals are given parts to read)
  - sequential (speaking lines one after another)
  - cumulative (voices are added as the story or poem develops).
- The reading is *repeated* several times to improve fluency and expression.
- Props, sound effects and movements can be added.
- Perform for a real audience if possible.
- (Shared reading often includes some choral reading.)

ECHO READING

Materials needed

A short children's book or poem.

Description

This strategy involves the teacher, parent or caregiver reading short sections of texts, usually a single clause or sentence at a time, and then the children repeating this text while reading the text. It is not merely a memory game; children need to read the text as they pronounce the words.

Procedure

- The teacher or parent reads one line, clause or phrase from the book, reading with expression and paying attention to phrase boundaries.
- The child reads along silently as the adult reads.

- The child now 'echoes' the adult's reading, while reading the text at the same time. He or she tries to read the text with the same expression and phrasing as the adult did.
- Continue in this fashion until the end of the text.
- Start again and do it again (if appropriate) *or* read the whole text together in choral reading.

PAIRED READING

Materials

A book at an appropriate reading level (not difficult). Picture books are best for young children.

Description

Paired reading involves an experienced reader (parent, caregiver, teacher or older peer) reading together with a child. The experienced reader 'fades out' when the child is reading comfortably alone and resumes reading when needed. This technique facilitates fluency and can increase reading confidence and motivation.

Procedure

- Choose an appropriate text and carry out some simple pre-reading activities such as predicting what will be in the text, discussing the topic or flicking through the pictures.
- Decide on a signal (often a nudge or a hand tap) for the child to give when they feel confident to read alone.
- Start reading the text together.
- When the child gives the signal, the adult fades out gradually by using a softer voice. Often, even if the child does not signal, the experienced reader can lower her voice and let the child's voice dominate.
- Give encouragement and praise, as appropriate.
- When the child begins to falter, mispronounces a word or pauses for more than four or five seconds, the adult begins to read along again, until the next hand tap or nudge is received.

ORAL RECITATION LESSON (ORL)

(Hoffman & Crone, 1985; Hoffman & Isaacs, 1991)

Materials needed

Story book in big book format *or* book each for each child in group

Description

ORL involves the teacher doing modelled reading of a text with a focus on comprehension and expression, prior to children engaging in choral reading of sections of the text. The first parts of ORL (parts 1–3) should be done for approximately four days per text, for thirty minutes per day (small groups). The indirect instruction should be done on a daily basis (whole class), for approximately ten minutes per day.

Procedure

Part 1: Read, discuss, summarise
- Read the story to the children (small group).
- With the children's input, create a story map of the story (in enlarged format).
- Write a summary of the story. The story map should guide the writing of the summary. Children can make suggestions.

Part 2: Focus on fluency
- Select a section of the story to use for the focus on fluency. It may be a few paragraphs or a few pages, depending on the text and the children.
- Do a 'mini-lesson' on an aspect of fluency (or several aspects of fluency) that you wish to focus on, such as expression, pace or phrasing. A mini-lesson only takes a few minutes to present.
- Read the section of text aloud, modelling fluency.
- In pairs or as a small group, children practise reading the section of text fluently. Give corrective and constructive feedback.

Part 3: Practice and performance
- In small groups, children select a portion of the story. After plenty of practice, they read the section aloud to the rest of the class. Practice should involve all children reading aloud together. Mumble reading or reading in a 'soft voice' allows children to practise without disturbing each other.

+ 10 minutes per day indirect teaching
- Students reread the story or a portion of the story independently (soft oral reading) for ten minutes a day.
- The teacher checks for mastery by ensuring that all children have achieved a 98 per cent accuracy rate and 75 words per minute (rate).

READERS THEATRE

Materials needed

A children's book, to be turned into a readers theatre script or a prepared script. A few simple props can be used, if appropriate.

Description

Children read and rehearse scripts in groups of four to approximately twelve in order to perform them to an audience. They read from the script during the performance and do not memorise lines. Few, if any, props are used as the focus is on the reading. Allow approximately a week for each script to be learnt.

Suggested procedure

- Teacher reads the script aloud to the children in a shared reading session. During this time, comprehension strategies may be modelled and word meanings discussed.
- Teacher reads script again, modelling fluent reading and discussing what this sounds like. The role of punctuation may also be discussed. Children join in (choral reading) where appropriate.

- Children read the whole script—this can be done as choral reading or paired reading.
- Children read the whole text independently. This may be done at home.
- A part is allocated to each child.
- In groups, children read scripts. Each child reads his or her part. Children discuss expression and phrasing with reference to the meaning of the script. The teacher 'visits' the group and participates in discussion and offers feedback.
- Children rehearse the script several times until they can read it fluently.
- Children decide on any gestures, facial expressions and props to be used. These will be minimal.
- Performance of the story is done in front of audience.

PART 3

Learning to Write

CHAPTER 15

Introduction to Writing

CHAPTER OBJECTIVES

This chapter will increase your understanding of:

- the knowledge, skills and strategies involved in competent written communication
- the components and qualities that comprise written texts
- the various steps involved in the process of writing
- the phases that depict children's growth as writers
- the phases and key areas of learning that occur for children as they develop as writers
- the key practices and experiences important to young children's growth in writing.

This chapter is the first of a sequence of chapters dealing with written language and with developing the knowledge, understanding, strategies and skills that children need for effective written communication. It provides a general introduction to written language, describing the various features of written texts and the practices of competent writers. The more you understand about written language, the more you are able to set up learning environments that most benefit children's growth as writers. As you read about written language, consider the implications for working with both younger and older children. The chapter also deals with the phases of writing development; that is, the pathway that many children follow and the achievements they reach along the way, as they develop as writers.

WRITTEN COMMUNICATION

Writing is the use of written language to compose a text for the purpose of communicating information. It might involve, for example, the composition of a procedural text that gives instructions on how to do something, a descriptive text that details the features of something or someone, a narrative that serves to entertain through story or perhaps a newspaper article that reports on an event. It might entail composing smaller texts such as the captions for a picture, the labels for a diagram or signs and messages.

Learning to write is a gradual process and involves knowledge and a range of skills which are built up over time.

Writing is a complex activity that requires an appropriate level of knowledge about written composition and the application of a range of skills and strategies. In order to compose a text that effectively communicates meaning, the writer must:

- consider the purpose of communicating, the information to be conveyed and the type of text to be used
- conceptualise ideas and translate them from oral to written form
- select, combine, arrange and develop ideas into effective sentences and paragraphs (Walsche, 1981)
- review what has been written and evaluate its effectiveness in conveying the ideas (Olsen, 2007, p. 195) and in achieving the communicative purpose
- apply the conventions of grammar, spelling and punctuation.

Learning to write is a gradual process and children need time to accumulate the knowledge, skills and strategies required to become effective writers. Children need to develop a capacity to write words and sentences and to construct suitably sequenced and comprehensible texts. They should be given frequent opportunities to experiment with writing as they learn about and gain control of the various features of written language, and they require regular instruction in the skills and techniques that will enhance their development in this area.

There are a number of practices that are important to young children's growth in writing and which should regularly occur in early childhood. These are:

- *Oral language experiences*: oral language is the foundation of writing (Cunningham & Moore, 2004). There needs to be a continual focus on conversation, dramatic play, storytelling and other oral language experiences. As children's oral language develops—as they develop more words in their speaking vocabulary and new and accurate ways to combine words to form sentences—they will have a greater range of language knowledge that they can bring to writing tasks.
- *Book reading*: children need the regular experience of having books read to them or, when able, to read books independently. Repeated exposure to different books develops children's understanding about the features of written language and increases their knowledge about the ways that language can be used in written communication.
- *Demonstration*: children need to observe teachers as they write, witnessing the processes used by a competent writer in composing a text. For instance, they can learn that writers read back what they have written, ensuring that there is a logical sequence in the next idea or sentence which they compose.
- *Practice*: children need continuous experience in writing. They need the chance to experiment using what they know about writing and the opportunity to apply and practise their developing skills and knowledge. The opportunities to write should be available during free play. For older children their writing development is also well served when they receive individual guidance from the teacher. The guidance can take many forms depending on the children's needs; examples include reminding a child to reread their writing to check for clarity of meaning, assisting a child to form full sentences as they compose their text or working with a child to read through their written text and revise it for necessary detail.

FOUR COMPONENTS OF WRITING

Writing can be viewed as a set of four interrelated components. They are:

1. the writing context
2. the text form
3. the process and strategies
4. the conventions.

Good writers have a depth of knowledge of all four **writing components** which they make use of when composing written texts. Children need to learn about all four components in order to develop a comprehensive understanding and competency in writing.

THE WRITING CONTEXT

The **writing context** refers to the features of the writing situation. It includes the purpose (reason) for writing, the audience (the person/people for whom the text is being written) and the topic (the subject matter of the text). Proficient writers take these features into consideration when they decide how a text should be composed. They produce texts that are structured to suit the communicative purpose, the audience (readership) and the subject.

Learning to write involves learning about the influence of context on text production. There are some fundamental understandings that need to be established for children to be able to produce texts in a way that shows consideration of purpose, audience and subject. Children need to develop the understanding that:

- Writing is a social activity. It involves communicating information to others.
- People write for many different reasons (purposes). The information in a text has to serve its particular communicative purpose.
- There are different types of written texts. Each is structured or formatted to best serve the purpose for which it is written.
- People write for a particular person or group of people (though this can sometimes be oneself such as when writing a journal or a shopping list). Someone will have to read the text and they need to be able to comprehend it.

With the right learning environment many of these understandings can be fostered at a young age.

THE TEXT FORM

Text form refers to the way in which the information in a text is organised and the features of the language used. Written language can be set out in many different text forms; the one used being that which is most appropriate for the purpose. Recipes, stories, letters, diaries and reports are all in different text forms and each is appropriate to the purpose. For example, a text using a recount format is used for the purpose of writing to tell someone about a recent holiday and a recipe format is used in order to provide someone with the information needed for making lamingtons. The form that a written text takes is determined by the communicative intention.

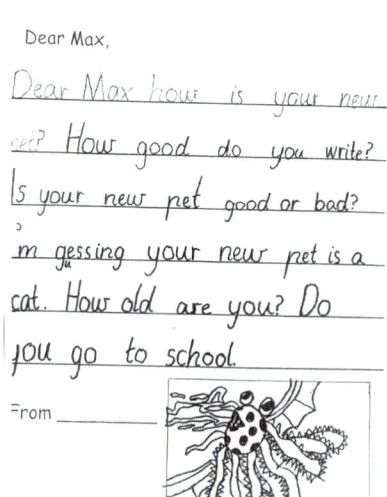

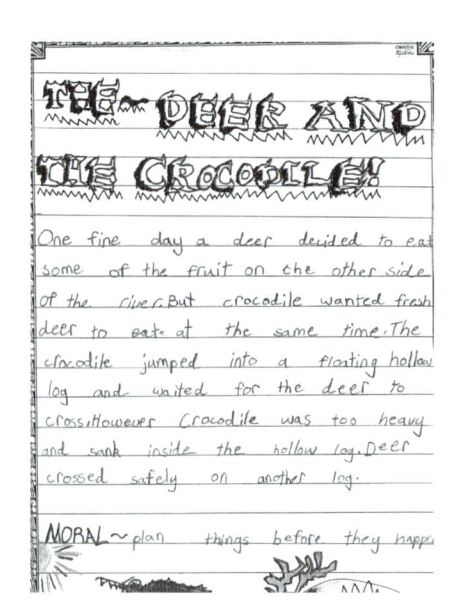

Written language is set out in a particular type of text depending on the purpose for writing.

There is a customary way in which information should be presented for the various text forms. For instance, a report would generally present an overview followed by a series of descriptions of different aspects of the topic. A recount text would organise information so that the events of the experience being conveyed were presented in the appropriate time order, while an instructional text would provide the necessary directions for completing a specific task. These organisational features are not obligatory, but they are useful for working with beginning writers who as developing writers need to learn how to organise written information to suit the communicative purpose.

Learning to write includes learning about different text forms. In early childhood, the focus should initially be on developing children's familiarity with the more common text forms. As children's writing fluency increases, they can be taught how to apply the organisational and language features of these and other text forms to their writing. Account should be taken of the overall writing ability of children in setting the requirements for the use of text forms.

In learning this component of writing:

- Children need to develop an understanding that there are different text forms, each of which is related to the communicative purpose of the text.
- Children should be taught how to write different text forms using the conventional organisational patterns.

Chapter 16 provides more detailed information about the range of text forms and their organisational and language requirements. It also explains how children can be taught about text forms and how their ability to control the organisational and language features can be developed.

THE PROCESSES AND STRATEGIES

Writing processes and strategies refer to the techniques that writers use as they compose texts. For instance, they might draw a picture or jot down ideas for the content of a text before they start writing and they might read over their text at the end and make some improvements. Tompkins (2008) identifies eight strategies that good writers utilise as they carry out the task of composing a text. These are explained by Tompkins as.

- *Generating*: this involves gathering the ideas and words for the writing task. It can involve thinking about the topic and recalling information or reading to expand information already known. Writers might draw pictures, take notes or write lists to remember their ideas.
- *Organising*: this involves planning the way in which the information should be organised to enable its comprehension.
- *Visualising*: this involves the use of the senses to inspire more detail to their writing.
- *Monitoring*: this involves the writer checking on how well the written text is evolving.
- *Playing with language*: This involves incorporating figurative and novel language in the text.
- *Proofreading*: this involves identifying and correcting misspelt words, punctuation errors and grammar mistakes in the written text.
- *Evaluation*: this involves a review of the written text and judging its effectiveness in achieving its purpose.

Of course, in teaching different writing strategies, teachers need to take into account the various other aspects of writing with which children are grappling. They need to introduce writing strategies when it is appropriate to children's phase of writing development.

THE CONVENTIONS

Writing conventions are the technical aspects to be applied in writing texts. These include punctuation, spelling, grammar, sentence and paragraphing structure. Writers must use these in ways that conform to the accepted standards for written English. However, for young beginning writers, their experiences with writing should not be restrained by an overemphasis on their use of conventional writing. Learning to write requires experimentation. Over time, children should learn to adopt the technical aspects of written composition and to understand their importance to the production of texts that are readily comprehended by others. Children need to learn about:

- the principles and practices that apply to ordering words in sentences
- the way words can be modified (e.g. run, running, ran)
- the different forms of punctuation that can be used in sentences
- the correct way to spell words
- the way to structure cohesive paragraphs.

Chapters 17 and 18 address the conventions of written texts in greater detail.

THE PHYSICAL ASPECT OF WRITING

Effective writing requires children to have achieved a certain degree of fine muscle control, hand–eye coordination and wrist and hand muscle strength. Writing experiences that make demands on children beyond their physical readiness will often result in children's disengagement with the act of writing. Writing experiences should be geared to children's physical as well as cognitive development.

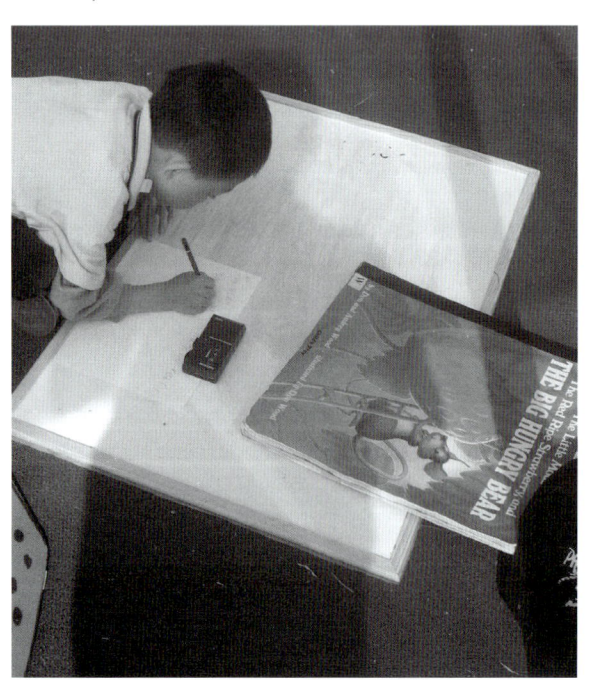

Writing experiences should be geared to children's physical as well as cognitive development.

WRITING TRAITS

Spandel (2009), in her book *Creating writers through 6 trait writing,* proposes a view of the components of written texts. She outlines a model of six good **writing traits** which can be used to measure the quality of children's writing. The six traits are:

- ideas
- organisation
- voice
- word choice
- sentence fluency
- conventions.

The *ideas* trait refers to the main ideas or storyline of a writer's text and the detail that is used to support or expand them. Children need to be taught how to clearly and comprehensively achieve the full intended meaning in a text.

The *organisation* trait refers to the writer's use of text design, structure and organisational patterns to put across information. It involves the writer presenting ideas in an appropriate and logical order (Spandel, 2008). Children need to be taught how to structure a text so that the information is arranged in an organised fashion and flows in a logical order.

The *voice* trait refers to the individual way a person expresses themselves in writing. It has to do with the tone such as whether it is friendly, formal, technical, chatty or distant, and it comes across through the types of words and patterns of sentences used. Children need to be taught to use a voice which is appropriate to the topic and the audience.

The *word choice* trait refers to the writer's use of words and phrases that most clearly portray meaning and that evoke feeling and mood. Children's vocabulary should be expanded continually so that they develop a strong repertoire from which they can choose the most appropriate words for their writing. They need to be taught how to select an appropriate word to convey the intended meaning.

The *sentence fluency* trait refers to the writer's use of various sentence types and lengths, and different ways to begin and join sentences so that a text is produced which flows naturally and is easy and enjoyable to read. Children need to develop competency in composing different types of sentences.

The *conventions* trait refers to the writer's use of standard forms of punctuation, spelling and grammar to ensure text readability. Children should be taught conventional spelling and the correct use of punctuation.

THE WRITING PROCESS

An understanding of the writing process is most relevant to those working with children who have achieved a certain degree of understanding and skill in writing, most likely children in the early years of school.

The writing process (Graves, 1983) refers to the steps that a writer carries out in order to produce an effective written text so that it clearly communicates the intended meaning. When the steps of the writing process are followed with skill and competency, the text produced should achieve its purpose and be easily comprehended by the reader. When teaching children in the early years of school to become effective writers, it is important to teach them to compose a text with regard to the steps of the writing process. The steps themselves need to be taught and competency in using them needs to be developed. The steps of the writing process are:

1 preparing to write
2 writing
3 revising
4 editing
5 publishing and sharing with an audience.

Children should be taught each step of the writing process and provided with the opportunity to practise these steps. However, it must be remembered that it takes a long time for children to develop competency, and the ability to implement each of the steps necessitates a certain degree of competency in other writing skills and knowledge. For instance, the revision step requires an ability to form different sentence types (simple, complex and compound) and to rearrange sentences, while the editing step requires a level of competency with spelling and punctuation and an ability to identify grammatically incorrect sentences. It may therefore be necessary to modify the various steps as well as the expectations held about the extent to which different groups of children will achieve reasonable fluency in their endeavours. Children should be expected to master the writing process only to the level of their capabilities.

Below are descriptions of each of the steps of the writing process, together with activities that can be used to assist children with each step.

PREPARING TO WRITE

To begin the writing process, writers should deliberate over, and make decisions about, the topic and purpose of their writing. They need time to consider and work out the information to be expressed. At this step, writers might also wish to find out more about the topic. They also need to determine how they will organise the information when writing it.

When writing, children benefit from regular opportunities to choose their own topic, purpose and audience. However, of equal benefit to their growth as writers is that teachers frequently make these decisions; that is, that they provide certain writing experiences with an established topic, purpose (communicative goal) and audience (readership). Teachers might also provide guidelines for the way in which children can organise their writing to shape the text. Children need a balance of different types of writing experiences and they need specific types that can best support the achievement of learning goals; for instance, if there is a need to focus on developing children's ability to write more descriptive sentences, then a suitable writing experience such as a character description can be planned.

It is important for children to be provided with balance in the types of writing experiences which they are given. Providing children with a balanced array of writing tasks is important to the comprehensive development of their writing. Different types of writing experiences (for example, a recipe for fruit kebabs, description of a zoo animal, recount of a story and letter to a friend) support the development of different writing knowledge and skills. Different tasks call for the application of different writing strategies and knowledge, and provide different ways in which the teacher can focus learning; for example, how to set out a letter, the elements of a story (narrative) and the use of adjectives and adverbs in creating more descriptive language.

Teachers should also teach children certain methods in planning the content ideas and information. This will expose them to different means by which they can plan their writing. The method which is espoused will depend on the nature of the writing task and those which are most appropriate to their age and present writing skills. Planning to write could include any one or more of the following methods:

- *Drawing*: this method calls for children to create a visual record of their ideas for the writing topic or, more specifically, to create a series of drawings which indicate content and the order in which the ideas should be presented. This method is useful when the written text involves writing about a sequence of events as, for instance, in a story, a recount or an instructional text.
- *Questions and answers*: this method calls for children to record answers to a series of questions which have been provided to them. If necessary they can find the answers by researching books or websites or watching informational films. This method is appropriate to planning a report. The questions could become the headings for the report which will in turn assist in structuring the text.
- *Text framework*: this method involves the provision of a planning document which sets down a number of headings that together constitute an outline of the proposed text. The children can then make notes, write words or draw pictures under each heading as a way of expanding on the content of their text. For example, if young children are to write a story, their text framework might contain the headings 'Beginning', 'Middle' and 'End'. For older children, the headings might be a little more complex.
- *Graphic organisers*: similar to text frameworks, graphic organisers help children to plan the content of their writing by listing ideas under a set of prompts. For instance, when writing about spiders, children might be provided with a graphic organiser containing the following prompts—'what they look like', 'where they live' and 'what they eat'.
- *Talking*: when children talk through their ideas they are better prepared to write about them. Before writing, children could be asked to discuss their ideas with someone else. For instance, if the writing task was to recount a recent class trip to the zoo, they might first work with a partner to orally recount the event. Photos could be used to support the children's recall of the experience.

WRITING

Once the preparation is complete, a draft of the text should be written. The children should write the full text from beginning to end. They should not, at this stage, be required to be overly concerned with technical accuracy or with achieving an optimal level of clarity, but rather with getting the content written in conformity with their plan.

Although teachers can assist children with this step, it is important to the development of their writing fluency that they first be allowed time to write on their own without interruption. When it is noticed that a child has stalled, the teacher can help to get him or her back on track by reading through what has been written and perhaps asking a question or making a comment or suggestion.

It is fairly common for young children to want to stop writing to ask about the spelling of a word. However, they should instead be encouraged to attempt to spell the words for themselves. This is a far better practice, as stopping to ascertain the spelling of a word or to ask about other technical aspects of writing interrupts the flow of ideas onto paper and the production of a good draft text (Ogle & Beers, 2009; Tompkins, 2008). Spelling and other technical errors can be addressed later.

REVISING

At the review stage, writers should read through their draft texts and make such changes, deletions or additions to the content as they consider would improve its accuracy and clarity. Words, sentences, paragraphs and the overall structure should all be addressed and adjustments made where needed. At this stage, writers should place themselves in the shoes of the readers to determine if the intended meanings are being accurately conveyed.

This is a difficult step for the young writer. A certain level of writing skill has to be brought to bear to be able effectively to reflect on one's own writing and to make useful changes to sentences, words and other aspects of a text. In fact, the demands of this task are such that, when children are first developing as writers, little if any attention should be given to this step of the writing process. Perhaps it should come into play at about the age of about seven or eight. Initially, children's learning is best served if revision mainly involves observation of the teacher revising a written draft and even then attending to only a few aspects at a time.

Teachers need to explicitly instruct children in how to revise their writing and they should consider the children's level of writing knowledge and skill in determining the expectations for text revision practices. There are a number of methods that can be employed to develop children's ability with text revision. These include:

- *Investigating the features of good texts*: teach children about the qualities of good writing through the examination of appropriately levelled texts. Read different texts aloud, and together with the children identify their good features. Such scrutiny should focus on one or two features at a time; for instance, the use of complete sentences, sentence beginnings, different sentence types, long and short sentences, conjunctions in compound sentences, text connectives and vocabulary.
- *Demonstration*: teach children what it means to 'revise writing' by demonstrating the process to them.
- *Question prompts*: provide questions that children can reflect on when they read through their draft text and that will guide them with the aspects of text to be revised, e.g. Does each sentence make sense? Is there enough detail so that someone reading it will know what you mean? Do you need to add anything in to your writing? The guiding questions should be determined by the children's level of skill and knowledge. Start small—don't aim for children to revise all aspects. The skills and knowledge should be slowly built up over time.
- *Reading aloud*: have children read their texts aloud to each other and seek responses to the content. Provide a focus for responses, e.g. What did you like about the writing? Was there anything that you didn't understand?
- **Conferencing**: work one-to-one with individual children, jointly revising their text.

EDITING

At this editing stage, writers critically review the overall quality of their writing. They edit it by identifying and correcting technical errors such as those associated with the grammatical structures of sentences, word usage, spelling and punctuation.

As with revising, editing is a difficult assignment for young writers with fledgling writing skills. It requires, among other things, an ability to identify when a word is spelt incorrectly or when a sentence is not structured properly. Yet the young novice writer is still learning how to spell and is still developing knowledge about sentence structures. Teachers need to match editing expectations with what they know of the children's writing skills. For instance, if children have been taught how to construct a complete sentence and about the placement of capital letters and full stops, then these two aspects can be included in the things which they are required to edit. However, there is little use in asking children to, for instance, attend to the placement of commas if they have no knowledge about the use of commas.

In supporting children to develop an ability to edit their writing for technical accuracy, teachers can:

- create checklists that can be used as guides by children in reviewing their writing. This should include only those editing tasks for which the children have the appropriate knowledge
- demonstrate how to identify and correct technical errors using a suitable written draft and focus on only those areas of the text about which the children have some knowledge
- work with individual children to help them to edit their text for technical accuracy
- utilise these editing experiences to develop children's spelling and punctuation, and the knowledge of sentence and word usage.

Table 15.1: Example of a checklist for early writers

Year 2 Checking your writing	✓
Do all sentences begin with a capital letter and end with a full stop?	
Do you have a title for your writing?	
Have you used a capital letter for the names of people and places?	
Do all your sentences make sense?	

PUBLISHING AND SHARING WITH AN AUDIENCE

Publishing occurs when writers prepare a final presentation of their written text for an audience (the person or people who will be reading it). A good copy is written or typed so that it is readable and appealing to the audience. Attention should be given to the setting out and overall design of the presentation. Artwork, graphics or photographs might be added as might an index or content page, depending on the type of text.

The communicative nature of writing is reinforced when children have the opportunity to 'publish' their writing.

This is an important step for children as it reinforces the communicative nature of writing and motivates them to produce their best writing. They will be encouraged to take pride in their efforts and to enjoy knowing that their writing will be read by people.

There are a number of formats that can be used for publishing children's writing, including the following:

- Provide the children with blank pages stapled together like a book and have them write their text in it. Include illustrations and design a cover page.
- Make a class book (a poetry anthology, a recipe book, a series of short stories etc.) by combining children's individual texts into one book and including an index and pictures.
- Place finished texts in the class library for other children to borrow and read.
- Display the children's writing on a notice board in the classroom or in another area of the school. Include illustrations and, where possible, photos to complete the display and to add further meaning to the writing.
- Draw visitor's attention to displays of children's writing by including a sign that explains the topic of the writing and invites them to read the texts. For instance, a sign might say, 'Year 3 have been learning about insects. Please feel free to read their descriptions of various insects.'
- Invite the children's parents to the classroom for an 'authors' morning' that involves children reading their written texts aloud.
- Start a class newsletter that is sent home to family members and given to other classes and teachers and staff in the school. Include some of the children's written texts in each newsletter.
- Send children's written texts to community organisations if the topic is relevant. For example, if the children write letters outlining suggestions for improving the neighbouring park, send them to the local council. If they write reports on different animals, forward these to the local zoo.

- Record children as they read their writing and place these readings in the listening corner for others to hear.
- Partner children with those from another class so that they can share their writing with each other. This could become a regular event over the year for the two classes.

CHILDREN'S GROWTH IN WRITTEN COMMUNICATION

The development of children as writers begins at an early age when, through the home and community, they first start noticing, and showing an interest in, written texts (for instance, signs, notes, books, pamphlets and catalogues) and they begin to realise that writing has meaning and conveys information. They observe the writing efforts of adults and other writers and they create their own texts using scribbles as their attempt at copying. As children move into the pre-school and school they are provided with teaching and learning experiences that put them on the path to becoming competent writers.

Learning to write occurs over time. It is a gradual process whereby knowledge, skills and strategies are progressively acquired. In order for children to improve as writers they need to be provided with effective learning experiences that span an appropriate range of the skills, knowledge and strategies to be learnt.

In early childhood, children's growth as writers can be depicted through a series of five **phases of writing development**—*beginning, emergent, early, transitional* and *fluent* (National Association for the Education of Young Children, 1998). The key areas of learning that occur at each phase of development and the ways in which teachers can support children's further progress as writers are outlined below. The age ranges suggested for the different phases are purposely broad; there are a variety of factors that influence children's development as writers, and teachers need to be mindful of the reality that the nature and rate of learning will likely be different for different children.

BEGINNING PHASE OF WRITING DEVELOPMENT (AGE RANGE: TWO TO FIVE YEARS)

Children at the beginning phase of their writing development:

- display an awareness of writing as a form of communication
- notice written texts in the environment and show interest in their use and meaning
- know that writing is different from drawing
- understand that it is the 'marks' (print) on the page that represent information
- use scribbles, symbols that simulate letters and some actual letters (randomly chosen) to 'write' (pretend) texts with the intention of representing meaning
- apply a few print concepts when they write; for example, they might show that they understand the left to right and top to bottom directionality of written text
- understand the nature of writing by stating a purpose for their writing (e.g. 'Here is a letter for you') and assigning meaning to their writing by 'reading' it or asking someone else to read it, thus assuming it can be understood
- develop the writing mechanisms of hand–eye coordination, wrist and hand muscle control and grasp strength.

Teachers can support beginning writers to further develop their writing by:

- regularly reading and talking about books with them
- introducing then to the letters of the alphabet using the letter name and the common sound of each letter
- displaying lots of different forms of writing in the classroom environment; for example, cards, pictures with captions, labels and information charts
- involving them in language games and other activities that further develop their oral language
- ensuring that they engage in a variety of play activities that incorporate reading and writing; for example, a dramatic play in a pretend post office which has writing instruments, forms, signs and other texts typical of a 'real' post office
- highlighting print concepts, letters and sounds when reading or demonstrating the process of writing
- providing a writing centre in the classroom and encouraging children to experiment with writing
- providing activities that further develop the children's hand–eye coordination, wrist and hand muscle control and grip strength.

THE EMERGENT PHASE OF WRITING DEVELOPMENT (AGE RANGE: FOUR TO SIX YEARS)

Children at the emergent phase of writing development:

- know that writing is spoken language that has been written down
- demonstrate a one-to-one association between written and spoken word (point to words in a sentence one at a time and verbalise them as spoken words)
- recognise and can write the letters of the alphabet
- are familiar with rhyming words and can identify the beginning phonemes (smallest sound units) of words, e.g. /s/ in 'sat' and /p/ in 'pot'
- sound out words when writing them down
- use one, two or three letters of the alphabet to represent a word in writing
- assign the right letter to only some of the phonemes in words
- represent only some of the phonemes (sound units) of words, e.g. dog might be written as 'dg' and kitten might be written as 'kt' or 'ktn'
- use upper and lower case letters indiscriminately when they write words, e.g. they might write kitten as 'kTn' or cat as 'cAT'
- are familiar with a few simple text forms such as a narrative (story) and a recount
- use simple sentence structures—mostly complete
- have a few sight words (words they can spell from visual memory, e.g. 'at', 'the')
- understand, and are beginning to apply, a few print conventions but will often overdo things, e.g. they might put full stops after every word.

Teachers can support emergent writers to further develop their writing by:

- encouraging them to talk about their writing
- using reading and writing demonstrations to reveal writing processes and to further their knowledge of sound–letter relationships

- explicitly teaching and developing children's phonemic awareness and graphophonic (letter–sound association) knowledge
- assisting them to segment (cat = /c/-/a/-/t/) individual phonemes when writing words
- regularly reading interesting and language-rich books
- providing daily opportunities for writing
- encouraging the 'sounding out' of words when writing
- establishing a classroom environment where children can go to write independently
- providing a classroom environment with materials and resources that support them as they write, e.g. charts of common sight words, alphabet charts and displays of writing around the room.

EARLY PHASE OF WRITING DEVELOPMENT (AGE RANGE: SIX TO SEVEN YEARS)

Children at the early phase of writing development:

- write for a small range of purposes, e.g. to tell a story, to provide instructions for doing or making something, to recount an experience or to describe something or someone
- use some of the basic organisational features of a few text forms
- write about topics that are significant to them
- write about their experiences as well as their feelings
- segment words into phonemes (individual sound units; e.g. /sh/-/e/-/ll/) and choose the most likely letter or letters to represent the different phonemes
- 'sound out' and represent all significant sounds when 'spelling' a word
- have a small collection of sight words
- recognise and name all the letters of the alphabet and identify their common sounds
- apply some simple phonics rules to words where a phoneme is represented by more than one letter; e.g., th, sh, ai
- write simple sentences, often with correct use of full stops and capital letters and some experimentation with other forms of punctuation
- write a number of sentences about a topic
- with the teacher's support, edit their writing in regards to a few simple elements.

Teachers can support early writers to further develop their writing by:

- providing experiences that develop oral vocabulary (their knowledge of words and their meanings)
- providing regular opportunities for children to write independently
- reading different types of books
- demonstrating the writing of a range of different text types and teaching about the organisational features of them
- teaching spelling patterns, rules and strategies
- regularly carrying out activities that explicitly teach phonological awareness, phonemic awareness and graphophonic knowledge
- developing sight words for writing.

TRANSITIONAL PHASE OF WRITING DEVELOPMENT (AGE RANGE: SEVEN TO EIGHT YEARS)

Children at the transitional phase of writing development:

- display greater control over spelling, punctuation and text organisation
- write using a range of text types
- display awareness of purpose and audience in writing
- have greater graphophonic knowledge (sound–letter association)
- spell words with common letter patterns
- use a few spelling strategies other than sounding-out words to write them
- use an expanded vocabulary to make their writing interesting
- have a large bank of sight words
- use simple and compound sentences
- apply a range of punctuation to their writing and punctuate simple sentences correctly
- revise and edit for some basic elements of their writing
- write about a range of topics to suit different audiences.

Teachers can support transitional writers to further develop their writing by:

- providing guidance in the use of text types for different writing purposes and teaching the basic organisational structures
- reading different types of books aloud and ensuring that their independent reading encompasses a range of types
- teaching children how to revise and edit the texts that they write
- teaching spelling, developing an ability to use a range of strategies to be used in spelling words.

FLUENT PHASE OF WRITING DEVELOPMENT (AGE RANGE: EIGHT TO NINE YEARS)

Children at the fluent phase of writing development:

- recognise and discuss the organisational features of a variety of text types
- write using a range of different types of text and apply many of the organisational features
- use a variety of vocabulary and sentence structures appropriate to the text being written
- with the teacher's support, revise and edit their writing in a growing number of aspects
- use conventional spelling for a range of words.
  Teachers can support fluent writers to further develop their writing by:
- providing the opportunity for writing to be used as a tool for learning and thinking in other curriculum areas
- extending knowledge about the correct use of different writing conventions (punctuation, grammar, spelling, sentence structure)
- teaching different strategies to be used in spelling words
- emphasising the importance of correct spelling in finished writing products
- reading and examining the organisational features of texts written for a variety of purposes.

> ### WRITING AND CHILDREN WHO SPEAK ENGLISH AS AN ADDITIONAL LANGUAGE (EAL)
>
> Children for whom English is an additional language generally have a different developmental path for learning to write. Some important points to consider when working with EAL children are:
>
> - Children who have some literacy understanding in their first language will make quicker progress in learning to write (and read) than those who do not. They have acquired knowledge about writing (literacy) when they learnt to write in their first language and they bring this to bear when learning to write in English.
> - Sometimes the features of the written texts of their first language are different from those of English (e.g. different script or directionality of print) and so they will need time and additional support to develop the print concepts particular to English.
> - EAL children require the opportunity to talk and write in their first language as well as in English. Continued first-language literacy growth supports the development of written English.
> - There is often a strong need to provide additional focus on phonemic awareness; the pronunciation of some of the sounds of English words will be different from the sounds that make up words in their first language. Phoneme articulation is important to their writing ability and development.
> - Some grammatical errors in writing are likely to occur as part of writing development. The types of errors are generally unique to EAL children (e.g. errors in verb tense/time orientation, subject/verb agreement, pronouns, prepositions, articles and singular/plural form of words).
> - The development of EAL children's oral language is critical to their development as writers.
> - Writing activities should involve EAL children writing about topics and experiences that are familiar to them (family, school, home, friends, pets).

USING THE PHASES OF WRITING DEVELOPMENT

The phases of writing development can be used by teachers to make choices about what to focus on when teaching children to write and as a guide to monitoring children's progress as writers. However, it is important to realise that the age ranges assigned to each phase of writing development are not hard and fast; they are merely guides. Children will start pre-school and school having had different experiences that have led to different levels of knowledge about, and skill in, writing. Different children will progress in their development as writers at different rates and will require different experiences, different levels of support and different degrees of instruction for them to learn and progress as writers.

It is also important to remember that, while the writing of different children will usually progress along much the same pathway, it does so in different ways. Children will not necessarily display all the competencies of one phase of development before having to grapple with the next phase; for instance, they might begin to display skills and knowledge that are characteristics of transitional writers well before displaying all those of early writers (that is, the previous phase).

SUMMARY

There is a range of knowledge, understandings and skills that comprise effective written communication and which, over time, children should be assisted to learn and develop competency in. Teaching, experiences and activities should be chosen to align with children's phase of writing development and to focus on those areas of learning and development that will assist them to progress towards competency in writing.

QUESTIONS AND ACTIVITIES

1. Why is oral language so important to children's written language development?
2. Create a chart that provides a summary of the steps of the writing process.
3. Consider the importance of the 'preparing to write' step of the writing process. Why is this such a significant step for young writers?
4. Learning to write begins at a young age. What can toddlers learn about writing from the home or childcare setting?
5. Refer to the phases of development for writing. Identify and discuss any statements about the abilities of children at the different phases that you do not fully understand.
6. Consider what has been discussed about the competencies of beginner writers; then draw a map showing how you would establish the environment of a childcare or pre-school setting to support beginner writers.
7. How should you set up a writing corner/play area so that children are provided with choices and visual supports for experimenting with written communication?

KEY TERMS

conferencing
phases of writing development
writing components
writing context
writing conventions
writing traits

KEY REFERENCES

Cunningham, P., Moore, S., Cunningham, J. & Moore, D. (2004). *Reading and writing: Research based K–4 instruction.* Boston: Allyn & Bacon.

Graves, D. (1983). *Writing: Teachers and children at work.* Portsmouth, NH: Heinemann.

National Association for the Education of Young Children (1998). Learning to read and write: Developmentally appropriate practices for young children. *Young Children, 53*(4), 30–46.

Ogle, D. & Beers, J. W. (2009). *Engaging the language arts: Exploring the power of language.* Boston: Pearson.

Olsen, C. B. (2007). *The reading/writing connection.* Boston: Pearson.

Spandel, V. (2009). *Creating writers through 6-trait writing: Assessment and instruction.* Boston: Allyn & Bacon.

Tompkins, G. E. (2008). *Teaching writing: Balancing process and product.* Boston: Pearson Education.

Walsche, R. D. (1981). *Every Child Can Write: learning and teaching written expression in the 1980s.* Rozelle, Australia: PETA.

CHAPTER 16

Writing Purpose and Text Organisation

CHAPTER OBJECTIVES

This chapter will increase your understanding of:

- the communicative function of written language
- the purposeful nature of writing
- different purposes for which texts are written
- the concept of audience in writing and establishing audiences for the written texts that children produce
- categories of text and the key characteristics of different text forms
- significant experiences for developing children's ability with purposeful writing and the use of different text forms.

This chapter is about the written text. It presents information that will assist you to understand about purposes (reasons for writing) and audiences in written communication, as well as about some different types of written texts. In considering these topics, you should keep in mind the different ways that children can learn about written texts; the emphasis should be on providing them with lots of experiences with texts—listening to and reading different types of fiction and non-fiction texts and experimenting with writing for different communicative purposes. The chapter also provides a number of ideas for teaching children how to write for different purposes and how to organise information into particular types of texts. It is important to appreciate that the use of a strict text structure for writing should be of concern only when children are ready. This will most likely be towards the end of early childhood.

INTRODUCTION

One of the first things that children should learn about writing is that it is a mode of communication. Like oral language, it is a means by which information, ideas, opinions and thoughts are shared between people but, in this instance, using the written rather than the oral form of language. Children will usually develop this fundamental understanding about writing at a young age, provided that they have the opportunity to observe others carrying out purposeful everyday writing tasks such as the writing of shopping lists, letters, lists, labels and notes. They will often first observe such writing tasks in the home and consequently develop a sense of the communicative nature of the written **text**. However, for some children, the home situation provides little opportunity to observe written communication and so classroom experiences must provide for this. A classroom or childcare centre that integrates the use of authentic texts for genuine communicative purposes supports children's understanding of the practical nature of writing.

WRITING PURPOSE

Additional to ensuring children's appreciation for the general communicative function of writing is the need to develop their awareness of the more precise purposes for which texts are written. For instance, a text might be written to give an account of a personal experience (writing a diary entry, a journal or a personal recount), to socialise (writing a personal letter or a note), to entertain (writing a story, a play or a poem), to explain how to do something (writing the set of instructions for a game or a recipe) or to convey facts on a particular topic (writing a report). It might also be written to identify things (writing labels) or as a personal reminder (writing a reminder note) and for a range of other purposes.

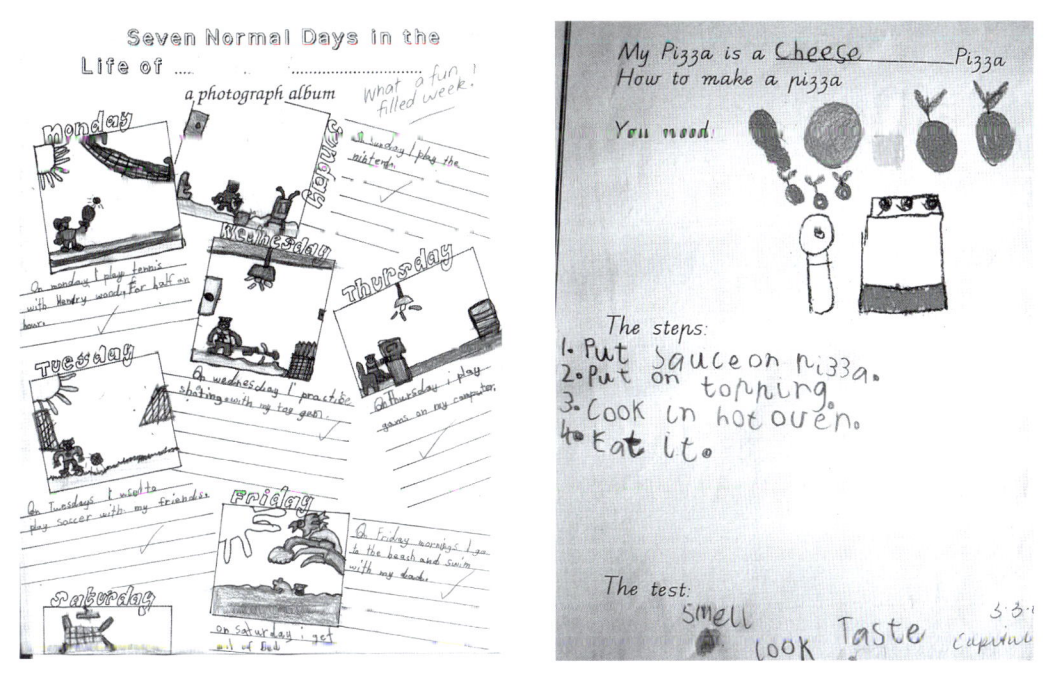

Written texts can be classified into different types according to the purposes they achieve.

The writing tasks in which children engage should be for purposes relevant to their lives and interests. Examples include:

- writing the procedure for the biscuits that are made during a class cooking experience
- preparing for an excursion by writing a reminder list of the things to be taken
- writing a thank you letter to a recent visiting speaker
- talking and then writing about favourite places at home and assembling them together to make a book for the classroom reading corner
- writing labels for the material containers and special areas of the classroom so as to assist people to easily locate them
- writing a sign to go over the fish tank advising people about required behaviour when dealing with the fish.

Depending on the children's abilities and needs, such tasks could be done independently by children or in conjunction with an adult who might scribe the text provided by children. The understanding that writing can be used to achieve different communicative goals should be continually reinforced.

AUDIENCES

Children also need to be assisted to understand that texts are written for certain **audiences**; that is, they are written to communicate with a particular person or a range of people. The audience reads the written text or listens to it being read aloud. Children's writing

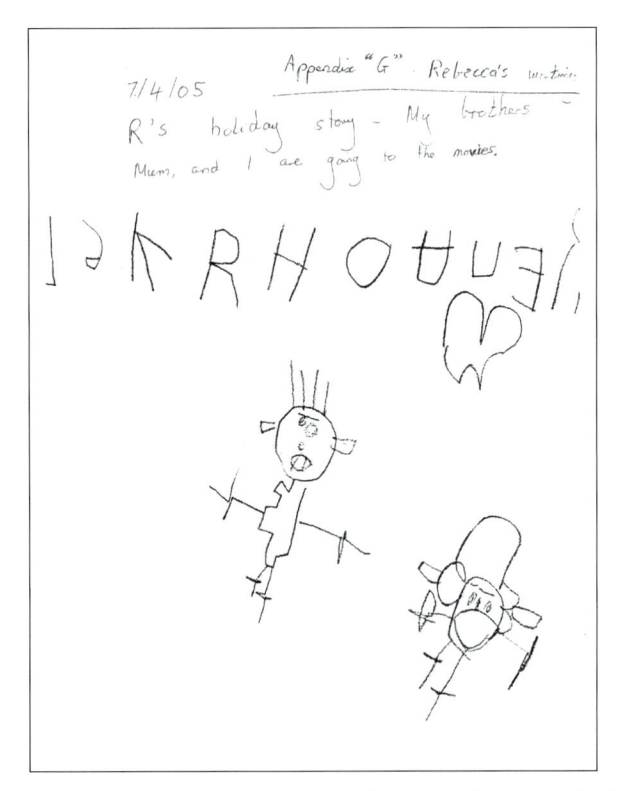

Children experiment with creating written texts for communicative purposes.

experiences should involve having real audiences for whom to write. Parents and other family members, members of the community, classmates, children from other classes, teachers, other school staff and visitors to the class are just a few of the range of people who might provide authentic audiences for the texts children write.

Children's knowledge about the purposes for writing and intended audiences can be developed spontaneously during reading and writing experiences. Children should be assisted to consider such issues as 'when and how [written] texts are used; who uses them; in what situations they are used and why; and when, how, by whom and why they were written' (Curriculum Council, 1998, p. 13).

With an understanding of the communicative and purposeful nature of written communication, and with the right opportunities and resources, children will likely begin to experiment with writing their own texts for different purposes. Even very young children who have not yet developed understanding of the alphabetic system of written English should be observed to write purposefully using what is referred to as 'role play' writing. They will behave as writers, composing purposeful texts using scribbles, pictures or a series of letter-like graphics to communicate with others.

WRITTEN TEXTS

The composition of a text is essential to achieving the purpose of written communication, and children's development as writers requires that they are eventually taught how to shape texts so that they achieve the purposes for which they are written.

For instructional purposes, written texts are classified into different types according to the purposes they achieve (for example, recount text, explanation text, story text, procedure text and so on). Each category or type of text has distinct compositional features which relate to:

a the topic and content
b the way the information is organised in the text (text structure)
c sentences (e.g. use of present or past tense, cohesive devices, grammatical constructions) and other language features
d vocabulary.

For example, if the purpose for writing was to *tell what happened* during a holiday experience, a *recount text* would be composed. The structure would very likely involve:

1 an introduction to the experience in general
2 a description of the events in the sequence in which they occurred
3 a conclusion that rounds off the topic and perhaps includes an evaluation.

Additionally, it would contain certain language features; typically:

- written in the first person ('I', 'my', 'we', 'us');
- words that indicated time order (e.g. 'first', 'then', 'as soon as possible', 'eventually', 'later', 'soon after')
- description of specific people and places.

Yet again, if the purpose for writing were *to tell [others] how to make something* (for example, chocolate crackles) a *procedure* text would be composed, which would likely be structured to include:

1. an introduction that establishes the goal—that is, what is to be made
2. a list of the materials (equipment and ingredients) needed
3. the method or steps to be used to make the item.

It also would likely contain the following language features:

- use of action verbs (e.g. 'put', 'stir', 'turn', 'spread', 'combine', 'bake')
- linking words to do with time (e.g. 'first', 'after a while', 'finally')
- tense as timeless (e.g. 'pour the butter into the bowl')
- use of precise vocabulary (e.g. 'slowly stir until butter is soft').

The categories of texts and the associated standards for composition should be used to support children to structure texts for particular purposes. They are a useful starting point in developing ability with the text-organisation aspect of writing. However, their use should be flexible so as not to restrict children's creativity as writers.

It is important to understand that, in reality, text composition rarely completely conforms to a single model standard. Communicative purposes are achieved by means of more interesting and dynamic texts when compositional flexibility is applied. Proficient writers will typically compose texts with a great deal more complexity and creativity.

Over time and with the right experiences, children will likely develop a more innate ability to apply structure to the texts they write, and a more sophisticated and flexible command of the organisational and language requirements.

The act of writing requires the orchestration of multiple processes, strategies and conventions (Annandale et al., 2005). When the focus during classroom writing experiences is on teaching about standard forms for structuring texts, it must be done in such a way that the challenges presented do not unduly distract the writer from being able to attend to all the other important elements of writing a text. The emphasis should not be such that children get so caught up with complying with the **text form** requirements that other important elements of good written communication are abandoned (Resnick & Hampton, 2009). Text forms are flexible and good writers use them flexibly.

TYPES OF TEXTS

Texts can first of all, be broadly categorised into three main types, which are:

1. *personal* (expressive writing)
2. *literary* (imaginative writing)
3. *expository* (factual writing).

Personal writing involves writing about the experiences, events and people in one's own life and about the issues and topics that are of personal interest and concern. It involves writing not just to describe or recount, but also to explore reactions or to express mood, feeling and opinion (Norton, 2007). Diaries, journals, letters and learning journals are all forms of personal writing.

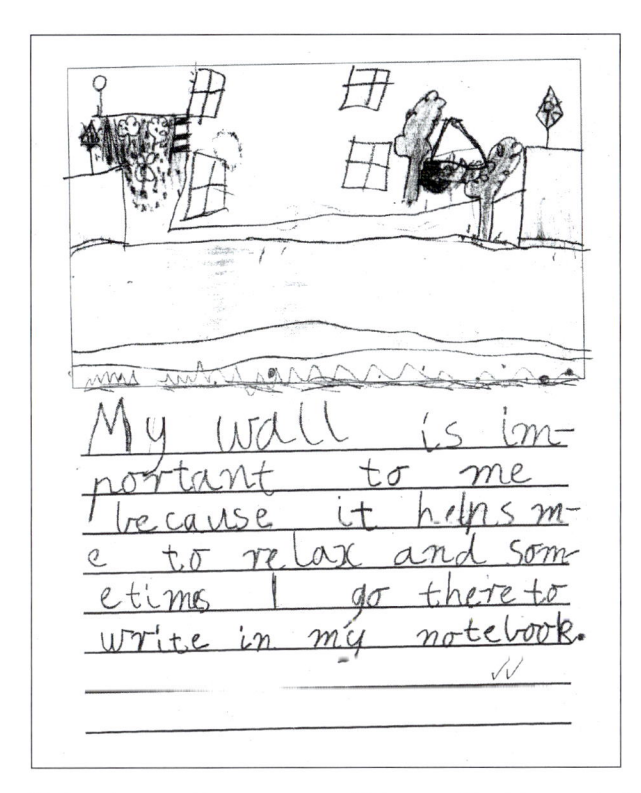

Topics of personal importance to children provide rich opportunities for writing.

Literary writing, which is sometimes referred to as creative or imaginary writing (Tompkins, 2008), means the writing of fiction texts. Narratives (stories), fairy tales, poems and play scripts are all types of literary writing.

Expository writing involves the writer presenting facts, ideas or opinions about non-fiction subjects. Texts include reports, explanations and procedures. They are important to children's academic learning and to other school subject areas.

Within each of these three broad categories there are different varieties of texts (or text forms), each of which serves a more precise purpose. Following is an overview of different text forms common to each of the three categories: personal, imaginary and expository.

PERSONAL WRITING

Personal writing involves writing about topics and experiences of personal significance. Writers recount and describe experiences and events of their own lives and they express their reactions to, and feelings and opinions about these.

Text forms used for personal writing purposes include:

- *Diary*: writing that depicts personal experiences, observations, thoughts and feelings. They can also include the use of recount, description and other text forms.
- *Journal*: writing that records responses to, and thought about, topics, issues, experiences and books read.
- A *dialogue journal*: a variation of the standard journal that involves the children writing informally about something of interest or concern and then the teacher or another student responding (also in writing) to what they wrote.

- *Reading response log*: writing that is done in response to stories or other books read or which the teacher has read aloud. It involves the children expressing reactions to the overall content of a book or some aspect of the content or topic, rather than a simple recount of what it was about.
- *Learning log*: writing about, or in response to, the learning experiences of content area lessons such as Mathematics, Science or Society and Environment.
- *Personal letters*: writing to share news, ask questions, offer advice and opinion, or invite or thank a family member, friend or someone familiar. Pen pals, community members and book authors are regular audiences for children's letters. Greeting cards are also forms of personal letters.

> **WRITING IN RESPONSE TO LITERATURE**
>
> Children should be given plenty of opportunity to respond in writing to the different types of literature that they read or have read to them. These experiences will often use one of the text methods already outlined but can also involve:
>
> - *Story recount*: writing a recount of a story; that is, retelling the story in own words.
> - *Literary description*: writing a description of a character, scene or event in a story (description as a text form is described under expository writing).
> - *Review*: writing a summary and analysis of a story and providing opinion about its appeal.

Personal texts can be attempted by children whatever their level of writing. They can be pictures and labels, words, a sentence, a series of sentences or more extensive texts. They can be dictated to the teacher who writes them or children can write them independently. They focus on personal experience, known people and immediate events.

Personal writing provides a good opportunity for children to write for well-understood reasons and serves to develop their understanding of the communicative nature of writing. Texts can be adapted to suit the children's phase of writing development and associated writing resources. For instance, a beginner writer might write a response to a story that comprises a picture or a random line of letters, while a more advanced writer might write a sentence and yet at another phase a child might write a series of well-ordered sentences or paragraphs.

Many of the different types of personal writing texts can also be used for imaginative or exploratory writing. For instance, a diary can be written imaginatively when written for a fictional character or it can be written factually from the perspective of a scientist, explorer, sportsperson, community member or the like.

LITERARY WRITING

Literary writing involves writing where the ideas and information presented are the original creation of the writer and come from the writer's imagination. Literary writing is sometimes referred to as creative or imaginary writing.

Text forms used for literary purposes include:

- *Narrative*: writing that tells a story containing original characters, settings and events. One or more of these elements might reflect reality or a story which has been read but at least one element should be the writer's original idea. Narratives contain description and might also contain dialogue between characters (direct speech). A narrative is usually intended to entertain but might also contain a message or a life lesson.

Table 16.1: Features of a narrative text

Structural features	Language features
- Introduction, orienting reader to the story, introduction of setting and characters - Develop the story through a sequence of events with a problem or complication occurring. Resolution or solving of the problem - There can be a series of problems and solutions.	- Nouns and pronouns particular to the characters and things in the story - Adjectives to describe characters and things - First- or third-person storyteller voice - Action verbs (events) - Verbs which indicate that a character is saying or thinking something - Usually past tense. Less often present tense - Varied sentence types (simple, compound and complex) and length - Time words to connect events (e.g. 'after', 'then', 'later') - Can contain direct speech/dialogue

- *Traditional narrative*: the writing of specific types of stories such as fairy tales, fables, myths and legends that reflect time-honoured storytelling styles of other cultures. They often serve to reinforce a cultural practice or ideal, or to explain a phenomenon. They can feature certain elements such as the use of a specific type of character, repeated or patterned language or certain topic categories (e.g. quests, journeys, good and evil, wise and foolish).
- *Poetry*: writing that allows readers to hear, see or feel the subject being described using particular language elements such as rhythm, rhyme, alliteration (repeating initial consonants in consecutive words), assonance (repeating vowel sounds in consecutive words), onomatopoeia (where the sound of a word, or words, closely mimics the sound being portrayed, e.g. 'hiss', 'splash', 'buzz'), repetition of words, phrases, lines or whole verses, and imagery. There are many different poetry forms, some of which are free verse, limericks, acrostics, ballads, haikus, couplets and cinquains. Poetry can also be a form of personal writing, depending on the topic.

Play scripts and some song lyrics are also forms of imaginative texts.

Children's picture books are predominantly composed of imaginary stories, sometimes based on real life or involving an aspect of life or a theme to which children can relate. Many children at quite a young age become familiar with several of the features of these types of texts. This is reflected when children pick up a book and pretend to read it. They might begin with, 'Once upon a time' or, 'One day' or another typical narrative starting point and proceed to 'read' the story demonstrating some of the language features typical of a narrative text.

Like personal writing, imaginary writing of stories is a good starting point for children's experience with writing. It draws on what they know, the types of books they will likely have experienced and on their natural inclination for imaginary play and creativity.

The written stories of children at the emergent phase of writing will regularly involve pictures as well as either letters, words or one or two sentences. Over time and with plenty of opportunities to hear and talk about narrative texts and with a developing understanding of the detail in narratives as well as writing skill and fluency, children's stories will progressively display a greater application of the text organisational and language features.

Other texts can also be imaginary; for instance, a letter might be written to a story book character or an imaginary space creature. A recount could be written about a pretend event and a diary could involve humanising an object (such as a tennis ball) and writing about its adventures.

EXPOSITORY WRITING

Expository writing involves the writing of texts about factual topics—events, people and things. It is the presentation of facts, ideas and sometimes opinions about non-fiction subjects. Expository writing is sometimes referred to as 'content area' writing.

Texts of expository writing include:

- *Recount*: writing that involves telling about an actual event or experience. It may also involve evaluation of the event or experience. A recount might, for instance, cover writing about a visit to the dentist or a day at the zoo or relating an event in history.

Table 16.2: Features of a recount text

Structural features	Language features
• Introduction to the event or experience—Who? What? Where? When? • Description of events in the sequence in which they occurred • Conclusion by rounding off the events and perhaps adding an evaluative or personal response	• First person (personal event) or third person (about someone else's experience) • Pronouns—people, animals, things and places involved • Past tense—locate events in time and use of action verbs • Words to show time order (e.g. 'first', 'then', 'as soon as', 'eventually', 'later', 'soon after') • Precise detail—adjectives, adverbs describing people and places

- *Description*: writing that involves the creating of a vivid picture of a person, place, object or event. For instance, writing to describe an animal, a family member or the scene from the classroom window. Descriptions can be texts in themselves but they are more often part of other text forms such as a narrative, report or a recount. Labels and captions are forms of descriptive writing.

Table 16.3: Features of a description text

Structural features	Language features
• Introduce the topic to be described • Describe different aspects of the topic—appearance, qualities, behavior, attributes etc. • Conclude with an overall statement about the topic being described	• Various sentence beginnings for writing fluency • Nouns and adjectives/adjectival phrases • Adverbs and adverbial phrases • Often present tense • Sometimes subjective language

- *Procedure*: writing that is about how to do or make something (an activity). It is often a set of instructions or directions for achieving a particular outcome (e.g. playing a game, baking a cake, making a model aeroplane). Procedural texts often list information and use diagrams or pictures.

Table 16.4: Features of a procedure text

Structural features	Language features
• Statement of aim or goal • List of materials needed • Sequence of steps (what to do/procedure to follow), sometimes numbered • Can include diagrams or pictures	• Action verbs ('put', 'chop', 'cut', 'stick') • Precise detail (e.g. 'two large teaspoons') • Indications of time order (e.g. 'first', 'second', 'third', 'finally' or numbered steps) • Adverbs of time and place (e.g. 'for two minutes', 'in the top, left corner') • Non-specific audience (e.g. 'You need to … then you …')

- *Explanation*: writing that explains why or how something happens or why something is like it is. It aims to make a phenomenon clear; for instance, the production of milk or the life cycle of a frog.

Table 16.5: Features of an explanation text

Structural features	Language features
• State the topic/phenomenon to be explained (this is sometimes written as a question to be answered) • Explain the process/occurrence (sequence the information/ group using subheadings) • Conclude by summarising main content or recapping on topic/phenomenon • May includes pictures, graphs, diagrams, flow charts	• Written in the third person • Timeless present tense • Passive voice (e.g. 'Milk is processed and put in containers') • Subject-specific or technical vocabulary • Sequence expressed using linking words (e.g. 'then', 'next', 'afterwards', 'finally')

- *Report*: writing that conveys certain information about something or someone; for instance, a report on the African elephant or life in the desert. Reports often include a large component of description writing.

Table 16.6: Features of a report text

Structural features	Language features
• State, define and classify the topic being reported on • Describe features—group information around sub-topics • Use topic sentences, which are followed by more detailed information for an aspect • Conclude by summarising the areas of information presented or with a general statement • Can include visuals—diagrams, charts, pictures, maps	• Nouns and pronouns for generalised participants (elephants, they) • Subject-specific language (e.g. mammals) • Descriptive factual language • Formal and impersonal • Present tense • Often use of passive voice • Verbs 'to be' and 'to have' used often • Repeated use of sentences that link with the topic (e.g. 'the elephant is …')

- *Discussion*: writing that presents a line of reasoning from different perspectives on a particular topic or issue. It might provide facts that support as well as those that disagree with an opinion on a topic, or simply explore various viewpoints and arrive at a conclusion.

Table 16.7: Features of a discussion text

Structural features	Language features
• State, the issue/topic and outline some background information • Present different points relating to the different points of view, for and against, and provide evidence or examples to support each point • Conclude by summarising the different points of view	• Thinking verbs (e.g. '… believes that', 'feels', 'hopes to …') • Connectives linking points of view (e.g. 'similarly', 'on the other hand', 'likewise', 'however') • Modal verbs (e.g. 'might', 'should', 'must', 'could', 'perhaps') • Adverbs (e.g. 'deliberately')

- *Experimental report*: writing that is often used in science and that describes experiments or research and explains the results.
- *Lists*: writing a list of items or events. Lists are sometimes written in a particular order—chronological, alphabetical or time order.

TEACHING ABOUT TEXTS: BEGINNING AND EMERGENT

The focus for children at the beginning or emergent phase of their development as writers should be on:

- understanding that written texts should be meaningful and communicate information, and that the meaning of a text stays the same each time the text is read
- understanding that the content of a written text comes from the thoughts and ideas of the writer
- knowing that there are different purposes and different types of texts for writing and that an author writes for an audience
- the purpose and nature of some familiar types of text, e.g. letter, list, telephone message, stories and greeting cards (and have a go at writing such texts during various play activities)
- print and text concepts such as writing from left to right and from top to bottom on the page, spaces between words, and the concepts of a word, sentence and punctuation mark.

PLAY EXPERIENCES AND TEXT FORMS

Young children learn about written communication and the social uses of written texts when they have the opportunity to read and write them for 'real' reasons in the different social contexts of their regular play activities. Teachers should ensure that the classroom learning centres provide for the purposeful use of texts. The different areas of the classroom should include plenty of writing materials as well as appropriate examples of written texts. For instance, the *blocks and construction area* of the classroom might be resourced with markers and various types of paper and cardboard so that the writing of building plans (pictures and/or print), signs and descriptive labels become a natural part of the children's experiences.

Young children should be provided with plenty of opportunity to explore and experiment with writing.

Children's learning about written texts is further enhanced when learning centres include examples of written texts. For the constructions and block area, this might be labelled pictures of other block constructions and books about building and construction. There might also be charts (with pictures) that list the types of blocks and signs that provide directions for packing away.

The classroom's dramatic play area provides a good opportunity to include different texts for purposeful reading and writing by children. For instance, if the dramatic play centre was to be set up as a supermarket, the relevant writing tasks might include shopping lists, labelling food items and making signs for the different areas. In this way children are able to reinforce their understanding of the communicative value of written texts and also to experiment with the writing of texts as part of their pretend play.

The classroom should include a writing centre and a reading centre, thus further providing children with the opportunity to explore and experiment with the writing of texts and apply their developing writing skills and understanding of the nature of texts. A functional and inviting writing centre should include a variety of writing instruments (different coloured and sized pencils, crayons, textas, markers) and different kinds of paper (cardboard and paper of different types, shapes and sizes, little blank books and cards). It should also have prominently displayed examples of written texts, including those that the children have composed and texts from shared and modelled writing which have been completed with the teacher. A chart depicting letter formations is also useful. There might also be pictures that provide the children with ideas for their writing when they visit the writing centre.

The classroom's reading centre should be a comfortable and inviting place where children can go to read books. It should contain a variety of story and information books. Children's learning about texts is enhanced when they get to explore books—look through them, talk about the pictures with other children and 'role play' the reading of books like 'real' readers.

TEACHER-DIRECTED LEARNING EXPERIENCES

The development of children's knowledge about written texts necessitates that learning opportunities beyond those provided through play, and exploratory experiences are eventually provided. Time should be given over to writing activities that involve the teacher using different teaching approaches to enhance children's understanding of writing purposes and written texts (as well as other writing knowledge, skills and strategies). Modelled and shared writing (explained in Chapter 19), and listening to and discussing books read by the teacher, present opportunities to highlight the purpose and audience of different texts and to draw children's attention to some basic structural and language features.

TEACHING ABOUT TEXTS IN THE EARLY YEARS OF SCHOOL

In the early years of school, children's writing development continues to progress and they develop competency with the use of different written texts. Their learning should involve a focus on developing:

- an ability to attend to the organisational patterns and language features of a range of different text forms: the range of text forms should be progressively addressed, beginning with the more familiar (letters, stories, recipes, recounts and lists) to the less familiar (explanation, procedure, discussion and report).
- an awareness of the needs of the audience (ensure that texts make sense, convey the intended meaning and include an appropriate level of detail): they should reread their writing to ensure that it will make sense to the reader.

- the need to group sentences together that express related information: the organisation of their writing should be supported by the use of headings and subheadings.
- vocabulary and topic knowledge: children should possess enough knowledge about the topic to permit confidence in writing about it, and a vocabulary that is adequate for the writing task.

READING AND TEXT FORMS

The experience of reading and discussion of different texts should continue during the early years of a child's schooling. Through these experiences, teachers can focus on the way authors have structured texts. For instance, in the case of a report text, the children can be shown how it is structured: how it begins with an introduction of the topic and then develops with the presentation of information about it and concludes with some finding. They can also be taught to identify other text features such as the use of headings and subheadings, and diagrams, pictures and charts.

Of course, there will be a great many variations to the organisation features of different texts and it might sometimes be necessary for teachers to choose texts at a level of form complexity appropriate to the writing development of the group of children being taught.

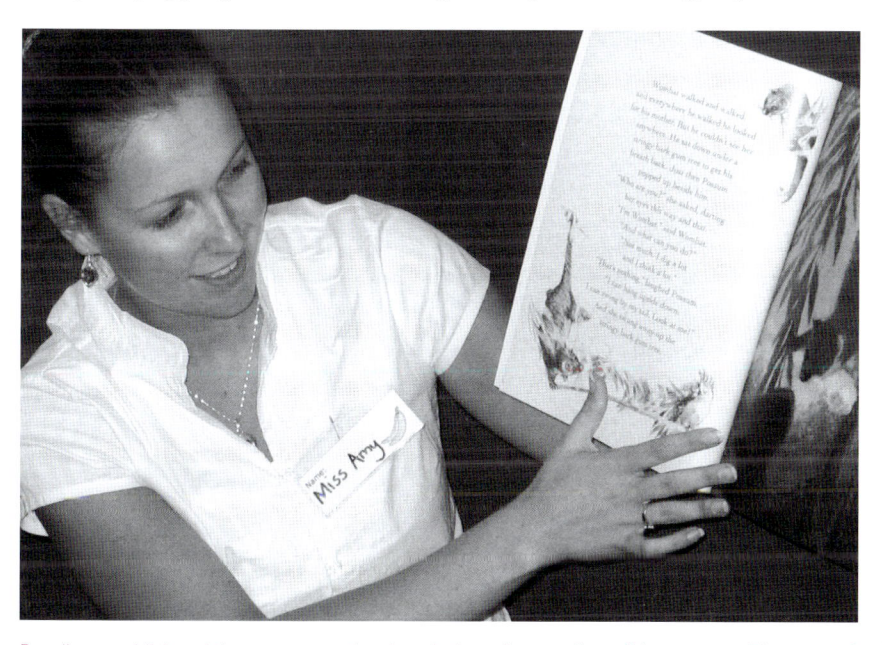

Reading to children is important to develop their understanding of the purposeful nature of written language.

THE CLASSROOM ENVIRONMENT AND WRITTEN TEXTS

Classrooms should display a variety of written texts. These might be ones written by the children themselves, by the teacher or those that the teacher and children have written together. They might also include commercially produced texts that present good examples for the children's own writing. Texts that relate to the functioning of the classroom, such as labels that indicate where materials are located, or posters that outline important writing behaviours or that outline how to go about the process of composing a text, should also be displayed.

Classrooms should also have a reading centre. As with pre-school, the reading centre should be set up as an inviting place where children can go to quietly read different books. By having the reading centre equipped with a variety of different types of books, the children have the opportunity to explore independently the text form of different books.

WRITING LESSONS AND TEXT FORMS

In the early years of primary school, lessons that focus on children's writing development should be a daily event. The lessons should be aimed at achieving specific goals and appropriate teaching methods should be used for this purpose.

Writing lessons might involve the teacher showing children how to structure (or form) a text or perhaps children composing their own written text using a particular text form. There are various ways in which the teacher can assist children with the application of particular features of a text form during writing, including:

- demonstration
- text analysis
- the use of text planning frameworks.

Demonstration and text analysis

Demonstration and **text analysis** provide useful means by which to teach children about the structuring of particular text forms. Demonstration involves children observing teachers as they write texts and highlight the structural and language features. Text analysis involves the display and scrutiny of ready-made texts and might possibly include the teacher:

- explaining the parts of the text on display
- underlining phrases or words that are typical of the text form
- circling or colour-coding different sections of the text to highlight the different organisational parts
- making annotations along the side of the text to explain about the elements being highlighted
- cutting a text up and separating the structural sections and working with the children to put them back in the correct order.

Analysis might also involve comparing books. A set of books of the same text form (for example, reports, narratives or explanation) are collected. They should be of an appropriate theme and reading level for the children. The books are read and examined and the form is identified. A flow chart or table might be completed as a way of identifying the content and organisation of the content of each book.

Independent writing and planning frameworks

A **planning framework** is a skeleton outline of a type of text or text form. It provides well-spaced headings indicating the information to be included in the text and the order in which it should be set out. Planning frameworks provide children with direction in composing a text of a particular form. For instance, a planning framework using the headings 'Aim', 'Materials' and 'Steps' would help children to organise the information for a procedural text.

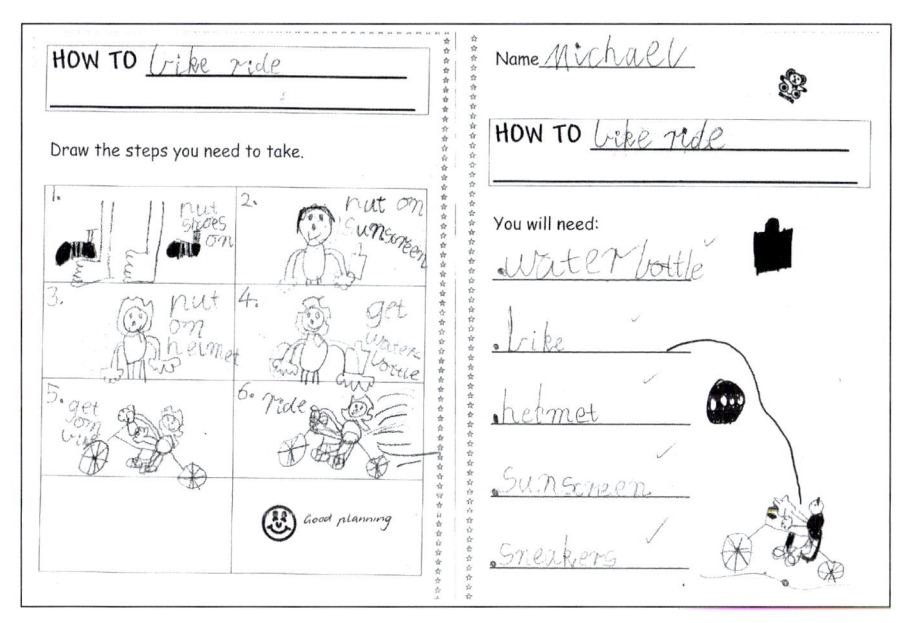

Planning frameworks can be used by children as they prepare the ideas for their writing.

Planning frameworks can be used by children as they prepare the ideas for their writing. They can draw pictures, write key words and phrases or write whole sentences under each heading and then use these as a guide for the actual writing of the text. Alternatively, the framework can be used to record the actual text itself.

Different frameworks should be constructed for children at different phases of writing. For children just beginning to experiment with text forms, writing frameworks should contain the most basic of headings. They might also pose questions underneath each heading to elicit the sort of information that should be included throughout the text. The headings might also have a picture or symbol to provide additional clues for the children. A planning framework might be designed using sentence starters instead of (or as well as) headings.

Table 16.8: A sample planning framework for a recount text

My Day	
Introduction	This is about …
Go to school	First …
At school	Then …
At school	Later …
Go home	Finally …
Ending	I felt … about my day.

Planning frameworks are useful supports for children as they learn about text forms because they focus them on the direction to take in composing a text. They assist them to organise the text content clearly and in a logical way.

An ability to manipulate texts to suit writing purposes is developmental and occurs gradually over time. The focus with young children should be on developing their awareness of, and ability with, a small range of **text types** that serve different communication goals. Children should be provided with regular experiences of reading and talking about books and teacher-demonstrated writing, and they should be given the opportunity to freely experiment with the writing of their own texts.

In the early years of school, the focus for children's writing is likely to involve:

- awareness of the connection between the purpose for writing and the structural and language features of a text
- awareness of the organisational and language features of a small range of text types with the range gradually increasing
- the ability to use certain frameworks to apply simple organisational and language features when writing texts for different purposes
- gradual increase in the types of texts that can be written using text structure frameworks
- the ability to structure some familiar text types with increased sophistication.

In the early years of school, children are acquiring important fundamental writing knowledge and developing a range of writing skills and strategies. The requirement for attending to the organisational aspect of a text (the form of the text) needs to be carefully considered in light of the children's overall writing ability. Writing tasks that place too great a cognitive and physical demand on children may well result in their lack of enthusiasm towards classroom writing experiences and thus affect their overall development as writers.

SUMMARY

Children require experiences with written texts that lead them to understand the communicative nature of written language and develop an awareness of specific purposes for which texts can be written. When writing texts, clear purposes should be established and real audiences should be involved. At an appropriate time in their development as writers, children should be assisted to compose texts that apply the structural and linguistic features of different text forms. The demands of such tasks should be modified to suit the children's writing ability and they should involve the use of various supports such as models and writing frameworks.

QUESTIONS AND ACTIVITIES

1. What do you consider to be appropriate goals for teaching about text types at different phases of early childhood?
2. What strategies might be used to promote writing for different purposes with pre-school and school-aged children?
3. List a variety of suitable ways to promote toddlers' understanding of the communicative nature of written texts.
4. Examine the written texts produced by children at different ages (three, five and seven years). Consider what these texts display about the children's knowledge of purposeful writing and text types.
5. Discuss the ways in which writing experiences for children in the early years of school can ensure that children have audiences for the texts that they write.

6 It seems that by the age of eight or nine years some children have developed a negative attitude to writing. Why do you think this is the case? What do you think could be done to ensure that all children remain motivated to write?
7 Choose three different themes for socio-dramatic play areas (for example, post office) and decide how written texts can be incorporated into these different areas.

KEY TERMS

audience
expository writing
literary writing
personal writing
planning framework
text
text analysis
text form
text types

KEY REFERENCES

Annandale, K., Bindon, R., Broz, J., Handley, K., Johnston, A., Lockett, L. et al. (2005). *Writing map of development: Addressing current literacy challenges* (2nd edn). Port Melbourne: Reed International.

Curriculum Council (1998). *Curriculum framework for kindergarten to year 12 education in Western Australia*. Osborne Park: Curriculum Council.

Norton, D. E. (2007). *Literacy for life*. Boston: Pearson Education.

Resnick, L. B. & Hampton, S. (2009). *Reading and writing grade by grade*. Washington: The National Centre on Education and the Economy.

Tompkins, G. E. (2008). *Teaching writing: Balancing process and product*. Boston: Pearson Education.

CHAPTER 17

The Writing Conventions: Grammar and Punctuation

CHAPTER OBJECTIVES

This chapter will increase your understanding of:

- the importance of grammar knowledge to good written language
- the grammar practices of Standard Australian English
- types of punctuation
- developing the grammar and punctuation knowledge of young children
- the structuring of paragraphs in written texts.

This chapter provides an overview of the writing conventions of grammar, punctuation, the use of capital letters and paragraphing. It explains some of the basics of these aspects of written language. Your knowledge of writing conventions is fundamental to being able to assist children to become competent writers capable of composing clear texts. Additionally, the understandings presented here should serve to assist your own writing. The texts you design (posters, charts, labels etc.) for children's learning environments should consistently model clear and accurate written structures. The chapter concludes by outlining some important principles for the teaching of writing conventions; in doing so, the emphasis is placed on the use of whole texts.

WRITING CONVENTIONS

When writers have a sufficient command of language, including a familiarity with **grammar** and the skills of punctuation, the use of capital letters, spelling and paragraphing, they are able to more effortlessly produce texts that convey a clear meaning. When texts are written with grammatical or technical errors (for example, inconsistent use of tense, incomplete sentences, punctuation and capital letter omissions or spelling errors) the writer's line of thought can become difficult to comprehend and a reading of the text is likely to be an arduous exercise.

WHAT IS GRAMMAR?

Grammar is an important element of both oral and written language, but the focus here is on the role of grammar in written communication and in developing children's ability to write effectively. In describing different grammatical components, a pedagogical approach (Deriwianka, 2001) has been used, that is, the information presented has drawn on different theories of grammar and has been chosen in terms of its relevance to teaching and learning.

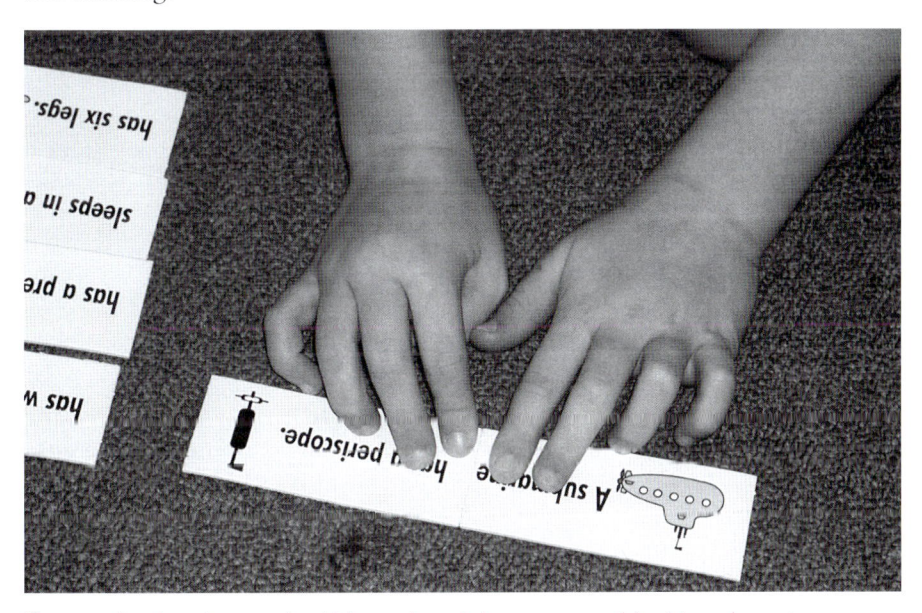

Grammar involves the ways in which words and phrases are combined to make sentences.

Grammar is a system for organising language. It is concerned with the parts of a **sentence** and with the ways in which words and phrases (word groups) can be combined and arranged in sentences to convey meaning. If written language is to be understood it should adhere to the language's grammatical system. Without grammar, written communication would not extend to anything much more complicated than a shopping list (Crow, 2010, p. 7).

Standard Australian English, like other languages (and dialects), has its own grammar and children should learn to write (and speak) using Standard Australian English in order to participate fully in the different spheres of Australian society.

Grammar comprises:

1. **Syntax**: the principles or standard practices for the arrangement of words and word groups into sentences. The sentence, 'The boy is wearing the red shirt', uses Standard English syntax. For a reader who is familiar with this grammatical system, meaning is easily established. When the words are arranged without regard for the grammatical system (for example, 'The boy the red shirt is wearing', or 'The red shirt is wearing the boy') the meaning is compromised or difficult to determine. The words, while individually understood, do not come together to present a clear and instantly understood meaning. More detailed information about sentences and about the principles that apply to the writing of sentences using Standard Australian English is provided in Chapter 1.
2. **Parts of speech** (sometimes referred to as word classes): words are divided into categories or types depending on their specific role in conveying the meaning of a sentence (Ogle & Beers, 2009). For example, when a word serves to name a person, place or thing it is part of the noun category and when it expresses action it is in the verb category. Other categories are adjectives, adverbs, prepositions, pronouns, articles and conjunctions. Each word in a category (or a word class) serves much the same purpose regardless of the sentence in which it is used. The different parts of speech are explained later in this chapter.
3. **Morphology**: it is sometimes necessary to modify a word by adding an inflectional ending (e.g. s, ed, ing) depending on its role in a sentence. Nouns are modified when a writer wants to indicate plural, e.g. 'dog'/'dogs'; verbs are modified to specify past tense, e.g. 'jump'/'jumped'; and adjectives and adverbs are modified when making comparisons, e.g. 'hot'/'hotter'/'hottest'. Morphology is described in more detail on later in this chapter.

ORAL LANGUAGE AND GRAMMAR AS A PRELUDE TO WRITING

Children intuitively learn the grammar of a language as they acquire oral language. By school age, their oral communication displays a breadth of grammatical knowledge and they are able to adapt this knowledge to cope with a wide range of oral communication settings.

Children's ability with regards to the grammatical system of English should continue to grow during their school years. They should gradually learn to say things in a more precise way and to use more elaborate sentence forms; they should expand on the sentence forms they already use and acquire new ones (Ogle & Beers, 2009, p. 46). Over time, children's spoken language should provide evidence of a greater breadth of grammatical knowledge.

Initially, when learning to write, children write in the same way as they speak; they construct sentences that replicate their speaking competency. However, they should eventually develop the realisation that written language is often different from spoken language; it regularly involves the use of sentence forms that are unlike those used when speaking. In order to learn about the unique ways that language is used in written communication, children should be given extensive exposure to written texts (through being read to, modelled writing etc.). With the right experiences their writing should eventually feature the use of language in ways that are different from that used in spoken communication.

Teachers should also be mindful of the need to provide experiences that will develop children's versatility with oral language; teachers need to support children in developing the ability to construct sentences in different ways and with growing grammatical complexity. This is important because oral language provides the foundation on which a competency in writing can be built. Teachers who nurture children's oral language development provide them with an important skill to take to the task of writing.

When children talk with teachers, other adults or peers about their writing ideas, they can be assisted to generate clear, well-formed sentences which are appropriate for written communication and which convey the meaning they want to express. Talk as a precursor to writing helps children in the use of written structures of English.

> It is important to remember that many children will arrive at school speaking another language or a dialect of English and their grammar knowledge will be about the language or dialect they speak rather than that of Standard Australian English. School might be the only time in which they regularly hear standard Australian English. They will need additional support to develop Standard Australian English. However, their first language or dialect should be supported and valued.

UNDERSTANDING ENGLISH GRAMMAR

In order for teachers to be fully equipped to support children's writing development, they require a firm grounding in the grammatical system of Standard English. They should be confident in making reference to the grammatical and technical elements of written texts when they talk to children about their writing or when they demonstrate the writing of texts or discuss books with children.

The following provides an overview of various components of the grammar of Standard English.

THE SENTENCE

The sentence, the main element of the written text, is made up of words and punctuation. The words must be produced in some sort of sequence (obviously they cannot all be produced at once) (Celce-Murcia & Larsen-Freeman, 1999). A properly structured sentence that observes the rules of the English language is most easily defined by the various features which it displays. These defining and necessary features are:

- A sentence is a group of words that expresses a complete thought.
- In a written text, a sentence starts with a capital letter and ends with a punctuation mark.
- It always has a subject and a verb.
- It is made up of two parts which are referred to as the subject and the predicate—e.g. Rachel (subject) eats bananas (predicate). The subject is the word or group of words

which identify who or what the sentence is about and the predicate is the verb and any other words that complete or modify it; basically, the words that are not part of the subject are part of the predicate.

When young children are being assisted to develop as writers, one of the first grammatical concepts on which to focus is the constitution of a sentence. When reading books, demonstrating writing or talking to children about their own writing, teachers should help them to recognise when a group of words constitutes a sentence and should assist them to construct complete sentences. Children soon show consistency in writing texts that contain complete and well-structured simple sentences.

CLAUSES

- A **clause** is any group of words containing a subject–verb relationship.
- An independent clause can stand alone as a sentence.
- A subordinate clause cannot stand alone as a sentence.

SENTENCE STRUCTURES

Sentences can be classified according to how they are put together (or formed). This is based on the number of clauses and how these clauses are combined. There are three main sentence forms—*simple, compound* and *complex*. These are explained and demonstrated in the chart below.

Table 17.1: Main sentence forms

A *simple sentence* is made up of a single clause only. It contains a subject and a verb. Examples of simple sentences are: *The car was parked. She wrote him a letter. Christopher's my friend.*	*Compound sentences* are made up of two or more independent clauses. They are often linked together by a conjunction. Examples of compound sentences are: *He went to the shops while I went to the movies. David was eating an ice cream when his friend rode past. Yesterday it rained so today I wore my raincoat.*	*Complex sentences* are made up of a main clause and one or more subordinate clauses. Examples of complex sentences are: *That he was not happy to be there was made obvious by the look on his face. The dog that had just eaten the goldfish was still hungry. The children were playing quietly by the swings at the far end of the park.*

Writing flows better and makes for better reading when it is made up of a combination of sentence forms. Too many simple sentences can make a written text mundane, tiresome to read and sometimes difficult to understand. When simple sentences predominate, the reader has to decide how the different ideas in each sentence connect whereas the use of compound and complex sentences can establish these connections. The following two versions of a text demonstrate the effect of sentence variety on text fluency, meaning and interest.

My Birthday, version 1: using simple sentences only

The sun was strong. I was hot. I rode my bike to school. It was two kilometres away. I had been walking to school for two years. This was since I started at Central Primary school. Mum hadn't wanted me to ride. She wanted me to catch the bus. I had convinced her to let me ride. Today was my birthday. I was riding fast. I wanted to get to school to see my friends. I wanted to see my friends before the bell rang.

My Birthday, version 2: using sentence variety

The sun was strong and I was hot as I rode my bike the usual three kilometres to school. I had been riding to school ever since I started at Central Primary School two years ago. Mum hadn't wanted me to ride. She wanted me to catch the bus but I had convinced her to let me ride. Today was my birthday and I was riding fast because I wanted to get to school to see my friends before the bell rang.

SENTENCE VOICE

The **voice** of a sentence is referred to as being either *active* or *passive*. When a sentence is written in the active voice (for example, 'Millions of people buy the magazine'), it shows that the subject of the sentence (millions of people) performs the action (buy the magazine). When a sentence is written in the passive voice (for example, 'The magazine is bought by millions of people') the subject of the sentence is acted upon (Martin, 2000). A sentence will maintain the same meaning whether written in the active or passive voice, but the emphasis that is given to the subject of the sentence will be different.

An examination of the following sentences shows the way in which a sentence can be ordered to exhibit active or passive voice.

Many people speak English. *(active)*

English is spoken by many people. *(passive)*

A green monster washes my car. *(active)*

My car is washed by a green monster. *(passive)*

Brazil produces coffee beans. *(active)*

Coffee beans are produced in Brazil. *(passive)*

My school purchased ten new computers. *(active)*

Ten new computers were purchased by my school. *(passive)*

There are a number of important features of sentences. These include:

1. A complete sentence must contain a *verb* and a *subject*. It might also contain other information but these two elements must be present.

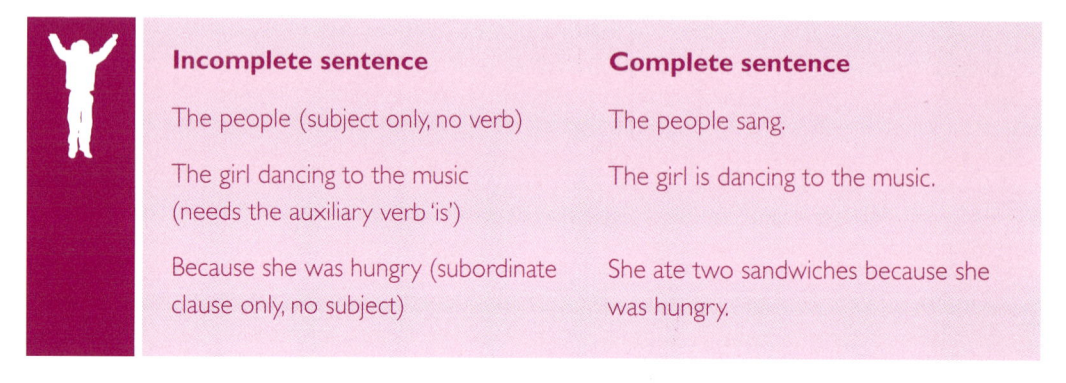

Incomplete sentence	Complete sentence
The people (subject only, no verb)	The people sang.
The girl dancing to the music (needs the auxiliary verb 'is')	The girl is dancing to the music.
Because she was hungry (subordinate clause only, no subject)	She ate two sandwiches because she was hungry.

2. The *verb* in a sentence *must always be compatible with the subject* of the sentence. This relates to the whether it is first, second or third person and to whether it is singular or plural. In the following sentences the verb is 'ride' and the subjects are 'I', 'she', 'we', 'they'.

> I ride my bike. (first person singular)
>
> She rides her bike. (third person singular)
>
> We ride our bikes. (first person plural)
>
> They ride their bikes. (third person plural)

3. A *pronoun* is used in a sentence to replace a *noun*. There needs to be a noun to which it is clearly referring. The noun is said to be the *antecedent* of the pronoun.

> The boy sat down because he was very tired.
>   noun   pronoun
>
> Note: The antecedent of the pronoun 'he' is 'boy'.
>
> Tomorrow the children will go to the zoo and they know that it will be fun.
>
> Note: 'they' refers to the children and 'it' refers to going to the zoo.

4. A pronoun, which is used instead of a preceding noun, needs to agree with that noun—in terms of number (singular or plural), person (first, second or third person) and gender (masculine or feminine).

> Noel is eating the lamb chops that his mum cooked for dinner.
>
> When the lady went shopping she bought some new shoes.

> Yesterday Sam and Sally started school. They enjoyed it.
>
> My grandma and I were talking on the phone. We were laughing a lot.
>
> Tomorrow Jean will visit the dentist with her mum.
>
> This belongs to Jimmy and his three brothers. It is their new football.
>
> Jackie, Gail and I will be going to London. It will be our first trip overseas.

5   It must be clear what *noun* the pronoun has taken the place of. In the following sentence it is not clear and this makes the meaning confusing.

> Yesterday Beth spoke to Dora about the bad news. She was not happy.
>
> Note: It is not clear as to whether she refers to Beth or Dora and so it is unclear as to who is not happy.

6   Different *forms of pronouns* are used depending on what *person* the sentence is written in. There are three persons. These are:
   - first person—this is the person talking (I, me, mine)
   - second person—this is the person spoken to (you, you (plural), yours)
   - third person—this is the person or thing being spoken about (he, him, his or she, her, hers, it, its).

7   Writers need to be careful to use a *verb tense* (past, present, future) consistently throughout a written text. Accidental changes to tense cause confusion for readers.

> The bear was looking for some honey. He arrived at the tree and looked up to see a large bee hive.
>
> The bear is looking for some honey. He arrives at the tree and looks up to see a large beehive.

TYPES OF SENTENCES

Sentences can be classified according to the purpose they serve. In English we have four basic sentence types—*statement, question, exclamation* and *command*. Each sentence type corresponds to the main communicative functions of language:

- statement—telling someone something
- question—asking someone something
- exclamation—expressing feelings about something
- command—getting someone to do something (Allen & Widdowson, 1975, cited in Celce-Murcia & Larsen-Freeman, 1999).

Children need to understand the purpose that each sentence type serves. The following examples demonstrate each of the four sentence types.

Table 17.2: The four types of sentences

Statement	Question	Command	Exclamation
A statement informs Examples: *Today is Monday.* *If I were fit, I would run in the marathon.* *I am thirsty.*	A question enquires Examples: *What day is it today?* *Why are you running in the marathon?*	A command directs or instructs Examples: *Pass the sugar.* *Don't do that.* *Stop right here.*	An exclamation expresses feelings Example: *What a beautiful day!* *How fantastic!*

PARTS OF SPEECH

There are eight parts of speech. They are nouns, verbs, adjectives and adverbs (which carry most of the meaning of a sentence and for this reason are sometimes termed the content words) and prepositions, pronouns, articles and conjunctions (which play more of a structural role in a sentence and are sometimes termed the structural or connecting words) (Beazley & Marr, 2001).

In the sentence, 'The <u>pen</u> which is used for <u>signing</u> the <u>certificates</u> is on <u>my</u> <u>table</u>', the underlined words are content words and those not underlined are structural words.

Definitions for each of the eight parts of speech and their roles in creating meaning in sentences are provided in Table 17.3.

Teaching children parts of speech is important for teachers to be able to able to talk with children about their writing. It provides a common and consistent language for conversations

Knowing the parts of speech is important. It provides a language for talking about language.

about the features of sentences in written texts and for helping children see the grammatical options for the production of clear and interesting sentences. Teachers can, for example, suggest to a child to 'Add an adjective here' or 'Let's think of a pronoun to use instead of this word'. Knowing about word classes provides children with a language to talk about language (this is referred to as a *metalanguage*). Bear in mind that the task of considering language as a thing in itself is tied to cognitive development and the young child might not be ready for the task.

Table 17.3: Parts of speech

Category and definition	Examples
Nouns *name a person, place, thing or idea* Frequently preceded by an article (a, an, the) or pronoun (my, his) Different types: (1) *Common nouns* refer to a kind of person, thing or idea (e.g. girl, ball) (2) *Proper nouns* refer to names for particular places or individuals (e.g. Perth, Sam) (3) *Collective nouns* refer to collections of things that we think of as one whole thing (e.g. herd (of cows), constellation (of stars), bunch (of grapes)) (4) *Abstract nouns* refer to a feeling or emotion and are derived from adjectives (e.g. happiness, derived from happy)	Jack drove to Melbourne, the capital of Victoria, which is located on the Yarra River. A gang of thieves stole his car which was clearly in need of a wash. He walked to the football game and when his team lost, his sadness was apparent. He caught three buses to return to his hotel. He arrived after dark. Jack's keys had fallen out of his coat pocket and he cried.
Verbs *denote an action or state of being* Two qualities—*tense* (the time the action occurred (past, present or future) and *aspect* (whether it already happened or is occurring now)	He reads the newspaper. He read the newspaper. His is reading the newspaper. He has been reading the newspaper. He was reading the newspaper. He has read the newspaper.
Adjectives *describe or denote the qualities of something* Serve to *modify* or *complement* a noun Commonly precede a noun, though in some instances can occur after	My cotton shirt lost a button. He became angry at the thought. The three small children sat in the front row. The youngest sister was the tallest.
Adverbs modify verbs and contribute meaning of various sorts to sentences Serve to modify verbs Most common types are those of direction, location, manner, time and frequency Flexible in terms of location in a sentence (beginning, middle or end)	Jim pointed there. (direction) Francis swims nearby. (location) The children sang joyfully at the concert. (manner) Aunty May will arrive soon. (time) Soon, Aunty May will arrive. We often ride to work. (frequency)

Category and definition	Examples
Pronouns *refer to or replace nouns or noun phrases within a text* Occupy same position in a sentence as a noun or noun phrase Different kinds of pronouns which are distinguished by number, person, gender: Subject—I, you, he, she, it, we, they Object—me, you, him, her, it, us, them Reflexive—myself, yourself, himself, herself, itself, ourselves, themselves Demonstrative—this, that, these, those	Mary is late for the bus so <u>she</u> is running. I found Jack's wallet and took it to <u>him</u>. The cat washed <u>itself</u> by licking its fur. '<u>These</u> are mine', she said, pointing to the pens. <u>That</u> has to stop before you hurt <u>yourself</u>.
Prepositions *connect words to other parts of a sentence and have a close relationship with the word that follows, which is usually a noun* Usually one word (e.g. in, to, at) Can sometimes be two or three words (e.g. next to, on top of) Typically signify spatial relationships but sometimes depict the role relationship between words (time, manner, place) A preposition and a noun comprise a prepositional phrase (e.g. at the shops, on top of the cupboard) Note: a phrase is a group of words that occur together in a sentence. They stick together for meaning	The box is <u>under</u> the table. ('under' signifies spatial relationship between box and table) Gavin gave the money <u>to</u> Fred. Fred got the money <u>from</u> Gavin. *('to' and 'from' depict role relationship)* The dog is sitting <u>next to</u> the tree. I live <u>at</u> 2 Parker Street. I work <u>in</u> the city. She was born <u>in</u> November. He went to work <u>on</u> Friday.
Determiners *are the category of words that limit the nouns that come after them. They include articles (a, an, the), demonstratives (this, that, these, those) and possessive determiners (my, your, his, her, its, our, their)* They precede an adjective if one is present (e.g. <u>the</u> blue coat) and if not they come directly before the noun	Margaret ate <u>the</u> juicy apple. Jan would like <u>a</u> sandwich for lunch. He drew a picture of <u>an</u> elephant. <u>That</u> book is mine. He wants <u>those</u> flowers in particular. <u>These</u> items are to be returned. We took <u>our</u> lunch. They took <u>their</u> shoes off. I want to use <u>my</u> pen. This must be <u>your</u> blue dress.
Conjunctions *are words that join ideas in a sentence* Can join two or more ideas of the same kind (and, but)—coordinating conjunctions Can join a subordinate clause to a main one (e.g. after, than, before, whenever, because, although)—subordinating conjunction. One part of the sentence (the subordinate clause) depends on the other Note: Any construction containing a subject–verb relationship is a clause. Some clauses can stand alone as sentences but subordinate clauses cannot	*Coordinating conjunction:* Justin <u>and</u> Keith went to the shops. *Subordinating conjunctions:* Kate was tired <u>because</u> she had just run a marathon. David watched television <u>while</u> Anna read a book. Mr Parsons decided to have lunch <u>although</u> he was not the least bit hungry.

Source: Beazley & Marr (2001); Celce-Murcia & Larsen-Freeman (1999)

> ## PARTS OF SPEECH: QUICK REFERENCE
>
> - **Nouns** name persons, places, things, qualities or acts,
>   e.g. *Mr Jones, Adelaide, courage, dog, beauty, execution*
> - **Pronouns** are substituted for nouns,
>   e.g. *he, she, them, it, their, her, his, they*
> - **Verbs** tell what a person, place or thing does. They express action or existence. Verbs change their form (endings are added or the word itself changes) according to whether something happens, happened is happening or will happen,
>   e.g. *run and runs, ran; stop and stops, stopped, stopping; laugh and laughs, laughed, laughing*
> - **Adverbs** describe verbs. They provide more information—time, frequency and manner—about a verb. They often end in *ly*,
>   e.g. *play the piano badly, run swiftly, sing off-key, cycle often, was born yesterday*
> - **Adjectives** describe or provide more information about nouns or pronouns— their size, colour, number and type,
>   e.g. *happy (people), five (oranges), red (dress), large (house), ('he is) happy, (it is) big*
> - **Prepositions** show words in relation to others in a sentence and show relationships of direction, time, place and manner,
>   e.g. *The book is under the table; He was born on Friday; They live in Sydney*
> - **Conjunctions** connect words, phrases (groups of words) or sentences,
>   e.g. *(and, but. or, because), It is blue and yellow, I will eat because I am hungry.*
> - **Articles** are words that are always used in the presence of a noun,
>   e.g. *a, an, the; an apple, the apple, a goat, the goat.*
>
> Source: Ogle & Beers (2009); Annandale et al (2005)

GRAMMAR AND WRITING

When children have achieved a certain level of writing ability, they should be assisted to develop a more detailed knowledge of grammar and sentences. Writers who are equipped with grammar knowledge have a better understanding of the principles and practices for building sentences; they have available to them a resource important to the achieve-ment of clear, precise and interesting written texts. They are able to accurately and meaningfully shape a range of simple as well as intricate sentences in order to achieve their communication goals.

PUNCTUATION

Punctuation refers to the marks placed in written texts that assist an understanding of the text:

- to signal the natural breaks between sentences and clauses
- to show expression (e.g. exclamation)
- to indicate questions
- to show pauses and stops

- for lists of items or ideas
- for abbreviations of words (Martin, 2007, pp. 263–6).

Learning to write texts requires an understanding of, and ability to use, a variety of types of punctuation correctly. Children should be introduced gradually to different punctuation marks and should be given the opportunity to notice and identify them. Table 17.4 explains the different types of punctuation.

Children's understanding of punctuation is enhanced when it is taught using the written texts that they produce.

Table 17.4: Different types of punctuation

Type	Examples
Full stop (.) Signals the end of a sentence	We went to a show last night. It lasted for five hours.
Question mark (?) Signals the end of a sentence that is asking a question	Did you know it was his birthday yesterday?
Exclamation mark (!) Signals the end of a sentence that is showing a strong feeling	What a beautiful day! How fantastic!
Comma (,) Used to separate words, phrases and clauses in sentences and to indicate a pause to the reader	I bought milk, bread, cheese and tomatoes at the shop. The cat, which was lying by the gate, didn't belong to us. While Marlee sang in the choir, I waited outside and read my book.

Type	Examples
Colon (:) Used to introduce a list of items	The collection of insects consisted of: • snails • caterpillars • slugs • beetles, and • grasshoppers.
Used to separate a sentence from additional information that is provided (a dash can also be used for this purpose)	When I went to the farm I noticed there were three different animals: cows, sheep and pigs. When I went to the farm I noticed there were three different animals—cows, sheep, pigs.
Semi colon (;) Used to link the ideas of two sentences or clauses	Last night I was unwell; I had been unwell all day.
Apostrophe (') Used to show where the letters have been left out in contracted words	was not = wasn't I will = I'll they are = they're
Used to show possession (when someone owns something)	Hillary's book the people's boat the two dogs' bones
Hyphen (-) Used to connect words or word parts; to show when two or more words should be read as a single word and to write fractions and numbers of more than one word	I didn't notice the sign and went down a one-way road. He ate two-thirds of the pizza. They were celebrating her twenty-first birthday.
Dashes (—) Used to separate parts of a sentence, to add additional detail or thoughts to a sentence, to introduce a list of items (as for a colon) and instead of brackets	Bill worked only three days this week—Monday, Wednesday and Thursday. Kate found the missing dog—a Labrador—by the gate of the school.
Brackets ( ) Used to enclose additional information, numbers, quotations	She counted the cards that had arrived for her birthday (there were 46) while she waited for her friend to arrive.
Ellipses (…) Used to show incomplete lines in a text and words left out of quotes	Once upon a time … 'The cat … didn't belong to us.'

PARAGRAPHING

Paragraphs are most often used in writing to indicate a change in the topic or idea. However, they can also show when there is a change in the time, place or speaker (Annandale et al., 2005).

A paragraph usually begins with a general sentence which indicates the main idea of the paragraph and is followed by other sentences which provide more detailed information. The sentences in a paragraph should present information on the same aspect of the paragraph topic.

A written text must indicate where one paragraph finishes and another one starts. This can be done in either of two ways: by placing an extra space between the different paragraphs of a text or by indenting (set in slightly from the left margin) the first line of each new paragraph. The task of reading and comprehending a text is made easier if paragraphs are used to group related information and the paragraphs are visibly distinguishable from each other.

> **THE PARAGRAPH**
>
> The different parts to a paragraph are:
> - *The topic sentence*: this is the sentence at or near the beginning of the paragraph which describes the main idea of the paragraph.
> - *The detail sentences*: these are sentences which follow the topic sentence. They provide more elaborate information and expand on the main idea.
> - *The concluding sentence*: this is the last sentence of the paragraph which usually provides a summary of the points made in the paragraph. Not all paragraphs have summary sentences.

Children are not ready to learn about paragraphs until their writing displays a high level of fluency; that is, when they write texts of a reasonable length and which cover a range of different ideas on the one topic.

Learning to write well-structured paragraphs occurs gradually. The first step is the development of children's awareness of paragraphing in written texts. A useful context for this is provided by the shared reading session. Eventually children can be taught to group sentences which address the same topic and, finally, to write a properly structured paragraph that includes a topic sentence and supporting detail.

When children's writing shows different ideas on the one topic they are usually ready to learn about paragraphing.

Like other conventions, children best learn about paragraphing when the teaching is directed at their own writing. This might first involve working with the whole class to examine a piece of writing and to determine appropriate paragraphing. The teacher can then work with each child and show how paragraphs should be created in their own texts. In order to provide a visual reminder for when children do their own writing, texts that use paragraphs should be displayed.

TEACHING THE WRITING CONVENTIONS

When writers are equipped with grammar and punctuation knowledge—when they understand the standard practices for structuring and punctuating sentences—they have available to them a resource important to the achievement of clear, precise and interesting written texts. They are able to accurately and meaningfully shape and punctuate a range of simple and more intricate sentences in an effort to achieve their communication goals.

Children will be supported in their development as writers when they are taught about the grammar of Standard Australian written English and the accurate application of punctuation and use of capital letters in their written texts. The central focus for such teaching should be on providing children with the tools to achieve clear coherent sentences and written texts that serve to achieve their communication goals.

Table 17.5: Scope and sequence of grammar topics and the early years of school

Level	Topics
Level One	• Concept of the sentence (and words and spaces) • Simple sentences • Word order in sentences • Nouns and verbs and their functions in sentences • Capital letters to begin sentences, full stops and question marks
Level Two	• Sequencing sentences logically in a written text • Word classes (nouns, verbs, adjectives, adverbs and conjunctives) and their functions in sentences • Compound sentences • Capital letters to begin sentences and for names of people and the 'I' pronoun • Full stops, question marks and exclamation marks • Singular and plural nouns and singular possessive • Sentence clarity and precision
Level Three	• Simple, compound and complex sentences • Word classes (nouns, verbs, adjectives, adverbs, conjunctives, articles and prepositions) and their functions in sentences • Sentences, phrases and clauses • Subject–verb agreement and noun–pronoun agreement • Adding words or phrases to a sentence to enhance meaning • Formal impersonal style in written texts—third person and passive voice • Punctuation

It is likely that an explicit focus on grammar and punctuation will not begin until the early years of primary school or at the stage when children have achieved a certain level of understanding about the nature of written communication and sentences.

Table 17.5 outlines a range of topics that might be the focus for the early years of school. The topics should be primarily addressed in the context of reading and writing. The choices about what to teach should be considerate of the children's current level of writing development as determined from the features of the written texts they currently produce.

Teaching the writing conventions of grammar as well as punctuation and the use of capital letters will serve to support children's development as writers when the instructional practices used are founded on the following important principles.

- Teaching children about grammar should occur in the context of written texts (Fellowes, 2006; Weaver, 1996). The teaching of punctuation and the use of capital letters should also occur in reading and writing situations. Children need to see how the application of different grammatical concepts and skills affects the meaning, clarity and flow of written texts. Writing demonstrations, discussions about example texts and student–teacher conferences during independent writing are all useful contexts for teaching children about the grammar of written language.
- Children will develop an intrinsic understanding of many different grammatical structures when they are regularly read to. Reading aloud exposes children to sentence structuring which, after a time, they will begin to incorporate in their writing (Polette, 2008, p. xv).
- Grammar teaching requires helping children to understand and apply those aspects of grammar that are most relevant to effective writing (Weaver, 1996).
- The cognitive development of young children should be considered when dealing with the grammatical system of written language.
- The teaching of grammar and punctuation should occur at the point of need. Teachers should examine children's writing to determine the knowledge or skills that would assist their writing development. Choices about what to teach should be based on the children's developmental readiness and learning needs.

Grammar teaching should involve teaching about how grammar affects the meaning of a text.

- Children's learning needs in regards to the conventions of written English will likely be varied. Teachers will need to ensure regular time working with small groups and with individual children so as to provide appropriately differentiated teaching.
- Knowledge and skills will need to be repeatedly addressed. Children will need constant practical support in applying what they know to their writing.
- Children should be assisted to revise and edit their writing with a focus on achieving accurate, clear and interesting sentences. They should be assisted to see that working to improve the sentences they write is about finding the clearest and most precise way to achieve meaning.

Modelled and shared writing, student conferencing and mini-lessons are all strategies that can be used to develop children's grammar and punctuation knowledge and their skill in using that knowledge to structure meaningful, clear and grammatically accurate sentences and to appropriately apply punctuation and capital letters. These strategies are explained in Chapter 19. They can be used to teach children about grammar and how to use grammar knowledge to write effectively. They might involve the teacher highlighting and talking with children about different words and their roles in sentences; highlighting different types of punctuation and different types of sentences (simple, compound, complex); demonstrating the skill of joining sentences to improve the flow of writing; or adding (or deleting) information to sentences so as to achieve clearer meaning.

SUMMARY

Grammar is a system for organising language, and its application to the composition of written texts is fundamental to the achievement of proficiency with written language. Children's growth as writers necessitates the gradual development of their grammatical knowledge and of their ability to apply it to written language. Likewise, it requires a vocabulary of grammatical terms thereby allowing children to engage in conversations about written language. Learning to write also calls for an understanding of, and ability to use, a variety of types of punctuation correctly. Grammar and punctuation are best taught in the context of the written text rather than through the use of isolated practice exercises. The central idea should be that there are fundamental grammar and punctuation practices that are to be applied to gain clear and accurate writing, and also that grammar is a writer's tool—it is the means by which effective, interesting and precise written language can be achieved.

QUESTIONS AND ACTIVITIES

1. Consider your own primary school experience of grammar and punctuation. How was it taught and what do you remember about it?
2. Discuss the following:
   a. Why is the teaching of grammar important?
   b. How can you ensure that children see the relevance of grammar knowledge to their writing?
   c. At what age does it seem appropriate to begin using the language of grammar with children?
   d. Investigate curriculum documents to determine the degree to which grammar in writing is addressed in the early childhood years.

3   Look through children's books and find examples of the different grammar and punctuation concepts outlined in this chapter.
4   Design an activity that could be used to enhance children's understanding of what constitutes a sentence.
5   Choose a story book that you might read to a group of seven-year-old children. Consider how you might highlight and teach one aspect of punctuation (for example, full stops or question marks) so the children understand its use in written language.

KEY TERMS

clause
grammar
morphology
parts of speech
sentence
syntax
voice

KEY REFERENCES

Annandale, K., Bindon, R., Broz, J., Dougan, J., Handley, K., Johnston, A., Lockett, L., Lynch, P. & Rourke, R. (2005). *Writing resource book: Addressing current literacy challenges.* Port Melbourne: Reed International.

Beazley, M. & Marr, G. (2001). *Writers handbook.* Putney, NSW: Phoenix Education.

Celce-Murcia, M. & Larsen-Freeman, D. (1999). *The grammar book* (2nd edn). USA: Heinle & Heinle Publishers.

Coffin, C. (eds) (2001). *Analysing English in a global context: A reader.* New York: Routledge.

Crow, J. T. (2010). *Unleashing your language wizards: A brain-based approach to effective editing and writing.* Boston: Pearson Education.

Deriwianka, B. (2001) Pedagogical grammars: Their role in English language teaching. In Burns, A. & Coffin, C. (eds), *Analysing English in a global context: A reader.* New York: Routledge.

Fellowes, J. (2006). Grammar knowledge and students writing. *Practically Primary, 11*(3), 40–3.

Martin, R. (2007). *Young writers guide* (4th edn). Flinders Park: ERA Publications.

Ogle, D. & Beers, J. W. (2009). *Engaging the language arts: Exploring the power of language.* Boston: Pearson.

Polette, K. (2007). *Teaching grammar through writing: Activities to develop craft in all student grades 4–12.* Boston: Pearson Education.

Weaver, C. (1996). Teaching grammar in the context of writing. *English Journal, 85*(7).

CHAPTER 18

Spelling and Handwriting

CHAPTER OBJECTIVES

This chapter will increase your understanding of:

- the English spelling system
- important spelling knowledge and strategies
- the nature of children's spelling development
- invented spelling and its importance to children's spelling development
- ways in which to assist children to develop spelling ability
- handwriting
- ways in which to support children to develop handwriting.

This chapter begins with a discussion of the spelling system of English and goes on to explain the areas of knowledge and key strategies that are important to developing proficiency in spelling. The knowledge and strategies outlined should form the basis of any approach taken in assisting children to develop as competent spellers. It is important that you develop a good understanding of these. The chapter uses a range of spelling terminology and you might want to spend some time revising it and developing a clear understanding of each term. The chapter concludes by outlining a large range of spelling activities that can be drawn on in developing the spelling knowledge and strategies of pre-school and school-aged children. The importance and development of handwriting is discussed at the end of the chapter.

THE IMPORTANCE OF GOOD SPELLING

Spelling involves the encoding of spoken words into written language by arranging letters in a way that adheres to the accepted conventions of the English language. The degree to which the spelling conventions are correctly applied when words are written is important to the effectiveness of written communication.

Learning to spell accurately is an important aspect of learning to write. A written text in which correct spelling is used contributes to the reader being easily able to decode and comprehend it. On the other hand, when a text contains words spelt incorrectly, reading and comprehension are compromised. Incorrect spelling obliges the reader to focus on decoding the words rather than on comprehending the meaning of the text. Correct spelling is about 'audience courtesy' (Biggam & Itterley, 2009). It is about the writer being considerate of the readers' task.

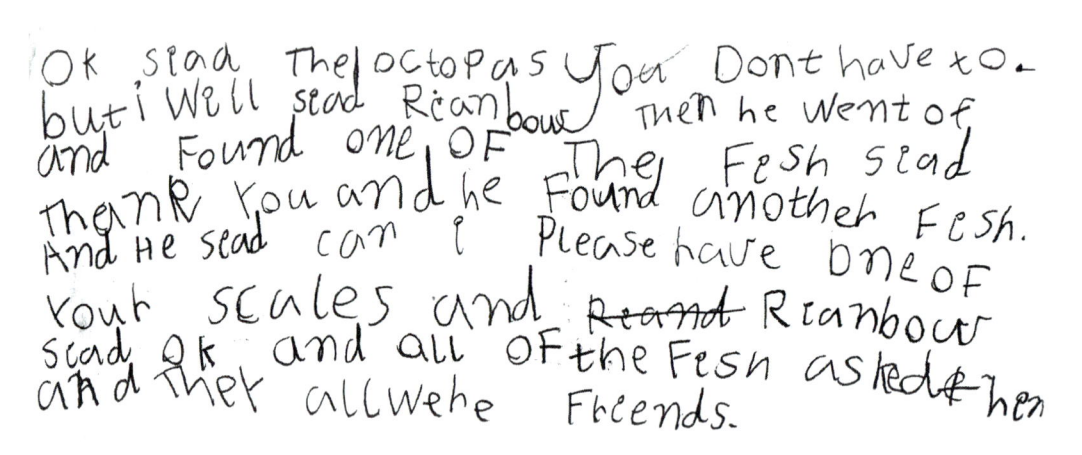

Learning to spell accurately is an important aspect of learning to write.

Society in general values accurate spelling and when writing contains misspelt words it is usually viewed unfavourably. People will often deem spelling errors to be indicative of a writer's lack of diligence and mental effort. They will tend to judge this defect in a person's writing as a measure of the writer's literacy credibility. As Templeton (1996, p. 102) states, 'spelling is so visible, so obvious, that it often assumes the role of a proxy for literacy and in that role is bound to generate controversy.'

Spelling competency contributes to writing fluency. Accomplished writers know how to spell or can quickly work out the spelling for most of the words that they want to use. They are less inclined to hesitate over spelling as they write and are therefore free to concentrate on using language effectively. Good spellers are competent with self-monitoring and self-correction when writing (Westwood, 2005, p. 6).

Spelling ability also has a bearing on students' reading development. Children who are good at spelling are also good at figuring out (decoding) words when reading (Cox, 2008, p. 355). The more students are familiar with the visual features of words, the more they are able to easily recognise them when reading texts.

INTRODUCTION TO THE ENGLISH ORTHOGRAPHIC SYSTEM

Different languages have different orthographic (spelling) systems. They have defined sets of symbols and rules for using the symbols to **encode** spoken words into written form.

The orthographic system of the English language is an *alphabetic system*. It employs a set of **graphemes** (letters of the alphabet) to represent the **phonemes** (individual speech sounds) of words. Many other languages also use an alphabetic system. Some are completely phonetic—that is, there is a consistent correspondence between letters and the phonemes of words. The same letter or combination of letters is always used for a particular sound regardless of the word. Italian, Spanish and Finnish are examples of phonetic languages.

The orthographic system of the English language is an alphabetic system

However, although the English alphabetic system is generally phonetically consistent, it is far from being so entirely. In some instances there are several different letter combinations that can be used to encode an individual phoneme into its written form. For instance, when spelling a word containing the /ae/ phoneme, any one of the letter combinations—a, ay, ey, eigh, ai or a-e—may have to be used. The choice of which letter combination to use will depend on the actual word; for example, tod**ay**, pr**ey**, sl**eigh**, r**ai**n and l**ate** (refer to Table 18.1). Moreover, the exact same letter or combination of letters can be used for different phonemes. For example, the letter 'c' can be used for each of two discrete beginning phonemes of the words 'cat' and 'cent'. Other examples can are the words **ch**aracter and **ch**eap, and the words en**ough**, b**ough**, thor**ough** and tr**ough.**

As noted in Chapter 10 (phonological awareness), there are an estimated forty-four different phonemes (individual sound units of words) that comprise all spoken words, of which there are about half a million, in the English language. The forty-four different phonemes are represented in writing from the twenty-six letters of the alphabet, used either individually or in combination. For a more elaborate description of phonemes and phonemic knowledge (this is an understanding that is contained within the broader topic of phonological awareness) refer to Chapter 10. There are about 120 variations in the use of letters to represent the forty-four phonemes. Learning to spell involves learning to make the right decision about the letters to use to generate written words.

Table 18.1: Examples of different spelling patterns used in written English for some of the phonemes of spoken words

sit	ma**de**	la**mb**	**r**un
pa**ss**	s**ay**	su**m**	**wr**ite
circle	b**ai**t	ha**mm**er	bo**rr**ow
lau**gh**	st**or**k	t**ea**m	**k**ing
tele**ph**one	f**our**	m**e**	du**ck**
su**ff**er	s**aw**	f**ee**t	**qu**een
fan	**Au**gust	laz**y**	**c**at
	d**oor**	ke**y**	**ch**aracter
t**igh**t	t**u**be	**j**am	b**oa**t
b**ye**	gl**ue**	fu**dge**	co**mb**
fl**y**	b**oo**t	**g**em	t**o**ne
b**i**te	st**ew**	gara**ge**	sl**ow**
van	**n**ut	h**er**	b**oy**
lo**ve**	**kn**ife	d**ir**t	s**oi**l
	ba**nn**er	t**ur**tle	

The alphabetic spelling system of English is derived from the ancient Hebrew, Greek and Roman languages (Cox, 2008, p. 347). Present-day spelling has been developed through a multitude of changes and additions over time.

At different times throughout history, modifications have been made to the pronunciation of words but not to their spelling. One such modification occurred at the start of the middle ages involving the removal of the /k/ sound from spoken words when the /k/ occurred before a consonant at the beginning of a word. However, the letter 'k' continued to be used when writing these words and we now have words with a silent 'k' (for example, **k**nife, **k**now).

Other languages have influenced the English language. For example, the words 'tree', 'birth', 'egg' and 'reindeer' were added to English from the language of the Vikings, and the French-based words 'ballet', 'bouquet' and 'restaurant' came into the English language during a Norman invasion of the British Isles (Cox, 2008, p. 347). Today, the English language continues to evolve as it continues to embrace words from other languages. The words 'pizza', 'spaghetti' and 'pasta' have been acquired from the Italian language.

Despite the disparity that might suggest little regularity in the way in which words are spelt in English, there is actually a fairly high degree of consistency in the English spelling system.

> Not all languages use an **alphabetic system** to write. For instance, the Chinese language is written using a logographic system, which entails using a unique symbol for each word. The Japanese language uses a syllabic system whereby a different symbol is used for each of the syllables in a word.

SPELLING KNOWLEDGE

Learning to spell is a complex process which develops over time. It involves children gradually accumulating **orthographic** (spelling) **knowledge** and learning strategies which help them to spell different word forms.

The use of rote learning and memorisation holds minimal benefit in learning and remembering the spelling of words (Tompkins, 2009). Learning to spell is more of a thinking process than a task of memorisation. It requires the regular and systematic analysis of word forms that focus on the connections between the phonological, visual and meaning layers of words (Wheatley, 2005, p. 7). The teaching of spelling is most effective and enduring when the goal is to develop children's understanding of the layers of word knowledge—phonological, visual, morphological and etymological knowledge as detailed below.

> The adequacy of children's spelling development will depend on their teachers having a sound understanding of the English spelling system and being fully acquainted with the standard rules and conventions that apply to the spelling of words in English.

LEVEL 1: PHONOLOGICAL KNOWLEDGE (HOW WORDS SOUND)

The **phonological** level of knowledge about the spelling of words has an oral application. It relates to children becoming aware of, and using, words in spoken language and the units of sounds (**syllables** and phonemes) of which they are composed. It involves understanding of, and skill with:

- *Syllables*   segmenting words into syllables or units of sound.

> el - e - phant   rab - bit   di - no - saur
> mu - se - um   cat - er - pil - lar

- *Onsets and rimes*—separating the beginning consonant of a one syllable word from the rest of the word.

r - at	c - at	f - at
b - at	h - at	m - at

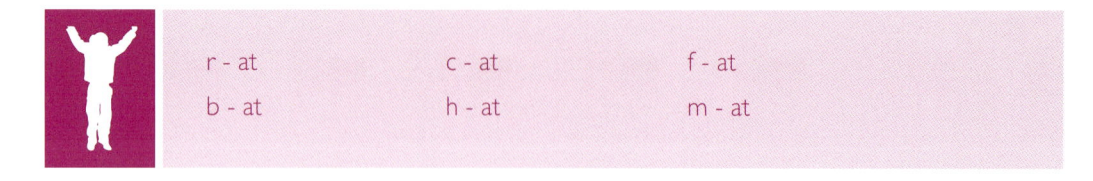

- *Phonemes*—identifying and being able to manipulate the individual speech sounds of words (e.g. hearing /d/, /o/ and /g/ as separate sounds in the word 'dog').

LEVEL 2: VISUAL KNOWLEDGE (HOW WORDS LOOK)

Visual knowledge as it relates to spelling is concerned with the appearance of words; specifically, the ordering of letters in words or parts of words. It refers to the alphabetic nature of written English and involves:

- *Print concepts*—the basic principles of written language such as:
  - Print is spoken language which has been written down.
  - Spaces are used to separate words from each other.
  - Sound parts of spoken words are represented by letters of the alphabet.
- *Letters of the alphabet*—the twenty-six written symbols that comprise the English alphabet (lower and upper case).
- **Letter–sound relationships**—the correspondence between phonemes (the individual sound units in spoken words) and the graphemes (the letters of the alphabet). This involves knowing that phonemes are represented by one or more letters of the alphabet when writing and that the same sound can be represented by different letters (s**ee**n, b**ea**n) and the same letter or letters can represent different sounds (r**ou**gh, pl**ou**gh).
- **Spelling patterns**—words contain patterns of letters representing specific phonemes that can be grouped together on this basis (e.g. 'heat', 'meat', 'feat', 'beat', 'mean', 'leap', 'lean', 'seat').

Words are made of units of sound (phonemes) which are represented by letters (graphemes) when writing.

The phonological and visual layers of English word knowledge are important aspects of the early phases of spelling development. The progressive development of these two areas should occur simultaneously and the association between the phonological and visual features of words should be emphasised.

LEVEL 3: MORPHEMIC KNOWLEDGE (HOW WORDS CHANGE FORM)

Morphemic knowledge is concerned with the internal structures of words and the different units of meaning (**morphemes**) which together make up individual words. It involves understanding how words can be separated into morphemes—meaningful *chunks* or parts (smallest units of words that hold meaning). For example, in the word 'deliberately' there are two morphemes. They are deliberate + ly. Morphemic knowledge involves understanding and skill with:

- *Morphemic units of words*—words are made up of morphemes. A word may be one morpheme ('run', 'money' and 'boy') or two or more morphemes such as 'redesign' (re + design), 'sadly' (sad + ly) and 'recreation' (re + create + ion). A morpheme is a word or a meaningful piece of a word (ly, un, pre, anti, less).
- *Morphemes and meaning*—most words with the same spelling base (e.g. *great, great*ness, *great*ly, *great*er) have the same meaning base.
- **Root words**—this is a word (one morpheme) to which another morpheme is attached to produce a new word. The root of the word 'happily' is 'happy'.
- *Suffixes and prefixes*—morphemes are added to words to produce new words. **Prefixes** are added to the beginning of words (e.g. pre, re, un) and **suffixes** are added to the end of words (e.g. ness, ly, tion). Suffixes include inflectional endings (ed, ing, s, es).
- **Compound words**—made up of two words (morphemes), e.g. 'wheelbarrow', 'cardboard'.
- *Rules*—there are rules that direct the conventional way of changing words when adding prefixes and suffixes (including inflectional endings).

LEVEL 4: ETYMOLOGICAL KNOWLEDGE (WHERE WORDS COME FROM)

Etymological knowledge of spelling is concerned with the origin of words. It requires an appreciation that many English words have been derived from another language and an understanding of their base or original meaning.

The spelling of many words is due to the fact that they have come from other languages, for example, 'garage', 'montage', 'collage' (from French) and 'photograph', 'photocopy' ('photo' from Greek). Words derived from other languages with common meanings will often have common letter clusters (parts of the word spelt the same way).

The four layers of word knowledge provide the base for children to become competent spellers. As children increase their knowledge, their ability to tackle the spelling of a greater variety of words improves. Over time they develop the understanding and skill required to achieve an increasingly higher level of accuracy with the spelling of all types of words.

In early childhood the focus is primarily on the teaching of the phonological and visual elements of words and about the relationships between them. In the early years of school, children's spelling ability will often progress to the stage where further progress should involve learning about the morphemic layer of spelling knowledge.

SPELLING STRATEGIES

Good spellers draw on a repertoire of strategies to learn the spelling of new words, to recall the spelling of words and to tackle the spelling of unfamiliar words. Most of these strategies draw on the different levels of knowledge or features of the spelling system—phonological knowledge (sounds within words), visual knowledge (letters and letter sequences in words), morphemic knowledge (root words and affixes) and etymological knowledge (origins of words). Several such strategies are:

- *Visualising*: retrieving an image of a word and recalling the significant visual features or letter patterns.
- *Chunking*: breaking a word into smaller 'chunks' and then spelling each 'chunk' of the word.
- *Using analogy*: making parallels between the visual, phonological or meaning features of words and drawing on this to spell a new word.
- *Applying morphemic principles*: applying knowledge of base words and affixes (prefixes, suffixes and inflectional endings) and of the rules that apply to forming new words by adding an affix.
- *Mnemonics*: using a learnt memory aid to recall the spelling of a difficult or irregularly spelt word.
- *Use of meaning origin*: using the meaning of words and making connections to words with similar meaning.
- *Source*: referring to a dictionary or some other source to check the spelling of a word.

CHILDREN'S SPELLING DEVELOPMENT

Learning to spell first requires an understanding of a few basic concepts of the English writing system. Children need to understand that:

- Written language is spoken language expressed in writing.
- Spoken language is made up of sounds which can be recorded as written letters.
- Written English takes a left to right direction.
- Spaces are used to separate words from each other in written texts.

Children move through various phases of spelling competency on their way to becoming **conventional** and accomplished spellers. Their progress through the various phases of development reflects increased knowledge of the orthographic system. At each phase, children's spelling ability will reflect an enhanced understanding of the correspondence between letters and sounds and of letter and syllable patterns in words. It will indicate an increased knowledge of the relationship between spelling and word meanings and of the use of different spelling strategies.

The level of children's spelling development should be apparent from their writing. When children are at the beginning phase of learning to spell, their writing is generally characterised by random shapes and letters used in no particular sequence to signify a message. From this point progress in spelling is enhanced by an awareness of the alphabetic principle and the basic concepts of written language and understanding of the association between written letters and the phonemes of words. A continued and systematic development of spelling knowledge, skills and strategies will assist further spelling progress. The phases of spelling development, which are typical of the way in which many children progress in spelling knowledge and skills (although at different rates), are outlined in Table 18.2.

Table 18.2: Phases of children's spelling development

Phase	Spelling attributes
Phase 1 Beginning (3–5 years)	The child's writing shows: • the random use of numerals, letters and letter-like shapes • increased use of alphabet letters—more likely to be upper case than lower case • no association between letters and phonemes, though towards the end of this phase there is some association between the letters and phonemes
Phase 2 Emergent (4–6 years)	The child's writing shows: • a consistent use of alphabet letters • an understanding of alphabetic principle and letter–phoneme correspondence • only a few phonemes in words represented, e.g. 'ct' for cat, 'kn' for kitten, 'lefnt' for elephant (beginning phoneme awareness) • more consonant sounds than vowel sounds in words, e.g. 'ct' (cat), 'lft' (elephant) • a knowledge of a few simple common letter patterns (e.g. 'ch') and some blends (e.g. cr—crib) • dominant use of the *sounding-out strategy* to spell words (apply phoneme segmentation skill) • whole words copied from environmental print of the classroom
Phase 3 Early (5–7 years)	The child's writing shows: • a more accurate use of standard letter–phoneme correspondence (reflecting phonemic awareness development). This develops as children progress within this phase • some difficulty in distinguishing certain sounds noted in spelling, e.g. 'chrain' for train and 'grive' for drive • use of some simple vowel and consonant letter patterns (digraphs) such as when two letters are used to represent one phoneme, e.g. ch, sh, th, ee • irregular words written as if regular, e.g. 'sed' for said • some letter pattern reversals ('siad' for said) and confusion when there are different letter patterns for the same sound, e.g. feet/feat and same/saym • the correct spelling for a small bank of high-frequency sight words • use of the *sounding-out strategy* as well as the *chunking strategy*—breaking words up into smaller parts/syllables (e.g. flow - er) to spell words

Phase	Spelling attributes
Phase 4 Fluent (7–10 years)	The child's writing displays: • more advanced understanding of word structure • a good range of words that are spelt correctly • the phonemes in words accurately represented using a range of common letter patterns and some less common letter patterns • application of different spelling generalisations and rules • correct inflectional endings (ed, es, ing) and consonant doubling • use of the *sounding-out*, *chunking*, *visual memory* and *analogy* strategies to spell words • understanding of homophones, compound words and use of prefixes and suffixes • all syllables represented in a word when writing • all letters included, but may still write some letters in reverse order, e.g. 'raelly' • good automaticity in the correct spelling of common words
Phase 5 Independent 11–12 years	The child's writing displays: • application of a wide range of letter–sound association rules and principles • large bank of words spelt correctly and automatically • knowledge of less common letter patterns, e.g. 'aisle', 'reign' • a variety of spelling rules and generalisations applied accurately • words with inflectional endings spelt correctly • the use of a variety of strategies for spelling unknown words including those derived from knowledge of word meanings and word history (**etymology**) • recognition of misspelt words and self-correction

Source: adapted from Westwood (2005) and Tompkins (2006)

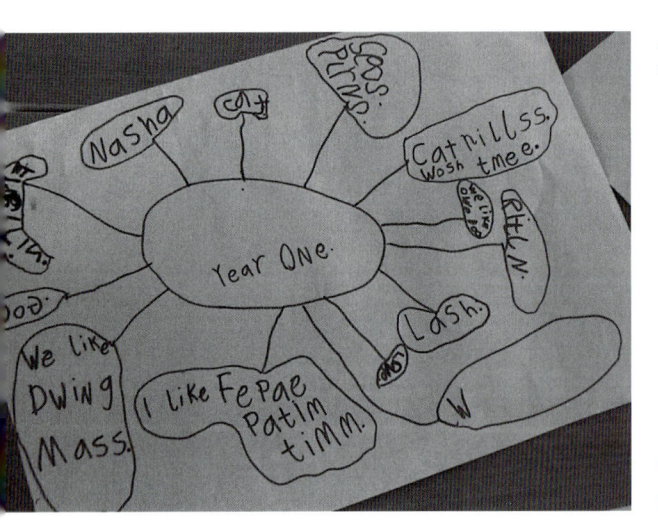

Children move through various phases of spelling competency on their way to becoming conventional and accomplished spellers.

Teachers' appreciation of the developmental nature of learning to spell and their familiarity with the different phases of spelling development is important. An ability to recognise the spelling knowledge and skills of children in their classes and to design instruction that appropriately builds on what children already know and can do is important to the children's overall development of spelling competence.

While most children will progress through the same sequence of phases as they develop spelling competency, not all will progress at the same rate. It is likely even that the children in a single class will be at different phases of learning and development and will therefore have different teaching and learning requirements. It is important for a spelling program to be devised on the basis of the spelling ability of different groups of children and for the provision of different instruction.

INVENTED SPELLING

Young children, will often want to write words which they do not yet know how to spell. They should be encouraged to use what is often referred to as **invented spelling**: to apply whatever knowledge they have acquired about spelling to arrive at their best judgment of the spelling of unknown words. Invented spelling is a temporary approach to spelling. Its encouragement is important as it enhances children's spelling development and overall writing ability.

Writing development is assisted when children regularly engage in the fluent and unrestricted expression of ideas and thoughts in writing. This should not be restricted by too strong an emphasis on spelling correctness. Otherwise they will limit themselves to using only those words for which they know the correct spelling or will too often stop writing to ask how to spell a word. These restrictions impede writing development. Children who are encouraged to attempt the spelling of words regardless of success are able to focus more clearly on the various other elements of written communication.

Invented spelling obliges children to think about the way in which words work—the sounds within words and the letters used to represent these sounds. They get to practise the segmenting of words into phonemes and to make decisions about the letters required to represent each phoneme. Attempts at invented spelling also provide useful information about a child's spelling development and learning needs. Teachers can determine the degree to which children have developed phonemic awareness, graphophonic understanding and other important aspects of spelling knowledge. Over time and with appropriate learning experiences, children's writing will progressively demonstrate a greater degree of correctness in spelling.

The encouragement of invented spelling when writing is important to children's spelling and overall writing development.

TEACHING SPELLING

The adequacy of children's spelling development will depend on their teachers having a sound understanding of the English spelling system and being fully acquainted with the standard rules and conventions that apply to the spelling of words in English. It will also depend on teachers providing an appropriate range of experiences in which good spelling can be nurtured. There are various principles to guide teachers in ensuring that important practices are implemented. The following principles should be addressed through classroom practices.

1. *Learning to spell is supported when there are opportunities to regularly engage in writing.*
   Learning to spell is not an end in itself; it is a means of achieving effective written communication. A significant goal of literacy teaching is the development of children's ability to use written language effectively, and learning to spell supports this goal. Texts written with accurate spelling enable readers more easily to identify meaning.

   Regular writing experiences give children plenty of opportunity to apply their developing spelling knowledge and skills. Children can apply what they know about sounds, letters and words as they work out the spelling of words while also attending to other elements of a writing activity. Teachers can use writing experiences to help students make links between the spelling patterns they already know and the spelling patterns of new words they want to use.

2. *Learning to spell requires that children receive regular experience with reading books and other texts.*
   Children are able to learn about letter–sound patterns in words and about other aspects of spelling when they are encouraged and assisted to explore words and word parts when reading texts. Shared reading is a perfect opportunity to explore words and spelling patterns as it involves the use of a large book and all children can thus view the text as the teacher guides them in the analysis of words and the discovery of spelling patterns in words. Any books used should feature words appropriate to the learning of spelling at the right developmental level.

3. *Learning to spell is supported when the classroom environment is established as a rich print resource.*
   The classroom writing environment should feature a special writing area as well as various charts, posters and labels and other written texts. The writing area should be well resourced with different types and colours of writing implements and different coloured paper, cards and other materials for the children to write on. It should also contain charts and pictures that children can use as they write. The classroom walls should display the children's writing efforts as well as the written texts created by the teacher. There should be alphabet cards, lists of words categorised according to their spelling and word charts that show new and interesting words. Children should be immersed in writing. They should be encouraged to refer to the print in the environment when spelling words and writing texts.

4. *Spelling instruction must take into account the children's current phase of spelling development and build on it to further progress spelling competency.*
   Spelling programs should be designed having regard to what has been learnt about children's spelling strengths and needs. Teachers should endeavour to gain a strong understanding of the developmental phase at which each child in the class is currently operating. They should be mindful of the fact that children's spelling competency develops at different rates and in different ways, and the design of a teaching program should represent the various needs of the children in the class.

5   *In learning to spell, children should be given regular, direct and systematic teaching that caters for their individual spelling needs.*

Learning to spell should involve much more than learning the spelling of a set group of words each week. Such practices have been shown to have little effect on children's long-term spelling ability (Tompkins, 2009). Learning to spell requires learners to engage in the study of words; to examine and learn about the structure and composition of words and about the phonological (sound), graphemic (visual) and meaning characteristics of words and groups of words. A spelling program should involve an approach to the teaching of spelling that systematically builds up knowledge of the spelling system and of the strategies and skills necessary to becoming a competent speller. Children's spelling ability will not progress efficiently if it relies just on incidental learning.

6   *Learning to spell involves learning a range of strategies for spelling words.*

Children need to be taught how to use the strategies of visualising, chunking, analogy and so on if they are to become competent spellers. Spelling strategies call for the application of the various levels of knowledge of the spelling system. The strategies that children are taught should align with the spelling knowledge to which they presently have access.

SPELLING ACTIVITIES

There is a variety of spelling activities that, when incorporated into a spelling program, serve to enhance children's understanding of the English spelling system and to support them in their development as competent spellers. Different spelling activities will be suitable for different groups of learners. Their place in an overall spelling program needs to be determined on the basis of the phase of spelling development at which a group of children is currently operating. Some activities will best provide for the learning needs of children at the beginning, pre-phonetic and phonetic phases where the development of children's phonological and graphemic knowledge is paramount. Others might best suit children whose spelling development requires learning more about the morphological features of words, while yet many others can be adapted to suit different groups of learners. A number of different spelling activities are outlined below. Teachers need to carefully select those for which the learning focus suits the spelling needs of the children with whom they are working.

WORD SORTS

Word sorts involve children being given sets of words (often written on individual cards) that they are required to compare and sort into groups on the basis common sounds or spelling patterns (e.g. Bear, Invernessi, Templeton & Johnston, 2004). Children might be given the category to be used or they can identify a category themselves. The category to be used will depend on the children's phase of spelling development, but it may involve such things as the beginning sounds or letters, vowel patterns, the spelling of the vowel sound or a syllable structure. Word-sort activities enable children to notice the visual patterns in words and the sounds associated with these patterns. They can involve children in comparing groups of words that are related with others that are not, and identifying any generalisations for spelling words.

For example, a group of children were asked to sort the words 'feed', 'said', 'weed', 'read', 'fail', 'beam', 'drain', 'peel' and 'bed'. They did so on the basis of the medial phoneme and without regard for the different spelling options, as shown.

Group One	Group Two
feed, weed, read, beam, peel	said, fail, drain, bed

An additional categorisation resulted in three groups being formed whereby the spelling of the medial /ee/ phoneme became important.

Group One	Group Two	Group Three
feed, weed, peel	read, beam	said, fail, drain, bed

Tierney and Readence (2005, p. 98) provide the following guiding principles for carrying out word sorts:

- Use words the children can read.
- Compare groups of words that relate to each other with those that do not.
- Sort words by both sight and sound so the focus is on phonemes (sound) as well as visual patterns.
- Begin with obvious contrasts.
- Don't hide exceptions.
- Focus on the identifying of generalisations and patterns.
- Provide repetition and aim for automaticity whereby children can sort with both fluency and accuracy.

Fountas and Pinnell (1999) identify various types of word sorts and some of those suggested include the following.

Picture sorts

Children look at a set of pictures that represent words and they identify the initial phoneme for each word. They sort the picture cards on this basis, grouping all those pictures together where the words they represent have the same beginning phoneme. This activity can also be done with medial or final phonemes. Picture sorts can be used to address various other phonological elements such as:

- number of syllables
- rhyme
- long and short vowel sounds.

Spelling sorts

Words can be sorted on the basis of phoneme–grapheme (letter) correspondence, letter patterns or meaning and spelling. The type of spelling sort will depend on the type of spelling knowledge being developed. Spelling sorts are effective in focusing children's attention on the critical parts of words, which is necessary to carry out a sort. Examples of specific spelling sorts include those based on:

- the sound that the letter 'c' makes when words are pronounced
- the different visual patterns for the /ou/ sound: ow ('cow') and ou ('flour')
- common prefixes or suffixes.

Blind sort

The teacher calls out a word with a particular spelling or sound feature. The children point to the category shown on a chart in which it belongs. Alternatively, the children are asked to write the word under the right category as indicated by a key word at the top of a column on a chart

ch as in chart	c as in carriage	ch as in choir	c as cent

WORD TRACE

Word trace activities assist children in recalling the visual features of words. They involve children carrying out the following steps with a select word or list of words:

1. Look at the word.
2. Read it aloud.
3. Trace the word, spelling out the letters at the same time.
4. Take a mind photograph of the word.

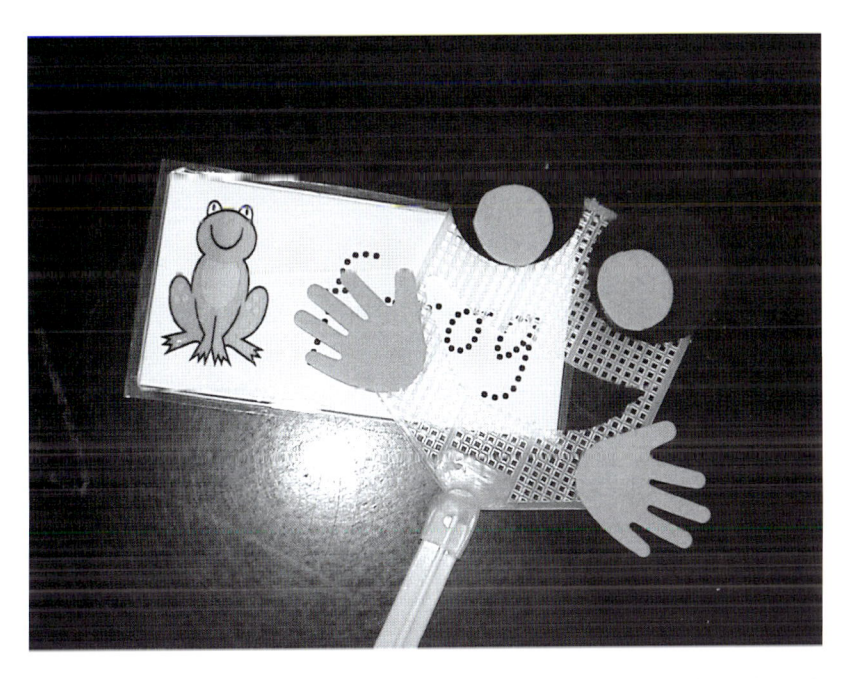

Spelling activities should focus on assisting children to recall the visual features of words.

5. Cover the word.
6. Write the word from memory, saying the letters at the same time.
7. Check the spelling.

HIGHLIGHTING CRITICAL FEATURES

Children identify and highlight the **critical feature** (most significant element) of a word or list of words; for example, h**eigh**t, fr**eigh**t, sl**ow**. After the examination of the word, they write the word from memory using a different coloured pencil (or underlining) to draw attention to the critical feature.

THE WORD WALL

The word wall is both a spelling resource for children and an activity that can be used to develop their spelling ability. It is particularly useful for learning to spell high-frequency words, topic words, words with common spelling patterns or words relating to specific spelling knowledge. The words being taught are written on a large chart on which the letters of the alphabet are shown across the top. New words are added to the word wall by being written under the letter with which they start. New words are added to the chart on a regular basis so that the collection being learnt is gradually increased. Each day, time is dedicated to learning these words. The teacher guides the children in various activities involving an examination of, and familiarity with, their spelling. Useful activities include:

- reading words aloud
- clapping the syllables
- pronouncing slowly, separating the word parts
- analysing words in relation to their spelling
- writing words and indicating the critical parts
- discussing the meanings
- putting into context—make sentence strips, with new words in a different colour
- categorising the words based on a sound, visual or meaning criteria
- making the words using magnets
- conveying the meaning of words in visual form
- playing the game 'Which word?' where five clues are provided about a word and the children have to use these clues to determine the word. The clues provided might be: It has four letters. It begins with a 'sh' sound. It has a short vowel sound in the middle. It sounds similar to the word 'fed'.

LOOK—COVER—WRITE—CHECK

This activity begins with children recording the words from their designated spelling list and slowly pronouncing each phoneme or syllable as they do so. The children then examine each word focusing on the sequence of letters, the critical letter patterns (the tricky parts of the word) and the shape of the word outline. Then, dealing again with each word, one at a time, they close their eyes and visualise them, attempting to recall the features. Next, each word is covered and written out from memory, and finally the spelling is checked. It is useful for the child to also 'say' the word after looking at it.

SYLLABIFICATION OF WORDS

This involves children identifying syllables in words. It can involve children using a method (pencil line, different colour or cutting up words) to highlight the letters that comprise each syllable of a word. This supports their ability to 'chunk' words for ease of spelling—a strategy used for the spelling of longer, more sophisticated words.

WORD HUNTS

Word hunts involve children looking at charts and posters around the room and in books to find words that contain the same letter patterns as those words in their spelling word list. This activity assists children to view words in terms of letter patterns and, when spelling, to use the strategy of analogy. They are encouraged to create and remember categories of words that share a similar sound and spelling pattern. Through finding words with common sound–spelling patterns, children develop the knowledge required to spell words on the basis of the common features in the spelling of different words with common sounds.

ee	ch	ea	sw	ai	er
street	chin	leak	swell	train	her
beet	chest	heal	sweep	chain	father
feet	cheek	peak	sweet	rain	water
green	cheap	weak	swim	wait	later
keel	rich	heat	swat	tail	brother
feel	chew	team	swig	nail	better
peel	much	meat	swallow	rail	letter
wheel	chain	cheat		vain	mother
week		beat			jumper
seek		wheat			

FINDING WORDS

Children look through magazines to find words of a given criteria; for example, words containing silent letters, compound words or words with a particular prefix such as 'un'.

ILLUSTRATING WORDS

Children demonstrate their understanding of the meaning of words by drawing pictures of the objects represented by words.

PARALLEL CHARTS

Children write some of their spelling list words, and for each they find or come up with words that sound similar (contain some of the same sounds) and words that look similar (contain the same visual pattern—part of the word spelt the same way).

Words that sound similar			Spelling list word	Words that look similar		
			light			
			jump			

ANALOGY CHARTS

Children examine groups of words on the basis of onset-rime; that is, words which rhyme but which have different initial sounds. They group words where the rime has the same spelling pattern. Activities can be carried out that involve separating the onset from the rime and making new words by changing the onset.

- ack	- ink	- it	- ip	- ice	- op	- ill	- ake
st - ack	p- ink	s - it	t - ip	m - ice	sh - op	f - ill	c - ake
p - ack	dr - ink	f - it	l - ip	pr - ice	t - op	w - ill	b - ake
l - ack	s - ink	l - it	wh - ip	d - ice	m - op	p - ill	r - ake
tr - ack	th - ink	sp - it	s - ip	sl - ice	dr - op	st - ill	m - ake
cr - ack	w - ink	b - it	z - ip	r - ice	h - op	dr - ill	w - ake

SHAPES OF WORDS

Children are assisted to visualise the shapes made by the collection of letters used to spell words. They draw around the outside of each of their spelling words to make the shape. Alternatively, they visually examine the shape of each of their words and match them to the right word shapes from those provided.

CHUNK—EXPLORE—VISUALISE—WRITE

The following steps can be used regularly for learning new words. They have been adapted from *Spelling recovery: Pathway to success* (Roberts, 2001). Children follow the steps outlined below for each new word.

1. *Chunk* the word by breaking it into sections of sound as determined by its pronunciation. Count the chunks, e.g. hap – pi – ness (3).
2. *Explore* the meaning of the word and of other words with a similar base (happy, happily, happiness, unhappy) or visual pattern (restart, revisit, reunite); say the word slowly and listen to how it sounds. Look at the spelling, notice letter patterns within each word part, decide on the trickiest part of the word and highlight it, and think about how to remember it.
3. *Visualise* the word by closing eyes and picturing the 'chunks' of the word as if written on a large screen. Spell the word while visualising its parts.
4. *Write* the word and say each chunk aloud as it is being written.

FINDING THE RULE

Work with children to help them to determine the rules and generalisations that apply to the spelling of many different words. For instance, when teaching the rule for adding inflectional endings such as 'ing' to base words, display examples of words (verbs) where the final consonant has been doubled when adding the 'ing' (running, hopping, batting) and examples where the 'ing' has been added without doubling the final consonant (singing, waiting, keeping). Have the children examine the words and work out the rule.

Root word	+ 'ing'	Rule
run	running	Final consonant is doubled when it follows a short vowel sound
hop	hopping	
bat	batting	
wait	waiting	Final consonant is not doubled because it follows a long vowel sound
keep	keeping	
sing	singing	Final consonant is not doubled because it follows another consonant
drink	drinking	

This method can be used for many other spelling patterns and generalisations. The rule, '*i* before *e* except after *c*', can, for instance, be demonstrated.

Words	
Re**cei**ve	Bel**ie**ve
Rule:	

MNEMONICS

Children can be taught or shown how to design memory triggers for the spelling of words for which the spelling is difficult to remember or is easily confused with other words. The following are some well-known mnemonics used to remember how to spell particular words.

- A **pie**ce of pie.
- There is a rat in sepa**rat**e.
- You h**ear** with your ear.
- You'll always be my fri**end** to the end.
- The princi**pal** is my main pal.
- The car is station**ar**y.
- Ne**cess**ary has one collar and two socks.

WORD OPERATIONS

Children begin with a word and 'operate on' it to produce new words by removing and adding elements. For example, the word 'sit' can be 'operated on' to form a new word by removing the letter 't' and replacing it with the letter 'p'. The new words thus generated are written down with the changed elements underlined (Ganske, 2000).

PHONEME FRAMES (ELKONIN BOXES)

Children are given a phoneme frame (made up of four boxes sitting side by side) and on hearing a word spoken by the teacher, they place counters in the boxes of their phoneme frame to represent the number of phonemes they identify in the word. To help the children to hear the word in terms of its separate phonemes, encourage them to verbally 'stretch' the word. This process can be followed by having the children place the appropriate letters (plastic letter or letter cards) for each phoneme in the separate boxes on the phoneme frame.

Phoneme frames can be used to assist children to segment words into individual sounds and letters.

An alternative is for the teacher, after following the process above, to say another word which is only one phoneme different from the previous word, and require the children to replace only one letter with another to make the new word; for example, cat—hat; dog—dig. The words used will depend on the children's phase of development.

MISSING LETTERS

The missing letters activity involves the use of a class text which has been written during a writing session but from which specific letters have been removed. The letters removed might relate to a beginning, middle or end phoneme of words. The removed letters are placed on another part of the board for the children to see (magnetic letters or letter cards can be used). The activity involves the children reading the text with the teacher and identifying any word which is missing a letter or letters, then correcting the word by replacing the missing letters from the collection of letters at the side of the board.

> Yesterday we m___d___ popc___n. We had to be c___r___ful because it w___ hot. The c___n popped and po___ed. Luckily there w___ a lid so the popc___n didn't go ever___where. When the corn had fini___ed popping we t___k the lid off so   at it could c   l down. Then we   t it. It w___ delicious.

SPELLING JOURNALS

Spelling journal are folders containing children's weekly spelling words and a set of spelling activities, as well as other information that is needed for the children to work independently and to learn spelling, including appropriate spelling knowledge, skills and strategies. They provide a way in which to organise for the teaching of spelling and are a key element of a teaching approach that aims to cater for different developmental levels and the specific learning needs of groups of learners in a class.

Spelling journals should generally include:

- *List of words*: children need to be provided with a set of words which are central to their weekly spelling activities. The words chosen for each group of children should serve to achieve the appropriate level of spelling learning and development. They should have the phonological, visual and/or meaning characteristics that support children in learning, not just how to spell the words but also general spelling knowledge, strategies and skills important to their spelling development. This development is enhanced when weekly spelling words are compiled from various sources such as:
    - *personal words*—words that children use in their writing but that they often spell incorrectly
    - *content words*—words relevant to the class topic or to the topics of learning in other curriculum areas
    - *sight words*—words that are frequently used when writing but that may not be easy to spell or be spelt conventionally
    - *words with similar features*—words chosen on the basis of the common spelling pattern or rule for forming. For example, words containing the 'ai' spelling, words containing the /ae/ phoneme or words with the inflectional ending 'ed'.

- *Weekly learning activities*: the teacher includes a selection of activities in each of the children's spelling journals. The activities chosen should support the children not just in learning to correctly spell a list of words, but also in learning about the phonological, visual and meaning features of words, as well as different spelling strategies.
- *Tests*: space is set aside in spelling journals for children to record their words when tested mid-week by a peer and at the end of the week by the teacher. It is also useful to provide a means by which children can record their test results, such as a bar graph.
- *Other materials*: specialised sheets and materials for carrying out the various learning activities are included. For instance, there might be a chart for carrying out the 'look—cover—write—check' activity with words.

Spelling journals are designed to address the different learning needs of the different spelling groups in a class. Different groups will be provided with different word lists and the learning activities will vary across the groups. There may be some overlap as many of the activities can serve all groups of learners regardless of their developmental level and the weekly word list.

Spelling journals do not remain constant. They are dynamic, flexible resources that need to be adjusted regularly so as to be an effective resource in a comprehensive and balanced spelling program. The groups' list words should be changed weekly or fortnightly and the learning activities and other materials should change as the need arises.

Table 18.3: Creating a weekly or fortnightly plan for children's spelling development

Group and phase of development	Current knowledge and skill	Teaching focus			
		Spelling knowledge	Spelling strategy	List words	Journal activities
1					
2					
3					
4					

SPELLING LESSONS

Spelling lessons should be conducted regularly and they should be designed so as to cater for the learning needs of the different spelling groups in the class. They should largely involve children working with their spelling group on the activities in their spelling journals while the teacher works to assist other groups or individuals. However, they should also include regular time when the teacher works with each spelling group and conducts a mini-lesson related to a specific area of knowledge or a **spelling strategy**.

Spelling lessons should also involve spelling tests. After a few days of working on their journal activities, the children are required to test each other on their list words. This is done for the purpose of providing additional practice in writing the words and the opportunity for children to self-monitor and be aware of their progress. At the end of the week, the teacher tests each child on his/her spelling words.

Although there is a variety of ways in which teachers can structure weekly spelling lessons, the tables below provide two examples. The important thing is to keep in mind the necessary elements; that is, to:

- Cater for the different needs of groups of learners.
- Provide regular, direct and explicit instruction to spelling groups where the focus is on knowledge and strategy development, highlighting a spelling pattern or a generalisation related to the spelling of a group of words.
- Provide guided spelling, involving working with one spelling group at a time with regard to their spelling journal activities.
- Support children with their spelling journal activities and their learning as they work in their spelling groups; provide **direct teaching** when observation indicates that this is needed.
- Emphasise the importance of spelling to good writing and develop a positive attitude to learning to spell.
- Observe and monitor children during spelling lessons and continue to examine their writing in terms of their spelling development, skills and needs.
- Continually apply what is learnt in spelling lessons when writing texts.
- Demonstrate and explain the use of any new materials or activities used in spelling journals.

Table 18.4: The spelling lesson 1

Time	Group One	Group Two	Group Three
MONDAY (new words and activities)			
10 mins	Class spelling game or word wall activity		
10 mins	Work with teacher	Spelling journals	Spelling journals
10 mins	Spelling journals		
WEDNESDAY			
10 mins	Spelling journals	Work with teacher	Spelling journals
10 mins		Spelling journals	
10 mins			Work with teacher
FRIDAY			
10 mins	Spelling journals/test	Spelling journals/test	Spelling journals/test
10 mins			
10 mins	Class spelling game or other class activity		

Table 18.5: The spelling lesson 2

1	2	3
Teacher carries out a *small group mini-lesson* while rest of class work on *Individual Spelling* (using Spelling Journal).	*Whole class mini-lesson*—introduce or revise a spelling strategy/rule/skill	Whole class spelling game
Whole class mini-lesson—introduce or revise a spelling strategy/rule/skill	Teacher carries out a *small group mini-lesson* while rest of class work on *Individual Spelling* (using Spelling Journal).	Teacher carries out a *small group mini-lesson* while rest of class work on *Individual Spelling* (using Spelling Journal).
Game—application of rule strategy	*Individual Spelling* continues Teacher works with individual children on spelling journal activities. Monitors all children's progress	

HANDWRITING

Handwriting is a basic skill of written communication. Despite the influence of modern technology it is an essential skill for young children and its development should be seen as an important and necessary goal of education. Children should be assisted to develop fluent and legible handwriting. This involves them learning how to:

- comfortably hold a writing instrument
- form upper- and lower-case letters legibly (using the specific vertical, horizontal and slanted lines and circular shapes, loops and curves appropriate to each letter of the alphabet)
- proportion the size of upper and lower case letters
- apply appropriate spacing between letters, words and sentences
- use joins to legibly produce cursive handwriting
- write fluently. (Tompkins, 2008, pp. 61, 66)

Learning to write legibly and fluently is a development process which requires experimentation, instruction and practice. Children's handwriting skill progresses from the initial experimentation with writing letters and words, to forming letters correctly and consistently, to applying other features of legible fluent handwriting such as correct spacing, evenness of size and placing letters on the line. At about eight years, children should be assisted to move to cursive handwriting (using connected letters). Their handwriting development continues as they gain control over the different types of joins and develop greater fluency in producing cursive writing.

The play experiences of toddlers should provide them with many opportunities for the early physical and motor development important to their eventual handwriting ability. Toddlers require lots of experiences manipulating objects and materials, building with blocks and other toys, assembling puzzles, playing with small objects and manipulating their parts etc.

Other activities might include scribbling, painting and drawing, and using different writing and painting implements, as well as threading, pouring liquids, spooning sand, drawing pathways, tracing around objects or over lines, finger plays and puppetry. These experiences assist to develop their ability with such physical tasks as grasping and manipulating materials, the coordination of eyes and hand movement, and fine motor control.

In the pre-school years, experiences that support children's physical and motor development should continue; fine motor skill, wrist and hand strength and coordinated eye–hand movement should continue to be a strong focus. Children should also be provided with the opportunity and encouragement to experiment with letter formations. Music or rhymes to assist with rhythmic control are useful. At this age (four to six years) a preference for left or right handedness should begin to emerge.

Teachers should also model handwriting. They should regularly write in front of the children and demonstrate correct letter formations and other features of good handwriting. Their handmade charts and posters and other resources for teaching and learning should demonstrate good handwriting.

In the early years of school, children should be provided with focused handwriting lessons that systematically and directly teach the skills of good handwriting. Handwriting lessons should involve the teacher demonstrating how to correctly form upper and lower case letters (starting point, directionality, movement and finishing point) and highlighting the features important to handwriting legibility; for example, size, slope, letter and word spacing. They should also involve the children practising their handwriting while being guided by the teacher. The correct posture and paper position and the technique for comfortably holding a writing instrument should also be taught and consistently reinforced. Handwriting development is also supported when:

- alphabet cards and charts, word banks, theme charts etc. are clearly displayed in the classroom

HANDWRITING LESSON: MODEL 1

1. *Warm up* (finger rhyme or game).
2. *Pre-writing pattern*: to develop fluent movements.
3. *Teacher demonstration*: the teacher demonstrates how to form the letter (upper and lower case) while also describing the steps in doing so (e.g. 'I start at the top line and go down, up and around') and the children observe.
4. *Guided practice*: the children practise the letter a number of times while the teacher provides individual guidance and explicit feedback.
5. *Demonstration and guided practice*: steps 3 and 4 are repeated twice but using words and then sentences containing the focus letter.
6. *Self-evaluation*: the children are encouraged to critique their efforts and handwriting results. This might involve them putting a tick above their 'best letter' or at the end of their best line. It might involve them setting a goal they would like to achieve.

- alphabet strips are fixed to desk tops (these could also use coloured dots on each letter to indicate the starting points)
- teachers' board work and charts model good handwriting.

In the early years of school, children's handwriting will also continue to benefit from various hand–eye coordination and fine motor activities.

Once children have developed a level of fluency with the formation of the upper- and lower-case letters, they should be taught the joins that are used to produce cursive writing. For most children this occurs at about the age of eight or nine. Handwriting lessons should involve the teacher demonstrating different joins and the children practising their cursive handwriting. Teachers should continue to support children in furthering their ability to produce legible and fluent handwriting. The various areas of handwriting development—posture, technique for holding a pen or pencil, size, slope and spacing—should continue to receive attention. Examples of good cursive handwriting should be made available through the teachers' board work and posters and charts.

HANDWRITING LESSON: MODEL 2

1. Whole class:
   - Warm-up activity, e.g. finger rhyme or game.
   - Teacher demonstration: how to form the letter.
2. Rotating groups:
   - *Group 1*: working with teacher to practise formations.
   - *Other groups*: manipulative activities, e.g. making plasticine letters, gluing macaroni on letter shapes, tracing around templates, tracing around letter shapes, and experimenting with letters and writing.

SUMMARY

An effective spelling program for children involves developing their knowledge of the spelling system of the English language and ability with key spelling strategies. Spelling proficiency develops over time, and the goals of any spelling program and the activities and learning experiences used to achieve them should be carefully chosen to suit children's phase of spelling development. It is also likely that any one group of children will be at different phases of spelling and development and this should be catered for. Additionally, handwriting is a skill that develops over time and children require opportunity to develop fine motor skills and coordinated hand–eye movement. They should be given a lot of opportunity to manipulate objects and to experiment with writing implements and, later, more formal experiences that focus on assisting them with letter formations as well as size, slope and fluency in handwriting.

QUESTIONS AND ACTIVITIES

1. Investigate the spelling system of two other languages (include one that is not an alphabetic system). Make comparisons between these two systems of spelling and English.
2. Carry out a discussion about how society views people who do not spell words correctly. Why do you think this is?
3. From the spelling activities provided, choose three and carry them out with a group of school-age children. Reflect on how the children responded to the activities and on the learning that resulted.
4. Critically examine different commercial spelling books that have been produced for use by young children (level 1 or 2). Consider the lists of words and the activities they contain.
5. Explain the importance of encouraging young children to use invented spelling when they write.
6. What methods can you use to support children's spelling growth when they engage in the writing of texts?
7. Design a simple spelling portfolio that could be used with a group of Year 2 children.
8. Examine the written texts of different children and identify the spelling understanding and skills displayed.

KEY TERMS

alphabetic system
compound word
conventional spelling
critical feature
direct teaching
encode
etymology
etymological knowledge
grapheme
invented spelling
letter–sound relationship
morpheme

morphemic knowledge
orthographic knowledge
orthography
phoneme
phonological knowledge
prefix
root word
spelling pattern
spelling strategy
suffix
syllable
visual knowledge

KEY REFERENCES

Bear, D., Invernessi, M., Templeton, S. & Johnston, F. (2004). *Word their way: Word study for phonics, vocabulary and spelling instruction.* New Jersey: Pearson, Merrill Prentice Hall.

Biggam, S. & Itterley, K. (2009). *Literacy profiles: A framework to guide assessment, instructional strategies and intervention, K–4.* Boston: Allyn & Bacon.

Cox, C. (2008). *Teaching Language Arts: A student centred classroom.* Boston: Pearson Education.

Fountas, I. C. & Pinnell, G. S. (1999). *Voices on word matters: Learning about phonics and spelling in the literacy classroom.* Portsmouth, NH: Heinemann.

Roberts, J. (2001). *Spelling recovery: The pathway to spelling success.* Camberwell, Victoria: ACER Press.

Templeton, S. (1996). Spelling: The foundation of word knowledge for the less-proficient reader. In L. Putnam (ed.), *How to become a better reading teacher* (pp. 317–29). Toronto: Prentice Hall.
Tierney, R. & Readence, J. (2005). *Reading strategies and practices: A compendium.* Boston: Pearson Education.
Tompkins, G. E. (2008). *Teaching writing: Balancing process and product.* Boston: Pearson Education.
Westwood, P. (2005). *Spelling: Approaches to teaching and assessment.* Camberwell, Victoria: ACER.
Wheatley, J. P. (2005). *Strategic spelling: Moving beyond word memorization in the middle grades.* Newark, DE: International Reading Association.

CHAPTER 19

Key Strategies for Teaching Writing

CHAPTER OBJECTIVES

This chapter will increase your understanding of:

- key strategies to support children's writing development and learning—modelled, shared, guided and independent writing as well as language experience
- the main features and learning supports of each of the key strategies identified
- adapting the different strategies to different groups of children with different writing competencies and learning and development needs.

This chapter introduces you to some important and useful strategies for the teaching of writing; the strategies draw on the principles of scaffolding and the importance of supporting children in carrying out writing activities that they are not yet able to do independently. A key practice is modelling or the demonstrating of writing to children which is a powerful means by which to assist them to learn about writing. When teachers write a sentence underneath children's drawings or write notes which are displayed on the message board for parents, they are demonstrating much about writing for children. At the end of the chapter there are examples of lessons for some of the teaching strategies presented. These tend to be more formal in nature and focus more on the pre-school and early years of school. As you read, consider how each of the teaching strategies outlined might be modified to the different groups of early childhood learners and the different learning settings, and that the environment and the teachers' and parents' writing practices are powerful means by which children can learn about writing.

INTRODUCTION

The development of children as writers is strongly enhanced when the learning of knowledge, skills and processes occurs during the composition of written texts. However, the discrete skills of phonics, spelling and handwriting should also be taught and practised separately and, when appropriate, direct, systematic and explicit methods should be used to ensure their comprehensive development. Although it is beneficial to teach these skills separately from the actual process of writing, they should still be highlighted and reinforced during text writing experiences. In this way children can see how they are applied when writing.

There are teaching strategies—*modelled, shared, guided* and *independent writing*—that are effective in developing children's writing competencies. These strategies all centre on the writing of texts but involve different types and degrees of teacher support. Each teaching practice plays a different role in helping children to understand the process of writing and in developing their writing skills. A teacher's goal, drawn from what the children need to learn to become better writers, will determine the way the teacher uses each of these four teaching strategies.

Modelled writing is when the teacher does the actual writing of the text while the children observe. Shared writing also entails the teacher writing the text, but in this instance the children are invited to contribute ideas and make suggestions for its content and composition. Shared writing can also incorporate an additional level of involvement from the children by having individual children doing some of the actual writing. When the teacher is writing a text, a child can be called upon to write a word, phrase or small part of the text. This is referred to as *interactive writing* and is best done when working with small groups of children rather than the whole class.

In guided writing children write their own texts. As they do so, the teacher works with small groups guiding them with aspects of writing particular to their learning needs. Independent writing also requires children to write their own texts. A significant aspect of this teaching practice is the **writing conference** where the teacher spends time with individual children discussing their progress. These four teaching strategies and the writing conference are explained in greater detail later in the chapter.

The four teaching strategies are effective in supporting children's writing development when they are part of a balanced program that draws on a variety of teaching and learning experiences. They are based on the **gradual release of responsibility** model (Pearson & Gallagher, 1983), a framework for moving children from a strongly supported text-writing experience, where the teacher has a high degree of responsibility for the writing task, to a more independent experience where the children assume most of the control in writing a text.

Writing is a cognitively demanding and highly skilled task. When children are relieved from responsibility for the entire writing task they are better able to focus on a particular aspect of writing which is important to their progress as writers. As children's understanding is established, greater responsibility for writing a text can be shifted to them so that they become the main players in the writing experience. Because so many different elements are to be considered (for example, spelling, ideas, handwriting and content) when children write, they often 'lose track' of where they are at. They should be encouraged to rehearse each sentence before committing it to paper, to read it back after they have written it and to read 'from the top' every so often to ensure that cohesion has been maintained.

Table 19.1: Summary of the four teaching strategies for writing

	Description	Features	Benefits	Adaptations
Modelled writing	Teacher writes a text as children observe. Uses 'thinking aloud' as a tool for making the processes and skills transparent	Demonstration of all facets of writing a text. Teacher does thinking and writing. One or a few specific aspects of writing become the teaching focus.	Children free from considering all the complex skills that go into writing and able to focus on learning specific skills and processes.	Text form, topic and length chosen in light of children's writing competency. Teaching focus chosen according to specific learning needs.
Shared (and Interactive) writing	Teacher and children write a text together. Children contribute ideas and teacher writes. Sometimes combined with interactive writing—individual children record some words or sentences.	Discussion used to assist children in thinking about text content and making decisions about what to include next. Children have sense of ownership of the text.	Children get to focus on the content and language aspect of writing. Learn about the 'thinking-speaking-writing' practice in writing	Can implement with small groups or individuals to provide focused instruction. Text form, topic and length adapted to suit children's abilities. Can include pre-writing discussion to develop topic knowledge
Guided writing	Teacher presents a writing task which children complete by taking responsibility for the content and actual writing. Teacher works with small groups of children instructing them in a specific skill or strategy.	Children responsible for all facets of text composition. Teacher supports and instructs at the group and individual level. Instruction occurs as part of text writing experience.	Opportunity for children to apply and reinforce new skills and processes. Children receive more individually focused assistance from the teacher.	Text form and topic adapted to suit children's abilities and experiences. Instruction to suit specific learning needs of a group. The degree of teacher support can be varied according to needs.
Independent writing	Teacher presents a writing task which children complete independently. Teacher assists individual children at the point of need. Teacher takes time to talk to children about their writing.	Children responsible for all facets of text composition. Conferences (one-to-one conversations) carried out throughout the lesson.	Opportunity for children to apply and practise skills. Own text created from beginning to end.	Text form and topic adapted to suit children's abilities and experiences. All facets of writing can be supported to varying degrees depending on children's needs.

The four teaching strategies are appropriate for use with children at all phases of their development—although, of course, they need to be adapted to different groups of children so they are being implemented in a manner that best suits their skill level and competencies and are directed towards each group's specific learning requirements.

A more comprehensive description of each of the four strategies and the way in which they can be used to support children's writing development is provided in the sections to follow.

MODELLED WRITING

Modelled writing involves the teacher writing a text while the whole class or a smaller group observes. Every child must be able to see exactly what the teacher is doing; they need to see all the words as they are written and they need to see how ideas are put together to create a meaningful text. The text written during modelled writing can be any type and length depending on the children's writing ability and the learning needs which are being addressed. Modelled writing lessons should not continue for too long; ten to fifteen minutes is usually adequate for young children, with a little more time given to older children. If a text does not get completed in one session, it can be continued the next day.

During modelled writing the teacher writes and 'thinks aloud' while the children observe.

In modelled writing lessons a clear teaching focus should be determined. Children will tend to be overwhelmed and their learning compromised if the teacher tries to highlight every aspect of text composition. The lesson should focus on only one, or perhaps a few, specific skills or processes. For instance, a modelled writing lesson might be conducted with the intention of teaching or improving children's competency with a particular type of text (for example, a recount), with an aspect of punctuation, with the use of adjectives to enrich text imagery or with the writing of compound sentences. Or it might involve instructing children on the steps of the writing process, or with one step such as revising or editing. The important thing is that a clear teaching goal should be determined in relation to children's writing development.

Children will learn more about writing when a writing demonstration is accompanied by an explanation of the thinking behind it. When teachers do this they are using what is referred to as the **think aloud** technique. Children are given the opportunity to 'hear' what is going on in the writer's mind—the decisions the writer makes about what to write next, the strategies to use (for example, rereading and stopping to think about the next point to be made) and the skills to apply when they write. In this way, they are taught that writing involves thinking; the way in which writers think in order to produce effective writing is revealed.

The 'thinking aloud' should generally be limited to that which supports the achievement of the specific goals of the lesson. For instance, if the lesson focuses on reviewing some basic print concepts for beginners, the teacher might say, 'This is the end of the sentence. I must remember to put a full stop.' Or, if the focus of the lesson is to teach the structure of a procedural text, an example of the associated thinking might be, 'I've listed the materials, now I need to write down what to do.'

By thinking aloud the teacher makes it obvious what the practices are for generating ideas and organising sentences and words in a text. Thinking aloud allows the teacher to demonstrate more effectively how the writer should apply skills, knowledge, processes and strategies when writing. It might focus on decisions about correct text structure, grammar, punctuation and spelling, or it might focus on the process of writing; for example, writing a draft, revising, editing and publishing. This does not mean that other learning does not take place, but it ensures that certain necessary learning does take place.

It is important that the children have knowledge of, or experience with, the topic which is to be written about during the modelled writing lesson. Such topics as family, friends, school, food or pets would usually be familiar to the children. Alternatively, a shared class experience can provide a relevant topic; for example, a cooking experience, a game played, a visiting speaker at the school or an art activity. The topic could also be drawn from other curriculum areas, such as magnets, electricity, transport or weather. Topic choice is important to children's learning during modelled writing. The selection of a suitable topic enables the children to more easily understand the text and to follow the teacher's musings and decisions as the text unfolds.

Like all teaching strategies, modelled writing should be adjusted so that it is done appropriately for the learning context and the needs and capacities of the children. For instance, teachers working with beginner writers might simply model the writing of a sentence that communicates something about the day's events or activities. The motivation would be to reinforce the communicative nature of writing and introduce some print concepts (for example, the concept of words and sentences and the left-to-right directionality of print).

Modelling writing is an important practice for children's learning about writing, regardless of the age of the children or the early childhood setting. Of course, with very young children, the texts written will be less involved and the attention given to them will be less formal than the examples provided previously. For toddlers (as well as for older children), modelled writing (that is, writing so that children can see it being done) might involve such things as:

- sentences underneath children's drawings and paintings or to accompany photos taken
- labels for items or areas in the room
- messages on the parent notice board
- signs for children's constructions.

Modelling writing is an effective practice for children's learning about writing.

Modelled writing with beginner writers can serve to develop children's awareness of writing as a form of communication, to assist them to learn about the use and meaning of written texts and to understand that it is the marks on the page that are used to represent information in writing.

THE FORMAT OF A MODELLED WRITING LESSON

1. Before writing

- Determine the teaching focus:
  - What do the children need to learn about or improve in order to develop as writers?
  - What will I write about (topic) that will be relevant and will make sense to the children?
  - What reason (communicative purpose) will I establish for my writing?
  - Who will be the intended audience (reader)?
  - What is the appropriate type of text to use?
- Consider the support techniques to be used:
  - For what parts of the text will I use 'think aloud' methods?
  - How will I word my 'think alouds'?
- Select the teaching aids to be used in the lesson:
  - Will I write the text on the board, the overhead, the computer or on a large sheet of paper?

- Do I need a marker?
- Will all the children be able to see what I am doing?

2. Writing

- Tune the children in to the topic of the writing. Make links to their knowledge and experiences; for instance:
  - Show and discuss suitable photos.
  - Read an appropriate story.
  - Bring relevant objects out of a surprise bag.
  - Read a letter to which you are going to respond.
  - Share relevant experiences and knowledge.
- Create a writing scenario—introduce the proposed writing task in a way that motivates the children to embrace the topic and the task that is about to be undertaken, including information about the:
  - topic
  - purpose (to entertain, to instruct, to recount)
  - audience (who the text is for)
  - text type to be used (e.g. recount, procedure).
- Write the text ensuring that all children can see. Incorporate techniques that are directed towards the lesson focus. For instance:
  - Think aloud (in relation to the predetermined teaching focus).
  - Stop every now and then to reread what has been written so far.
  - Pause occasionally and invite children to consider what might be written next.
  - Ask a question (without necessarily demanding an answer) to prompt the children's thinking about the writing task.
- Read the text from beginning to end and revise the teaching focus with the children— what they did and what they learnt.

3. In conclusion

- Display the written text prominently in the classroom.
- Children can illustrate it if appropriate.
- Have the modelled writing text available as an example when the children do their own writing.

USING MODELS OF GOOD WRITING

In addition to observing the creation of a written text, children can be shown good models of texts already written (commercially published or written by the teacher). The text selected should clearly illustrate writing features which are currently the focus of learning. The teacher might, for example, use a text model to teach children about the use of punctuation. The children's attention would be focused on direct speech in the text and the writer's use of quotation marks (speech marks) as punctuation. Below is an example of the use of a text model to demonstrate the use of quotation marks in writing. It shows how the teacher has highlighted this feature of the text.

> Alice was usually a happy little tugboat with a big smile on her face. But Alice's face changed when her funnel began to itch. 'Aa-toot!', sneezed Alice loudly, 'Aa-toot! Aa-toot! Aa-toot!'
>
> 'You can't stay here if you're going to make so much noise!', said the big ships, so poor Alice had to move. Alice sailed over to a little jetty.
>
> 'Aa-toot! Aa-toot!', sneezed Alice.
>
> 'You can't stay here', said the people. 'You are disturbing all the fish!' Alice sailed on to where the water was deep.
>
> 'Aa-toot! Aa-toot!', she sneezed.
>
> 'You can't stay here', said the gulls. 'This is where we dive for our dinner.' Poor Alice pulled up her anchor and sailed out to sea.

SHARED WRITING

Shared writing (McKenzie, 1985) involves the teacher and the children working together to compose a written text. The teacher scribes the text while the children, with the teacher's help, supply the content. The teacher assists the children to think about and then clearly verbalise the information that should be recorded.

In shared writing any type of writing can be undertaken, whether it be a narrative, a report or whatever. The goal of the lesson is to create a text that is well written in both content and form (Morrow, 2009). The effectiveness of the exercise will depend, to a large extent, on the relevance of the topic to the children; that is, whether they have sufficient knowledge to enable them to contribute the information required for the text. It might be that an experience in another curriculum area (for example, carrying out a science experiment) is selected as the topic. In this instance the shared writing lesson would involve the writing of a report on the experiment: outlining what was done and the results achieved.

Shared writing is of particular benefit to children's writing development because it allows them to focus on developing the content of a text without the task of simultaneously recording ideas. Children can devote their cognitive energies into thinking about the topic, generating and organising ideas and information, and orally producing the necessary sentences. Shared writing becomes the first step in the development of their writing skills.

Discussions are central to the shared writing lesson. They stimulate children in making decisions about what should be included in the text and how it should be expressed. The teacher should question, suggest and provide feedback during discussions in order to encourage the children to:

- express their ideas in a clear, logically ordered manner that maintains the communicative goal of the writing
- consider a range of alternative or additional ideas, sentences or words
- convert ideas into the language of a writer
- refine their ability to apply thought processes (e.g. reasoning, making judgments) integral to writing
- explore the choices that writers make, e.g. What next? How will I say that? Is that the best word to use? Can I say that differently so that it is clearer?
- use language to achieve particular effects in writing such as the use of adjectives or adverbs, the ordering of information in a sentence, the insertion of a clause to include additional information to a sentence, and the use of a simile to describe something or someone.

The teacher's role in discussions is important to ensure that the children are developing an understanding about the processes and strategies for composing texts. However, it is also important that these discussions do not detract from children feeling a sense of ownership of the text. Teachers should not impose their ideas but rather they should lead the children in considering different possibilities (Combs, 2006).

Shared writing texts can be illustrated by children and made into class books.

The actions of the teacher as a text is recorded provide another learning opportunity for children. For instance, watching as the teacher repeats a child's sentence and slowly records it assists the children in learning about the connection between thinking, oral language and written language. Again, when the teacher regularly rereads and evaluates the text as it is being written down, this important process is impressed on the children. Of course, there are many other things about the process of writing and written texts that the children can learn through the actions of the teacher when writing. What they learn will depend on the current phase of their writing development and on what they are ready to learn next. Beginner writers might learn about the concept of left-to-right and top-to-bottom writing, spaces between words and other basic aspects of writing. More advanced writers might learn about the use of spelling strategies or the use of various types of sentences and punctuation. While recording the text, teachers should talk to the children about some of the innovative things that they are doing.

THE FORMAT OF A SHARED WRITING LESSON

1. Before writing

- Determine the teaching focus:
  - What do the children need to learn about concerning the composition of writing?
- Identify the topic, the writing purpose and the type of text that will be written:
  - Do the children have sufficient knowledge about the topic to be covered?
  - What will be the purpose (communicative goal) and who will be the audience (the people for whom the text is written)?
  - What type of text (which suits the writing purpose and task) will be written?
- Select the materials to be used in the lesson:
  - Should the text be written on the board, the overhead, the computer or on a large sheet of paper?
  - Is a marker required?
  - Will all the children be able to see the text?

2. Writing

- Tune the children in to the topic of the writing. Make links to their knowledge and experiences; for instance:
  - Show and discuss suitable photos.
  - Read an appropriate story.
  - Bring relevant objects out of a surprise bag.
  - Read a letter to which you are going to respond.
  - Share relevant experiences and knowledge.
- Create a writing scenario—introduce the proposed writing task in a way that motivates the children to embrace the topic and the task that is about to be undertaken, including information about the:
  - topic
  - purpose (to entertain, to instruct, to recount)
  - audience (who the text is for)
  - text type to be used (e.g. recount, procedure).
- Write the text ensuring all children can see, and maintain a discussion with the children which guides them with the composition of the text. Incorporate other techniques that are directed towards the lesson focus. For instance:
  - Use questions and prompts (to direct thinking).
  - Stop every now and then to reread what is written so far and consider what comes next.
  - Provide time for children to talk together and to think about the content and how to word it.
  - Repeat contributing sentences back before writing.
  - Focus on sentence sense and text organisation.

- When finished, read the text from beginning to end and, together with the children, reflect on the writing experience—what they did and what they learnt about writing.

3. In conclusion

- Provide an audience to read and respond to the text. Display the text and have it available to be used as a reference for children for future writing.

Source: Adapted from Annandale, Bindon, Broz, Dougan, Handley, Johnston, Lockett et al. (2005)

WORKING WITH THE TEXTS PRODUCED IN SHARED AND MODELLED WRITING

The texts produced as a result of shared and modelled writing lessons can be later used as central resources for further literacy learning. Activities that draw on the features of the texts could be designed around sight-word knowledge, phonemic awareness, decoding skill, fluency, and so on. Using texts which children played a key role in creating serves to harness children's engagement and motivation.

The text below, about the snails that a particular Year 1 class was keeping, was written during a shared writing lesson. The teaching activities that followed from the writing of this text provide examples of the way in which class-produced texts provide opportunities for further literacy teaching.

Figure 19.1: Shared writing text produced by a Year 1 class

Our Snails

By Year 1 Green

We have three pet snails in our classroom. We have named them Jack, Thelma and Raffy. Thelma moves a lot but the other two are very still. When we pick one up it shrinks into its shell. Our snails sleep a lot. They eat the plants we give them. Raffy is always chewing the leaves. It is nice having our pet snails but we have to put them back in the garden soon. That is their home and where their family is.

Cloze activity

Focus: Initial phoneme identification, letter–sound correspondence

The text can be used to conduct a cloze activity whereby some letters are omitted from the words of the text (see example) and plastic letter shapes, representing the missing letters, are displayed. The cloze activity proceeds with the teacher asking the children to help put them back. The teacher reads the text, reading the words as they are now incorrectly written (that is, with beginning sounds missing) and then again, pausing where a letter is missing, whereupon the children identify the phoneme (sound unit) and the missing letter represented. A child is invited to choose a letter from those displayed and place it in the space where it belongs. The process continues until all the letters had been replaced and the text is then reread to make sure that it makes sense again.

> **Our Snails**
> **by Year One Green**
>
> We have three …nails in our classroom.
>
> We have …amed them Jack, Thelma and …affy.
>
> Thelma moves a …ot but the other two are very still. When …e pick one up it shrinks into its …ell. Our snails sleep a …ot. They eat the plants we …ive them. Raffy is always …ewing the leaves. It is nice having our …et snails but we have to put them …ack in the garden …oon. That is their …ome and where their …amily is.

Text reconstruction

Focus: Text organisation and fluency, reading fluency, comprehension

The sentences from the text are each written onto a separate strip of cardboard and placed in random order on the board. The children work with the teacher to put the sentences back into the correct order of the text. First, each sentence is read and then decisions are made about which to put first, second, third etc. Each time a sentence is brought into the text, the updated text is read before a decision is made about the next sentence to be incorporated.

| We have named them Jack, Thelma and Raffy. |

| Our snails sleep a lot. |

| It is nice having our pet snails but we have to put them back in the garden soon. |

| They eat the plants we give them. |

| That is their home and where their family is. |

| We have three pet snails in our classroom. |

| Thelma moves a lot but the other two are very still. |

| Raffy is always chewing the leaves. |

| When we pick one up it shrinks into its shell. |

Sentence reconstruction

Focus: Sight words, syntax, punctuation

The children are each given an envelope. Inside the envelope is one sentence from the *Snail* text, written on cardboard but cut up into individual words. There is also a picture that matches the sentence. The children place the words onto their work area and, with a partner, start to put them back into sentence order. The teacher assists with the task. After gluing the reconstructed sentence and the picture onto paper, they read their sentence to the others. This can be extended to having the children work together to put all the sentences back into the correct text order.

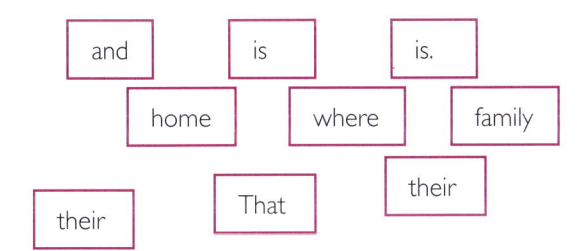

and	is	is.
home	where	family
their	That	their

INTERACTIVE WRITING

Interactive writing involves the composition and recording of a short text jointly by a small group of children and the teacher. The use of short texts—as short even as a single sentence—is best fitted to the practice. The focus of the instruction is the writing and spelling of individual words. Although the teacher may record some words in the sentence, the pen is handed to individual children at different times so they can take a turn at recording a word. As a child writes a word, the teacher should focus the child on attending to the spelling. With early writers this might involve them having to segment (sound out) the individual sounds as they write a word, while with more advanced writers it may require them to recall and apply a different strategy in spelling the word. Children could be asked to place punctuation into the text.

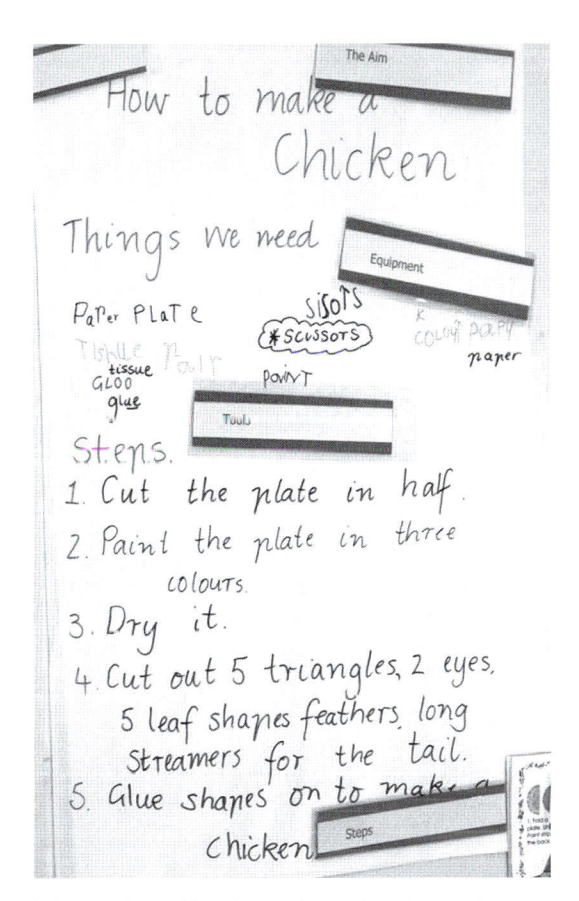

In interactive writing the teacher writes the text but individual children write some of the words.

LANGUAGE EXPERIENCE APPROACH

The Language Experience Approach (LEA) (Stauffer, 1970) is useful for developing a range of literacy skills and understandings, from oral language through to reading, writing and viewing. It particularly suits the beginning and emergent writer. The foundation of LEA is oral language and the key concept is the relationship between speaking and writing. *Writing is oral language written down, it has meaning and it can be read back.* The sequence for a language experience session is described below but, while each step is important, it should be adapted to the features of the early childhood setting and the particular needs of the children. Experience is at the heart of early childhood education and so language experience opportunities should be plentiful.

THE EXPERIENCE

This teaching strategy begins with children participating in a stimulating, authentic, multi-sensory experience. Suitable experiences include cooking activities, playing with new materials, excursions, science experiments, dressing up, and so on.

During the experience, the teacher scaffolds the children's use of oral language by introducing new vocabulary relating to the context and encouraging the children to use it. Within the context of the experience, teachers encourage children to use languages for different purposes, such as language to describe, to get things done, to interact socially, to hypothesise, to express feelings and to enquire. The teacher models language and uses questioning and various other means to elicit talk from the children. It is useful to employ Joan Tough's (1977) language functions and teacher strategies when talking to children during such experiences. After the experience, the teacher and the children have further conversations to extend and consolidate language used.

The giraffe was reaching for the leaves to eat. *Jade*

The zebra was shy. I liked its stripes. *Sam*

Excursions provide a rich starting point for the language experience approach.

DISCUSSION AND RETELLING OF THE EXPERIENCE

After the multi-sensory experience, the teacher gets the children to retell what happened, and to discuss the experience. This phase of LEA is important because it enables children to learn how to sequence events, use appropriate descriptive vocabulary and practise using the past tense. The teacher takes the opportunity to model appropriate sentence structures and to expand and rephrase what the children have said, modelling the correct form. They should also make comments about and respond to the child's message to emphasise the importance of meaning-making and the use of language to communicate.

THE VISUAL REPRESENTATION

Next, individual children draw or paint a picture to represent a salient part of the experience. They talk about their picture with the teacher, who asks questions about the child's recollections of and feelings about the experience. This constitutes another opportunity for teachers to model and extend oral language. If the child does not use the standard form of the language (Standard Australian English), the teacher can at this point paraphrase or respond to what the child has said using the standard form. For example, if the child says, 'The kite flied high in the sky', the teacher can say, 'Yes, the kite flew really high, didn't it?'

WRITING THE TEXT

The teacher then asks the child to make up a sentence or two to go with the picture, to describe the experience. During this part of LEA, the child utters the sentence(s) and the teacher may repeat them and ask the child if they want to make any changes. The teacher then writes the words down beneath the picture that the child has drawn.

When doing this scribing, it is important that the teacher writes down the child's words exactly as spoken. Now is not the time to be changing the child's language and syntax, since this would defeat a central rationale of the strategy—that is, that the child needs to come to understand that their language can be written down. During the scribing, the teacher may discuss concepts about print such as directionality and spaces between words, as well as how to represent sounds with letters.

READING BACK

Finally, the teacher reads the story back and then the child reads it. The text should be highly readable to the child because she wrote it, using her own words. The story (or written recount) should ideally be made available in the classroom library for the child to reread, and for other children to read.

LANGUAGE EXPERIENCE APPROACH VARIATIONS

Language experience is suitable for use with emergent literacy learners, for ESL/EAL children, and for children who are experiencing literacy difficulties. The Electronic Language Experience Approach (E-LEA) (Oakley, 2001, 2008) is a modification of the Language Experience Approach that employs the use of ICT. E-LEA and its rationale are described in Chapter 24.

LANGUAGE EXPERIENCE APPROACH (LEA)

Summary of steps

1. Experience—language stimulus
   Excursion, cooking, visitor, pet, surprise object, food, reading a story, making something, personal experience.
   Can use drama and movement to consolidate experience.
2. Oral language
   Encourage talk about the experience—how it looks, sounds, feels, tastes, smells.
   Use good questioning to stimulate talk; expand oral language/vocabulary.
3. Visual representation
   Children draw/paint or 'make' some aspect of the experience.
4. Child's oral statement
   The children are assisted to make an oral statement about the visual version of the original experience.
5. Teacher scribes
   The teacher writes the statement for the child, ensuring that it is clear, well spaced and of large print.
6. Teacher models reading
   The teacher reads back the child's statement (perhaps a few times) and points to words while the child listens and follows the text.
   The child 'reads' the statement, often from memory.
   Highly predictable text based on child's own language, supported by a picture and modelled by a competent reader.
7. Follow-up activity/activities
   The text can be used to further the children's literacy knowledge, e.g. print concepts, word identification, letter identification, letter–sound matching, syntax.

GUIDED WRITING

In guided writing the children write their own text as the teacher works with small groups having a similar writing level or with similar learning and development needs. In this way the teacher can assist where needed with an element of the writing task (for example, planning what to include and in what order) or with a specific writing skill (for example, joining short sentences to make longer ones) that they are not yet able to achieve independently. Guided writing provides an opportunity for children to use their own initiative when writing. They can apply what they have learnt about writing, including any new skills and techniques learnt during recent modelled and shared writing experiences. It also provides the opportunity to target the specific needs of small groups of children.

There are many skills and strategies that could be the focus for a small-group session during guided writing. For instance:

- choosing what information to include in a text
- translating ideas into clear and complete sentences

- using different sentence types—simple, compound and complex
- moving from one thought to another and developing the flow of a written text
- combining short sentences into a longer one
- using precise words.

Source: Gunning (2010, p. 526)

The choice will depend on the children's current writing ability and the skills required for their further development.

The teacher sets a writing task appropriate to the general competency of the class and provides the necessary information about what the children are required to do. The teacher should stimulate the children's knowledge about the topic and their ideas for the text, and provide them with guidelines for the task. The time that should be taken at this phase will depend on the support the children require to understand what they are required to do to be able to complete the task.

All the children should set about the writing while the teacher identifies individuals who require support. The teacher also works with different groups of children, concentrating on helping them with their specific writing needs. It may be that in one lesson the teacher's time is divided between working with one or a number of different groups and helping individual children with specific needs.

THE FORMAT OF A GUIDED WRITING LESSON

1. Before writing

- Determine the teaching focus.
- Identify the group of children to receive more focused guidance as they carry out the writing.
  - What is the particular writing skill or strategy to be developed with a group of children?
  - Who are the children who I need to work more intently with in order to develop this?
- Identify the writing task—the topic, the writing purpose and the type of text that will be written.
  - What is the topic to be covered about which the children have sufficient knowledge?
  - What will be the purpose (communicative goal) and who will be the audience (the people for whom the text is written)?
  - What type of text (suits the writing purpose and task) will be written?
  - What writing task is appropriate for the class for practising their writing skills and strategies?
- Select the materials to be used in the lesson.
- Consider the support techniques to be used.
  - Will the children be provided with a planning framework?
  - Will the children benefit from seeing an example of the text form in which they are going to write?

- Is there any aspect of the task that needs clarification or revision through the use of demonstration?

2. Writing

- Tune the children in to the topic of the writing. Make links to their knowledge and experiences; for instance:
    - Show and discuss suitable photos.
    - Read an appropriate story.
    - Bring relevant objects out of a surprise bag.
    - Read a letter to which you are going to respond.
    - Share relevant experiences and knowledge.
- Create a writing scenario—introduce the proposed writing task in a way that motivates the children to embrace the topic and the task that is about to be undertaken, including information about the:
    - topic
    - purpose (to entertain, to instruct, to recount)
    - audience (who the text is for)
    - text type to be used (e.g. recount, procedure).
- The children are provided with time to share their ideas with each other and the teacher before they begin writing. The children write their texts independently, working through the steps of the writing process—*plan, write, revise, edit, publish*—to the degree which they are able. Adherence to the steps of the writing process and the independence in using them is in accordance with the children's phase of development.
- The teacher works with a small identified group, while the others continue to do their writing independently. Various techniques can be used to assist the group with the writing task with particular focus on an identified area. The techniques used will depend on the focused teaching area, but might include:
    - having children read their writing aloud
    - asking questions
    - giving explicit feedback
    - demonstrating
    - making suggestions
    - highlighting features of a text.
- When finished (small group sessions should not be too long), the teacher might work with another group or assist and provide feedback to individuals as the group continues to work independently on their writing.

3. In conclusion

- When the children finish their written texts, an audience should be provided—someone should read the texts and respond to them.

INDEPENDENT WRITING

Independent writing is another strategy where children write their own texts, thus providing opportunity for them to apply and practise new skills, strategies and knowledge already learnt in other writing activities such as modelled or shared writing.

Independent writing provides children with sustained practice in orchestrating the various components of writing and thus encourages writing fluency.

During independent writing, teachers should monitor the children's progress and assist individuals as required. This assistance usually takes the form of what is often referred to as the *writing conference*.

THE WRITING CONFERENCE

A feature of independent writing is the use of the writing conference (Graves, 1983), which involves the teacher talking with children one at a time about their writing

> **The Two Horses**
>
> by   year 3
>
> On the farm there were two horses. One of the horses, which was a riding horse, had the name Speed. The other horse, which just ate and slept, was called Ly-Lo. One day when Speed had just returned from a long hot, tiring ride, he noticed Ly-Lo just sleeping in the cool shade of the barn. That made Speed furious, so he walked up to Ly-Lo and said, "It just isn't fair. Why do I have to do all the work? You just eat and sleep." With that he gave Ly-Lo a great big thump. Ly-Lo then said, "you shouldn't hit me. You should hit my master for it is he who has taught me my job."
>
> Moral: Don't blame the child. Blame the parent.

During independent writing children write their own texts. They might sometimes be word processed.

and assisting them in whatever way may be necessary. For older children this is often about helping them to revise and edit their work. The writing conference support takes place at the point of need while the children are writing. Teachers can also use this conference time to monitor and assess the children's progress and make note of their strengths and weaknesses.

A writing conference can be tackled in a number of ways, but it is generally best to begin by having a child read their writing to you and then providing them with feedback. The conference should generally focus on providing specific responses to the child's writing and to addressing any areas of need. Following a conference the child should continue with the writing task.

Writing conferences can involve interaction between the children. A pair, or other small group of children, work together and read what they have written to each other (Cox, 2008). They respond to each others' writing by commenting on what they found interesting or liked and perhaps by asking questions about the content. More advanced writers can assist each other with revising their work, although this can be difficult and children usually need quite a few opportunities to learn how to do it effectively (Ruddell, 2006).

THE TEACHING STRATEGIES IN USE

Following are three examples of writing activities that use modelled, shared and guided writing with either pre-school or school-aged children. They should assist in understanding how the **teaching strategies** outlined in this chapter might be used. The emphasis is again placed on the adaptive nature of the teaching strategies and their use in a way that aligns with where the children are at in regards to their learning about writing and with the features of the early childhood education setting.

Table 19.2: An example of a modelled writing lesson: Year 3

Preparation	
Teaching focus:	The use of adjectives with nouns to add to the interest and clarity of sentences
Topic:	Zoo animals
Purpose, audience:	To recount the zoo trip for sharing with parents
Techniques:	*'Think alouds'* (1) When writing nouns, particularly when describing animals and other things seen Examples: *What adjective can I use to describe what the giraffe [elephant, etc …] looked like? Is that the best adjective? Is there a better adjective? Do I need to add another adjective? If I read this back does it sound right? I need to put the adjective here in front of the noun. This is a noun. Do I need an adjective in front of it?* (2) Other: *What shall I write next? I need to read this through—does it sound right?*
	Pausing. Stop writing after a few sentences and provide children with time to consider what has been written. Model stopping to think; revisit nouns to insert appropriate adjectives; ponder what next
Materials:	Black felt marker, sheet of large paper taped to board
Implementation	
Motivation for, and knowledge about, the topic:	Use the photos taken from yesterday's zoo trip to stimulate discussion about the experience—what was done/seen, the different animals seen, what they looked like. Select an animal—write the name on the board under the heading 'noun'. Provide a corresponding adjective. Write it on board under the heading 'adjective'
Explain task	For example: *I am going to write about what we did and the different animals we saw when we went to the zoo yesterday. Then our parents can read it and they will learn about our lovely day. I want to use some adjectives to describe the animals we saw so they will know what they were like. The text I am using is a recount*
Write:	First write the heading *Our Day at the Zoo*. Then begin writing the text. For example: *Yesterday we went to the zoo. We saw animals and we had a lot of fun. The bus trip was really long and we were very excited and noisy. We were happy when we finally arrived at the zoo. First we went to see the Australian animals. We saw a kangaroo and a koala* Reread and in front of the nouns—*animals, kangaroo, koala*—insert appropriate adjectives, e.g. *many interesting animals; large, grey kangaroo, sleepy koala* Continue writing using techniques planned to highlight the teaching focus—use of adjectives as well as some general strategies that writers use

Implementation	
Reread and revise teaching focus:	When complete (can be in one sitting or a little bit at a time over a few days), reread the written text aloud from beginning to end. Use voice to emphasise the adjectives and then revise the teaching focus with the children. Identify nouns and accompanying adjectives in the text; write these in the chart Read a sentence first without, and then with, the adjectives—highlight the difference they make
Display:	Place the *Our Day at the Zoo* recount on the outside bulletin board for parents to read when they collect their children. Display the photos with the text
Audience response:	Put a blank piece of paper and a marker near the text as well as a note inviting parents to read it and to respond to the content
Display as an exemplar	Display the *Our Day at the Zoo* recount in the classroom so the children can use it as a model for their own writing experiences. Add a sign—'We know how to use adjectives to describe things'. Display the nouns and adjectives chart here too. When relevant, draw attention to the text and the chart when children are doing their own writing

Table 19.3: An example of a shared writing lesson: Year 1

Preparation	
Teaching focus:	The transfer of ideas into written sentences. The use of complete sentences
Topic:	The story book *Mrs Wishy Washy*, farm animals, cleanliness
Purpose and audience:	A letter to Mrs Wishy Washy to offer suggestions for keeping her farm animals clean and neat
Discussion techniques to be used:	Such techniques as: • Ask the children to suggest sentences as the text is being composed • Before taking suggestions for a sentence to be written, have the children share their ideas with each other • When sentence suggestions are made from the children, repeat back to them and when necessary recast into correct form • Make suggestions to expand on the children's suggestion—substituting one word for another, adding more information, deleting some information, extending the sentence etc. • Continually reread what has been written and ask, 'What comes next?' • When writing, emphasise the recording process
Implementation	
Motivation and knowledge	Read the story and have the children identify the problem Mrs Wishy Washy faced (keeping animals clean). Children draw and share ideas about solutions to the problem.
Explain task:	*We are going to write a letter to Mrs Wishy Washy and share with her some of our ideas about what she can do to keep her animals clean. When we have written the letter …*

Implementation	
Write:	Write the greeting, 'Dear Mrs Wishy Washy', and then ask the children to make suggestions for the rest of the letter • Continually focus on the way the information should be organised, e.g. first identify Mrs Wishy Washy's problem (keeping her farm animals clean), explain why she is being written to, outline different solutions one at a time and then summarise at the finish • Give the children the chance to talk with each other before making a suggestion about what to write • Prompt their thinking through questions—What do we write next? Do we need to give any more information so she knows what to do? We have given her lots of ideas; now we need to think about how to finish. Think about what we could say to finish our letter. • Guide the children's use of language: Can we say that in a different way? Is there another word we can use here? When finished, read the letter out
Audience	A good copy of the letter is typed on the computer and put in an envelope which is addressed and 'sent' to Mrs Wishy Washy.
Response	The teacher could prepare a reply from Mrs Wishy Washy and have it arrive a few days later.
Display	The original letter and Mrs Wishy Washy's response are placed on the classroom display board. They are used as models for future letter-writing experiences.

SUMMARY

Modelled and shared writing are teaching strategies useful to the development of children's writing ability. They involve the teacher demonstrating and focusing on the skills, strategies and knowledge necessary for the children's growth as writers. Language experience also involves demonstration. It is a teaching strategy that serves to provide children with an understanding of the relationship between spoken and written language, and to develop print and text concepts and other important foundational writing concepts. The strategy centres on making connections between children's experiences, their talk about the experiences and the composition of written texts. In interactive writing, the teacher works with a small group of children and assists them to compose a text. The teacher takes the main responsibility for writing the text, but at different stages individual children in the group are invited to help by writing some of the words or phrases. The teaching strategies of guided and independent writing involve children composing written texts and the teacher working with small groups or individuals to support their competency in doing so.

QUESTIONS AND ACTIVITIES

1. Create a chart that highlights the main features of each of the strategies of modelled, shared, guided and independent writing.
2. Consider how you could use modelled writing in a childcare program with toddlers. You might need to refer to information about the childcare setting (Chapter 3) and the beginner phase of writing development (Chapter 15).
3. Adapt the example of the shared writing experience earlier in this chapter to the writing development needs of a group of children at the emergent phase of writing development.
4. Brainstorm to compile a list of some of the different types of written texts that should be included as part of the environments of childcare, pre-school and school.

KEY TERMS

gradual release of responsibility
teaching strategies
think aloud
writing conference

KEY REFERENCES

Combs, M. (2006). *Readers and writers in primary grades: A balanced and integrated approach, K–4.* Upper Saddle River, NJ: Pearson Prentice Hall.

Gunning, T.G. (2010). *Creating literacy instruction for all children for all students* (7th edn). Boston: Pearson Education.

McKenzie, M. G. (1985). *Shared writing: Apprenticeship in written language matters.* London: Centre for Language in Primary Education.

Morrow, L. M. (2009). *Literacy development in the early years* (6th edn). Boston: Pearson.

Oakley, G. (2001). *12 things young children can do with an electronic talking book.* Paper presented at the Joint National Conference of the Australian Association for the Teaching of English and the Australian Literacy Educators' Association. Hobart, Tasmania.

Pearson, P. D. & Gallagher, M. C. (1983). The gradual release of responsibility model of instruction. *Contemporary Educational Psychology, 8*, 112–23.

Ruddell, R. B. (2006). *Teaching children to read and write: Becoming an effective teacher.* Boston: Pearson Education.

Stauffer, R. G. (1970). *The Language Experience Approach to the teaching of reading.* NY: Harper & Row.

Tough, J. (1977). *Teachers' strategies in dialogue.* London: Ward Lock Educational.

CHAPTER 20

Writing Experiences and Activities

CHAPTER OBJECTIVES

This chapter will increase your understanding of:

- foundational writing knowledge and experiences
- emergent writing
- experiences and activities for writing development.

This chapter begins with a focus on beginning and emergent writing and presents different ways in which to support children's growth as writers in these important foundational phases. The information presented should assist you in knowing how to create environments and experiences for infants, toddlers and pre-schoolers so that they understand about written communication. The chapter also considers the writing development of children beyond the emergent phase. Additionally, the chapter outlines a range of activities and experiences that you might use to support children to develop the knowledge, understanding and skill for writing competency. As with any learning and development activities, they should be chosen and modified to suit the context, which includes the learners, the setting and the learning goals.

THE EMERGENCE OF WRITING

Learning to write commences well before the start of formal schooling. The years from birth to five are important for children to learn many concepts that are the foundation of writing. Childcare and pre-school educators should be familiar with the conditions and experiences necessary for children to build sound writing foundations and they should work together with families in order to develop these important foundations.

Young children first learn about writing as they interact with other people and observe the actions of competent writers. Their understanding of written communication develops as they gain experience with story books and other written texts and when they get to experiment or 'play' with writing themselves. This understanding further evolves when they learn more about the use of symbols to communicate meaning in written language.

Young children's growth as writers can be seen to emerge when, in imitating the act of writing, they produce 'texts' that comprise drawings, scribbles, shapes and letters of the alphabet in an effort to communicate ideas and information. They do not at this phase write in a conventional manner, but engage in '*writing like*' behaviours and begin to display insights about writing as a mode of communication.

Children first use drawings as a substitute for writing, but as their learning progresses their writing gradually takes on more conventional qualities. This is apparent from an examination of the visual features of children's writing at different phases of learning, a summary of which is outlined by Sulzby (1985) as follows.

1. Children *draw pictures when asked to write* something. Writing and drawing are seen as the same thing. Children understand that the purpose of drawing/writing is to communicate a specific message. They 'read' their drawings as if they were written messages.
2. Children *scribble but intend it to be writing*. They may 'scribble' from left to right. They will move the pencil as an adult does. The scribble bears some resemblance to writing.
3. Shapes in children's writing *resemble letters*. However, on close observation they are not properly formed and are quite often unique letter-like creations.

4   Children use *letter strings or random letters* to write. The letters are learnt from such sources as first name or words in the environment. Children may write the same letters in different ways or write long strings of the same letter.

5   Children write using *invented spellings of words*. There are many levels within this phase. Not all sounds in a word are represented with letters. To start with, one or a few letters may represent an entire word or syllable (for example, 'b' for ball, 'ct' for cat, 'fr' for flower). The letters used do, however, match the sounds in the word; usually the beginning sound is first represented. Words may run into each other and not be properly spaced. Eventually more and more sounds (phonemes) in a word are represented with a letter or letters. Over time the match between sounds and letters is more accurate.

6   Children's writing displays use of *conventional spelling*.

SUPPORTING THE EMERGENCE OF WRITING

It is important to remember that, for young children, learning should be considered holistically; the experiences with which they are provided should be designed not just to support learning about written communication, but also to facilitate understanding of other forms of communication (reading, oral and visual) as well as other important areas of learning. *The Early Years Learning Framework for Australia* (DEEWR, 2009, p. 8) identifies five areas which should be the focus for children's development and learning between the years of birth to five. The outcomes highlighted are as follows:

- Children have a strong sense of identity.
- Children are connected with and contribute to their world.
- Children have a strong sense of wellbeing.
- Children are confident and involved learners.
- Children are effective communicators.

Play, exploration, investigation and **intentional teaching** activities (DEEWR, 2009, p. 15) should allow for the integration of learning across a range of cognitive, social, emotional, creative and physical domains.

There are many ways in which educators can support young children in learning foundational writing concepts and assist them to emerge as writers. They primarily comprise a print-rich learning environment, play experiences that incorporate written texts and writing, and activities where the focus is on written communication.

THE LEARNING ENVIRONMENT

Young children learn new knowledge and develop new skills when their learning environment lends itself to their natural inclination to observe and imitate and to explore objects and materials. Learning about writing is supported when the learning environment features:

- the display of written texts that are relevant to the children and that connect to their daily experiences. They might involve sentences written to describe each child's art and craft work, to describe the steps of a class cooking experience or to explain what was done on an excursion. They might also incorporate writing about different play situations or about the children's reactions to a story book reading

- the use of signs and labels to denote play areas and to identify the location of different materials
- charts showing letters of the alphabet displayed on the walls and positioned so that children can easily see and read them
- alphabet blocks, puzzles, games, play-dough cutters, magnets, stamps and books so children can create letters using the different materials
- pictures and writing efforts of the children
- a variety of children's literature and suitable information texts about topics in which the children are interested
- charts depicting the words to the rhymes and songs that are familiar to the children.

LEARNING CENTRES

Learning centres are areas set up in classrooms containing materials and activities to support children's active, playful and exploratory learning. They should include materials that support children to experiment with writing. For example, a classroom might have a science learning centre which includes paper, pens, pencils, clipboards, labels and forms, and a blocks centre in which strips of paper and marker pens are provided so children can make signs for their constructions. Learning centres should be designed so that children can work either independently or in cooperation with others as they explore the available materials or carry out unstructured, open-ended activities. They should include opportunities for children to write. They can be placed in both the indoor and outdoor areas of the learning environment, and written texts should be incorporated in both. The outdoor area might contain different written signs, charts, labels and even books, as well as materials that specifically encourage children to engage in writing within particular learning centres.

Literacy related learning centres should also be set up as part of the learning environment; that is, centres or areas in the classroom where children can try out reading and writing and explore texts.

A *writing centre* should contain various materials that encourage children to explore writing in a relaxed and playful way. The available materials should facilitate their experimentation with writing and should include different writing tools (e.g. crayons, textas, pencils, chalk and paint brushes) and different materials on which children can write (e.g. unlined paper and cardboard of different shapes and sizes, chalkboards, blank books, index cards, envelopes and postcards). Other items such as clipboards and display boards might also be included.

A letter box is also a worthwhile addition to the writing corner. Young children are motivated by the opportunity to write letters to each other and to others they know. They can be encouraged to write letters by having their own class letter box in which they can post letters to each other or to children in other classes. The letter box should be emptied and the letters distributed at a set time each day in order to keep the children motivated. Perhaps different children could take it in turns each week to be the mail delivery person where their job is to empty the letter box and distribute the letters.

The benefit of having a writing centre is enhanced when children also get to observe and learn from teachers and other adults writing. They will be more inclined to attempt purposeful writing and, when they have seen what people do when they write, it is usually the case that they will have gained new knowledge and understanding that they can apply to their own attempts at writing.

Table 20.1: Establishing learning centres to support learning about writing and written texts

Learning centre	Writing materials	Literacy possibilities
The block centre (including brief description)	Texts about buildings and other constructions Visuals of different constructions Paper, index cards, pencils and textas, tape, clipboards Photos and written descriptions of constructions made by children	Create labels and signs for their block structures Draw plans of what they are going to build Refer to books and pictures for ideas and to find similar structures to those they make Talk about what they have made and how they made it
The music centre	Large sheets of paper and crayons Musical instruments—drums, tambourines, sticks Songs/music with repetition, rhythm, rhyme Display words to songs—books, charts or song cards	Write, draw patterns to the beat of the music Experiment with musical instruments (listening, phonological) Tap, bang or strum to the beat of the music Listen to songs and follow along in the song word book Draw a picture that tells a story about the music listened to
Puzzles and manipulatives	Pens, pencils, crayons, paper, cardboard, scissors, coloured plastic letters, large letter shapes, word shapes, different types of paper/cardboard, clipboards, pattern books and pattern pictures displayed Play dough, alphabet cutters, stamp pad and stamps	
Science area	Books related to the topic of interest/theme—fiction and non-fiction Pictures, information charts and tables displayed. Captions written under objects and pictures (full sentence) Blank booklets and markers, pencils, crayons Blank charts and tables Felt board—felt shapes (items/things related to theme and words (sentence maker)	Be a scientist and record discoveries Draw and add a caption underneath Draw and label Match captions to objects
Socio-dramatic play		'Real' reasons for reading and writing Functional literacy

A *reading centre* should contain a variety of books and other types of texts. It should provide a good balance of children's literature and information texts, including different types of everyday texts such as pamphlets, brochures and catalogues. It might also include class-made books and texts from shared reading sessions and perhaps a listening post with taped stories. The reading centre should be an inviting and comfortable place where children can go to explore books and other texts either by themselves or with others and thus have the opportunity to learn more about written texts and communication.

An *alphabet centre* is another possibility for a literacy-focused learning centre. It should provide young children with the opportunity to explore and play with letters of the alphabet and so build up some early alphabetic knowledge. The alphabet centre might include magnetic letters and small magnetic boards, a set of letter stamps, stamp pad and paper, sponge letter shapes, paint and paper, alphabet tracing stencils, alphabet lace-up cards, pictures, alphabet books and picture dictionaries.

SOCIO-DRAMATIC PLAY

Play provides a highly motivating situation for young children to learn about and practise writing. When given the opportunity, they will explore writing in a way that involves behaving like writers: trying out the things they have seen adults do when writing (for example, putting marks on the page, creating a text by going from left to right and top to bottom, reading their writing back).

In order to support understanding about writing during socio-dramatic play, the resources provided should include writing materials that can be naturally incorporated into their play efforts. The resources might include note pads, various kinds of forms, cards, pencils, markers, blackboards and clipboards. In a hospital play setting that has appropriate writing materials, children's pretend play might involve them completing check-in forms at reception, taking notes after patient examinations, writing make-believe prescriptions and filling out appointment cards. In a restaurant, pretend play might involve the children writing customers' orders into a note pad. The integration of writing into children's play supports the development and enhancement of their writing knowledge, skills and understanding. The key consideration is that the materials are appropriate for the play setting and that they are able to be used by the children to carry out writing tasks.

Children's understanding of written communication is further supported when socio-dramatic play areas also incorporate actual written texts that, as far as possible, resemble those of the literacy environments that the children would likely encounter at home and in their communities (Christie, Enz & Vukelich, 2007). It might be that the area contains advertisements, signs, job descriptions, maps, directions, notices, menus or magazines—whatever is relevant to the play theme. Table 20.2 outlines examples of socio-dramatic play themes that could be established and suggests materials relevant to the themes that would serve to develop children's understanding of written texts and encourage their use of writing as they engage in pretend play.

The choice of effectively themed play settings in the classroom requires that consideration be given to the community settings that are familiar to children. Children need to be knowledgeable about the events and activities that are applicable to the theme of their play setting. They need to know what type of things typically occur. For instance, play in a post-office themed setting requires that children have visited a post office and have gained some knowledge of what goes on; for example, buying stamps, posting letters, paying bills, completing forms. Obviously, they cannot act out something they have no knowledge about. Children's experiences are also important considerations when deciding on the writing materials to be incorporated in the play area. The use of these materials by children as they play requires that they have seen other people use them. For example, if they have observed wait staff at a restaurant write meal orders in their note pads, then it is likely that they will act out this activity when note pads are included in the restaurant-themed play area of the classroom.

Table 20.2: Socio-dramatic play themes, and suggestions for materials to foster the use of written texts

Socio-dramatic play area themes	Writing materials and written texts
Hospital	• Prescription pad • Clipboards and paper for taking notes • Book for scheduling appointments
Restaurant	• Menus • Sign showing restaurant name • Book for noting bookings
Post office	• Envelopes and paper for writing letters • Forms to be completed and submitted • Pencils and pens • Phone message pads • File folders • Post box
Shop	• Note pads and pens for making shopping lists • Sales dockets for recording items bought • Cardboard for making signs for items on special
Bank	• Pencils and markers • Passbooks to record transactions • Forms to complete for deposits and withdrawals
Home corner	• Pencils and markers • Paper • Message board • Note pad
Airport	• Pencils and markers • Paper • Luggage tags • Maps • Signs

There are a number of ways in which teachers can help children to utilise writing in socio-dramatic play. They can become co-players: taking on a role and joining with the children as they play (Christie, Enz & Vukelich. 2007). For instance, in a shop-themed play area, the teacher might take on the role of a customer and write a shopping list which is then referred to when role-playing goods being selected from the shelves. Alternatively, the role might be that of a shop assistant who writes the notices needed to indicate where various items are located in the shop. When teachers participate in children's socio-dramatic play they are able to demonstrate the different ways in which written communication can function in the differently themed play areas and there is the potential for children to replicate the writing activities that they carry out.

Teachers should be available to assist children with the writing activities that they choose to carry out in their pretend play. They might observe children's play and step in and assist when necessary. This might involve helping children to write the signs and labels that they decide are needed in different parts of their themed play area.

READING AND TALKING ABOUT BOOKS

Children discover and learn about written language when they have books read to them. Their learning can be further enhanced when they can view the print as the teacher reads and when teachers occasionally highlight certain features of the written language.

INTENTIONAL TEACHING ACTIVITIES

Intentional teaching (DEEWR, 2009) involves teachers working with children on activities that serve a specific teaching and learning focus and that include suitable teaching strategies (for example, modelling and demonstration, questioning, speculating and explaining, shared thinking and problem solving) for children's achievement of the intended learning. In order for teachers to advance children's development as writers, teaching and learning programs should include a component of intentional teaching. The writing development of children in pre-school and in the early years of school benefits from a degree of intentional teaching.

Outlined below are a range of activities that have a specific teaching intention in regards to children's writing and that are suitable for working with emergent writers. However, in order to optimise children's learning, teachers should make decisions regarding a number of factors when employing these activities. They should consider:

- children's current knowledge and writing skills and modify the activities accordingly
- the incorporation of teaching strategies (e.g. demonstration, questioning and explaining) suitable to the activities and to optimising children's learning.

The class message board

A daily message written by the teacher for the children provides a good way to get children curious about decoding written texts and to engage them with the communicative function of writing. The teacher writes a short message to the class or to an individual child on a message board and places it where the children will easily see it. A picture can be used to assist the children to understand the message. The message might be about:

- an activity to be done during that day
- a special visitor coming to the classroom

- a reminder about when something is happening, e.g. assembly
- someone's birthday.

When the children arrive they read the message or the teacher reads it to them. An alternative but more time-consuming method is for the teacher to write a short message to each child and place these in their individual folders which are attached to the message board.

The 'All about us' book

The 'All about us' book is a large scrap book in which each child has been designated their own double page. At the beginning of the year, the book is sent home with each child one at a time and families create an information page for their child. It can include photographs, drawings, writing or anything else that helps to tell the others in the class about the child. The teacher also attaches an envelope to each child's page and they put a note from the teacher inside the envelope. The children take the messages out from their envelope and, with the teacher's help, read them. When finished, the book can be made available for the children to read and look at and for families to read.

Take-home bear

Each child has a turn at taking home a small teddy bear (or a similar cuddly toy) which is accompanied by its special diary. At home, the child dictates a sentence for a parent to write in the bear's diary. The sentence should tell about something that the bear did during the home visit. On return to school, the bear's diary should be read to the other children. Following this, questions and a discussion of the event written about should be encouraged.

Noticing environmental print

Children learn a lot about written communication when they are assisted to pay attention to it in the school or community environment. They particularly come to understand the various functions it serves as a form of communication. During excursions, teachers should draw the children's attention to various forms of written language in the environment—the signs, labels and advertisements that are situated on buildings, roads, crosswalks and in other outdoor locations. An excursion can be as simple as a walk around the neighbourhood or the grounds of the school or centre. The teacher can read them out and talk with the children about their messages and purposes.

Labelling the classroom

In this activity children identify where signs and labels might be needed in the classroom and, with the teacher's assistance, write them. The writing could be done using the teaching strategy of shared writing (refer to Chapter 19) where the children provide the ideas and information and the teacher writes them down. The children might be required to add symbols or pictures to the labels, providing the opportunity to focus their learning on the use of visual texts to communicate.

Dictated sentences

The dictated sentences activity involves the children drawing or painting a picture about an experience, event or item and the teacher writing a sentence underneath. The sentences written should be derived from the children's explanation of their pictures, although, depending on their ability, children can specifically dictate the sentences for the teacher to write. The teacher should verbalise each of the children's sentences as it is being written to assist the children to see the connection between oral and written language. The experience provides an opportunity for the children to observe and learn about the use of symbols (letters) to represent oral language in written form. The children also become familiar with certain writing behaviours such as the left-to-right directionality of writing and the association between spoken and written words.

Pocket texts

Pocket texts are created in a similar way to dictated stories (above) or language experience texts (refer to Chapter 19). They involve each child drawing a picture on an A4 sheet of cardboard and then dictating a sentence about their drawing which the teacher writes underneath their picture. The teacher also writes each word of the children's sentences onto separate cards which are stored in an envelope or pocket attached to the back of the child's picture. The sentence words can be used for various related activities such as having the children put the words in the right order to make the sentence, matching two word cards where the words contain one of the same letters, or categorising the word cards according to the number of letters in each of the words.

Daily modelled writing

Daily modelled writing occurs when the teacher writes a sentence or a short text each day while the children watch. The sentence or text written should hold meaning for the children: it might be about something they are going to do in the day, someone's birthday, a special visitor or another special event. It might be of general relevance to the class or of significance to one child in the class. For example, 'Yesterday was Moira's birthday. She had four candles on her cake', or 'Later today a fire truck is coming to our school'. Daily modelled writing serves much of the same learning values as dictated writing. Chapter 19 provides a more expanded description of the strategy of modelled writing and how it can be practised with children at all levels of writing ability.

Class photo books

Class photo books are created using photographs and written texts that recall different activities which have been experienced by the children. For instance, should the class visit the local fire station, photographs can be taken of the children and of what they see and experience and then placed, one per page, into a blank scrap book. The children should then write (or dictate what to write while the teacher writes) underneath the photograph, explaining what it is about. The books can be read and reread to the children and they can be made available for them to explore independently or can be sent home to share with families. Class photo books can be made about many different school and classroom activities; for example, the sports carnival or the events of a typical school day.

Making sentences

Children can compose their own sentences by using words that are shown on cards which have been prepared by the teacher. The children look at the words and choose those they want to use to compose a sentence. They might then read their sentences to the teacher or to another child or they might copy their sentence by writing it down.

Patterned stories

Patterned stories are generally implemented using modelled or shared writing (refer to Chapter 19). However, if appropriate to the children's ability and learning needs, they can be supported to write their own. Patterned stories are about playing with language. They involve creating a text where the sentences of the text follow a repetitive pattern. Two different types include:

- repeated use of the same sentence but with changes to one or two of the words (most often adjectives and nouns); for instance, 'I can see a red flower. I can see a bright flower.'
- starting with a simple phrase (e.g. 'the ball') and building a text that comprises the phrase continually repeated but with an adjective added each time (e.g. 'the blue ball'; 'the blue bouncy ball'; 'the yellow and blue bouncy ball'; 'the yellow and blue soft bouncy ball').

The apple	The house	I can see a flower
The red apple	The house has a door.	I can see a red flower.
The shiny red apple	The house has a window.	I can see a blue flower.
The delicious shiny red apple	The house has a chimney.	I can see a green flower etc.

Patterned stories are written onto large sheets of cardboard that the teacher has prepared in the shapes of the objects that are being written about; for example, the cardboard would be prepared in the shape of an apple when an apple is to be written about.

Patterned stories can be written by the teacher using the modelled or shared writing strategies. Alternatively, the children can write their own in a book of blank pages prepared in the shape of the object to be written about. They write one of the sentences of their patterned story on each page and illustrate it.

The repetition of the basic phrase or sentence and the addition of, or change to, words in patterned stories provides an effective language enrichment activity (specifically vocabulary) for young children, and is particularly relevant to the language learning needs of children who are learning English as an additional language.

Magazine picture booklet

The preparation of a magazine picture booklet begins with each child selecting pictures from magazines and gluing one onto each of the pages in a blank booklet. The teacher assists the children to write a title for their booklet and to write a sentence that is relevant to the picture on each page. The children can read the books to each other or take them home.

Journal writing

Journal writing involves the children writing freely about their lives or a topic of personal interest to them. They might convey their feeling and thoughts, recount personal experiences, express their ideas or reflect on their understanding of something. However, there might be times when the teacher sets a topic for the children to respond to or write about. This could be a response to a story read or information learnt. The writing in journals is done independently and without interruption and is often done a number of times a week. The writing is not subject to corrections and children apply whatever writing knowledge and skills they hold; they might use pictures, scribbles, random letters, invented spelling or more conventional spelling and they might write one sentence, many sentences or a lengthy text.

The writing that children do in their journals is for not for any particular audience, though it might be that it is read by the teacher who makes a written response to the content. The children's writing benefits from the opportunity afforded them to write freely and spontaneously about something they are interested in and without concern for accuracy of writing conventions.

SUPPORTING CHILDREN'S FURTHER PROGRESS AS WRITERS

The experiences suggested for beginner and emergent writers as discussed so far are also important for children who have moved beyond the emergent phase and whose writing knowledge and skills are being further extended. However, for children beyond the emergent phase, instruction that more explicitly addresses different aspects of writing is also needed, and their learning about writing should extend to the areas of:

- writing for a range of purposes
- text organisation
- graphophonics (letter–sound association) and spelling
- punctuation and sentence knowledge
- use of the writing process (prepare, draft, revise, edit, publish) for producing written texts
- strategies for writing
- topics written about.

Children's writing ability is enhanced when they are provided with a range of writing experiences and focused teaching about the different aspects of writing. Their knowledge of written communication and texts, and writing skills, is increased when the teaching and learning experiences encompass:

- independent writing activities appropriate to their phase of writing development that are accompanied by suitable teaching strategies, supports and guidance and regular writing discussions with the teacher
- the use of relevant experiences and discussion for developing the ideas and information to be included in a written text before writing it
- watching teachers write, or working with the teacher to write, a text with the teacher also using the strategies or techniques of explanation, thinking aloud, asking questions and highlighting text features and thereby focusing attention on different aspects of writing
- reading various types of books and other texts and listening to them being read
- shared reading sessions that highlight the authors' use of written language—for instance, sentences, vocabulary and text structure (ordering and setting out the information) and the use of different types of punctuation
- learning about the segmenting of words into phonemes (individual sounds) and the relationship between the phonemes and letters in words
- learning how to spell words and the strategies that can be used to spell new words
- experiences that develop vocabulary.

DEVELOPING WRITING LESSONS FOR CHILDREN IN THE EARLY YEARS OF SCHOOL

In their early school years, it is important that children be provided with daily opportunities to write. This should include regular occasions when the children are allowed to choose their own writing topics and decide on how they will write about these (Cunningham & Allington, 2008, p. 141). It should also frequently involve lessons in which all the children complete the same writing activity, thereby allowing the teacher to develop children's ability with particular text forms. Whatever the situation, children's writing endeavours should consistently involve teacher guidance so that writing experiences serve to further their writing competency.

Moreover, the more focused teaching of writing skills and strategies can be undertaken through the use of 'mini-lessons' (Cunningham & Allington, 2008; Cooper & Kiger, 1997). These are short teaching sessions, of about ten to fifteen minutes, which are used to teach or clarify specific aspects of writing. The focus for a mini-lesson should be small enough to enable the children to understand it and apply it to their writing within a short time. A mini-lesson might, for instance, focus on writing an introduction for a report or understanding the difference between weak and strong verbs and how each contributes to clarity. Mini-lessons can be undertaken with the whole class or can be employed to give more focused attention to smaller groups of children who have common writing development needs.

Writing lessons that involve the composition of written texts should be planned with consideration given to the following important elements:

1 *The writing stimulus*: a writing lesson should begin with an activity that provides the topic for the writing and which will stimulate the children to engage in the writing. The activity might be reading a story, cooking, carrying out a scientific experiment, or a visit to the local park. The opportunities are endless for ways to select a stimulating activity, as outlined in the next section.
2 Writing rehearsal *using talk*: in order to make the task of writing easier for children, the lesson should be preceded by adequate time for discussion. When children get the time to talk with others about the writing topic (and the specific content for the activity) their writing is more likely to be completed with greater clarity. Discussion before writing helps children to write with appropriate sequence and structure and to be clear about where their writing is leading.
3 *The specific teaching focus:* writing lessons should focus on teaching one or two aspects of children's writing.
4 *The teaching strategies and supports*: writing activities should provide a vehicle for children's writing development. However, learning is dependent on teachers providing appropriate input and employing suitable teaching strategies when implementing writing lessons. Modelled, shared and guided writing, writing conferences (teacher–child conversations) and mini-lessons are some examples of the teacher's role in ensuring that the children's experience of writing a text leads to their learning—to increased understanding and knowledge of and skill in writing. Children's writing development will be optimised if

the teaching strategies are selected after careful consideration of the particular writing task which is to be undertaken by the children.

These elements should be considered with a view to ensuring that the children fully engage themselves and that they have the best possible chance of absorbing the skills and understandings that the text writing activity is intended to convey.

ESTABLISHING THE STIMULUS FOR WRITING ACTIVITIES

There are three main categories from which the stimulus for writing activities can be chosen. The first involves children's literature, the second non-fiction texts and the third children's own school or home experiences.

1. USING CHILDREN'S LITERATURE AS A STIMULUS FOR WRITING

Children's literature provides a natural and stimulating topic for children's writing. Children are motivated by good stories and enjoy sharing their impressions with others. Teachers can harness this natural interest by using stories as the basis for writing activities.

There are many enjoyable writing activities that can spring from reading a story to children. The activities are generally of two types—realistic or imaginative. Realistic writing activities involve children writing about the ideas, events and characters in the story; for example, writing a recount or summary of a story or a description of one of the characters. Imaginative writing activities involve children writing as if the story, characters and events are real; for example, writing a letter to one of the characters.

There are many different realistic writing activities that can follow from story reading. The following are just some:

- rewriting a story or part of it, telling it from the viewpoint of one of the characters
- writing an advertisement for a story book
- writing a story as a poem
- writing a letter to a story's author
- drawing a coat of arms or a banner for a character from a story and writing to explain the design and symbols used
- constructing a timeline (sequence of events arranged in order and presented along a line) using pictures and sentences that depict and order the main events in the story
- retelling a story using pictures and written text
- writing a character description
- using pictures and written text to create a story map which shows different scenes and associated events
- writing a personal reaction to an element of a story as an entry in their literature response journals (notebooks used to for children to record their responses to stories). The focus for the response can be left open or set by the teacher; for example, 'What do you think about…?' 'Which of the characters was the most clever/cunning/lazy?'

The following are some of the many imaginative writing activities that can arise from reading stories.

- writing letters to a character from the story
- writing as if one character from a story is addressing another
- writing diary entries for one of the characters in a story
- writing stories or parts of stories as feature news articles.

Not all these activities will work with all story books. Different books will lend themselves to particular activities. Teachers should familiarise themselves with the books they will use to stimulate children's writing and carefully design appropriate writing activities. The table below provides examples of children's story books and outlines possible writing activities for each book.

Table 20.3: Children's story books and example writing activities

Children's literature	Writing activities
Belinda by Pamela Allen	• Use the chart provided to develop a story summary using written text • Write a letter from Belinda the cow to Bessy, telling her what Tom did while she was away • Write character descriptions of Tom and Bessy • Write the instructions for milking a cow to give to Tom • Write a list that outlines all the things about Bessy that Belinda the cow missed while she was away • Write a recipe for making butter
Dear zoo by Rod Campbell	• Write a list of the different animals that the boy received from the zoo and, next to each animal, write why it wasn't suitable • Write about the boy's response for each animal he received from the zoo • Write a story based on the plot of *Dear zoo* but, instead of different animals arriving from the zoo, make it about different food items arriving from the supermarket
The rainbow fish by Marcus Pfister	• Write one scene of the story as a comic strip • Write a description of the rainbow fish • Write a list of questions to ask the rainbow fish during an interview

Children's literature	Writing activities
Who sank the boat? by Pamela Allen 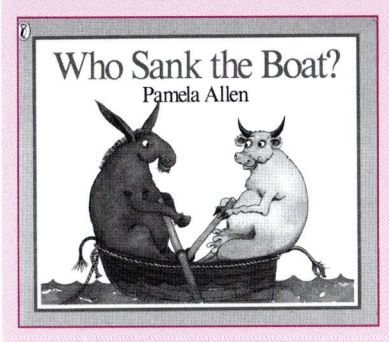	• Continue the story by writing about what happens when the animals return to the farm • Write the story from the point of view of one of the animals involved • Write the thoughts of each of the animals when the mouse got into the boat and it sank • Construct a story-wheel (circle divided into quadrants) that summarises the story in four parts using pictures and written text • Write a letter from the farmer to the animals explaining why they cannot return to the farm
The hidden forest by Jeannie Baker 	• Rewrite part of the story from the point of view of either Sophie or Ben • Write a letter from Ben to Sophie or vice versa • Write an advertisement to sell the underwater garden • Write Ben's diary entry for the day he went diving • Rewrite the beginning of the story but changing the main characters and setting
Magic beach by Alison Lester 	• Create a two-column chart and in one column write all the things the children did at the beach and, in the other, all the associated imaginative activities. Write a story about what happens when the children do actually find pirate treasure at the beach or the sandcastle they are building becomes real • Draw a picture of the beach (or use the one in the book) and label all the parts of the beach and the things the children did there

Text innovation

In text innovation a children's story which has a repetitive sentence pattern is selected and used as the basis for writing another story. It entails substituting some of the elements of the original story—often the characters and actions—with other elements. The story *Brown bear, brown bear, what do you see?* (Martin, 1984) is an example of a story that provides a repetitive sentence pattern appropriate for a text innovation. The story begins with the sentences, 'Brown bear, brown bear, what do you see? I see a yellow bird looking at me'. This is then repeated but with the question being put to the bird, which answers by naming yet another animal. The repetition continues with different animals being introduced and being asked the question, 'What do you see?' The box below shows the words to the brown bear story and a text innovation that has been written using the shared writing strategy with a Year 1 class. The use of shared writing for the text innovation allows the teacher to assist the children to understand the technique. However, children can also write their own text innovations independently.

Brown bear by Bill Martin and Eric Carle

Brown bear, brown bear
what do you see?
I see a red bird looking at me

Red bird, red bird
what do you see?
I see yellow duck looking at me

Yellow duck, yellow duck
what do you see?
I see a blue horse looking at me

Blue horse, blue horse
what do you see?
I see a green frog looking at me

Squeaking mouse by Year 1

Squeaking mouse, squeaking mouse
what do you hear?
I hear a meowing cat looking for me

Meowing cat, meowing cat
what do you hear?
I hear a barking dog looking for me

Barking dog, barking dog
what do you hear?
I hear a growling bear looking for me

Growling bear, growling bear
what do you hear?
I hear a hunter rustling in the trees

To town (Cowley, 2005) is another example of a children's story that is suitable for a text innovation. The story uses a repetitive sentence pattern to describe various forms of transport that the author uses to travel to town. The same repetitive sentence pattern can be used but with changes to the place and the forms of transport. The right-hand column below shows the beginning of such a text produced by Year 2 children.

To town by Cowley

I will go to town on my bulldozer,
my big yellow bulldozer.
Brr-rrr, Brr-rrr,
all the way to town.

I will go to town in my fire-engine,
my big red fire-engine.
Ooooo-aaaah – ooooo – aaaah,
all the way to town.

To the moon by 2F

I will go to the moon in my rocket,
my shiny grey rocket
swoosh swoosh,
all the way to the moon.

I will go to the moon in my hot air balloon
my colourful round hot air balloon
h-wooh h-wooh,
all the way to the moon.

I will go to the moon on my magic broomstick
my new brown magic broomstick
sweep sweep,
all the way to the moon.

I will go to the moon in my space ship
my sparkling silver space ship
zoom zoom,
all the way to the moon,
and all the way home again.

2. USING NON-FICTION TEXTS AS THE STIMULUS FOR WRITING

It is important for children to be given writing activities using information sourced from non-fiction books. Good writing development requires that children be taught to summarise information and write reports and other non-fiction texts, such as explanations, procedures and descriptions. They should also learn to organise information into various forms of presentation such as charts, tables and diagrams.

There are many interesting writing activities that can be carried out using information provided in non-fiction books. The books should be chosen carefully to ensure that they are appropriate to the children's current level of writing knowledge and skill. Suitable teaching strategies and techniques should be employed—modelling, demonstrating, providing writing frameworks, and so on (refer to Chapters 15 and 19)—to ensure that the activities serve to support learning goals and extend the children's ability as writers. When the writing activities provided for children are too difficult or are not accompanied by appropriate teaching techniques, young developing writers can become frustrated and disengaged with the task.

The non-fiction books chosen as the basis for writing activities should appeal to the children's interests. They should be examined to ensure that the information presented is set out in a way that is intelligible to the children; for instance, the use of headings and subheadings, simple sentence structures, pictures and diagrams.

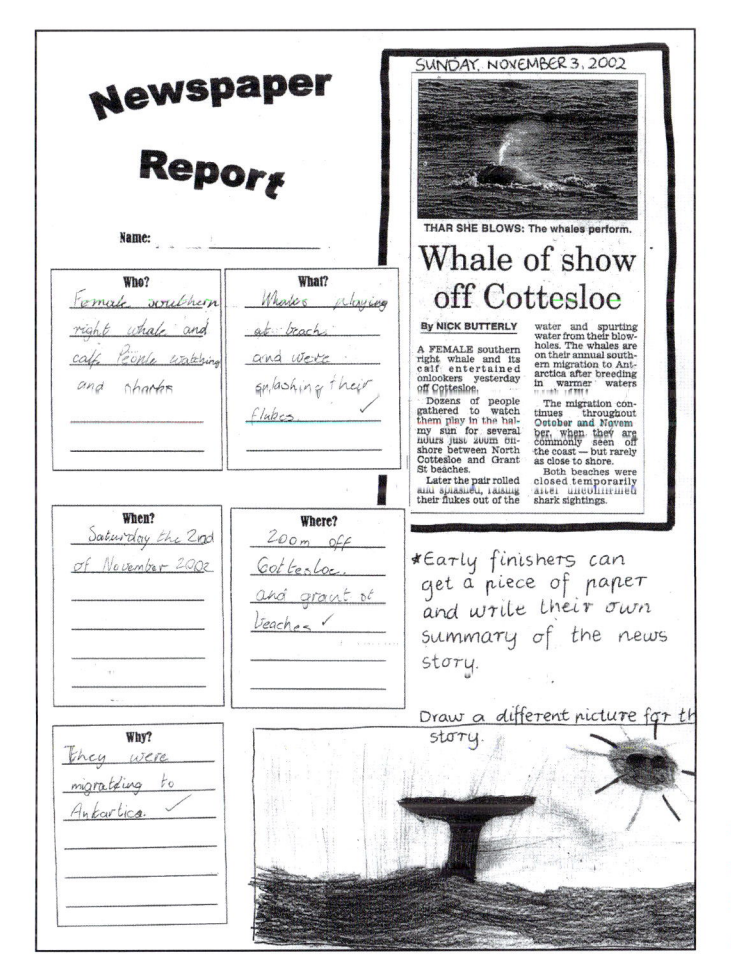

Children's writing experiences should include those that require information being sourced from non-fiction texts.

Table 20.5: Non-fiction texts and example writing activities

Children's non-fiction texts	Writing activities
Why is the sky blue? by Geraldine Taylor and Amy Schimler	• Create a poster that poses four of the questions from the book and provides the answers in summary form • Write a list of questions similar to those contained in the book but on different topics • Write a different book using a similar structure to this one • Draw and label a diagram that depicts the answer to one of the questions in the book
Elephants by Edel Wignall	• Write a diary entry: 'A day in the life of an elephant' • Draw a representation of the features of an elephant as described in the text and add labels that help to explain the drawing • Summarise the information about elephants which is provided in the book by writing appropriate sentences or phrases under headings which are shown on a chart • Using the summary chart as a source, write a report about elephants
Eating fruit and vegetables by Claire llewellyn	• Create a quiz by writing questions and answers about fruit and vegetables using the information found in the text • Create a poster using visual and written information about the importance of eating fruit and vegetables • Find information from the book about eating fruit and vegetables and write notes (words and phrases). Then use these notes to write a summary paragraph • Create a menu for a day's meals, ensuring the appropriate balance of fruit and vegetables is included

Writing activities based on non-fiction texts might include:

- making notes into a chart or table using an abbreviated form (words and phrases)
- creating posters that use a combination of visual and written texts
- labelling diagrams or pictures
- creating a summary paragraph or series of paragraphs
- compiling brochures using a combination of pictures and written text
- writing information from an appropriate text (an historical biography) in summary form on a timeline (sequence of events arranged in order and presented along a line)
- writing a report
- writing a biography or diary entry
- writing a poem.

3. USING CHILDREN'S EXPERIENCES AS A STIMULUS FOR WRITING

When children write about their own lives and experiences, the topic is of personal significance and interest and the content is readily available. Because the experiences are personal they should have little difficulty in recalling information that is required for the text. Topics based on life experiences therefore provide children with the opportunity to write freely without the distraction of having to assemble information and decide on sequence.

Activities that involve children writing about their experiences can take two forms: about the children's lives and experiences outside of school or about the experiences that teachers provide in the classroom. Topics requiring children to write about their home, family or community lives might cover family members, events and celebrations, leisure activities or hobbies, home and favourite places and things. Classroom experiences that would lend themselves to writing activities include art and craft projects, guest speakers, science investigations, class celebrations and excursions, and school assemblies. The teacher may organise a particular experience for the main purpose of providing the content and stimulus for a writing activity. This can be useful when children's writing development requires the teacher to implement a specific writing activity to achieve a certain learning goal. A teacher might, for instance, need to teach the children about writing instructional texts and so the provision of, say, a cooking experience becomes the topic and stimulus for writing.

Children's experiences provide a wide variety of possibilities for writing activities. The type of writing will depend on the experience which has to be written about, but could easily include recounts, reports, instructional texts, descriptions, diaries, personal journals and so on.

SUMMARY

Learning to write begins well before school, and the learning environment and experiences provided for young children are important to establishing important foundational concepts from which further understandings and skills can be built. There are many experiences that can be provided for children to develop their ability as writers. They should be chosen, adapted and implemented so that they are appropriate to the present competency of the children and support their particular writing development and learning needs. They should primarily involve writing texts for different purposes and audiences and involve the use of different teacher supports to ensure children's learning and progress. Children's literature, non-fiction texts and the experiences of children provide motivating starting points for children's writing.

QUESTIONS AND ACTIVITIES

1. Choose one or two of the writing activities listed in this chapter and consider how you could implement them with pre-school children. If possible, work with a group of pre-school children to carry out the activities.

2 Choose a children's story book suitable for six- or seven-year-olds. Create a chart that shows the ways in which the story book can be used as a springboard for writing activities.
3 Choose three different activities from those listed in this chapter and consider what aspects of written communication each would best support.
4 In choosing the experiences and activities to suit the needs of the learners, what factors should be taken into account?

KEY TERMS

intentional teaching
writing rehearsal

KEY REFERENCES

Christie, J. F., Enz, B. J. & Vukelich, C. (2007). *Teaching language and literacy: Preschool through elementary grades.* Boston: Pearson Education.

Cooper, D. J. & Kiger, N. D. (1997). *Literacy: Helping students construct meaning.* Boston: Houghton Mifflin Company.

Cunningham, P. M. & Allington, R. L. (2008). *Classrooms that work: They can all read and write* (5th edn). Boston: Pearson Education.

Cunningham, P., Moore, S., Cunningham, J. & Moore, D. (2004). *Reading and writing: Research based K–4 instruction.* Boston: Allyn & Bacon.

Department of Education, Employment and Workplace Relations (DEEWR) (2009). *Belonging, being and becoming: The Early Years Learning Framework for Australia.* Barton, ACT: Commonwealth of Australia.

Sulzby, E. (1985). Kindergartners as writers and readers. In M. Farr (ed.), *Advances in writing research. Vol. 1: Children's early writing development* (pp. 127–99). Norwood, NJ: Ablex.

CHAPTER 21

Writing: Assessment and Evaluation

CHAPTER OBJECTIVES

This chapter will increase your understanding of:

- the knowledge, skills and understandings of writing to be assessed
- methods to collect information about children's knowledge, skills and understandings of writing
- how to use information gathered to evaluate children's development and learning
- the application of various record-keeping methods.

This chapter provides information that, when considered in light of the previous writing chapters, prepares you to be able to monitor children's learning and development as writers. Many of the fundamental skills and understandings necessary for writing (knowledge of letters of the alphabet, concepts of print, vocabulary and phonics) are also essential for reading and their assessment has been discussed in Chapter 10. In early childhood, observation, examination of children's written texts and conversations with children and their parents provide the most relevant methods for collecting information about writing development. The assessment of writing is complex and it is unfortunately beyond the scope of this chapter to go into great detail. However, the information we present here should provide you with the basic information you will need to get started with the effective assessment and evaluation of children's writing.

Remember that assessment information should be used to inform teaching, to report to others or to provide feedback to children.

WHAT TO ASSESS?

In order to determine what needs to be assessed and how it might be assessed, it is necessary to be familiar with the requirements of the curriculum for the children concerned and to have a thorough understanding of what writing learning and development entails. **Assessment** should also take place in light of program goals. It should provide a means by which teachers can adapt their programs; that is, modify or change the learning and development goals, the learning environment and the approaches taken in supporting children's progress as writers.

The areas of writing that were discussed in earlier chapters form the basis of assessment of children's writing, but the specifics of assessment will depend on the age and developmental phase of the children concerned, the particular early childhood setting in which learning is taking place, the requirements of the relevant curriculum and the goals of learning programs.

When assessing what *toddlers and pre-school children* know, understand and can do in regards to written communication, the following are some questions that might be considered:

- Does the child understand writing as a type of communication between people?
- Does the child understand that what we say, think and feel can be written down?
- Does the child understand that the print in books and other types of written texts (e.g. signs, labels) represents meaning?
- Does the child give meaning to what he/she 'writes'?
- Does the child know that writing is different from drawing?
- Does the child use any letter formations or letter-like formations when writing?
- Does the child choose to 'write' during free play?
- Is the child showing increased hand–eye coordination, wrist and hand muscle control and grasp strength?

In order to determine the writing development of *pre-school children*, the following additional questions might be asked:

- Does the child show awareness of different purposes (reasons) and audiences for writing?
- Does the child use written texts for different purposes during socio-dramatic play?
- What letters of the alphabet can the child recognise, name and write?
- Is the child able to use one-to-one correspondence in matching spoken to written words in texts?
- Does the child have an understanding of any phoneme–grapheme links (the links between the sounds of spoken words and the letters of written words)? Does the child accurately represent any phonemes with the right letters?
- What level of phoneme awareness and letter–sound knowledge is displayed in the child's use of invented spelling?
- Does the child's writing show appropriate text directionality and the use of other basic print concepts?
- Is the child aware of some different types of written texts (story, poem, recount) and their broad structural and linguistic characteristics?
- Does the child use written texts for different purposes during socio-dramatic play?
- Does the child experiment with punctuation (such as full stops) and capital letters when writing?

- Does the child use complete sentences in their writing?
- Does the child write any simple common words by sight (e.g. 'and', 'the', 'an')?

For children in the *early years of school*, similar questions can be asked to ascertain their writing knowledge, skills and understandings. The information gained would likely demonstrate increased knowledge and more consistent and comprehensive use of the different skills. Assessment for children in the early years of school should be considered in light of the four broad areas of:

- *The writing context*
    - Does the child produce written texts for different purposes and audiences?
    - Do the written texts that the child produces contain information, structures and language features that suit each of a variety of purposes for writing?
- *The written text*
    - Is the child aware that texts written for different purposes contain a particular type of information and are organised differently?
    - Does the child have knowledge of the language and structural features of some different text forms?
- *Strategies and processes*
    - What methods does the child use to generate ideas before writing and how effective are the methods used?
    - Does the child monitor his/her writing as they write (e.g. read it back to remember how it is evolving and as a reminder of what should come next)?
    - What editing or proofreading techniques to 'fix up' or 'polish' writing does the child use?
- *Conventions*
    - What punctuation, capital letters and sentence structures are used when writing?
    - What spelling knowledge and strategies does the child use when spelling words?
    - Does the child have a collection of words that can be spelt automatically?
    - What types of words can the child write using conventional spelling?
    - Does the child use appropriate grammatical structures for the sentences produced?
    - Does the child use various sentence types and lengths, and different ways to begin and join sentences?
    - Does the child produce a written text which flows naturally and is easy to comprehend?

Other areas that might provide a focus for the assessment of children's writing include vocabulary and word choice, as well as general writing fluency.

COLLECTING INFORMATION ABOUT CHILDREN'S WRITING

There are many ways to collect information with regards to the assessment of children's writing development and learning. The methods used should allow teachers to determine children's understanding about, and knowledge of, writing and written communication, and of the skills and strategies that they use in composing a text. The methods that are most significant to early childhood are observation, the analysis of children's written texts, conversations with children and with their families, and writing conferences. It is also important to involve children in the self-assessment of their writing.

OBSERVATION

This is sometimes referred to as 'surface observation' (Martin, 2010) of writing. It involves watching children as they write and recording what is seen, and is useful for determining children's writing knowledge and ability, their motivation towards writing activities and their particular writing interests. Observation alone does not reveal everything that there is to know about children's writing development and learning; it does not, for instance, uncover the thinking that goes on during the composition of written texts. Knowing how children think as they write is important. It provides information about children's writing knowledge and about the strategies they apply when they write. Observation as an assessment tool is most dynamic when it is accompanied by conversation with children. It should be guided by, but not limited to, the goals of the teaching and learning program.

Observation enables teachers to acquire information about what children do as they write during specific times and in specific situations. The observation of children at one particular moment in the day and in one situation is limiting in the establishment of a comprehensive and accurate profile of them as writers. Observations should be carried out in a variety of situations and at different times in the day or week. The observation, for instance, of children at the writing centre should be supplemented with observations made as they participate in other writing situations such as the socio-dramatic play area and perhaps during a dictated or modelled writing activity with the teacher.

It is useful to establish a system for recording observations. There are a number of ways in which this can be done. In early childhood, the most common and useful of these include anecdotal notes, checklists and **rubrics**. These recording methods are explained in Chapter 7, which deals with the assessment of speaking and listening. Examples of each of these for recording observations of children as they engage in writing experiences are shown throughout this section.

THE ANALYSIS OF CHILDREN'S WRITTEN TEXTS

This involves collecting samples of the written texts that children produce during different writing activities and free and structured play situations. It involves using the evidence provided in the children's written texts to determine their writing knowledge and skills. They might reveal competency with such things as phonemic awareness, letter–sound matching, spelling, sentence structures, punctuation and vocabulary. The focus of the **analysis** should be drawn from the goals and objectives of the literacy learning program. In order to ensure accurate assessment and evaluation, the analysis of children's written texts should involve a range of samples. Texts written for different purposes and in different writing situations provide varied information about the children's writing competency and help to determine the consistency of children's application of particular writing skills.

There are various methods that might be used to record the information gleaned from the analysis of children's written texts. Some of these are annotations (written comments), checklists and rubrics. Teachers should devise their own checklists and rubrics with reference

Table 21.1: Example of a rubric that facilitates the assessment of the writing process (Years 2 and 3)

Writing process rubric Name:_____			
Writing process and strategies rubric			
	1	2	3
Planning	No planning observed	Plans a little by talking with others about ideas, writing brief notes, drawing pictures, referring to charts and other resources	Plans well by talking with others, writing notes, simple story maps and graphic organisers. Looks in books for ideas
Composing	Writes a little (a few sentences at most) but does not use processes that would help drafting/composing	Refers to notes, charts and word wall when writing. Asks others for help	Refers to plans when writing and uses a range of other resources such as word walls, charts and dictionary
Revising	No revision observed	Little revision but sometimes crosses out parts of text not wanted	Revises by crossing out parts not wanted and adding in new sentences and paragraphs Sometimes changes the position of parts of the text. Changes words to improve meaning
Editing	No editing observed	Reads through writing to search for spelling and punctuation errors but misses many	Reads through writing several times and edits for punctuation and spelling errors. Uses dictionaries and other references when needed
Publishing	Work rarely finished	Finishes many pieces of work but little attention to presentation. Still has little sense of audience	Takes a pride in finishing many pieces to publishable standard. High standard of presentation

to the expected outcomes of the children in their class. These should relate to curriculum requirements, the children's phases of writing development and the teaching and learning program.

The annotative comments, checklists or rubrics should focus on what the text reveals that children know and what they do well or what skills or strategies they are beginning to apply to their writing. When viewed in a **portfolio**, children's ongoing writing development is able to be clearly identified and easily accessed when communicating with families about their children's learning and development.

The use of **annotations**, checklists and rubrics for recording information about children's learning and development is more comprehensively explained in Chapter 7. The following examples demonstrate their use with the assessment and evaluation of children's writing.

Table 21.2: Example of a checklist that can be used to record information about children's written texts

Writing checklist James Allen Age: 5 years 9 months Year Level: Pre-primary Term 4		
Accomplishments	Consistently demonstrated	Comments
Mostly uses invented spelling to write words. Includes some vowels	✓	Represents initial and (usually) end consonants when spelling words. Vowel sometimes included in CVC words. Knows letters for common phonemes like /t/ /s/ /k/
Can spell a few words conventionally		Hit and miss. Not consistent
Can write own name (first and family name) and some other names		Can write own first name and attempts to write family name. Can write 'Sam' (brother)
Can write most of the letters of the alphabet in lower or upper case	✓	Have seen James write most letters of the alphabet. Mixture of upper and lower case. Letters to work on: B, G, P, Q, R, Y, Z
Other: Emerging audience awareness	✓	James is beginning to take writing home to share with parents. Likes to read his stories to his mum

The practice of analysing and evaluating children's written texts might also involve the use of exemplars (models of writing that display skills at different developmental levels). Exemplars assist in making judgments about the quality of children's writing by supporting the use of comparisons between the exemplars and the children's written texts. Examples of writing samples at different levels can be found on the websites of various Education Departments. There are also published books containing writing exemplars, such as the *PM exemplars for teaching writing* (Cengage Learning).

The analysis of children's written texts as a method of assessment is restrictive and is best used in combination with other assessment methods. It does not allow for complete pictures of the children as writers to be established. For instance, the strategies and processes used when writing are often not able to be determined or they are only minimally revealed. Furthermore, the written texts of young children might involve scribbles, pictures or a series of letter-like shapes. While the information contained within these texts is useful, it is often the children's behaviours and conversations while creating these texts, as well as what they do with them afterwards, that is most relevant to gaining an understanding of what they know about writing and written communication. Conversations and observations are likely to be more appropriate in determining the understanding about writing that is held by younger learners.

Table 21.3: Extract of the BWC rating guide, which shows criteria for rating the 'ideas' trait of children's written texts

Ideas				
Experimenting 1	Emerging 2	Developing 3	Capable 4	Experienced 5
• Uses scribbles for writing • Dictates labels or a story • Shapes that look like letters • Line forms that imitate text • Writes letters randomly	• Some recognisable words present • Labels pictures • Uses drawings that show detail • Pictures are supported by some words	• Attempts a story or to make a point • Illustration supports the writing • Meaning of the general idea is recognisable/ understandable • Some ideas clear but some are still fuzzy	• Writing tells a story or makes a point • Illustration (if present) enhances the writing • Idea is generally on topic • Details are present but not developed (lists)	• Presents a fresh/ original idea • Topic is narrowed and focused • Develops one clear, main idea • Uses interesting, important details for support • Writer understands topic well

Once upon a time there was a very rich family and they had servants that did whatever they said. There was a brother a sister and a baby and a Mum and Dad, they were all happy Except the sister her name was Kate she did'like her home at all. She did't like it because every room had two piles of gold and Diamons, She did't have a garden so she had no where to play. One day Kate was lying in her bed and Jack came in her brother. Jack took her to a secret garden and they played there every day. The End.

Capable writer (Level 4 of BWC Rating Guide)

CONVERSATIONS WITH CHILDREN

This involves talking with children and asking them questions to find out what they know about writing. They can occur as children are actually carrying out writing activities or at a different time when it is useful to have some of the children's writing at hand. Questions should be directed towards particular writing experiences and to children's actual written texts; young children will find them easier to answer than questions that focus on writing in general. The questions listed below provide examples of those that might be asked to gain insights about children's writing knowledge processes and strategies.

- Tell me about what you did when you wrote this story?
- Who is it for?
- Did you like writing it?
- What was hard?
- What was easy?
- How did you work out how to spell these words [pointing]?
- How did you come up with the ideas for your story?
- When you had finished writing the story what did you do?

As with other methods of assessment, the information gleaned from conversations about children's writing knowledge and understandings should be recorded using the most appropriate system. Many of the methods already discussed are useful. It might sometimes be useful to create an audio recording that then allows for later analysis and evaluation.

CONVERSATIONS WITH CHILDREN'S FAMILIES

Talking with parents and families is important in establishing a comprehensive understanding of children's development as writers and in determining the experiences that will best support their writing development. Parents and families can impart information about the types of writing that their children see in the home and community and about their children's interest in writing and written texts. Additionally, when sharing with parents about their children's engagement with writing (at school, pre-school or childcare) and about their development as writers, parents can often offer useful insights.

THE WRITING CONFERENCE

The writing conference is a discussion between teachers and individual children about aspects of the children's writing. It is a central part of the writing process and significant to writing lessons in the early years of school. There might be a particular focus, for instance, on writing ideas, forming sentences or structuring a text and on setting some goals for improvement. Conferences should be kept reasonably short, and they should involve highlighting the positive aspects of the children's writing. As developing writers, children can become overwhelmed and disheartened when the errors in their written texts are the overriding focus of discussions. It is important to highlight the many achievements and it is far better to have a specific focus, or a few focus areas, for each conference.

SELF-ASSESSMENT

As indicated in previous chapters, self-assessment by children is extremely powerful because it encourages them to think about their achievements and their goals. It might also motivate them to take more responsibility for their own learning. Self-assessment involves children considering the written texts they produce as well as what they do when they are writing the texts.

Children in pre-school and the early years of school can be assisted to develop some self-assessment methods. In pre-school it should take a fairly informal approach; perhaps involving a few questions to direct the children's thinking towards their writing and their engagement in a writing activity; for example, 'Have a look at your writing. What do you think you are really good at?'

Children in the early years of school should be provided with charts and checklists that can be used to assist them with self-assessment. Teachers should model self-assessment and the use of the wall charts in self-assessment.

Table 21.4: Extract of a self-assessment checklist

My writing Name: Benjamin (Year 1)	
I always read through my writing to check that it makes sense.	✓
I try to use interesting words.	✓
I use my word book to help me spell well.	✗
[Continued …]	

LETTER IDENTIFICATION

The learning experiences with which children are provided to support their writing development can be considerably enhanced when teachers design them using specific information about certain fundamental skills of writing. Such information can be gleaned from observation as well as from other informal assessment methods. More formal assessment tasks might also be designed to gather the required information.

Table 21.5: Checklist for noting children's development with letter identification

Writing of alphabet letters: Class profile Date:	James	Anna	Zoe	Cher	Ling
Writes mainly scribble and/or squiggles					
Uses primarily drawing as writing					
Writes letter-like shapes					
Writes a few letters conventionally (up to 5)					
Writes several letters conventionally (6–15)					
Writes most letters conventionally (16 +)					

An important skill in children's writing development is that of letter identification. The assessment of children's ability to write each of the letters of the alphabet can be done using informal observations of children engaged in experiences that involve writing, or through the use of a focused assessment task that requires them to write specified letters (McGee, 2007). The checklist provides an efficient way to record information about children's ability with letter identification and about their development towards the use of conventional letters when writing.

Checklists also provide a useful means of recording letter identification skill as gleaned from a more formal assessment task.

SPELLING

Spelling tests do not provide the most reliable information about children's spelling knowledge or about the strategies that they use to spell words. There are times when the information they provide is useful, but a more complete picture of children's spelling ability is gained when tests are supported by information gathered from the analysis of children's writing. This method provides information that is useful for the design of experiences and activities that most accurately address children's needs in learning to spell. Table 21.6 outlines the steps to be taken in collecting information about children's spelling development using the analysis of their written texts., while Table 21.7 shows an example spelling analysis chart.

Table 21.6: Analysing children's writing to assess spelling

Step	Description
1. Select several writing samples	Samples should be of at least fifty words each, if possible. Most of the words must be readable or decipherable.
2. Identify words spelt incorrectly	The teacher identifies incorrectly spelt words. It may be necessary to ask children what some of the words say.
3. Make or select spelling analysis chart	Depending on what type of analysis is to be done, the teacher draws up or selects a spelling analysis chart. An example of a spelling analysis chart is shown below.
4. Categorise the spelling errors	Categorise the errors. The categories will depend on the type of analysis.
5. Count/tally the errors	Counting/tallying the errors will help the teacher see patterns in where errors are being made. It is important to note that a child who makes many errors is not necessarily a poor speller but may be taking risks and attempting to write difficult words. Some children with few errors may be 'playing it safe' and only using words they know. *For this reason it can be useful to assess spelling through dictation, where the teacher reads a short text aloud and the children write it down.*
6. Interpret results to identify spelling instruction needed	Careful analysis of errors and patterns of errors will help teachers plan instruction for individual children and small groups.

Source: based on Tompkins (2007, p. 83)

Table 21.7: Spelling error analysis chart

			Spelling error analysis					
Name: Harry Winters			Age: 6:10	Year/Class: 1/2			Date: Nov 2009	Teacher: P. Delbosi
Word spelt incorrectly	Type of word		Type of error				Other	
	High frequency word (for age)	Irregular word	Using phonetic spelling – all phonemes represented	Misuse of spelling rule or pattern	Syllable error	Morpheme error (base word or affix)	Wrong choice of letters to represent sound	Omission/ substitutions/ wrong order (suggesting phonological awareness issues)	Notes and comments
creem (cream)			✓				ee chosen instead of ea		
biscet (biscuit)		biscuit	✓						
strorbury (strawberry)			✓				'or' used instead of 'aw' 'ur' instead of 'er'		
lollys (lollies)			✓	lollies					
praty (party)								Reversals of 'a' and 'r'	I believe this was lack of care – Harry can orally segment this word into phonemes.
danserg (dancing)			✓			-ing dance			

SPELLING TESTS

Spelling texts should be viewed with a degree of caution in early childhood, not least because raw scores from spelling tests give teachers limited information. For example, two children might get exactly the same score, but their (incorrect) spelling attempts may be very different; one child may be making errors that indicate he is spelling semi-phonetically while the other may be spelling phonetically but making other types of errors. Each of these children will require different experiences for their spelling development. The Developmental Spelling Test, shown below, encourages the teacher to analyse children's spelling errors in order to ascertain their developmental level.

Another test, the Writing Vocabulary Test, requires children to write as many words as they can think of in ten minutes. They are not allowed to copy from charts or other aids (Clay, 2002). This test is norm referenced, although the norms may not be appropriate for all children around Australia. In this individually administered assessment, young children (often Year 1 children) are asked to write all the words they know how to write. If they run out of ideas the teacher may prompt them by asking questions such as, 'Can you write the names of any animals?', 'Can you write the names of any people you know?' or 'Can you write the word "on"?' Words written should be spelt correctly in order to be credited with a point. Words not spelt correctly can be analysed to assist the teacher in planning spelling and phonics lessons for the child.

Words Their Way (Bear, Invernessi, Templeton & Johnston, 2004) is a comprehensive word study program and its Primary Spelling Inventory (PSI) is intended to help teachers analyse the spelling of children from the later part of pre-school to Year 3. The PSI tests children on twenty-six words in order of difficulty, starting with the words 'fan', 'pet' and 'dig' and ending

Table 21.8: A Developmental Spelling Test

Name:		Date:			
Word	Sentence	Child's spelling	Semi-phonetic	Phonetic	Transitional
monster	The boy chased a monster.		MTR	MOSTA	MONSTIR
uniform	The girl wore her school uniform.		U	UNIFM	YUNIFORM
dress	The lady wore a new dress.		JRS	JRAS	DRES
bottom	A big fish lives at the bottom of the sea.		BT	BODM	BOTTAM
biked	We biked to the top of the mountain.		B	BIKT	BICKED
human	Shrek is not a human.		UM	HUMN	HUMUM
eagle	An eagle is a beautiful bird.		EL	EGL	EGUL
closed	The little girl closed the door.		KD	KLOSD	CLOSSED
bumped	The car bumped into the bus.		B	BOPT	BUMMPED
type	Type your story on the computer		TP	TIP	TIPE

Source: based on Gentry and Gillet (1993)

with 'camped', 'tries', 'clapping' and 'riding'. For children in the year prior to Year 1, it will only be necessary for the teacher to call out approximately five (beginning of year) to fifteen (end of year) of the words. All twenty-six words should be called out for children in Years 1–3. If Year 3 children get more than twenty of the twenty-six words correct, it may be advantageous to use the Elementary Spelling Inventory (ESI) to find out more about their spelling. Once the PSI (or ESI) has been administered, the children's attempts are assessed with reference to a feature guide, which assists teachers to find out which spelling features children have control of, which they are attempting, and which are still beyond them. Features in the analysis include initial and final consonants, short vowels, digraphs, blends, long-vowel patterns, other vowels, and inflected endings. Analysing children's spelling in this way can help teachers tailor teaching to match children's needs with precision.

ASSESSMENT OF HANDWRITING

Handwriting style and fluency is important and ongoing assessment is essential to ensure that children do not slip into bad habits (such as incorrect grip) which can be very difficult to rectify. Depending on the age and development of the children, areas to assess through ongoing observation and analysis of writing samples include:

- Grip: child should grip pencil using the tripod grip.
- Posture: child should be sitting up straight with feet on the ground.
- Positioning: the paper should be correctly positioned.
- Letters: size, shape, spacing, formation, direction.
- Fluency: the child should write at an appropriate speed.
- Joins: letters are joined at the correct points.
- Affective factors: takes pride in writing neatly and legibly.

CHILDREN'S SELF-ASSESSMENT OF SPELLING

Self-assessment of spelling can be extremely powerful. Children can self-test and peer-test words they have learnt through the week from their spelling journal words. This can help them take responsibility for their spelling and allows for them to be tested on their personalised lists. Children can also self-assess the strategies they use to spell (see Table 21.9).

Table 21.9: Self-assessment checklist

How did I learn to spell this word?	
I used mnemonics	
I looked at the word parts	
I compared it with a word I already knew	
I sounded it out	
I did Look, Say, Cover, Write, Check until I got it right	
I thought about the meaning of the word and looked for the base word	

ASSESSMENT OF WRITING INTEREST AND MOTIVATION

Interest inventories have been developed by several authors and it is possible for teachers to modify these to suit their specific situation. In the Writing Attitude Survey (Kear, Coffman, McKenna & Ambrosio, 2000), children are asked to circle the 'Garfield' character that best describes how they feel about the different aspects of writing and what writing activities they enjoy during their spare time. Romeo (2008) has also devised an interest inventory that is suitable for young children, which features an appealing puppy. For each statement, children must circle the puppy that best represents their feelings about a writing activity (out of five drawings, which range from a very excited puppy to an unhappy one). The twenty-five questions asked include: 'How do you feel about writing stories?', 'How do you feel about writing letters and cards?' and, 'How do you feel about reading over something you wrote and trying to find any mistakes that you made?'

SUMMARY

Written communication involves the coordination of a range of skills, concepts and understandings, and the assessment of children's writing development and learning requires determining their knowledge and ability across a range of areas. The assessment methods of observation, analysis of children's written texts and conversations with children and their parents are effective for acquiring relevant and varied information. However, a clear and accurate picture of children's ability with written language and learning and development needs is more likely to be achieved with the additional use of more formal tests that focus in on explicit areas of written language.

QUESTIONS AND ACTIVITIES

1. Examine different formal assessments for writing and discuss their benefit or otherwise to the design of learning programs for young children that cater for children's writing development.
2. What do you view to be the most useful method to assess children's ability to write for different purposes?
3. Examine the written texts of different children and consider the type of feedback that you might provide the children that will motivate them with their writing efforts.
4. In what ways do the assessments of reading and writing overlap?
5. Why is it important to discuss children's writing efforts and ability with their family?
6. Create a chart that lists some appropriate writing outcomes for toddlers and that indicates the aspects of the learning environment and experiences that serve to help achieve the outcomes.
7. Design a recording sheet that you might use with a group of Year 2 or Year 3 children to record information that you glean from observing them as they write.

KEY TERMS

assessment
analysis
annotations
portfolio
rubrics

KEY REFERENCES

Bear, D. R., Invernessi, M., Templeton, S. & Johnston, F. (2004). *Words their way: Word study for phonics, vocabulary and spelling instruction*. Upper Saddle River: Pearson Education.

Clay, M. (2002). *An observation survey of early literacy* (2nd edn). Auckland: Heinemann.

Gentry, R. J. & Gillet, J. W. (1993). *Teaching Kids to Spell*. Portsmouth, NH: Heinemann.

Kear, D. J., Coffman, G. A., McKenna, M. C. & Ambrosio, A. L. (2000). Measuring attitude for writing: A new tool for teachers. *The Reading Teacher, 54*, 110–23.

Martin, S. (2010). *Take a look: Observation and portfolio assessment in early childhood*. Ontario: Pearson Education.

McGee, L. M. (2007). Language and literacy assessment in preschool. In J. R. Paratore & R. L. McCormack (eds), *Classroom literacy assessment: Making sense of what children know and do* (pp. 65–84). New York: The Guilford Press.

Romeo, L. (2008). Informal writing assessment linked to instruction: A continuous process for teachers, students, and parents. *Reading and Writing Quarterly, 24*(1), 25–51.

Tompkins, G. E. (2007). *Literacy for the 21st century: Teaching reading and writing in prekindergarten through grade 4*. Upper Saddle River, NJ: Pearson, Merrill Prentice Hall.

PART 4

Framing Language and Literacy Learning

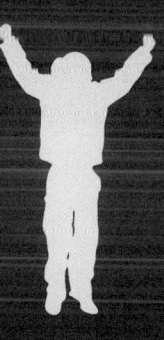

CHAPTER 22

Children's Literature

Helen Adam

CHAPTER OBJECTIVES

This chapter will increase your understanding of:

- the nature of children's literature and different types of books
- the role of literature in children's development and learning
- ways in which to assist children to respond to children's literature.

In this chapter, the role of literature in children's development and learning is explored with reference to several theoretical positions. Children's literature goes well beyond playing a major part in the development of literacy; it also has a role in developing children's sense of identity and self, their understandings about other people, and about values, society and the world. As you read this chapter, consider how literature can be used not just to teach literacy, but also to help each child's growth as a whole person. The chapter provides many practical ideas for teachers and childcare professionals which extend on the ideas presented in other chapters. However, there is plenty of scope for you to expand on these suggestions. A main focus of the chapter is 'reader response' and how to foster, encourage and develop reader response in order to enhance the development of the child as a whole.

WHAT IS CHILDREN'S LITERATURE?

Not all texts for children 'count' as children's literature, and there is some controversy about what 'children's literature' is. Hancock (2008, p. 33) suggests the following definition:

> Children's literature can be defined as literature that appeals to the interests, needs and reading preferences of children and captivates children as its major audience. Children's literature may be fictional, poetic or factual, or a combination of any of these.

Winch, Johnston, March, Ljungdahl and Holliday (2006) state that: 'Children's literature is usually defined as *literature for children*, or, less commonly, as *literature of children*.' They examine the challenges raised in defining the term, given the varying views of the stakeholders involved in children's literature—namely, the author, who writes from their own experience and position; those who select the books for children; and, of course, the children themselves, who make choices and respond to texts each in their own unique way. It is small wonder that the term children's literature is difficult to encapsulate in one firm definition.

It is, perhaps, Saxby (1997, p. 35) who enlightens us most by telling us what good literature *does,* rather than what it is:

> Literature entertains. It allows, too, for the re-creation of thoughts, sensations, dreams, feelings, fears, aspirations. It causes awe and wonder. It can bring joy. It can set off reverberations that are echoes of far-off, distant insights from times past. It can propel the reader into a more secure future as self-awareness and understanding is nourished and grows. Literature is life, illuminated and sweetened by the artist.

From the definitions above, it is clear that children's literature can be either fictional or informational, and it appears that the distinction between children's literature and other books has something to do with aesthetic quality and, perhaps, its ability to engage the reader on an emotional level. Quality children's literature engages the 'whole person' of the reader or listener, and children are drawn into the world created by the writer and are free to respond through their own feelings, emotions, senses and imaginations. Times and places in history, or other countries and cultures, become real to the reader and they can experience for themselves these other lives and times.

In terms of the teaching of literacy, children's literature constitutes a powerful resource for the teaching of reading and writing, provides tools for the teaching of critical and visual literacy skills, and provides an engaging medium for the development of speaking and listening skills. These vital literacy skills are covered in the other chapters of this book.

But above and beyond these, children's literature gives us the means to educate children about human behaviour, values, morals, and other cultures and times in history. Children's literature exposes children to a depth of life experience that they could otherwise not experience due to practical constraints.

THE PLACE OF CHILDREN'S LITERATURE IN THE CURRICULUM

LITERATURE AND LITERACY

In the Australian context, the *National English Curriculum Framing Paper* (National Curriculum Board, 2009) identifies literature as one of three key elements in the English curriculum, while, at the same time, recognising and highlighting the importance of literature to the overall learning and development of the child:

> Engaging with literary texts is worthwhile in its own right, but, importantly, it is also valuable in developing the imaginative application of ideas, flexibility of thought, ethical reflection, and motivation to learn. (p. 11)

Here, the value of literature is deemed to be in developing the child as a 'learner of life'. Emphasis is placed on the role of literature in developing the child's ability to think, reason and grow in logical and ethical understandings and applications.

> Literary texts engage students in a large part because of what they might learn about the human condition and, in conjunction with this, what they might learn about how language has been used to create particular emotional, intellectual, or philosophical effects. (p. 11)

In the above statement it is recognised that literature contributes more than just intellectual material to be learnt and studied. Literature has value in the personal and social development of the child and provides many aesthetic experiences that can develop and engage the child as a person. Recognition is rightly made of the essential aspect of enhancing language learning through experience of literature, but this framework stresses the role of literature in teaching children about the human condition.

Another key Australian curriculum document is *The Early Years Learning Framework for Australia* (EYLF) (DEEWR, 2009), which states as its key vision for children up to the age of five: 'All children experience learning that is engaging and builds success for life' (p. 7). The EYLF considers this in terms of the three key areas of *Belonging, Being* and *Becoming*:

- Belonging: 'Experiencing *belonging*—knowing where and with whom you belong—is integral to human existence …'
- Being: 'Childhood is a time to be, to seek and make meaning of the world'
- Becoming: 'Children's identities, knowledge, understandings, capacities, skills and relationships change during childhood … Becoming … emphasises learning to participate fully and actively in society.' (p. 7)

It is not difficult to see how children's literature can play a key role in helping children grow in the three areas, which are broken down further and elaborated on through the Learning Outcomes, Principles and Practice which form the Elements of the EYLF. While Outcome Five (Children are Effective Communicators) contains a clear focus on the role of texts in developing children's communication skills with specific regard to literacy. Frequent use of quality literature within the early years can make a valuable contribution to all of the outcomes and principles of the EYLF.

Good children's literature can provide children with models and understandings of *belonging*. Books written from different cultural perspectives can enhance a child's awareness of and tolerance for the diversity in their world. Furthermore, the use of such literature can ensure that the cultural and family background of each child is represented, assisting in the development of positive self-concept.

Books such as Maurice Sendak's (1963) *Where the wild things are* touch on the feelings experienced by children as they seek to find their place of belonging in their world. Young Max goes on his imaginative journey to a place where he is king and in control, but the poignant return to his room where his supper awaited him ('and it was still hot') encompasses the human desire of belonging and the security of knowing who we are.

Children's literature can also play a great part in developing the key area of *being*. Books that cover the themes of building and maintaining relationships with others can be of enormous benefit in exposing children to understandings of relationship with others. Books exploring life's joys and complexities can guide children in the development of their own sense of being, while at the same time gently leading them to an awareness of others and the wonder of diversity and variety in our world.

Careful selection and use of children's literature can greatly assist educators in encouraging respect for diversity. *Whoever you are* by Mem Fox (1998) is a book that sensitively takes children on a journey of discovery of the differences and, more importantly, the similarities, between all human beings.

The area of *becoming* is well encompassed in good quality children's literature. The EYLF states that, 'Children's identities, knowledge, understandings, capacities, skills and relationships change during childhood … Becoming reflects this process of rapid and significant change that occurs in the early years as young children learn and grow' (p. 7). Quality children's literature is carefully crafted to connect with the growing and developing child—children's authors connect with the child where they are and gently lead them through a journey of discovery of themselves and the world in which they live.

One of many such authors is Paulette Bourgeois who, in her series of Franklin books, deals with many common childhood issues such as: new classmates in *Franklin's new friend* (1997), keeping up with others in *Hurry up Franklin* (1989), honesty in *Franklin fibs* (1991), childhood fears in *Franklin in the dark* (1987), and many others. Children delight in the humour, the stories and the characters that are beautifully portrayed in the words and enhanced with the illustrative skills of Brenda Clark. While engaging with these stories, children can connect with the characters and the issues, subconsciously learning new ways to deal with life and to grow in confidence and understanding. The chart at the end of this chapter illustrates how children's literature might be used to help teachers address other EYLF outcomes.

THE ROLE OF THE TEACHER

It is the responsibility of every teacher, childcare professional and parent to lay the foundations for each child to access literature. Children need to enjoy literature, to hear it frequently and to engage with it in meaningful contexts. Also, they need to learn to read and interpret children's literature and to appreciate and understand the language of literature. By making literature a central and everyday part of a young child's experience, educators can pave the way for a child's learning journey and provide them with deep insight into what it means to be human.

Making literature a central part of every day can foster a lifelong love of literature and language.

Few would dispute the significant body of research that shows the relationship between young children's exposure to reading and literature and the development of their own literacy skills. The years prior to the commencement of formal learning have been recognised as being vital in laying the foundations for literacy development and, indeed, engagement in learning itself. Children who enter formal learning with a background depleted of exposure to, and enjoyment of, literature are less likely to succeed in literacy and more likely to disengage from learning. Ultimately, this affects the child for the whole of their life (Centre for Community Child Health, 2006).

Thus, the exposure of children to the love, learning and experience of literature must begin in a child's early years. In fact, it should begin with the life of the child itself and become an everyday part of their existence and life experience. With many children now spending some part of their early years in childcare, it is important for childcare professionals to understand the importance of this exposure and how best to implement literature and literature-based activities in their centres and daily routines. By understanding that, not only are they caring for the child, but they also have a significant role to play in the development of the child's learning journey. Childcare professionals can strive to give children in their care an enriching experience of literature that can and should begin when they are babies.

RESPONSE TO LITERATURE

Having explored and understood the value and importance of children's literature in supporting children in their overall social, emotional and learning development, it is necessary for educators and caregivers to consider how best to use literature with this end in mind.

The most important aspect that teachers and carers must consider with children's literature is that of **reader/listener response**. The child must be allowed to be drawn into the text and respond through their own senses, imagination and feelings. This interaction of text, reader and/or listener is a different and unique experience for each participant and even varies with multiple readings of the same text.

Maurice Saxby (1997) draws on several past examples of research when he discusses what happens when we read (or are read to) in terms of three key theories:

1. Psychological theories—the psychological response is broken into the subcategories of:
   - identification, in which the reader 'identifies with a fictional character and is able to see, feel and think through that persona' (Saxby, 1997, p. 67)
   - projection, in which the reader 'may also well turn a character into an echo of themselves, projecting their own feelings and motivation onto the character' (Saxby, 1997, p. 67)
   - the spectator role, in which the reader 'takes on the role of an onlooker or bystander' (Saxby, 1997, p. 67). The reader responds to the text with differing emotions or insights which can vary with the text and the reader.
2. Psychoanalytic theories—the psychoanalytic response theorists believe that readers can allow themselves to be drawn emotionally into the archetypal struggles apparent in literature, and, through 'surrendering' to the experience, they can gain resolution or reconciliation to their own life struggles and experiences or, at least, comfort in knowing that 'they are not alone'.

3   Psycholinguistic theory: transactional theory—the response to a text is dependent on the reader as much as the text and the interplay between the two.

It is this third theory that most strongly guides educators in their efforts to understand and encourage reader response. Louise Rosenblatt (1978) is well known for her **transactional theory** of reader response: 'The theory focuses on the reciprocal relationship between the reader and the literature that results in individual responses to the text during and following engaged reading of literature' (Hancock, 2008, p. 5). It is the work of Rosenblatt that has led to the recognition and acknowledgment by educators of the importance of literature as an essential part of the whole learning curriculum and not just an isolated part of the teaching of literacy.

The written word can only truly 'come to life' in the mind of the reader or the listener, and much depends on their prior experiences. The writer writes with their own purposes, thoughts and ideas, but it is the mind and response of the audience which enlivens and translates the writing. As explained in Chapters 8 and 9, readers and listeners make meaning by using information from the text and relating this to what they already know: 'Each reader thus evokes his or her own meaning from the same text' (Hancock, 2008, p. 248). Hancock uses the words of Sebesta (2001) to sum up the relationship of the participant (reader/listener) and the writer: 'The author isn't boss anymore, but neither is the reader. It's what they come up with together that makes the literary experience.'

Chase and Hynd (1987, p. 537) give us this summary of the consensus of thought regarding reader response:

> 1. Meaning is not 'contained' in the text but is derived from an interaction between the content and the structure of the author's message and the experience and prior knowledge of the reader.
> 2. Readers comprehend differently because every reader is culturally and individually unique.
> 3. Examining readers' response to text is more valid than establishing one correct interpretation of text meaning.

THE ENVIRONMENT FOR READING AND RESPONSE

To provide an environment that promotes and encourages response to literature, educators must consider and plan for the following elements.

TYPES OF BOOKS

The environment of the childcare centre, kindergarten, pre-school centre or classroom should have plenty of accessible, high-quality children's literature. As the child grows they will begin to make their own choices about qualities and types of stories and books they prefer. The greater the depth and variety of books, the greater the opportunity to expose the children to a wealth of children's literature.

Machado (2007), Saxby (1997) and many other experts tell us that the literature environment of the young child should incorporate high-quality books from the following categories (note that many books fit into more than one category).

Story books (picture books)

These will include nursery rhymes, fairy tales, animal tales, folk tales, adventure and mystery, and so on. These books should contain a variety of themes and exposure to other cultures and times in history as well as Australian literature.

Non-fiction or content books

These books can expand the child's knowledge and stimulate their natural curiosity about the world around them. New vocabulary and concepts will be learnt through these books. Children will begin to discover how to read to learn.

Wordless books

These books provide the child with the opportunity to 'tell' the story; in doing so they are experimenting with their vocabulary, sequencing and imagination.

Interactive books

Pop-up books, flap books, flip books, touch and feel books etc. can delight and engage the child by encouraging them to interact with the story and the pages. The kinaesthetic qualities of these books build the multi-sensory learning of the child as well as provide opportunities for fine motor development.

Concept books—with a central concept or theme

These books can help develop categorisation and help children build on knowledge and understandings.

Predictable books

Books containing repetition and reinforcement encourage and reward the children intrinsically. Children can grow in confidence as they can predict what will happen, or what the next word is. They learn that books make sense. They can tell the story accurately in their own words as they turn the pages, thus enabling retell and recall. It is these books that enable children to begin to read along and, therefore, the children will pick these books up themselves and 'imitate' the reading process. Before long many children will successfully recognise and point to the correct words as they say them, thus giving them their first 'real' reading experiences.

Reference books

Books that can be accessed to answer questions provide opportunities for one-on-one sharing between the teacher and child. Individual learning can be promoted and children can find areas that are of particular interest to them. The teacher can enhance children's understanding of reading to learn by accessing these books frequently.

Alphabet, counting and word books

These simple bright books are also often sturdy and designed for the child to handle frequently. The child can see models of letters, numbers and words and can often begin to identify these through these books.

Novelty books

These can include pop-up books, fold outs, electronic books, activity books that include pasting, gluing or colouring, electronic talking books, and so on. These provide another series of interactive opportunities which stimulate and engage the child as well as drawing on their five senses and promoting kinaesthetic learning and fine motor coordination.

Paperback books and magazines

These books are relatively inexpensive and contain many classic stories (for example, Little Golden Books) and a wide variety of story types.

Real-life themes and multicultural/cross-cultural books

Many children's books deal with real-life issues in a sensitive way, offering understanding, empathy and solutions. Issues such as separated families, death, new babies and moving house are covered in well-written fictional stories. Stories about other cultures and lifestyles help increase understanding and positive attitudes towards diversity in society. They can assist children to discuss and work through their own feelings, fears and experiences. In addition, they present to children accurate reflections of the diverse society in which they live.

Seasonal and holiday books

Books that centre on the seasons, both climatic and cultural, assist children in understanding and anticipating the cycles and variety of their lives. Celebrations such as Christmas, birthdays and the like are of relevance and interest to the child and can be added into the program at appropriate times of the year.

Board, fabric or plastic books

Babies, toddlers and young children should have access to these well-constructed books. As well as being resistant to damage, they are easier to hold and manipulate.

Bilingual or multilingual books

There is an increasing number of children's books being produced with text in both English and other languages, including several of the Indigenous Australian languages. These books are of great use in promoting diversity and inclusivity and encouraging understanding of other cultures, traditions and histories.

Many of these books are also produced in big book format which provide wonderful opportunities to share books with larger groups of children. Other useful formats are audiovisual combinations of books with tapes, DVDs etc., each of which provides additional ways for children to experience and engage in literature.

Other types of texts

Movies, cartoons, educational programs, audio resources, CD-ROMs and web-based multimedia stories etc. provide other text types to engage and stimulate children. These can enhance their learning and understanding by linking with different learning preferences. Many popular stories are available in these formats and this provides opportunities for children to compare different media, even at a very young age.

CHOOSING BOOKS FOR BABIES AND TODDLERS

The types of books to have in the environment of the baby and young toddler need to be selected with the following points in mind. Not each book will fit all points, but this is a guide as to what to look for when stocking the bookshelves in a childcare centre:

- Books that contain bright, simple, bold pictures—these books help the young child to focus clearly and to learn to identify familiar objects and scenes.
- Books that contain repetitive rhymes and rhythm—these can be poems, nursery rhymes, songs or simple stories, all of which can expose children to the variety and rhythm of language sounds.
- Books that the carer enjoys—this should not be overlooked. If the reader enjoys a book, then they can find it easier to pass on their natural enthusiasm to the children in their care.
- Books that can safely be left in the child's reach, even in their cot.
- Books that are appropriate to the child's age.

'Careful consideration should be given to selecting books that are appropriate to the child's age. Children younger than three (and many older than this age) enjoy physical closeness, the visual changes of illustrations, and the sound of the human voice reading text. The rhythms and poetry of picture books intrigue them. Experts point out that very young children's "syntactic dependence" is displayed by their obvious delight in recognised word order. The sounds of language in picture books may be far more important than the meanings conveyed to the very young child.' (Machado, 2007)

Reading is a great way for family members to engage and relate to a child of any age.

READING AND READING RESPONSE

First, the reader must consider their own attitude to the task—here is an opportunity to engage and relate to the child. Not only that, but here is a chance for the educator to actively enjoy reading and engaging with the child. Reading time should be an enjoyable time for both the educator and the child. This is the time when positive attitudes can be modelled and passed on to the child. Reading to the child should never be simply a task that needs to be ticked off on a daily duties list.

> ### THE CHILD AS A READER
>
> The importance of making suitable books accessible for the very young child must not be underestimated. By being permitted and encouraged to handle books the child will be able to naturally develop their interest in books and reading. As stated previously, children love to imitate and learn by doing so; by having access to books these young children will begin to imitate the reading process—the turning of pages and the babbling of words as they do so. In time this will lead to them recognising, first, pictures and later words, giving them great pleasure, pride and motivation. The carer must not only ensure this access to books but also actively encourage the children to engage with them. The youngster should be praised for their efforts whenever possible.

Reading

The reader needs to read the book clearly and with expression—not forced or condescending but in a natural melodious voice showing rhythm and expression. The reader, by familiarising themselves with the book beforehand, can enhance the whole reading experience. With a good source of quality literature the reader should select a book that they enjoy themselves as reader attitude has a powerful effect on the listener.

Reading can be varied to achieve different purposes—at times read the whole book in a melodious expressive voice and allow the child to enjoy the sounds and rhythm of different kinds of language as they look and listen. At other times point to the objects or words and actively engage the child or children by questioning them and allowing them to respond and contribute.

Oral response to texts can take a variety of forms which the teacher or carer can utilise to encourage and develop the children's abilities to process and respond to literature.

The very young child can be encouraged to respond to literature through three simple questions improvised by David Bleich (1978, cited in Hancock, 2008, p. 253):

- What did you notice in the story?
- How did the story make you feel?
- What does the story remind you of from your own life?

Other questions and reader 'think alouds' can also be used; for example:

- I wonder why Sam did that?
- What do you think will happen next?

- I think I would do …
- Who do you like in this story?

These questions allow individual responses—each child is free to respond in their own context and from their own experience. Over time, this will scaffold the children's understanding and assist in their ability to respond orally. Children will discover the joy of delving into a text themselves and recognise that their response is valued and encouraged. By providing many opportunities for 'book talk', children will become increasingly comfortable with expressing their response. Their enjoyment of story time and literature will increase accordingly.

Encouraging response

Encouraging the child to be an active participant in the reading process has already been discussed, but there is much more that can be done in response to reading. Following the reading, the educator can involve the children in games, song and dance to extend the fun and encourage children to respond to the literature. Children could stomp around like a giant or tiptoe like a mouse following the reading of a relevant story. Children can often provide the ideas and incentive here. The role of the teacher could be to provide shared time for a response: ask questions, play 'Guess who I am?' by acting out a character etc. Any activity can take place that enables the children to recall and respond to the story, whether teacher- or child-initiated. Recordings of nursery rhymes and stories can also be played for infants and children to listen to and respond to in their own manner and time. The emphasis with very young children should be on enjoyment, and spontaneity should be encouraged.

RESPONSE THROUGH INTEGRATED ACTIVITIES

Many of the everyday type of activities of the early childhood environment can be adjusted or adapted to create an opportunity for response to children's literature.

DRESS UPS

Most young children love the opportunity to play dress ups. A dress-up box or corner is easy to set up, often at little cost with the donation of old clothing, shoes, hats etc. Simple costumes can be made at reasonable cost, often by willing parent helpers. Giving the children access on a regular basis to the dress-up box provides a stimulating opportunity for them to use their imagination and engage in role play. The teacher or carer often needs to do no more than provide the opportunity, since most children will naturally engage and motivate themselves and each other. Many children that can usually seem quite reticent can be transformed with a mask or costume. Children will often interact and re-create stories together.

This gives them the opportunity to respond to literature in an informal and unstructured way. The teacher or carer can join in with this response through dressing up also or encouraging the play through questioning and guiding or making suggestions for direction of play. At other times the dress ups could be used as a more structured response in which the teacher directs the children to act out different characters or scenarios. This could include text reconstruction or innovation in which parts of the story are changed or added to. As described earlier, the educator can 'think aloud', model or ask questions to encourage the children.

Dress-ups give children a chance to retell a story.

SOCIO-DRAMATIC PLAY

Consider transforming part or all of the room into a castle, a cave, a deserted island, a fairy kingdom or a dragon's lair for a period of time. With a little imagination and easily sourced materials such as tulle, netting, cardboard and egg cartons the room can be changed into many different environments. As with the dress-up box, the children then have a stimulus for spontaneous response to children's literature in which the teacher may simply need to provide prompts, ideas or encouragement for the children to use their recall and their imaginations through their play. Without even realising it, the children are developing their ability to retell a story and to reconstruct a story or engage in text innovation.

ART AND CRAFT RESPONSE

With a ready supply of art and craft materials such as those available in most pre-school centres and classrooms, many children will spontaneously respond to literature through art and craft. Paintings, drawings, play-dough figures, collage and the like can be produced by the child by their own choice and design. The teacher and carer can enhance this activity by discussing the child's work and questioning them on the content and its meaning—this takes the visual work and enhances it with dialogue. The teacher can ask the child if they would like the teacher to write the child's version or description of the work onto the work itself. Older children can attempt to write their own text. This can be integrated into writing activities within the classroom.

In addition to this opportunity for spontaneous artistic response, the teacher and carer can plan activities to allow artistic response to literature. This can be done by providing pre-prepared sheets/drawing/collage materials and the like that relate to a book that is shared with the children. The children are then guided to respond artistically through such activities as:

- Illustrate the story, or part of the story—retell in pictures.
- Re-create or draw an aspect of the story—e.g. character, setting—through different materials, e.g. painting, clay, 'box corner', cutting/gluing, and so on.
- Draw an alternative ending to the story—or create another character through art, and so on.

Whole group art and craft activities can be carried out with input from children as they wish. A large collage could be made of a scene from a story; a story could be recreated with each child illustrating one scene or page; a model of setting and characters can be made as a group. During each of these activities, much discussion, decision making, recall and response will take place as a matter of course.

The teacher or carer can guide response through 'think alouds' and questions such as:

- 'I wonder what the princess's dress would look like.'
- 'Where do you think the frog pond would go?'
- 'How can we make the cave seem dark and scary?'
- 'What do you think it would feel like if you lived in the castle we have made?'

All of this enhances and encourages the children's response to and enjoyment of literature.

THEME DAYS

Occasional theme days can be held in which the children, and hopefully the teachers and carers, dress up as characters from a particular story or theme. This can lead to a day of activities such as role play, retell, drama and constant spontaneous response.

BOOK CORNER

The book corner is a vital part of the early childhood environment of a child. Well stocked with a variety of books drawn from the types mentioned previously, it provides children with the opportunity to develop their understanding and love of literature through self-selection of books. Children should be encouraged to look at the books and read to whatever ability they have as often as possible. The teacher can engage incidentally with children through sharing books, discussing them, questioning or simply showing interest in the child's choice of book.

OTHER ACTIVITIES

Many other common activities can be used as an opportunity to encourage response to literature:

- shapes for play-dough cut-outs, e.g. stars, three bears and
- outdoor play such as building sand castles, forts, tents with sheets and
- children's spontaneous play.

These and many others can be turned into valuable opportunities with the teacher or carer engaging with the children and encouraging them through joining in, suggesting alternative ideas, and questioning them reflectively.

Table 22.1: Using children's literature to address Australian EYLF Outcomes 1–4

Outcomes and contexts of each outcome	Books	Themes/ content	Examples of how this can assist educators to promote the child's learning (from EYLF)
Outcome 1: Children have a strong sense of identity			
Children feel safe, secure and supported.	*A home for Bilby* by Joanne Crawford (2004)	Feelings Friendship Belonging	• Acknowledge each child's uniqueness in positive ways • Support children's expressions of their thoughts and feelings
Children develop their emerging autonomy, interdependence, resilience and sense of agency.	*Koala Lou* by Mem Fox (1988)	Belonging Individual achievements Persistence	• Promote children's sense of wellbeing, connectedness and belonging • Display delight, encouragement and enthusiasm for children's attempts • Motivate and encourage children to succeed when faced with challenges
Children develop knowledgeable and confident self-identities.	*Dougal the garbage dump bear* by Matt Dray (2004)	Self-esteem Friendship Identity	• Talk with children in respectful ways about similarities and differences in people • Promote in all children a strong sense of who they are
Children learn to interact in relation to others with care, empathy and respect.	*Just a joke* by Karen Sapp (2007)	Friendship Tolerance Forgiveness	• Acknowledge children's complex relationships and sensitively intervene in ways that promote consideration of alternative perspectives and social inclusion
Outcome 2: Children are connected with and contribute to their world			
Children develop a sense of belonging to groups and communities and an understanding of reciprocal rights and responsibilities necessary for active community participation.	*Greetings from Sandy Beach* by Bob Graham (1990)	Concern for others Diversity Tolerance Inclusivity	• Encourage children to respect diverse perspectives • Promote a sense of community • Provide opportunities for children to investigate ideas, complex concepts and ethical issues that are relevant to their lives and the local community
Children respond to diversity with respect.	*Whoever you are* by Mem Fox (1998)	Similarities and differences between people Diversity Respect	• Reflect on their own responses to diversity • Engage in interactions with children that promote respect for diversity and value distinctiveness • Demonstrate positive responses to diversity

Outcomes and contexts of each outcome	Books	Themes/content	Examples of how this can assist educators to promote the child's learning (from EYLF)
Children become aware of fairness.	*Franklin's secret club* By Paulette Bourgeois (1998)	Fairness Compassion Friendship Inclusion	• Discuss diverse perspectives on issues of inclusion and exclusion and fair and unfair behaviour • Draw children's attention to issues of fairness relevant to them in the early childhood setting and community
Children become socially responsible and show respect for the environment.	*The hidden forest* by Jeannie Baker (2000)	Understanding and respect for the natural environment Environmental relationships	• Model respect, care and appreciation for the natural environment • Share information and provide resources about the environment, and the impact of human activities on the environment
Outcome 3: Children have a strong sense of wellbeing			
Children become strong in their social and emotional wellbeing.	*Together* by Jane Simmons (2006)	Friendship Sharing humour, happiness and satisfaction Personal achievements	• Promote children's sense of belonging, connectedness and wellbeing • Talk with children about their responses to events with a view to supporting their understandings of emotional regulation and control
Children take increasing responsibility for their own health and physical wellbeing.	*Chocolatina* by Erik Kraft (2003)	Desires Nutrition Care for oneself	• Engage children in experiences and conversations that promote healthy lifestyles and good nutrition • Model and reinforce health and nutrition practices
Outcome 4: Children are confident and involved learners			
Children develop dispositions for learning such as curiosity, cooperation, confidence, enthusiasm, persistence, imagination and reflexivity.	*Harry's box* by Angela McAllister (2003)	Imagination Play Curiosity Confidence Enthusiasm	• Recognise and value children's involvement in learning • Encourage children to engage in both individual and collaborative explorative learning processes • Model enquiry processes, including wonder, curiosity and imagination, try new ideas and take in new challenges

Outcomes and contexts of each outcome	Books	Themes/content	Examples of how this can assist educators to promote the child's learning (from EYLF)
Children develop a range of skills and processes such as problem solving, enquiry, experimentation, hypothesising, researching and investigating.	*All about magnifying glasses* by Melvin Berger (1993)	Enquiry Experimentation Hypothesising Investigating	• Provide resources that offer challenge, intrigue and surprise, support their investigations and share their enjoyment • Provide opportunities for involvement in experiences that support the investigation of ideas, concepts and thinking, reasoning and hypothesising
Children transfer and adapt what they have learnt from one context to another.	*If* by Sarah Perry (1995)	Visual stimulation Imagination Reflection 'What if'	• Provide learning environments that are flexible and open ended • Listen carefully to children's ideas • Provide opportunities for children to revisit their ideas and extend their thinking
Children resource their own learning through connecting with people, places, technologies and natural and processed materials.	*Killer plants and how to grow them* by Gordon Cheers and Julie Silk (1996)	• Nature • Investigation • Cultivation	• Provide opportunities and support for children to engage in meaningful learning relationships • Provide sensory and exploratory experiences with natural and processed materials

SUMMARY

In this chapter the importance of children's literature as a tool for facilitating child development has been discussed: children's literature has a significant role to play in the cognitive, social and emotional, language and literacy, and moral development of young children.

It has been noted that 'what counts' as children's literature is contested, but most definitions refer to the aesthetic qualities of children's literature. Children need to be given opportunities to engage with literature and to respond to it freely. Most importantly, it has been argued in this chapter that enjoyment is paramount, and that teachers should ensure that children use children's literature as a means of developing positive attitudes to reading.

QUESTIONS AND ACTIVITIES

1. What is 'reader response' and how can teachers ensure that young children are able to respond in meaningful and diverse ways to the literature they hear or read?
2. How would you define children's literature? Which kinds of texts would you *not* include in your definition, and why? Should all texts intended for children be included?
3. How can children's literature be used to teach concepts across the curriculum? Locate and analyse some children's stories that might be used to teach science concepts, for example.
4. Go to the children's section of your local library and select three fictional books that show different cultures. How might you use these in your centre or classroom to help children understand cultural diversity?
5. Refer to the earlier chapters on comprehension and vocabulary. How might you use children's literature to teach comprehension strategies such as predicting, visualising and summarising? How might you use children's literature to enhance children's vocabulary and oral language?

KEY TERMS

reader/listener response
transactional theory

KEY REFERENCES

Centre for Community Child Health (2006). *Literacy promotion*. Available on www.rch.org.au/emplibrary/ccch/PR_Literacy_S1.pdf.

Chase, N. D. & Hynd, C. R. (1987). Reader response: An alternative way to teach children to think about text. *Journal of Reading, 30*, 530–40.

Department of Education, Employment and Workplace Relations (DEEWR) (2009). *Belonging, being and becoming: The Early Years Learning Framework for Australia*. Barton, ACT: Commonwealth of Australia.

Hancock, M. R. (2008). *A celebration of children's literature and response* (3rd edn). New Jersey: Pearson.

Machado, J. M. (2007). *Early childhood experiences in language arts: Early literacy*. Emerita: Thomson.

National Curriculum Board (2009). *The shape of the Australian Curriculum: English*. Retrieved 4/12/2009 from www.acara.edu.au/verve/_resources/Australian_Curriculum_-_English.pdf.

Rosenblatt, L. M. (1978). *The reader, the text, the poem: The transactional theory of the literary work*. Carbondale: Southern Illinois University Press.

Saxby, M. H. (1997). *Books in the life of a child*. South Yarra: Macmillan.

Sebasta, S. (2001). What do teachers need to know about children's literature? *The New Advocate, 14*, 241–49.

Winch, G., Johnston, R. R., March, P., Ljungdahl, L. & Holliday, M. (2006). *Literacy: Reading, writing and children's literature* (3rd edn). South Melbourne: OUP.

CHAPTER 23

Visual and Critical Literacy

CHAPTER OBJECTIVES

This chapter will increase your understanding of:

- the terms 'critical literacy' and 'viewing'
- why it is important to teach critical literacy and viewing
- various elements of images, both static and moving
- appropriate teaching strategies for viewing and critical literacy in the early years.

In this chapter, you will learn about aspects of literacy that were not traditionally taught in early childhood contexts. Indeed, they were often not taught at all until the notion of 'multiliteracies' changed the agenda in literacy teaching. These aspects of literacy are now part and parcel of reading and writing and should not be thought of as separable. However, they have been discussed separately in this book for reasons of clarity.

MULTILITERACIES

Multiliteracies theory arose when the New London Group (NLG) (1996) argued that the notion of literacy should be broadened to reflect linguistic and cultural diversity as well as the multiplicity of communication channels at people's disposal with which to make and transmit meaning. In other words, the increase in the prevalence of computer-based multimedia texts, DVDs and picture books, along with the reduced cost of technologies with which to create such texts, has changed the textual landscape dramatically. Because multimodal texts can be very complex, children need to be explicitly taught how to read and write them. Since the mid 1990s, educators and researchers have significantly extended the work of the NLG and have devised exciting practices that can assist children in becoming multiliterate.

Another aspect of being multiliterate involves being able to understand that people from different cultures and social groups have different ways of 'doing' literacy and valuing literacy. In our increasingly globalised world, it is important that children come to appreciate this.

The Muliliteracies Map (Table 23.1), developed in South Australia (DECS, 2010), is a useful framework that can be used to conceptualise what needs to be taught in early childhood contexts as far as multiliteracies is concerned. The framework is loosely based on Luke and Freebody's four resources (Luke & Freebody, 1999), which have been discussed earlier in this book.

Table 23.1: Muliliteracies Map

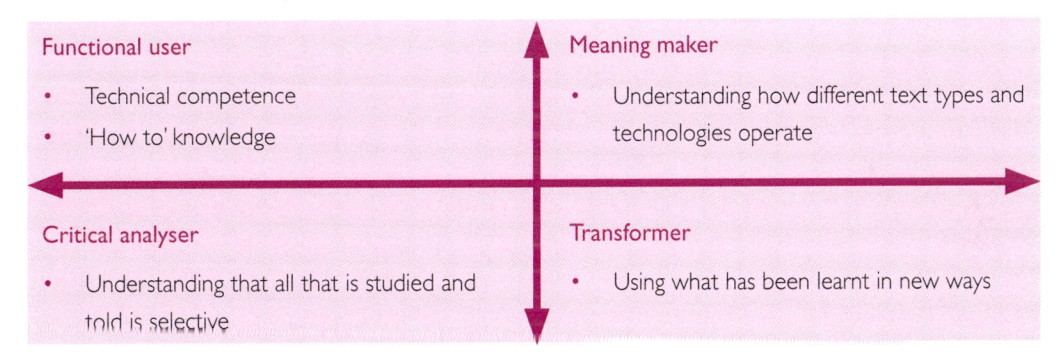

Functional user	Meaning maker
• Technical competence • 'How to' knowledge	• Understanding how different text types and technologies operate
Critical analyser	**Transformer**
• Understanding that all that is studied and told is selective	• Using what has been learnt in new ways

- The *functional* dimension is to do with acquiring technical competence and 'how to' knowledge. This might involve knowing how to use computers or video cameras, recognising and understanding icons when using the computer, or knowing how to decode sounds and symbols (including letter–sound correspondences).
- The *meaning-making* dimension is to do with understanding how to make meaning from different text types and technologies and how they can be used for a variety of purposes. Here, it is particularly important to draw children's attention to the form of text and how this links to the purpose.
- The *critical* dimension is to do with building an understanding that there can be multiple ways of looking at things and that there is no 'universal truth' in any text; authors select what to include for particular reasons, and these must be considered when reading or writing a text. Also, the critical dimension involves being able to select appropriate tools, texts and technology for a particular literacy task.
- The *transformative* dimension is very important and is to do with learning how to use what has been learnt in novel ways and situations.

It is beyond the scope of this chapter to discuss all elements of multiliteracies so the focus will be on critical literacy and viewing. You will find that the chapter in this book on Literacy and ICT is also relevant to multiliteracies.

Viewing (visual literacy) and critical literacy involve reading and viewing texts in a critical way, thinking about the author or illustrator's craft and intentions, and evaluating texts in the light of information about the author's or illustrator's background and known beliefs. Being critical also involves interrogating one's own values, beliefs and assumptions and becoming aware of how these may affect our interpretation of texts. A critical stance towards texts is necessary to minimise the possibility of being manipulated or misled, and to ensure a full appreciation of how authors and illustrators carefully craft texts in order to fulfil particular purposes and to encourage particular responses. Without this critical element, full comprehension of texts cannot occur.

According to Annandale et al. (2004, p. 59), children need to learn that:

- Authors and illustrators present a view of the world that can be challenged.
- Authors and illustrators represent facts, events, characters and people in different ways.
- Authors and illustrators use devices to achieve a specific purpose.

As noted above, viewing and critical literacy involve identifying and analysing **devices** used by authors and illustrators to create particular meanings or moods. A device can be seen as a 'trick of the trade' or a way of crafting an image or written text (using codes and conventions) to encourage the reader or viewer to feel, think or act in a particular way. Children need to be able to recognise and discuss the devices used by authors and illustrators, and be able to understand how these devices affect people's responses to texts. They also need to learn how to use such devices when creating their own texts. Not all people will respond to a particular text in the same way, and children need to understand why this may be so.

For children in their early childhood years, the above understandings can reach a surprisingly sophisticated level, although it is of course necessary for educators to gear teaching and learning activities towards the particular needs, interests and abilities of the children concerned. The use of terminology may be adjusted for very young (pre-school) children in favour of more everyday language, even though it is necessary for children to acquire the language of visual and critical literacy in the longer term. For reasons of clarity, we are discussing visual and critical literacy separately in this chapter, although it should be noted that these will more often than not be taught and discussed together, since written and visual texts interact with each other to create meaning.

CRITICAL LITERACY

> Critical literacy is an approach to literacy that involves analysing and questioning texts to reveal the beliefs and values behind the surface meanings, and to see how a reader can be influenced and affected. By interrogating texts, readers become aware of how language is used to position particular social and cultural groups and practices, often preserving relationships of power. (Annandale et al., 2004b, p. 56)

Not everyone agrees what critical literacy *is* because 'doing' critical literacy changes from one context to another (Knobel & Healy, 1998), and it has even been suggested that the term 'critical literacies' may be appropriate. However, there does appear to be general agreement that critical literacy involves questioning texts and challenging what is presented by the author, even (especially) when the author's message seems to be quite straightforward, neutral and unbiased. Building children's ability to recognise that *no* text is neutral, and that all authors have values, perspectives and agendas, is one of the main aims of critical literacy teaching.

Children need to learn how to analyse and 'problematise' texts so that bias, values and unequal power relationships are exposed (Comber, 1993). Also, they need to become aware that they are *positioned* by texts; texts encourage readers, often in very subtle ways, to think and feel a certain way, and even to perceive themselves in a particular way. Children need to come to realise that texts can be interpreted in multiple ways, and that different people will often 'read' texts and respond to them in different ways. Ultimately, people who are critically literate are able to: critique texts; detect bias, assumptions and values in texts; think about their own interpretations of texts and compare them with the interpretations of others; and take social action as a means of challenging or changing the status quo. In terms of the four reader resources or practices, described in Chapter 8, critical literacy aligns with the **text analyst** practice (Freebody & Luke, 1992).

CRITICAL LITERACY INVOLVES:

- seeing texts as social constructions that are not neutral
- doing 'alternative readings' (from different positions) to find multiple perspectives
- thinking about the author's beliefs and values
- thinking about one's own beliefs and values
- asking questions of texts
- uncovering and challenging values and assumptions in texts
- identifying and questioning stereotypes in texts
- understanding that texts are 'powerful'
- using texts as a springboard to advocate for social justice and change.

Some educators argue that it is not necessary and appropriate to teach critical literacy to young children, and that the focus should be squarely on 'the basics' such as the ability to decode words. Indeed, many textbooks on literacy learning in the early years barely mention critical literacy. A number of educators express the fear that critical literacy may somehow spoil children's enjoyment of literature, or detract from the 'magic' of stories. It can be immensely difficult and confronting for educators to break away from choosing 'safe, happy books' (Hefferman, 2004, p. 4) to read to children. Despite all this, a body of educators and researchers maintain that the teaching of literacy should take in a broad definition of literacy right from the start (Hassett, 2006) and that children as young as three years of age are perfectly capable of talking about 'difficult topics or issues' if teachers and caregivers enable this by opening up the discourses used (Vasquez, 2007, p. 6). Indeed, reading, writing and talking about real issues that matter to the children can result in more motivated readers and writers (Hefferman, 2004). Our own view is that critical literacy is an aspect of comprehension and is integral to learning about purposes of texts, so it can and should be introduced early, primarily through questioning and discussion. However, it is not desirable or necessary to deconstruct every single text read. In the section that follows, we describe some teaching procedures for 'doing' critical literacy in early childhood contexts, although it is unfortunately beyond the scope of this chapter to go into great depth.

TEACHING CRITICAL LITERACY

Critical literacy can be taught through three broad approaches: deconstruction, reconstruction and juxtaposition of texts. Deconstruction involves the analysis of texts, or 'taking them apart' to see how they have been crafted. Key questions include:

- What effect does the text have?
- How did the author manage to achieve this?
- What devices has the author used?

Reconstruction involves changing a text in some way to see how this alters the meaning and the effect. A simple example of this involves asking children to change some of the adjectives or 'describing words' in a text. This can be done either orally or in writing.

Juxtaposition is to do with the comparison of texts. Children can compare two versions of the same story, for example, and then discuss what the differences and similarities are, and how the differences impact on the meaning and on their response.

BROAD APPROACHES TO TEACHING CRITICAL LITERACY

- *deconstruction*: analysis of texts (language features, pictures, structure)
- *reconstruction*: putting texts together again in a different way and analysing the effects
- *juxtaposition*: comparing texts.

Questioning and discussion is a key means of developing critical literacy. During shared reading there is ample scope for early childhood educators to make comments (think aloud) and to ask questions about texts and how they have been crafted. There are some generic questions that can be used with a wide variety of texts (Annandale et al., 2004a, p. 65). Examples are shown below:

- 'Do you know anyone like this character? How are they like the character? How are they different?'
- 'Do you think this could really happen? Why/why not?'
- 'Why did the author use the words "flopped down" and not "sat down"?'
- 'Why do you think the author has chosen the name Doris as this character's name?'
- 'Is there anything important you know about that the author has left out?'
- 'Who/what seems important in this story? How did the author make this character look important?'

- 'How do you feel about this story? Why do you think you feel that way?'
- 'Have we read any other books by this author? What do you think this author might be like as a person? Where did he grow up?'

Questions encouraging children to make comparisons between texts are also powerful in terms of helping children build their critical awareness. An example would be: 'We read another version of *The three bears* last week, didn't we? Which version do you like better? Why is that?'

For young children who are still role-play or experimental-phase readers, Annandale et al. (2004a, pp. 66–8) suggest such activities as the *goodies and baddies ratings scale, catalogue searches, changing places, like or unlike* and *text innovation*, which will be briefly described below. All of these activities involve deconstruction, reconstruction or juxtaposition. For maximum usefulness, a good deal of discussion and questioning should be incorporated in all of these activities. Apart from the generic approaches described above, there are structured experiences that can be used. Many of these are more appropriate for children in lower primary than for pre-school children. Some of these are outlined below.

The *goodies and baddies ratings scale* involves children judging the characteristics or traits of characters in books using information from the text in conjunction with their own personal experiences. Children are asked to rate characters according to traits—for example, 'happiest', 'smartest', 'sneakiest' or 'nastiest'. They must then justify their ratings. This activity encourages children to search the text for clues that the author has given (or devices he or she has used). As with other critical literacy activities, this activity is most beneficial if it entails discussion between children. Not everybody will have come to the same conclusions or will have made the same interpretations, and discussions around these multiple perspectives can deepen children's understandings.

Table 23.2: Goodies and baddies ratings scale

Who was the:	Character ranking	I/We thought this because …
Scariest	1. Terrible tongued dragon	He has fire coming out of his mouth. He is big and fierce.
	2. General Min	She can pounce and she can sneak.
Book: *Drac and the gremlin* by Allan Baillie and Jane Tanner	3. Gremlin of the groaning grotto	He is dangerous and quick and quiet as a spider.

Catalogue searches are a useful means of helping children think about the impact advertising material can have on people and the devices, both written and visual, that advertisers use to persuade people to desire or buy their products. For this activity, children are given a variety of catalogues, such as Mothers Day or toys catalogues (junk mail), and asked to discuss the types of items that are for sale, the words and pictures the advertisers have used, who might buy the products in the catalogues, and how the people and objects have been represented in the catalogues.

Changing places is an activity that asks young readers to select a story character whom they would like to 'change places' with. It is important that they justify their choice. An example might be, 'I would like to be the ugly duckling because he surprises everybody when he turns into a pretty swan.' This activity encourages children to make a personal connection with the text, which is an essential element of comprehension and critical literacy.

Like or unlike encourages children to examine texts and compare them with real life. The teacher selects a character from a book who may be, for example, a mother, a doctor, a scientist, a teacher or a princess. Prior to reading the book to the children (or prior to the children reading the book), the teacher should ask them to brainstorm what they know about this category of people (for example, dentists). A class chart is drawn up, which may look like the chart illustrated in Table 23.3.

Table 23.3: Like or unlike

This is what we know about dentists	This is what the book says about dentists
Dentists take teeth out.	They spend a lot of time cleaning and polishing teeth.
There is a lot of blood.	There are women and men dentists.
They wear a mask.	Dentists study for a long time.
They do injections.	Dentists wear a mask and gloves.
They charge a lot of money.	They have nurses helping them.
They have a drill.	The nurses can be men or women.

Text innovation is an activity that involves the text being changed slightly, or reconstructed. Before 'innovating' a text, it is necessary for it to be read to the children several times so that they can become thoroughly familiar with the characters, plot and settings.

The teacher or the children then select an aspect of the text to be changed—this is likely to be a character, a character trait or the setting. The story is then rewritten or, if more appropriate, retold orally. For young children, the context for rewriting will often be interactive writing, where the teacher and the children jointly make decisions about what will be written and the teacher scribes.

After the story has been reconstructed, it is necessary to discuss the impact this had, and to compare it with the original story. For example, 'We made Cinderella bossy and mean in our story. How did that change the way the story went? How do we feel about Cinderella now?'

Clever cloze is another way of reconstructing texts to change the effect. Here, the teacher simply removes selected words from a text. The children supply words to write in the spaces. They then compare with the original text and discuss what kinds of words were changed to create the new effect. This can also build their awareness of word classes and syntax (grammar).

CLEVER CLOZE EXAMPLE

Original version

Little Red Riding Hood <u>skipped</u> through the woods one <u>sunny</u> morning. Her grandmother was <u>ill</u> so Red Riding Hood was taking her some <u>tasty</u> food. Little Red didn't know that a <u>clever</u> wolf was watching her. The wolf was feeling very <u>hungry</u>. He <u>rubbed</u> his <u>hands together</u> and ran ahead to Grandma's house.

> **Example of a clever cloze version**
>
> Little Red Riding Hood <u>ran</u> through the woods one <u>rainy</u> morning. Her grandmother was <u>lazy</u> so Red Riding Hood was taking her some <u>microwave</u> food. Little Red didn't know that a <u>sneaky</u> wolf was watching her. The wolf was feeling very <u>mean</u>. He <u>licked</u> his <u>teeth</u> and <u>skipped</u> ahead to Grandma's house.

Literary letters involves children writing, so is most appropriate for children in the second half of Year 1 and onwards. For younger children, the teacher can scribe for small groups in an interactive writing format. The activity involves writing letters to characters in the book. For example, some children could take on the role of the woodcutter and write to Red Riding Hood's mother to ask why she allowed Red Riding Hood to wander around the woods alone when everybody knew full well there was a dangerous wolf at large. Other children in the class could write from the perspective of the wolf. The wolf could, perhaps, apologise for his behaviour but explain that, being a wolf, he was very tempted to eat people. The children in the class could compare the letters and discuss the differing points of view of the two characters.

VISUAL LITERACY AND ITS IMPORTANCE IN THE TWENTY-FIRST CENTURY

New technologies are largely accountable for the fact that young children are increasingly encountering multimodal forms of texts (Kress, 2003), or texts that are made up of more than one symbol or sign system. (A symbol or sign system can be thought of as a 'mode' of communication. Symbol systems can be written, pictorial, spoken or musical.) Moreover, pictures and diagrams in modern texts often have a different role from that which they had in the past; the visual mode of text used to be mainly illustrative in that pictures were primarily used to decorate or support words—words carried most of the meaning. These days, visual texts do so much more than this. Sometimes images have meanings that support written text, but at other times they may tell a different or parallel story, or may even be accompanied by no written text at all ('wordless' picture books). In wordless texts, images, whether still or moving, carry all of the meaning.

In today's world, children need to learn how to critically make sense of the visual texts that surround them, some of which are immensely sophisticated. There are visual texts for a range of different purposes, such as to entertain, to persuade and to describe; children need to learn what visual texts are *for*. Furthermore, they need to learn how to construct and create visual texts themselves for a range of purposes and audiences. Anstey and Bull (2000, pp. 5–6) propose that: 'Communication has changed over time so that the cognitive and intellectual demands made by the syntax of the language is lessened while there has been an increasing sophistication demanded by the visual medium … Increasing technological advances means, among other things, increasing use of visual text and iconic language.'

DEFINING VIEWING OR VISUAL LITERACY

It will probably come as no surprise that an agreed upon definition of visual literacy does not exist (Williams, 2007). However, Frey and Fisher (2008, p. 1) venture: 'We think of visual literacy as describing the complex act of meaning-making using still or moving images. As with reading comprehension, visually literate learners are able to make connections, determine importance, synthesise information, evaluate and critique.'

This definition highlights the importance of *processes* of meaning-making. As in comprehending or writing traditional written texts, the creation and comprehension of visual texts involves the employment of cognitive processes, such as questioning, predicting and clarifying.

It can be useful to think of visual literacy or viewing in a similar fashion to the way in which we think of reading and writing: there are **visual codes** and conventions to be understood, audiences and purposes to be taken into account, and it is necessary to use a variety of processes and strategies in order to make meaning, whether this is expressive or receptive. Also, the viewer's cultural and experiential background will impact upon (receptive) meaning-making, as will their ability to think critically about the creator's craft and intentions.

It is important not to see viewing as completely separable from reading and writing. In reality, these are all elements of literacy and meaning-making, and multimodal texts require readers (or 'consumers') to pull together a variety of meaning-making strategies and resources. Reading and viewing often go hand in hand and are interdependent. Children need to learn how to read and create multimodal texts and to understand the role of the various symbol systems involved, and how these systems impact upon each other. It must be stressed that we are dealing with them separately in this book for reasons of clarity only.

LEVELS OF VISUAL COMPREHENSION

Just as there are levels of comprehension in reading comprehension (for example, literal, inferential and evaluative/critical), there are levels of comprehension of images, whether still or moving. In early childhood contexts, it is a good idea to begin with literal understanding, or to ask children to describe what is actually shown in the image. In order to facilitate this, the teacher can ask questions such as, 'Where is the wolf hiding?', 'What colour is the ball?' or 'How many mice are shown in the picture?'

A little later on, children may learn to make inferences about what the illustrator *means* by the illustration, rather than what is explicitly stated. For example, 'Why is the wolf's mouth watering?', 'Why is the wolf hiding?' or 'Why is Rosie looking so happy?'

Evaluative judgments and analysis of the techniques used by the illustrator to convey ideas and elicit responses may come still later, as this level requires viewers to orchestrate their knowledge about codes, conventions and contextual influences, among other things. Questions that teachers could ask to help young children develop this capacity would be of the following type:

- 'How does the yellow background make you feel? Why is that?'
- 'What did you look at first in the picture? Why did you look at that part first?'

- 'Which picture of Beauty and the Beast do you like better, the Disney picture or the other one? Why is that?'
- 'Which picture do you think your grandma/brother/friend would like better? Why do you think that?'

UNDERSTANDING VISUAL ELEMENTS (CODES)

In order to help children read, comprehend, view or 'consume' (Bull & Anstey, 2007; Callow, 1999) and write, draw, create, construct or produce images, it is necessary for them to learn about the codes of visual communication. Visual codes are 'the tools that the author employs to establish the specific message' (Fellowes, 2007, p. 30). They include such things as angle and distance of shot, the use of colour and line, distance of shot, framing, line and colour.

Angle

The angle of an image affects the way the viewer and the 'character' (whether this is a living character or an inanimate object) interrelate. A *high angle* has the reader looking down on the object or character, making it appear relatively powerless or unimportant, or somewhat vulnerable, while a *low angle* has the viewer looking up at the character, giving the impression that it has power or importance. An *equal (eye-level) angle* involves the viewer looking at the character 'straight on', and leads to no power differential. Sometimes an angle is oblique and this can have the effect of unsettling or disorienting the viewer.

Framing or distance of shot

When a *close up* of a character is shown, the illustrator is often seeking to establish a close relationship between the viewer and the character. This results in a strong emotional response from the viewer towards the character's feelings, actions or experiences (Fellowes, 2002). A *close up* is usually just head and shoulders, whereas a *medium* shot shows people from about the waist up (Quin, McMahon & Quin, 1997). A *long-distance* shot typically elicits a less powerful response from the viewer and establishes a less intimate (and thus more public) relationship.

Close-up shot

Here, the viewer can take in the whole scene and see 'the big picture'. According to Callow (1999), viewers may see characters in close up as friends, whereas characters in long shots are likely to be perceived as distant strangers.

Distance of shot is related to *framing*. A close-up shot necessarily crops out large areas of the surrounding scene, whereas a distant shot allows the viewer to see more of the scene. However, even with distant shots, framing may still be used to cut out particular characters or objects. In this way, illustrators reveal to viewers only what they wish to reveal, while other aspects of the picture are highlighted or emphasised through the use of framing. Characters and objects can also be framed by lines or boundaries within the scene.

Media

Images may be in the form of drawings, paintings, photographs, cartoons and charcoal or pastel drawing. The brushstrokes or pen-strokes used can have an impact on the way in which the image is perceived and the impact it has on the viewer. Photographs can appear more 'realistic' than other media types, such as watercolours.

Shape and line

Different shapes can represent concepts or ideals. Circles can represent continuity or infinity or 'wholeness', whereas squares can represent honesty, morality and truthfulness (according to the ancient Greeks), as well as strength and stability. To young children, different shapes may represent a range of things, depending on their socio-cultural background.

Lines are used in particular ways by illustrators in order to elicit responses or to lead the viewer's eyes along a particular path. Lines can also indicate movement. Most images are composed of many lines of differing weights, some of which are straight and some of which are curved. Some lines are real and others are implied, for example, through the eye contact between characters and objects in the image (Evans, Griffiths, Stokes & Tuckey, 2008). The direction and curve of lines can convey meaning, but it is beyond the scope of this book to go into further detail.

Vectors

A vector is a line that leads the eye to particular parts of the image. They can be actual lines, such as a lane or a river or someone's outstretched arm, or they can be invisible lines, such as when the viewer follows a represented participant's gaze. Sometimes a vector is known as a 'line of action'.

Mood

When the character seems to be looking directly at the viewer, a powerful emotional attachment is more readily established. This direct gaze tends to demand the viewer's attention and has thus been termed a *demand* (Callow, 1999). On the other hand, when there is no direct gaze towards the viewer, and the character is looking elsewhere, the viewer is invited to follow the gaze of the character to see what he or she is looking at. This has been termed an *offer*.

Modality

Features such as colour, background, detail, sharpness and blurriness, the media used and texture can affect the level of 'realism' that an image conveys. A very realistic looking image is said to have *high modality*, and can appear to be 'beyond question'. On the other hand, images such as cartoons and some types of drawings and paintings do not appear realistic, and are said to have *low modality*.

Symbolism

Within cultures, certain objects or icons have connotations or culturally agreed upon symbolic meaning. For example, birds in flight often signify freedom, spectacles are often used to signify intelligence or eccentricity, and rings signify commitment or eternity. Clothing and hairstyles can also have symbolic meanings in images. For example, characters dressed in long, flowery skirts and headbands might be associated with peace or vegetarianism. Symbolism is often used to portray stereotypes.

Colour

Colours are often used to symbolise emotions or moods. However, these symbolic meanings may vary from culture to culture. Furthermore, different text types or genres have different ways of using colour (Callow, 1999). Thus, a particular colour does not have a universal meaning. The value (lightness or darkness) and saturation (brightness or dullness) of colours also influence meanings that viewers assign to images.

COLOURS—SOME COMMON CONNOTATIONS AND MEANINGS

- red—danger, excitement, passion, love, strength
- blue—coolness, serenity, sadness
- pink—tranquillity, relaxation, femininity, baby girls
- green—fertility, creativity, natural
- yellow—happiness, energy, sunshine
- black—wickedness, mysterious, high quality
- white—purity, cleanliness
- purple—royalty, religion, luxury

Facial expression and body language

Facial expressions of characters in images can affect the response of the viewer, as can body language or gestures. Children can have a lot of fun making their own picture books using photographs they have taken themselves with a digital camera. They can experiment with body language and facial expression and choose those that best fit the meaning they want to convey.

Music and sound effects

Movies, television programs, advertisements and animations, as well as many websites, include music and sound effects as part of the message. It may seem illogical that sounds are deemed to be part of 'viewing' but, as indicated above, multimodal texts are difficult if not impossible to disentangle into separate symbol systems. One of the best ways for children to come to understand these elements is to use them in their own multimodal texts, which they can create using programs such as Microsoft PowerPoint or Photostory (see Chapter 24 for more detail of using ICT in early literacy contexts).

Composition

An image is composed using the elements described above. The way in which an illustrator uses the elements and puts them together can create a variety of effects. For example, the use of white space in newspapers can draw the eye to certain areas of text or to specific pictures. The composition can encourage a 'preferred' reading path; that is, the illustrator can use visual elements strategically to persuade the viewer to look at the image in a certain way, and view particular elements in a pre-specified order. The size and position of characters or objects in the image can also have an impact: the larger elements of an image will generally command more attention, as will elements that have a central position or elements that have lines drawing the eye towards them.

WHAT KIND OF TEXTS?

When teaching viewing, there is a large and exciting range of visual texts to choose from, many of which come from outside the classroom. Indeed, visual and critical literacy teaching are more effective when real, authentic texts are used as opposed to texts published especially for the classroom. For a list of suggestions, see the box below.

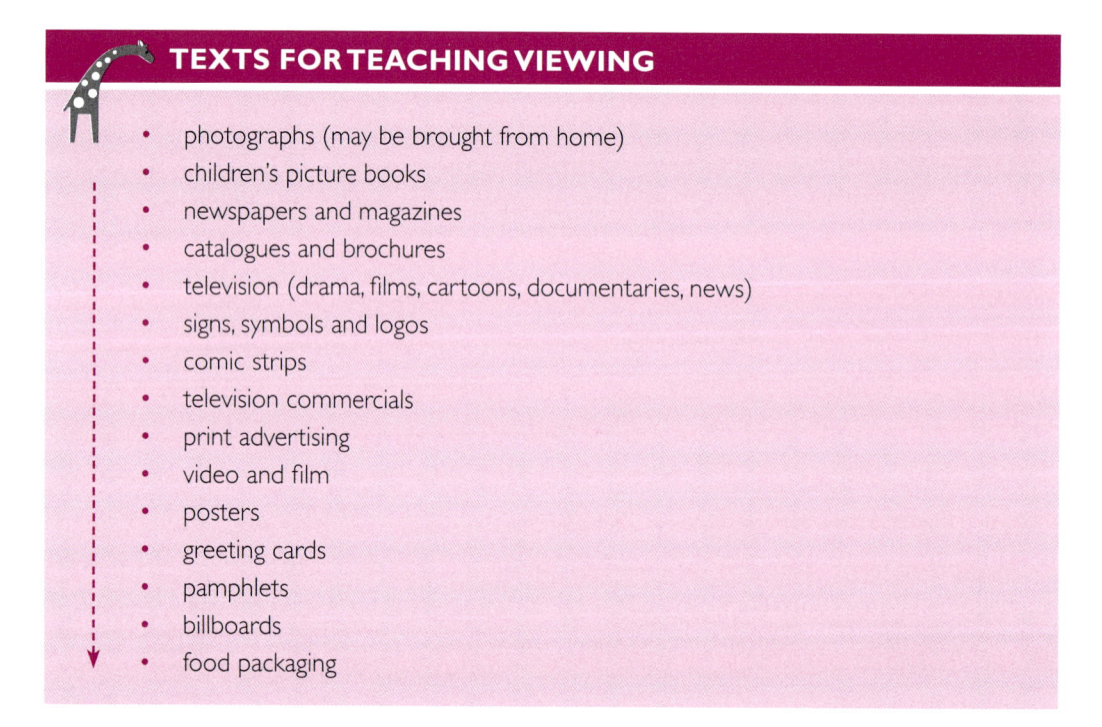

TEXTS FOR TEACHING VIEWING

- photographs (may be brought from home)
- children's picture books
- newspapers and magazines
- catalogues and brochures
- television (drama, films, cartoons, documentaries, news)
- signs, symbols and logos
- comic strips
- television commercials
- print advertising
- video and film
- posters
- greeting cards
- pamphlets
- billboards
- food packaging

MOVING IMAGES

Moving images are prevalent in today's world, on the television and on computers and hand-held games. Some of the techniques used are the same as for still images (such as angle and distance of shot, framing and colour) but there are additional elements to be taken into account such as sequencing, location, lighting, casting, movements, and transitions from one scene to another. Unfortunately, it is beyond the scope of this text to go into detail about moving images.

VIEWERS SEE DIFFERENT THINGS

As indicated above, factors such as age and cultural background influence viewers' interpretations of images. Callow (1999) has pointed out that visual texts or images are social constructions and, as such, can be difficult to understand for people from another culture. He uses as an example the symbols below from Poland. Most Australian children would struggle to know their meaning, even if they were placed in context, on toilet doors. The triangle signifies 'ladies' and the circle signifies 'men'.

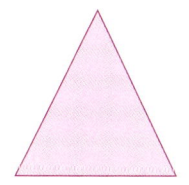

BROAD APPROACHES TO TEACHING VIEWING

As in the teaching of critical literacy, there are three general techniques that children can be taught to help them view pictures critically.

- *deconstruction*: analysing the image in terms of the codes and conventions used
- *juxtaposition*: comparing the image with other images
- *construction* and *reconstruction*: creating images (still or moving).

ACTIVITIES FOR TEACHING VIEWING

Fellowes (1997, pp. 31–2) suggests a range of activities for helping young children understand images and how they may be used to create meaning. You will notice that they all involve deconstruction, reconstruction or juxtaposition. Educators can use the gradual release of responsibility model to help children.

- Orally construct a story using the images from a story (the written text should be covered up) then compare this with the original.
- Respond to various pictures in story books. Discuss how the image is constructed to elicit this affective response.
- Draw the illustrations to match the text of a picture book, where the images have been covered up. Then compare with the original.
- After examining birthday cards for girls and boys, men and women, make cards that represent a broader view of gender.
- Compare a number of books presenting a different point of view on a particular theme—e.g. families, the environment or friendship—and identify the different viewpoints, and the role of the images in constructing the different viewpoints.
- Create a tableau (freeze frame) of a picture from a children's story book and then vary it by changing the way the different visual codes are used. Photographs can be taken of each for comparison.

- Discuss the portrayal of fathers and mothers in Father's Day (or Mother's Day) catalogues and their design, and compose catalogues where the images used are different and portrayals of mothers and fathers are thus different.
- Compare the visual images of two story books.
- Children work in pairs and order a set of visual images from books—from lowest to highest modality. Children then explain their choices.
- Children categorise or sort images according to use of angle or distance of shot. Discuss the way angle or distance of shot influences the viewer's interpretation or response.
- Draw a picture to accompany the written text of one page of a familiar story and do so by applying distance of shot in various ways.
- Take different photos of students applying different distance of shot and discuss the effects.
- Create a dialogue between a character in a story book image and the viewer.
- Represent a written text, such as a recount or narrative, as a comic strip.
- Children examine the use of symbols and visual signs in the school and then design their own to be placed in appropriate locations in the classroom or school grounds.

QUESTIONS TO ASK ABOUT IMAGES

- Who produced (drew/painted/photographed) this picture?
- What do we know about the person who created this picture?
- Why did they put a picture here?
- Why did they make the picture look this way?
- Why did they use this colour?
- How does the picture make you feel?
- Why does it make you feel that way?
- How could we change the picture so that it makes you feel a different way?

Cropping

- Children find and classify images using the criteria angle of shot, distance of shot, mood or modality.
- Children design posters and include symbols to convey the meaning.
- Children examine magazine advertisements and identify the use of colour and other symbols to portray a message about a product.

USING PHOTOGRAPHS CHILDREN BRING FROM HOME

- Discuss the photographs and the context.
- Where, when and why was the photograph taken?
- Where was the photographer standing?
- Discuss the clothes worn in the photos.
- Scan the photographs into the computer and manipulate them (crop, expand, recolour) using photo software or a cardboard viewfinder.
- Write a story or caption to go with the photo.

SUGGESTED THEMES FOR CRITICAL AND VISUAL LITERACY

FAIRY TALES

Fairy tales, because they contain so many stereotypes, are an excellent place to start critical literacy.

Stereotypes in fairy tales include wicked witches (who are typically old and ugly), helpless females, beautiful young princesses, handsome princes and unintelligent poor people (such as Jack from *Jack and the beanstalk*). Gender roles are also stereotyped in many fairy tales; girls and women are often represented as powerless and dependent on men, who often make the important decisions or come to the rescue. The ways in which males and females are represented in fairy tales can be discussed with young children.

The visuals in fairy tales can vary dramatically, with older versions featuring illustrations that are unlike modern day versions, in which characters are often cartooned and unrealistic. A version from 1856 shows Red Riding Hood to be realistic, quite mature and certainly not naïve looking, and the wolf looking like a real wolf as opposed to a wolf with a host of human qualities (see the Red Riding Hood Project at www.usm.edu/english/fairytales/lrrh/lrrhfi.htm). Children can learn a lot through the comparison of different versions of the same fairy tale.

Little Red Riding Bananas is a lift-the-flap book, written by Richard Tulloch and illustrated by Paul Pattie (1999), that features the popular children's television characters, Bananas in Pyjamas, acting out the *Little Red Riding Hood* story. Even very young children could successfully participate in discussing the differences between this version of the story and other versions, such as the online version on DLTK's Fairy Tales and Nursery Rhymes (www.dltk-teach.com/rhymes/) or the animated version on the British Council's website (www.britishcouncil.org/kids-stories-red-riding-hood.htm). The movie *Hoodwinked* also features a version of Red Riding Hood, in which the main character is not gullible and helpless.

ANIMALS IN TEXTS

Animals in children's texts are often portrayed as almost human. This personification of animals, or bestowing upon them human qualities, is called anthropomorphism. While it is not the intention to spoil young children's enjoyment of books and stories, it is a worthwhile exercise to discuss the ways that animals are represented in stories. This can be done by comparing pictures of animals in various picture books, such as the dogs in *Let's get a pup* (Graham, 2001), *Spot* (Hill, 1996), *Hairy Maclary* (Dodd, 1983), *Come away from the water, Shirley* (Burningham, 1977), *John Brown, Rose and the midnight cat* (Wagner, 1979), *Black dog* (Pamela Allen, 1991) and *Drac and the gremlin* (Baillie, 1988). The dogs can be compared in terms of modality, colours, demand and offer, whether they look important, scary or cute, and so on. Picture book dogs can then be compared with photographs of real dogs in non-fiction texts and television programs and advertisements. Children can even bring in photographs of their own pet dogs. Examples of questions that can be asked of young children are:

- How do you feel about the dog in the picture?
- What makes you feel that way?
- How has the artist made the dog look friendly/happy/sad?
- How does a real dog look when it's happy?
- What would happen if the dog in the story looked like this? (Show children another picture.)
- How real does the dog in this picture look? Why do you think that?
- How could we make it look more/less real?
- How has the illustrator managed to make us like the dog so much?
- Why has the illustrator drawn human clothes on the dog?

Kate's feet are no longer lonely under the blankets.

It seems like Dave and Rosy have always been there. Their weight is comfortable and reliable, and will stop Kate's bed floating away into the night.

Let's get a pup! by Bob Graham (Illustration © 2001 Blackbird Design Pty Ltd, reproduced by permission of Walker Books Australia on behalf of Walker Books Ltd, London SE11 5HJ)

REPRESENTATIONS OF FAMILIES

Young children can actively engage in interrogating the ways in which families and family members are represented in various texts.

Mothers

The ways in which mothers are presented, for example, can be examined through a range of critical and visual literacy activities. There are still many picture books available that show mothers in rather stereotyped ways. For example, in *My mum and dad make me laugh* (Sharratt, 1994), the mother is portrayed in a slightly stereotypical way. She lies on the sofa reading a beauty magazine and she lets her husband do the driving.

There are now some wonderful books showing mothers in a different light. *The trouble with mum* (Cole, 2004) tells of a mother who is rather different and is not good at baking cakes. *My Aussie mum* (Morrison & Bright, 2009) shows an Aussie mum who is involved in a whole range of activities, including martial arts, cooking and (worryingly) bingeing on sweets. *Supermum* (Manning & Granstrom, 1999) shows mothers of a variety of racial backgrounds and species, all valiantly caring for their children: swans will fight to protect their young, as will human mothers; osprey mums know what to feed their babies, as do human mothers. The picture book *My mum* (Browne, 2006) shows many different facets of a mother—she's soft, she's tough, she's powerful, she's many things. Representations of mothers can be investigated by examining advertising materials such as brochures and advertisements in magazines and on television, on greetings cards such as birthday cards and Mother's Day cards, and in movies. Children can compare mothers in these texts with real mothers they know.

A critical literacy question asked by Australian teacher Jenny O'Brien of her lower primary children, who had not yet mastered decoding, was:

> If you knew about families only from reading this book, what would you know about what mothers do? What would you know about what fathers do? (cited in Comber, 1993, p. 76)

Grandparents

Old people in our society are often presented in a stereotyped way. However, there are some lovely children's books that portray grandparents in a broader way. For example, *Grandpa and Thomas* by Pamela Allen (2003) tells a delightful story about young Thomas going to the beach for the day with his grandfather. In this book, the grandfather is fairly active, well built and modern. He wears the same clothes that a younger man might, and is gentle natured and happy to spend time with his young grandson. Another book about grandfathers, *Granpa* (Burningham, 1988), shows the relationship between and grandfather and granddaughter, moving from one scene to another, until the grandfather dies. The pictures in this book are watercolours and embedded in these are sepia pictures that represent the grandfather's thoughts and memories of the past. There is an interesting use of fonts to distinguish the grandfather's speech from the girl's. There are many other picture books featuring grandparents that children can enjoy and discuss.

FOOD PACKAGING

In *Belonging, being and becoming: The Early Years Learning Framework for Australia* (DEEWR, 2009, p. 41), early childhood educators are advised to 'support children to analyse ways in which texts are constructed to present particular views and to sell products'. One way of looking at how texts are constructed to sell products is through the analysis of food packaging.

Vasquez (2007) describes work she has done with pre-school children around food packaging and how it is designed to influence potential purchasers. The teaching arose because one of the children had brought in a particular snack, the packaging of which aroused interest in the children. Vasquez saw a teaching opportunity and used this 'everyday' text as a context to talk about visual and linguistic features used on food packaging. She asked the children to suggest some 'good ideas' and 'bad ideas' for food packaging, and the young children made some excellent suggestions. For example, Emily drew a happy family and said, 'People like to be happy and this is happy' (p. 9). After discussion and deconstruction of the original packaging, the children set about redesigning it.

ASSESSMENT OF VISUAL LITERACY

In the visual literacy area, there is little guidance for teachers about what to assess and how to assess it (Callow, 2008). Callow has suggested a 'show me' framework as a tool for assessment for children in K–6. He suggests that the three dimensions to be assessed should be the *affective*, the *compositional* and the *critical*.

- Affective responses are an important part of viewing, and can be assessed by observation of the child's body language when they are viewing images, as well as through discussions, questioning and other behaviours such as choice of picture books. Example questions would include: 'How does this image make you feel?', 'Which is your favourite picture?' and, 'Which part of the image do you like best? Why?'
- Compositional knowledge includes concepts such as angle and distance of shot, use of colour and line, gaze, layout, symbols and vectors. Possible questions to ask are: 'What is happening in this picture?', 'Are we looking at this picture at eye level, from above or from below?' and, 'Which part of this picture did you look at first? Why was that?'
- The critical dimension is to do with understanding how the illustrator has crafted the image to elicit a particular audience response. Discussion and questioning are effective means of finding out what children's understandings are. Helpful questions would include: 'Why do you think the illustrator made the character look like this?' and, 'Do you think the illustrator's picture of a family looks like a real family?'

These three dimensions should be assessed as part and parcel of authentic learning experiences, be assessed on an ongoing basis as well as summatively (at the end of a unit of work), be assessed by a variety of means in a variety of contexts, and involve children using the 'metalanguage' or terminology of visual literacy (Callow, 2008, p. 619). These principles of assessment are in line with the principles for assessing any literacy activity. Children should also be encouraged to self-assess, or to talk and think about their own understandings in the area of viewing.

SUMMARY

This chapter has defined and outlined critical literacy and viewing. It has also suggested some ways of teaching these important aspects of literacy to children in their early years. Because of space constraints, there is much that we had to omit from this chapter. Readers are encouraged to consult some of the references in order to deepen and broaden their knowledge.

QUESTIONS AND ACTIVITIES

1. How can critical literacy be defined and how do you think it might fit in with Freebody and Luke's 'four resources or practices'?
2. How are critical literacy and viewing related?
3. How might you explain the purpose of teaching critical literacy and viewing to the parents of young children?
4. Go to the library or a children's bookshop and select three books for young children that you could use to teach some important viewing concepts. How would you use the books in the classroom?
5. Study the Multiliteracies Map and think about how some of the activities described in this chapter relate to this.

KEY TERMS

devices
multiliteracies
text analyst
visual codes

KEY REFERENCES

Annandale, K., Bindon, R., Handley, K., Johnston, A., Lockett, L. & Lynch, P. (2004b). *Reading resource book: Addressing current literacy challenges* (2nd edn). Port Melbourne: Reed International.

Anstey, M. & Bull, G. (2000). *Reading the visual*. Sydney: Harcourt.

Callow, J. (1999). *Image matters: Visual texts in the classroom*. Sydney: Primary English Teachers Association.

Callow, J. (2008). Show me: Principles for assessing students' visual literacy. *The Reading Teacher*, 61(8), 616–26.

Department of Education and Children Services (2010). The multiliteracies map. Retrieved 20/3/2010, from www.earlyyearsliteracy.sa.edu.au/pages/resource/21402/.

Department of Education, Employment and Workplace Relations (DEEWR) (2009). *Belonging, being and becoming: The Early Years Learning Framework for Australia*. Barton, ACT: Commonwealth of Australia.

Evans, D., Griffiths, A., Stokes, D. & Tuckey, J. (2008). *Viewing resource book: addressing current literacy challenges* Port Melbourne, Vic: Rigby Pearson Education.

Fellowes, J. (2007). Viewing: An important component of the English curriculum. *Practically Primary, 12*(3), 29–32.

Knobel, M. & Healy, A. (1998). Critical literacies: An introduction. In M. Knobel & A. Healy (eds), *Critical literacies in the primary classroom* (pp. 1–12). Newtown, NSW: Primary English Teaching Association.

New London Group (1996). A pedagogy of multiliteracies: Designing social futures. *Harvard Education Review, 66*(1).

Vasquez, V. (2007). Using the everyday to engage in critical literacy with young children. *New England Reading Association Journal, 43*(2), 6–11.

CHAPTER 24

Literacy and Information and Communication Technologies (ICT)

CHAPTER OBJECTIVES

This chapter will increase your understanding of:

- classroom practices involving the use of ICT to enhance literacy learning
- the notion of developmentally appropriate technology in early childhood
- the fact that literacy and ICT are constantly changing and have an interactive relationship
- the importance of 'cyber smartness'.

In this chapter you will learn about the importance of ICT in the early childhood years. As an aspect of multiliteracies, which was discussed in the previous chapter, it is a highly important part of the curriculum. You will learn how to use ICT in classrooms to enable children to become multiliterate. Also, you will consider ways in which ICT might be used to enhance children's literacy learning in a traditional sense; for example, their spelling. ICT and its applications in educational contexts changes rapidly, so this is an area in which you need to keep abreast of new developments and be creative in thinking of new ways to apply emerging technologies to enhance children's learning

YOUNG CHILDREN'S ENGAGEMENT WITH ICT IN THE MODERN WORLD

Many children start childcare or school with some knowledge of information and communications technologies (ICT) (Turbill & Murray, 2006; Zevenbergen & Logan, 2007). They may have seen their parents and older siblings use computers to send and receive emails, to search the internet, to download music or to socialise with others through social networking websites. In addition, they may have seen people play electronic games, either on the computer or using other electronic devices such as Nintendo Wii, X-Box or Nintendo DS. Most children will also have seen sophisticated electronic checkouts in shops, and may have observed delivery people asking adults to sign for deliveries electronically. In addition, they may have seen doctors and other professionals using ICT to help them go about their business. There are also sophisticated hand-held devices such as mobile phones, MP3 players, digital games and 'pets' such as Tamagotchis, as well as a host of other digital tools and toys that people use on an everyday basis. Many young children will not only have observed others using ICT for a variety of purposes, but will have participated themselves.

Because the majority of Australian children are born into communities that use ICT for many purposes, they do not seem to be intimidated by such technologies in the way that older people sometimes are. They are usually willing to 'have a go' and to experiment with electronic devices that can appear complicated to many adults; their ability to rapidly come to grips with remote controls for televisions and DVD players comes to mind. Because of this propensity to embrace new technologies, and because ICT seems natural to them, they have been referred to as **digital natives** (Prensky, 2001). In fact, Prensky argues that new technologies have resulted in today's youngsters, who have grown up with digital technologies all around them, *thinking* differently. Whether Prensky's assertion is true or not—and it has been pointed out that the notion of digital natives is not backed by research (Bennett, Maton & Kervin, 2008)—many children do seem to gravitate towards ICT and it would probably be unwise of educators not to capitalise on this fact. *Being, becoming and belonging: The Early Years Learning Framework for Australia* (DEEWR, 2009, p. 38), clearly states that: 'Children benefit from opportunities to explore their world using technologies and to develop confidence in using digital media.' It also states that, in order to become effective communicators, young children need to 'use information and communication technologies to access information, investigate ideas and represent their thinking' (p. 44).

Brooker and Siraj-Blachford (2002, p. 267) point out that the use of computers in early childhood can be highly appropriate because 'the manipulation of symbols and images on the computer screen represents a new form of symbolic play, which the children themselves seem to treat as equally "concrete" as the manipulation of blocks and small-world toys'. They describe children engaging in rich symbolic play around the computer, 'grabbing' apples and pears from the screen and then sharing them with each other, biting into them, and licking their lips afterwards.

The use of ICT in early childhood contexts is not uncontested, however; some authors claim that it can be harmful and can inhibit social interaction, hands-on exploration and play, and that it can be damaging to children's cognitive, social and emotional development (e.g. Healy, 1998). This debate is ongoing but the weight of evidence seems to be emphasising the benefits of ICT use in early childhood, *if used appropriately*, as opposed to any negative effects. Having said this, it is clear that more research needs to be carried out in the area of literacy learning and ICT use in the early childhood years.

Another issue is the *digital divide*, which cannot be ignored. Although the majority of children have experiences with, or access to, ICT outside of school, many others are disadvantaged in that they do not have technologies such as computers and internet access at home. In Australia, Indigenous children and children from lower socio-economic backgrounds often fall into the category of those disadvantaged in this way. It is necessary for teachers to find out about children's home literacy practices and experiences, including electronic literacies, and to avoid making assumptions. All children should be given opportunities to participate in a wide range of literacies, and those whose home literacy experiences do not include digital literacies need to be given special consideration. Childcare professionals and teachers should communicate with parents to find out about their views on computer use with young children, and these views should be taken into account in planning for a child's learning (Morrison, 2008).

As well as being at ease with digital technologies, today's young children are usually exposed to a range of *multimodal texts* prior to the school years. This means that they are used to accessing texts that use a variety of symbol systems, such as sound, video and graphics. They bring to educational contexts 'funds of knowledge' (Moll, Amanti, Neff & Gonzales, 1992) that need to be recognised and built upon.

It has been found that many children in pre-school years are confident about 'reading' on screen, yet somehow lose this confidence during Year 1 (Levy, 2009). Clearly, children's knowledge and positive attitudes are not being effectively built upon in such instances. It appears that we, as educators, need to find ways of introducing children to paper-based and conventional literacy without alienating them from their screen-based funds of knowledge brought from home. Indeed, screen-based literacy should be seen as every bit as important as paper-based literacy and should be celebrated and taught in its own right.

These days, it would be difficult to find an early childhood classroom without a computer. Likewise, many childcare centres now have computers for children to use. For teachers and childcare professionals, it is important to be able to select appropriate software and learning activities for children. Having a computer in the corner that only has 'drill and practice'

DEVELOPMENTALLY APPROPRIATE TECHNOLOGY

Developmentally appropriate technology in early childhood should:
1. *Be educational*—clear learning aims should be identifiable.
2. *Encourage collaboration*—children should be able to use the technology in pairs or small groups.
3. *Support integration*—technology should be integrated into a range of curriculum areas.
4. *Support play*—technology should encourage role play.
5. *Give control*—the child should be in control of the software; not the other way round.
6. *Be transparent and intuitive*—the child should be able to see the purpose of the software and its functions should be intuitive.
7. *Contain no violence or stereotyping.*
8. *Support the development of an awareness of health and safety issues.*
9. *Support the involvement of parents.*

Source: Siraj-Blatchford and Siraj-Blatchford (2006, p. 9)

programs installed on it is certainly not the ideal. Instead, the use of *developmentally appropriate software* (Haugland & Wright, 1997) in supported, scaffolded ways is advised. Unfortunately, though, there are many schools and centres in Australia, and around the developed world, where ICT is not yet being used as effectively as it might be. There are many legitimate reasons for this, and one of them is insufficient training and professional development for staff. In this chapter, we provide some pointers for practice that will hopefully assist.

Criteria for developmentally appropriate software for early childhood is briefly summarised in the textbox above. These principles of developmentally appropriate software were constructed in the light of a large UK-based study called DATEC, which concluded that it is crucial that software has clear educational aims, is amenable to integration across the curriculum, and supports play. Play has been defined in different ways in the literature but DATEC emphasise discussion, creativity, problem solving, risk-taking and flexible thinking as important elements of play that can be stimulated through the use of ICT (see the DATEC website at www.datec.org.uk/curricguide.htm). It is also important that children are taught about health and safety issues such as correct posture at the computer, limiting time looking at the computer screen and observing 'cybersmartness' (see below). Also, software should be such that parents can participate and engage with their child's learning.

Before going on to discuss how ICT might be used to facilitate literacy learning in early childhood contexts, it is necessary to remark upon the reality that ICT is changing the very nature of literacy and also the nature of readers and writers (Kress, 2003). That is, not only is ICT changing the ways in which literacy is *done*, but it is also changing what literacy is *for*. Unless children in their early years are involved in what has been referred to as *digital literacy* (Glister, 1997), *electronic literacy*, *new literacies* (Lankshear & Knobel, 2003) or *technoliteracies*, they will not be able to develop understandings about the full range of literacies they will need to function in today's world. ICT has changed literacy, and how and why it is 'done'. Literacy has also changed ICT; technologies are often developed to fulfil literacy needs. In this way, literacy and ICT are reciprocal and constantly changing each other.

USING ICT TO FACILITATE LITERACY LEARNING IN CLASSROOMS

There is some literature about the ways in which young children use ICT to *transform* literacy. That is, children are creative in using language and technologies in new ways for new purposes, and in melding and reshaping home and school literacies to form completely new practices. This capacity should be encouraged, and teachers and caregivers can learn a lot from observing how young children use ICT for creative and communicative purposes. The focus in this chapter, though, is largely on using ICT to enhance learning of existing literacies, not on the transformation of literacy. This is because research on the transformation of literacy through young children's use of ICT is still very scanty. To supplement information in this chapter, throughout this book we have provided material about using ICT for specific aspects of literacy learning in the relevant chapters.

The use of ICT can help young children learn much about literacy. It can support their learning about concepts of print and purposes of literacy, and it can help them learn about letter–sound correspondences, comprehension, vocabulary, spelling and viewing. It can be used to facilitate writing and it can be used as a means of developing oral language. Also,

ICT can be highly motivational because it involves multiple media and interactivity. It is important, though, that ICT is embedded in the program of literacy learning and not be seen by teachers and caregivers as a reward, an add-on or some kind of 'extra' that is not integral to the learning environment (Turbill & Murray, 2006). This integration requires a degree of knowledge about how children best learn using ICT, as well as knowledge about available software and its features. It also requires that computers are located in the classroom and not in a computer laboratory.

As noted above, research into the use of ICT in early childhood contexts needs to be furthered. Because technology, literacy and the experiences and interests of children are constantly changing, it can be difficult for researchers and authors to keep up with the pace of change and to ensure relevance. Thus, it can be difficult for teachers and other professionals in the field of education to make informed decisions about this area. In this chapter we attempt to provide some broad strategies that teachers can use, with references to research and theory where possible. However, it is beyond the scope of this text to describe every possible use of ICT in early childhood literacy learning.

ELECTRONIC LANGUAGE EXPERIENCE APPROACH

The Electronic Language Experience Approach (e-LEA) (Oakley, 2001, 2008), also known as Digital Language Experience Approach (D-LEA) (Labbo, Eakle & Montero, 2002), is an excellent way of using ICT to improve and expand a tried and trusted approach. E-LEA is carried out in the same way as 'traditional' LEA (Stauffer, 1970), which has been fully described in Chapter 11. E-LEA differs from traditional LEA in two main ways:

- The teacher scribes using the computer, after the child has recorded her or his story digitally and listened to it to ensure that it 'sounds right' and 'makes sense'.
- The illustration accompanying the text is produced digitally. It can either be a photograph taken with a digital camera, a movie clip, or a picture created using art or painting software. If a traditional drawing is preferred, this can be scanned into the computer.

The steps of e-LEA are outlined below.

1. The multi-sensory experience

The Language Experience Approach (LEA) commences with a stimulating multi-sensory experience. Throughout, the caregiver or teacher talks with children about elements of the experience in an attempt to extend their oral language and conceptual knowledge. Teachers can use modelling, questioning or paraphrasing to extend children's vocabulary and syntactic knowledge. During the multi-sensory experience, the teacher or the children can take digital photographs or record videos.

2. Elaboration of the experience

The next step involves elaboration of the experience. The teacher and caregiver may talk about it, dramatise it, set it to music, think about it, hear about it or view and discuss the digital photographs and video clips. As well as encouraging children to listen to and use particular words and structures, this may also help them remember the experience, sequence it and visualise it—all important skills in writing. Photographs and video clips can be particularly helpful in facilitating this step.

3. Detailed discussion and retelling

The third step of e-LEA involves teachers helping children create an oral retell of the experience, using appropriate vocabulary and syntax. A central rationale of LEA is that the child's own language is used, although the teacher may model conventional forms of language. The oral retell can be digitally recorded and played back, if required.

4. Producing the illustration

In traditional LEA, the child draws or paints a picture to illustrate a salient part of the experience, and this is used as a context for scaffolded talk. However, some young children are not proficient or confident about representing their experiences through drawing. As a consequence, they may draw 'easy' things that do not faithfully represent their experience. With e-LEA, digital photographs or video clips can be used instead of drawings. The child can then describe what is happening in the picture and talk about how the experience felt.

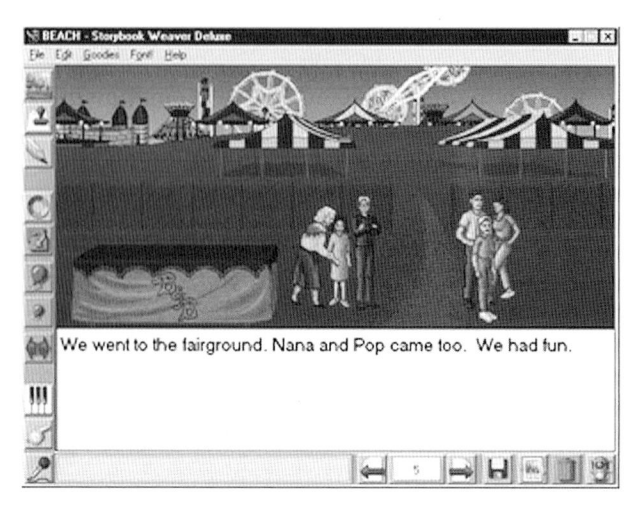

e-LEA using Storybook Weaver Deluxe software and PowerPoint

5. Eliciting the oral story

This part of e-LEA involves the teacher eliciting a story or recount from the child. Here, the teacher can lay out the digital photos in sequence and discuss them with the child, if necessary. At this stage of e-LEA, the teacher once again scaffolds and prompts the child's talk. Depending on the age and capabilities of the child, the electronic talking text may range from a single page with only one or two sentences to several pages.

The oral story is recorded on the computer (usually only one or two sentences per page), using sound recording software. Audacity (download free from audacity.sourceforge.net/) can be used for this; if not the built in 'record' feature of whatever software is used. The child's oral story can be played back so that she or he can decide if it makes sense and sounds right. At this point they may decide to try again and record some new words and sentences.

6. Scribing the story

The teacher and the child listen to the recorded sentences and the teacher repeats them and scribes them, discussing spelling, spaces between words, punctuation, and so on. Although the teacher does most of the transcribing, the text can be written interactively, with the child doing part of the transcribing, if appropriate.

Which software can be used for e-LEA?
Software such as Microsoft PowerPoint can be used to make the electronic talking text. Other software, such as Storybook Weaver Deluxe, Clicker 5, 2Create A Story or Kidpix can also be used.

7. Rereading the story

Finally, the child rereads the story. This can be done along with the recorded narration or with the volume turned off. The text can be listened to and read repeatedly by the author, as well as by other children.

Advantages of e-LEA
- Children can hear recordings of their speech before it is scribed—they can listen to ensure that it 'sounds right' and 'makes sense'. After hearing the recording, they may wish to change the syntax or the vocabulary used.
- Children can listen to the text as well as read it afterwards.
- Other children can listen to and read the electronic texts produced.
- Digital images can be used.

Possible disadvantages of e-LEA
- Young children's speech may not be loud or clear enough to record well.
- e-LEA may be slightly more time consuming than traditional LEA.

ELECTRONIC TALKING BOOKS

Electronic talking books (ETBs), also known as digital storybooks or CD storybooks, are stories that are narrated by a computer. These texts are usually distributed in CD or DVD format, but some such stories can be accessed on the internet. Although the features of ETBs vary, they generally contain roughly the same number of pages as a traditional paper-based picture book. Indeed, many ETBs are based on printed stories, a fact that may change as the ETB genre evolves.

As each 'page' of an ETB is presented on the computer screen, written text is accompanied by a range of media options, which almost always include pictures, either still or animated. Sometimes there are 'hotspots', which are animations that need to be clicked on to be activated. A defining feature of ETBs is the fact that they include text narration that children can listen to as they are presented with the written text. The written text is often highlighted in synchronisation with the spoken narration. Sound effects, as well as music, are also common features.

Selecting appropriate ETBs

Because ETBs vary from publisher to publisher, it is necessary for teachers to evaluate them carefully in order to ascertain their suitability for meeting the learning needs of the children concerned (Shamir & Korat, 2006). This involves a degree of analysis of available software, which quite often does not meet educational standards (De Jong & Bus, 2003).

For example, some ETBs contain numerous hotspots and sound effects which may distract children's attention away from the story itself. Teachers can place restrictions on the way in which children use them, although it should be noted that some research findings exist that indicate that clicking on a lot of hotspots does *not* necessarily adversely affect children's comprehension or story recall of ETBs (De Jong & Bus, 2002). In fact, hotspots that relate closely to the story can improve comprehension (Labbo & Kuhn, 2000).

Just me and my mom by Big Tuna Multimedia. Image courtesy of MobyGames.

To help teachers evaluate ETBs, Shamir and Korat (2006) have devised a checklist, based on Haugland and Wright's (1997) criteria for developmentally appropriate software. Most ETBs will not fulfil all of the criteria in the checklist, but the more that can be ticked off, the better. Questions that education practitioners should ask include:

- Is the software open-ended and exploratory?
- Does the software allow children a high degree of control?
- Does the software require children to solve problems?
- Are people, animals and objects represented realistically?
- Is the software easy to use and intuitive?
- Do the features of the software match the instructional goals?

How can using ETBs help young children?

ETBs can be advantageous to young children in many ways. First, they make stories easy to access so that children can enjoy them and learn to appreciate them relatively independently. In order to hear a particular story on an ETB, a young child does not need to wait for an adult or proficient reader to find time to read it aloud—he or she can access it independently. This may enhance feelings of 'ownership' of stories and control over the learning environment (Lefever-Davis & Pearson, 2005), factors that are important to motivation.

Also, ETBs offer children models of fluent reading. Stories are read fluently and expressively by the narrators, allowing children to learn what fluent reading sounds like; it is difficult for children to learn to read fluently without knowing that fluent reading involves smoothness, expression and an appropriate speed or pace.

Text highlighting, which may highlight individual words, phrases or sentences (depending on the publisher and/or the settings selected) can help children learn much about literacy. Concepts of print such as directionality, concept of word and correspondences between written and spoken words can be reinforced through seeing text highlighted as it is spoken.

DIGITAL STORYTELLING USING PHOTO STORY

1. Download Microsoft Photo Story 3 from www.microsoft.com and install. This software is free.
2. Launch Photo Story and click 'Begin a new story' then click Next.
3. Click on the Import Pictures button. Import desired images/photos from source folder/s (use browse to locate images).
4. Images will be imported into a 'film strip' or timeline. You can change the sequence of the images by dragging and dropping. You can easily delete pictures you decide not to include.
5. Edit the images, if necessary, and click Next.
6. Add titles and text to images by selecting image on timeline. Type in the textbox that will appear. Click on the appropriate buttons to alter font and text layout. Click Next.

7. Record narration by clicking on desired images and then following on-screen directions. If your computer does not have a built in microphone you will need plug one in.
8. Customise motion and transition effects. Here, you set the timings and framing for each image.
9. Add background music. You can browse to locate music on your computer or create music.
10. Preview the digital story and then, if happy with the story, click Save.

Seeing individual words highlighted as they are spoken may also assist children in developing a bank of sight words, especially if the ETB is repeatedly accessed. Text highlighting can also help children become fluent readers through showing them how groups of words can be 'chunked' together into phrases (Oakley, 2003).

Talking books that partially 'sound out' words that the user clicks on (**onset and rime** are sounded out to help children decode by analogy) have been developed, although this sounding-out feature is not yet available widely. Chera and Wood (2003) evaluated this type of software and found that the phonological awareness of the four- to six-year-old users was significantly improved after relatively short periods of use (ten ten-minute sessions).

For children who are a little older and more proficient at reading, full text narration may be dispensed with. Many ETBs support children's independent reading by pronouncing individual words (when clicked on). This facility can remove decoding barriers that may impede fluent reading and comprehension (McKenna, 1998). A difficulty here is that some children are 'underclickers' (and do not click when they should) and some children are 'overclickers' (and click on far more things than necessary). Education practitioners should help children become metacognitive, and show how to make good decisions about when and why something should be clicked.

Some studies have found that the use of ETBs can help children improve their comprehension. Animation, pictures and sound effects can help children make meaning and build a more elaborated, or 'deeper', understanding (Labbo & Kuhn, 2000). De Jong and Bus (2004) found that kindergarten-aged children could retell ETB stories just as well as they could repeat stories that were told by teachers.

It is important to *set a purpose* for reading ETBs, as is the case for any other text. Labbo (2000) wrote an article about using ETBs with children in early childhood contexts. The ideas in her article are worth considering. Children can:

- listen to the e-story purely for enjoyment
- chorally read the story
- look for known letters and sounds
- look (and listen) for rhyming words
- tell how one screen fits with other screens
- tell how special effects fit the story
- tell about similar stories.

The ability to appreciate, understand and respond to multimedia texts such as ETBs is essential, since such texts are becoming more and more prevalent in today's world. *The Early Years Learning Framework for Australia* (EYLF) (DEEWR, 2009) has pointed out the importance of children being given the opportunity to 'engage with technology for fun and to make meaning'. Educators should provide modelled and guided reading experiences of ETBs to help children make meaning from them. After reading, children should be given opportunities to respond to ETBs in a range of ways, such as discussion, wondering, role play, art, dance, music or writing.

Possible disadvantages of ETBs

There are potential disadvantages in young children using ETBs. Several authors have articulated the fear that ETBs could make children dependent on assistive features, actually impeding the development of independent strategies in important areas such as decoding and comprehension. To ensure that this does not happen, teachers should ensure that they use a variety of texts, not just ETBs.

Kim and Anderson (2008), in their small study, found that parent–child interactions in ETB contexts differ from those when reading traditional printed texts; more interaction and sharing appears to take place with traditional texts. If this is the case, parents need to be advised to read a variety of texts with children.

There may also be difficulties in sourcing and selecting ETBs that are suitable for the context. It can be time consuming to thoroughly evaluate software, although there are some useful websites that provide helpful reviews. Check your state Education Department's website as it is likely that there will be software reviews for you to refer to.

In order to minimise problems of finding suitable ETBs, teachers can make their own using simple software such as PowerPoint, Clicker 5 or 2Create A Story. It is beyond the scope of this book, however, to provide technical instructions on how to do this. A Google search will return many sites containing instructions on how to make talking books using PowerPoint.

CREATING TALKING BOOKS AND DIGITAL STORIES

Children, either independently or in collaboration with teachers, can create ETBs or *digital stories* themselves. This is a highly creative and exciting experience that can involve speaking and listening, reading and writing, as well as visual literacy. It fulfils all of the requirements of **developmentally appropriate technology** for early childhood.

In modelled ETB writing, teachers write the ETB and think aloud about writing-related choices they make as the children observe. This can be done on a large screen (interactive whiteboard or data projector) if it is being presented to a whole class or group. If PowerPoint is being used to create an ETB, it is recommended that a template is used to begin with so that children can concentrate on the creation of the message, rather than on the technicalities of setting up page layouts and so on. It is advisable that all pictures, graphics and sounds that are going to be needed for the ETB are sourced before writing begins and placed in an easily accessible folder.

In interactive writing, the teacher and children jointly construct the ETB. As in traditional interactive writing, the children are given opportunities to 'hold the pen' (or the keyboard), as well as suggest ideas. Guided and independent writing of ETBs can follow.

USING ICT TO HELP CHILDREN LEARN WORD IDENTIFICATION AND GRAPHOPHONIC RELATIONSHIPS

Research has shown that ICT can be used to help children learn sight words. Levandowski, Begany and Rogers (2006) found that matching words with their pronunciations (these can be termed 'talking flashcards') using a computer helped (3rd Grade) children learn sight words and improve reading fluency just as effectively as did one-on-one tuition. Five to ten words were taken from each text to be read and children learnt to recognise the words using the computer, prior to reading the text. They did this by repeatedly viewing the words and simultaneously listening to pronunciations. Although drill and practice type activities are not usually recommended as a central part of literacy learning in the early years, it is clear that they do have a place in the teacher's repertoire of approaches. PowerPoint has also been used successfully, using a direct instruction (DI) model, to teach sight words to children at risk (Parette, Blum, Boeckmann & Watts, 2009). Again, the words were shown in isolation and the pronunciation of each word was simultaneous with the visual presentation.

There is a range of software available to help children learn phonological awareness and graphophonic relationships. The Phonics Alive! software clearly explains how letters and sounds work and provides opportunities for children to practise matching letters with sounds. Sound effects and animations are used as amusing 'rewards' when children get it right.

Phonics Alive! is excellent Australian software that can be used to teach phonological awareness, phonics and spelling.

CONCEPT MAPPING

Concept mapping is a means of graphically representing ideas and their interrelationships and has been mentioned in other chapters of this book. ICT presents children with the opportunity of mapping their ideas using software such as Kidspiration. The use of such software facilitates the 'moving about' and changing of elements of the concept map, whereas on paper the need to manually rub out, rearrange and rewrite can often result in concept maps that do not fully represent children's ideas. Further, ICT-based concept maps, because they can be changed so easily, can facilitate group work: children can discuss their thoughts and ideas and collaboratively make changes, try out new representations, solve problems together and jointly construct concept maps.

As in traditional reading contexts, ICT-based concept maps can be used as a means of representing ideas and events from the texts that children have read. This is excellent for developing comprehension skills such as sequencing, relating ideas to each other (main ideas and supporting ideas) and representing top-level structures (cause–effect, problem–solution etc.). Concept maps can be an excellent means of describing characters from books and also doing literary sociograms, which show relationships between characters in stories. Because children can add audio, these concept maps can be supplemented with important sound effects and recordings of children's comments. For children who are not good writers, this can be an excellent means of helping them demonstrate their comprehension of texts.

ICT-based concept maps can be useful to support young children's writing: children can use them to record and organise ideas as they brainstorm, to plan characters and their traits, and to sequence ideas. Kidspiration includes many templates, such as the story starter. Story starters can help children plan main characters and some of the main events in stories to be written. Teachers can easily create their own templates to cater for specific needs.

WORD PROCESSORS

Research shows that the use of word processors can lead to better writing processes and products in young children (Jones, 1994) and may also improve motivation for writing, especially for those who struggle in this area (Kelly, Kratcoski & McClain, 2006). Many examples can be found of young children using ICT to write and create multimodal texts and we have all heard, anecdotally, of young children amazing their parents and teachers with what they can do on the computer. For some, writing using the computer seems to be much easier than writing using pencil and paper. Zevenbergen and Logan (2007) give the example of a barely four-year-old child who did not have the fine motor skills to write (form letters) using traditional writing instruments but was able to use a word processor to write his own name and his sister's name, and change the fonts and colours of the text.

In terms of research into word processors and effective practice in early childhood contexts, there is still a very long way to go. There is a lot we do not know, right down to the best age to begin teaching keyboarding skills. The use of word processors designed for adults may have limited usefulness for young children, not least because word processors such as Microsoft Word have become very complex and 'bloated' with features. For young children, specially designed software with word processing features, such as Kidpix, Clicker 5 and Storybook Weaver Deluxe, seems preferable. Such programs are easy and intuitive to use, make good use of multimedia, and include many attractive features such as sound effects, pictures and graphics.

The EYLF (2009) states that young children should be given opportunities to 'use information and communication technologies as tools for designing, drawing, editing, reflecting and composing', so it is essential that educators find ways of doing this that are appropriate for the children in their care.

TALKING WORD PROCESSORS

Clicker 5 (Crick software)

Clicker 5 is a writing support and multimedia tool that can be used to help children write. It has also been shown to facilitate word recognition and grapheme awareness in young children (Karemaker, Pitchford & O'Malley, 2008). This software, which includes a talking

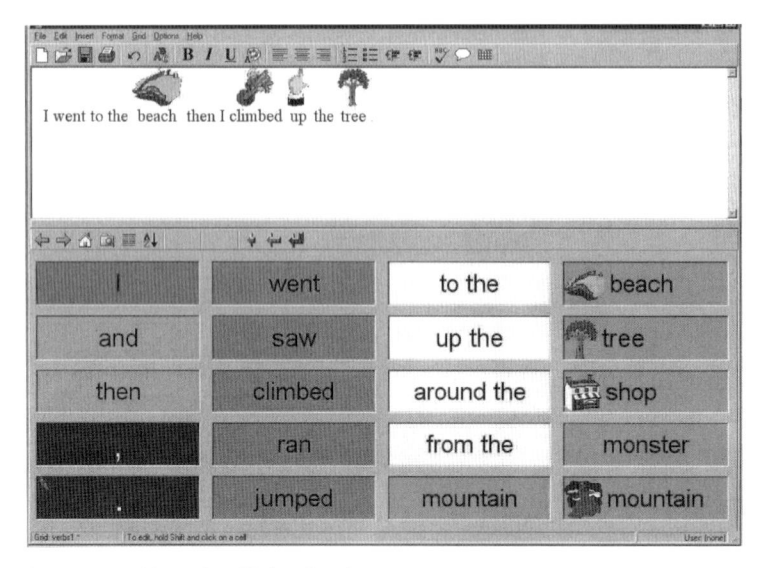

Sentence making using Clicker 5 software

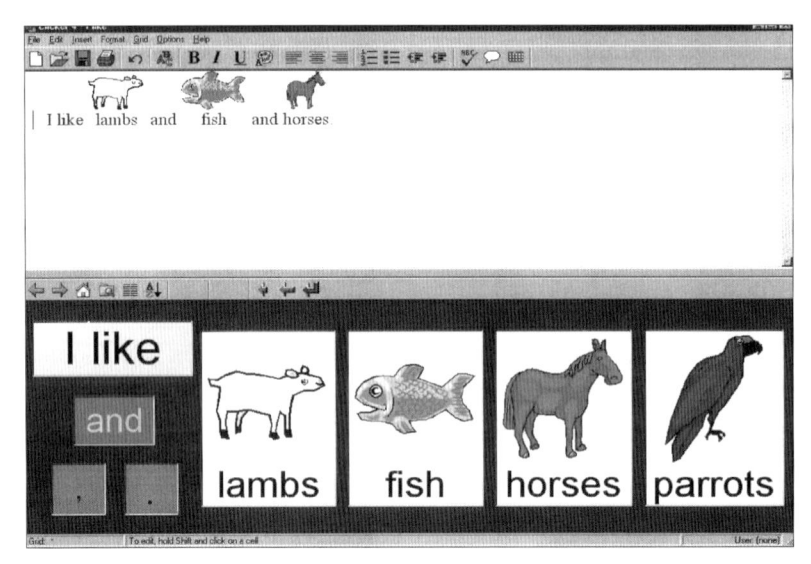

Sentence frame using Clicker 5 software

word processor, provides writing support, primarily through the provision of text to speech features. When children have written a sentence and pressed the 'enter' key, the sentence is read back to them. Children can then think about whether it sounds right and makes sense. This can help them decide whether they need to edit or revise, and what to write next.

Children can also click on the words or pictures provided in the grid at the bottom of the screen, whereupon the corresponding word will appear in the text they are composing in the writing space above the grid. Grids can be either teacher created or downloaded from the internet from a large repository uploaded by teachers from around the world.

Grids can help children write through giving children prompts or choices (Parette, Hourcade, Dinelli & Boeckmann, 2009). Although they are at liberty to type in whatever words they wish to in the normal way, children can also click on preselected words in the grid. This speeds up the writing process for them and means that they are not 'overloaded' with choices, such as what words to use, what sentence structure to use and how to spell the words.

In the illustration above, Clicker 5 has been used to make sentence frames. Children can select from the choices provided in the grids to make sentences, such as 'I like fish and horses' or 'I like horses, lambs and parrots'. Using the grid with more choices, they can make compound sentences such as 'I climbed up the mountain then ran around the tree'. The teacher has listed or colour-coded word choices according to word classes, which should help children understand elements of sentence structure and grammar. Children who are struggling with writing and ESL children can find Clicker 5 and other talking word processors, especially those with grids, very useful. For a full guide about Clicker 5 and its features, see www.cricksoft.com/us/products/clicker/guide/Clicker5guideUS.pdf.

Kidpix Deluxe

Kidpix Deluxe is another word processor and drawing/painting computer program for young children (recommended for ages four and above). Using this software, it is possible for young children to create multimedia texts that include words and letters, sound effects, drawings, animations, 'stamps' (children can stamp the page using a range of pictures and letters) and other effects.

Children can also use Kidpix Deluxe to make slide shows, or very simple digital stories using a sequence of pages set to music and sound effects.

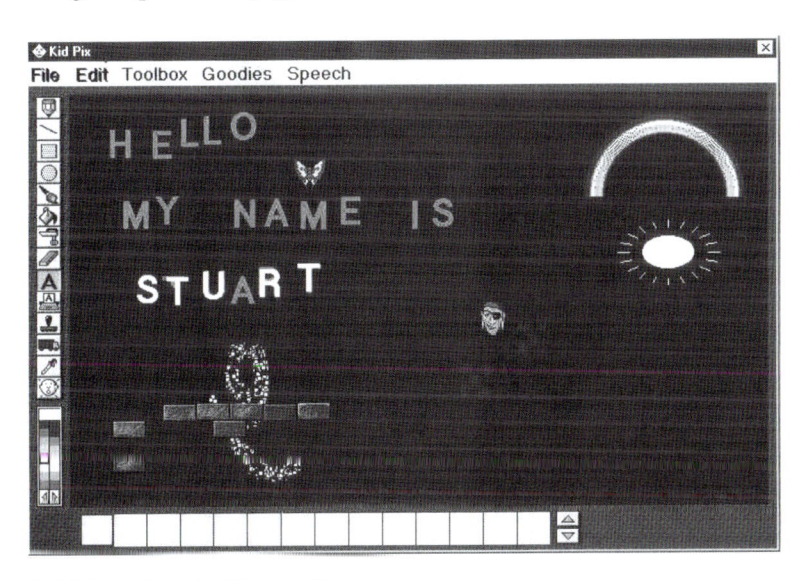

A child's writing using Kidpix software

DEDICATED SPELLING SOFTWARE

There is a variety of software available that can be used to help children improve their spelling (Oakley, 2007) and research has shown that such software can play a part in helping children learn to spell at least as effectively as traditional methods can (Torgeson & Elbourne, 2002). The Phonics Alive! software family has already been mentioned above. Phonics Alive 3 (The Speller) focuses on how to spell and on spelling rules in a systematic and engaging way.

Superspell—A Day at the Beach (Hoopers Multimedia) was created by Australian teachers, and the words to be learnt are pronounced in Standard Australian English. There are over

3200 words to learn in this spelling program, which has seven different games that children (Year 1 onwards) can play to help them master the spellings. Teachers can make customised spelling lists to suit individual children and can add words that are not already in the Superspell database. This software, and others like it, can be used to supplement child-centred spelling approaches, which have been discussed in Chapter 18. We would not necessarily recommend the use of spelling software as a main approach to spelling, since children need to use multiple strategies, and many computer-based spelling programs focus largely on memorisation.

Word Wizard (Macroworks) is another spelling and word study program for children aged five and above. It helps children learn spelling through twenty interactive learning games. Among other things, it covers phonics, homophones, spelling rules, suffixes and prefixes. Children can do a 'placement test' the first time they use the software so that they can use the software at the right level for them. There are many other software packages to help children learn to spell, and caregivers and teachers can find out about these by monitoring educational software suppliers' websites.

USING THE INTERNET

Many young children use the internet at home for a variety of purposes. For example, they may play games, listen to music, watch video clips, look things up (hopefully with the help and supervision of parents), listen to talking books or read stories. The EYLF (2009) states that young children should learn to 'use information and communication technologies to access images and information, explore diverse perspectives and make sense of their world', so the use of the internet and other ICT in early childhood educational contexts is no longer optional.

It is up to the educator to carefully select appropriate websites to suit children's learning needs. There are many worthwhile sites that have games, stories and information for young children, and we have already referred to several of these sites throughout this book. We list more of these towards the end of this chapter.

One of the most difficult aspects of using the internet with young children is harnessing its power to facilitate content-area reading. There are simply too many websites of varying quality, and setting young children 'research' tasks using the internet is fraught with difficulties. Indeed, setting older children research activities using the internet is also problematic in many ways due to difficulties they have in selecting search terms and assessing the suitability and readability of websites. A way to ensure that children quickly find relevant websites that are of an appropriate quality and readability, and that they have a clear purpose for reading them, is through the use of WebQuests.

WEBQUESTS

What is a WebQuest?

'A WebQuest is an inquiry-oriented activity, in which some or all of the information that students interact with comes from resources on the internet' (Chatel, 2003, p. 70). Or, to put it more simply, a WebQuest entails an investigation of a topic, using the internet. The

WebQuest asks some questions about a topic, requires a problem to be solved or sets a task. It then directs children to specific websites (links), where the necessary information can be found. WebQuests generally include a rubric to help children judge how well they have carried out the task. Tasks are often carried out in small groups, although WebQuests can be done individually. Although they may sound a little complicated, there are many simple WebQuests available online that are suitable for children from around five years of age. The best way to find out about WebQuests is to explore some. Have a look at some of those listed in the box below. Think about how you, as an educator, might be able to create your own WebQuests to suit the children in your class.

> **EXAMPLES OF WEBQUESTS FOR CHILDREN K–3**
>
> - *Fairytale Court: The True Story of the Three Little Pigs* by Rosalena Hefferle and Pamela Thompson: projects.edtech.sandi.net/king/investigatingacrime/index.htm
> - Eduscapes WebQuests (K–3): eduscapes.com/sessions/butter/k3webquests.htm
> - *Dinosaur WebQuest* by Ruth Elliott and Christine Todd: olc.spsd.sk.ca/de/webquests/dino/dinowq.htm
> - Literature Learning Ladders—literature-based WebQuests: eduscapes.com/ladders/themes/w1.htm
> - Pets: www.teacherweb.com/IN/PNC/Cassady/
> - Filamentality—make your own WebQuests (a site for teachers): www.kn.sbc.com/wired/fil/

Benefits of WebQuests

- WebQuests give children a clear *purpose* for reading texts on the internet.
- WebQuests give children specific *directions* about where to go on the internet.
- Only suitable websites are included in WebQuests—no 'too difficult', inappropriate or irrelevant sites will be accessed.
- The set tasks can be carried out collaboratively or on an individual basis, whichever best suits the learning needs of the children.
- Children are encouraged to self-evaluate (which helps them build metacognitive skills).
- WebQuests can be integrated with broader classroom themes.
- The principles of developmentally appropriate technology in early childhood are met.

To learn about making WebQuests, go to the well-known website run by the grandfather of WebQuests, Bernie Dodge: www.webquest.org.

SEARCHING THE WEB

Children in lower primary school sometimes need to search for information on the internet, but, not surprisingly, a lot of time can be wasted if they are not furnished with appropriate support. It is helpful to discuss with children prior to the web search which search terms they might enter into the search engine. It is also useful to direct young children to children's search engines such as Ask Kids at www.askkids.com/. This engine allows users to type in questions in plain English and will return appropriate information for children. Kids Click at www.kidsclick.org/ is a search engine and directory for children, as is Kids.Net.Au at www.kids.net.au/.

HELPING YOUNG CHILDREN BECOME 'CYBER SMART'

It is crucial that children are safe on the internet and realise that 'stranger danger' is just as much an issue in the cyber world as it is in the real world. Also, they need to realise that they are potentially subject to persuasion, exploitation and deceit when they go on the internet. An excellent website to explore in order to familiarise yourself with cyber smartness is the Australian Government website, Cyber smart: www.cybersmart.gov.au/Schools.aspx.

Among other things, this website provides teacher resources to facilitate teaching children in lower primary (five- to seven-year-olds) about becoming cyber smart. Three main foci are:

- *Digital media literacy*—defined as the ability to access, understand and participate in, or create, content by using digital media.
- *Positive online behaviours*—defined as positive, appropriate and constructive online relationships with peers, family and strangers in a variety of mediums. Key concepts associated with positive online behaviour include 'netiquette', appropriate contact and communication with others, as well as consideration of issues such as 'cyber bullying'.
- *Peer and personal safety*, or developing protective behaviours while using a range of online media including social networking—these behaviours include protecting personal information to safeguard privacy, identifying when feeling unsafe and recognising 'grooming' tactics used by online sexual predators.

USEFUL WEBSITES FOR YOUNG CHILDREN

Storybee	www.storybee.org/
CBeebies	www.bbc.co.uk/cbeebies/
Science Postcards	www.sciencepostcards.com/
Storyline Online	www.storylineonline.net/
Boowakwala	www.boowakwala.com/kids/boowakwala-home.html
Playschool	www.abc.net.au/children/play/
Songs for Little Kids	www.britishcouncil.org/kids-songs-little-kids.htm
Fun with Spot	www.funwithspot.com/au/

CRITERIA FOR SELECTING WEBSITES

When selecting websites to use with children, there are several things that educators must think about, including suitability for the pedagogical goals, navigability and usability, credibility, accuracy and bias (see Table 24.1). Eventually, children themselves need to be able to assess the credibility and quality of websites using similar criteria.

Table 24.1: Criteria for selecting websites: checklist

Pedagogical suitability	1. Will the website help the children concerned reach specified learning outcomes?
	2. Is the website of an appropriate 'readability' for the children concerned?
	3. Is the website easy to navigate?
Credibility and accuracy	4. Is it possible to tell who wrote/produced the site?
	5. Is the author/producer a reliable, well-known organisation or person?
	6. Is it possible to check the qualifications/credentials of the author?
	7. Do I already know anything about this person/organisation that might help me critically analyse the information on the site?
	8. Is it possible to cross-check the information given? (Has the author provided sources?)
	9. Is the website up to date?
	10. Does the information on the site conflict with information I have already gathered from other sources? (How?)
Bias	11. Has any relevant information been omitted?
	12. Has anyone or any group been 'marginalised'?
	13. Are there advertisements on the website? (Whose advertisements?)
	14. What sort of websites does this site link to? (Are they trustworthy?)

INTERACTIVE WHITEBOARDS

Interactive whiteboards (IWBs) are fast becoming the norm in classrooms. These allow teachers to present information to children in new, interactive ways. Essentially, children and teachers can do with their finger or special pen on the IWB what they can do with a mouse or a stylus on a (tablet) computer. IWBs allow small groups or even the whole class to *interact* around an enlarged computer screen (the IWB), and it is through this interaction that scaffolding is supplied and talk between children about their learning can be encouraged.

Although little, if any, research has been conducted on the use of IWBs in early childhood contexts, many positive practices have been observed (Siraj-Blatchford & Siraj-Blatchford, 2006), including situations where individuals or groups of children independently use the IWBs, employing a variety of software. The large screen facilitates working in groups and the fact that IWBs are operated by touch (instead of a mouse) make them accessible to young children whose fine motor control is not yet fully developed. Blatchford and Blatchford note that the use of games on an IWB can facilitate teamwork, talk and collaborative problem-solving.

IWBs are also an excellent means of offering interactive writing experiences, where both the teacher and individual children can 'share the pen' and build a text. Unlike interactive writing on a traditional whiteboard or on butchers' paper, the writing process can be better demonstrated using an IWB. For example, changes can easily be made, annotations can be added, and copies of the screen can be printed out for small groups or individual children to work on.

Reading can be modelled using IWBs. A large range of texts can be read aloud by the teacher, and 'think-alouds' can be included to assist children in understanding reading processes. Using the IWB, the teacher can annotate parts of the text to draw children's attention to particular features. The use of the IWB to do shared reading allows a great deal of flexibility in terms of texts used, since the teacher does not have to rely totally on (expensive) commercial big books or (relatively time-consuming) teacher-made paper ones.

Teachers can make their own 'electronic big books' and display them using the IWB. This can be highly economical, and teachers can ensure that texts are 'just right' in terms of level and relevance. The teacher reads 'electronic big books' aloud just as she or he would read a traditional paper-based big book. An advantage is that, with an IWB, annotations can be made. Individual copies can easily be printed out or sent to children electronically.

SUMMARY

We have seen in this chapter that there are many ways in which ICT can be used to facilitate literacy learning. Indeed, the use of ICT has become a *part* of literacy and must therefore be included in literacy teaching. Although young children are not advised to spend a great deal of time 'at the screen', because it is important to engage in many other activities, there is a growing body of research evidence to show that the use of ICT can be beneficial to them.

QUESTIONS AND ACTIVITIES

1. On your next school experience, observe how teachers use ICT to enhance children's language and literacy learning. What software do they use and how do they manage children's use of computers?
2. How do you think that the terms 'digital natives' and 'digital immigrants' might help you understand the interactions young children and adults might engage in when using ICT?
3. Is the notion of developmentally appropriate technology useful? Substantiate your answer.
4. Using PowerPoint, create a short digital story for young children, using written text, pictures and audio. If possible, use this resource on your next school experience.

KEY TERMS

digital natives
developmentally appropriate technologies
onset and rime

KEY REFERENCES

Brooker, L. & Siraj-Blatchford, J. (2002). 'Click on Miaow!': How children of three and four years experience the nursery computer. *Contemporary Issues in Early Childhood, 3*(2), 251–73.

Chera, P. & Wood, C. (2003). Animated multimedia 'talking books' can promote phonological awareness in children beginning to read. *Learning and Instruction, 13*, 33–52.

Kim, J. E. & Anderson, J. (2008). Mother–child shared reading with print and digital texts. *Journal of Early Childhood Literacy, 8*(2), 213–45.

Lefever-Davis, S. & Pearson, C. (2005). Early readers and electronic texts: CD-ROM storybook features that influence reading behaviors. *The Reading Teacher, 58*(5), 446–54.

Levy, R. (2009). 'You have to understand words … but not read them': Young children becoming readers in a digital age. *Journal of Research in Reading, 32*(1), 75–91.

Morrison, T. (2008). Computers in childcare. *Putting children first, 27*(Sept), 14–16.

Oakley, G. (2003). Improving oral reading fluency (and comprehension) through the creation of electronic talking books. *Reading Online, 6*(7).

Oakley, G. (2008). e-LEA: Multimodal writing. *Practically Primary, 13*(1), 23–4.

Prensky, M. (2001). Digital natives, digital immigrants. *On the Horizon, 9*(9).

Shamir, A. & Korat, O. (2006). How to select CD-ROM storybooks for young children: The teacher's role. *The Reading Teacher, 59*(6), 532–45.

Siraj-Blatchford, J. & Siraj-Blatchford, I. (2006). *A guide to developing the ICT curriculum for early childhood education.* Stoke on Trent: Trentham Books.

Zevenbergen, R. & Logan, H. (2007). Computer use by preschool children: Rethinking practice as digital natives come to preschool. *Contemporary Issues in Early Childhood, 8*(8), 19–29.

CHAPTER 25

Connecting with Families

CHAPTER OBJECTIVES

This chapter will increase your understanding of:

- the role of the family in children's language and literacy development and learning
- the diversity of children's experiences in written and oral communication in the home and community
- a range of successful initiatives for supporting children's home literacy
- the importance of establishing and maintaining strong partnerships with families
- practices that support effective partnerships with families
- the language and cultural diversity of Australian families
- working with families from diverse language and cultural backgrounds.

This chapter is about families. It presents information that should assist you in realising the diversity among Australian families and the different communication practices of children's homes and communities. Such knowledge is important to ensuring a strong language and literacy program that values and connects to what children bring to the learning setting and that works in partnership with the families and communities to which children belong. The chapter provides you with ideas and suggestions for the important early childhood practice of working in partnership with families and has a particular focus in working with families from diverse cultural and linguistic backgrounds including Indigenous Australian families. This is a starting point but you should continue to seek understanding of, and ways in which to ensure, strong collaborative partnerships between early childhood educators and parents and families.

FAMILY LITERACY PRACTICES

Family literacy refers to the way families, children and extended family members use literacy during the home and community activities of their everyday lives (Morrow, 2009). Literacy can play a huge part in the day-to-day life of a family: writing reminder notes, reading the mail, following the directions of a recipe, writing cards, keeping records, following the instructions on street signs, and so on. Family literacy also encompasses those home activities that are purposely extended to enhance children's literacy learning (for example, demonstrating how to write letters of the alphabet). It is also concerned with oral communication.

FAMILY LITERACY PRACTICES AND EMERGING LITERACY

Children begin to develop their literacy competency well before they enter school. From early in life the everyday experiences of family and community can provide them with the opportunity to gain important insights into literacy and to acquire reading and writing concepts and skills. When children grow up in an environment where they are able to observe family members engaging in reading and writing tasks (for example, reading the newspaper, referring to the television guide or the bus timetable, writing a thank-you note or a shopping list, or sending and receiving party invitations), the foundation for literacy development is laid. They gradually build an understanding of the role played by literacy in daily life. They begin to realise that reading and writing are all about communicating meaning.

When family members read and talk about stories with children, and engage them in songs, rhymes, games and activities with a literacy focus (teaching the alphabet, for example), children's literacy knowledge will be further raised.

ORAL LANGUAGE AS A COMPONENT OF FAMILY LITERACY

When the home provides children with certain oral language experiences, it is helping not just to increase children's oral language competency, but also to develop the knowledge and skills which children need for learning to read and write. The actual types of oral language interactions that children experience at home will have a significant bearing on their literacy abilities at pre-school and Year 1 (Snow, Dickenson & Tabors, 2001). Of greatest influence are parent and child discussions during story book reading, extended conversations at meal and play time, a focus on new and interesting words, and explanation and discussion of things (people, places, events) beyond the child's immediate environment or situation (Snow et al., 1999). The home speaking and literacy practices that support literacy development include:

- extended oral interactions with young children during play
- conversations during meal time, in the car etc.
- exposure to new vocabulary within conversations
- use of explanation within conversations

- modelling of conversation and listening behaviours by parents and other family members and the use of a variety of morphological and syntactic forms in oral language
- asking children questions about different shared experiences or about what they are doing and about events not part of the immediate situation
- encouraging children to use language for different purposes—to describe, explain, instruct, recount or reason
- talk time that encourages children to make up stories or to tell about stories they have read
- questioning that promotes critical and creative thought processes.

FAMILY LITERACY AND EMERGENT LITERACY

Print-rich environments and family literacy practices—reading books and other texts, plus songs, rhymes, games and conversations—support children's literacy development in a number of areas. Although there can be a wide variation, depending on the types of experiences and interactions around these experiences, they might include:

- identification of letter names and sounds and identification of some words by their shape or initial letter/sound
- understanding that letters make words and words make sentences
- phonological awareness (familiarity with rhythms, intonations and prosody of language)
- book concepts (e.g. how to hold a book, concept of reading from front to back, turning pages)
- print concepts (the words read come from the printed text, print is oral language mapped to letters and words, print is read from left to right and from top to bottom of the page)
- having a substantial expressive and receptive vocabulary (words and their meanings)
- familiarity with story language (for example, 'Once upon a time …', 'One day …' or 'Finally the bear came upon a large cave') and story structure
- listening skills (listening with concentration, understanding and remembering)
- purposes of reading and writing (understanding of the functional uses of print in life)
- type of texts and communicative purposes (narratives are imaginary texts; they are primarily written to entertain people and non-fiction texts are written to present facts or true information about a topic or topics)
- comprehension (reading is about making meaning) and comprehension strategies (visualise, summarise, self-question and connect own knowledge to book content)
- oral language proficiency (e.g. vocabulary, morphology, syntax).

These early literacy skills and understandings are the building blocks for success in learning to read and write and they are part of what is often referred to as 'emergent literacy' (Clay, 1987). Emergent literacy is a phase of literacy learning that paves the way for, and eventually progresses to, standard reading and writing.

Literacy is a developmental process and children move through different phases of the development. Each phase is characterised by the achievement of certain understandings about literacy and of particular literacy skills. The degree to which children receive experiences in the family that support emergent literacy strongly correlates to their success in learning to read and write at school (Morrow, 2009; Snow, Burn & Griffith, 1999).

FAMILY LITERACY DIVERSITY

It is important to understand that no typical family experience of oral and written communication applies to all children. Children grow up in very diverse homes, families and communities, each characterised by its own unique set of social and cultural features. It cannot, therefore, be assumed that all children are provided with the experiences, the types of literacy models and the oral interactions that satisfactorily develop emergent literacy and contribute to later literacy success.

Family contexts will vary in terms of family unit structures, routines (for example, meal times, bed times, leisure activities, parenting roles of the adults), social and economic conditions, parent literacy levels, family stresses, child rearing and other cultural practices and values, and beliefs. All these factors interact to shape the literacy practices of the home.

Differences in literacy practices from family to family might lie in the amount and type of book reading and the use of written texts, the amount and style of interpersonal communication, and the level of parental guidance in building up knowledge about literacy. For some children, family literacy might be more oriented towards oral communication and involve less engagement with print-based texts. For some there might be rich and varied oral interactions, but for others a limited access to new vocabulary and different patterns of language. Some children might be raised in environments where talk is at a minimum. Daily story book reading may be a part of some family routines but not of others or there may be countless experiences with oral storytelling but not with the reading of books.

A significant difference in family literacy relates to children's access to books and the amount and type of book reading at home.

RESPONDING TO FAMILY DIVERSITY

In order to ensure that all children are given the best opportunity to successfully learn to read and write, pre-school and school literacy programs should be designed in light of family (and childcare) literacy experiences and children's literacy learning prior to school. It cannot be assumed that all children will be at the same starting point in their literacy development on arrival at pre-school or Year 1 and so teachers must determine the children's current literacy levels and the types of family literacy that they have experienced. Children with minimal emergent literacy skills and understandings, and with family literacy experiences that are incongruent to the experiences of 'school literacy', require particular literacy learning opportunities. Effective teaching programs build on children's existing strengths; they start with what children already know, what they can do and what they have experienced and then work towards teaching the things that are not yet known or able to be done.

Literacy learning is enhanced when teachers recognise that all children come to school with their own individual expertise or '**funds of knowledge**' (Moll, 1992). Their family life and community experiences nurture certain understandings, abilities, practices and interests. For instance, some children might be knowledgeable about football because attending games is a regular family event. Others might have special ability with computer games or with fixing things or they might have an interest in cooking, motorbikes or cars. Alternatively, visits to art galleries, holidays by the beach or time with grandparents might be integral to the family lives of children. Whatever it is, when these 'funds of knowledge' are validated by being used as the vehicles for literacy learning, the children's ability to make sense of classroom literacy activities and their level of motivation and engagement are enhanced.

One example of making use of children's funds of knowledge comes from the practices of a teacher in a country community. She developed a program for making links between children's home experiences and the literacy teaching practices of her classroom. Children took turns taking digital cameras home and, with the help of their parents, photographed different family, home and community activities. The photos were used as a springboard for a variety of oral language, reading and writing activities of the classroom. Conversations, oral language games, vocabulary extension tasks and writing activities were all implemented using the photos. She used the pictures to develop small reading books for the children to read and to develop word and sentence knowledge and phonics skill. Other literacy texts, linking to the topic, were brought into the program—visuals, shared reading books, videos and word cards.

Another example involves a teacher who had been working in a remote Indigenous community. In getting to know his class, he became aware that, for many of the children, leisure time regularly involved fishing. He noticed the enthusiasm with which they talked about these experiences so he decided to use them as the stepping stone for classroom literacy. He began with a class excursion to the local fishing spot. For many days after, the children were engaged in a great deal of talking and writing about the experience. He continued with the topic for a number of weeks, extending on it by bringing in new areas of learning that highlighted new topic concepts and literacy skills. The activities were developed to encompass other curriculum areas and additional resources—books, posters, photographs, videos and the internet were used. In discussing the program, he reported that the most profound learning for him had to do with the level of motivation and engagement that came from working with a topic of relevance to the children and their lives outside of school.

FAMILY LITERACY INITIATIVES

Because of the significance of children's family literacy to the learning of reading and writing, a large number of community and school programs have been established that assist parents to provide their young children with important family literacy experiences. They are usually designed for parents of children in the years before formal schooling and are often set up within a community health centre or library. Many childcare centres, pre-schools and primary schools also provide families with an understanding of home literacy practices for their young children. The impetus to support family literacy is founded on the now well-established understanding of the relationship between home literacy and learning to read and write, and of the diversity of young children's literacy experiences in the family. These programs serve to support families to engage their children in family experiences that foster the development of emergent literacy at home and work towards closing the gap between the literacy learning of all children.

Better Beginnings (Barratt-Pugh, Rohl, Oakley & Elderfield, 2005) is one successful home literacy support program. It aims to foster parents' understanding of their roles as children's first teachers and to increase their understanding of emergent literacy development and of appropriate home literacy experiences for children in the first three years of their life. Through the Better Beginnings program, parents of newborns are provided with a variety of resources that support emergent family literacy practices—information about the value of sharing books with children, a children's book, recommendations of other good books for infants and toddlers, a growth chart depicting the words of a number of nursery rhymes, and information about useful library resources. Additionally, parents are provided with access to childcare, child development workshops and a wealth of ideas for incorporating literacy learning experiences into the everyday home and community experiences of families. The ideas are 'flexible and varied enough to connect with all families including those that do not share a reading culture and whose children are at the greatest risk of not developing [emergent] literacy skills' (Barratt-Pugh et al., 2005).

Another program which is designed to support family literacy is Bridging the Gap (Freeman & Bochner, 2008). It was developed to meet the specific needs of a particular community. The impetus for the establishment of this program was a teacher's concern that, with a family culture of oral rather than written communication, her Indigenous students were not adequately prepared to deal with the literacy learning demands of the school. Bridging the Gap served to expand the home literacy experiences of young Indigenous children, through shared book reading and child–parent literacy interactions.

The Bridging the Gap program is a combination of resources and parent training that focuses on developing children's emergent literacy skills and understandings. The resources comprise a set of culturally appropriate books for reading to children, together with tape recordings prepared by members of the local Indigenous community that accompany each book. A series of literacy games and activities are also supplied for each book. In order to assist parents' with use of the resources, the school's Indigenous education assistant demonstrates different reading techniques as well as the format of the literacy games. An evaluation of the program has shown it to be effective in producing positive outcomes in regard to children's emergent literacy skills. These included an increased ability with listening comprehension, story recall and sequencing; development in phonological awareness and letter identification; and an increased knowledge of different print concepts (Freeman & Bochner, 2008).

Research supports the fact that more needs to be done to 'bridge the gap' between Indigenous children's learning at home and that which needs to take place at school. Many Indigenous children come to school with different knowledge bases and different ways of learning.

PARENT–TEACHER PARTNERSHIPS

Parent–teacher partnerships entail teachers and parents working together to provide the best opportunity for children to achieve optimal development and learning. Partnerships involve a high degree of collaboration between parents and teachers in addressing important issues and requirements for children's language and literacy development, and establishing practices that promote parents' involvement in their children's care and education. The underlying principle is that both parents and teachers have a role to perform in children's development and learning and that when they work together children have a greater chance of success. Parent–teacher partnerships are most effective in supporting children's progress when they have the following characteristics.

TWO-WAY COMMUNICATION

Reciprocal communication between parents and teachers brings a wealth of information that supports the work of both families and teachers. Teachers need to create a variety of means by which they can convey information about, for example, the curriculum and the program, children's language and literacy development and learning in general, as well as opportunities for sharing with individual parents about their child's progress and needs. Teachers should also create the means by which parents share their own knowledge about their children—their experiences, interests, likes, concerns and needs—and about the home and family culture. Teachers should value the insights that parents can offer about their children.

MUTUAL RESPECT

The teacher and parents view each other as having valuable contributions to make to children's language and literacy development and learning. Teachers tap into the rich source of information and expertise that parents have about their children, which results in a greater potential for programs to be more effective. Families and parents respect the teachers' professional expertise and their work in supporting the children's progress.

COMMON LITERACY LEARNING GOALS

The goals for children's development are established from a comprehensive understanding of each child. This requires drawing on parents' knowledge as well as on teacher assessments and observations. Parents' expectations for their children and their views on their children's development and learning needs are brought into play in setting goals.

OPPORTUNITIES FOR PARENT PARTICIPATION

Parents are invited to participate in decision making and to become involved in learning programs. Surveys, questionnaires, committee membership or workshops are used to give parents a voice in the decisions of the centre or school and to seek their assistance in the implementation of programs. Parents should be made to feel welcome and comfortable when they become involved and help out.

FLEXIBILITY AND VARIETY IN PARTNERSHIP PRACTICES

Parents are provided with different ways and times for learning about, and becoming involved in, the children's day and with the activities and experiences with which the children are provided. They are given various alternatives for involvement. Opportunities might include helping out with activities, making resources, attending information evenings or coordinating special projects or activities. Family ideas sheets and newsletters can be used to support parent–teacher links and parent involvement.

RESPECT FOR DIVERSITY

The different family experiences and their cultural and social backgrounds are responded to positively, and development and learning programs take into account **family diversity**. Parents will feel validated and will more likely feel comfortable in coming to the centre or school.

THE BENEFITS OF PARENT–TEACHER PARTNERSHIPS

When parents and teachers work in partnership, there are a great many advantages for children's development and learning, some of which include the following.

- When parents are involved in their children's out-of-home care and education, and when teachers draw on parents' knowledge of their children, children's transition from home to childcare, pre-school or school is made easier. Teachers are more easily able to ensure that development and learning programs take account of the diversity between families and respond positively to their cultural and social backgrounds.
- When teachers work in collaboration with parents, there are strong positive effects on children's development and learning. Partnerships allow for children's emergent literacy knowledge and skills to be more readily enhanced.
- Parents have a strong influence on their children's attitude to the centre or school, and partnerships can influence parents in encouraging their children's development and learning in and out of these settings.
- When partnerships lead to parents being in a more informed position, they are more likely to support teachers' goals for their children and their care and education practices.
- Because the home environment becomes an element in the totality of language and literacy programs, parent–teacher partnerships can assist in supporting children's interest in, and engagement with, development and learning activities and experiences.

- Parent–teacher partnerships work to enhance parents' understandings about the culture (values, attitudes, practices, behaviours) of the centre or school as well as teachers' insights about the culture of the home. This helps to counteract the effect of any cultural mismatches between each domain.
- When parents are involved in the activities of child care, pre-school or school, they bring a new set of skills and expertise which can complement those of the teacher and thus enhance outcomes for children.
- When parents contribute their time to assist with childcare, pre-school and school programs, more can be achieved and children can be given more adult support.
- When parents assist they get to see and understand the way language and literacy is defined, and its development and learning is supported; what they learn can guide them in their support for children's language and literacy at home.
- When parent–teacher partnerships include various practices for regular communication, teachers and parents are more easily able to access each other, and important aspects about children's development and learning can be more readily discussed.

PARTNERSHIP PRACTICES

There is no standard model for **parent partnership programs** but, rather, there is a number of practices which are worthwhile. Any such practice should play a part in successful language and literacy learning for all children. It is important to follow a program that emphasises the significant role of parents in their children's childcare, pre-school or school. Parents are their children's first and most enduring teachers and they exert a strong influence on their children's values, attitudes, aspirations and learning. The following are a range of valuable practices for inclusion in parent partnership programs.

PARENTS HELPING IN THE CENTRE OR CLASSROOM

Parents (and grandparents) can be asked to help with learning activities and experiences. They can be given a number of opportunities to be involved; however, the type of involvement will naturally depend on the setting and the children involved. In regards to language and literacy, parents might read and talk about stories with children, transcribe children's oral stories or join in a play experience and, in so doing, initiate and support children's use of language and their engagement with and understanding of texts. Parents might share their special skills, talents or experience or they might talk with children about a topic of expertise in which they have some aptitude (for example, a job or hobby). They might hear children read, guide them as they write or lead a small group in writing a text together. The opportunities for, and the benefits of, parent participation are abundant. Children's language and literacy development and learning can be well supported when parents are involved in childcare and education settings and when a range of adults support and guide children in their endeavours.

Before approaching parents, a teacher should plan the various tasks and activities in which parents' involvement would be useful. The focus should always be the children's development and learning, but this might include developing parents' understanding of the approaches to children's language and literacy development. Once the tasks are established, a letter can be written to parents or a meeting called to ascertain their availability and interest in becoming involved.

When parents are provided with information about the activities they might help with and how best to nurture children's language and literacy, they are in a better position to enhance the children's development and learning and they are likely to be more confident in their role in the centre's or school's program. An information card might be provided ahead of time, whereby the nature of the activity and the materials to be used are indicated. Additionally, it might provide some guidelines as to the way in which children can be encouraged to think and talk so as to support their literacy learning.

Parents and extended family members can provide time, energy and expertise which can support children's language and literacy development in many ways. However, it is important to provide choice and flexibility and to ensure parents' confidence in being involved in the development and learning activities and experiences.

EXAMPLE YEAR 1 INFORMATION CARD FOR PARENT INVOLVEMENT

THANK YOU for coming in
to help with our
Language and Literacy Program

This week you will be reading a story to _____

The name of the story is _____

Helpful hints:

- Make sure all children can see the book while you are reading.
- Before reading ask the following questions:
  _____
  _____
  _____

- Read the story and:
  - Show children the pictures and help the children get additional information from the pictures.
  - Use an animated voice that brings the story alive.
  - Stop every so often to ask a question about the story, the characters or the setting.
  - Encourage the children to join in when you read the repeated sentences.
  - When you have finished reading the story, ask the children to tell you what happened (____ events in order).
  - Ask questions that encourage them to provide detail as they describe the events.
- The children can then move to their group work area and complete the _____ activity (provided).

COMMUNICATION ABOUT CHILDREN'S LITERACY PROGRESS

It is essential to ensure that families are informed about and understand their child's progress. They should be kept up to date about their children's language and literacy development and be involved in finding solutions to any problems that might arise. Communication between parents and teachers should be encouraged and a variety of different formal and informal communication procedures established. These could include:

- *The parent–teacher conference* involves a meeting between a child's parent/s and the teacher in person to discuss the child's development needs, interests and problems and solutions. It is useful to schedule conferences soon after the year commences to enable the teacher to get to know the children and their families. Any important information can be shared. There should also be regular conferences with parents throughout the year. The teacher can take the opportunity to provide observations and assessments and together parents and teachers can set goals which can be reinforced at home and at school. Effective parent–teacher conferences call for a quiet space, comfortable seating and adequate planning. It is important to allow enough time for adequate parent input. The scheduling of conferences should ideally be flexible in regards to time and venue so as to give all parents the opportunity to attend. Where parents do not speak English, a translator should attend if at all possible.
- *Home–centre/school messages*, a less formal approach to communication than the parent–teacher conference, are an important method of regular ongoing communication between the home and the teacher. They might take the form of letters or notes or they might involve the establishment of a specific communication book that travels back and forth between the home and the centre or school. Home–centre/school messages should

Meetings between a child's parent/s and the teacher are important for ensuring that the child's development, learning and interests, and emotional and social needs are well catered for.

serve to strengthen the working partnership between parents and teachers and to extend parents' understanding of their children's development and learning and of the experiences and activities in which their children engage. They are most useful in dealing with daily incidental communication; for instance, information about children's engagement with particular activities, new interests or their day-to-day language and literacy successes.

- *Literacy portfolios* are organised collections of photographs, samples of the children's work, transcribed conversations, teacher observations and notes, as well as other sources providing information about children's language and literacy growth and achievements. They serve to demonstrate the different dimensions of children's development and learning—what they can understand and can do. The main purpose of the portfolio is to inform parents and families about their children's progress. However, they also provide a means by which teachers, when working with older children, can foster their self-assessment and goal setting. Each item in a portfolio is annotated with the date and a description of the experience from which the sample came. Other information signifying children's language and literacy progress might be included such as the teachers' observational notes, and a checklist indicating skills. The portfolio is sent home for review and response by parents. It might also be used as a focus of discussion during parent–teacher conferences. Literacy portfolios should be sent home regularly as they provide an important means of keeping parents abreast about their children's progress.

- *Sharing and celebrating* the achievements and milestones of children's language and literacy development are essential for their continued motivation and sense of esteem as literacy learners. Parents are also motivated when communication from teachers involves children's successes. What children are able to understand and do in oral and written communication can be shared with parents in many different ways. A newsletter explaining activities and containing copies or photographs of children's work might be sent home each month. A bulletin board outside the centre or classroom could display photographs taken of the children as they carry out activities and associated descriptions. These could be changed regularly. Morning teas, open days or end-of-term celebrations provide the opportunity for children to share experiences and for older children to show and explain their language and literacy experiences and achievements to family members.

PARENT SURVEYS

A parent survey comprises a written list of questions for the purpose of gathering information from parents about their children. It might have questions about children's favourite home activities and their competencies and expertise, parents' perceptions about children's oral communication as well as the home literacy environment and family literacy practices. Surveys should be designed so that they can easily be completed by parents. This might involve the use of checklists or multiple choice answers or questions requiring yes/no answers. Parent surveys are useful for gathering family information that is important to teachers in designing and implementing learning programs that make connections to children's lives outside of the centre or classroom. A parent observation sheet is a different type of survey which can be used for parents to record their observations about their child's language and literacy growth.

PARENTAL AWARENESS

Parents can be empowered to adopt a positive and proactive approach to their children's language and literacy development when they are provided with information about language and literacy and about the development and learning experiences of their children's care and education setting. The information provided will depend on the needs and priorities of the parents and of childcare, pre-school or school. The enhancement of parents' knowledge about language and literacy can take place through workshops, information sheets and the establishment of a parent resource room.

- *The literacy workshop* is a centre- or school-based short course (one session or a series of sessions) run by teachers or other education professionals for the purpose of explaining or demonstrating aspects of the language and literacy curriculum and related development and learning experiences. They might also serve to explain and discuss policy or to talk about methods with parents who have volunteered to assist with the learning and development program. Parents may also wish to use these sessions to discuss their own family literacy practices. Workshops should usually be designed in consultation with parents. A needs assessment survey could be sent out to determine parents' interests and needs.
- *The parent resource room* is a place in the care and education setting where parents can borrow books or articles about language and literacy. There is a variety of topics, such as family literacy, beginning and emergent literacy, reading, comprehension, writing, oral language, methods, choosing books for children etc. which might be covered. Parents should have the opportunity for input into the types of information to which they would like to have access.
- *Information sheets*, like other parental awareness techniques, are used to provide parents with language and literacy information. They are a simple and convenient means of informing parents. An information sheet might be sent home regularly and the topics might include those that arose from the parental survey or from discussions at parent conferences. Wherever possible, if the parents' first language is not English the information sheets should be translated into their first language.

DECISION MAKING

It is important to provide opportunities for parents to work with teachers in arriving at decisions in areas that effect their children's care and education. Committees can be established whereby parents work with teachers to choose topics and resources for learning and development programs. Surveys can be sent home that call for parents to indicate topics that would likely interest their children.

TAKE-HOME LITERACY RESOURCES

Parent–teacher partnerships and children's language and literacy development can be promoted by the use of carefully designed resources for families to take home to use with their children. They are a way in which children and families can participate in enjoyable language and literacy activities that support the experiences and development and learning goals of

Family literacy can be supported through the supply of different literacy resource packages for families to take home to use with their children.

the care and education setting. Resources might include story books, writing materials, games, tapes of songs and rhymes, or recipes and other texts. To maximise involvement and success, each pack should contain a letter to parents, explaining the purpose of the pack and the ways in which children should be engaged with the activities and resources.

- *Literacy bags* contain different books, book audio tapes and other literacy resources that promote enjoyable and relevant reading and writing experiences for children to undertake with their families. There might be a set of different bags, each of which contains different books, resources and activities. Different bags might be suitable for children at different development levels. Children and families borrow the bags to take home for a week or so at a time.

> ### THE TAKE-HOME LITERACY BAG
>
> The bags consist of:
>
> - sets of books (fiction and non-fiction) on a theme of interest to the children
> - related activities/materials—link to books or topic
> - activities for developing literacy knowledge, emergent literacy skills and a positive attitude to story books and literacy learning
> - games, craft and play-type activities (suited to the learning style of the age group).
>
> Bags are borrowed by families and kept for a week or two.
> Families read the books with their children and choose and carry out some of the activities.
>
> **Example**
>
> Topic: ducks
> Literacy level: emergent/early
> Texts: *Duckling, Six little ducks, Do like a duck does.*
> Activities:
> After reading the *Duckling* book, the parent/child:
>
> - writes one thing learnt about ducks in the record book provided
> - records (draw or write) in the diary provided the things Oliver Duck does with the family
> - uses the pictures provided to sequence and retell the events from the story
> - uses the letter cards to experiment with making words.

- *A lending library* can be set up for parents to borrow books, puppets and recorded stories and other language and literacy learning resources for their children's use at home. There should be materials that cater for the different interests of children, books that parents can read aloud and those that are appropriate to the group of children involved.

WORKING WITH FAMILIES FROM CULTURALLY AND LINGUISTICALLY DIVERSE BACKGROUNDS

AUSTRALIA IS A MULTICULTURAL SOCIETY

Australian people represent a rich variety of language and cultures. Approximately 2.5 per cent of Australia's people are Indigenous Australians, many of whom have a home language that is not English; it might be one of the approximately 250 traditional Indigenous languages, or Aboriginal English or Creole, or it might be another dialect of English. The practices, beliefs and values of many of Australia's Indigenous people reflect their traditional culture.

The population of Australia also includes around 2.5 million people who have migrated from non-English speaking countries and who have brought with them their own culture and language. Approximately 200 languages, other than English, are spoken by these migrants (Australian Bureau of Statistics, 2006).

Considering the diversity of cultures and language in Australian society, early childhood teachers will inevitably work with families and children of different cultural backgrounds and those for whom English is not their home language. Culture refers to:

> … the values; traditions; social and political relationships; and world view created, shared and transformed by a group of people bound together by a common history, geographic location, language, social class and/or religion. (Nieto, 2004, p. 436)

Cultural diversity in families yields differences in such things as the roles of the different family members, communication practices, attitudes to education, religious beliefs and practices, family ritual, and food and child-rearing practices.

Differences in child-rearing practices might involve the type of play encouraged, teaching and discipline methods, the time spent by parents with their children, the regularity of family activities, the type and frequency of communication between parents and children, and the level of freedom granted to children.

Cultural diversity is also reflected by differences in the language spoken at home. Language is integral to culture.

While it is important to understand that there can be many differences between families of different cultures, it is equally important to be aware of their shared values and practices; principal among these shared values is that parents of all cultures generally want what is best for their children. They want them to be healthy and to develop skills for a good life.

Children for whom Standard Australian English (SAE) is not their home language are understandably prone to an inadequate development of their reading and writing of English. In the case of Indigenous children, levels of literacy learning are frequently well below that of non-Indigenous children. Although there has been some degree of improvement over the past few years, the gap between the literacy achievements of Indigenous and non-Indigenous children still remains, with the discrepancy usually being wider in remote locations. The discrepancy in literacy achievement can, to a large degree, be attributed to the disparity between the cultural practices of the home and those of the childcare centre or school. Teachers should endeavour to acknowledge and take account of the diversity of the languages and cultures of the children's families. Literacy learning and development is more likely to be fostered when family culture is understood and respected and when there is a degree of consistency between the practices and expectations for success in the home and childcare or school contexts.

IMPORTANT PRACTICES

Endeavours to promote the involvement of parents and families without the benefit of a shared language, or when cultural practices and ideals are not clearly understood, can present something of a challenge. However, there are a number of practices which foster successful partnerships with families from culturally and linguistically diverse backgrounds. Teachers should be mindful of the following.

- Understand and respect the differences between their own culture and the culture of the families with whom they are working; that is, they should recognise and respond to the individual nature of different families—who they are, how they do things, what they believe and what they need.
- Be aware of the children's home environment and consistently demonstrate to families and children that the home language is valued. The maintenance and use of the home language is important to children's participation in family life and to their sense of identity and self-esteem.
- Encourage the use and development of the child's home language within and outside of the centre or school. A number of benefits flow from children maintaining fluency and developing literacy skills in their home language. Their learning is enhanced and, because literacy skills and comprehension have been built up in the child's first language, English literacy skills are more readily embraced. In other words, the skills first learnt benefit English literacy learning.
- Use various sources of information to gain an understanding of different cultural practices. While a general understanding can be gained from books and organisations, the most substantial and distinctive source of knowledge is the families themselves.
- Avoid cultural stereotypes and generalisations and display non-judgmental attitudes. 'Dealing with your preconceptions and being careful of your judgments is vitally important if you are to build strong relationships with the parents of your students. It is as much about working with your own thoughts and assumptions as it is about working with them' (Harrison, 2008, p. 120).
- Make adjustments to the general practices of parent–teacher partnerships (outlined earlier in the chapter) so they cater for the needs of families from different cultural and language backgrounds. The use of translators and interpreters may be one such adjustment. If interpreters are not readily available from official sources, a member of the community who speaks both languages may be able to assist. Wherever possible, written information to parents (newsletters, information sheets, surveys etc.) should be translated and conferences should involve the use of a translator.
- Include aspects of family culture and the home language in the classroom. Notices, posters, charts and signs can be displayed in both English and the home language. The centre and schools materials and resources should reflect family cultural diversity. When parents visit, their sense of belonging and level of comfort can be heightened when the environment partly reflects their own language and culture.
- Ensure that plans for centre and school events take account of cultural or religious festivals that may affect the involvement of some parents.
- Adapt take-home literacy material (e.g. home literacy bags) in ways that take into account the English language capacity of the parents and children. Resources that include audio-taped readings of story books or bilingual books and dictionaries might be added.

> It is important to 'stretch' the existing childcare or school culture to reflect the culture of the children. How can this be done?

FACTORS AFFECTING THE INVOLVEMENT OF INDIGENOUS PARENTS

Teachers should understand the reticence of some Indigenous parents to become involved in their children's care and education outside of the home. Any lack of involvement should not be judged as disinterest; it can be influenced by any of a number of different factors, examples of which might be:

- family histories that involve a burden of unfair treatment or unequal relationships between Indigenous and non-Indigenous people
- the language/dialect difference between parents and teachers and discomfort with teacher's use of Standard Australian English and with the formality of the childcare or school meetings and other events
- the parents' own negative experiences of school or limited school experience
- a lack of cultural understanding on the part of the childcare centre and school or a generalised view of Indigenous families that does not take account of any difference within the group
- poverty and illness making it difficult for parents to attend activities and functions
- a lack of effort by centres and schools to engage parents, or contact from centres and schools that is limited purely to the discussion of problems
- a lack of consultation about the celebrations of Indigenous culture at school.

Source: Sanagavarapu, Skattebol and Woodrow (2008) and Harrrison (2008)

COMMUNICATING WITH INDIGENOUS FAMILIES

As with all families, successful communication with Indigenous families is about building strong, respectful relationships with parents and sharing knowledge and experiences. Any barriers to successful communication should be identified and genuine attempts need to be made to address them.

> One day, when talking to Rose, an elderly member of the Indigenous community where I was teaching, I told her how much I enjoyed fishing. The very next day, and every day after school for a week, she came around to my home, fishing rod in hand, and told me that she was going fishing. I couldn't understand why she came to tell me. I would have loved to have gone with her. I eventually realised; she was offering to take me fishing. But rather than ask directly, she was allowing me the comfort of not having to decline but to simply take up the offer. What I should have said is, 'I will come too.'

Communication with Indigenous parents is enhanced when teachers take into account the interaction styles of the culture. However, it is important to remember that, although it is useful to be aware of the general practices of Indigenous culture, there will always be variations in the ways in which individual Indigenous people interact. The following are some suggestions to assist in establishing good communication practices with Indigenous parents.

- Use a personal approach—first names, be casual, engage in social talk before getting to the business at hand.
- Indicate equal status—do not assert position or come across as having superior knowledge.
- Be a little ambiguous in seeking and giving information—circle around the topic; learn by using indirect questions or comments. For many Indigenous people indirectness is more courteous than candour.
- Avoid being assertive or aggressive—to intimate rather than impose ideas is a more sensitive approach; be non-confrontational and if disagreement must be expressed do it without discrediting the opinion of the other person.
- Ensure speech is kept free of educational jargon.
- Take plenty of time; do not rush conversations.

The engagement of parents, of whatever cultural background, in the life of the childcare centre or school and good parent–teacher communication are invaluable strategies for helping all children achieve optimal language and literacy outcomes. Understanding each individual family is an important first step.

SUMMARY

Children grow up in diverse families and communities, each characterised by its own unique set of social and cultural features including communication practices. Getting to know families and communities and being familiar with the language and literacy practices valued by families is important to the effectiveness of the language and literacy programs of the childcare, pre-school and school settings. Working in partnership with parents where planning and implementation involves strong collaborations is important to children's learning and development success. There is a range of practices that can be adopted to foster effective partnerships. Of significance is the establishment of regular effective communication, which requires building strong, respectful relationships and sharing knowledge and experiences.

QUESTIONS AND ACTIVITIES

1. Locate and summarise the suggested methods for working towards strong and effective parent–teacher partnerships. Then investigate and determine other methods that might also support this purpose.
2. Create a chart that depicts the ways in which the features of each of the settings of childcare, pre-school and school might influence parent involvement.
3. How might a person's cultural and linguistic background influence their communication with a childcare centre, pre-school or school?
4. Decide on the possible content of take-home literacy packs for different groups of learners—toddlers, pre-schoolers and children in the early years of school.

5 Find out about state or nationwide Australian family and community programs that have been developed to support young children's language development and early experiences with books and other written texts.
6 How might you set up the childcare environment for a group of three-year-olds so that the topics, materials, experiences and activities build on the children's prior knowledge, family and community experiences and interests?

KEY TERMS

cultural diversity
family diversity
family (or home) literacy
funds of knowledge
parent partnership programs
parent–teacher partnerships
two-way communication

KEY REFERENCES

Barratt-Pugh, C., Rohl, M., Oakley, G. & Elderfield, J. (2005) *Better beginnings: An Evaluation from two communities*. Edith Cowan University.

Burns, M., Griffin, P. & Snow, C. E. (eds) (1999). *Starting out right: A guide to promoting children's reading success*. USA: Committee on the Prevention of Reading Difficulties in Young Children.

Clay, M. (1987) *Writing begins at home: Preparing children for writing before they go to school*. Auckland: Heinemann.

Docket, S., Perry, B., Mason, T., Simpson, T., Howard, P., Whitton, D., Gilbert, S., Pearce, S., Sanagavarapu, P., Skattebol, J. & Woordrow, C. (2008). *Successful transitions from prior-to-school for Aboriginal and Torres Strait Islander children*. Carlton South, Vic: Ministerial Council on Education, Employment and Youth Affairs.

Freeman, L. & Bochner, S. (2008). Bridging the gap: Improving literacy outcomes for Indigenous students. *Australian Journal of Early Childhood 33*(4), 9–16.

Harrison, N. (2008). *Teaching and learning in Indigenous education*. Melbourne: Oxford University Press.

Morrow, L. M. (2009). *Literacy development in the early years: Helping children read and write*. Boston: Pearson Education.

Nieto. S. (2004). *Affirming diversity: The socio-political context of multicultural education*. Boston: Pearson Education.

Snow, C., Dickenson. D. & Tabors, P. (2001) Language development in the preschool years (pp. 1–26). In D. Dickenson & P. Tabors (eds), *Beginning literacy with language: Young children learning at home and school*. Baltimore: Paul H. Brookes.

CHAPTER 26

Planning for Language and Literacy Learning and Development

With contributions by Tracy Heldt

CHAPTER OBJECTIVES

This chapter will increase your understanding of:

- important features of good learning programs
- important features of language and literacy learning programs for infants, toddlers, pre-schoolers and school-age children
- developing an integrated program for language and literacy learning
- developing a stand-alone English program
- the importance of children's attitude and motivation to their language and literacy development and learning.

In order to effectively cater for children's language and literacy development, teaching and learning programs need to be planned and written. This chapter provides you with information about developing language and literacy programs for different groups of early childhood learners. It presents information important to effective long-term planning and provides a specific focus on the use of integrated and stand-alone programs for language and literacy. This chapter provides some insight into how to draw together the information from previous chapters so as to be able to set up learning environments and learning spaces and implement experiences and activities in a cohesive and considered way.

PLANNING DEVELOPMENT AND LEARNING PROGRAMS

Learning programs are produced to map the different ways in which children's learning and development needs will be addressed over a set period of time. Their production involves making decisions about the outcomes, content, learning experiences, teaching strategies and practices, and the resources and assessment methods to be used (Annandale, Bindon, Handley, Johnston, Locket & Lynch, 2003, p. 141). They are generally developed with either a short-term (two weeks) focus or for a longer period of time (five to ten weeks) and are important to ensuring continuity and cohesiveness in the provisions made for children's learning and development. They should be underpinned by a sound knowledge of the children and their families.

There are a number of important factors to be taken into account to develop an effective learning program; these include:

- the prior learning, developmental phases and learning needs of the children
- the diversity of the children's learning needs at a particular phase of development; whole group, small groups and individual learning and development needs should be provided for
- the different learning styles, interests, ideas and strengths of the children
- the outcomes for children (birth to five years) of *The Early Years Learning Framework for Australia* (DEEWR, 2009, p. 9):
    - Children have a strong sense of identity
    - Children are connected with and contribute to their world
    - Children have a strong sense of wellbeing
    - Children are confident and involved learners
    - Children are effective communicators
- national and state curricula outcomes for the relevant learning areas
- the features of the setting in which the children's learning is taking place, i.e. childcare, pre-school or early years of school
- the developmental domains:
    - Physical Development
    - Cognitive Development
    - Language and Literacy Development
    - Personal and Emotional Development
    - Social and Moral Development
- working with and involving families and the wider community
- the language and cultural backgrounds of the children
- children's family and community experiences
- research-based knowledge about how young children learn and best practices for children's learning and development
- the central role of communication and interaction, critical thinking and problem-solving skills
- the people available to assist with program implementation
- the importance of developing children's confidence, enthusiasm, enjoyment and independence.

In regards to language and literacy, program design should be considerate of:

- the various modes—reading, writing, speaking and listening, viewing and critical literacy
- children's phases of development within each of reading, writing, listening and speaking, and viewing, and the skills, knowledge and understandings to be developed
- the different aspects of:
  - oral and written texts
  - contextual understanding (the use of oral and written language in different situations and different socio-cultural contexts)
  - conventions (structures, systems and patterns of oral and written language)
  - processes and strategies (approaches and techniques to ensure effective use of oral and written language)
- the materials and resources to support children's language and literacy learning, as well as their engagement and motivation
- experiences to promote children's confidence, enthusiasm, enjoyment and independence in language and literacy
- the language and cultural backgrounds of the children
- the oral communication and literacy practices of the families.

CREATING A LEARNING PROGRAM

There is no one way to create programs for children birth to eight years; different approaches are required depending on whether they are for infants, toddlers, pre-schoolers or school-age children. The program goals and outcomes and the learning experiences and activities should be established with due consideration given to the children's age, developmental capacities, learning needs, and language and culture, as well as the features of the setting (childcare, pre-school or school) in which children's learning is to take place.

Play, exploration and **holistic learning** should be central to the experiences provided for early childhood, regardless of the setting. However, there will be groups of children who, for optimal growth and development, require a degree of **intentional teaching** as well as **explicit systematically organised teaching**. For instance, to fully support the literacy development of emergent learners (when learning is often taking place in the pre-school setting), a degree of explicit systematic teaching is required; and, when working with children in the early literacy development phase and beyond (most likely when in the school setting), it is beneficial to implement a daily literacy session where reading, writing, listening and speaking, and viewing are individually addressed in a cohesive and connected framework. When developing learning programs it is necessary to bear in mind when such approaches are important to ensuring the best possible opportunity for children to learn and develop.

KEY FEATURES OF A LEARNING PROGRAM

A good early childhood learning program will contain certain key elements, though there might be some variation depending on the group of children for whom the program is being developed. Key program elements include the following.

A COMPREHENSIVE OVERVIEW OF THE CHILDREN

- Speak with families and learn about the children—their home and community experiences, dispositions and learning styles, interests, language spoken at home, family and community cultural practices etc.
- Observe children and talk with them and get to know them—what they enjoy doing, what they do well, and what they need to further develop. For older children this might also involve carrying out some formal assessments.

RELEVANT AND REALISTIC GOALS FOR THE CHILDREN'S LEARNING AND DEVELOPMENT

- Consult state and national documents (e.g. *The Early Years Learning Framework for Australia* and/or national and state curricula) and other professional support material and consider what children should know, understand and be able to do.
- Keep in mind what children's prior experiences are and what they currently know, understand and can do, as well as the goals and aspirations of their families.
- Consider the various domains or learning areas and the 'development paths that children typically follow' (NAEYC, 2009, p. 21).

A TOPIC FOCUS

- Consider the potential for integration across learning domains and/or learning areas.
- Consider the children's interests or decide on the topic in consultation with the children.
- Establish the main concepts within the topic—create a flow chart or explosion chart to determine the concepts within the topic and the various directions in which the topic can be taken.

PRINCIPLES (SET OF BELIEFS ABOUT TEACHING, LEARNING AND DEVELOPMENT)

- These should shape the practices to be employed in supporting children's learning and development.
- Refer to current research-based information about how children best learn and about best practices for young children's development and learning.
- Consider the features of the setting and the expectations of the key stakeholders.

THE LEARNING PROGRAM

- Plan the environment, the schedule and the experiences and activities.
- Consider such things as the indoor and outdoor environment; the materials and resources; the learning centres or areas; the routines and transitions; whole class, small group and individual experiences; the roles of adults; intentional teaching; oral interactions; and investigation and problem solving.
- Where appropriate, consider the explicit systematic teaching to be carried out and other teaching strategies to be employed.

- Ensure all components are appropriate to the developmental phase of the children and that they serve to clearly and comprehensively address the established goals and outcomes.

METHODS TO BE USED TO MONITOR (ASSESS AND EVALUATE) CHILDREN'S DEVELOPMENT AND LEARNING

- Ensure manageable and systematic methods are used.
- Ensure that an understanding of children's learning and development in relation to the established goals and outcomes is able to be clearly gained.

LANGUAGE AND LITERACY LEARNING PROGRAMS

INFANTS

When developing a program for infants there should be a strong focus on establishing security, creating opportunities for infant and caregiver interactions and on providing for the infants' exploration of the environment (NAEYC, 2003). Carers should give individual attention to the infants and support their development during the routine activities of their day; for instance, when settling them to sleep and during meal and nappy-changing times.

In order to ensure their language and literacy development is addressed, a program for infants should include the following:

- The one-to-one interactions between carers and infants should involve reading and telling stories, reciting rhymes, talking to them about experiences and things in the environment, and responding orally to their babbles and sounds.
- Environments should be provided and materials with which they can interact and explore, including a variety of durable books.

TODDLERS

A program for toddlers should include a variety of flexible play experiences that 'integrate children's learning within and across the domains' (NAEYC, 2009, p. 21) and that cater for their different interests, abilities and needs. It should support free interaction and engagement with the environment and materials and allow for individual and group exploration and play.

In addressing language and literacy, a program for toddlers should include:

- a strong emphasis on oral communication and support for children's oral language development by way of adult role models and adult–child interactions. Adults should draw on various techniques to nurture and extend the children's use of language
- the provision of literacy-focused materials such as crayons and pencils and other writing implements for children to draw and scribble; magazines, books, brochures, pamphlets and so on; and the integration of functional texts in the environment (labels, posters and charts, written messages)

- displays and message boards for parents; these could include such things as photos and written descriptions that serve to share children's experiences
- reading stories aloud to the children and involving them in simple action rhymes, songs and finger plays.

PRE-SCHOOLERS

The pre-school program should include different free and structured play experiences and an environment that supports holistic and continuous development across the domains or learning areas. Moreover, there should be a balance of different types of play opportunities for the children: exploratory, socio-dramatic, games with rules etc. The program should include investigations and problem-solving activities in relation to children's interests and their growing competencies and knowledge. Individual, small group and large group experiences should be provided for and there should be opportunities for focused teacher-directed learning.

In order to ensure that language and literacy is appropriately addressed, a program for pre-schoolers should include:

- language and literacy within a holistic learning framework that also includes children's cognitive, social, emotional, physical and creative development
- children's language and literacy development as integral to the environment and the experiences of the day
- strategies and experiences that purposely cater for children's language and literacy development and learning (e.g. writing and reading centres, shared reading and modelled writing)
- a strong emphasis on experiences that develop children's oral language and communication competency and, in so doing, increase their vocabulary and syntactic ability
- the provision of experiences that make connections between oral and written language

Language and literacy development and learning occurs within a holistic learning framework.

- teaching strategies that support the development of emergent literacy knowledge, understanding and skills (e.g. modelled and shared writing, shared reading and explicit and systematic teaching of some fundamental skills)
- daily, explicit and teacher-directed experiences that support the children to develop phonological and phonemic awareness, letter knowledge and letter–sound association.

The following timetable for a class of pre-school children (five- to six-year-olds) shows how one teacher, Jane Crowley, has scheduled the experiences and activities for the day.

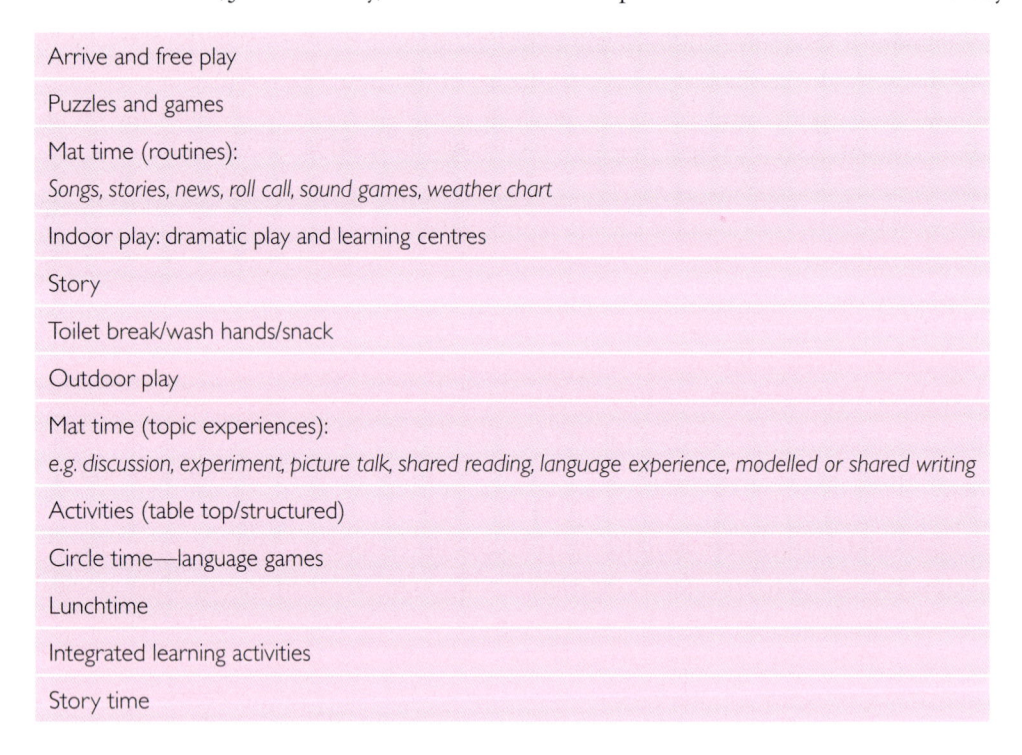

Arrive and free play
Puzzles and games
Mat time (routines): *Songs, stories, news, roll call, sound games, weather chart*
Indoor play: dramatic play and learning centres
Story
Toilet break/wash hands/snack
Outdoor play
Mat time (topic experiences): *e.g. discussion, experiment, picture talk, shared reading, language experience, modelled or shared writing*
Activities (table top/structured)
Circle time—language games
Lunchtime
Integrated learning activities
Story time

Table 26.1: Pre-school settings—balancing integrated language and literacy learning with focused literacy learning experiences

Balanced approaches	Integrate literacy into daily experiences	Focused literacy experiences
• Whole class • Small groups • Individuals • Teacher supported • Teacher directed	• Arrive and free play • Attendance • Mat time • Circle time • Dramatic play • Outdoor play • Learning centres • Interest areas • Special literacy areas • The environment • Games and activities • Activities (groups/structured) Transitions	• Modelled and shared writing • Language experience • Shared reading • Story time • Mat time (songs, rhymes, stories, other) • Small group literacy time • Reading and writing centres • Activities and experiences for developing phonological and phonemic awareness • Letters and words activities

Balanced approaches	Integrate literacy into daily experiences	Focused literacy experiences
	• Other • Problem-solving tasks • Topic activities	

The following tables highlight how the pre-school (five- to six-year-olds) teacher Jane Crowley has carefully planned the environment and experiences so that language and literacy learning is an integral part of the day. Additionally, it shows the provision of activities that more directly deal with achieving language and literacy outcomes. These language and literacy activities occur daily; they are short in duration, focused and involve the use of methods and activities appropriate to the children's age, development and needs.

Table 26.2: Language and literacy and the experiences of the pre-school

Whole Class Mat Session (routines)	
Activities and experiences	**Language and literacy**
Rhymes: I had a little nut tree; One-ery, two-ery Ziccary zan; A-B-C tumble down D; In a tree I see a bee; I saw a pretty flower; Five little monkey's swinging in the tree **Roll call:** (daily) identify initial phoneme in name; object—recognise when same starting phoneme as name **Weather chart:** (daily) complete sentences by placing right word to describe weather **Morning message:** (modelled writing) teacher writes to class on board, 'Dear class, Today we are going to plant sunflowers. Love Mrs Brown' **Morning message follow-up:** Each day use the message text—cloze, letter matching, segment and blend words. Word matching	• Phonological awareness • Phoneme identification • Sentences and words • Concepts of print • Writing as communication • Syntax and semantic cues in reading • Sight words • Letter identification • Letter–sound matching
Whole Class Mat Session (topic experiences) For example, discussion, experiment, picture talk, shared reading, language experience, modelled or shared writing	
Activities and experiences	**Language and literacy**
Shared reading: Big book—*From seed to plant*; *Flower garden* **Picture talk:** different plants, trees, flowers in nature **Nature walk:** observe, describe, collect fallen leaves, take photos **Shared writing:** using pictures from nature walk, write a recount, make a class big book **Language experience:** plant flower seedlings, record observations regularly in science journal	• Concepts of print • Reading comprehension • Understanding a non-fiction text • Oral language: vocabulary, using descriptive language, answering questions, recalling and verbalising recount of flower planting activity • Using visual and written texts to record ideas

Table Top Activities/Learning Centres	
Activities and experiences	**Language and literacy**
Activities (rotate over the week): **Order big book pictures:** glue down and write underneath (or dictate) **Sunflower petal counting:** place spots on flower petals (1–10) **Flower collage:** cut pictures from magazine, categorise according to colour, make collage **Leaf prints:** use paint to print or do crayon rubbings, using leaves collected on nature walk **Computer story:** Children listen and watch to story online—*Exploring the secret life of trees* **Leaf shape book:** work with representational materials to make a book about leaves **'L' is for leaf:** match item or picture with a foam letter according to initial phoneme	• Comprehension • Written communication • Experimental writing • Oral language: vocabulary, listening to and recalling steps of instructions • Reading and reading comprehension • Book concepts • Letter–sound correspondence • Letter identification
Snack Time and Transitions	
Activities and experiences	**Language and literacy**
To do while transitioning from one task to another or to snack or lunchtime: Rhymes and songs (from mat session) Find the letter (on wall) Identify words with a particular beginning sound Use charts and labels for locating areas and items	• Phonological awareness • Letter knowledge • Phoneme awareness • Text purposes
Indoor Learning Centres	
Activities and experiences	**Language and literacy**
Construction: using the large 2D and 3D shapes **Reading corner:** story and non-fiction texts on trees, plants and leaves; Listening post story—*The giving tree* **Writing centre:** pictures to label, leaf, flower and tree-shape paper and card. Examples of texts about nature displayed. Blank leaf-shape book **Puzzles/manipulatives:** threading/felt sewing to make a flower/tree; nature puzzles **Dramatic play:** plant shop/gardening—soil, pots, gardening trowel, spoons, large seeds, watering can, gloves, hats and gardening aprons. Literacy resources e.g. seed packets, labels for plants, signs for shop … **Painting/collage:** leaf symmetry; use crayon to complete other half of a leaf picture	• Role-play reading: applying print and text concepts • Writing for a purpose and an audience • Applying known print and text concepts and alphabetic principle • Understanding the function of written texts

Outdoor Learning Centres	
Activities and experiences	**Language and literacy**
Groups play in different areas over week: **Sand:** alphabet dig—bury letters, and children use shovels to dig up. Hang on alphabet tree (close by on board). Prepare pots for planting and plant bulbs **Water:** water plants in class garden; use different plant pots for water play. Coloured water—spray onto cardboard leaf shapes. Compare wood sawdust and shavings and how they interact with water (also do with different types of paper) **Climbing:** climbing frame, obstacle course—collect the flowers along the way. Tunnel; play hut **Games:** Don's dugout; 'Giant trees (down) and ladders (up)'—like 'Snakes and ladders'. Giant ball games; parachute games **Fundamental movement:** balance beam, moving in different ways and in different directions. High and low movements. Hop/jump/crawl/skip in hoops and around cones	• Letter recognition • Purposeful use of written texts (labels and signs in outdoor environment) • Oral communication (to instruct, compare and describe)

THE INTEGRATED PROGRAM

Integrated programs use a teaching approach where the traditional subject (learning area) boundaries disappear and learning occurs around themes or topics, real-life issues and student questions. An integrated program is a suitable way to consider the development and learning of toddlers, pre-schoolers and children in the early years of school.

When using an integrated approach to planning for children's development and learning, such methods as **inquiry-based learning**, projects and learning centres should be used. These methods enable children to make connections and develop understandings across learning areas. For example, the focus of setting up a classroom aquarium can provide opportunities for children to:

- reflect on what they know about fish and generate questions about what they want to know
- read fiction and non-fiction books to gain insights and information
- discuss and list roles and responsibilities for looking after fish
- plan and write about fish and how to care for them
- draw, paint, and create fish in art
- learn about pollution in waterways and how it impacts on fish life
- visit a pet shop to buy fish and equipment.

Through this example children are developing knowledge, skills and understandings in the areas of reading, writing, spelling, oral language, Art, Mathematics, and Society and Environment to accomplish their project. An integrated curriculum links learning to the real world, providing a meaningful context for concepts and skills to be developed.

It is important to note that an integrated curriculum does not replace the need to teach individual learning areas. It aims to provide a meaning context where children can learn and apply skills and develop conceptual understandings.

THE BENEFITS OF AN INTEGRATED CURRICULUM

There are many benefits to using an integrated curriculum in an early childhood setting. They include the following:

- It is physiologically compatible with how the brain functions. Links to prior information, patterns in information and webs of information are readily processed by our brains. An integrated curriculum brings these aspects into the planning of development and learning experiences for children.
- It provides a realistic context for learning, which is important to enhancing children's recall and memory.
- A wide variety of skills are employed in a meaningful manner. Learning occurs through the combined application of reading, writing, speaking and listening practices, as well those of other learning areas (e.g. mathematics, science).
- It is child-centred. Children are directly involved in the process; they pose questions, collect and sort data and form conclusions about the concepts that emerge. If children discover key concepts and ideas for themselves they are more likely to retain this knowledge.
- It places an emphasis on concept development and serves to build children's knowledge and understanding. Without this concept focus there is the danger that facts may be taught in isolation.
- The task of covering a full curriculum is made more manageable as a variety of key learning areas or domains and multiple outcomes are able to be covered in one integrated learning unit.
- It caters for a range of interests, learning styles and levels of understanding.
- It provides exposure to a process (of problem solving and investigation) that supports continued and independent learning.

In addition, integrated programs, when designed appropriately, provide strong support for children's language and literacy development. In order to ensure children's language and literacy development and learning is well catered for, it is important to:

- establish and address specific language and literacy (English learning area) outcomes
- use methods (e.g. modelling, demonstration, guided practice, reinforcement and independent practice) appropriate to enhancing language and literacy knowledge and skills
- assist children to distinguish between using literacy for learning and using literacy for communication
- provide children with ample instruction, guidance and practice in the application of language and literacy skills so that they achieve success with established English outcomes.

FINDING THE STARTING POINT FOR THE INTEGRATED LEARNING PROGRAM

There are many starting points for the design of an integrated learning program. One starting point might be the curiosities and interests of children. A teacher might observe children's fascination with the light reflected in a puddle of water and so use this as the way into experiences and activities that integrate areas of development and learning.

The design of an integrated learning program might be in response to an excursion or another shared experience such as a visitor to the classroom, a walk through the local community or a recent hail storm, or it might begin with the reading of a book (fiction or non-fiction). Alternatively, a specific learning area outcome or concept might provide an appropriate starting point for the integrated learning program. Whatever the case, an approach to planning that involves an integrated approach to children's learning and development involves activities and experiences in which outcomes across learning areas and domains are simultaneously addressed.

When using an integrated curriculum for the first time it is better to use a starting point that is directly related to a learning area or outcome. This will provide a focus for planning and learning. As you become more proficient with this form of planning you will be able to link student interests and experiences with the curriculum areas and outcomes.

INTEGRATED LEARNING AND THE INQUIRY APPROACH

Significant to the integrated learning program is the design of activities and experiences which involve children investigating and problem solving to answer questions and develop understandings. These type of experiences are part of what is commonly referred to as the inquiry approach to learning. As Macdonald (1991, p. 1) states, 'if we inquire into something we are directing our thoughts and actions towards a better understanding of the issue'.

Inquiry can be done in many ways. It can be quite unstructured, as is often the case when supporting young children with their investigations. However, there are various models of inquiry which present steps to guide a more structured approach to investigations and which serve to develop children's understanding of practices important to effective learning through inquiry. A useful model is presented by Marsh (1998) who sets out explicit steps to be followed in inquiring into a topic or issue. The steps which serve to guide children's investigations and learning are:

1. tuning in
2. finding out
3. sorting out
4. drawing conclusions
5. taking action
6. reflection and evaluation.

The different steps are child-centred and involve the teacher facilitating experiences and acting as motivator, organiser, reader and scribe. The steps are detailed in Table 26.3 on the next page.

Inquiry is a process and, as such, it will likely require several sessions where the focus is simply on ensuring that the steps are understood and able to be implemented by the children. It is necessary for teachers to demonstrate each of the inquiry steps and for the children to get plenty of opportunity to practise them. These early practice sessions should also focus on making the connection between the experiences and the initial question or inquiry topic. When working with older children the purpose for each step is made clear to the children.

Table 26.3: Steps of the inquiry approach to children's learning

Inquiry steps	Purpose/what happens
Tuning in	• To motivate and engage students • To arouse curiosity and activate prior knowledge • Students generate who, what where, how, why questions
Finding out	• Collect resources, allocate jobs, form groups, collect data
Sorting out	• Organise data in a graphic form
Drawing conclusions	• Analyse data to reach a generalisation or understanding
Taking action	• Decide on a plan of action which allows children to become involved in wider community
Reflection and evaluation	• Reflect on and asses their personal learning journey

Source: Marsh (1998)

LANGUAGE, LITERACY AND THE INTEGRATED CURRICULUM

Speaking, listening, reading, writing and viewing are fundamental experiences that are carried out at each step of an inquiry. This is demonstrated in Table 26.4 in which examples of the use of language and literacy at each step of an inquiry are outlined.

Table 26.4: The inquiry steps and language and literacy

Inquiry step	Language and literacy
Tuning in	Children generate where, how, what, when questions. Children orally express what they already know about a topic or issue.
Finding out	Children engage in modelled, shared and guided reading as they investigate into and learn about a topic or issue. Children ask questions, listen to others, hear and learn new vocabulary, record their findings. They observe, discuss and write lists and ideas.
Sorting out	Children sort and categorise information, using an appropriate graphic organiser, e.g. flow chart. They record information using an appropriate format, e.g. a graphic organiser.
Drawing conclusions	Children orally explain findings—what they learnt and know. Children engage in group discussion and use different methods to write (or draw) about what they have learnt.

Inquiry step	Language and literacy
Taking action	Children create posters, labels, plays, speeches to share new understandings and concept knowledge. Children write letters, reports, poetry and create different multimedia presentations that incorporate new information.
Reflection and evaluation	Children write and talk about their inquiry and the inquiry process. They share their thoughts and evaluative comments and judgments, using various oral and written modes of communication.

Oral and written communication is significant to the inquiry model, and the type and extent of, and supports for, talking, listening, reading, writing and viewing should be determined by the age and skill of the children as well as the type of inquiry being carried out.

Table 26.5 provides an example of an integrated program in which the inquiry model is used with pre-primary. The program focuses on an exploration of the children's local park and lake and has as its central topic 'The Lake is Our Home'. This unit addresses children's learning and development in an integrated fashion, integrating Geography, Mathematics, Science, reading, writing, listening and speaking through the experiences and activities.

Table 26.5: 'The Lake is Our Home': An integrated pre-primary learning program

Stage of inquiry	Literacy learning
Tuning in	• Excursion to the lake • Take photographs of tadpoles and rubbish/pollution • Generating where, how, what, when questions • KWL chart
Finding out	• Read non-fiction texts on pollution, tadpoles and frogs • Photograph and collect examples of rubbish • Draw and label life cycle of tadpoles • Modelled/shared/guided reading • Asking questions, listening and recording answers using key words • Observing, discussing and writing lists
Sorting out	• Classify rubbish found, tally and record in a bar graph • Draw a flow chart of what would happen to the wildlife at the lake if the rubbish is not cleared away
Drawing conclusions	• Explain in own words what their flow chart means • Write and draw about the effect pollution has on a tadpole or frog
Taking action	• Create posters to display at the lake • Pick up rubbish on 'Clean up Australia Day' • Write a letter to the local council for more rubbish bins
Reflection and evaluation	• Revisit KWL chart to record new learning • Written reflection on how you use the lake

READING AND WRITING IN AN INTEGRATED LEARNING PROGRAM

A well-developed integrated learning program involves children reading, listening and writing information texts. The ERICA model (Effective Reading in Content Areas) (Morris & Stewart-Dore, 1984) provides teachers with a method for supporting children's ability to access and translate written information. It outlines teaching strategies that assist children with the skills and techniques for reading and writing informational texts. There are four stages to the model and each addresses an important practice for reading purposefully and for using a different medium (for example, chart, poster, letter, report) to represent information. Through the use of the four stages of the model, teachers can guide children with the reading and writing tasks of an integrated learning program; they can scaffold the learning of effective research skills. The four stages of the ERICA model (elaborated in Table 26.6) are:

1. Preparing for reading
2. Thinking through the reading
3. Extracting and organising information
4. Translating.

Inquiry-based learning projects involve children using literacy to learn.

Table 26.6: The ERICA model and using non-fiction texts with children

ERICA stage	Purpose/what happens
Stage 1: Preparing for reading	• Develop or activate prior knowledge/schema • Set a purpose for reading the text • Arouse interest and curiosity • Motivate • Teach new vocabulary that will be found in the text (reading and meaning) • Introduce ideas, concepts and text format

ERICA stage	Purpose/what happens
Stage 2: Thinking through the reading	• Assist students to make meaning from the text • Develop their ability to use specific comprehension strategies • Focus attention on text content relating to the reading purpose • Shared reading or individual reading of the text • Ask and answer questions • Small group/whole class discussion • Small group/individual activities designed to develop literal, inferential and evaluative levels of comprehension
Stage 3: Extracting and organising information	• Identify and select relevant information • Sort out and organise the information that was found in the text • Reflect on what has been read—relevance to reading purpose • Prepare to represent the information in another form— report, summary, newspaper article, poster, illustration or labels
Stage 4: Translating	• Communicate or represent ideas in another form using their own words • Represent knowledge for an intended audience • Use of a written or oral report, letter, illustration, poster, chart

Source: Morris and Stewart-Dore (1984)

THE ERICA MODEL AND LANGUAGE AND LITERACY

Each step of the procedure of the ERICA model requires that children are involved in various language and literacy activities; for instance, in Step 1(Preparing to read) children use oral and written communication as they discuss their predictions about a text and consider the meanings of words in the text. Activities might include brainstorms, before and after charts, interesting word charts, graphic outlines and semantic grids. The different activities should be implemented with the degree of teacher support appropriate to the skills and learning and development needs of the children. They might be carried out using the modelled, shared, guided or independent strategy. Table 26.7 provides an overview of a range of literacy learning activities that can be employed at each step of the ERICA model.

Table 26.7: The ERICA model and language and literacy activities

ERICA stage	Suggested activity	Literacy learning
Stage 1: Preparing for reading	• Brainstorm/prediction • Before and after chart • Interesting word chart • Graphic outline • Semantic grid	Generating where, how, what, when questions. Verbally explaining knowledge about a topic

ERICA stage	Suggested activity	Literacy learning
Stage 2: Thinking through the reading	• Modelled and shared reading • Cloze • Sentence completion • Three level guide (comprehension questions)	Reading and comprehension, asking questions, listening, oral and written answers to questions, observing, discussing, writing lists
Stage 3: Extracting and organising information	• Retrieval chart • Semantic grid • Flow chart • Structured overview • 'Was, had, did' chart • Main idea and supporting detail • Problem/solution chart	Oral explanations, group discussion, drawing and labelling, identifying key words, skimming and scanning the text
Stage 4: Translating	• Poster • Write letter • Speeches • Report writing • Newspaper report • 'Did you know?' chart	Posters, labels, role plays, letter writing, written and oral reports, multimedia presentations

CHILDREN IN THE EARLY YEARS OF SCHOOL (SIX- TO EIGHT-YEAR-OLDS)

In the early years of school, children's language and literacy development benefits from integrated programs in which topics, units of work and investigations are used to address outcomes from a number of learning areas. Through integrated programs, children are

A stand alone program exclusively addresses the outcomes for reading, writing, listening, speaking and viewing.

provided with the experience of *using* language and literacy to investigate and learn; written, oral and visual communication is employed as a tool of investigation and learning. However, in an integrated program some areas of language and literacy development are not easily catered for; in order to ensure that language and literacy is able to be comprehensively addressed, **stand-alone English programs**—where the outcomes for reading, writing, listening and speaking, and viewing are exclusively addressed—should also be developed.

THE STAND-ALONE ENGLISH PROGRAM AND THE DAILY LITERACY SESSION

Stand-alone English (language and literacy) programs, with their absolute focus on reading, writing, speaking and listening, and viewing, are more likely to provide for the many layers of literacy learning to be addressed. They should involve structuring the teaching and learning experiences into a daily block of continuous time, or a daily literacy session framework

Table 26.8: Example of a daily literacy session framework for Year 2

Monday	Tuesday	Wednesday	Thursday	Friday
Oral language (news telling, barrier games, discussion groups, story retelling)				
Reciprocal reading or readers' theatre	Shared reading			Language experience
	Guided reading groups and literacy centres			
Writing (modelled, shared, guided and independent writing)				
Explicit systematic phonics teaching (including phonological and phonemic awareness, graphophonics)				
Handwriting	Spelling	Handwriting	Spelling	Handwriting
Reading aloud to children				

THE IMPORTANCE OF BALANCE

Stand-alone language and literacy programs should be developed with a view to achieving balance with the various facets of teaching and learning; they should include the following features:

- Children's learning occurs by means of facilitative experiences and activities as well as by explicit systematic teaching experiences.
- Learning in the different modes of English—reading, writing, listening and speaking, and viewing—is provided for.

- Whole class, small group and individual teaching and learning situations are utilised.
- Modelled, shared and guided teaching strategies are employed to provide different levels of support for children as they move to independence with certain skills, concepts or tasks.
- There is a focus on purposeful reading, writing and viewing of whole texts, as well as on developing skills and understanding in relation to particular text elements (e.g. sentences, vocabulary/words, letters and sounds).
- The areas of phonics, spelling and handwriting are taught using systematic and explicit methods as well as through embedded processes that involve reading and writing whole texts.
- Materials and resources are varied and chosen to support learning as well as motivation and engagement.

ATTITUDE AND MOTIVATION

It is recognised that motivation plays an important role in children's literacy development (Fang, 2005; NZ Ministry of Education, 2003). The Australian study of effective early years literacy practices, *In teachers' hands* (Louden et al., 2005) indicates that a defining characteristic of effective literacy teaching is an ability to create 'energetic and exciting classrooms, in which pleasure in literacy learning [is] evident' (p. 181) and that this leads to greater levels of student participation, effort and attention. The more effective literacy teachers identified in the study had well-developed strategies for motivating children to partake in the literacy learning experiences of the classroom.

Research into literacy motivation (Paris & Turner, 1995; Bruning & Horn, 2000) provides an understanding of the features of the teaching context that best promote children's motivation for reading and writing.

Challenge, ownership and collaboration

Literacy learning experiences of the classroom should provide the learner with genuine *challenge* while at the same time being attainable. They should provide children with *choice*, a sense of *ownership* and opportunities to *collaborate* with peers and the teacher.

Focus on the 'big picture'

Literacy learning goals and related teaching and learning experiences should be considerate of the specific skills, concepts and strategies important to reading and writing development; however, they should also link to the *big picture* of reading and writing—that is, use of texts for communicative purposes. Literacy experiences should promote a *functional understanding* of texts, whereby children see reading and writing as having a relevant communicative and social purpose.

Feedback and guidance

Teachers should provide explicit, focused and regular feedback to children in a way that supports their progress towards the learning goal of the literacy tasks and that maintains their motivation for, and desire to persist with, the task.

Classroom climate

Teachers need to establish a classroom climate whereby children are geared towards *successful completion* of a learning experience rather than getting something right or wrong. They need to be supported to use concentration, persistence and effort when applying newly learnt skills and strategies and to adapt strategies and skills rather than giving up.

Teacher's attitude

Important to children's attitude to, and motivation for, literacy are the behaviours and the attitudes of teachers. Children's motivation is influenced when they observe teachers read and write with enjoyment and enthusiasm.

FOUR SPHERES OF INFLUENCE

Good language and literacy teachers maintain current knowledge in each of the following four spheres of influence:

Theoretical knowledge
- language and literacy
- language and literacy learning
- successful language users.

Curriculum
- literacy learning outcomes
- literacy knowledge, skills
- concepts to be developed.

Pedagogy
- teaching strategies
- literacy learning experiences
- literacy teaching methods and approaches
- materials and resources.

Evaluation
- literacy learning
- development of students.

Social and emotional

When children's social and emotional needs are not met, they find it difficult to engage in reading and writing and literacy learning experiences. If their minds are occupied with social and emotional concerns, motivation is diminished. The literacy classroom should provide for children's self-esteem, safety, security, belonging and relatedness with others.

Literacy learning contexts which positively contribute to motivation to learn feature:

- acknowledgment of children's successes
- acceptance of their mistakes
- routine and order
- teamwork and collaboration
- the promotion of respectful relationships
- recognition from the teacher
- active listening.

THE INFORMED EARLY CHILDHOOD PROFESSIONAL

In 2005, the National Inquiry into the Teaching of Literacy (Department of Education, Science and Training, 2005) determined that:

> … many teaching approaches used in schools are not informed by findings from evidence-based research, and that too many teachers do not have a clear understanding of why, how, what and when to use particular strategies.

The inquiry emphasised the need for teachers' decisions about children's learning and development to arise from rigorous evidence-based research about effective literacy teaching and learning.

Good language and literacy education requires that early childhood professionals possess up-to-date knowledge of research into how children learn language and literacy, and the best practices for language and literacy teaching. Knowing what is important and what works for different groups of children and having the repertoire of skills and teaching strategies is fundamental to effective literacy teaching.

INFORMATION ON LANGUAGE AND LITERACY TEACHING AND LEARNING

There are a number of professional organisations which provide teachers with information about language and literacy teaching and learning:

- Australian Literacy Education Association
- Australian Early Childhood Association
- The International Reading Association
- The National Association for the Education of Young Children (NAEYC)
- Centre for the Improvement of Early Reading Achievement.

In teachers hands (Louden et al., 2005) provides an understanding of the important characteristics of an effective literacy teacher. The research project, which sought to examine the link between children's literacy learning in the early years of school and their classroom teachers' teaching practices, identified effective early literacy teaching as requiring teachers who:

- are deeply knowledgeable about literacy learning
- ensure high levels of student participation
- can simultaneously orchestrate the complex demands of the classroom
- can support and scaffold learners at word and text levels
- can target and differentiate instruction
- create classrooms characterised by mutual respect.

Table 26.9: The six dimensions of effective early years' literacy teachers

Participation: ways in which the teacher organises for and motivates children's participation in classroom [literacy] tasks	*Orchestration*: ways in which the teacher manages or orchestrates the demands of the [literacy] classroom	*Knowledge*: ways in which the teachers uses his/her knowledge [of literacy] to effectively teach significant [literacy] concepts and skills
Support: ways in which teachers support children's [literacy] learning	*Differentiation*: how the teacher differentiates tasks and instructions for individual learners, providing individual levels of challenge	*Respect*: ways in which the teacher gains the respect of the children and in which the children demonstrate respect for the teacher

Source: Louden et al. (2005)

SUMMARY

The development of teaching and learning programs should provide information that clearly shows how children's language and literacy learning and development are supported over time. They should be useful in guiding the teacher or carer in the achievement of relevant learning and development goals for the children. Programs should be developed in response to careful and comprehensive assessment that identifies children's current ability and their learning and development needs. The goals, learning environment, experiences, activities and other information contained in programs should clearly link to what the assessments have revealed about what children are ready to learn and develop. There are various ways in which to approach the development of language and literacy programs, and the approach taken will depend on a number of factors including the setting and the children's age and phases of development. An integrated program involves considering language and literacy alongside other learning and development areas, while a stand-alone English program involves the separate consideration of language and literacy.

QUESTIONS AND ACTIVITIES

1. Why is it important to plan children's learning and development over an extended period of time?
2. Consider the key features of a learning program (outlined earlier in this chapter) and devise a pro forma that you could use to write a program for toddlers' learning and development.
3. How might you determine a program's topic focus? What factors should be taken into account?

4 Discuss the positives and negatives of an integrated curriculum to children's language and literacy learning.
5 What are the benefits of a stand-alone English program and a daily literacy session for children in the early years of school? Consider whether such an approach would be appropriate for pre-schoolers.
6 How can the diverse learning needs of children be catered for in an integrated curriculum/program and in a stand-alone English program?
7 Locate and examine two websites for different Australian and international professional organisations where information on early childhood language and literacy is provided. List the ways in which each might serve to inform the practices of early childhood language and literacy educators.
8 Using the websites of the previous activity, find an informative document or section of information and share it with other students.

KEY TERMS

explicit systematically-organised teaching
holistic learning
integrated programs
intentional teaching
inquiry-based learning
stand-alone English programs

KEY REFERENCES

Annandale, K., Bindon, R., Handley, K., Johnston, A., Locket, L. & Lynch, P. (2003). *Linking assessment teaching and learning*. Port Melbourne: Rigby Heinemann.

Bruning, R & Horn, C. (2000). Developing motivation to write. *Educational Psychologists 35*(1), 25–37.

Department of Education, Employment and Workplace Relations (2009). *Belonging, being and becoming: The Early Years Learning Framework for Australia*. Canberra: Commonwealth of Australia.

Department of Education, Science and Training (2005). *National inquiry into the teaching of literacy*. Barton, ACT: Australian Government Department of Education, Science and Training.

Fang, Z. (2005). *Literacy teaching and learning: Current issues and trends.* Upper Saddle River, NJ: Pearson Education.

Louden, W., Rohl, M., Barratt Pugh, C., Brown, C., Cairney, T., Elderfield, J., et al. (2005). *In teachers' hands: Effective literacy teaching practices in the early years of schooling*. Commonwealth of Australia.

Marsh, C. (1998). *Teaching studies of society and environment*. Sydney: Prentice Hall.

Morris & N. Stewart-Dore (1984) *Learning to learn from text*. North Ryde, NSW: Addison-Wesley.

National Association for the Education of Young Children (2009). *Developmentally appropriate practice in early childhood programs serving children birth through 8*. Washington, DC: NAEYC.

Nettles, D. H. (2006). *Comprehensive literacy instruction in today's classroom: The whole, the parts, and the heart.* Boston: Pearson Education.

NZ Ministry of Education (2003). *Effective literacy practices in K–4.* Wellington, NZ: Learning Media Ltd.

Paris, S. & Turner, J. (1995). How literacy tasks influence children's motivation for literacy. *The Reading Teacher, 48*(8), 662–73.

APPENDIX: OXFORD WORDLIST

Oxford Australia's *Oxford Wordlist* contains the 307 most frequently used words collected from over 4000 writing samples from students in the first three years of school. The research was conducted in Australian schools throughout 2007, and gathered under the guidance of, and endorsed by, the University of Melbourne. The list is arranged by frequency of use, in this order: 1–100, 101–200 and 201–307.

A full *Oxford Wordlist* research summary by the University of Melbourne is available at www.oup.com.au/thesuccessfulteacher.

WORDS 1–100

I	she	weekend	Sunday	them
the	said	time	upon	bed
and	played	her	Saturday	made
to	one	go	did	name
a	is	came	school	too
was	were	because	two	next
my	day	up	very	dog
went	so	his	back	lots
we	when	once	ate	night
on	home	after	get	not
it	you	fun	lived	friends
then	at	like	am	into
he	me	some	him	an
had	mum	have	watched	park
in	for	are	little	will
they	dad	out	can	car
with	but	going	bought	our
of	saw	called	brother	do
there	house	all	big	sister
got	that	play	birthday	be

WORDS 101–200

people	your	eat	wanted	inside
didn't	off	fish	bike	it's
friend	three	this	no	tree

Appendix: Oxford Wordlist

their	dinner	ran	lost	cake
put	liked	first	TV	best
gave	won	by	fairy	fell
found	morning	food	cousin	long
from	playing	named	stayed	movie
down	want	baby	Friday	soccer
water	happy	cat	games	how
party	what	outside	old	also
about	as	away	woke	know
took	love	favourite	ball	last
good	if	has	come	sleep
other	again	family	ever	swimming
see	game	lunch	new	don't
girl	really	man	room	just
boy	could	shops	nice	told
over	shop	football	scared	yes
us	would	looked	who	around

WORDS 201–307

lot	I'm	work	horse	monster
today	happily	coming	movies	slide
beach	started	someone	names	thank
finished	dragon	team	bit	white
funny	much	thing	race	buy
book	rabbit	always	sad	dressed
bad	five	boat	snake	fast
things	turned	red	jumped	head
yesterday	another	teacher	place	walking
computer	make	its	show	why
help	cousin's	princess	where	blue
zoo	breakfast	shopping	everyone	dogs
now	chips	until	or	footy
ride	door	only	shark	here
castle	couldn't	black	something	killed
toy	present	garden	asked	need
cousins	together	still	OK	playground
look	walk	beautiful	scary	that's
more	great	pool	every	watch
tried	ice cream	take	walked	
find	loved	well	read	
four	magic	animals	world	

Oxford Wordlist © Oxford University Press 2008. The *Oxford Wordlist* may be used for instructional purposes. If you wish to use the *Oxford Wordlist* in any other way, you must seek written permission from Oxford University Press.

BIBLIOGRAPHY

Adams, M. J. (1990). *Beginning to read: Thinking and learning about print.* Cambridge, MA: MIT Press.

Ahlberg, J. & Ahlberg, A. (1989). *Each peach pear plum.* London: Puffin.

Alborough, J. (1994). *Where's my teddy?* London: Walker.

Allen, P. (1991). *Black dog.* Ringwood, Victoria: Viking.

Allen, P. (2003). *Grandpa and Thomas.* Camberwell, Victoria: Puffin Books.

Allen, P. (2006). *My first ABC.* Camberwell, Victoria: Puffin Baby.

Allen, P. (2009). *Our daft dog Danny.* Camberwell, Victoria: Viking.

Allington, R. (1977). If they don't read much, how they gonna get good? *Journal of Reading,* October (1977), 57–61.

Anderson, J. (1983). Lix and Rix: Variations on a little-known readability index. *Journal of Reading, 26*(6), 490–6.

Annandale, K., Bindon, R., Broz, J., Handley, K., Johnston, A., Lockett, L., et al. (2005). *Writing map of development: Addressing current literacy challenges* (2nd edn). Port Melbourne: Reed International.

Annandale, K., Bindon, R., Handley, K., Johnston, A., Lockett, L. & Lynch, P. (2004a). *Reading map of development: Addressing current literacy challenges* (2nd edn). Port Melbourne: Reed International.

Annandale, K., Bindon, R., Handley, K., Johnston, A., Lockett, L. & Lynch, P. (2004b). *Reading resource book: Addressing current literacy challenges* (2nd edn). Port Melbourne: Reed International.

Anstey, M. & Bull, G. (2000). *Reading the visual.* Sydney: Harcourt.

Anstey, M. & Bull, G. (2004). *The literacy labyrynth.* Frenchs Forest: Pearson Education.

Anstey, M. & Bull, G. (2005). *The literacy landscape.* Frenchs Forest: Pearson Education.

Australian Council of Educational Research (2008). *Progressive achievement test in reading—revised (PAT-R).* ACER Press.

Ayrey, H. (1999). *Informal prose inventory 1.* Christchurch, NZ: Handy Resources.

Baillie, A. (1988). *Drac and the gremlin.* Ringwood, Victoria: VikingKestrel.

Baker, J. (2000). *The hidden forest.* London: Walker Books.

Barclay, K. (2009). Click, clack, moo: Designing effective reading instruction for children in preschool and early primary grades. *Childhood Education, 85*(3), 167–72.

Barratt-Pugh, C. (1998). The socio-cultural context of literacy learning. In C. Barratt-Pugh & M. Rohl (eds), *Literacy learning in the early years.* Crow's Nest, Australia: Allen & Unwin.

Barratt-Pugh, C., Rivalland, J., Hamer, J. & Adams, P. (2005). *Literacy learning in Australia: Practical ideas for early childhood educators.* Melbourne: Thomson Dunsmore Press.

Base, G. (1986). *Animalia.* Camberwell, Victoria: Puffin.

Bear, D., Invernessi, M., Templeton, S. & Johnston, F. (2004). *Word their way: Word study for phonics, vocabulary and spelling instruction*. New Jersey: Pearson, Merrill Prentice Hall.

Beaty, J. J. (2009). *50 early childhood literacy strategies*. Upper Saddle River: Pearson.

Beazley, M. & Marr, G. (2001). *Writers handbook*. Putney, NSW: Phoenix Education.

Beimiller, A. & Slonim, N. (2001). Estimating root word vocabulary growth in normative and advantaged populations: Evidence for a common sequence of vocabulary acquisition. *Journal of Educational Psychology, 93*, 498–520.

Bemelmans, L. (1956). *Madeline and the bad hat*. London: Scholastic.

Bennett, S., Maton, K. & Kervin, L. (2008). The 'digital natives' debate: A critical review of the evidence. *British Journal of Educational Technology, 39*(5), 775–86.

Berger, M. (1993). *All about magnifying glasses*. New York: Scholastic.

Berry, R. & Hudson, J. (1997). *Making the jump: A resource book for teachers of Aboriginal students*. Broome: Catholic Education Commission of Western Australia.

Biggam, S. & Itterley, K. (2009). *Literacy profiles: A framework to guide assessment, instructional strategies and intervention, K–4*. Boston: Allyn & Bacon.

Blachowicz, C. L. Z., Fisher, P. J. & Watts-Taffe, S. (2005). *Integrated vocabulary instruction: Meeting the needs of diverse learners in grades K–5*. Naperville, Illinois: Learning Point Associates.

Blaiklock, K. E. (2003). *A Critique of running records*. Paper presented at the New Zealand Association for Research in Education/Australian Association for Research in Education Conference, Auckland, New Zealand. www.aare.edu.au/03pap/bla03738.pdf

Blank, M., Rose, S.A. & Berlin, L.J. (1978). *The language of learning: The preschool years*. New York: Grune & Stratton.

Block, C. C. & Dellamura, R. J. (2001). Better book buddies. *The Reading Teacher, 54*(1), 364–70.

Bloodgood, J. W. (1999). What's in a name? Children's name writing and literacy acquisition. *Reading Research Quarterly, 34*, 342–67.

Bourdieu, P. (1977). *Outline of a theory of practice*. Cambridge: Cambridge University Press.

Bourgeois, P. (1987). *Franklin in the dark*. Gosford: Scholastic Australia.

Bourgeois, P. (1989). *Hurry up, Franklin*. Gosford: Scholastic Australia.

Bourgeois, P. (1991). *Franklin fibs*. Gosford: Scholastic Australia.

Bourgeois, P. (1997). *Franklin's new friend*. Gosford: Scholastic Australia.

Bourgeois, P. (1998). *Franklin's secret club*. Gosford: Scholastic Australia.

Boyd Batstone, P. (2004). Focused anecdotal assessment: A tool for standards based assessment methods. *The Reading Teacher, 58*(3), 230–9.

Brace, J., Brockhoff, V., Sparkes, N. & Tuckey, J. (2006). *Speaking and listening map of development: Addressing current literacy challenges* (2nd edn). Port Melbourne: Rigby Harcourt Education.

Brantley, D. K. (2007). *Instructional assessment of English language learners in the K–8 classroom*. Boston: Pearson.

Brooker, L. & Siraj-Blatchford, J. (2002). 'Click on Miaow!': How children of three and four years experience the nursery computer. *Contemporary Issues in Early Childhood, 3*(2), 251–73.

Browne, A. (2006). *My mum*. London: Picture Corgi.

Bruce, T. & Spratt, J. (2008). *Essentials of literacy from 0–7*. London: Sage.
Bruner, J. (1990). *Acts of meaning*. Cambridge, Mass: Harvard University Press.
Bruning, R. & Horn, C. (2000). Developing motivation to write. *Educational Psychologist, 35*(1), 25–37.
Bull, G. & Anstey, M. (2007). Exploring visual literacy through a range of texts. *Practically Primary, 12*(3), 4–7.
Burningham, J. (1977). *Come away from the water, Shirley*. New York: Crowell.
Burningham, J. (1988). *Granpa*. London: Puffin.
Burns, M. S., Griffin, P. & Snow, C. (eds) (1999). *Starting out right: A guide to promoting children's reading success*. Washington, DC: National Academy Press.
Burns, P. C. & Roe, B. D. (1999). *Burns-Roe informal reading inventory* (5th edn). Boston: Houghton Mifflin.
Butler, A. (1987). *Shared book experience: An introduction*. Melbourne: Rigby Education.
California State Department of Education and San Jose (California) Unified School District (n.d.). Student Oral Language Observation Matrix (SOLOM). California: CSTE.
Callahan, E. (n.d.). Conductive hearing loss in the classroom. *Class Ideas K–3*, from www.det.wa.edu.au/education/Abled/docs/RICPubClassIdeasK3.pdf.
Callow, J. (1999). *Image matters: Visual texts in the classroom*. Sydney: Primary English Teachers Association.
Callow, J. (2008). Show me: Principles for assessing students' visual literacy. *The Reading Teacher, 61*(8), 616–26.
Cambourne, B. (1988). *The whole story: Natural learning and the acquisition of literacy in the classroom*. New York: Ashton Scholastic.
Campbell, J. (2005). *G is for galaxy: An out of this world alphabet*. Chelsea, Michigan: Sleeping Bear Press.
Campbell, R. & Baker, C. (2003). Children learning language. In R. Campbell & D. Green (eds), *Literacies and learners: Current perspectives* (2nd edn). NSW: Prentice Hall.
Carle, E. (1973). *Have you seen my cat?* New York: Watts.
Carle, E. (2002). *"Slowly, slowly, slowly", said the sloth*. New York: Philomel Books.
Carnine, D. W., Silbert, J. & Kameenui, E. K. (1997). *Direct instruction reading* (3rd edn). Upper Saddle River, New Jersey: Prentice Hall.
Carrow-Woolfolk, E. (1999). *The Comprehensive Assessment of Spoken Language (CASL)*. Circle Pines, Min: WPS/Pearson.
Carter, D. (1994). *Alpha bugs: A pop-up alphabet*. London: Orchard Books.
Celce-Murcia, M. & Larsen-Freeman, D. (1999). *The grammar book* (2nd edn). USA: Heinle & Heinle Publishers.
Centre for Community Child Health. (2006). Literacy promotion, from www.rch.org.au/emplibrary/ccch/PR_Literacy_S1.pdf.
Chall, J. S. (1983). *Stages of reading development*. New York: McGraw-Hill.
Chase, N. D. & Hynd, C. R. (1987). Reader response: An alternative way to teach children to think about text. *Journal of Reading, 30*, 530–40.
Chatel, R. (2003). Developing literacy in the technological age: Expanding the boundaries of reader–text interactions. *New England Reading Association Journal, 39*(2), 67–73.
Cheers, G. & Silk, J. (1996). *Killer plants and how to grow them*. Ringwood, Victoria: Puffin.

Chera, P. & Wood, C. (2003). Animated multimedia 'talking books' can promote phonological awareness in children beginning to read. *Learning and Instruction, 13*, 33–52.
Chomsky, N. (1975). *Reflections on Language*. New York: Pantheon.
Chomsky, N. (1982). *Lectures on government and binding*. NY: Foris.
Christelow, E. (2006). *Five little monkeys jumping on the bed*. New York: Clarion Books.
Christie, F. (2005). *Language education in the primary years*. Sydney: UNSW Press.
Christie, J., Enz, B. & Vukelich, C. (2007). *Teaching language and literacy: Preschool through the elementary grades* (3rd edn). Boston: Allyn and Bacon.
Clay, M., M. (2002). *An observation survey of early literacy* (2nd edn). Auckland: Heinemann.
Clay, M. M. (1979). *Reading: the patterning of complex behaviour*. Portsmouth: Exeter, NH.
Clay, M. M. (1991). *Becoming literate: The construction of inner control*. Auckland: Heinemann.
Cohen, J. H. & Wiener, R. B. (2003). *Literacy portfolios: Improving assessment, teaching, and learning*. Upper Saddle River, NJ: Merrill Prentice Hall.
Cole, B. (2004). *The trouble with mum*. London: Egmont.
Comber, B. (1993). Classroom explorations in critical literacy. *Australian Journal of Language and Literacy, 16*(1), 73–83.
Combs, M. (2006). *Readers and writers in primary grades: A balanced and integrated approach, K–4*. Upper Saddle River, NJ: Pearson Prentice Hall.
Cook, R. E., Klein, M. D., Tessier, A. & Daley, S. E. (2004). *Adapting early childhood curricula for children in inclusive settings* (6th edn). Boston: Pearson.
Cousins, L. (2006). *Maisy's ABC*. London: Walker Books.
Cowley, J. (1980). *Mrs Wishy Washy*. Auckland: Shortland.
Cowley, J. (2005). *To town*. Hawthorne, Victoria: Mimosa McGraw Hill.
Cox, C. (2008). *Teaching Language Arts: A student centered classroom*. Boston: Pearson Education.
Cramer, E. D. (2006). In the beginning: Phonological awareness. In J. S. Schumm (ed.), *Reading assessment and instruction for all learners* (pp. 89–119). New York: The Guilford Press.
Cramer, R. L. (2004). *The language arts: A balanced approach to teaching reading, writing, listening, talking, and thinking*. Boston: Allyn & Bacon.
Crawford, J. (2004). *A home for Bilby*. Broome, Western Australia: Magabala Books Aboriginal Corporation.
Crow, J. T. (2010). *Unleashing your language wizards: A brain based approach to effective editing and writing*. Boston: Pearson Education.
Crowther, R. (2005). *The most amazing hide and seek alphabet book*. London: Walker Books.
Cummings, P. (1989). *Goodness gracious*. Norwood, South Australia: Omnibus Books.
Cummins, J. (1996). *Negotiating identities: Education for empowerment in a diverse society*. Ontario, CA: California Association for Bilingual Education.
Cunningham, A. & Shagoury, R. (2005). *Starting with comprehension: Reading strategies for the youngest learners*. Portland, Maine: Stenhouse Publishers.
Cunningham, P., Moore, S., Cunningham, J. & Moore, D. (2004). *Reading and writing: Research based K–4 instruction*. Boston: Allyn & Bacon.
Cunningham, P. M. & Allington, R. L. (2008). *Classrooms that work: They can all read and write* (5th edn). Boston: Pearson Education.
Cunningham, P. M. & Cunningham, J. (2002). What we know about how to teach phonics. In A. E. Farstrup & S. J. Samuels (eds), *What research has to say about reading instruction* (pp. 87–109). Newark: DE: International Reading Association.

Curriculum Council. (1998). *Curriculum framework for kindergarten to year 12 education in Western Australia*. Osborne Park: Curriculum Council.

Curtis, C. & Jay, A. (2004). *I took the moon for a walk*. Cambridge, MA: Barefoot Books.

Dahl, K. L. & Scharer, P. L. (2000). Phonics teaching and learning in whole language classrooms: New evidence from research. *The Reading Teacher, 53*(7), 584–94.

De Jong, M. T. & Bus, A. G. (2002). The efficacy of electronic books in fostering kindergartners' story recall. *Reading Research Quarterly, 39*(4), 378–93.

De Jong, M. T. & Bus, A. G. (2003). How well suited are electronic books to supporting literacy? *Journal of Early Childhood Literacy, 3*(2), 147–64.

DeKonty Applegate, M., Benson Quinn, K. & Applegate, A. J. (2008). *The critical reading inventory: Assessing students' reading and thinking*. Upper Saddle River, NJ: Pearson Merrill Prentice-Hall.

Department for Education and Skills (DfES). (2007). *Letters and sounds: Principles and practice of high quality phonics*. Norwich: DfES.

Department of Education and Children Services. (2010). The multiliteracies map. Retrieved 20/3/2010, from www.earlyyearsliteracy.sa.edu.au/pages/resource/21402/.

Department of Education and Training (2006). *Literacy and numeracy review: The final report*. Department of Education and Training, Western Australia.

Department of Education, Employment and Workplace Relations (DEEWR) (2009). *Belonging, being and becoming: The Early Years Learning Framework for Australia*. Barton, ACT: Commonwealth of Australia.

Department of Education Western Australia (2002). *Ways of being, ways of talk*. Perth: Department of Education Western Australia.

Diaz-Rico, L. T. & Weed, K. Z. (2006). *The cross cultural language and academic development handbook: A complete K–12 reference guide*. Boston: Pearson.

Dickinson, D., McCabe, A. & Sprague, K. (2003). Teacher rating of oral language and literacy (TROLL): Individualising early literacy instruction with a standards-based tool. *The Reading Teacher, 56*(6), 554–64.

Docket, S., Perry, B., Mason, T., Simpson, T., Howard, P., Whitton, D., et al. (2008). *Successful transitions from prior-to-school for Aboriginal and Torres Strait Islander children*. Carlton South, Vic: Ministerial Council on Education, Employment and Youth Affairs.

Dodd, L. (1983). *Hairy Maclary from Donaldson's dairy*. Flinders Park, SA: Keystone Picture Books.

Dodd, L. (1985). *Hairy Maclary from Donaldson's dairy*. Harmondsworth: Puffin.

Dougherty Stahl, K. A. (2009). Assessing the comprehension of young children. In S. E. Israel & G. G. Duffy (eds), *Handbook of research on reading comprehension* (pp. 428–48). New York: Routledge.

Dray, M. (2004). *Dougal the garbage dump bear*. Camberwell, Victoria: Penguin.

Driscoll, A. & Nagel, N. (2008). *Early childhood education, birth–8: The world of children, families and educators*. Boston: Pearson Education.

Duke, N. K. & Pearson, P. D. (2002). Effective practices for developing reading comprehension. In A. E. Farstrup & S. J. Samuels (eds), *What research has to say about reading instruction* (3rd edn, pp. 205–42). Newark, Delaware: International Reading Association.

Dunn, L. M. & Dunn, L. (1997). *Peabody Picture Vocabulary Test III (PPVT-lll)* (3rd edn). Circle Pines, Minn: American Guidance Service.

Early childhood Australia (n.d.). Cultural diversity position statement. Retrieved 12/12/2009 from www.earlychildhoodaustralia.org.au/index.php\.

Education Department of Western Australia (1999). *Solid English*. East Perth: EDWA.

Ehlert, L. (1989). *Eating the alphabet*. USA: Harcourt Brace Jovanovich.

Ehri, L. C. (1995). Stages of development in learning to read by sight. *Journal of Research in Reading, 18*, 116–25.

Emmitt, M., Komesaroff, L. & Pollack, J. (2006). *Language and learning: An introduction for teaching* (4th edn). South Melbourne: Oxford University Press.

Estes, L. (2004). *Essentials of child care and early childhood education*. Boston: Pearson Education.

Evans, D., Griffiths, A., Stokes, D. & Tuckey, J. (2008). *Viewing resource book: addressing current literacy challenges*. Port Melbourne, Victoria: Rigby Pearson Education.

Factor, J. (1995a). *All right, vegemite! A new collection of Australian children's chants and rhymes*. Rydalmere, NSW: Hodder.

Factor, J. (1995b). *Real keen baked bean! A fourth collection of Australian children's chants and rhymes*. Rydalmere, NSW: Hodder.

Fang, Z. (2005). *Literacy teaching and learning: Current issues and trends*. Upper Saddle River, NJ: Pearson Education.

Fawson, P. C., Reutzel, D. R., Smith, J. A., Ludlow, B. C. & Sudweeks, R. (2006) Examining the reliability of running records: Attaining generalizable results. *The Journal of Educational Research, 100*(2), 113–26.

Fellowes, J. (2002). Helping children become visually literate. *Class Ideas K–3, 19*, 8–9.

Fellowes, J. (2007). Viewing: An important component of the English curriculum. *Practically Primary, 12*(3), 29–32.

Fisher, D., Flood, J., Lapp, D. & Frey, N. (2004). Interactive read alouds: Is there a common set of implementation practices? *The Reading Teacher, 58*(1), 8–17.

Fleer, M. & Raban, B. (2007). *Early childhood literacy and numeracy: building good practice*. Canberra.

Foley, J. & Thompson, L. (2007). *Language learning: A lifelong process*. London: Oxford University Press.

Ford, M. P. & Opitz, M. F. (2002). Using centers to engage children during guided reading time: Intensifying learning experiences away from the teacher. *The Reading Teacher, 55*(5), 710–17.

Fountas, I. C. & Pinnell, G. S. (1996). *Guided reading: good first teaching for all children*. Portsmouth, NH: Heinemann.

Fountas, I. C. & Pinnell, G. S. (1999a). *Matching books to readers: Using leveled books in guided reading, K–3*. Portsouth, NH: Heinemann.

Fountas, I. C. & Pinnell, G. S. (1999b). *Voices on word matters: Learning about phonics and spelling in the literacy classroom*. Portsmouth, NH: Heinemann.

Fox, B. J. (2008). *Word identification strategies* (4th edn). Upper Saddle River, New Jersey: Pearson.

Fox, M. (1988). *Koala Lou*. Melbourne: Ian Drakeford Publishing.

Fox, M. (1991). *Possum magic*. Norwood, South Australia: Omnibus Books.

Fox, M. (1998). *Whoever you are*. Sydney: Hodder Headline.

Fox, M. (2001a). *Boo to a goose*. New York: Puffin Books.

Fox, M. (2001b). *Reading magic: How your child can learn to read before school and other read aloud miracles*. Sydney: Pan Macmillan.

Freebody, P. & Luke, A. (1992). A socio-cultural approach: Resourcing four roles as a literacy learner. In A. J. Watson & A. M. Badenhop (eds), *Prevention of reading failure*. Sydney: Ashton Scholastic.

Frey, N. & Fisher, D. (2008). *Teaching visual literacy: Using comic books, graphic novels, anime, cartoons, and more to develop comprehension and thinking skills*. Thousand Oaks, California: Corwin Press.

Fry, E. B., Polk, J. K. & Fountoukidis, D. (2000). *The reading teacher's book of lists*. Paramus, NJ: Prentice Hall.

Gaiman, N. (2008). *The dangerous alphabet*. London: Bloomsbury.

Ganske, K. (2000). *Word journeys*. New York: The Guilford Press.

Gelber, L. (2007). *P is for peanut: A photographic ABC*. Los Angeles: J Paul Getty Museum.

Gesell, A. (1928). *Infancy and human growth*. New York: Macmillan.

Gill, S. R. (2006). Teaching rimes with shared reading. *The Reading Teacher, 60*(2), 191–3.

Gillham, B. (2006). *Early literacy test*. Abingdon: Hodder and Stoughton.

Gleason, J. B. (2005). *The development of language*. Boston: Allyn and Bacon.

Glister, P. (1997). *Digital literacy*. New York: Wiley Computer Pub.

Gold, I. (2006). *Bugs and beasts ABC*. Canberra: National Library of Australia.

Good, R. H., Kaminski, R. A., Smith, S., Laimon, D. & Dill, S. (2001). *Dynamic Indicator of Basic Early Literacy Skills* (5th edn). Eugene: University of Oregon.

Goodman, K. S. (1973). *Psycholinguistics and reading*. New York: Holt, Rinehart and Winston.

Goswami, U. & Bryant, P. (1990). *Phonological skills and learning to read*. Hove, UK: Laurence Erlbaum

Gough, P. B. (1996). How children learn to read and why they fail. *Annals of Dyslexia, 46*, 3–20.

Graham, B. (1990). *Greetings from sandy beach*. Melbourne, Victoria: Lothian Books.

Graham, B. (2001). *Let's get a pup!* London: Walker Books.

Graves, D. (1983). *Writing: Teachers and children at work*. Portsmouth, NH: Heinemann.

Graves, M. F., Juel, C. & Graves, B. B. (2004). *Teaching reading in the 21st century*. Boston: Pearson.

Graves, M. F., Juel, C. & Graves, B. B. (2007). *Teaching reading in the 21st century* (4th edn). Boston: Pearson Education.

Greene Brabham, E. & Villaume, S. K. (2000). Continuing conversations about literature circles. *The Reading Teacher, 54*(3), 278–80.

Gregory, A. E. & Cahill, M. A. (2010). Kindergartners can do it, too! Comprehension strategies for early readers. *The Reading Teacher, 63*(6), 515–20.

Grisham Brown, J., Hallem, R. & Brookshire, R. (2006). Using authentic assessment to evidence children's progress toward early learning standards. *Early Childhood Education Journal, 34*(1).

Guastello, F. E. & Lenz, C. (2005). Student accountability: Guided reading kidstations. *The Reading Teacher, 59*(2), 144–56.

Gunning, T. G. (2006). *Assessing and correcting reading and writing difficulties*. Boston: Pearson.

Gunning, T. G. (2010). *Creating literacy instruction for all students* (7th edn). Boston: Pearson Education.

Guthrie, J. T., Wigfield, A. & Perencevich, K. C. (2004). Scaffolding for motivation and engagement in reading. In J. T. Guthrie, A. Wigfield & K. C. Perencevich (eds), *Motivating reading comprehension: Concept oriented reading instruction*. Mahwah, NJ: Erlbaum & Associates.

Halliday, M. A. K. (1964). Comparison and translation. In M. A. K. Halliday, M. McIntosh & P. Strevens (eds), *The linguistic sciences and language teaching*. London: Longman.
Halliday, M. A. K. (1973). *Explorations in the function of language*. London: Edward Arnold.
Halliday, M. A. K. (1975). *Learning how to mean: Exploration in the development of language*. London: Edward Arnold.
Hancock, M. R. (2008). *A celebration of children's literature and response* (3rd edn). New Jersey: Pearson.
Harmon, J. M., Hedrick, W. B., Soares, L. & Gress, M. (2007). Assessing vocabulary: Examining knowledge about words and word learning. In J. R. Paratore & R. L. McCormack (eds), *Classroom literacy assessment: Making sense of what students know and do*. New York: The Guilford Press.
Harrison, N. (2008). *Teaching and learning in Indigenous education*. Melbourne: Oxford University Press.
Hart, B. & Risley, T. R. (1999). *The social world of children learning to talk*. Baltimore: Brooks.
Hassett, D. (2006). Signs of the times: The governance of alphabetic print over 'appropriate' and 'natural' reading development. *Journal of Early Childhood Literacy, 6*(1), 77–103.
Hattie, J. A. C. (2003). *Teachers make a difference: What is the research evidence?* Paper presented at the Building Teacher Quality: ACER Annual Conference, Melbourne.
Haugland, S. W. & Wright, L. (1997). *Young children and technology: A world of discovery*. London: Allyn & Bacon.
Healy, J. A. (1998). *Failure to connect: How computers affect our children's minds … for better or worse*. New York: Simon & Schuster.
Heap, S. & Sharratt, N. (2007). *Alphabet ice cream*. London: Puffin.
Heath, S., Fletcher, J. M. & Hogben, J. (2006). *Catch them before they fall 2003–05: Cost effective screening for children at risk for literacy problems*. Child Study Centre, University of Western Australia and Department of Education and Training Western Australia.
Hedge, T. (2000). *Teaching and learning in the language classroom*. Oxford: Oxford University Press.
Heffernan, L. (2004). *Critical literacy and writer's workshop: Bringing purpose and passion to student writing*. Newark, DE: International Reading Association.
Hernandez Sheets, R. (2005). *Diversity pedagogy: Examining the role of culture in the teaching learning process*. Boston: Pearson Education.
Herrel, A. & Jordon, M. (2004). *Fifty strategies for teaching English language learners* (2nd edn). Upper Saddle River, New Jersey: Pearson.
Herrera, S. G., Murray, K. G. & Morales Cabral, R. (2007). *Assessment accommodations for classroom teachers of culturally and linguistically diverse learners*. Boston: Pearson.
Hiebert, E. H., Pearson, P. D., Taylor, B. M., Richardson, V. & Paris, S. G. (1998). Every child a reader: CIERA.
Hill, E. (1996). *Spot bakes a cake*. New York: Penguin.
Hill, S. (1999). 100 children go to school: Connecting between literacy development in the prior to school period and first year of schooling. *Queensland Journal of Educational research, 15*(1), 35–42.
Hill, S. (2007). *Developing early literacy: Assessment and teaching*. Prahran, Victoria: Eleanor Curtain.
Hissey, J. (2000). *Little bear's alphabet*. London: Hutchinson.
Holdaway, D. (1979). *The foundations of literacy*. Sydney: Ashton Scholastic.

Hornsby, D. (2000). *A closer look at guided reading*. Armadale, Victoria: Eleanor Curtain.

Hulit, L. M. & Howard, M. R. (2006). *Born to talk: An introduction to speech and language development* (4th edn). Boston: Pearson.

Hutchins, P. (1978). *Don't forget the bacon*. Harmondsworth: Puffin.

International Reading Association (1999). *Using multiple methods of beginning reading instruction: A position statement of the International Reading Association*.

International Reading Association (2002). *Family–school partnerships: Essential elements of literacy instruction in the United States*.

Irwin, J. W. (1991). *Teaching reading comprehension processes* (2nd edn). Englewood Cliffs, NJ: Prentice Hall.

Jalongo, M. R. (2007). *Early childhood language arts*. Boston: Pearson.

Johns, J. (2005). *Basic reading inventory: Pre-primer through grade twelve and early literacy assessments*. Dubuque: Kendall Hunt.

Johnston, R. S. & Watson, J. E. (2005). A seven year study of the effects of synthetic phonics teaching on reading and spelling attainment. *Insight, 17*, 1–9.

Jones, I. (1994). The effect of a word processor on the written composition of second-grade pupils. *Computers in the Schools, 11*, 43–54.

Jonson, K. F. (2006). *Sixty strategies for improving reading comprehension in grades K–8*. Thousand Oaks, CA: Corwin Press.

Juel, C. (1988). Learning to read and write: A longitudinal study of 54 children from first through fourth grade. *Journal of Educational Psychology, 80*, 437–47.

Justice, L. M. & Pence, K. L. (2005). *Scaffolding with storybooks*. Newark: Delaware: International Reading Association.

Karemaker, A., Pitchford, N. J. & O'Malley, C. (2008). Using whole word multimedia software to support literacy acquisition: A comparison with traditional books. *Educational and Child Psychology, 25*, 97–118.

Kearns, K. & Austin, B. (2007). *Working in children's services series: Frameworks for learning and development*. Boston: Pearson Education.

Keene, E. & Zimmerman, S. (2007). *Mosaic of thought: The power of comprehension strategy instruction* (2nd edn). Portsmouth, New Hampshire: Heinemann.

Kelly, J., Kratcoski, A. & McClain, K. (2006). The effects of word processing software on the writing of students with special needs. *Journal of the Research Center for Educational Technology, 2*(2), n.p.

Kennedy, A. (2009). Let's talk: Having meaningful conversations with children. In N. C. A. Council (ed.), *Putting children first*. Surry Hills: NCAC.

Kidd, W. (2002). *Culture and identity*. New York: Pelgrave MacMillan.

Kim, J. E. & Anderson, J. (2008). Mother–child shared reading with print and digital texts. *Journal of Early Childhood Literacy, 8*(2), 213–45.

Klein, T. P., Wirth, D. & Linas, K. (2004). Play: Children's context for development. In D. Koralek (ed.), *Spotlight on young children and play*. USA: National Association for the Education of Young Children.

Knobel, M. & Healy, A. (1998). Critical literacies: An introduction. In M. Knobel & A. Healy (eds), *Critical literacies in the primary classroom* (pp. 1–12). Newtown, NSW: Primary English Teaching Association.

Kontis, A. (2006). *Alpha oops! The day Z went first*. Cambridge, MA: Candlewick Press.

Kozulin, A. (1986). *Thought and language: Lev Vygotsky*. Cambridge: The MIT Press.
Kraft, E. (2003). *Chocolatina*. Melbourne: Hinkler Books.
Kresner, I. M. (2005). *Alphabet wings*. South Melbourne: Lothian.
Kress, G. (2003). *Literacy in the new media age*. London: Routledge.
Labbo, L. D. (2000). Twelve things young children can do with a talking book in a classroom learning center. *The Reading Teacher, 53*(7), 542–6.
Labbo, L. D., Eakle, A. T. & Montero, M. K. (2002). Digital Language Experience Approach: Using digital photographs and software as a Language Experience Approach initiative. *Reading Online, 8*(8).
Labbo, L. D. & Kuhn, M. (2000). Weaving chains of affect and cognition: A young child's understanding of a CD-ROM talking book. *Journal of Literacy Research, 32*, 187–210.
Lamb, S. (2006). Being realistic, being scientific. *Linguistic Association of Canada and the United States (LACUS) forum, (32)*. Retrieved November 29, 2009 from www.lacus.org/volumes/.
Lane, H. B., Pullen, P. C., Eisele, M. R. & Jordan, L. (2002). Preventing reading failure: phonological awareness and instruction. *Preventing School Failure, 46*(3), 101–10.
Lankshear, C. & Knobel, M. (2003). New technologies in early childhood literacy research: A review of research. *Journal of Early Childhood Literacy, 3*(1), 59–82.
Lefever-Davis, S. & Pearson, C. (2005). Early readers and electronic texts: CD-ROM storybook features that influence reading behaviors. *The Reading Teacher, 58*(5), 446–54.
Levy, R. (2009). 'You have to understand words … but not read them': Young children becoming readers in a digital age. *Journal of Research in Reading, 32*(1), 75–91.
Lewandowski, L., Begeny, J. & Rogers, C. (2006). Word-recognition training: Computer versus tutor. *Reading & Writing Quarterly, 22*(4), 395–410.
Lightbown, P. & Spada, N. (1993). *How languages are learned*. Oxford: Oxford University Press.
Lobel, A. (1989). *On Market Street*. NY: Greenwillow Books.
Louden, W. (1999). Literacy in its place: Literacy practices in urban and rural communities. *Queensland Journal of Educational Research, 15*(1), 91–5.
Louden, W., Rohl, M., Barratt Pugh, C., Brown, C., Cairney, T., Elderfield, J., et al (2005). *In teachers' hands: Effective literacy teaching practices in the early years of schooling*. Commonwealth of Australia.
Louden, W., Rohl, M. & Hopkins, S. (2008). *Teaching for growth: Effective teaching of literacy and numeracy*. Perth: DET.
Luke, A. (2001). *A map of possible practices: A non-reductionist approach to making state literacy policy*. Paper presented at the Leading Literate Lives Conference, Hobart, Tasmania.
Luke, A. & Freebody, P. (1999). A map of possible practices: Further notes on the four resources model. *Practically Primary, 4*(2), 5–8.
Machado, J. M. (2007). *Early childhood experiences in Language Arts: Early literacy*. Emerita: Thomson.
Machado, J. M. (2010). *Early childhood experiences in Language Arts: Early literacy* (9th edn). Emerita: Thomson.
Maclean, M., Bryant, P. & Bradley, L. (1987). Rhymes, nursery rhymes, and reading in early childhood. *Meril-Palmer Quarterly, 33*(3), 255–81.

Majod, E. & Kendall, P. (2008). *A sausage went for a walk*. Fremantle, Western Australia: Fremantle Press.

Makin, L., Campbell, J. & Jones Diaz, C. (1995). *One childhood many languages: Guidelines for early childhood education in Australia*. Pymble, NSW: Harper Education.

Makin, L. & Whitehead, M. (2004). *How to develop children's early literacy: A guide for professional carers and educators*. London: Paul Chapman Publishing.

Manning, M. & Granstrom, B. (1999). *Supermum*. London: Frankin Watts.

Manzo, A. V., Manzo, U. C. & McKenna, M. C. (1995). *Informal reading-thinking inventory*. Fort Worth: Harcourt Brace College Publishers.

Martin, B. (1984). *Brown bear, brown bear, what do you see?* London: Hamilton.

Massey, S. L. (2004). Teacher-child conversation in the preschool classroom. *Early Childhood Education Journal* (31), 4.

McAfee, O. & Leong, D. J. (2002). *Assessing and guiding young children's development and learning*. Boston: Allyn and Bacon.

McAllister, A. (2003). *Harry's box*. London: Bloomsbury.

McGee, L. M. (2007). Language and literacy assessment in preschool. In J. R. Paratore & R. L. McCormack (eds), *Classroom literacy assessment: Making sense of what children know and do* (pp. 65–84). New York: The Guilford Press.

McGee, L. M. & Richgels, D. J. (2008). *Literacy beginnings: Supporting young readers and writers*. Boston: Pearson Education

McKenna, M. C. (1998). Electronic texts and the transformation of beginning reading. In D. Reinking, M. C. McKenna, L. D. Labbo & R. D. Kieffer (eds), *The handbook of literacy and technology: Transformations in a post-typographic world*. Mahwah, NJ: Lawrence Erlbaum Associates.

McKenna, M. C. & Kear, D. J. (1990). Measuring attitudes towards reading: A new tool for teachers. *The Reading Teacher,* May, 626–39.

McKenna, M. C. & Stahl, E. (2003). *Assessment for reading instruction*. NY: The Guilford Press.

McKenzie, M. G. (1985). *Shared writing: Apprenticeship in written language matters*. London: Centre for Language in Primary Education.

Meyers, P. A. (2006). The Princess Storyteller, Clara Clarifyer, Quincy Questioner, and the wizard: Reciprocal teaching adapted for kindergarten students. *The Reading Teacher, 59*(4), 314–24.

Moats, L. C. (1998). Teaching decoding. *American Educator,* 1998 (Spring/Summer).

Moll, L., Amanti, C., Niff, D. & Gonzales, N. (1992). Funds of knowledge for teaching: Using a qualitative approach to connect homes and classrooms. *Theory into Practice, 31*(2), 132–41.

Morris, A. & Stewart-Dore, N. (1984). *Learning to learn from text: Effective reading in content areas*. North Ryde, NSW: Addison-Wesley.

Morrison, T. (2008). Computers in childcare. *Putting children first, 27*(September), 14–16.

Morrison, Y. & Bright, N. (2009). *My Aussie mum*. Gosford, NSW: Scholastic Australia.

Morrow, L. M. (2009). *Literacy development in the early years* (6th edn). Boston: Pearson.

Munro, J. (1998). *Assessing and teaching phonological knowledge*. Camberwell, Victoria: ACER.

Nagy, N. M. & Scott, J. A. (2000). Vocabulary processes. In M. B. Kamil, P. B. Mosenthal, P. D. Pearson & R. Barr (eds), *Handbook of reading research: Volume III* (pp. 269–84). New York: Longman.

Nation, K. & Snowling, M. J. (1997). Assessing reading difficulties: The validity and utility of current measures of reading skill. *British Journal of Educational Psychology, 67*, 359–70.

National Association for the Education of Young Children. (1998a). *Learning to read and write: A joint position statement of the International Reading Association and the National Association for the Education of Young Children*. Retrieved 15/12/2009 from www.naeyc.org/positionstatements.

National Association for the Education of Young Children. (1998b). Learning to read and write: Developmentally appropriate practices for young children. *Young Children, 53*(4), 30–46.

National Association for the Education of Young Children. (2009). *Where we stand on learning to read and write*. Retrieved 15/12/2009 from www.naeyc.org/positionstatements/learning_readwritehigh.

National Curriculum Board. (2009). *The shape of the Australian Curriculum: English*. Commonwealth of Australia. Retrieved from www.acara.edu.au/verve/_resources/Australian_Curriculum_-_English.pdf.

National Inquiry into the Teaching of Literacy (2006). *Teaching reading: Report and recommendations*. Barton, ACT: Australian Government Department of Education, Science and Training.

National Institute of Child Health and Human Development (2000). *Report of the National Reading Panel. Teaching children to read: An evidence-based assessment of the scientific research literature on reading and its implications for reading instruction*. Washington, DC: Government Printing Office.

Nettles, D. H. (2006). *Comprehensive literacy instruction in today's classroom: The whole, the parts, and the heart*. Boston: Pearson Education.

Neuman, S. & Roskos, K. (eds). (1998). *Children achieving: Best practices in early literacy*. Newark, DE: International Reading Association.

New London Group. (1996). A pedagogy of multiliteracies: Designing social futures. *Harvard Education Review, 66*(1).

NICHD Early Child Care Research Network. (2005). Pathways to reading: The role of oral language in the transition to reading. *Developmental Psychology, 41*(2), 428–42.

Nieto, S. (2004). *Affirming diversity: The socio-political context of multicultural education*. Boston: Pearson Education.

Nilson, B. A. (2004). *Week by week: Documenting the development of young children*. Clifton Park: Thomson Delmar Learning.

Norman, K. (ed.). (1992). *Thinking voices: The work of the national oracy project*. Kent, UK: Hodder and Staughton.

Norton, D. E. (2007). *Literacy for life*. Boston: Pearson Education.

Nunes, T., Bryant, P., Pretzlik, U. & Hurry, J. (eds). (2006). *Improving literacy by teaching morphemes*. New York: Routledge.

Oakley, G. (2001). *12 things young children can do with an electronic talking book…maybe*. Paper presented at the Joint National Conference of the Australian Association for the Teaching of English and the Australian Literacy Educators' Association. Hobart, Tasmania.

Oakley, G. (2003). Improving oral reading fluency (and comprehension) through the creation of electronic talking books. *Reading Online, 6*(7) n.p.

Oakley, G. (2006a). Assessing reading comprehension. *Practically Primary, 11*(2).

Oakley, G. (2006b). From theory to practice: motivating children to engage in reading. *Practically Primary, 11*(1), 18–22.

Oakley, G. (2007). Can ICT help children spell? *Practically Primary, 12*(1), 45–7.

Oakley, G. (2008). e-LEA: Multimodal writing. *Practically Primary, 13*(1), 23–4.

Ogle, D. (1986). K-W-L: A teaching model that develops active reading of expository text. *The Reading Teacher, 39*, 564–70.

Ogle, D. & Beers, J. W. (2009). *Engaging the language arts: Exploring the power of language.* Boston: Pearson.

Olsen, C. B. (2007). *The reading writing connection.* Boston: Pearson.

O'Neill, S. & Gish, A. (2008). *Teaching English as a second language.* Melbourne: Oxford University Press.

Otto, B. (2010). *Language development in early childhood* (3rd edn). Upper Saddle River, New Jersey: Pearson Education.

Owens, R. E. (2005). *Language development: An introduction* (6th edn). Boston: Allyn and Bacon Pearson.

Owocki, G. (2001). *Make way for literacy! Teaching the way young children learn.* Portsmouth, NH: Heinemann.

Palincsar, A. S. & Brown, A. L. (1984). Reciprocal teaching of comprehension-fostering and comprehension-monitoring activities. *Cognition and Instruction, 1*, 117–75.

Pallotta, J. (1989). *Icky bug alphabet book.* Charlesbridge Publishing.

Parette, H. P., Blum, C., Boeckmann, N. M. & Watts, E. H. (2009). Teaching word recognition to young children who are at risk using Microsoft PowerPoint coupled with direct instruction. *Early Childhood Education Journal, 36*, 393–401.

Parette, H. P., Hourcade, J. J., Dinelli, J. M. & Boeckmann, N. M. (2009). Using Clicker 5 to enhance emergent literacy in young learners. *Early Childhood Education Journal, 36*, 355–63.

Paris, S. C. (2005). Reinterpreting the development of reading skills. *Reading Research Quarterly, 40*(2), 184–202.

Paris, S. C. & Carpenter, R. D. (2003). FAQs about IRIs. *The Reading Teacher, 56*, 2–4.

Paris, S. & Turner, J. (1995). How literacy tasks influence children's motivation for literacy. *The Reading Teacher, 48*(8), 662–73.

Patz, N. (1983). *Moses supposes his toeses are roses and 7 other silly old rhymes.* San Diego: Harcourt Brace Jovanovich.

Pearson, P. D. & Gallagher, M. C. (1983). The gradual release of responsibility model of instruction. *Contemporary Educational Psychology, 8*, 112–23.

Perry, S. (1995). *If.* California: Getty Trust Publications.

Pitcher, B. & Fang, Z. (2007). Can we trust levelled texts? An examination of their reliability and quality from a linguistic perspective. *Literacy, 41*(1), 43–51.

Prensky, M. (2001). Digital natives, digital immigrants. *On the Horizon, 9*(5), 1–6.

Pressley, M. (2002). Metacognition and self-regulated comprehension. In A. E. Farstrup & S. J. Samuels (eds), *What research has to say about reading instruction* (3rd edn, pp. 291–309). Newark, Delaware: International Reading Association.

Pressley, M. (2006). *Reading instruction that works: The case for balanced teaching.* New York: The Guilford Press.

Primary National Strategy. (2005). *The new conceptual framework for teaching reading: the 'simple view of reading'—overview for literacy leaders and managers in schools and Early Years settings.*

Retrieved 25/11/2008 from DfES www.standards.dfes.gov.uk/primaryframework/downloads/PDF/Paper_on_searchlights_model.pdf.

Primary National Strategy (2007a). *Letters and sounds: Principles and practice of high quality phonics.* Retrieved 1/10/2007, from www.standards.dfes.gov.uk/clld/las.html.

Quin, R., McMahon, B. & Quin, R. (1997). *Picture this: Reading visual language.* Carlton, Victoria: Curriculum Corporation.

Raban, B. & Coates, H. (2004). Literacy in the early years: A follow up study. *Journal of Research in Reading, 27*(1), 15–29.

Raphael, T. E. (1984). Teaching learners about sources of information for answering comprehension questions. *Journal of Reading, 30*(7), 632–6.

Raphael, T. E. & Au, K. H. (2005). QAR: Enhancing comprehension and test taking across grades and content areas. *The Reading Teacher, 59*(3), 206–21.

Rasinski, T. & Padak, N. (2008). *From phonics to fluency: Effective teaching of decoding and reading fluency in the elementary school.* Boston: Pearson.

Rathvon, N. (2004). *Early reading assessment.* New York: The Guilford Press.

Raver, S. A. (2004). Monitoring progress in early childhood special education settings. *Teaching Exceptional Children, 36*(6)

Resnick, L. B. & Hampton, S. (2009). *Reading and writing grade by grade.* Washington: The National Centre on Education and the Economy.

Riley, J. (2006). *Language and literacy 3–7: Creative approaches to teaching.* London: Sage.

Roberts, J. (2001). *Spelling recovery: The pathway to spelling success.* Camberwell, Victoria: ACER Press.

Roberts, V. & Nicholl, V. (1996). Making the most of traditional newstime. In P. Jones (ed.), *Talking to learn.* Sydney: Primary English Teaching Association.

Robinshaw, H. (2007). Acquisition of hearing, listening and speech skills by and during key stage 1. *Early Child Development and Care, 177*(6), 661–76.

Rog, L. J. & Burton, W. (2002). Matching texts and readers: Leveling early reading materials for assessment and instruction. *The Reading Teacher, 55*(4), 348–56.

Rohl, M. (2000). Learning about words, sounds and letters. In M. Rohl & C. Barratt-Pugh (eds), *Literacy learning in the early years.* Crows Nest, NSW: Allen & Unwin.

Rose, J. (2006). *Independent review of the teaching of early reading.* Nottingham: Department for Educations and Skills (DfES).

Rosen, M (1989) *We're going on a bear hunt.* London: Walker Books.

Rosen, M. (2004). *Alphabet poem.* London: Milet Publishing Limited.

Rosenblatt, L. M. (1978). *The reader, the text, the poem: The transactional theory of the literary work.* Carbondale: Southern Illinois University Press.

Rosenthal, R. & Jacobson, L. (1968). *Pygmalion in the classroom: Teacher expectations and pupils' intellectual development.* New York: Holt, Rinehart and Winston.

Roth, F. P., Speece, D. L. & Cooper, D. H. (2002). A longitudinal analysis of the connection between oral language and early reading. *Journal of Educational Research, 95*(5), 259.

Ruddell, R. B. (2006). *Teaching children to read and write: Becoming an effective teacher.* Boston: Pearson Education.

Samuels, S. J. (1979). The method of repeated readings. *The Reading Teacher, 21*, 360–407.

Sapp, K. (2007). *Just a joke.* Heatherton, Victoria: Hinkler Books.

Saxby, M. H. (1997). *Books in the life of a child.* South Yarra: Macmillan.

Scafer, R. E., Staab, C. & Smith, K. (1983). *Language functions and school success.* Illinois: Scott, Foreman and Company.

Scanlon, D. M. & Vellutino, F. R. (1996). Prerequisite skills, early instruction, and success in first-grade reading: Selected results from a longitudinal study. *Mental Retardation and Developmental Disabilities Research Reviews, 2,* 54–63.

Scraper, K. (2005). *It's game time.* Greenboro: NC: Carson-Dellosa Publishing Company, Inc.

Sebasta, S. (2001). What do teachers need to know about children's literature? *The New Advocate, 14,* 241–9.

Sendak, M. (1963). *Where the wild things are.* London: Random House.

Senghas, A. & Coppola, M. (2001). Children creating language: How Nicaraguan sign language acquired a spatial grammar. *Psychological Science, 12,* 323–8.

Seuss, D. (1958). *The cat in the hat comes back.* New York: Random House.

Seuss, D. (1963). *Dr Seuss's ABC.* New York: Random House.

Seuss, D. (1974). *There's a wocket in my pocket.* New York: Random House.

Seuss, D. (2003). *Dr Seuss' ABC.* London: Harper Collins.

Shamir, A. & Korat, O. (2006). How to select CD-ROM storybooks for young children: The teacher's role. *The Reading Teacher, 59*(6), 532–45.

Sharratt, N. (1994). *My mum and dad make me laugh.* London: Walker Books.

Sheward, T. (2006). *Little Aussie alphabet book.* Sydney: Macmillan.

Simmons, J. (2006). *Together.* London: Orchard books.

Sipe, L. R. (2002). Talking back and taking over: Young children's expressive engagement during storybook read-alouds. *The Reading Teacher, 55*(5), 476–83.

Siraj-Blatchford, J. & Siraj-Blatchford, I. (2006). *A guide to developing the ICT curriculum for early childhood education.* Stoke on Trent: Trentham books.

Skinner, B. F. (1957). *Verbal behavior.* Upper Saddle River: Prentice Hall.

Smith, F. (1971). *Understanding reading: A psycholinguistic analysis of reading and learning to read.* New York: Holt, Rinehart & Winston.

Snow, C. (2002). *Reading for understanding: Towards an R & D program in reading comprehension.* Santa Monica, CA: RAND.

Snow, C., Burns, S. M. & Griffin, P. (1998). *Preventing reading difficulties in young children.* Washington, DC: National Research Council. National Academy Press.

Snow, C. & Jordan, G. (2001). Project ease: A US success story. *Literacy Today, 29.* Retrieved on 25/9/07 from www.literacytrust.org.uk.

Spandel, V. (2009). *Creating writers through 6-trait writing: Assessment and instruction.* Boston: Allyn & Bacon.

Splitter, L. J. & Sharp, A. M. (1995). *Teaching for better thinking.* Melbourne: ACER.

Stahl, S. & Yaden, D. B. (2004). The development of literacy in preschool and primary grades: Work by the Center for the Improvement of Early Reading Achievement. *The Elementary School Journal, 105*(2), 141–65.

Stauffer, R. G. (1970). *The language experience approach to the teaching of reading.* NY: Harper & Row.

Stauffer, R. G. (1975). *Directing the reading-thinking process.* New York: Harper & Row.

Stuart, M. (2005). Phonemic analysis and reading development: Some current issues. *Journal of Research in Reading, 28*(1), 39–49.

Sulzby, E. (1984). Children's emergent reading of favourite storybooks: A developmental study. *Reading Research Quarterly, 20*(4), 458–81.

Sulzby, E. (1985). Kindergarteners as writers and readers. In M. Farr (ed.), *Advances in writing research: Vol. 1. Children's early writing development*. Norwood, NJ: Ablex.

Taback, S. (1997). *There was an old lady who swallowed a fly*. New York: Penguin.

Temple, C., Crawford, A. & Gillet, J. W. (2009). *Developmental literacy inventory*. Boston: Pearson Education.

Templeton, S. (1996). Spelling: The foundation of word knowledge for the less-proficient reader. In L. Putnam (ed.), *How to become a better reading teacher* (pp. 317–29). Toronto: Prentice Hall.

Thames, D. G. & York, K. C. (2004). Disciplinary border crossing: Adopting a broader, richer view of literacy. *The Reading Teacher, 56*(7), 602–10.

Tompkins, G. E. (2006). *Language Arts essentials*. Upper Saddle River, New Jersey: Pearson Education.

Tompkins, G. E. (2007). *Literacy for the 21st century: Teaching reading and writing in prekindergarten through grade 4*. Upper Saddle River, NJ: Pearson, Merrill Prentice Hall.

Tompkins, G. E. (2008). *Teaching writing: Balancing process and product*. Boston: Pearson Education.

Tompkins, G. E. (2009). *Language Arts: Patterns of practice* (7th edn). Upper Saddle River: Pearson.

Torgerson, C., Brooks, G. & Hall, J. (2006). *A systematic review of the research literature on the use of phonics in the teaching of reading and spelling*. London: Department for Education and Skills.

Torgeson, J. K. & Elbourne, D. (2002). A systematic review and meta-analysis of the effectiveness of information and communication technology (ICT) on the teaching of spelling. *Journal of Research in Reading, 25*, 129–43.

Torgeson, J. K. & Mathes, P. G. (2000). *A basic guide to understanding, assessing and teaching phonological awareness*. Austin, TX: Pro-ed.

Tough, J. (1976). *Listening to children talk: A guide to the appraisal of children's use of language*. London: Ward Lock Educational.

Tough, J. (1977). *Teachers' strategies in dialogue*. London: Ward Lock Educational.

Tough, J. (1979). *Talk for teaching and learning*. London: Ward Lock Educational.

Trask, R. L. & Stockwell, P. (eds). (2007). *Language and linguistics: The key concepts*. Abingdon, Oxon: Routledge.

Trelease, J. (1995). *The read aloud handbook* (4th edn). New York: Penguin.

Tulloch, R. & Pattie, P. (1999). *Little Red Riding Bananas*. Sydney: Australian Broadcasting Corporation.

Turbill, J. & Murray, J. (2006). Early literacy and new technologies in Australian schools: Policy, research and practice. In M. C. McKenna (ed.), *International handbook of literacy and technology* (vol. 2, pp. 93–108). Mahway, NJ: Laurence Erlbaum & Associates.

Van Allsburg, C. (1987). *The X was zapped*. Boston, MA: Houghton Mifflin.

Vasquez, V. (2007). Using the everyday to engage in critical literacy with young children. *New England Reading Association Journal, 43*(2), 6–11.

Victorian Department of Education. (1998). *Teaching readers in the early years: Keys to Life early literacy program*. Melbourne: Longman.

Victorian Department of Education (2009). *Victorian early years learning and development framework for all children from birth to eight years*. Retrieved 15/3/2010 from www.vcaa.vic.edu.au/earlyyears/index.html.

Vincent, D. & Crumpler, M. (1997). *Reading progress tests (RPT)*. London: Hodder & Stoughton.

Vukelich, C., Christie, J. & Enz, B. (2008). *Helping young children learn language and literacy: Birth through kindergarten*. Boston: Pearson.

Vygotsky, L. (1978). *Mind in society: The development of higher psychological processes*. Cambridge: Harvard University Press.

Waddell, M. & Wojtowycz, D. (2000). *Baabooom*. Oxford: Rigby Education.

Wade, B. & Moore, M. (1998). An early start with books: Literacy and mathematical evidence from a longitudinal study. *Educational Review, 50*, 135–45.

Wade, B. & Moore, M. (2000). A sure start with books. *Early Years, 20*, 39–46.

Wagner, J. (1979). *John Brown, Rose and the midnight cat*. Harmondsworth: Puffin.

Walpole, S. & McKenna, M. (2004). *The literacy coach's handbook: A guide to research-based practice*. New York: The Guilford Press.

Walpole, S. & McKenna, M. C. (2006). The role of informal reading inventories in assessing word recognition. *The Reading Teacher, 59*(6), 592–4.

Walsche, R. D. (1981). *Every child can write: learning and teaching written expression in the 1980s*. Rozelle, Australia: PETA.

Weaver, C. (1990). *Understanding whole language: From principles to practice*. Portsmouth, NH: Heinemann.

Weaver, C. (1996). Teaching grammar in the context of writing. *English Journal, 85*(7).

West, C. (1996). *'I don't care!' said the bear*. London: Walker.

Westwood, P. (2005). *Spelling: Approaches to teaching and assessment*. Camberwell, Victoria: ACER.

Wheatley, J. P. (2005). *Strategic spelling: Moving beyond word memorization in the middle grades*. Newark, DE: International Reading Association.

Whitehead, M. (2007). *Developing langauge and literacy with young children: 0–8 years* (3rd edn). Los Angeles: Paul Chapman Publishing.

Wilkins, V. (1993). *ABC I can be*. Camberley, UK: Tamarind.

Williams, K. T. (1997). *Expressive Vocabulary Test (EVT)*. Circle Pines: American Guidance Service.

Williams, T. L. (2007). 'Reading' the painting: Exploring visual literacy in the primary grades. *The Reading Teacher, 60*(7), 636–42.

Winch, G., Johnston, R. R., March, P., Ljungdahl, L. & Holliday, M. (2006). *Literacy: Reading, writing and children's literature*. South Melbourne: OUP.

Wood, K., Lapp, D. & Flood, J. (1992). *Guiding readers through text*. Newark, DE: International Reading Association.

Wren, S. (2001). Reading and the three cueing systems: Topics in early reading coherence. Austin, Texas: Southwest Educational Development Laboratory.

Yopp, H. K. (1995). A test for assessing phonemic awareness in young children. *The Reading Teacher, 49*(1), 20–9.

Yopp, H. K. & Yopp, R. H. (2009). Phonological awareness is child's play. *Young Children, 61*(1), 12–21.

Zevenbergen, R. & Logan, H. (2007). Computer use by preschool children: Rethinking practice as digital natives come to preschool. *Contemporary Issues in Early Childhood, 8*(8), 19–29.

Zimmerman, S. & Keene, E. O. (1997). *Mosaic of thought: Teaching comprehension in a readers workshop*. Portsmouth, NH: Heinemann.

INDEX

Aboriginal English   24
academic language   113–14
adult talk and children's learning   114–16
affective factors, assessing   159–60
affixes   10, 255–6
alphabet   174–5
alphabet centre   437
alphabetic principle   170, 176
alphabetic system   383–5
anecdotal notes   137–9, 141, 145, 171, 202, 290, 456
animals in text   504
annotations   458
anticipation guides (reading comprehension)   293
antonyms   254
approximation and literacy learning   156
art and craft response (children's literature)   482–3
assessment *see* oral language assessment; self-assessment; visual literacy; writing, assessment
attitude and literacy development   158–9, 568–70
audiences   346–7
audio recordings   140
Australian National Curriculum   152
automaticity of word recognition   269, 302, 303, 305, 315

babies and childcare   49–50
base word   10
behaviourist perspective and language development   32–3
Better Beginnings (home literacy support program)   535
bilingualism   25–6
bingo (wordo)   220–1
Blank, Marion   117–20
Bleich, David   480
blind sort   395
blurb writing (reading comprehension)   294
book corner   483
book handling   168–9
books
    audio recordings of   308
    children's literature   476–86
    children's (rhyme or alliteration)   198–9
    creating talking   519
    digital/electronic talking   312–13
    electronic talking   515–19
    infants/toddlers   226, 479, 555–6
    selection for shared reading   230
    story (vocabulary building)   249–50, 477
    writing digital   313
    see also children's literature; literature
books and print, concepts about   168–70
Bourgeois, Paulette   474
brain development and language use   108
Bridging the Gap (home literacy support program)   535
buddy reading   238

Cambourne, Brian   155–6
Cambourne's seven conditions of literacy learning   155–6
character mapping (reading comprehension)   294
character ranking (reading comprehension)   294
checklists   140–2
child care setting
    and babies   49–50
    and language development   49–54
    and toddlers   50–1
children
    and conversations about writing   459–60
    how they learn   110–11
    and language functions   19–20
    learning and adult talk   114–16
    as writers   443, 445–51
    writing lessons, developing   444–5
children's books with rhyme or alliteration   198–9
children's literature   241, 471–86
    and curriculum   472–5
    definition   472
    infants/toddlers   226, 479, 555–6
    and integrated activities   481–6
    reader/listener response   476
    reading and response   476–86
    response to literature   475–6
    teacher role   474–5
    see also books; literature
children's reading interests   241–2
children's self-evaluation and oral language assessment   130, 135–6
children's work and oral language assessment   130, 135
choral reading   306–7, 319
class message board   439–40
class photo book   441
classical conditioning   33

classroom environment and written texts 357–8
Clay, Marie 155, 169, 171–2, 240, 289
Clicker 5 (Crick software) 521–3
cloze
    clever 495
    and reading comprehension 286
    and writing 419–20
code switching 26
cognition
    and language 107, 108–10
    and questioning 116–24
cognitive development 107, 108
cognitive developmental perspective and language development 35–6, 155
cognitive processes 112, 267
communication
    with families 130, 136
    and language 4–5
    and oral language 55, 76, 80, 126, 129, 136, 140, 555
    written 326–7, 337–41
competency in speaking and listening 100–3, 130, 131, 135, 141–2, 146
compound words 252, 387
comprehension
    children's 226, 239, 267
    of informal texts 281–3
    levels of 271–2
    processes and strategies 281
    strategies 293–300
    see also reading comprehension
Comprehensive Assessment of Spoken Language (CASL) 137
concept mapping and ICT 520–1
concepts 111
    about books and print 168–70
    about print, assessment of 170–2
    about print, teaching 170
    letter 170
    word 169–70
conferencing 334
consonant riddles 201
conversation
    oral language assessment 130, 134–5
    oral language learning and development 61, 71–2, 534, 554, 555
    and reading comprehension 287
cooperative learning 113
core questions 122–4
creating titles (reading comprehension) 294
critical literacy 490–5
    themes for 503–6
cueing systems and text use 167
cultural diversity 545
culture and language 22–3
cyber smart, helping young children become 526

decoding words strategically 216
dedicated spelling software 523–5

demonstration
    and literacy learning 155
    and text analysis 358
developmental perspective on literacy learning 154
developmentally appropriate software/technology 512, 519
dialect 23
dictionaries 257–8
Digital Language Experience Approach (D-LEA) 513
digital natives 510
digital stories 519
Directed Reading Thinking Activity (DRTA) 295–6
directionality for reading and writing 169
discussion
    and critical literacy 492–3
    and oral language learning and development 72–5
    types of 74–5
diversity and listening 104
drama (vocabulary building) 250
dress ups 481–2

early childhood professional 570–1
early childhood settings
    and language diversity 26–7
    oral language development 42–3
early years
    language and literacy development 566–8
    and vocabulary development 248
Early Years Learning Framework for Australia (EYLF) 152, 165, 518, 434, 473, 484–6, 518, 551
echo reading 307–8, 319
editing 335
Effective Reading in Content Areas (ERICA model) 564–6
Electronic Language Experience Approach (e-LEA) 513–15
electronic literacy 512
electronic talking books 515–19
Elkonin boxes 400–1
emergence of writing 433–43
emergent literacy 532–3
emergent perspective on literacy learning 155
encoding 383
English
    Aboriginal 24
    lessons in primary school setting 54–7
    programs, stand-alone 567
    standard 23
etymological knowledge (spelling) 387–8
evidence-based approaches to teaching literacy 158
expectation and literacy learning 156
explicit systematically organised teaching 552
exploratory play 62
expository writing 349, 352–4
expressive engagement 226–8
expressive modes of oral language 6
expressive vocabulary 245, 261

fairy tales 503
families
    connecting with 530–48
    and conversations about writing 460
    culturally and linguistically diverse
        backgrounds 544–8
    emergent literacy 532–3
    family literacy 531–3
    family literacy diversity 533–4
    family literacy initiatives 535–6
    Indigenous 547–8
    and oral language 130, 136, 531–2, 542
    parent–teacher partnerships 536–8
    partnership practices 538–44
    take-home literacy resources 542–4
    in texts 505–6
family literacy 531–2
    diversity 533–4
    and emergent literacy 532–3
    initiatives 535–6
    and oral language 531–2
    practices 531
    practices and emergent literacy 531
feedback and literacy learning 156
figurative meanings 256
first-wave teaching 246
fluency see reading fluency
formal tests and oral language assessment 130, 136
funds of knowledge 534

games
    barrier games 82–4
    electronic 285
    matching 221
    syllable clapping 193, 194
    for teaching phonics 212–14
    and word consciousness 259, 260
    word recognition 232, 315
gradual release of responsibility 225, 230, 281, 410
grammar
    definition 363–4
    as a prelude to writing 364–5
    understanding English 366–73
    and writing 373–7
graphemes 206–7, 383
graphophonic knowledge 167, 172–3
graphophonic relationships
    assessing knowledge about 217–18
    and ICT 519–21
    teaching about 204–6
    what children need to know 206–9
    see also phonics
guided imagery (reading comprehension) 296
guided reading 225, 235–8
    appropriate text 235–6
    book introduction 236
    discussion 237
    follow-up activities 237–8

independent reading 236–7
    suggested procedure for 235
    and teacher organisation 238
    tuning in stage 236
guided writing 410, 411, 424–6

handwriting 404–6
Hearing and Recording Sounds in Words Test (Dictation
    Test) 217
high-frequency words 179
Holdaway, Don 228, 230, 231, 232
holistic learning 552
'home corner' 250
home setting and language development 47–9
home–centre school messages 540–1
homonyms 254–5
homophones 254–5
hot-seating (reading comprehension) 296–7

idioms 256
immersion and literacy learning 155
independent reading 239, 250–1
independent writing 358–60, 411, 427
Indigenous families 547–8
indirect instruction (vocabulary learning) 249–51
infants (language and literacy) 226, 479, 555–6
inferential level of comprehension 271
informal reading inventories (IRIs) 289–90, 315
informal texts, comprehension of 281–4
information and computer technologies (ICT)
        509–28
    and concept mapping 520–1
    cyber smart, helping young children become
        526
    dedicated spelling software 523–5
    and graphophonic relationships 519–21
    interactive whiteboards 527–8
    and literacy learning in the classroom 512–19
    and teaching fluency 312–13
    using the internet 524–7
    webquests 524–5
    websites, criteria for selecting 526–7
    and word identification 519–21
    word processors 521–3
inner speech 110
inquiry-based learning 559
integrated curriculum 560, 562–3
integrated learning 561–2
integrated programs 559, 560–1, 564–6
intentional teaching 133, 165, 552, 553
    activities 434, 439–43
interactionist perspective and language
        development 36–7
interactive whiteboards 527–8
interactive writing 411, 421
internet 524–7
intonation 8
interviews and reading comprehension 287

invented spelling   391
investigations
    and oral language learning and development   76–7

Jolly Phonics   218
journal writing   442–3

Kidpix Delux   523
K-W-L charts (reading comprehension)   297

language
    academic   113–14
    and cognition   107, 108–10
    and communication   4–5
    and culture   22–3
    diversity and early childhood settings   26–7
    is functional   14–20
    and learning   110–16
    learning programs   554–9
    metalanguage   216
    phonological component   8–10, 129
    play (home corner)   250
    pragmatic component   13–14, 129
    properties of   6–7
    semantic component   11–13, 129
    social   114
    and speech   5–6
    syntactic component   10–11, 129
    use and brain development   108
    variations   23–5
    see also oral language; spoken language
language acquisition device (LAD)   34, 36
language acquisition support system (LASS)   36
language development
    behaviourist perspective   32–3
    child care setting   49–54
    cognitive developmental perspective   35–6, 154
    home setting   47–9
    infants/toddlers   226, 479, 555–6
    interactionist perspective   36–7
    maturational perspective   35, 154
    nativist perspective   34
    neurobiological perspective   37–8
    pre-schoolers   555–9
    primary school setting   54–6
    theoretical perspectives   32–8, 154–8
    see also oral language development
Language Experience Approach (LEA)   169, 228, 422–4, 513
language register   20–2
learning
    experiences   55, 56
    experiences, teacher-directed   356
    holistic   552
    and language   110–16
    and oral language   111–16
    and questioning   116–24
    to read   179–84

learning centres   59, 238, 435–7
learning environments   46, 434–5
learning programs
    attitude and motivation   568–70
    creating   552
    and early childhood professional   570–1
    early years of school   566–8
    key features of   552–4
    integrated   559–63
    integrated, reading and writing in an   564–6
    language and literacy   554–9
    planning   551–2
letter identification   461–2
letter names, teaching   175–6
letter–sound relationships   177, 210–11, 386
letters
    concept of   170
    knowledge about   174–7
    missing   401
    most common sounds of   209
    and sounds order   210–11
    and sounds phases   210–11
    working with   214–16
levelled texts   240–1
listening
    competency   100–3, 130, 131, 135, 141–2, 146
    contexts   132
    cooperative   113
    and diversity   104
    and function   18–19
    importance of   99–103
    reading while   306–8
    see also oral language assessment; speaking and listening activities
listening posts   90–1, 306
literacy
    assessing affective factors   159–60
    Cambourne's seven conditions of literacy learning   155–6
    constituents   158
    critical   490–5
    definition   152–3
    development, attitude and motivation   158–9, 568–70
    developmental perspective   154
    electronic   512
    emergent   155, 532–3
    evidence-based approaches   158
    and ICT   313, 512–19
    infants/toddlers   226, 479, 555–6
    initiatives, family   535–6
    learning   534
    learning, importance of motivation   158–9
    and literature   472–4
    maturational perspective   154
    portfolios   541
    related learning centres   435
    resources, take-home   542–4

socio-cultural perspectives 157–8
and stand-alone English programs 567
teachers, practice of highly effective 160–1
visual 490, 495–501
writing 350–2
see also family literacy
literal level of comprehension 271
literary writing 349
literature
    and integrated activities 481–6
    and literacy 472–4
    psychoanalytic theories 475
    psycholinguistic theories 476
    psychological theories 475
    reading and response 476–86
    response to 475–6
    see also books; children's literature
literature circles 239–40

magazine picture booklet 442
manipulation 77
maturational perspective and language development 35, 154
meaning vocabulary 245
meanings
    figurative 256
    multiple 256
mental imagery (texts) 276
message boards 439–40
metalanguage 216
metaphors 256
mnemonics 400
modelled reading 225, 250, 258–9, 278, 305–6, 320
modelled writing 215, 410, 412–16
morphemes 255–6, 387
morphemic knowledge (spelling) 387
morphology 10, 364
motivation and literacy learning 158–9, 568–70
moving images 500
Multidimensional Fluency Scale (MS) 316–17
multilingualism 25
multiliteracies theory 489–90
multimodal texts 284–5, 511
multiple meanings 256
multi-syllabic words 216

NAEP Oral Reading Scale 315–16
National English Curriculum Framing Paper 472
National Inquiry into the Teaching of Literacy (NITL) 158
nativist perspective and language development 34
neurobiological perspective and language development 37–8
news-telling
    and oral language learning and development 91–3, 567
nonsense words 191
noun 368–9

observation
    and oral language assessment 130, 131–4
    and writing assessment 456
Observation Survey 217
onset-rime awareness 188, 518
onset-rime level of phonic awareness 194–5
onset-rime word spinners 213
onsets 385
operant conditioning 33
oral communication 6, 9, 19, 20, 23, 46, 55, 60, 66–7, 70, 80–1, 99, 129, 135, 145, 364, 541, 552, 554, 555
oral language
    ability 4, 86, 128, 130, 135, 141
    activities 52, 56, 80, 85, 100, 131, 135, 145
    children's, collecting information about 130–7, 146
    children's strengths 133, 135
    children's use of 86, 137–8
    collecting information about 130–7
    competencies 21, 63, 135, 138, 141, 142, 531
    and core questions 122
    and communication 55, 76, 126, 136, 140, 554, 555
    and discussion 72–5
    experiences 100, 108, 327
    expressive and receptive modes 6
    and families 130, 136, 531–2, 542
    and family literacy 531–2
    fluency 69
    information interpretation 146
    investigations 76–7
    knowledge 166–7
    and learning 111–16
    and parental awareness 542
    and play 59–65
    and print 532
    and reading 166–7
    skills 4, 67, 70, 131, 133, 138, 141, 166
    speaking and listening activities 81–98
    tests 136–7
    and text 90, 166–7
    and writing 166–7, 327, 364–5, 417, 422, 423, 441
oral language assessment 127–46
    anecdotal notes 137–9, 141, 145
    audio recordings 140
    checklists 140–2
    children's self-evaluations 130, 135–6
    communication with families 130, 136
    conversations 130, 134–5
    documentation of information 137–45
    formal tests 130, 136–7
    goals 128
    information collection 130–7
    information interpretation 146
    observation 130, 131–4
    portfolios 145
    rating scales 142–3
    rubrics 143–5
    samples of children's work 130, 135

        story retelling   133–4
        video recordings   140
    oral language development
        and action rhymes   86–7
        activities   52, 85, 86–7
        in childcare and education settings   42–3
        children's level of   74
        in early childhood settings   46, 55–6, 61
        and conversation   61, 71–2, 534, 554, 555
        and discussion   72–5
        important considerations   80
        and investigations   76–7
        milestones   38–42
        and the learning experience   55
        and news-telling   91–3, 567
        nurturing   4
        phases   38–42
        and reading aloud to children   64–7
        rubrics   143–5
        and storytelling experiences   67–71, 567
        understanding   128
        see also language development
    oral language learning
        and action rhymes   86–7
        activities   85, 86–7
        anecdotal notes   137–9, 141, 145
        audio recording   140
        checklists   140–2
        and conversation   61, 71–2, 534, 554, 555
        documentation of   137–45
        in early childhood settings   46, 55–6, 61
        important considerations   80
        and investigations   76–7
        and the learning experience   55–6
        and news-telling   92, 567
        portfolios   145
        rating scales   142–3
        and reading aloud to children   64–5
        rubrics   143–5
        and storytelling experiences   67–71, 567
        video recording   140
    oral recitation lesson (ORL)   321–2
    orally blending sounds   201
    orally segmenting sounds   200
    orthographic knowledge   385
    orthographic system, English   283–4

    pace and reading fluency   302, 310–11
    paired reading   308, 320
    paragraphing   375–7
    parent partnership programs   538
    parent surveys   541
    parental awareness   542
    parent–teacher conference   540
    parent–teacher partnerships   536–8
    part-to-whole approach and reading   182–3
    passage comprehension assessments   285
    patterned stories   442

    personal texts   350
    personal writing   348, 349–50
    phoneme awareness   188, 383
    phoneme frames   400–1
    phoneme level of phonic awareness   195–7
    phonemes   8, 188, 196–7, 383–5, 386
    phonemic awareness   195
    phonics
        definition   204
        commercial programs   218
        knowledge, assessment of   217–19
        synthetic   206
        through spelling   206
    phonics, teaching   204, 209–14
        approaches   204–6
        possible sequences   209–11
        principles   211–12
        strategies and games   212–14
    phonological awareness   172–4, 188, 269
        assessment   202–3
        teaching   188–9, 202
        teaching at the syllable level   193–4
        principles for teaching   202
        word-level   189–202
    Phonological Awareness Literacy Screening
        (PALS)   202
    phonological component of language   8–10, 129
    phonological knowledge   385–6
    phrasing (reading fluency)   303, 310
    picture cards   199
    picture hunts   199
    picture labelling   250
    picture searches   202
    picture sorts   199, 394
    picture vocabulary   261
    picture walks (reading comprehension)   298
    Piaget, Jean   35, 108–9
    play
        experiences and text forms   355–6
        exploratory   62
        language (home corner)   250
        and oral language   59–65
        role   250
        spaces   51, 59
        socio-dramatic   63–4, 437–9, 482
        structures   51
        unstructured   51
    poems   194–5
    portfolios   145, 290, 457, 541
    pragmatic component of language   13–14, 129
    prefixes   387
    pre-school environment and language
        development   52–4
    pre-school setting and language development   51–2
    pre-schoolers and language/literacy learning
        programs   555–9
    primary school setting and language
        development   54–6

print
- assessment of concepts about 170–2
- and books, concepts about 168–70
- and oral language 532
- teaching concepts about 170

process questions 122–4
pronoun 368
prosody 303, 312, 315
psychoanalytic theories to literature 475
psycholinguistic theories to literature 476
psychological theories to literature 475
punctuation, reading and writing 170, 373–5

question frameworks 117–24
- Blank's Levels of Talk 117–20
- core and process 122–4
- Splitter and Sharp 120–2

question–answer relationships (WARs) 275–6
questioning
- and critical literacy 492–3
- for cognition and learning 116–24
- and reading comprehension 286

questioning texts 275–6

RAND Reading Study Group 268–9, 283–4
rating scales 142–3
read, learning to 179–84
read-alouds 64–7, 226, 227
reader response (transactional theory) 476
readers, assisting struggling beginning 314–15
readers theatre 309, 321–2
readiness (biological) 35
reading
- assessing affective factors 159–60
- buddy 238, 306
- Cambourne's seven conditions of literacy learning 155–6
- centre 437
- choral 306–7, 319
- concept of word 169–70
- conceptual knowledge 168–70
- definition 179–80
- development 180–2
- developmental perspective 154
- directionality 169
- echo 307–8, 319
- emergent perspective 155
- evidence-based approaches 158
- fluency 226
- foundations 165
- guided 225, 235–8
- independent 239, 250–1
- to infants 226, 479, 555
- in an integrated program 564–6
- interests, children's 241–2
- inventories, informal 289–90
- knowledge about letters and sounds 174–7
- learning 179–84

- maturational perspective 154
- modelled 225, 305–6
- non-fluent 306
- paired 308, 320
- part-to-whole approach 182–3
- perspectives on how to teach 182–4
- and phonological awareness 172–4
- and print 170–2
- and questioning text 275–6
- and response 476–86
- sight words 178–80, 221
- socio-cultural perspectives 157–8
- story book 249–50
- and talking about books 439
- and text forms 357
- text purposes 172
- text use and understanding 166–8
- theoretical perspectives 154–8
- to toddlers 227, 479, 555
- topic knowledge 168–70
- and vocabulary 245–6, 284
- while listening 306–8
- whole-to-part approach 183
- word recognition 177–8
- see also shared reading

reading, teaching 182–4, 224–42
- buddy reading 238
- guided reading 235–8
- independent reading 239
- language experience approach (LEA) 228
- literature circles 239–40
- matching texts to children 240–2
- part-to-whole approach 182–3
- reading aloud to children 225–8
- reciprocal teaching 239
- shared reading 228–34
- whole-to-part approach 183

reading aloud to children 64–7, 225–8
reading comprehension 226, 266–90
- analysis of written work 287
- anticipation guides 293
- appropriate texts 283–4
- assessment 285–90
- blurb writing 294
- character mapping 294
- character ranking 295
- cloze 286
- comprehension strategies 293–300
- and conversations 287
- creating titles 295
- definition 268–9
- determining importance 276–7
- developmental pathways 269–71
- directed reading thinking activity (DRTA) 295–6
- expository text structures 281–3
- fix-up strategies 278–9
- guided imagery 296

hot-seating/character interviews 296–7
informal reading inventories 289–90
informational texts 281–3
and interviews 287
K-W-L charts 297
levels 271–2
making connections 273–5
making inferences 277–8
making predictions 273
and mental imagery 276
multimodal texts 284–5
picture walks 298
and portfolios 290
process and strategies 281
and questioning 275–6, 286
and reciprocal teaching 279–81
response journal 298
retelling and synthesising 278, 286
running records 287–9
self-monitoring strategies 278–9
story mapping 299
strategic processes 273–81
summarising 278
tableaux 299
talk to the author 299–300
and text 269, 281–5
think-alouds 286
thought bubbles 300
and visualisation 277
vocabulary for reading 284
reading fluency 301–22
assessment 315–17
definition 302–3
development 304–5
elements 303, 310–11
encouraging, key practices for 305–10
expressiveness 312
facilitating 305
and ICT 312–13
importance 304
modelling 305–6
pace 302, 310–11
phrasing 303, 310
and practice 314
readability 313–14
readers' theatre (RT) 309
reading while listening 306–8
repeated readings 308–9
self-monitoring 314
and struggling beginning readers 314–15
texts, appropriate 313–14
Reading Recovery 240, 287, 314
reasoning 77
receptive modes of oral language 6
receptive vocabulary 245, 261
reciprocal teaching 239, 279–81
recorded/taped readings 308
repeated readings (reading fluency) 308–9

representation 77
response journals (reading comprehension) 298
responsibility and literacy learning 156
retellings and reading comprehension 286
rhymes 190–2
    children's books with 198–9
rhyming generation 191–2
rhyming names 191
rhyming riddles 191, 192
rhyming words 190–2
riddles 191, 192, 259
rimes 385
role play 250
root words 255, 387
Rose Report 158, 206, 211–12
Rosenblatt, Louise 476
rubrics 143–5, 456
running records and reading comprehension 287–9

Saxby, Maurice 475
scaffolding 36, 114–15, 281
schemata 111
self-assessment 317, 456, 460–1, 465, 541
self-evaluation and oral language assessment 130, 135–6
self-monitoring (reading comprehension) 278–9
semantic component of language 11–13, 129, 167
semantic feature analysis 263
semantic knowledge 167
semantic mapping 263–4
Sendak, Maurice 473
sentence(s)
    features of 365–6
    fluency 331
    and grammar 363, 365–6
    reconstruction (writing) 421
    strips 219
    structures 366–7
    types of 369–70
    voice 367–9
Shape of Australian Curriculum: English paper 152
Shared Book Experience (SBE) 175, 228–9, 232
shared reading 169, 183, 194, 228–34, 392, 437, 492, 557
    discovery stage 231
    elements of 230–4
    exploration 232
    independent experience and expression 232–3
    letters and sounds 215
    pre-reading 233
    and reading fluency 306
    reading while listening 306
    selecting books for 230
    sight words 221
    and vocabulary in story books 250
shared (interactive) writing 411, 416–19, 421

Sharp, A.M. 117, 120–2
sight words 177, 178–9
    assessment of 221–2
    reading 178–80, 221
    strategies for teaching 219–21
    teaching 219
similes 256
Slack, Jill 122, 123–4
social language 114
socio-cultural perspectives of literacy learning 157–8
socio-dramatic play 63–4, 437–9, 482
sound addition 201
sound deletion 201
sound shop 199
sound substitution 201–2
sounds
    isolating 197–9
    knowledge about 174–7
    and letters order 210–11
    and letters phases 210–11
    letter–sound relationships 177, 210–11, 386
    manipulating 201–2
    and oral language 167
    orally blending 201
    orally segmenting 200
    working with 214–16
speaking
    competency 130, 131, 135, 141–2, 146
    contexts 132
    see also oral language assessment
speaking and listening activities 81–98
    action rhymes 86–7
    activity sharing 98
    barrier games 82–4
    celebrity heads 94
    character interviews 82
    class meetings 93
    dictogloss 97
    hide the object 94
    listening post 90–1, 306
    listening walks 94–5
    making sounds 95
    memory tray 93
    news-telling 91–3
    paired improvisation 94
    pass it on 96–7
    phonological knowledge 385–6
    picture talks 85–6
    quick questions 97
    sequence chart 94
    Simon says 95–6
    sorting and classifying 84–5
    sound lotto 95
    surprise bag 87–9
    telephone role plays 81–2
    think, pair, share 93–4
    What am I? 97

speech
    inner 110
    and language 5–6
    parts of 364, 370–3
spelling
    ability 382
    activities 393–402
    analogy charts 398
    children's development 388–91
    chunk–explore–visualise–write 399
    competency 382
    dedicated spelling software 523–5
    English orthographic system 383–5
    etymological knowledge 387–8
    finding the rule 399
    importance of good 382
    invented 391
    journals 401–2
    knowledge 385–8
    lessons 402–4
    look–cover–write–check 396–7
    morphemic knowledge 387
    parallel charts 398
    patterns 386–7
    self-assessment of 465
    sorts 394–5
    strategies 388, 402
    teaching 392–3
    tests 462, 464–5
    visual knowledge 386–7
    and writing 462–6
Splitter, L.J. 117, 120–2
spoken language, components of 8–14
    phonological 8–10
    pragmatic 13–14
    semantic 11–13
    syntactic 10–11
stories, patterned 442
story book reading 249–50
story mapping (reading comprehension) 299
story retelling 133–4
storytelling
    and oral language learning and development 67–71, 567
stress (syllables in words) 8
Student Oral Language Observational Matrix (SOLOM) 143–4
suffixes 387
syllable awareness 188, 385
syllable clapping games 193, 194
syllable level of phonic awareness 192–4
synonym webs 264
synonyms 252–3
syntactic component of language 10–11, 129, 167
syntactic knowledge 167
syntax 364
synthetic phonics 206

tableaux (reading comprehension)   299
take-home bear   440
talk to the author (reading comprehension)   299–300
talking word processors   522–3
Teacher Rating of Oral Language and Literacy (TROLL)   136
teacher-directed learning experiences   356
teachers
    and children's literature   474–5
    early childhood professional   570–1
    practice of highly effective literacy   160–1
    see also parent–teacher partnerships
teaching
    critical literacy   492–5
    direct   403
    first-wave   246
    graphophonic relationships   204–6
    reciprocal   239
    spelling   392–3
    texts   354–6
    texts in the early years of school   356–60
    viewing, approaches to   501–3
    writing, key strategies   409–30
    the writing conventions   377–9
    see also intentional teaching; phonics, teaching; phonological awareness; reading, teaching
tense (sentences)   11
text analysis   358, 491
text forms   328, 348
    and play experiences   355–6
    and reading   357
    and written lessons   358–60
text innovation and writing   447–8, 494
text purposes, knowledge about   172
text reconstruction (writing)   420
text types   360
text use and understanding   166–8
    oral language   166–7
    vocabulary   167–8
text-to-self connections   274
text-to-text connections   274–5
text-to-world connections   274
texts
    animals in   504
    families in   505–6
    informal, comprehension of   281–3
    levelled   240–1
    and making connections   226, 273–5
    and making predictions   273
    matching to children   235, 240–2, 313–14
    multimodal   284–5, 511
    non-fiction   449–50
    personal   350
    planning framework   359–60
    and readability   313–14
    questioning   275–6
    teaching   354–6
    teaching in the early years of school   356–60

types of   348–54
written   347–8
think-alouds   216, 286, 413
thinking   110, 226, 267, 269
thought bubbles   300
toddlers (language and literacy)   226, 479, 555–6
toddlers and childcare   50–1
tracing activities (learning sight words)   220
transactional theory to reader response   476
tuning in to reading (guided reading)   236

universal grammar   34

verb   368
video recordings   140
viewing, approaches to teaching   501–3
viewing (visual literacy)   490
visual codes   496
visual comprehension   496–7
visual elements (codes)   497–500
visual knowledge (spelling)   386–7
visual literacy   490
    assessment of   506
    definition   496
    themes for   503–6
    in the twenty-first century   495–501
visual texts   500
visual work and oral language assessment   130, 135
visualising (texts)   276
vocabulary   167–8, 244–61
    antonyms   254
    cline   254
    compound words   252
    contextual clues, using   258–9
    drama   250
    definition   245
    development in early years   248–9
    explicit instruction   251
    expressive   245, 261
    figurative meanings   256
    home corner   250
    homonyms   254–5
    homophones   254–5
    independent reading   250–1
    indirect instruction   249–1
    knowledge, assessment of   260–1
    knowledge, development of   246
    knowledge, levels of   246–8
    making connections   257
    meaning   245
    morphemes, teaching about   255–6
    multiple meanings   256
    and reading   245–6, 284
    receptive   245, 261
    repeated exposure (story books)   249
    role play   250
    sight   245
    story book reading   249–50

strategies   263–5
synonyms   252–3
teaching, principles of   260
using dictionaries   257–8
visits   264–5
word consciousness, teaching   259–60
word sorts/classifications   258
word maps   265
word study   252–7
and writing   245–6
voice of sentence   367–9
Vygotsky, Lev   13, 108, 109–10

web, searching the   525–6
webquests   524–5
whole language philosophy   155, 183, 229
whole-to-part approach and reading   183
word charts   260
word comprehension assessments   285
word consciousness, teaching   259–60
word dominoes   220
word families   194, 212–13
word family posters   212–13
word hunts   397
word lists   251, 574–5
word maps   265
word operations   400
word play   259
word processors (ICT)   251–3
word shapes   219–20
word slides   213
word sorts   213, 214–15, 218, 220, 393–5
word spinners, onset-rime   213
word trace   395–6
word walls   220, 259–60, 396
word Wizard (Macroworks)   524
word-level phonological awareness   189–202
   isolating sounds   197–9
   manipulating sounds   201–2
   onset-rime level   194–5
   orally blending sounds   201
   orally segmenting sounds   200
   phoneme level   195–7
   rhymes   190–2
   syllable level   192–4
   words   189–90
words
   automatic recognition of   269, 302, 303, 305, 315
   awareness   188
   compound   252, 387
   concept of   169–70
   decoding strategically   216
   finding   397
   high-frequency   179
   how they change form   387
   how they look   386–7
   how they sound   385–6
   illustrating   397

making   215–16
multi-syllabic   216
nonsense   191
and phonological awareness   189–90
recognition   177–9
rhyming   190–1, 192
root   255, 387
shapes of   398
syllabification of   397
where they come from   387–8
working with   195
see also sight words; spelling
written communication   326–7, 337–41
written lessons and text forms   358–60
written texts   347–8
   analysis of children   456–9
   and classroom environment   357–8
written work
   and oral language assessment   130, 135
   and reading comprehension   287
writing
   ability   443
   activities   445–51
   assessment   454–66
   audiences   346–7
   Cambourne's seven conditions of literacy
         learning   155–6
   centre   435
   children's experiences   451
   children's progress   443
   collecting information about children's   455–61
   components   327–30
   conference   410, 427, 460
   context   327–8
   conventions   330, 363, 377–9
   development   391, 410
   development, phases of   337–42
   developmental perspective   154
   directionality   169
   and editing   335
   emergence of   433–43
   emergent perspective   155
   evidence-based approaches   158
   expository   349, 352–4
   foundations   165
   and grammar   364–5, 373–7
   guided   410, 411, 424–6
   independent   358–60, 411, 427
   in an integrated program   564–6
   interactive   411, 421
   lessons for early years of school   444–5
   letter identification   461–2
   literacy   349, 350–2
   language experience approach (LEA)   422–4
   maturational perspective   154
   modelled   215, 410, 411, 412–16, 419–21
   models of good   415–16
   observation   456

and oral language   166–7, 327, 364–5, 417, 422, 423, 441
paragraphing   375–7
physical aspects   330
personal   348, 349–50
portfolio   457
preparing to write   332–3
process   331–7
processes and strategies   329–30
publishing and sharing with an audience   335–7
punctuation   170, 373–5
purpose   345–6
revising   334
self-assessment   460–1
shared (interactive)   411, 416–21
socio-cultural perspectives   157–8
and spelling assessment   462–5
teaching strategies   427–30
text form   328–9, 348, 355–6
theoretical perspectives   154–8
traits   331
and vocabulary   245–6

zone of proximal development (ZPD)   235